W. JENKINS

A World Not to Come

A WORLD NOT TO COME

A History of Latino Writing and Print Culture

RAÚL CORONADO

HARVARD UNIVERSITY PRESS
Cambridge, Massachusetts
London, England
2013

Printed in the United States of America

Published with the generous assistance of the
William P. Clements Center for Southwest Studies,
Southern Methodist University.

Library of Congress Cataloging-in-Publication Data

Coronado, Raúl, 1972–
A World Not to Come : A History of Latino Writing and Print Culture /
Raúl Coronado.
pages cm
Includes bibliographical references and index.
ISBN 978-0-674-07261-9 (alk. paper)
1. American literature—Hispanic American authors—History and criticism.
2. American literature—19th century—History and criticism.
3. Hispanic Americans—Intellectual life. I. Title.
PS153.H56C68 2013
810.9'868073—dc23 2012040361

To my family,

here and in Mexico,

both related by blood and made from scratch

Contents

Illustrations

Note on Translations

All translations, unless otherwise noted, are mine. In the spirit of a more multilingual, comparativist approach to literary and intellectual history, I first quote the Spanish original of primary documents followed immediately by the English translation in brackets. I cite the original Spanish without modernizing orthography. The archives upon which this account is based are housed at the Dolph Briscoe Center for American History (Austin), the Nettie Lee Benson Latin American Collection, the Texas State Archives, Southern Methodist University's DeGolyer Library, the Bancroft Library, the Newberry Library, the New York Public Library, the Archivo General de la Nación de México, the Hemeroteca Nacional de México, the Biblioteca Nacional de México, the Instituto de Investigaciones Mora, as well as several online databases.

A World Not to Come

Introduction

Divergent Revolutionary Genealogies

As quickly as he printed them, Antonio Nariño set his pamphlets ablaze. On December 15, 1793, in Santa Fé de Bogotá, New Granada (what would become Colombia), Nariño had the audacity to translate and publish the Marquis de Lafayette's 1789 French Declaration of the Rights of Man and of the Citizen, hoping, he would later claim, not to provoke a revolution but to capitalize on the local penchant for European publications and earn a few extra *reales*. This would be the first printing of the declaration in Spanish America. Nariño had taken the declaration from a history of the French Revolution, a copy of which he had borrowed from the library of his dear friend the Viceroy of New Granada.[1]

Spanish royal authorities had desperately sought to prevent the circulation of the revolutionary thought that had convulsed the rest of the Atlantic world, and despite his burning the pamphlets Nariño now seemed well equipped to publicize the declaration throughout Spanish America. It appears, however, that a few copies of the declaration escaped his rushed immolation, for eight months later Nariño found himself charged with heresy. Throughout his trial, Nariño consistently pointed to the absence of any evidence; the court never included even a portion of this pamphlet as evidence. And yet the *audiencia* (high court) of New Granada ultimately sentenced Nariño to ten years in prison and exiled him to Spain.[2]

Figure 1. José María Espinosa, *Antonio Nariño* (1856).

Oil on canvas, 124 × 84 cm. No. registro 4. Colección Museo de la Independencia, Casa del Florero, Ministerio de Cultura, Bogotá, Colombia.

Only four years later, in 1797, a more radical edition of the French Declaration of the Rights of Man and Citizen, that of 1793, would be discovered in Venezuela (see Figure 2). This time the culprit was one Juan Mariano Picornell, a radical Spaniard who had been exiled to New Granada but had escaped to the Antilles where he began his revolutionary career as a printer. From there, he translated and published 10,000 copies of the declaration (with a false Madrid imprint), seeking to disperse them throughout Venezuela and Mexico. Picornell, like many revolutionary Spaniards and Spanish Americans of this period, would travel throughout the Atlantic world: from Spain to South America and the Caribbean, on to Philadelphia and Baltimore, to and from France, across to New Orleans and Texas, Mexico, and eventually to Cuba, where he would finally settle and die.[3] And like these other individuals he would also bring this new political language of rights to the places he visited, imbibing this political philosophy by reading and through conversations and discussions. Spanish-American *criollos* or creoles, those elite Americans of Spanish cultural descent that inhabited Spanish territory in what is the present-day U.S. Southwest down to the tips of South America, had long resented Spanish peninsular condescension. Spanish peninsular arrogance toward Spanish Americans had increased significantly since the mid-eighteenth century when Americans were denied positions of power within the colonial bureaucracy. But this resentment built on a much older discourse, what historians now describe as creole patriotism. It had emerged shortly after the Spanish colonization of the Americas, and lamented the devalued and demoted status of the conquerors and their descendants. Combined with this history, these revolutionary ideas would ultimately lead to action both profound and unexpected.[4]

The French declarations put into clear, stark, secular language an alternative model of sovereignty, one that rested solely in the people and not in a monarch or particular class. What made it even more attractive to Spanish-American creoles was the deep resentment they harbored toward the Spanish Bourbon monarch's reform policies of the eighteenth century.[5] These reforms, which began in the middle of the century, sought to rein in the kingdoms throughout the Hispanic world (composed of the Spanish Peninsula, Spanish America, and the Philippines) and undo the tradition of the Habsburg dynasty (1516–1700).

Under the Habsburg monarchs, Spain had emerged as a consolidated monarchy, a federation comprised of ancient Iberian kingdoms and the newly created sixteenth-century kingdoms in the Americas. But this consolidation was fueled by a wave of religious millenarianism that inundated the Spanish kingdoms. The long seven-hundred-year *Reconquista,* the wars

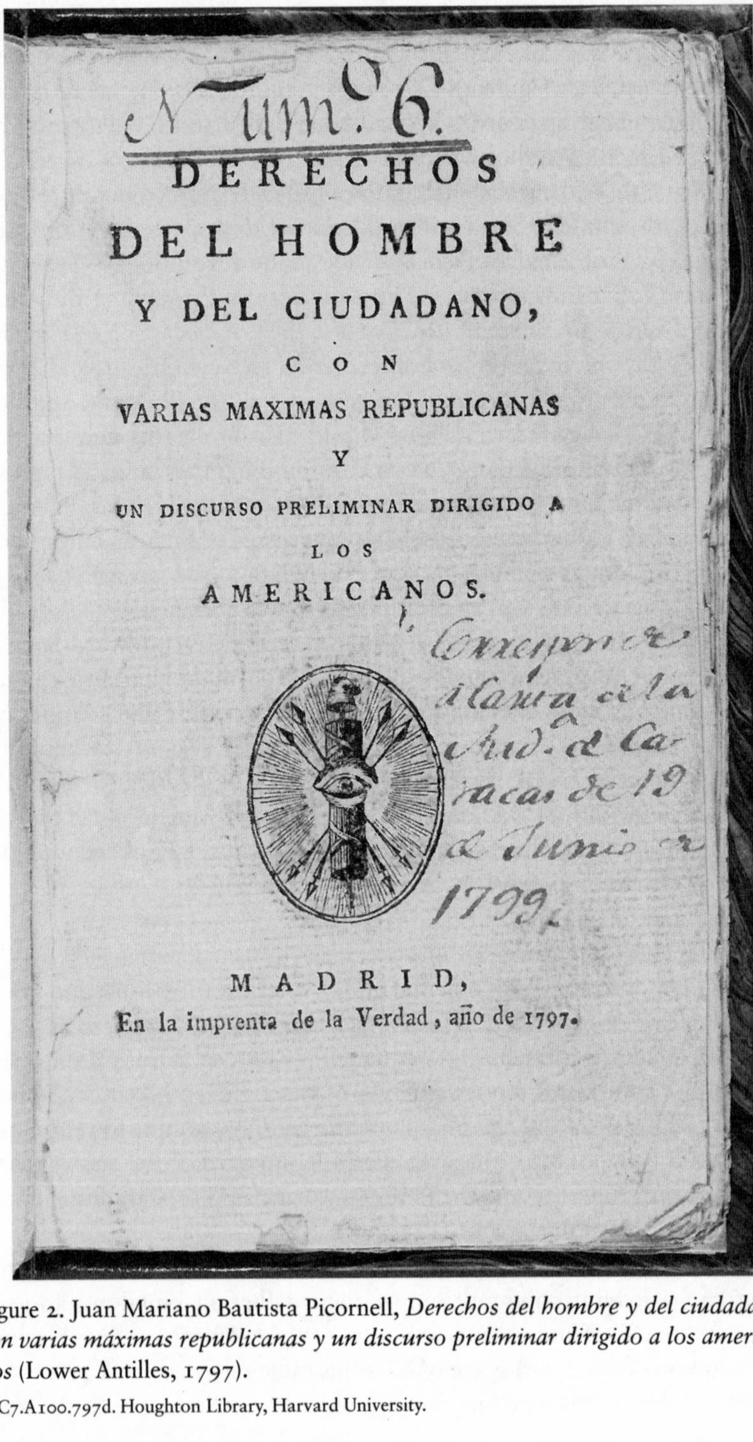

Figure 2. Juan Mariano Bautista Picornell, *Derechos del hombre y del ciudadano, con varias máximas republicanas y un discurso preliminar dirigido a los americanos* (Lower Antilles, 1797).

*SC7.A100.797d. Houghton Library, Harvard University.

led by various Catholic kingdoms in their attempt to wrest Muslim control of the Spanish Peninsula, had at long last ended in 1492 with the defeat of Al-Andalus and the expulsion of all Moors and Jews from the Peninsula. Then, Columbus's encounter with the Americas in the same year added fuel to a burgeoning sense of Spanish Catholic providentialism, only ostensibly confirmed with the astonishing conquest of the vastly superior Aztec and Inca civilizations in 1521 and 1532.[6]

Through this all, the Spanish monarchy was unwaveringly Catholic, named the "Catholic Kings" by the pope in 1494 and later designated as the protector of the Church during the trying years of the Protestant Reformation. From its very emergence, the monarchy and Catholicism were inseparable, yet, to be clear, Spain never conceded full authority to the Church, working instead in tandem. Indeed, the Spanish Inquisition, founded in 1480, was under direct control of the Spanish monarchy, and Spain held all final authority on ecclesiastical appointments in the Americas. Still, so enmeshed was Spain with Catholicism that the seventeenth-century prime minister Count-Duke Olivares declared, "God is Spanish."[7]

As a way to govern the Americas, Spain established the kingdoms of New Spain (comprising what is today Mexico, the U.S. Southwest, and Central America), Peru, New Granada, and Río de la Plata (modern Argentina and surrounding countries). And these New World kingdoms were equal to those recently united kingdoms of peninsular Spain. Though ruled by the Spanish monarch, the various kingdoms in Europe and America had functioned under some semblance of autonomy. They were governed by the monarch's representatives, a wide array of viceroys, other administrators, and various councils. The monarchy's quasi-federalist approach to ruling had cultivated a curious if dangerous sense of independence in the Americas—albeit de facto—which had led to a concentric sense of identification with their local kingdoms under which they were all united with the Spanish Catholic monarchy. But Habsburg policy eroded when the dynasty died out, and was replaced (after the 1701–1714 War of Spanish Succession) with the French Bourbon family.[8]

By the mid-eighteenth century and inspired by French Bourbon policy, the Spanish Bourbon monarchy attempted to create a rigid, bureaucratic order out of a massive monarchy. The Bourbons' focus on economic, administrative reform, and their desire to create a centralized state have been described as "Enlightened absolutism."[9] Along with their attempt to restrict greatly the Church's political and economic power, the Bourbon reforms limited the political and economic autonomy of the increasingly frustrated creoles by appointing only peninsular Spaniards to all positions of power (from political, ecclesiastical, commercial, and university appointments).

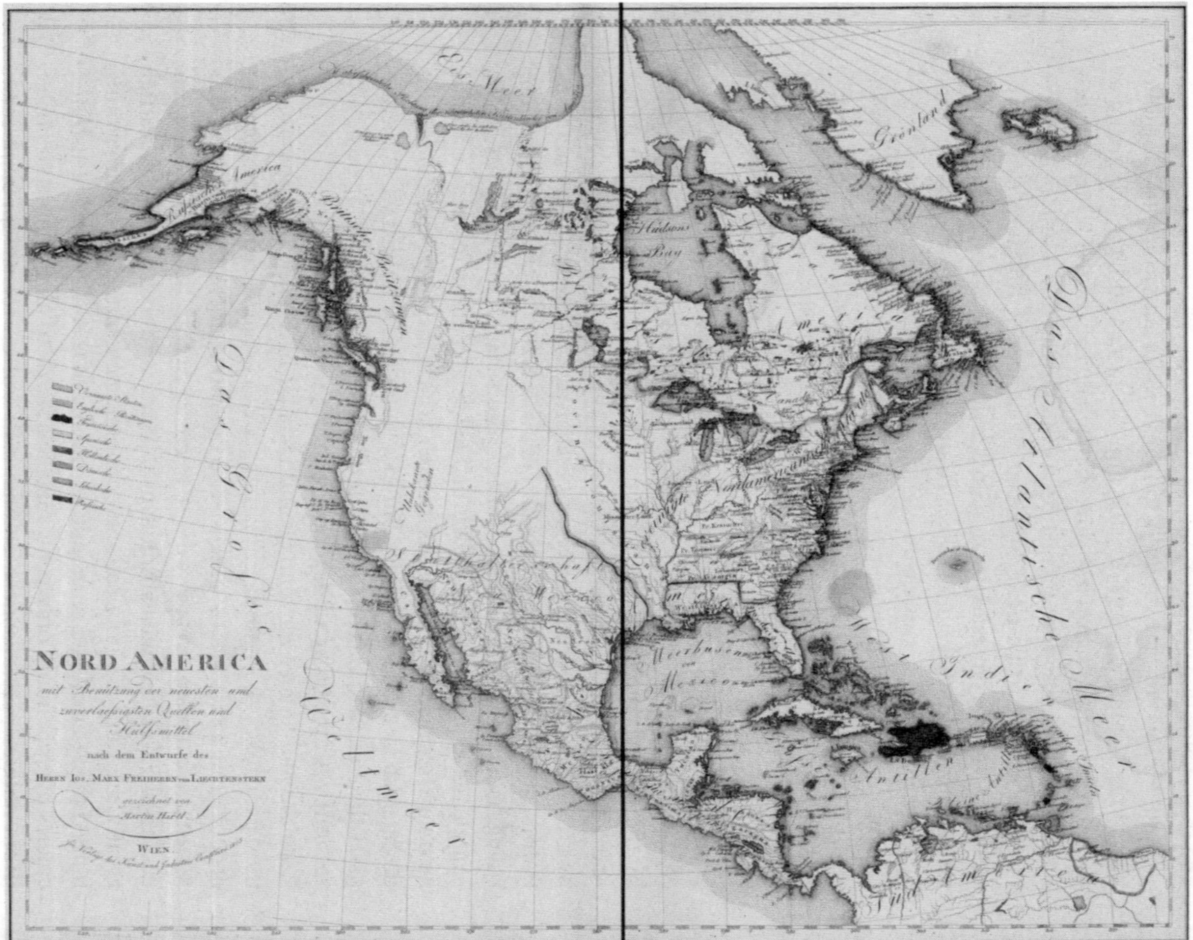

Figure 3. Joseph Marx Liechtenstern, "Nord America mit Benützung der neuesten und zuverlaessigsten Quellen und Hülfsmittel" [North America with the use of the latest and most reliable Sources and Aids] (1805).

48 × 59 cm. Digital ID http://hdl.loc.gov/loc.gmd/g3300.ct000175, Geography and Map Division, Library of Congress.

They increased taxation, implemented strict trade restrictions, stymied the development of industry in Spanish America, and, in effect, attempted to convert Spanish America from kingdoms of the mother country into a series of money-making colonies. Indeed, it was only in the late eighteenth century, and influenced by British and French practice, that the Spanish monarch began to refer to the Americas as "colonies." "Indicative of their attitude was the change in the monarch's title," writes the historian Jaime E. Rodríguez O. "In Habsburg times it had been *King of the Spains and of the Indies;* under the Bourbons it became *King of Spain and Emperor of America.*"[10] Creoles despised these reforms, and yearned to regain local political authority. It was during this last decade of the eighteenth century that we begin to see a syncretism of various political intellectual traditions and, fueled by creole resentment, the eruption of revolts throughout Spanish America.

The radically seditious ideas contained in what had been, in Nariño's case, a mere four pages, demanded vigilance. In November 1794 the royal forces sent out expeditions in search of his heretical pamphlet. One circular declared, "La señal del impreso son: hallarse en papel grande, grueso, y prieto en cuarto y con mucho margen; todo de letra bastardilla, y de tres clases de mayor a menor [The description of the printed document is: found on large thick dark paper, in quarto and with significant margins; all the letters are italicized, and in three decreasing font sizes]."[11] So dangerous was this new way of thinking that in 1797, after discovering yet another conspiracy and finding Picornell's edition of the declaration, the Caracas high court declared that "las dos [causas que influyeron la conspiración] mas descubiertas han consistido en la adhesion á varios libros, y papeles torpes y sediciosos, y papeles sueltos impresos y manuscritos, y en el empeño de los extrangeros en su introduccion y extension. [The two primary (causes leading to the recently discovered 1797 conspiracy) that have come to light consist of the adherence to various books, ignominious and seditious pamphlets, broadsheets, and manuscripts and of their introduction and circulation on the part of foreigners]."[12] In Nariño's case, the royal forces would never find a single copy. Nor, as they would soon discover, would they be able to prevent the flourishing of this way of thinking among their subjects.

As the eighteenth century lurched toward the nineteenth, books, pamphlets, broadsheets, and manuscripts launched a discursive war against Spanish imperial rule. These texts may have targeted Spain's specific reign over America, but they were birthed throughout the Atlantic world: in London, Philadelphia, France, the Caribbean, and even Spain herself. They were smuggled in as contraband, sometimes published within Spanish

America but often with false imprints as a way to evade authorities, and they circulated among reading groups, were posted in public spaces, and were read aloud to communities. A discursive history of these texts, describing the conditions of possibility that allowed for them to flourish, will go a long way toward offering an alternative model of modernity as it unfolded in the Americas. Exploring these documents, and the long-underappreciated world that accompanies them, enables us to witness alternative, if at times unfulfilled, paths to our modernity. These texts enable us to see no less than different visions of imagining communities that did not necessarily have to lead to nationalism, of conceptions of rights and subjectivity that do not genuflect to our now dominant account of possessive individualism, and of how writing and printing facilitated the processes of disenchantment, of imagining the world as a produced order rather than a received one.

This book offers, in other words, a historical-archaeological account of an alternative West, one that has its roots in Catholic thought. But it is a world that became increasingly marginalized within the West after the Protestant Reformation, so much so that the post-Reformation intellectual history of the Hispanic world—Spain and Spanish America—has become excised from dominant accounts of modernity, of the development of modern political sovereignty and of secularization, for example. In this regard, it shares a similar desire—with that of Latin American critics like Walter Mignolo and Enrique Dussel, among others—of "unveiling the imperial presuppositions that maintain a universal idea of humanity."[13] Such a model will pay careful attention to Spanish America's own intellectual heritage, rooted as it was in Spanish Catholic thought and local, creole epistemologies, even as this heritage was reconfigured by the arrival of ideas from Protestant northern Europe and Anglo-America.

Historians have long debated how to characterize (indeed, even periodize) the Hispanic Enlightenment and revolutions, which span from roughly the late eighteenth century to the 1820s.[14] During this period both Spain and Spanish America were roiled by debates on how to improve the well-being of the public, how to integrate the new modern philosophy with the dominant Scholastic thought that ruled over higher education, and, after the Spanish monarch was deposed in 1808, with the literal and philosophical question of the origin of sovereignty. Indeed, some have debated whether such a thing as the Enlightenment ever existed; and some, more recently, have rightly claimed that the initial Spanish-American rebellions were not wars of independence at all but, rather, part of a global Hispanic civil war.[15] In part, the difficulty in these debates has to do with how the Enlightenment has long been characterized: as a diverse, secular, anti-clerical intellectual movement where "Man," using his reason, became liberated from the chains of dogmatism and tyranny. The Enlightenment has been understood as what paved the road to our political modernity, leading to revolutions and to the establishment of republican forms of government.[16] But such a thing never occurred in such a way in the Hispanic world. Nonetheless, intellectual historians have sought to align the intellectual history of the Hispanic world with some of the familiar terms of the Enlightenment or of the U.S. and French revolutions. Thus, the definition of the Hispanic Enlightenment becomes so restricted—excising the virulent anti-Catholic thought of a Voltaire, say—that the ideas that did circulate during this period have become obscured.

The difficulty in trying to characterize this period of Hispanic intellectual thought has to do with the problem of comparison and the categories that we use to compare. In this instance, the dominant narrative of the Enlightenment and of revolutions, which emerged from the experience of Protestant northern Europe and British America, has become the standard essentialist model for thinking of the eighteenth century and, ultimately, of revolutions and independence. Historians then rummage through the Hispanic archive seeking out any trace of "Enlightenment" thought; or they parse the revolutionary Spanish-American print culture of the early nineteenth century, attributing this or that to the influence either of Anglo-American or of French revolutionary thought.[17] "As a result of this principle of classification," writes Harry Harootunian, societies are "invariably ranked according to spatial distance from an empowering model that radiated the achievement of industrial and technological supremacy—namely, the countries of Euro-America—and expected identification with it."[18] But these categories—the Enlightenment, revolution, independence—are susceptible to multiple temporalities that may lead to familiar forms but with contents that have had distinct genealogies. That is, while revolutions erupted throughout the turn-of-the-nineteenth-century Atlantic world, they all did so with their own particular ideological configurations with distinct intellectual genealogies that, while on the surface all ostensibly yearned for liberty and equality, often resulted in incommensurable understandings of those very terms, liberty and equality. For example, as we will see, when Spanish-American revolutionaries during the early nineteenth century declared themselves independent, at times using republican language, they "were at once deeply rooted in the Spanish past and at the same time appeared rather modern on the surface."[19] This weaving of the past into the present, of familiar forms with unfamiliar (again, to us) content, will be a pattern that emerges more than once in the pages that follow.

The tension is between form and content; or, as Harootunian puts it, between space and temporality. He takes critics to task for giving priority to space/place and what the *form* of, say, modernity is in a particular place; rather, he claims, critics must turn instead to temporality, to understanding the nuances of the *contents* of these forms, unraveling the minute processes entailed in the emergence of these forms or concepts—such as Enlightenment, revolution, and modernity.[20] What needs to be better understood are the genealogies, in the Foucauldian sense, of particular ideas even if it means radically redefining the overarching concept or, indeed, doing away with it.

Thus, the dominant account of the Enlightenment, revolution, and modernity emerges from the particular histories of Anglo America and Protestant northwestern Europe. In becoming dominant, they in fact become accepted as universal ideals, divorced from their particular historical contingencies and seen as the norm to which others should strive. Scholars then try, with a certain desperation, to fit the square peg of "Enlightenment" into the round hole of Spain and Spanish America, and, unable to do so, find Spain and Spanish America wanting.[21] But to force the dominant form or concept of the Enlightenment, for example, onto the Hispanic world would render the particularities of that world opaque at best or retrograde at worst. The Enlightenment, after all, or so the story goes, was seen as displacing what had remained of traditional, conservative Scholastic modes of inquiry. Scholasticism had been the dominant method of critical thought in Europe until it began to be replaced by the humanism of the Renaissance, the political philosophy of the Protestant Reformation, and scientific developments of the seventeenth century. But if Scholasticism by the late eighteenth century had become a minor figure in the intellectual world of (primarily) Protestant northwestern Europe, that was far from being the case in the Hispanic world.[22]

How, then, to reconcile these discordant histories without resorting to the language of belatedness, to a model where the Euro-Anglo world is seen as the origin of universal ideals and the Hispanic world is seen as always striving to catch up? A genealogical approach would eschew what Harootunian correctly criticized as a fetishizing of form over content, of understanding history as modular where certain categories are merely applied to the histories of various social formations. The emphasis instead would be on what Harootunian described as temporality, on working inductively from the nuances, details in order to arrive at larger conceptual claims without needing to accord these histories to some universal norm. In this sense, Foucault's concept of genealogy proves fruitful. "Genealogy," he writes,

> does not pretend to go back in time to restore an unbroken continuity that operates beyond the dispersion of forgotten things. . . . Genealogy does not resemble the evolution of a species and does not map the destiny of a people. On the contrary, to follow the complex course of descent is to maintain passing events in their proper dispersion; it is to identify the accidents, the minute deviations—or conversely, the complete reversals—the errors, the false appraisals, and the faulty calculations that gave birth to those things that continue to exist and have value for us.[23]

Instead of pursuing avenues that focus solely on some idealized form as the only basis from which to write history ("Here, at last! Spanish Americans use secular revolutionary language!" or "Look! There is the first Latino novel!" as if these instances signal for us the beginning of history), a genealogical approach pauses instead on those moments of ostensible contradiction where, for example, Catholic thought intransigently remains ensconced in revolutionary language, and it does so in order to reveal alternative possibilities for revolutionary thought. But even more to the point, a genealogical approach will allow us to produce a history that is not teleological, one that does not assume that previous generations consciously sought to arrive precisely at the world we inhabit today. Rather, even while paying close attention to those conscious efforts, to their writing, for example, genealogy will allow us instead to elaborate on how their efforts often led to completely unintended results. This is to say, genealogy allows us to move beyond obstinate analytical categories that obfuscate alternative histories, categories that line up neatly such as the Enlightenment, revolution, independence, and the modern nation-state. Hegemonic histories often narrate the coming into being of the modern nation-state, and in the account that I have been unfolding here, one would be forgiven if they expected this narrative to begin with colonial Spanish America, move through revolutions, and conclude with the independence of the various Spanish-American nations.

The Traumatic Origins of the Modern World

The late eighteenth-century circulation of revolutionary thought and increasing rebellions did not lead to revolution. Instead, revolution came from outside. A shift of global proportions occurred in early 1808. Napoleon Bonaparte invaded Spain, and on May 5 forced King Charles IV and his heir, Fernando VII, to abdicate, and placed his brother Joseph on the throne. Napoleon pummeled northern Spain first, forcing each region to submit as he made his way south. Faced with an immediate political vacuum, and with Napoleon on their heels, the political elites of the various ancient kingdoms of Spain all gathered in September in Aranjuez, just outside of Madrid and just far enough from Napoleon's grip. There, the fragments of a recently glorious and suddenly vulnerable monarchy voted to create the Junta Suprema Central y Gubernativa de España e Indias (Supreme Central Governing Council of Spain and the Indies). As news spread across the Hispanic world, the kingdoms of Spanish America and the Philippines, too, convened their own regional governing councils.[24] The choice of a new governing body was both anachronistic and fortuitous. The *juntas* or councils had a long-established precedent, created in the sixteenth century as a way to help govern each kingdom, but the Spanish monarch had all but done away with these forms of local control—quasi-autonomous, rather than centralized—by the eighteenth century. Napoleon chased the Supreme Central Junta all the way down south to the port of Cádiz. Surrounded by the French and desperate to unite the Hispanic world, the twenty-four-member Supreme Central Junta in Spain appealed even further to historical precedent. They revived the medieval political entity of the *cortes,* that parliamentary form of representation comprised of the three estates (clergy, nobles, and commoners). The *cortes* had emerged in the twelfth century, but, like the councils, had all but been done away with by the seventeenth. The Supreme Central Junta did the incredible, and called for the creation of the Cortes of Cádiz, Spain's first modern parliament.[25] We will have occasion to visit these momentous events in more detail.

If 1808 forced upon Hispanics an earth-shattering moment, producing immeasurable patriotism, then 1809 veered in the opposite direction, toward revolution. The Cortes were based in southern Spain's bustling commercial port of Cádiz, and were protected from Napoleon's forces by the British fleet. But their first move was a radical gesture: they called for representatives from Spain's provinces throughout the world. Even more revolutionary was their proclamation issued on January 22, 1809—the news would arrive in New Spain some two months later and would be published in the April 15 issue of the Mexico City *Gazeta* (see Figure 4)—declaring that "cesan ya los nombres de *colonias* de los dominios españoles de Indias, y toman los de parte *integrante* de la monarquia [the Spanish dominions in the Indies shall hereafter cease to be called *colonies* and shall be considered *integral* parts of the monarchy]."[26] The mid-eighteenth century Bourbon reforms, as noted earlier, had sought to convert Spanish-American and Pacific territories into colonies. Now, the Cortes not only boldly rejected Bourbon policy, but they also openly declared

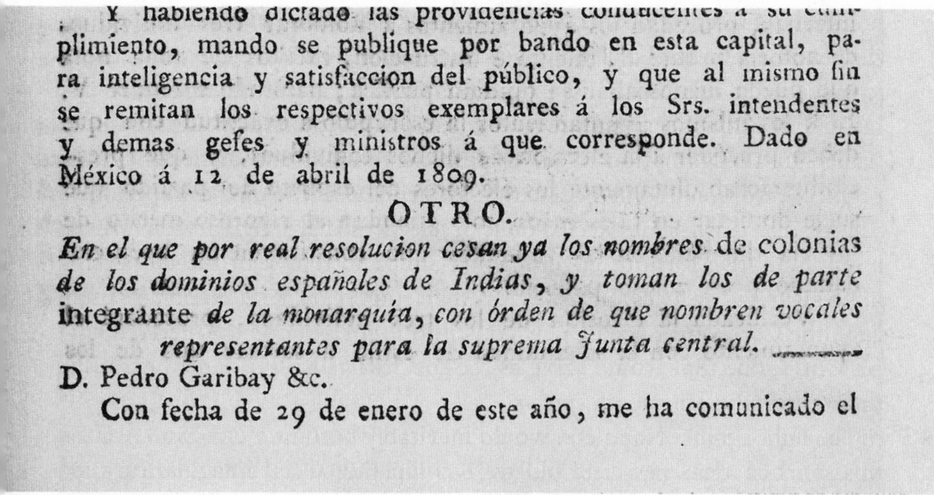
Y habiendo dictado las providencias conducentes á su cum-
plimiento, mando se publique por bando en esta capital, para inteligencia y satisfaccion del público, y que al mismo fin
se remitan los respectivos exemplares á los Srs. intendentes
y demas gefes y ministros á que corresponde. Dado en
México á 12 de abril de 1809.

OTRO.

En el que por real resolucion cesan ya los nombres de colonias *de los dominios españoles de Indias, y toman los de parte* integrante *de la monarquía, con órden de que nombren vocales representantes para la suprema Junta central.*

D. Pedro Garibay &c.

Con fecha de 29 de enero de este año, me ha comunicado el

Figure 4. The conservative, European Spaniard-controlled *Gazeta de Mexico* buried on the last page of the April 15, 1809, issue the news that Spanish America would no longer be referred to as colonies.

Vol. 16, no. 49 (April 15, 1809), p. 325. Nettie Lee Benson Latin American Collection, University of Texas Libraries, University of Texas at Austin.

Spanish-American and Pacific territories to be equal to those of peninsular Spain.

That such a move on the part of the Cortes may be seen as radical must be tempered by the fact that the Spanish government, sequestered in Cádiz while the rest of the Peninsula was occupied by Napoleon, sorely needed financial support from America in its struggle against its new ruler. New Spain, as the wealthiest viceroyalty in all of Spanish America, had over the course of the eighteenth century provided Spain with two-thirds of its entire imperial revenue; and this only increased with the silver boom by century's end. The Cortes were inspired, in part, by the centuries-long Habsburg tradition of thinking of the Spanish monarchy as a composite, or federation, of kingdoms, from the Spanish Peninsula to the Americas to the Philippines.[27] And they were inspired in part by a desperate need for usable assets in the expensive war against Napoleon.

Still, what had once been accepted practice—the Habsburg custom of electing local officials—became, immediately, de jure. The world of Enlightenment-era political philosophy had just a half century earlier been banned by the Spanish crown, in collaboration with the Catholic Inquisition; such ideas could only be contemplated in hushed, clandestine circles. But now, almost overnight, not only the philosophy but the practice of political representation became officially sanctioned; *ayuntamientos,* or the governing body of a city and its surrounding area, across Spanish America engaged in heated discussions as to how to go about electing representatives.[28] But this seemingly radical departure, like most new ideas, was in reality an amalgamation of novel political thought and ancient Spanish political traditions, some originating as far back as the medieval period.[29] The Spanish Cortes unleashed a radical, eclectic, social imaginary, one where a representative form of government claimed to represent the monarch's interests in his absence. In 1812, less than four years after Napoleon's seizure, the Cortes produced a new constitution for a suddenly altered Spanish world, one that would serve as the touchstone for Hispanic liberalism throughout the nineteenth century.[30]

The fight against Napoleon would inevitably become a civil war. Amidst this swirl of ideas new and old were competing social imaginaries, very different visions of what the Spanish world meant and how Hispanic society should be constructed.[31] Napoleon was defeated in 1813 and King Fernando VII restored to the throne. But restoration made things worse. The king abolished the Cortes and shredded the constitution, exercising his long-denied authoritarian power as if his actions alone could undo people's desire to produce new social relations. The king's repressive actions immediately inaugurated a regime of terror in Spain, but across Spanish America, it led to civil war; and that civil war would become wars of independence.

The king's restoration only inflamed tensions that had been simmering for decades. In New Spain in particular, long-existing conflicts between creoles and Peninsula-born Spaniards bubbled to the surface immediately after Napoleon seized the crown as the creole-dominated Mexico City *ayuntamiento* gestured toward home rule. The Spaniards acted quickly in September 1809 when the viceroy appeared to side with the creoles. They arrested him and replaced him with a more conservative viceroy. The Spanish minority now tightened its grip even further, persecuting all those who had intimated any thought of self-determination. While the urban creole elite chafed under the ever-more conservative regime, rural communities took a more aggressive approach.[32]

In the early hours of September 16, 1810, Father Miguel Hidalgo led a party of mostly mestizo and Indian peasants to revolt against the Spaniards, who had long been seen as oppressors and clearly, now, were seen as tyrants. The Mexican War of Independence had begun. Within six months Hidalgo's forces were being pursued by the royal army. Hidalgo attempted to flee north, confident that he would gain support in the United States. But on March 21, 1811, Hidalgo and his men were captured at the Wells of Baján, some 200 miles southwest of present-day Laredo, Texas. The insurrection, however, would not end that fateful day.[33]

Manuel Salcedo, the Spanish governor of Texas, had prevented Hidalgo and his minions from crossing into the United States. He and other officers captured Hidalgo, forced him back south, and promptly executed him.[34] But Governor Salcedo was unable to smother the embers of insurrection that quickly spread on both sides of what is today the Texas-Mexico border. One of these embers, in the person of José Bernardo Gutiérrez de Lara, eventually fulfilled Hidalgo's desire. Born into a prosperous and influential family in 1774, Gutiérrez de Lara hailed from Revilla, Nuevo Santander, located along today's Texas-Mexico border.

The province of Nuevo Santander (present-day Tamaulipas) formed part of the Eastern Interior Provinces, along with what are today Nuevo León, Coahuila, and the state of Texas. Of these, Texas served as a direct frontier buffer zone that separated New Spain from French, British, and, with the turn of the nineteenth century, U.S. imperial interests. Our story centers broadly on the Eastern Interior Provinces, and more specifically on the provinces of Texas and northern Nuevo Santander, since it was here that the modern crucible of Texas emerged, that discursive-physical location where nation-states came and went within decades, building hopes as quickly as they were snatched away.

Northern New Spain had been colonized as early as the sixteenth century. But by 1787, as a result of the Bourbon reforms, the territory had been consolidated into the Eastern and Western Interior Provinces; after independence they would become the vast northern territory that is now the Mexico-United States border. Over the course of the late eighteenth century, the provinces were divided and consolidated several times. But what made them unique in Spanish America is that they were continually ruled by a military commandant general. This general reported directly to the Spanish king rather than the viceroy of New Spain, though the general relied on the viceroy as a communication conduit with the king. Even more complicated, the judicial affairs of the provinces were addressed by the *audiencia* in Guadalajara, New Spain. In turn, each province had a governor who reported directly to the commandant general.[35]

As for the far northeastern province of Texas, it had emerged as a frontier line of defense, in good Spanish military tradition. Spain had relied on this strategy since the late fifteenth century reconquest of Moorish Spain, and it had worked well for them then. It involved creating a military buffer zone between the civilian settlements and the territory occupied by the enemy and then gradually expanding these civilian settlements until the entire territory was under Spanish control.[36] But the strategy failed miserably

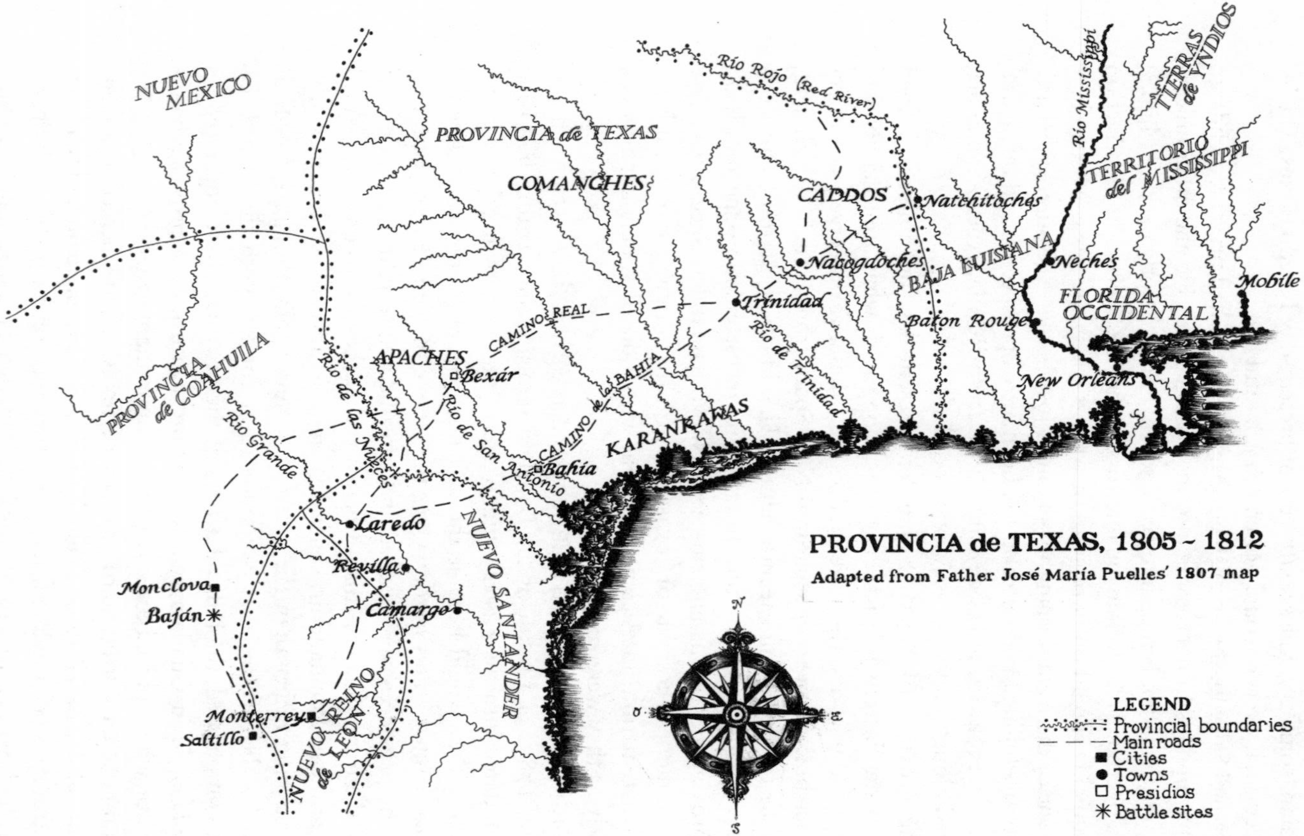

Figure 5. Anna Theresa Coronado de Rueda, "Provincia de Texas, 1805–1812." Based on Father José Maria Puelles's manuscript "Mapa Geographica de las Provincias Septentrionales de esta Nueva Espana" (1807?).

in Texas. Spanish Americans were never able to conquer the various Native American nations in Texas, the powerful Comanches to the north, Apaches and Tonkawas in the center, the Caddos in the northeast, and the Karankawas along the coast.[37] Spain's own economic policies, in turn, did much to stymie the immigration of Spanish Americans into Texas. Desperate to protect Spanish industry, Spain was unwilling to shift its mercantilist economic policies. It refused to allow Texas to engage in trade with Louisiana, rejected efforts to open ports along the Gulf Coast, and levied heavy tariffs on the trade that did exist with Mexican merchants.[38] The conditions were ripe, then, for social upheaval.

A History of Latino Textuality

Rather than tell a story about the splintering of the Spanish-American world and the coming into being of modern Spanish-American nations, this book tells a story of the historical accidents and reversals that led Spanish Americans to imagine themselves not as sovereigns of new nations but as an unexpected and, increasingly, racialized group of peoples within the United States. That is, it turns to the space of overlap between Spanish America and the United States, to the individuals and communities of "Latinos"[39] that circulated in the United States and throughout the Atlantic world. The book does so in order to tell a more complex story about a specific place: the geographic space that *would become* Mexico and the United States. It does so by centering on a story that both traverses continents and unfolds within a delimited place. It traces the circulation of ideas and texts as these relate to the making of Latino intellectual life in the United States. It is a history that spills over national boundaries, preceding, in fact, the emergence of nations. Rather than a story about the coming into being of a nation, I focus instead on Latinos who sought to engage with the discourses of modernity in order to produce a modern world that would supplant the *ancien régime.* Many of these individuals held, from our contemporary vantage point, problematic political stances, some embracing constitutional monarchies, others refusing to accept freedom of religious thought; and they have been duly judged and condemned by many critics.[40]

The story I narrate offers a different history of modernity as it unfolded via the dispersion of texts. More specifically, the geographic space I focus upon is that region that *would come to be recognized* as Texas, even as I zoom in on the towns of San Antonio de Béxar (referred to as "Béxar" until the early nineteenth century) and Nacogdoches in far east Texas, or zoom out to events in Louisiana, Philadelphia, Washington, D.C., Mexico, South America, London, Spain, and other places in the Atlantic. In claiming that this book will focus on the space that "would become" Mexico and the United States, I emphasize the future-in-past tense of the auxiliary "would" and inchoative aspect of "become," rather than the past tense proper ("the space that *became* Mexico, the United States, or Texas"); though cumbersome, I hope the focus here will help us call into question the inevitability of nation-formation.

The future-in-past tense draws out, unfolds, and lengthens the process of "becoming," which itself denotes the *processes* entailed in any radical shift in thought.[41] As a result, the consolidated nation-states of Mexico and the United States ("the territory that *became*"), are deemphasized, allowing us to trace the various routes of "becoming." But to elongate this history, in a sense, to stretch out the temporality of the phrase "would become," calls for a narrative filling of discursive space. The history that follows also draws attention to the processes by which the signifiers, "Mexico" and the "United States," came to signify what they do today. Yet, though I may refer to "Texas," "Mexico," and "the United States," I will do so while simultaneously emphasizing the slippage between signifier and signified. It is in this slippery realm, as we'll see, that the process of "becoming" occurs.

My narrative begins in Texas, around 1810, with the initial Spanish-American calls for independence from Spain; it ends a half century later, with the efforts on the part of Latinos in Texas to contest their racialization in the 1850s. In doing so, it follows a trans-Atlantic trail of manuscripts, pamphlets, proclamations, and manifestoes. During the early nineteenth century, the public sphere animated by Hispanophone print culture was at once small because of limited access to printing presses and quite vast, encompassing the entire Hispanophone Atlantic world. Editors published newspapers in London, for example, aimed at audiences in Spain and Spanish America, while readers in Philadelphia replied in kind by publishing pamphlets that vociferously disagreed with said editors. These documents circulated to and from Europe, Spanish America, and the United States, from Paris, London, and Spain, to New Granada, and from there to Philadelphia, Washington, D.C., Mexico, Louisiana, and Texas.

It was in the peripheries of these emerging nation-states that we see the movement of goods, and with them, of people and revolutionary ideas. We see the convergence of various political philosophies, theories of sovereignty, and no less than the development of new ways of imagining the world. In the case of Texas, we will see a geographic locale that witnessed waves of revolutions, of expatriates from Spain, Mexico, the Caribbean,

South America, the United States, and Europe, at times working in tandem with local Spanish Americans and Native Americans, all seeking to produce sovereign nation-states. But, in the end, in Texas we will witness a contested community of Spanish-Mexican Tejanos who will see themselves devolve from an elite community of "civilizing" conquerors into an embattled, pauperized, and racialized community.

I describe the ways in which Spanish Americans generated imagined communities in places that would overlap across several nation-states within a matter of decades. Texas becomes one of the focal points precisely because it was peripheral to the reconfiguring of empires of the nineteenth-century Americas and, because of its peripheral status, one of the places where the Spanish and U.S. empires met and clashed. Texas is where the leader of Mexican independence, Father Miguel Hidalgo, sought to make his way, fleeing the pursuing Spanish royal forces in 1811 in order ultimately to arrive in Washington, D.C., where he and other Spanish-American insurgents were sure they would receive support for their glorious cause. Then, in 1813, Texas would become the first province in New Spain to declare itself an independent republic with a written constitution. (Even when Mexico would finally declare its independence in 1821, it would do so as a monarchy.) For many revolutionary Spanish Americans, Texas emerged as a focal point for the independence of all of Spanish America: gain independence in Texas from Spain, and it would only be a matter of time before New Spain would fall, contributing to a domino effect across Spanish America. This helps explain the arrival in Texas of radical, expatriate Spaniards and Spanish Americans throughout the nineteenth century.

This story of revolution and print culture in Spanish Texas has been elided by both historians of Mexico and of the United States, and relegated to a footnote for several reasons.[42] In the case of Mexican historiography, the Texan attempts at Mexican independence from Spain failed to expand Hidalgo's revolution, adding little to the tale of the coming into being of the Mexican nation. But even more troubling is the tortured memory of Texas and the United States' defeat of Mexico in 1848. Texas serves as a bitter memory of conquest, and Mexican historians have long ignored the formative experience of Texas in Mexican history.[43] For historians of the United States, on the other hand, the narrative of democracy and expansion of the nation-state had long been paved over by racialist narratives that placed Anglo-Americans at the center of history. It was the Alamo, and the names of Stephen F. Austin, Sam Houston, Davy Crockett, and James Bowie that resounded and, in many ways, continue to resound there; and the foundation of an Anglo-American democratic republic had long taken center stage in narrative histories. The contributions by Spanish Americans were immediately excised. While the historiography has changed somewhat over the last decade, this racial narrative continues to be dominant in the popular imagination. Nonetheless, the goal here is not to reverse this discursive history by placing Spanish Americans at the center of a foundationalist history, one that sees Spanish Americans as the true and rightful originators of republican political thought. Indeed, it is precisely the absence of a foundational nationalist genealogy that is of interest here.[44] These individuals may have failed to establish a nation, but an alternative language of modernity began to sediment itself in particular ways, in part because of their activities. By returning to these moments of aspiration and failure, perhaps we, too, may be inspired to imagine our present and future in more capacious ways that move beyond possessive individualism and xenophobic nationalisms.

This history also forces us to imagine Texas not as we do today, as some behemoth of nationalist independent feeling; rather, we are called on to see it as a desolate, emerging interstitial colony, shaped by a long history of imperial jockeying among New Spain, French Louisiana, and the expanding United States. Thus, the social and economic networks that tied communities in Texas and Louisiana facilitated the circulation of peoples and ideas along a southwesterly-northeasterly direction, along the Texas Gulf Coast from San Antonio, to Nacogdoches, and then New Orleans (see Figures 5 and 6). From New Orleans, the communication network expanded to reach yet larger routes of trade and communication. While Spanish San Antonio, by contrast, remained officially limited to trade with Mexico, New Orleans opened its arms to Havana, Veracruz, and Philadelphia. This book pursues these various communication networks, at times taking a step back in order to provide a larger panoramic vision of intellectual circuits between metropoles. But it does so in order ultimately to focus in on the particular making of Latino intellectual thought. I analyze a variety of texts, from manuscripts, revolutionary pamphlets and broadsheets, to periodicals, petitions, essays, travel narratives, and official and personal correspondence. Based on the materiality of these texts—how they traveled, who carried them, and to what end—I unwind the dense, elaborate discursive networks that condensed in the area that would become the transnational space of Texas.

The result is a history of textuality: not just what is imprinted on a sheet of paper, but also the surrounding ideas that inform the production of that document and that, thus, may be seen as part of a broader tapestry of "writing." Instead of asking, "What was the status of the literary?"—with its presumption of high literacy rates along with its cognates of the genres

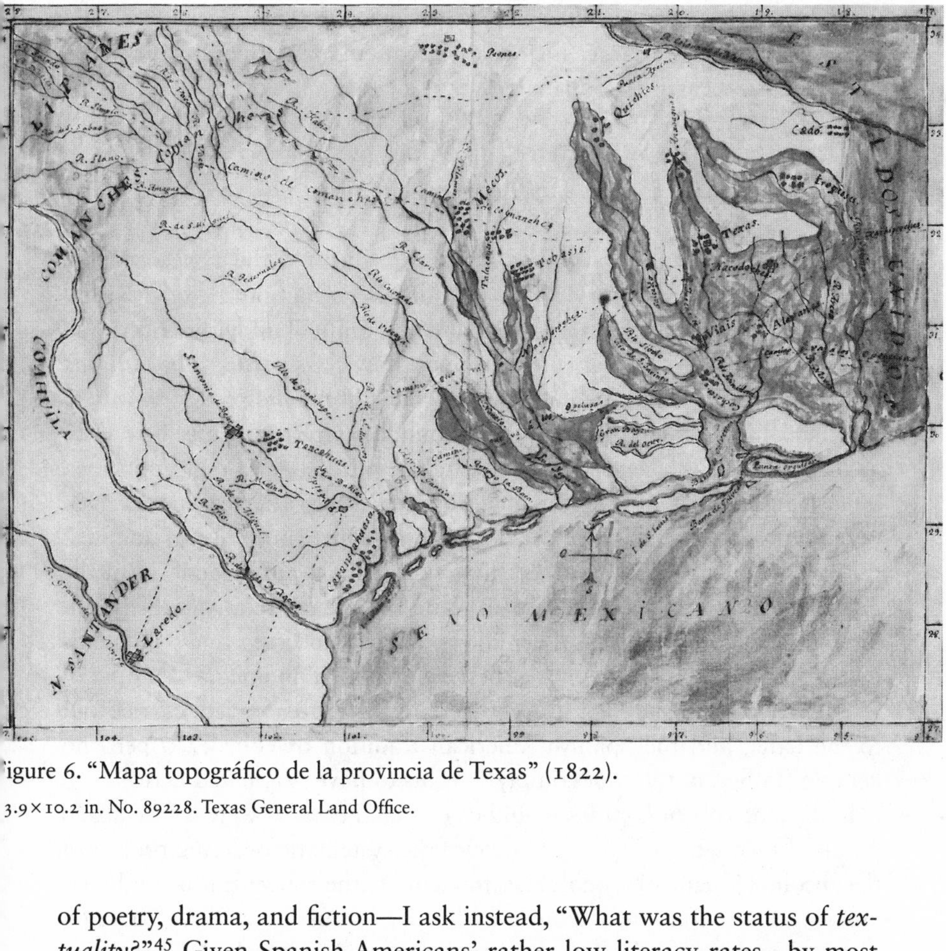

'igure 6. "Mapa topográfico de la provincia de Texas" (1822).
3.9 × 10.2 in. No. 89228. Texas General Land Office.

of poetry, drama, and fiction—I ask instead, "What was the status of *textuality?*"[45] Given Spanish Americans' rather low literacy rates—by most accounts, only around 10 percent during the early nineteenth century—how did individuals and communities relate to ideas and their transmission?[46] Thus, I will be concerned with who produced these texts and who carried them from, say, Nacogdoches to San Antonio, and I will do so, in great part, because even the history of this period is not well known. (Even less known, and unfortunately not fully addressed here, is the history of textuality of the various Native American nations in Texas.)[47] In the end, however, I will not be as concerned with the biographies of these individuals as I will be with the question of why they, collectively, committed their lives to ensuring that these ideas would circulate. However, the point must be made that rarely, if ever, did these ideas produce what their carriers intended. In fact, at times, these ideas produced results that their initial carriers could never have anticipated. Thus, I will strike a balance between narrating a story with its specific actors, texts, and networks of circulation, and narrating a larger history of the discursive formations to which these texts and carriers contributed.

Disenchantment

This history of textuality will take us back through the sixteenth- and seventeenth-century history of the Catholic Reformation in order to understand the elaborate relationship that communities had with writing and sovereignty.[48] As Angel Rama tells us in his now classic study *The Lettered City,* the Spanish-American colonial project had been first and foremost an imagined and discursive one, a project founded on paper, decreed by monarchies, transcribed by scribes, duplicated, triplicated, and quadruplicated by moving quills controlled by men of letters. Only after having received permission and orders on paper did Spanish-American political administrators set out to make them a reality, to put them into practice. But the division, Rama insists, between words and actions existed from the beginning of the colonial project; the millions of letters, decrees, and commands left in dusty archives represent, at best, remnants of an imagined utopia of an orderly colonial project. Rarely were these written orders carried out to the letter, and the Spanish-American tradition of "obedezco pero no cumplo [I obey, but do not comply]" seems to have originated here.[49]

In this, the role of *letrados* would be crucial. *Letrados* were a specialized group of men who worked "to advance the systematic ordering project of the absolute [Spanish] monarchies, to facilitate the concentration and hierarchical differentiation of power, and to carry out the civilizing mission assigned to them."[50] They were a conglomeration of royal administrators, military men, and ecclesiastical missionaries working in consort to secure epistemological and patriarchal authority over the masses. They saw themselves as a special class of men solely capable of manipulating, interpreting, and enacting the written word on behalf of the masses. Imagining themselves as individuals selected by Divine Providence, destined to put God's word into action, they embodied a form of sovereignty emanating downward in hierarchical fashion from the heavens to the monarch's scribes, and filtered further still through the plethora of printed decrees and manuscripts that circulated throughout Spain's vast dominions.[51] The archive became a fetishized object, a source of transcendental authority produced on the highest-quality paper—such that the colonial archives continue to withstand the test of time compared to the brittle, crumbling mess of late nineteenth-century Spanish-American newspapers.[52]

On their own, *letrados* wielded little political authority, but it was their intimate relationship with Spanish-American political figures and the juridical system, their finesse with the written word, and their tight grip on the production of all forms of official documents that allowed them to shape the political world in which they lived. *Letrados* had been crucial to the colonial enterprise from its inception, and their function was "to prescribe an order for the physical world, to construct norms for community life, to limit the development of spontaneous social innovations, and to prevent them from spreading in the body politic."[53] In effect, they helped consolidate the authority of the Hispanic Church and state.

Letrados sent and received a steady stream of written orders from all levels of government. Officials sent clear directives on the precise formatting of documents: all correspondence was numbered consecutively (and if a *letrado* made a mistake, he was immediately reminded of his egregious error); handwriting had to be immaculate or a *letrado* would risk being reprimanded. Documents contained a wide two-inch margin on the left that served as a space to provide commentary by various officials as the document made its course through the Hispanic world of authority, and calendars were made listing the archive's contents. Often, when a good *letrado,* able to keep his records in order, was transferred, authorities would futilely request his return.

Texas, remote though it may have been from Mexico City and Spain, formed a part of this towering library of Babel, a massive collection that exceeded even Jorge Luis Borges's fantasies. The Texas archives were initially stored in what had long been the capital of San Antonio de Béxar, and are now known as the Bexar Archives. Dating from 1717 (the year before the founding of the mission and presidio at San Antonio) through 1836 (the year that Texas declared itself an independent republic), the more than 300,000 pages, of which a mere 4,000 are of printed documents (comprising 172 reels of microfilm), have been described as "one of the great historical treasures of the American continent."[54] But this world of writing would end after 1836 when Texas tore itself apart from Mexico.

During the late eighteenth century but especially, as we will see, in the early nineteenth century, the Hispanic world would slowly become disenchanted. The world would cease to be God's, one that humans merely inhabited, and become one that humans actively, creatively produce. As such, sovereignty, too, would be reconfigured, and made accessible to an increasing number of people. But careful attention to both the form of the text and the ideas contained in them will lead us not toward the well-rehearsed Protestant, Weberian narrative of secularization, a mere Spanish-American imitation that would appear belated in relation to that of the United States and Protestant northern Europe.

If, for example, the explicit Catholic invocations of the Holy Family, conjoined with proclamations of independence and republican forms of government, have baffled critics, suggesting delayed or deviant forms of modernity, the path this book pursues will instead latch onto these seeming inconsistencies. What we find are the ways that "ghosts of a surviving past . . . return from a place out of time or a different temporality to haunt and disturb the historical present, to trouble the stable boundaries between past and present, subject and object, interior and exterior." It is in this sense that the history I offer denies the assumption of a singular, universal unfolding temporality, one defined by the United States and Protestant northern Europe, with which Spanish America would appear to be struggling to "catch up." Rather, this approach "requires a willingness to envision a structure . . . where past and present are not necessarily successive but . . . coexist as uneven temporalities."[55]

This history will lead us toward a typically ignored Hispanic worldview, one that had already been marginalized by the eighteenth century when the Spanish empire began its descent as a global political-economic power.[56] By then, the humanism of the Renaissance, the Protestant Reformation, and the new experimental methods of the scientific revolution had of course already created a fissure in the West, between Protestant northern Europe and a resolutely Catholic Hispanic world. In the course of the sixteenth and seventeenth centuries, the theologians of the Catholic Reformation united against their Protestant counterparts. But the struggle was also internal as they feverishly sought to rein in those dissident, strong humanistic impulses from within the Church. The theologians turned to Scholasticism, the method of close dialectical reasoning based on the exegesis of scripture and the writings of the Church fathers such as Augustine and, especially, Aquinas. In doing so, they revived Scholasticism, and used it against the tenets of Renaissance humanism, Protestant political thought, and the new sciences. This history, however, is not familiar to the nonspecialist. Thus, we will delve into this past in order to better understand why nineteenth-century Spanish-American insurgents referred to these specific intellectual transformations as shaping, in part, their desire to change their world.

What we have here are two divergent paths that modernity has taken. As the sociologist Norbert Lechner writes, speaking for many others, "Modernity is, above all, a process of secularization: the slow transition from *received order* to a *produced order*."[57] The shift from this received, God-given order to one in which humans become agential, able to comprehend nature for itself and create societies of their own free will, is the process

Max Weber famously described as the disenchantment of the world. A disenchanted world, which we now so utterly take for granted, was in fact the result of a long and wrenching process. Though its antecedent, the enchanted world, now seems bewilderingly naïve, nearly absurd in its simplicity, it was the norm for the first millennium and a half of Western history. It was built on the essential notion that humans inhabited a world produced by a higher power; this world was suffused by various forces, good and evil, sentient and not, that influenced the way events unfolded around us and which, therefore, makes it difficult to impossible for us to fully comprehend.

The Hispanic world fully entered this process of modernity—of disenchantment, of understanding oneself as able to shape and transform the world in which one lives—not at the time of the Reformation, as was the case with the more Protestant part of the world, but rather in the eighteenth century.[58] But if the Enlightenment, or the dominant account of it, was part of the long history of modernity in the Protestant Atlantic world stretching back to the Renaissance and Protestant Reformation that produced the modern individual subject with his or her own particular rights, then this concept of the Enlightenment proves less fruitful as a means to accurately describe the Hispanic intellectual world. "Modernity" becomes the concept that is more useful, compared to "Enlightenment," in that it captures the complex nuances and transformations that the Hispanic world was undergoing during the eighteenth century. As the late eminent Franco-Spanish historian François-Xavier Guerra writes, "Parallel to the development of [Bourbon] absolutism in the eighteenth century there also appeared the grand cultural mutation that we designate with the term Enlightenment, *but that we may also designate with the more capacious term of Modernity.*"[59] This is not to suggest that there were no cadres of elites who had started this process much earlier, that it was immediate and uniform, nor that this shift can be specified to the year. Rather, I mean that this process of disenchantment begins to seep into Hispanic society, beyond the elite, at a much broader, systemic level in the latter third of the eighteenth century through the early nineteenth century.

There are at least three causes that contributed to the unfolding of this shift in Spanish America, broadly, and, more specifically in northeastern New Spain. The Bourbon reforms of the mid-eighteenth century undid the Habsburg sociopolitical world that had structured Spanish-American society since its founding. These reforms, in effect, tightened the noose of Spanish Bourbon rule, choking the traditional forms of sovereignty under which Spanish Americans had long lived. Second, while the new modern sciences and philosophy along with their doctrine of rationalism and skepticism had long been studied by Hispanic Scholastics, it is not until the eighteenth century that these new methods begin to have a major impact on Scholastic thought. This development led to a vigorous debate among Hispanic Scholastics, leading one historian to describe the debate as "the last stand of the Schoolmen." The debate ultimately led to the reconfiguration of the university curriculum in the late eighteenth century.[60] This syncretic philosophy, combining Scholasticism with the modern philosophy, may have provided part of the impetus to think skeptically about the world and to imagine new social formations.

Finally, perhaps the obvious defining moment came with Napoleon in 1808. As we have seen, on May 5, 1808, Napoleon deposed the Spanish king, and placed his brother on the Spanish throne. Overnight, the Hispanic world—composed of the Spanish Peninsula, Spanish America, and the Philippines—was transformed forever. Throughout the Hispanic world, Spaniards, Spanish Americans, and Filipinos, including those living in what is today the United States, sought ways to buttress transcendental truth: If an unquestioned Catholicism and monarchical rule had been the basis for organizing society for a millennium, what would replace authority in the absence of the king and, possibly, God?[61] Immediately after Mexican independence in 1821, for example, the first Mexican governor of Texas turned to the printing press as a means to imagine a world where political authority rested in the inhabitants of the new nation-state. Latinos in the rest of the Southwest, too, began to seek out printing presses during this period, as did those in New Mexico and California in 1834.[62] The documents the first Mexican governor of Texas published, including a newspaper prospectus and broadsheets, reveal this desire to reconfigure sovereignty. For those Spanish Americans who lived in the United States, the problems would be compounded by U.S. imperial interests and expansion and, after the U.S.-Mexican War of 1846–1848, with conquest and racialization.

This, then, is modernity as historical trauma: the forced collapse of the Hispanic world brought about externally by a foreign invader followed by a search on the part of the Spanish monarch's subjects for a new source of transcendental political authority. This is why historians now see the initial wars of Spanish-American independence as a global Hispanic civil war: it was a war of competing social imaginaries, fighting to establish themselves as authority in the wake of the deposed king and, by extension, religion.[63] Immediately upon Napoleon's invasion, insurgent Hispanics descended upon Philadelphia and London, searching for support for their causes. They launched into a publishing frenzy, producing abundant visions of sovereignty and notions of the common good they thought should develop in the absence of the king. One may compare this to the experience of Anglo-Americans; the difference is that the Anglo-American trauma of modernity—the process of disenchantment and the creation of secular states—was brought about over more than a century (from the sixteenth-century Protestant Reformation, the mid-seventeenth century English Civil Wars, to the 1688 Glorious Revolution, through the struggles for sovereignty within the British-American colonies) while the Hispanic variant of modernity occurred literally overnight.[64] As we'll see, the consequences were at once devastating—resulting in spiritual-political uncertainty—yet thrilling—producing a world where one could imagine countless possibilities for the organization of life.

Writing and the circulation of ideas become a way of mitigating this transformation. With the declaration of freedom of the press in 1810, the Hispanic public sphere exploded, unleashing imprints on both sides of the Atlantic seeking to bring into being new worlds and radically shifting mentalities, all within a matter of years.[65] To be clear, the public sphere is not a generic analytical category that emerges anywhere. It is the product, as Jürgen Habermas painstakingly documents, of the reconfiguration of the *ancien régime* of Protestant northwestern Europe where mercantile capitalism began to yield to free-trade capitalism and where monarchical rule gave way to more representative forms of government. Here, "the emergent bourgeoisie gradually replaced a public sphere in which the ruler's power was merely represented *before* the people with a sphere in which state authority was publicly monitored through informed and critical discourse *by* the people."[66] Through the public sphere a more visible Spanish-American public emerges, one that had existed before, certainly, but one mediated by print in ways it had never been before. Writing and print, to be sure, are only components of the public sphere, along with the much more immediately felt effects of the market economy and unfolding political affairs. But one first has to *imagine* the world one wants to inhabit and then convince others of its value in order for those ideas to come to fruition. It is in the realm of the public sphere, through writing, publishing, and the circulation of ideas, that sovereignty becomes increasingly divorced from the monarch and displaced onto this amorphous public. Writing, as the literary critic Jean Franco argues, became the privileged site of reasoned debate for early nineteenth-century *letrados* as they sought to reconfigure sovereignty away from royal authorities.[67]

In the decades after Napoleon's earth-altering invasion, the rigorous development of the public would unleash the univocality of sovereignty, as a hierarchical, absolutist form of power descending down from God, the monarch, and his representatives. The official concept of the public had long been aligned with a univocal sovereign. In the aftermath of Napoleon's invasion, however, and the reconfiguration of the concept of the public, the concept of sovereignty, too, underwent transformation. Now, the public would become increasingly multivocal, allowing competing voices to emerge, and would likewise make sovereignty multiple. But this displacement would not necessarily mirror Protestant renderings of the social contract, the coming together of individuals and the giving up of their individual rights in order to inaugurate society. Instead, we can make out how the past seeps into the present. In the midst of what would be seen as a familiar rhetoric of revolution and independence, what reemerged was Catholic Scholastic theories of sovereignty.

Becoming Latino

Nineteenth-century Latino writing, then, operated as part of a larger and largely undifferentiated field of writing, one that included handwritten documents such as manuscripts and epistolary forms of all kinds, as well as revolutionary pamphlets and broadsheets, political journalism, memoirs, poetry, and histories. But this world of writing was firmly situated and part of an oral and visual culture. Each of these, in their vast diversity, sought to sustain a sense of immanence and belonging, of what Jacques Derrida following Martin Heidegger has described as transcendental-metaphysical-ontological authority and security, in the wake of an increasingly disenchanted world. Writing and publishing becomes an increasingly important means for communities to search for new sources of metaphysical certainty. They produce a self-sustaining knowledge that becomes ontologically foundational. Rather than a history of Latino literary culture, our history of textuality—a Derridean grammatology of sorts—does not reduce the plurality of textuality to the fetishized, aestheticized, polished forms of literature (that is, the novel, the short story, the poem, the play), but seeks instead to trace the discursive (trans)formations of textuality.[68]

What emerges from this archive is a yearning for new modes of being, a grasping for language that would allow these individuals to practice new personhoods, to enact new ways of imagining community, even as they used language long available within the Catholic tradition. But these newly, and feverishly, imagined communities would fail to take hold. That is, more often than not the aspirations articulated in Texas during the long nineteenth century did not produce the social cohesion that Spanish-Mexican Tejanos so desired. Instead, their grand efforts resulted in the literal annihilation of these voices through war or racial violence. Indeed, not only did the ideas in these texts fail to congeal, but the world from which they emerged was radically reconstituted in ways that the authors and their communities had never imagined.

Today, however, our own inability to reimagine these possible pasts remains just that: rarely imagined. We have inherited a very limited, juridically defined history of Texas specifically, and of Latino history more broadly. That is, U.S. Latino history is often seen as beginning after some form of U.S. invasion and conquest: from the 1836 annexation of Texas or the 1846–1848 U.S.-Mexican War. But this history, with its fetishization of war and national temporality (namely, the "birth" of the modern U.S.-Mexico borderlands) must be put into perspective. Though the United States would eventually conquer Mexico and annex what is today the Southwest, these epistemic questions would not go away. In the face of this history, the question of U.S. imperialism becomes secondary. Rather than victims writing against U.S. colonialism, we more often than not find elite male voices seeking to establish a metaphysics of presence, a sense of authority in the face of rapid sociopolitical transformations. Though elite, these voices have been ignored and forgotten, and will have to be read and analyzed in order to shed light on discursive realms just as complex, such as those of women, mestizos, Hispanicized Indians, and various Native American nations.

To do justice to these materials, the question we should ask is not "How were Latinos conquered and colonized?" or "How did they abet colonization?" but "How did Latinos become modern?" Or, to be even more precise: What discursive formations gave rise to Latinos? The term "Latino" may suggest some hidden history of *Latinidad* across the ages, buried and needing recovery; however, I use it proleptically. Throughout the nineteenth century, Spanish-Americans living in what is today the United States identified variously as creole, *Americano,* Spanish, Spanish American. The list goes on. What perhaps would be most appropriate for this period is the term "Spanish American," which is in fact the standard term used by historians. But "Spanish American" invokes an affiliation with inchoate Spanish-American nation-states. How do we come to understand the lives and experiences of Hispanic individuals and communities, Spanish and Spanish-American alike, who lived within the United States or what would become the United States? The difficulty is in tracking the shift in discursive formations that allowed individuals to identify in various ways, from Spanish American to Latino, an issue linked with the question of whether nation, race, or both serve as the ontological basis of identity.

What we need is an interplay among these various terms. I use "Spanish American" in discussing historical events and personages. At times, I use

"Hispanic" when I do not want to distinguish between peninsular Spaniards and American Spaniards (as the well-known late eighteenth-century Peruvian Jesuit writer Juan Pablo Viscardo identified himself). In turn, I use "Latino" as a way to conceptualize the experiences of these communities as they sedimented over time, a sedimentation that may also have had its detours and reverse-formations, but that nonetheless contributed to the formation of Latino literary and intellectual culture. "Latino," in this sense, refers less to a subject-position than it does to a literary and intellectual culture that emerges in the interstices between the United States and Spanish America. Because it emerged in that space it does not have clear temporal and spatial boundaries. The modern nation-states of Spanish America did not exist at the beginning of the nineteenth century, and much less so a congealed sense of a modern national consciousness that might constitute an imagined community.[69] However, given the fact that the term "Latino" transcends nationalist identifications (Latinos do not originate from any one specific nation), the term pushes us to think outside the framework of the nation. In contemporary parlance, "Latino" has also been used as a means to emphasize the historical racialization of specific Spanish-American communities within the United States, those with the longest history having Mexican, Puerto Rican, and Cuban origins, followed by Central American and Dominican communities.[70] I would submit that it is precisely the non-national specificity of "Latino" that makes the term particularly useful, given the intractability of the nation as an overpowering concept in organizing fields of knowledge.[71]

A Spiral Historical Narrative

In order to narrate this dispersed genealogical account, the book moves away from a straightforward linear narrative. Although organized chronologically, the chapters themselves move out in a spiral. We begin in Part I with a very specific event—the initial insurgency in the Eastern Interior Provinces—only to then produce a genealogy of that event, peeling back the discursive layers in order to understand the semantics of key operative terms such as *nación* (nation), *pueblo* (the people or town), *patria* (fatherland), and *felicidad* (happiness). At times the narrative will move back in time in order to see how the past seeps into the present, in order to see how the past is redesigned into a more invigorated future as our narrative curves back around and moves forward.

Part I begins with the moment of rupture in 1811 when Spanish Americans in what would become the Texas-Mexico border declared themselves in favor of revolution. It explores the language and intellectual resources they had at their disposal that allowed them to think of abandoning the world they had known for so long. Only weeks before Father Miguel Hidalgo was executed by the royal forces, two creole brothers committed themselves to the revolution. Father José Antonio Gutiérrez de Lara had been educated in Monterrey, and had served as a teacher and priest in the area that is now the south Texas-Mexico border. For several months he preached revolution and dispersed a widely circulated manuscript proclamation where he pronounced the birth of a new nation.

Chapter 1 begins with the background that informed the making of this proclamation and concludes by revealing the declaration's beautifully moving desire to reconfigure previous affective attachments to Spain in order to cathect them to the new nation. While Father José Antonio stayed in the area, his brother, the aforementioned José Bernardo, took as his mission Hidalgo's desire to seek support from the United States. Prior to Hidalgo's death, Bernardo was named ambassador to the United States. Like many revolutionary Spanish Americans of the early nineteenth century, Bernardo made his way to the United States in the hope of gaining support for the independence of Spanish America.

Chapter 2 focuses on Bernardo's travel diary, paying close attention to how he began to think of independence. If his brother worked rhetorically to reconfigure the emotional attachments people had to Spain, Bernardo began to imagine what, exactly, a nation should do. Still, while their work paved the way for bringing in a new world, they had not worked out the particular details of this new nation. Once Bernardo arrived in Washington, D.C., in December 1811, he encountered an emerging, and vibrant, Hispanophone print culture that shaped his political thinking. But this print culture was embedded within a much larger project of reform. Here, our story orbits once again, taking us back to the broad, rich world of Hispanic socioeconomic reform.

Part II focuses on how late eighteenth- through early nineteenth-century Hispanics turned to rethinking the purposes of the nation, initially as a monarchy and, later, as independent republics. Chapter 3 studies the prehistory and flourishing of the print culture Bernardo encountered on the U.S. East Coast. Reform had been a long desired goal, and late eighteenth-century Hispanic *letrados* latched onto the emerging field of political economy in order to secure the happiness of the nation. All this language of reform, however, was disrupted by the cataclysmic Napoleonic invasion of Spain in 1808. With Chapter 4, we return to the world of print culture that Bernardo encountered in Philadelphia. It traces the transformations in thought that led many to abandon the project of reform in favor of revolution. Paying attention to the Philadelphia-based documents, ones that Bernardo would have had access to, I argue that what emerges is political economy as a mode of social contract. That is, the breaking of the social contract and the need for revolution are not based on a language of natural rights or the rights of man, but rather on the rights of the social body.

Upon his return to the Louisiana-Texas border in 1812, Bernardo spent two months bombarding Spanish Texas with revolutionary documents *before* invading with his forces. Spanish royal commanders desperately attempted to prevent the circulation of these documents, which they feared would "seduce" the inhabitants of Texas. Part III focuses on this period, and reveals that the language used by royalists and revolutionaries invoked a profoundly Catholic Scholastic-inspired view of the world even as it reinvigorated it for present purposes. Chapter 5 pays particular attention to how royal commanders described these documents, with a focus on what it meant to describe the literature as seducing the Spanish subjects of Texas. The royalists' language reveals a thoroughly Catholic worldview, one that sees revolution as the cyclical return of the iniquitous Protestant Reformation.

In Chapter 6 we turn to the history of these documents, how they circulated, and the ideas they contained. Bernardo easily defeated the royal forces and declared independence on April 6, 1813. Texas thus became the first province in all of New Spain to do so and to create a republican government based on a written constitution. Historians have long dismissed these documents as mere mimicry of Anglo-American revolutionary thought. Upon closer reading, however, we see another thoroughly Catholic worldview, but one that was far more egalitarian than the royalists' vision. The political philosophy of these revolutionaries demonstrates the intellectual complexity of Catholic Hispanic thought. To fully comprehend this legacy requires that we return to the sixteenth and seventeenth centuries, the period during which Catholic political thought reached its peak, producing theories that would continue to reverberate across the Americas well into the nineteenth century. Having excavated this intellectual past, we come back to the revolutionary literature only to see that these documents reveal a hybridity as well, as they also reflect the then-dominant political thought of the United States. Independence, however, would be short-lived. The royal forces would regroup and, four months later, decimate the revolutionaries and their radical communities in Texas, forcing them to remain a part of New Spain. So brutal was the repression that the Mexican population in Texas decreased by at least 60 percent during these wars for independence.[72] Indeed, the takeover was so swift that some historians have concluded that by the time New Spain declared itself independent as the nation of Mexico in 1821, Texas, the dejected northeastern province of Mexico, merely acquiesced with neither objection nor jubilation.

Independence from Spain in 1821 required that the inhabitants of Texas and the rest of Mexico begin to see themselves as the sole authors of their sociopolitical world. That is, it continued the process of disenchantment begun with the Gutiérrez de Lara brothers, one where sovereignty did not rest in the monarch or his representatives. Political-metaphysical uncertainty required Tejanos to write and, certainly, act in order to create the foundation for their nations. Part IV elaborates these complex intellectual processes that reversed the order of things. Where God and king had long been the rationale for their social world, independence required that they place themselves front and center. Chapter 7 traces the various ideological significations of writing in 1820s and 1830s Texas. It begins by studying the imprints produced on some of the earliest printing presses to enter Texas in 1817 and then, again, in 1823. The chapter examines the relationship between printing and the reconfiguration of sovereignty, from one in which authority descended from God down to the sovereign to one in which people came to see themselves as the authors of the universe they inhabited.

But even while these transformations were occurring, by the 1830s it was clear to Tejanos that newly independent Mexico would continue Spain's own history of ignoring their needs. On the other hand, however, they were simultaneously weary of the rapidly increasing Anglo-American population in Texas, and feared being politically displaced. Refusing to sign a thinly veiled seditious Anglo-American petition to the Mexican government, Tejano representatives came together and collectively authored their own petition to the Mexican government asking for these concerns to be addressed. Chapter 7 concludes by examining their theorization of the social contract and the need to heal the injured "social body." But if the social body had once been a rigid hierarchy with the monarch at its head, the petition inverts the social relation by placing the inhabitants of Texas at the center of the new social contract. In doing so, it offers a nuanced, rhetorical "biography" of this new living entity, one that was born with the colonization of Texas and one that must be cared for by the state. It was nothing short of the entrance of life into history. Yet this moving petition fell on deaf ears in Mexico, and Anglo-Americans in Texas escalated their demands, leading to the 1835–1836 revolution (which many Tejanos supported) and the tearing of Texas from Mexico.

Because of the trauma and instabilities caused by wars (the Spanish-Texan war of independence between 1811 and 1814—itself a part of the Mexican War of Independence, the Texas Revolution of 1835–1836, and the U.S.-Mexican War between 1846 and 1848), a regular press and Spanish-language print culture did not emerge in Texas until the 1850s. After the annexation of Texas to the United States, Mexicans in Texas again used the printing press as a way to intervene in the public sphere. Chapter 8 pays attention to the first regularly published Spanish-language newspapers beginning in 1855 Texas. Journalists used these newspapers to map out the new modern world for Tejanos even as they sought to reconfigure previously existing concepts of publics to suit the needs of the new public sphere. Chapter 9, in turn, turns to the fascinating electoral debate that emerged a year later in 1856, and the way journalists sought to counteract the literal and rhetorical racialization of Tejanos. This is a story, ultimately, of fantastic failure; the struggles of this group of men were all for naught. Their initial efforts at establishing a Spanish-language print culture in the 1850s failed within a few years.

The visions that had been articulated throughout the first part of the nineteenth century would ultimately not come to be. Much like Nariño's immolated pamphlets and desire to bring a new world into being, their efforts, too, have been largely forgotten by history. The book concludes by turning to a unique document unlike anything else studied in this book. Amidst the increasing racialization of Mexicans in 1850s Texas, a young woman kept a journal in which she used writing to create a sense of belonging and connection. Using this journal as a keen reminder of our need to continue our archival research, I reflect on the history of Latina/o writing in order to make the case for a far more expansive, interdisciplinary enterprise that expands literary history beyond the confines of belletristic categories of fiction, poetry, or drama. Finally I ask, what after all may we, in the present, learn from the history of unrealized aspirations? As we will see, in order to understand or, indeed, reimagine our world we must also understand the history of other worlds that were not to be.

I

IMAGINING NEW FUTURES

CHAPTER ONE

Anxiously Desiring the Nation

The Skepticism of Scholasticism

The Beginning of the End

Spanish Texas governor Manuel Salcedo's world began to crumble in April 1812. The news arrived all at once, from multiple sources. Captain Bernardino Montero wasted no time in advising the governor that the insurgent José Bernardo Gutiérrez de Lara had returned from the United States, arriving in Natchitoches, Louisiana, a mere 120 miles due east of the Spanish town of Nacogdoches, on April 28 (see Figure 7).[1] Throughout that summer of 1812, Montero and other royal officers would continuously inform Salcedo of the ease with which Bernardo introduced his revolutionary documents into Spanish Texas, paving the revolutionary path with pamphlets and broadsheets, until finally, in August 1812, the insurgents followed the trail of revolutionary literature and invaded Nacogdoches.[2]

It all seemed terribly predictable to Governor Salcedo. He had spent endless amounts of precious ink and paper across the previous eighteen months writing to his superiors, pleading for aid against the inevitable military attack by insurgents—all to no avail.[3] The leader of Mexican independence, Father Miguel Hidalgo, had attempted to make his way to the United States via Spanish Texas, and easily persuaded many to join his cause. But the revolutionary movement had also caused deep consternation and confusion among the inhabitants of northern New Spain, including Texas. For some, the insurrection was aimed squarely at the Spanish-born administrators and governors who looked upon Spanish Americans with condescension, but it was certainly not directed at the king or the church. For others, it meant hatred of all things Napoleonic and French, and peninsular Spaniards were viewed with great suspicion since many had exhibited strong pro-French sympathy before the Napoleonic invasion. And for even more, revolution meant a complete break with Spain. As a result, specific revolutionary goals shifted depending upon region. Confusing matters even more, news, during this period, was transmitted through official dispatches from the viceroy and his delegates, read aloud in each town's public square, and then circulated by word of mouth, making it difficult—then as now—to discern the precise unfolding of events and shifting alliances during this tumultuous period.

In January 1811, a retired San Antonio de Béxar (hereafter "Béxar") officer by the name of Juan Bautista de las Casas had led a revolt and arrested Governor Salcedo. But the revolt was done in the name of the king. De las Casas falsely accused Salcedo of planning to abandon Texas and leave it in the hands of Hidalgo's hordes; the case, in fact, had been the exact opposite. Salcedo was humiliated, and sent in irons to Monclova, Coahuila, some 300 miles southwest. By December 1811, however, the short-lived, confused revolt had ended, and Salcedo again was at the royalist helm. But Salcedo would never be able to erase the memory of being humiliated in front of the residents of Béxar. Along with reporting on the revolutionary activities, Salcedo also spent the summer of 1812 writing, continuously, to his cantankerous and unfeeling uncle, the commandant general of the Interior Provinces, and ultimately to the viceroy, pleading without success for the restoration of his honor.[4]

And so it was that on August 17, 1812, in Béxar, Salcedo turned to his pen once again. With palpable exhaustion and perhaps resignation, he wrote to the governor of the neighboring province: "Llegó, pues, con este motivo el desagradable día para mi en que se ve enarbolado el omnoue estandarte de la rebelion en esta extremidad del Reino [Alas, with these events, that most dreaded day of mine has finally arrived in which the ominous standard of rebellion has been raised over this the remotest region of the Kingdom]."[5] Salcedo represented the *letrado* class, who, as we have seen, were central to Spanish monarchical rule. But along with using the pen, he also just as effectively used the sword to ensure the consolidation of Spanish sovereignty. Salcedo's correspondence comprises the majority of the Spanish Texas royal archive from this period, and throughout we find traces of his repeated, frustrated attempts to shore up Texas's defenses against the insurgents, and we will see later his own fascinatingly complex views on the unfolding insurgency. Still, for the moment, revolution had arrived: his royal troops in far east Texas were defeated. Despite his desperate attempts to stamp out the flame of rebellion, Salcedo had been able to do little to prevent its spread. When Bernardo had returned from the United States four months earlier, he was armed with pamphlets, broadsheets, and ammunition. And having spent the intervening months circulating his revolutionary literature, he had finally invaded Texas.

How did Bernardo and his brother Father José Antonio become insurgents? What inherited habits, what ruling-class language did they need to abandon in order to cultivate a new, revolutionary self? What intellectual resources did they draw from in understanding their world and the changes they sought? The path to revolution and independence is never straightforward, notwithstanding our teleological desire to construe such a linear narrative, in which "revolution" implies a clear and total rejection of the colonial order of things and a grasping for a new, modern world. As the German intellectual historian Reinhart Koselleck affirms, in the late eighteenth century the word "revolution" begins to assume "a transcendental significance; it becomes a regulative principle of knowledge, as well as of the actions of all those drawn into revolution. From this time on, the revolutionary process, and a consciousness which is both conditioned by it and reciprocally affects it, belong inseparably together."[6]

But how did they come to "belong inseparably together," this revolutionary "process" and "consciousness" itself? Historians have documented well most of the events ("the process") that occurred across the Eastern Interior Provinces, though we certainly know less about what exactly happened in Texas. Here, we turn more to the other diad in Koselleck's argument, that of consciousness, or more accurately, that of discursive formations. Though it will center on the Gutiérrez de Lara brothers, the analysis of this chapter will shift us back and forth from the events unfolding during this period to the larger semantic field from which the brothers' arguments emerged, in order to trace the transformations in thought—at once subtle yet radical—required in order to arrive at revolution. We will uncover, in other words, the epistemology of insurrection.

During the late eighteenth century, the Hispanic world was in the midst of radical intellectual transformation, producing vituperative debates between Aristotelian-based scholars and those embracing the methods of the experimental sciences. Though taking place primarily in the metropolitan centers of the Hispanic world, these changes were felt in New Spain's furthermost northeastern frontier, the four provinces of Nuevo Santander, Texas, Coahuila, and Nuevo León that comprised the administrative unit of the Eastern Interior Provinces. And they had radically altered Antonio's perspective on the world. But these changes were, in fact, signs of a much

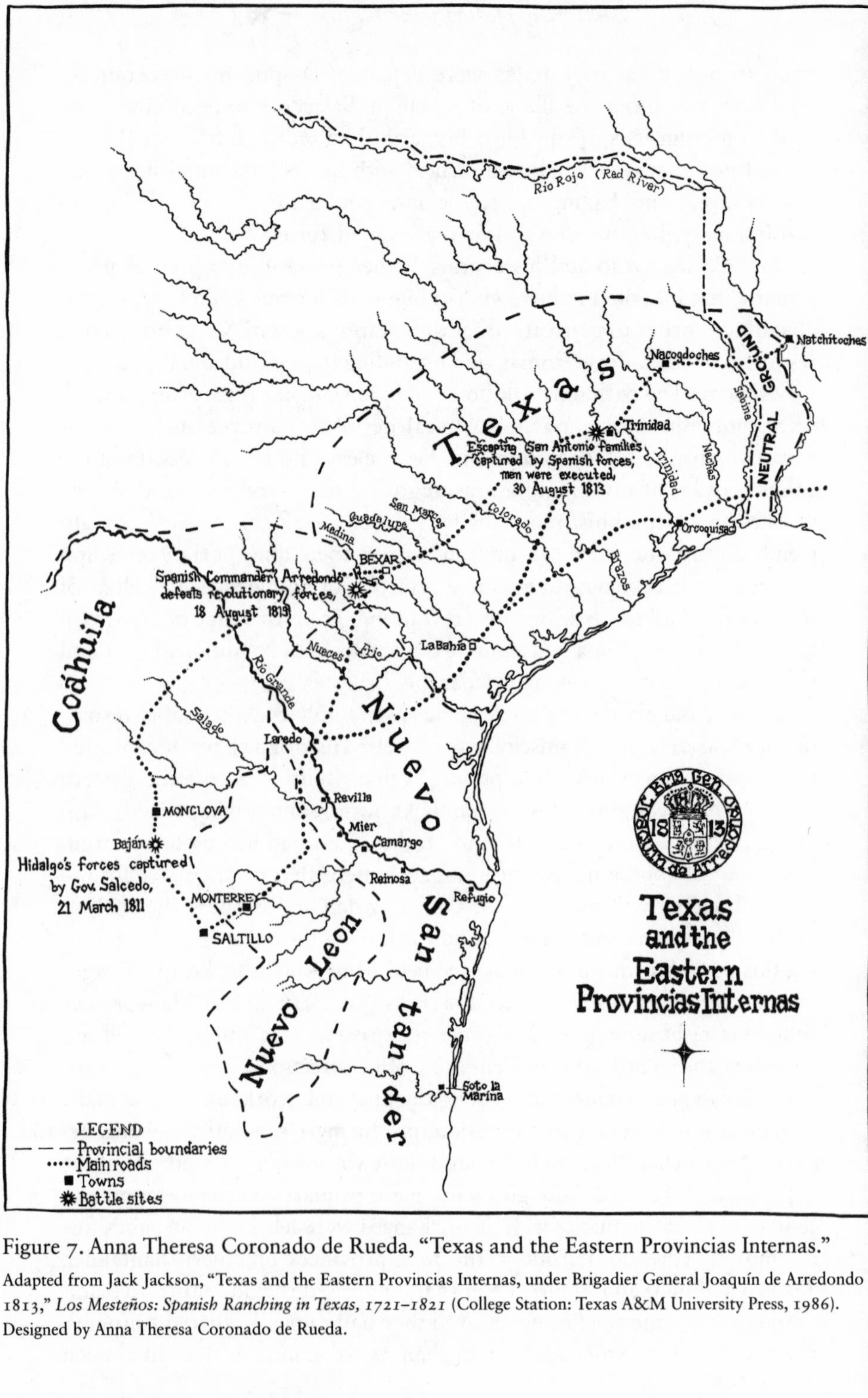

Figure 7. Anna Theresa Coronado de Rueda, "Texas and the Eastern Provincias Internas." Adapted from Jack Jackson, "Texas and the Eastern Provincias Internas, under Brigadier General Joaquín de Arredondo 1813," *Los Mesteños: Spanish Ranching in Texas, 1721–1821* (College Station: Texas A&M University Press, 1986). Designed by Anna Theresa Coronado de Rueda.

larger shift in epistemes, those unconscious structures that make knowledge possible.[7] How did these shifts, in his words, "move his spirits," and cause him to act? In tracing these discursive shifts—from a Scholastic curriculum to what they described as modern philosophy—we witness how Antonio began to think differently about his *patria.*

Upon Hidalgo's arrival in northeastern New Spain, Antonio set out to advocate for a new *nación.* But the shift from *patria* to *nación* was not without its complexities, and Antonio took this project head on. Throughout 1811, he traveled throughout what is today the south Texas–Mexico borderlands preaching and circulating handwritten manuscript versions of his proclamation in favor of the *nación* (see Appendix 1 for a translation). The proclamation beautifully reveals the intricate, torturous shifts of loyalty in this emergent nationalism. In Chapter 2, we will witness how Bernardo began to imagine the political rationale for this emergent nation. Let us start at the beginning of the end.

Provincial Education

José Antonio Apolinario Gutiérrez de Lara was born in Revilla, Nuevo Santander on June 13, 1770; his younger brother, José Bernardo Maximiliano, was born some eight months before the outbreak of the American Revolutionary War, on August 20, 1774. They had a younger brother by the name of Enrique and a younger sister whose name has been lost in the historical record. Originally from Nuevo León, the Gutiérrez de Laras had been one of the initial families who, in 1748, helped establish the Nuevo Santander colony.[8]

The colony was established by the Spanish empresario José de Escandón, and encompassed what is today portions of south Texas and the Mexican states of Tamaulipas and Veracruz along the Gulf Coast. Like the establishment of other colonial outposts in Texas, such as San Antonio de Béxar in 1718, Nuevo Santander was intended to continue the religious mission of proselytizing Native Americans and to fend off France's efforts to extend its dominion west from Louisiana. Significantly, Nuevo Santander was also unique from other Spanish colonization projects. It was established just as the Spanish throne was implementing the Enlightenment-inspired Bourbon reforms in the mid-eighteenth century that concentrated political authority in the hands of peninsular Spaniards; thus, the throne granted the Spaniard, Escandón, and other landed elites complete political, social, and economic control over the colonists. Seeking to ensure the success of the colony, Escandón established an austere military rule in alliance with the wealthy elite. Authority was so heavy-handed that permission was needed for even the most minor of activities. If a family sought to move, even within a town, they had to secure permission from political authorities or risk imprisonment.[9]

Figure 8. Matthew Carey, "Mexico or New Spain" (1814).
17.2 × 19.8 in. No. 79313. Texas General Land Office.

The Gutiérrez de Laras became increasingly prosperous and influential; the patriarch, Santiago Gutiérrez de Lara, for example, expanded his landholdings throughout the 1780s, and he served as one of the Revilla aldermen.[10] But nothing like the rich central Mexican silver mines that made the Spanish empire wealthy was found in Nuevo Santander. Instead, ranching and salt mines dominated the local economy. What is more, the Bourbon reforms, with their focus on shifting power solely to European-born Spaniards, only served to alienate the American-born creole elite. The absence of pecuniary wealth and the absolutist control exercised by Escandón and his allies delayed the development of social institutions.[11]

Nuevo Santander's social conditions, which grew more dire by the decade—much like the rest of the Eastern Interior Provinces of Texas, Coahuila, and Nuevo León—were enough to sway many of its settlers to support insurrection.[12] But, as noted above, insurrection did not always mean total upheaval: many wanted significant reform within the framework of monarchical rule, others sought to completely remake the social fabric, while most, perhaps, equivocated between both. Still, as Father Hidalgo's forces made their way toward Texas in early 1811, everywhere, it appeared, the inhabitants and soldiers of the Eastern Interior Provinces were joining the revolutionary wave. It was then that Antonio started corresponding with Hidalgo's men. He advocated for their support in his rural parish, and eagerly wrote a letter of introduction for his younger brother Bernardo. Antonio and Bernardo would work in tandem, spending the rest of their lives struggling to create a better world for themselves and those they referred to as their fellow "Americanos."[13]

Shortly after Antonio's first letter, Bernardo met with the leaders of the insurgency, and delivered another letter to them in which Antonio committed what he had at his disposal for the insurrection. The list included

> una carabina, una escopeta, una pistola, un gran fusil, cinco libras de pólvora, cuatro planchas de plomo, trescientos pesos que había logrado reunir del producto de una escuelita de niños que personalmente dirigía él, juntamente con las limosnas de las misas diarias, doscientos pesos en libros y a medio hacer una casa.
>
> [a rifle, shotgun, pistol, large rifle, five pounds of gunpowder, four sheets of lead, three hundred pesos he had collected through the boys' school he personally directed, together with the alms of the daily masses, two hundred pesos in books, and a half-built house.][14]

The social conditions were clearly enough to force the settlers' hands, and the great earnestness of Antonio's scrappy list of aid testifies to their dedication.

It is not clear how much education Bernardo received, but his activities, writings, and, later, foundational role as legislator and governor reveal the mind of one well read in politics. Given his father's role as an alderman, Bernardo certainly learned a significant amount about politics from him.[15] We do know that his older brother received extensive education.

Commentators have long noted, often with a sense of derision, the relative paucity of any intellectual community in the Eastern Interior Provinces. As historians have long told the story, the residents of the provinces, especially Texas, epitomized frontier stereotypes: backward, lazy, iniquitous; they could hardly be seen as engaging in a life of the mind, much less contribute to one. The Franciscan friar, Juan Agustín Morfí, may have been one of the earliest to inscribe the myth of intellectual backwardness in his *The History of Texas* (1782–1783), where he describes the residents of San Antonio de Béxar as "indolent and given to vice, and do not deserve the blessings of the land."[16] This complaint would be made in various versions by observers in the decades to come, thickening over time until it congealed into an all too familiar racial discourse that equated Mexicans with laziness.

Historians revised this narrative in the latter twentieth century.[17] We now know that at least two structural causes made it difficult to develop the frontier: the creoles' inability to conquer and defeat local Native American nations and Spain's mercantilist policy that forbade economic trade between the northern provinces and their much closer French, British, and U.S. neighbors in Louisiana and abroad. Relatively little is known about education, manuscript and print culture, or the history of the book along the frontier. The lack of research on these topics, rather than the lack of any proof, has led to the non sequitur that no intellectual culture existed.

Educational institutions may have been sparse, indeed rare; yet ideas and books did enter this sphere. Historians have long noted that the Franciscan convent of Monterrey, Nuevo León, was the most important intellectual center for the Eastern Interior Provinces, including Texas. The children of elite families, and many of those who would take a lead in the revolution, including Antonio, were educated there. While a number of schools had come and gone throughout the early eighteenth century, the mid-eighteenth-century discovery of mineral wealth in Nuevo León triggered an economic boom and the development of the arts, architecture, and education. But the school grew slowly. It was not until 1768 that the foundations of a seminary were established. In 1767 Leonor Gómez de Castro bequeathed $500 to finish construction of the parish church, $2,000 for the convent, and the staggering amount, for that period, of

$6,000 to the establishment of a chaplaincy in order to support a professorship in grammar. After her death in 1768, the professorship in grammar was established. Antonio, born in 1770, would have witnessed and benefitted from all this expansion in the arts and education. By 1787 Friar Cristóbal Bellido y Fajardo, the new guardian of the convent, commissioner of the mission, and synodal examiner, would teach rhetoric and philosophy.[18]

As the historian Israel Cavazos Garza notes, "It is in this school—that managed to stay open for twenty-five years until the founding of the present Seminary—that Servando Teresa de Mier, Miguel Ramos Arizpe, Bernardino Cantú, among others, initiated their studies, men who shone brightly during the beginning of Mexican independence," and several of these figures will reappear in our narrative here.[19] Antonio received degrees in canon and civil law from the seminary and became a professor of philosophy there as well.[20]

As it turns out, the Franciscan school had stirred in Antonio the desire to transform the world he inhabited. Years later, explaining his participation in the rebellion to his religious superiors, he wrote: "No, los que me han perseguido no saben el espíritu que me anima, como lo supo el M. I. y V. Sr. Dean y Cabildo, ya confiándome el desempeño del primer curso de Filosofía Moderna, ya honrándome con sus sabios argumentos y distinguida asistencia [No, those who have persecuted me do not know the spirit that moves me, the way the Most Venerable and Illustrious Sir Dean of the Collegiate Chapter knew. He who had entrusted me with teaching the first course in Modern Philosophy, honoring me with his wise arguments and distinguished presence]."[21]

Antonio was referring to Friar Bellido who, as mentioned above, taught the first modern philosophy course beginning in 1787. Antonio enrolled in the school precisely as the chair in grammar was established, and taught the philosophy course under the guidance of Bellido. Bellido, a Franciscan, was originally from Morón, in southern Spain, located on the outskirts of Seville. He took the habit in Seville and studied philosophy and theology, eventually leaving for New Spain to work in the missions.[22] It is precisely during this period of Bellido's education, in 1767, when the Jesuits were expelled from all of Spain's territories, that a massive "general housecleaning of the institutions of higher learning" began.[23]

As part of the Bourbon reforms' attempt to convert the Americas into colonies, the monarchy not only summarily removed all Spanish Americans from positions of power, but it also expelled anyone questioning even in part the concept of divine rule, a theory put forward by Protestant countries during the Reformation and which Spanish Scholastic theologians, with the support of the Church and Spanish monarchy, vehemently denounced at the time. But now the Bourbon monarch embraced the concept in the hope of wresting power from the Church, and expelled the Jesuits from his territories, largely because they had been the intellectual opponents of divine right and because—as an international religious order—they were seen as having no loyalty to Spain. The Bourbon monarch sought to crush them.

The Jesuits had controlled higher education in the Hispanic world, making them responsible for the education of Spanish Americans. As we will see, the Bourbon monarch was terrified of their theories, especially those of Francisco Suárez. Thus the Bourbon monarch in 1767 expelled the entire order from the Hispanic world. In the Americas, some 2,600 Jesuits, the vast majority American born, were given only a few days to pack their belongings before they were exiled forever to Italy, leaving behind empty school halls and cloisters. With their removal, the monarch's reformers slowly began to dismantle Scholasticism; they forbade the teaching of classic Scholastic political philosophy, especially Suárez and his critique of divine right, and ordered the universities to teach the modern sciences, including physics, mathematics, and the law of nature and nations, along with modern philosophy.[24]

The Scholastic Episteme

The sixteenth- and seventeenth-century Protestant and Catholic Reformations had split the West in half. This history, in turn, is inseparable from Spain's conquest and colonization of America. Spain had conquered the imperial Aztec civilization, headquartered in modern-day Mexico City, in 1521. A mere four years earlier, Martin Luther had nailed his *Ninety-Five Theses* to the church door, inaugurating what would become the Protestant Reformation. In turn, the Catholic Church initiated its own official Reformation with the convening of the Council of Trent in 1545, furthered by eighteen years of contentious meetings that produced a reformed vision of the Catholic Church. The council condemned Protestant heresies, even while seeking to address long-standing criticisms of the church. As the church historian John O'Malley has noted, the Reformation was a highly complex movement, beginning as an internal debate within the Catholic Church, only to fracture into Protestant and Catholic traditions, even while each had their own internal, often diverging ideological camps. Thus, even as we attempt to schematize the difference between Catholic and Protestant intellectual traditions, ultimately in order to better situate the early nineteenth century, we should be keenly aware that beneath these descriptions are worlds of differences.[25]

The Catholic Reformation offered a strident, though certainly revised, political defense of its worldview against that of Protestant Reformers. Among other things, the council's rulings addressed the serious concerns related to superstition and the "sensual appeal" associated with the veneration of sacred images. In doing so, however, they also reaffirmed the importance of visuality, orality, and community as a means of accessing the divine. Protestant Reformers had insisted that transcendental meaning or a sense of eternal salvation could only be achieved via a direct, unmediated relationship between the individual and biblical scripture. All other previous forms of metaphysical mediation—from relics, images, to festivals, and the "pantheon" of saints, angels, and the Virgin Mary—were significantly reduced, if not eliminated, in the Protestant attempt to achieve transcendental meaning. But the council vehemently criticized the Protestant emphasis on not only reading scripture but also translating it into the vernacular, fearing the masses would be overwhelmed by the power of the divine, at best, or misinterpret it, at worst. Instead, it placed emphasis on hierarchy, on the need for Church authorities to properly convey doctrine to the masses, and insisted instead that transcendental meaning, immanence, or salvation could be achieved by collectively listening to official doctrine and interpretations of scripture, contemplating religious art (such as sculpture and stained-glass paintings in churches), and participating in communal religious processions.[26]

In developing its intellectual armament, the Council of Trent returned to its foundational theologian, St. Thomas Aquinas (1225–1274), and embraced his school of thought, referred to as Thomism. Indeed, during the eighteen-year long council, Aquinas's magnum opus *Summa Theologica* was placed next to the Bible on the altar. Over that period, the Spanish Scholastics emerged as the intellectual avant-garde, and over the course of the sixteenth and seventeenth centuries they would produce some of the most innovative philosophy in Europe, developing, for example, the first sustained philosophical debate on what may anachronistically be termed human rights or laying the foundation for international law. Based primarily at the Spanish University of Salamanca, the premiere European university of the time, these theologians reformulated Aquinas's Aristotelian thought. This revival, termed in retrospect "Late Scholasticism," would become the pillar of the Catholic Church. Indeed, Aquinas's *Summa* remains, to this day, the basis of the Catholic vision of the cosmos.[27]

Scholasticism had been the dominant mode of intellectual inquiry in medieval Europe. But Aquinas radically transformed it in the thirteenth century. Aristotle's work, along with much of Greek literature, had been lost to medieval Europe, but Muslim scholars from Andalusia introduced Aristotle to Europe during this period. It was then that Aquinas undertook the great effort to integrate Aristotelian philosophy with Christian theology.[28] Written between 1265 and 1274, *Summa* offered a carefully argued interpretation of the cosmos, and became the foundation of natural law, the philosophical tradition that argued that there were universal truths that applied to everyone. The *Summa* "will tell you 'all you need to know,' " writes O'Malley. "It will neither omit anything nor dodge anything that is pertinent. . . . [It is] comprehensive, yes, but also coherent. All the parts fit. . . . The result is a system, an Aristotelian 'science,' an intellectually satisfying whole."[29]

To the Scholastics, the cosmos was a perfectly balanced order produced by God, where every being and object had its precise place in the world. In this world, the system of signs was ternary, writes Foucault, where meaning was produced by identifying resemblances between entities, such that A is to B as B is to C as C is to D, ad infinitum. There was, first, *logos,* God's word, directly unknowable, but its traces left everywhere in the sensual world around us. These traces became the second level of signs: the order of flora and fauna, for example, or the celestial movements, and, most immediately, the Christian canon where divine beings had been graced by God and were given an approximate knowledge of God's law which had been transliterated in scripture and passed on through the Church. Finally, there was Scholastic commentary or knowledge production, which sought to trace the vastly complex web of meaning that unified all these levels, from the smallest of beings to the many levels of angels, all in one unending string.[30] In this world, God had produced the cosmos, and the entirety of it was created in an intricately balanced, hierarchical fashion. And Aquinas's *Summa* had offered a movingly convincing, complete account of this world.[31]

A similarly moving account is that of the Franciscan historian from New Spain, Diego Valadés, who in 1579 developed the concept of the great chain of being as a way to describe God's world as one of resemblances, where each level served as a metaphor or translation of God's word.[32] Human language, then, was coextensive with (but not identical to) the language of God as represented in the universe: human words were immutably fixed to things through conjuncture, the idea that the divine had cemented together words and things. What emerged was a system of resemblances uniting one level of meaning to another into an infinite string of meaning.[33] The world was understood as a carefully woven tapestry, where everything and everyone had their station.

gure 9. Diego Valadés, "The Great Chain of Being."

his *Rhetorica Christiana* (Perugia, Italy: Petrutius, 1579).

The Council of Trent bolstered this worldview. According to this epistemological framework, knowledge was acquired and transmitted to the vast majority of people through the sensorial, communal world. Knowledge was organized by resemblances, the divine existed in the world and not only in script, and God's language was imprinted everywhere. It was one's duty to interpret the world, and to construct meaning by identifying similarities between objects: "There is no difference between marks and words in the sense that there is between observation and accepted authority, or between verifiable fact and tradition. The process is everywhere the same: that of the sign and its likeness, and this is why nature and the word can intertwine with one another to infinity, forming, for those who can read it, one vast single text."[34]

Scholasticism sought, through deduction, to understand how the world functioned in perfect harmony. Everything, everywhere contained God's signature embedded within it, and the Scholastics' task was to decipher the web of meaning surrounding us. Knowledge was produced by "commenting" on God's language as it had been imprinted in the world. It involved a hermeneutics of similitudes, of searching for allegorical relations between entities that could reveal God's fixed pattern. In this episteme, interpretations of the world are adjusted so that they fit canonical Catholic teachings, rather than the other way around. The Catholic canon—both scripture and knowledge passed on through the Church—becomes the blueprint for interpreting God's world precisely because it was a transliteration of God's law. The Church becomes the arbiter of *logos*. As a result, Scholasticism does not require innovation but interpretation, an ability to analyze the world that can help us search for God's signature. The Scholastic world "bristles with written signs; every page is seen to be filled with strange figures that intertwine and in some places repeat themselves. All that remains is to decipher them."[35]

In this sense, the post-Reformation world of Scholasticism—not necessarily the Scholastics themselves, but the Catholic social world in which they lived—was an enchanted one. An enchanted world is one inhabited not only by humans but also by spirits and unknown forces, good and evil. But, as the philosopher Charles Taylor emphasizes, this explanation "understates the strangeness of the enchanted world" in that we may think of spirits as almost human-like in their agency. Thus, for example, in the "cult of the saints, we can see how the forces were not all agents, subjectivities, who could decide to confer a favour. . . . [Rather,] power also resided in things," such as relics, temples, candles, and other objects. Proximity to the divine involves having a "porous" self, where meaning emerges not within autonomous individuals but relationally with the visible and invisible world around us; where spiritual transcendence could at times be experienced by a community coming together during trying times.[36] "In fact," continues Taylor,

> in the enchanted world, the line between personal agency and impersonal force was not at all clearly drawn. . . . [T]he enchanted world, in contrast to our universe of buffered selves and 'minds,' shows a perplexing absence of certain boundaries which seem to us essential. So in the pre-modern world, meanings are not only in minds, but can reside in things, or in various kinds of extra-human but intra-cosmic subjects. . . . Thus in the enchanted world, charged things can impose meanings, and bring about physical outcomes proportionate to their meanings.[37]

Thus, we should take the intransigent insurgent Fray Servando Teresa de Mier at his word when, in 1794, he preached to a Mexican congregation that the Gospel had arrived in the Americas prior to the Spaniards. Mier blasphemed, claiming that Thomas the Apostle had spread the Gospel to the Americas five years after Christ's death. According to Mier, Thomas arrived in the guise of the Aztec god Quetzalcoatl, and converted Native Americans to Christianity. Such sacrilegious arguments completely undermined the very basis of the Spanish rationale for the conquest and colonization of the Americas: to convert Native Americans to Christianity. In doing so, Mier gave voice to an emerging creole American consciousness, producing new narratives of origin that could provide a sense of belonging for Spanish Americans, but he did so using an adamantly Catholic epistemological worldview. This worldview, along with that of Spanish Texans, was one where God, the Holy Family, the apostles, saints, spirits, and demons coexisted with humans. In order to understand this Spanish-American Catholic modernity, we must undo teleologies of the modern.[38]

In this world, divine intervention was an active force; here, good and evil forces cohabited with and often *through* humans. In this pre-Cartesian world, there was no mind-body split, no *cogito ergo sum,* because meaning emerges from everywhere. "Once meanings are not exclusively in the mind, once we can fall under the spell, enter the zone of power of exogenous meaning," continues Taylor in his characterization of this world, "then we think of this meaning as including us, or perhaps penetrating us. We are in as it were a kind of space defined by this influence. The meaning can no longer be placed simply within; but nor can it be located exclusively without. Rather it is in a kind of interspace which straddles what for us is a clear boundary."[39] The point to be taken here is that the genealogy of individualism, of thinking of agency as embodied solely in human beings, follows a different path in the Catholic Hispanic world.[40] We will encounter later, for example, Spanish royalists simply unable to countenance the notion that their subjects could have their own agency.

But just as the Catholic Scholastic world became reinvigorated, a new threat emerged. This was the emerging *via moderna,* with its roots in the Scholastic nominalism of the thirteenth century, that emphasized logic and experience over speculation and abstraction, and which influenced the modern philosophy associated with humanism, the scientific revolution, and the political thought of the Protestant Reformation. In the sixteenth and seventeenth centuries, Galileo Galilei, Francis Bacon, René Descartes, and Isaac Newton inaugurated the new natural and empirical sciences. Rather than view the world as a perfect whole, these modern scholars began to work inductively, arriving at theories that eschewed abstract concepts of inanimate agential objects in favor of carefully observed experiments. Their radically new methods of skepticism and rationalism penetrated European universities, slowly though undeniably upsetting Aristotelian-based Scholastic interpretations of the world. Where before there was a received order, one ordained by God, fixed and unchanging, the new sciences revealed a natural world with its own laws at odds with Scholastic doctrine. Skepticism and rationalism, the hallmarks of the new sciences and modern philosophy began to seep deeply into Europe. It was during this period that words began to separate from things, the links in the great chain of being burst apart, and the written word no longer belonged in an infinite web of meaning but began to open up its signification into a universe of signs.[41]

Language came to be seen as something that could be manipulated, with a less anchored, less stable relationship between signifier and signified. In effect, meaning-making or the system of signs had radically transformed from a ternary to a binary system. Conjuncture, the idea that the divine had put together words and things and, thus, that resemblances between proximate entities could be discerned, no longer held its hegemony. The act of representing, of humans as the authors of knowledge as opposed to knowledge originating only from established Church doctrine, was now seen as an entirely human construct shaped by reason. The divine was decentered, and humans came to be seen as active agents, empowered to reconfigure the order of things. Now, "language occupied a fundamental situation in relation to all knowledge: it was only by the medium of language that things of the world could be known. Not because it was a part of the world [as it had been before], but because it was the first sketch of an order in representations of the world; because it was the initial, inevitable way of representing representations."[42]

Over the course of the sixteenth and seventeenth centuries, language no longer came to be seen as genuflecting to God; rather, it was a first order of representations upon which humans could objectively comprehend the world. For the first time, human subjects saw themselves as capable of understanding nature's system for itself through the use of science. The great metaphor is that of the table of life: where everything was laid out before our very own eyes, everything was knowable, waiting for the objectivity of our observations to finally produce a narrative of their order, very much as it had been for Carl Linnaeus. Instead of God, the observing human eye came to see itself as able to know everything; and soon, the eye would turn in on itself, yearning to search for the knowledge of its origin, to achieve transcendence through language. Life, as Foucault describes it, entered history.[43] It was the transformation from sovereign power to biopower, as "the right of the social body to ensure, maintain, or develop its life."[44]

But the world Foucault was describing was not the Catholic Hispanic world. It was instead that of northern and, increasingly Protestant, Europe. These were the centuries that also saw the rise of the modern state. Coextensive with the rise of the state, Machiavellianism slowly supplanted traditional Western European Christian virtues, at the same time as Christianity's hegemony splintered into various sects after the Reformation. It was also the period during which Cartesian skepticism and rationalism displaced received wisdom. That is, the world began to shift from a *received order* to a *produced order*, from a world defined by God to a world that is knowable and defined by humans.[45] Yet, all of these sources have drawn upon primarily Protestant northern European sources.

Perhaps there, in the Protestant world, Foucault's claim that the Scholastic episteme of resemblance shifted in the seventeenth century may hold true. There, language had become a binary system of signs, cut adrift from God's chain of signification. Metaphysical presence opened up into language and the fetishized written word. Salvation or transcendental meaning could now be arrived at by internalizing language, by engaging in a hermeneutic of scripture. One of the effects of the Protestant Reformation was its insistence in the silent, solitary reading of texts. This history of reading, too, served to heighten the sense of individuality as the subject reading the text attempted to arrive at meaning introspectively, through the silent acquisition of knowledge. "People were seeking a more personal religious life," writes Taylor. They "wanted a new kind of prayer, wanted to read and meditate the Bible themselves."[46]

Not so across the Hispanic world, however, where Catholicism reigned supreme, where, for example, teaching often involved *listening* to a teacher and memorization rather than following along with a primer.[47] Rather than bending to and accommodating the new sciences, the Catholic Reformation embraced this enchanted worldview even more, and insisted, in the tradition of Aquinas, on deriving metaphysical meaning not from human innovation but from the sensual world.[48] A sense of spiritual transcendence or what Jacques Derrida describes as a metaphysics of presence could be experienced by resting metaphysically secure knowing that one was a part of this infinite web of meaning.

This is not to say that the modern philosophy of the new sciences and humanism did not penetrate Spain, even as early as the sixteenth century. Certainly, they did, as Olga Victoria Quiroz-Martínez and, more recently, Jeremy Robbins have revealed.[49] Still, if and when they did circulate, these ideas were confined to the elite few, and for those who embraced them, they were forced to incorporate the new philosophy into Aristotelian methods, producing an eclectic philosophy that was never fully able to escape its Scholastic grip. The case was rather different in the Americas, especially New Spain, where Scholasticism proved itself much more resilient against any form of eclecticism.[50] This is to say that, at a much broader level, the new modern way of thinking had yet to permeate the social imaginary. Thus, just as the Renaissance was beginning to embrace humanism, science, and rational skepticism—in other words, to embrace intellectual exploration and minimize the senses for making truth claims—the Hispanic world tenaciously held onto sensuality, mysticism, and the inexplicable as a poetic, spiritual source of knowledge even as it slowly incorporated some of these new ideas. In other words, the standard historical narrative, of Scholasticism giving way to humanism, beginning with the Renaissance's dawn in the fifteenth century—complicated and nuanced though it may be—is a narrative more fitting for Protestant northern Europe. It certainly is not one that describes Spain or Spanish America.

Unlike universities in more Protestant regions of Europe, Hispanic universities in Spain and the Americas not only held fast to Scholasticism but saw it experience a robust resurgence. They resisted the new scientific methods, and would continue doing so until the late eighteenth century. Instead of capitulating to science, it absorbed it: "While the [Spanish] Peninsula participated in the general movement of scientific research as did other countries, . . . it tried successfully to assimilate the revolutionary spirit which the sciences evoked all over Europe, but it did not develop a natural system in the sense of Bacon, Descartes, Newton, and other principal thinkers of the century, or in political science, the absolutism of

Hobbes. For such was the strength of Late Scholasticism that it was able to absorb but it would not be absorbed."[51] Thus, while some Hispanic elites, particularly those living in urban areas, may have read the new scientists and philosophers, the Scholastic episteme continued to thrive. Indeed, as historians have noted, eighteenth-century Spanish America was more Scholastic than Spain, and this set of beliefs would dominate well into the early nineteenth century.[52] Even the first vice president of the Texas Republic, Lorenzo de Zavala, noted that it was only in the early nineteenth century, in his native Mérida, Yucatán, that Scholasticism began to be replaced with modern philosophy and the sciences: "modern philosophy, experimental physics, Newton's luminous principles, Condillac's logic, Loke's [*sic*] doctrines, penetrated even the halls of the cloisters and colleges."[53] Yet, though Scholasticism would dominate, it, too, underwent significant transformations.

The lines were far from rigid. Scholastics found ways to incorporate the new sciences just as the new humanists found ways to hold onto their "irrational" faith. The ambiguities here, the murky ways that faith and modern reason mixed with one another, are one of the many elements of our story that have been minimized by generations of scholarship. As we have long been taught, it was modern philosophy and the new sciences, founded on rationalism and skepticism as developed in the sixteenth and seventeenth centuries by Bacon, Descartes, and Newton, that cultivated a much broader, systemic skepticism toward not only claims about the natural world but about the social world as well.[54] Rather than assuming that canonical teachings could explain all natural phenomena, the emergent scientific method, fueled by Cartesian doubt, argued that natural phenomenon should be explained instead through empirical observation. But scientific skepticism crept into the realms of philosophy and theology as well, especially with the Protestant and Catholic Reformations. The birth of modern science and philosophy can be traced to these radical, heretical intellectual transformations, which slowly yet steadily called into question Catholic authority.[55] And yet, though this notion of scientific development is applicable in the Protestant world, and less so in the Catholic, this is not to say that the inverse holds true for the Catholic world, that the skepticism of the sciences or the rationalism of humanism never influenced that world. Instead, we must delve into the murkiness in order to appreciate the Catholic world, where Scholasticism reigned strong, but where the *via moderna* gained an unsteady foothold.[56]

The Catholic web of meaning began to shred in the eighteenth century. Hispanic Scholastics became increasingly vocal in their desire to engage with the new methods. Repercussions were severe; scholars were dismissed from universities, others were excommunicated, and not a few were unofficially banished from the Americas by being called to serve the monarch in Europe, as was the case with the recalcitrant Mexican prodigy Antonio López Portillo, rector of the national university in Mexico City; the peninsular archbishop of New Spain (what would become Mexico) thought "it was not advisable that such an intellectual of such stature live in Mexico."[57] But the hunger only grew.

In addition, the Bourbon reforms that began at midcentury were built on a great irony: just as they sought to create an absolutist state, they sought to create more room for the new scientific methods. By the latter part of the century, as mentioned earlier, the Bourbons were able to transform the university curriculum. Modern science and philosophy became mandatory fields of study not only for the elite few but also for all students enrolled in universities. The changes, however, were limited primarily to the sciences. When political philosophy was taught, the Bourbon reformers made sure to excise all references to the long Scholastic tradition, embodied in the work of Suárez, of critiques of divine right and theories of sovereignty as resting in the people. As for modern political philosophers, if they were included, their texts were amended, "with corrections according to the doctrine of the Catholics."[58] In this, as the intellectual historian John Tate Lanning notes, "There was always . . . a sharp contrast between natural and divine authority."[59]

Skepticism in the Eastern Interior Provinces of New Spain

After banishing the Jesuits, and their significant influence, from all Hispanic territory in 1767, the Bourbon administrators ordered universities to replace old Scholastic philosophical texts with *Institutiones philosophicae* (1757–1759), a six-volume work in Latin by the French Franciscan monk François Jacquier. *Institutiones* is a hybrid work, combining Scholasticism and the methods of scientific inquiry. While the first two volumes exuded Scholasticism, the last four were dedicated to arithmetic, algebra, geometry, physics, astronomy, geography, and moral philosophy.[60] Jacquier's text modified and reconfigured the modern philosophy to suit his worldview; it facilitated the dissemination of a Catholicized version of rationalist philosophy, including Bacon, Descartes, Locke, and others.[61] By the late eighteenth century Jacquier's *Institutiones* had become the standard university text for modern philosophy throughout the Hispanic world, though not without struggle.[62] So popular did the work become that it

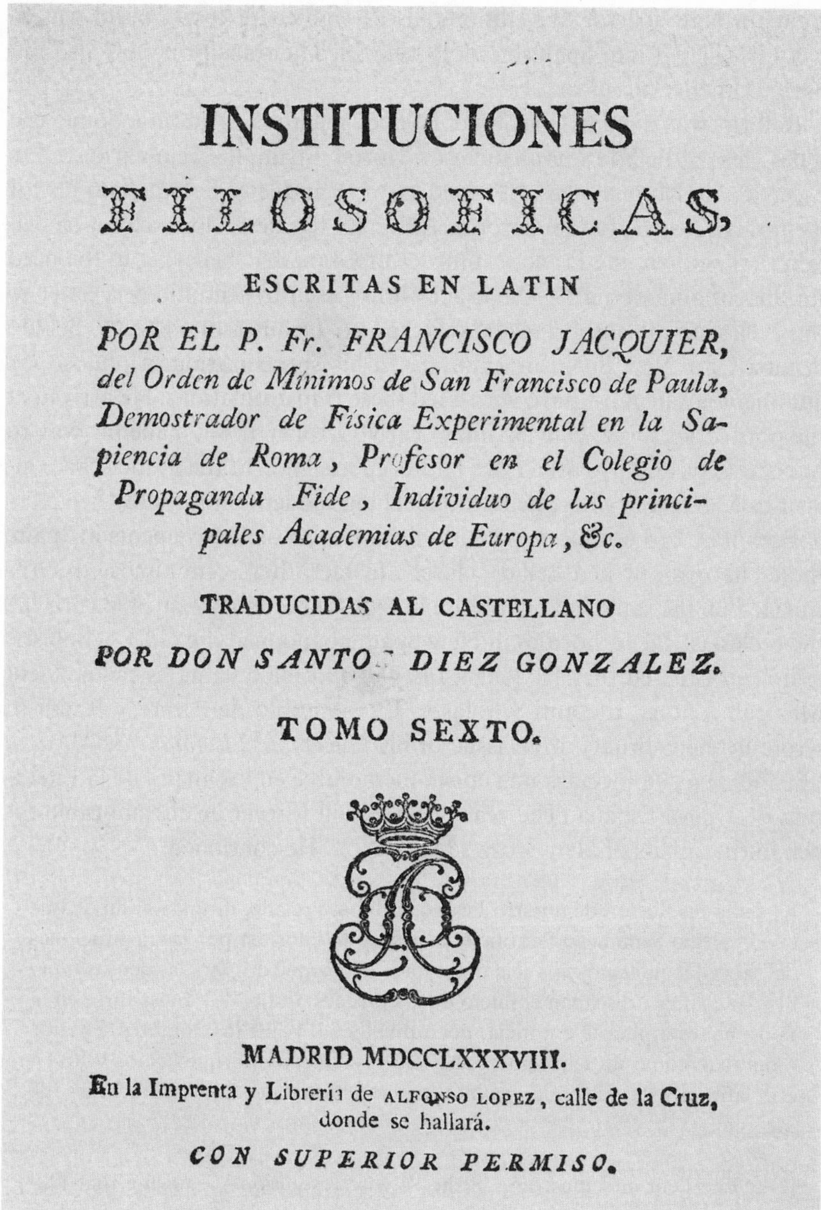

INSTITUCIONES

FILOSOFICAS,

ESCRITAS EN LATIN

POR EL P. Fr. FRANCISCO JACQUIER, del Orden de Mínimos de San Francisco de Paula, Demostrador de Física Experimental en la Sapiencia de Roma, Profesor en el Colegio de Propaganda Fide, Individuo de las principales Academias de Europa, &c.

TRADUCIDAS AL CASTELLANO

POR DON SANTOS DIEZ GONZALEZ.

TOMO SEXTO.

MADRID MDCCLXXXVIII.

En la Imprenta y Librería de ALFONSO LOPEZ, calle de la Cruz, donde se hallará.

CON SUPERIOR PERMISO.

Figure 10. François Jacquier, *Instituciones filosóficas* (Madrid, 1788).

University of Chicago Library, Special Collections Research Center.

went through at least five editions in the eighteenth century and was finally translated into Spanish in 1787–1788. The transformation also impacted other religious orders.

Reform was not far from Friar Bellido, mentor of Antonio. Some 300 miles west of Bellido's hometown of Morón, Spain, the Seminario de San Fulgencio in Murcia "was reformed in 1774 and later became famous for its modern instruction under progressive lay teachers." Even closer to Bellido's hometown, the Franciscan order of Granada, "believing in the need for 'filosofía moderna' "—the exact phrase used by Antonio in a letter to the ecclesiastical authorities—"switched to Jacquier in 1782."[63] Bellido departed for New Spain in 1786; given his specialization in philosophy and theology, he must have witnessed these transformations. He arrived at the port of Veracruz, New Spain, in early October 1786, made his way to Mexico City, and by early 1787 had been assigned to the Franciscan convent in Monterrey where he began teaching modern philosophy.[64]

Even if he had not participated in these intellectual movements in Spain, these changes pursued Bellido closely. In fact, they seem almost to have traveled on the same boat with him in 1786. That same year of his arrival, the ecclesiastical authorities in New Spain abandoned the older Scholastic texts and ordered that Jacquier's *Instituciones* be taught. As the eminent Mexican scholar, the anti-Scholastic José Antonio de Alzate y Ramírez, wrote in the February 1788 issue of his *Gaceta de Literatura de México:* "El año de 1786 formarà una època memorable en los anales de la Literatura de Nueva España [The year of 1786 will forever be a memorable epoch in the annals of New Spain's literature]." He continued:

> La sabia resolucion de nuestro Ecsmo. é Illmo. Prelado, dirigida al fin de que en el colegio Seminario Pontificio se enseñe la Filosofia por las instituciones del sabio Jacquier, nos anuncia una ràfaga de luz que disiparà las densas tinieblas que antes ofuscaban el juicio de los jòvenes destinados à instruirse en la Filosofia: esta plausible noticia, poco divulgada, y que los hombres sensatos reputaban como un feliz agüero, ha tenido su efecto; porque hemos visto en este año de 87, defender públicamente el método, las instituciones de Jacquier.
>
> [Our Excellent and Illustrious Bishop's wise resolution—requiring that Philosophy be taught utilizing *Instituciones* by the sage Jacquier—is a burst of light that will forever dispel the dense darkness that had obscured the wisdom of those youth destined to study Philosophy: this laudable news, poorly circulated as it is, and one that rational and judicious men have accepted as a joyful omen, has had its effect; because we have seen in this year of 87 the public defense of the methods in Jacquier's *Instituciones*.][65]

Institutiones was quickly adopted throughout New Spain and the rest of Spanish America. By the end of the eighteenth century, it was required reading at the Colegio de San Rosario in New Granada, at the University of San Carlos in Guatemala, at the University of Guadalajara in New Spain, and the Franciscan College of Guadalupe in Zacatecas, New Spain. The Franciscan College, in turn, had trained many of the ecclesiastics working in Texas and other territories in the Interior Provinces of New Spain. By 1802, both the Latin and Spanish editions of *Institutiones* were housed in a private library in Guanajuato, 240 miles northwest of Mexico City and 320 miles southwest of Monterrey, which suggests the extensive travel of these new ideas in an era when both books and their ideas moved slowly. Indeed, Enrique González González finds that Jacquier's text was recommended throughout seminaries and universities in New Spain, and that "its echo was heard well into the first decades of independent Mexico."[66]

The influence of these ideas, however, was far from radical, or immediate. The debate between Late Scholasticism and the new sciences continued to rage.[67] Change may have been slow to come, but the desire for modern philosophy had emerged within New Spain. The historian Carlos Stoetzer argues that during the first half of the eighteenth century the new natural science methods gradually entered Spanish America, but that the second half of the eighteenth century witnessed a much broader scientific skepticism; the seeds of Cartesian rationalism developed, accompanied with a strident critique of Scholasticism. It was this rationalism that began to challenge "dogmatism and traditional authority."[68]

Scientific skepticism and rationalism, then, were the harbingers of revolution, not the political philosophy of the eighteenth-century revolutions. For example, during the tumultuous, revolutionary decades of the late eighteenth century, when the Atlantic world was topsy-turvy, not one piece of information was published in any of the Mexican periodicals regarding the British-American revolution and its declaration of independence; and when British America was mentioned, if at all, it was to celebrate, for example, Benjamin Franklin's harnessing of the power of lightning.[69] But such careful control of the press merely points to the divergent path the Hispanic world had taken in the world of ideas. On the surface, the late eighteenth-century Hispanic intellectual world was embroiled in a debate between Scholasticism and those supporting the natural and experimental sciences. At a more profound level, the debate signified an epistemic shift of authority, from Scholastic doctrinal explanations of natural phenomenon to an authority based on reason, experimentation, and repeated observation. But if recent generations of contemporary scholars have focused on explicitly political writings in order to understand the era leading up to independence, they have done so by eliding the truly radically politicized epistemic shift from Scholasticism to modern philosophy, including the sciences.[70]

The Franciscan anti-Scholastic intellectual Juan Gamarra had paved the road with his 1774 publication in Mexico City of *Elementa Recentioris Philosophiae (Elements of Modern Philosophy)* which, though Scholastic in its explanations of philosophy, embraced modern experimental science over the Scholastic reliance on doctrine as authority. And again in 1781, five years prior to Bellido's arrival in Mexico City, Gamarra, clearly desiring to expand his readership beyond Scholastics, published not in Latin but in Spanish *Los errores del entendimiento humano (The Errors of Human Understanding)*, in which he reproached the conservative Scholastic educational system. But for these late eighteenth-century anti-Scholastic Scholastics, the desire for modern philosophy was really a desire for the experimental sciences. Modern philosophy was, ultimately, a desire to embrace skeptical rationalism as a way to understand the natural world. The debate would continue both in Catholic Europe and the Americas.[71]

What is yet more significant is that Jacquier was virtually unknown in predominantly Protestant northern Europe. The original Latin *Institutiones* was published at least once during each of the last five decades of the eighteenth century, and all were published in primarily Catholic countries: Italy (in Rome and Venice), Spain (in Valencia, the university town of Alcalá de Henares on the outskirts of Madrid, and Zaragoza), and France (in the southern Spanish-French border town of Perpignan). The fact that he was published in Italy, Spain, and southern France speaks to the influence that he had in the Catholic world over that of the Anglophone Atlantic. More striking, however, is that *Institutiones* was translated only once, into Spanish (Madrid, 1787–1788). Notwithstanding the fact that Latin continued to be the lingua franca among scholars during this period, and thus we may assume that Jacquier was read in Latin by non-Spanish speakers, not a single review or mention of *Institutiones* can be found in *British Periodicals, British Newspapers, 1600–1900, Eighteenth-Century Collections Online*, or *Archive of Americana*, all of which contain millions of digitized, searchable pages of periodicals. Nor was Jacquier read or even cited by Anglo-American revolutionaries.[72] Here, we have growing evidence of the split between the Protestant and Catholic West, one where the Catholic world would appear to pursue a different path to our modern world. But it would be a mistake to claim that the Hispanic world parted from northern, Protestant Europe and British America in the eighteenth century. One may say, in fact, that they had diverged centuries earlier. As Stoetzer notes, "Spain was that country which has had its own Reformation and its own Renaissance, and not those of the other European peoples, and experienced in its own way the fundamental renewal of Christian faith and of human culture and education."[73] It would, however, be just as egregious to suggest that the partition was a fixed barrier to the flow of ideas between the Hispanic world and other parts of the West.

Jacquier's text was a seed that would promulgate, disseminate, and articulate a new modern world, irresolutely Catholic and yet fully engaged, one that would give shape to a modernity different from the idiom which dominated—and continues to dominate—Western consciousness, that of a Protestant, and therefore secular, northern European and Anglo-American outlook. A world in which the supernatural, the sensual, and the mystical have little to no place in the temporal, political world of civic affairs. Jacquier's text is thus not an aberration of an idealized vision of the Enlightenment; it is, rather, a creative adaptation, one which refused the split between the rational mind and the spiritual life, that incorporated the sensuous and the supernatural as active agents into a rapidly changing world.

With Friar Bellido in Monterrey, then, we have something quite different from a centuries-long gradual shift from Scholasticism to science, from authority to skepticism. That narrative is one that the modern world has told itself in order to imagine a continual line of progress from darkness to light, with all the moralistic connotations of such "evolutions." Friar Bellido represents instead an epistemic rupture. The Scholastic world was an enchanted one, where everything remained fixed like a tableau, authored by God, inscribed in canonical texts, and therefore immutable. The modern world was one where divine authority had begun to slip, first in the realm of the natural world and soon in the realm of the social.

This break, however, was not clean but hybrid, one that sought to integrate both intellectual traditions. We will see this later especially in the ways that Scholastic theories of sovereignty reemerge. For now, the ambassadors of this break, particularly Jacquier and Bellido, helped shape Antonio's vision of the world, and eventually, of his modern philosophy course. Through this new, eclectic philosophy, Antonio learned the science-inspired methods of rationalism and skepticism, and began to question master narratives by asking particular questions about the local. This was the new episteme: a desire to arrive at a more precise understanding of the parts rather than finding functionalist reasons for how the whole came together. But he did more than learn this new philosophy; he taught it to his pupils and modeled it in his sermons as he preached to his congregations.

Imagining the Nation

If the "modern philosophy" course moved Antonio's spirits, as he had claimed, the material circumstances in the Eastern Interior Provinces were something those spirits needed to tend to. Governed by iron-willed and Bourbon-appointed royal administrators who, beginning in the latter eighteenth century were imported directly from Spain and thus knew nothing of local conditions or history, the residents of the provinces of Nuevo Santander, Texas, Coahuila, and Nuevo León, as we have seen, chafed under a heavy bureaucracy that sought to extend its rule over all matters. Where bureaucracy delayed development, the royal prohibition on foreign trade, even trading with their much closer neighbors in Louisiana than with those south in Mexico City, did its part to stymie the residents' ambitions. This was the world Antonio had known. His education in the 1780s, and then, continuing well into the early nineteenth century, his ministering and teaching of modern philosophy throughout the Eastern Interior Provinces, had provided him with new methods and reasons for imagining a new world.

Discontent with stern Bourbon rule had saturated Spanish America, and Napoleon Bonaparte's deposing of the Spanish king in May 1808 was the perfect impetus for this world to begin to unfold, especially for those who actively sought to end Spanish rule. Everywhere, everyone in the Hispanic world openly contemplated what to do in the absence of the "desired one," as the king of Spain was referred to. Still, the initial reasons for rebellion given by the insurgents, Hidalgo and Antonio alike, had not been the overthrow of monarchical rule. Rather, they had been motivated by a desire to reform the sociopolitical and economic system that had for half a century so successfully disempowered the creoles.[74] As Hidalgo's revolt swept across the Eastern Interior Provinces, New Spain's furthermost northeastern frontier, Antonio put his philosophy and rhetorical skills to work. He preached to his congregations the reasons for insurrection: not necessarily the end of monarchical rule, but reform where creoles would gain political power in the Americas.[75] Even here, though, prior to a declaration of independence, one can begin to trace the semantic shifts of loyalty, community, and belonging required *before* one could begin to imagine one's self as an autonomous nation.

Antonio proselytized throughout what is today the south Texas–Mexico border. But he apparently felt that his speaking alone was not enough. In March 1811, just as his brother Bernardo was presenting himself to Hidalgo's revolutionary forces, Antonio turned to pen and paper, produced many hand copies of a proclamation (a printing press would not arrive in the region for many years), and distributed them far and wide (see Appendix 1). So many were in circulation, in fact, that when a Spanish royal captain finally captured a copy, he forwarded it to his superiors with the note that the proclamation had been "dispersed throughout the four Eastern Interior Provinces by Father Gutiérrez, a schoolteacher from Revilla."[76]

The bold statement begins by daringly addressing his audience as "Americanos," and then declares, "Llegó la feliz época que muchos años ha, deseábamos con ansia y en que declaradamente tratemos los asuntos interesantes a nuestra nación [The felicitous epoch we have anxiously desired for so many years has finally arrived. Now we can openly deal with the matters of our nation's interest]." The proclamation begins with familiar language. Headlined with the single word "Americanos" and welcoming the new "felicitous epoch," Antonio appears to be invoking the sentiment of independence, the dawn of a new age. Indeed, his reference to "our nation" and a theoretically unified group of people seems to do just that. Yet even in the same breath that uttered "Americanos," Antonio declaims, "Si, americanos, la seguridad de nuestra religión católica, le guarda vasallaje a nuestro soberano augusto, el señor Fernando VII y la libertad a nuestra amada patria, consiste en la expulsion de los traidores europeos [Yes, *Americanos,* our unquestioning Catholic faith is a testament of our allegiance to our majestic sovereign King Fernando VII; and the liberty of our beloved homeland (also "fatherland") is secured through the expulsion of the European traitors]."[77] The mention of the deposed king throws the syntax off balance and renders foreign what to our ears sound like familiar revolutionary referents. How can he talk about the arrival of a "felicitous epoch" where his "nation's interests" can finally be addressed even while declaring loyalty to the king of Spain *and* advocating the expulsion of "European traitors"?

But the language was not unfamiliar to Antonio's contemporaries. Popular uprisings throughout the eighteenth century often declared, "Long live the King! Death to bad government!" putting into question not the king's authority but, rather, that of a political bureaucrat, such as a viceroy, which usually resulted in some form of a compromise.[78] Similar language had been used throughout Spanish America in response to that groundbreaking event three years earlier. It took six weeks for the news of King Fernando's forced abdication to make its way to the Americas, as mentioned earlier, but once it did cities and towns throughout Spanish America declared themselves vehemently against Napoleon and anything French, including those *afrancesado* (frenchified) Spaniards who had been at the helm of French-inspired Bourbon reforms. Spanish Americans also organized celebrations in honor of the deposed king. Sumptuous Baroque arches were built and poetry and pronouncements declaimed.[79]

Yet the celebration of King Fernando was marked by despondency as well. The editor of Mexico's first daily newspaper, the liberal Carlos María de Bustamante, reported on these processions with great enthusiasm. Like all other *Americanos,* Bustamante had responded with absolute patriotic support for his *patria,* though, like many of his fellow *Americanos,* he, too, would embrace independence and serve as one of postindependence Mexico's statesmen and historians. In the July 1808 issue of the *Diario de Mexico,* Bustamante concluded his report on the patriotic celebrations of King Fernando with an invocation:

> Dios de los Exércitos . . . no desampares jamás á una *nacion,* que confiesa humildemente tu Santo nombre, que sostiene los derechos de la Religion, como un tesoro infinito que tú mismo le has confiado para hacerla feliz, que clama por un Soberano, que tú, ó Dios justo, proteges como hechura de tus manos, y procura salvar á la *patria* que, sabe inmortalizar tu nombre aún en medio de la desolacion. Dios fuerte, Dios inmortal, en tí solo confian las dos Españas, cual otro Israel.
>
> [God of the Armies . . . never forsake a *nation* that humbly confesses your name, that maintains the rights of Religion, like an infinite treasure that you yourself have given in order to make her happy, that yearns for a Sovereign, that you, oh just Lord, protect as a product of your workmanship, and try to save the *fatherland* that knows how to immortalize your name even in the midst of desolation. Almighty God, immortal God, only in you do both of the Spains confide, as if it were another Israel.][80]

Antonio mirrored this language as well and intermingled *nación, patria,* king, and religion, each with different inflections. The intermingling reflects the ambivalence in the initial separation of the Americas from the Spanish monarchy.

For Bustamante, the nation is local, the viceroyalty of New Spain herself, and placed in a subordinate position to God, religion, and the fatherland, and thus "yearns for a Sovereign." Historians have demonstrated that, unlike *patria* (whose signification we will trace below), the meaning of *nación* was not fixed during the colonial period, and had a slippery, varied etymological history. José Carlos Chiaramonte and Mónica Quijada, for example, have found at least four denotations of *nación:* the oldest refers to distinct ethnic groups; a second denotes a group of people (of the same ethnic group or not) living in a specific geographic territory; a third refers to the emergent state in the seventeenth century (with no reference to ethnic groups); and, finally, in the early nineteenth century, all three meanings coalesce.[81]

At this point, in 1808, Bustamante appears to utilize the second denotation of *nación* to refer to the territory of New Spain and its inhabitants. Still, though subordinate, New Spain ostensibly resists this position, and is described, almost heretically it would seem, as one of two Spains. But rather than heresy, Bustamante in fact reveals the discursive trace of the Habsburg composite model of the Spanish monarchy as one that unites both Spains. There had never been one Spain, but several Españas. The Peninsula, for example, was comprised of several kingdoms, none of which were named Spain. The Hispanic monarchy cultivated, in essence, a concentric sense of loyalties, beginning with one's town, followed by province, then kingdom, and expanding out until one united with king and God, two inseparable entities, as discussed earlier, that had come together with the creation of Spain in the fifteenth century. Still, historians note that prior to 1808 the phrase "dos Españas" was rarely used in the American press. Only after Napoleon's invasion did the press more audaciously use the term and with greater frequency. We can see here, for example, how Bustamante gives it a different spin, between that of a Europeanized Spain and an Americanized Spain, a concept that would reverberate later in 1810 during the meetings of the Cortes of Cádiz.[82] For this editor, both Spains, both nations, still genuflected to the father, the *patria,* the sovereign.

Antonio, too, appears to use the second denotation of *nación,* as the territory where a specific group of people live. And yet, for Antonio, the nation not only refers to a territory and the people inhabiting it, but is also emergent, morphing from New Spain into some new unknown entity. It has torn itself apart from the *patria.* Antonio disregards the denotation of *nación* that refers to the global Hispanic monarchy with the monarch at the helm, the *patria.* In doing so, he begins to separate Mexico and *América* (Bustamante's Americanized Spain), from the Hispanic monarchy. His initial reference is to the inhabitants of the nation, and he refers to them consistently as *Americanos* and never as *Mexicanos.* Yet even though they are *Americanos,* the affinity he cultivates is concentric: "Poco tardará México en ser de nosotros, y lo mismo toda la América [Soon, Mexico will be ours, as will all of *América*]."[83] Mexico remains affectively cool, an object to be possessed and not to be identified with, but it appears to have a metonymical relationship to a much broader expanse, that of *América.* This concentric notion of belonging, as we will see in Chapter 6, has its seeds in the Scholastic political philosophy of the Catholic world.[84]

It was a worldview that had continued to reverberate in England as well, though its affective reach had become diminished. In his conservative critique of the French Revolution, Edmund Burke lambasted the Revolution's attempt to eliminate social hierarchies, and embraced what he saw to be natural social divisions: "To be attached to the subdivision, to love the little platoon we belong to in society, is the first principle (the germ as it were) of public affections. It is the first link in the series by which we proceed toward a love to our country, and to mankind."[85] But Burke's words may also have buried in them, and not too deeply, a sense of concentric, geographic (not just social) belonging, a sense of love for the local *patria chica* (hometown or province) even while imagining one's self as also belonging, as in a great chain of being, to larger communities. Yet his views, as we know, are associated with a conservative view of the world that refused to embrace the modern world of social equality that had engulfed him. Even more revealing, perhaps, is that Burke's mother was Catholic, and he repeatedly had to dodge accusations that he was Catholic.

In the Catholic Hispanic world, however, this concentric sense of the world remained dominant. Thus, while Antonio refers to the geographic place as Mexico, its inhabitants remain *Americanos,* part of the Spanish-American hemisphere. As a result, Antonio gives voice to that very common hemispheric sense of belonging that has not yet relinquished *América* to the United States. Antonio's struggle is local, and the immediate nation is that of Mexico; but this struggle must be related to the larger struggle across *América.*

Like its Latin root *nativitas,* meaning birth or nativity, which is also etymologically related to the Spanish verb *nacer* (to be born; from the Latin *nasci*), *nación* signifies a living entity whose shape is configured with each passing day. The Hispanic philologist Joan Corominas notes that the first documented use of *nación* is from a fifteenth-century translation of the book of Genesis, from a Hebrew word that meant both simultaneously "ancestry and posterity."[86] Thus, because Antonio's proclamation "finally" inaugurates an emergent, "felicitous epoch," "our nation" inspires optimism. The nation's future is as yet unwritten, and the propitious moment calls for its people to "openly deal with the matters of our nation's interest." The nation is something one gives birth to and possesses, and like a child, is something one regards with all the optimism of a parent. But it is also, as Benedict Anderson notes, something whose imagined history can—and will—be traced to the ancients, as Antonio's generation of revolutionary historians will do.[87]

Antonio, for example, begins by desperately seeking to bring the various *pueblos* (towns) of New Spain together in order to give birth to Mexico:

> ya el día 16 de septiembre de 1810, que será memorable eternamente entre nosotros, dimos principio a la gloriosa empresa de nuestra libertad en el

> pueblo de Los Dolores, villa de San Miguel el Grande. . . . Valladolid, Pátzcuaro, Salamanca, San Felipe, León, Irapuato, Silao y una numerosa porción de pueblos de la Nueva España, se han rendido ya a nuestro saludable partido.
>
> [on September 16, 1810, which we will forever remember, we began the glorious struggle for our liberty in the town of Los Dolores, the village of San Miguel el Grande. . . . Valladolid, Pátzcuaro, Salamanca, San Felipe, León, Irapuato, Silao, and numerous other towns of New Spain have already sided with our salubrious party.][88]

The English translation of *pueblo* here is "town," but since the medieval period *pueblo* has had a double denotation that refers to the combined entity of a group of people—or, more accurately, an indivisible collective—inhabiting a town or region. Still yet another denotation, since at least the early seventeenth century, is the derisive sense of *pueblo,* as in "the people," the masses, as in *populacho,* which is still used today to refer to the working classes or to a disorderly group of people. From the very first 1737 edition, the *Diccionario de la lengua española de la Real Academia Española* (*Dictionary of the Spanish Language of the Royal Spanish Academy* [*DRAE*]) offered as a tertiary denotation, "those people inhabiting a town who were not part of the nobility" (only in the 1899 edition is the reference to nobility replaced by "the common and humble people of a population").[89] But the continuing significance of *pueblo*—that is, the combined entity of town and collective of people—is in the Aristotelian-influenced Thomist theory of sovereignty emerging from the Greek *polis,* the city.

For Aquinas, humankind was, by nature, always social: we were born into families, shaped by groups of humans, and have never lived in isolation. Hence, *pueblo* continues, very much to this day, to connote an irreducible concept—the people rooted to a particular place, a visible town—in political thinking. The Latin roots of *pueblo* are *oppidum,* which Caesar used to describe the fortified towns colonized by the Roman empire, and *populus,* meaning the people. Yet both connote a sense of disorder or mayhem; *oppidum* refers to settlements that were in transition, spaces that had been enclosed as they became incorporated into the Roman empire, while *populus* can also connote the multitude. *Pueblo,* then, serves to continue to operate as an irreducible political entity, as the source of sovereignty.

Like his fellow revolutionary Spanish Americans, Antonio works to cement both connotations of "town" and "people" with the Scholastic theory that sovereignty emerges from the people. As a result, Antonio lists the names of countless towns where "the nation has been proclaimed," creating order out of chaos, and sutures them together with the affective language of an incipient nationalism.[90] But the transformation of *pueblo* (people) and *pueblos* (towns) into a *nación* is far from easy. Like the residual connotation of *pueblo,* the disordered, inchoate nature of "the people" must be transformed and tamed, its loyalty reconfigured from the *patria* of Spain to that of the new *nación.*

Historians have long emphasized that *patria* has meant the place of one's birth, but, curiously, they have disregarded that the word in fact has also had a much larger, catholic signification (in the more secular sense of the word). From the very first definition in the 1737 edition of the *DRAE* to the twenty-first edition of 2001, *patria* has meant the place, *pueblo* (town), or *país* in which one was born. *País* (which is usually translated as "country"), in turn, has likewise maintained a uniform meaning since 1737, denoting a "region, kingdom, or province." Astonishingly, it is not until the 1970 edition that *país* comes to be associated with *nación,* along with, in order, "region, kingdom, province, or territory."[91]

In effect, *patria* has been as much an abstract ontological concept as it has been a physical locale. The *patria* is a foundational concept, in the Derridean sense, providing a sense of stability, meaning, and order to the cosmos that allows one to link the specificity of their location of birth—no matter where in the Hispanic monarchy—to a much larger cosmos. The *patria* is a version of the great chain of being, providing that spiritual-ontological sense of security in the world, from one's hometown all the way up to the king and then God. François-Xavier Guerra is one of the few historians who has noted that during this period of instability *patria* immediately connotes, primarily, the catholic imagined community of the Hispanic monarchy.[92] In effect, the metaphysical meaning of *patria* as ontological, spiritual, political foundation did not shift; it was merely stripped of physicality (location) and was left with a desperate desiring for the *patria(rch).* It is as if the traumatic, (not so) theoretical beheading of the monarchy produced this metaphysical sense of instability, of foundering foundations, triggering, in response, a yearning for the Hispanic *nación cum patria.*

It is in this sense that the *pueblos* owe their loyalty, their very existence, to the *patria,* Spain, King Fernando, and the Catholic Church: "Ellos, no hay duda, cuando conquistaron este Nuevo Mundo, trajeron a él la cristiana religion que profesamos, las politícas leyes que seguimos y los más artes que ejercemos, para nuestra felicidad, gobierno y utilidad [There is no doubt that after they conquered this New World they brought to it the Christian religion that we profess, the political laws that we follow, and the other arts that we practice for our happiness, government, and utility]."[93] But these traditions—the religion, laws, and arts of the *patria*—will by necessity be transformed as the *pueblos* separate from the *patria,* Antonio suggests. The proclamation insists on a linear temporality punctuated by this "felicitous epoch" that founds the modern nation. The language looks forward to the nation's unfolding (its "becoming"), and it must do so by reconfiguring tradition and loyalty. Antonio's proclamation reveals the nation in medias res; the discursive echo of previous social formations rings throughout. These are the embers from which the nation will emerge.

The *pueblo,* therefore, is bracketed by two competing discourses. If the *pueblo* strives to move forward toward the emergent *nación,* a symbol of the future, the *patria* tenaciously holds onto the *pueblo.* The *patria* sings its siren song, luring the *pueblo* back to the familiar, dominant, father-figure discourse. The *patria* inspires, indeed requires, a mimicry of the past by holding on to and reenacting tradition (hence, the countless number of celebrations throughout Spanish America held in King Fernando's honor). Antonio's proclamation appears to perceive this tension between the emergent *nación* and the dominant *patria.* Quite similar to the incipient revolutionary language in other parts of Spanish America, the *nación* (much like "Mexico" in Antonio's proclamation) remains a passive object to be produced by the *pueblo.*[94] Even in a proclamation full of dependent clauses and elaborate, endless phrases, the proclamation refuses to place the words *nación* and *patria* in the same grammatical sentence. Instead, *nación* appears first, in the first sentence, and remains secular, with no invocation of father, God, or Catholicism; only the language of celebratory futurity may be found. In contrast, *patria* appears in the second sentence surrounded by the language of patriarchal tradition, that of religion and King Fernando. It is as if the rhetoric of religious messianism is giving way to a nationalist messianism.[95] But this is far from a facile, seamless transition from one form of belonging to another.

The *nación* is new and unknown, and thus anxiety-producing. The *patria* is dominant; it holds out the lure of security, belonging, intimacy, the known, what we have referred to as a metaphysics of presence, of a sense of origins. Antonio's proclamation strives to break the nation free from *patria* and religion, and thus the second sentence begins with "Americanos," metonymically invoking the nation, and proceeds to argue: "Yes, *Americanos,* our unquestioning Catholic faith is a testament of our allegiance to our majestic sovereign King Fernando VII; and the liberty of our beloved *patria* consists in the expulsion of European traitors." It is as if the language descends—from *nación* in the immediately prior sentence, to *Americanos,* king, and *patria*—peeling back the layers through which the *pueblo* comes to be united. The *pueblo* is filially related to both the new *nación* and the old *patria.* Yet, unlike the mothering relationship between *pueblo* and *nación,* where the *pueblo* gives birth to the *nación,* the relationship between *pueblo* and *patria* is a patriarchal inversion: the *pueblo* is subordinate to the *patria.*

But the concept of *patria* reflects Aquinas's Aristotelian-based political theory, and especially so when we consider the term, still in use to this day, of the *madre patria* ("the mother fatherland or country"). Here, we can trace Aquinas's theory of society as one that emerges from the family. The *madre patria* brings to life the unity of the community as the foundation of the *polis,* as one shaped by both the loving care of the mother and the patriarchal demands of the father as they work in unison to shape the *nación.* As one newspaper editor described it in 1808, "The true *patria* is 'a tender mother who equally loves all her children,' and therefore ensures that they are 'equal before the law,' have access to the same posts and enjoy the general well-being. . . . The *Patria* is . . . of a higher political authority, as old as societies, based on nature and order, it equally submits to its laws all those who rule as well as those who obey."[96] Enacting the very intransigence that it signifies, the Spanish word *patria* has not changed from its Latin and Greek origin and continues to denote "place of one's birth." But this place, as we have seen, is also a metaphor for the metaphysical yearning for foundation, a sense of one's ontological origins.[97] Thus, one refers to one's *patria* in this larger, abstract sense, but, even to this day, one may refer to one's *patria chica* ("small fatherland" as in homeland or hometown) as the literal place of one's birth.

The *patria* demands respect. It insists on its connection to the past, its ancestral origin, and provides a sense of stability, order, tradition. It is nostalgic, and like its Greek roots *nóstos,* "returning home," and *álgos,* "pain" or "ache," the *patria* is pessimistic, longing for a moment that will never return; indeed, this moment has never really existed. It is this desire, this Odyssean longing for the patriarchal home, that must be sublimated in the transition from the *patria* to the *nación.* Antonio's proclamation bears witness to the genesis of modern Spanish-American nationalism and reveals its discursive origins in the *patria.*

If the nation's discursive origins are in the *patria,* its literal origin is also discursive, which is to say it is oral, not textual. Antonio's proclamation may have circulated in manuscript form, but his was not part of a developed print culture. A printing press would not arrive in the region until 1817, six years *after* Antonio's proclamation circulated. This is not to say that there were no books in the Eastern Interior Provinces, which indeed there were. The Bourbon reforms, however, placed more restrictions on trade; and, working in tandem with the Church, authorities did their best to control the movement and circulation of books of any kind. While historians of the book have demonstrated that the Inquisition's *Index of Prohibited Books* hardly prevented the circulation of books between Europe and Spanish America, recent work on the history of the book in northern New Spain tells a different story. Gerardo Zapata Aguilar's groundbreaking work on the history of libraries in Nuevo León, one of the four Eastern Interior Provinces adjacent to Texas and Nuevo Santander, reveals how local royal bureaucrats held considerable power over the circulation of books. Individuals had to petition and pay a tax for each and every book that entered the Eastern Interior Provinces; books were often embargoed, forcing individuals to petition the authorities for their release.[98]

But even then the phantasmagorical circulation of censored books still managed to unleash their damage. In one instance, the Spanish soldier Joseph María de Aysa arrived from Spanish New Orleans in Arramberri, Nuevo León, in 1779, where he had been appointed mayor. Within years, he became known for allegedly hosting literary salons where the blasphemous texts of Machiavelli and Luther were discussed.[99] By 1783, however, he was denounced to the Inquisition by one of his guests, apparently in retribution over a heated argument. To be clear, however, the case of Aysa appears negatively, that is, as charges brought up against him by the Inquisition. Zapata Aguilar reveals that the authorities never found any of these censored books in Aysa's library, that in fact they only found authorized books there, and that it was quite unlikely that Aysa could have imported any censored books from New Orleans.[100] This case, however, reveals the power that the printed text had. Its power arguably became even more pronounced when its material evidence could not be found. The mere suggestion or rumor of someone harboring a censored book could lead them to immediate imprisonment. In these instances, it is the idea of the book itself, the idea of the form versus the content, which causes transformation. These phantasmal books, much like Antonio Nariño's immolated pamphlets, circulating in the imaginary and through gossip, come to exercise their own agency in the Eastern Interior Provinces. And they would continue to do so throughout the Americas.

The transformation of *pueblos* into the *nación* was not textualized; its origins are not in print. It was not something that was solipsistically read by individuals who would imagine themselves belonging to a nation. Rather, the emergence of the nation in the Eastern Interior Provinces, as in the rest of Spanish America, was oral and visual, a performance in the town square.[101] Antonio's ambivalent nation, or, perhaps better, his emergent nationalism, was declaimed. The archive has left the material evidence, the written proclamation itself, along with the testimony of the Spanish royal captain commander Pedro Herrera, that the proclamation was circulated throughout the Eastern Interior Provinces; but no testimony has yet been found describing the experience of witnessing the proclamation. One may imagine, however, the work that the proclamation did as it was offered before townspeople throughout the provinces.

As a performance, the emergent *nación* is a sensational affair that works to win the *pueblo*'s affection over from the *patria.* Beginning with all the promise that only a newborn can bring, Antonio celebrates the announcement of the new nation that his fellow *Americanos* "have anxiously desired for many years." But this emotional, celebratory work will not be enough, so Antonio implies. The nation's "interesting matters" must be dealt with.

Yet these matters do not include revolution or independence. Not once does Antonio utter these words. It may be that he refuses to use these words precisely because revolution, at this time, denotes "inquietude, unrest, sedition, turmoil," and he explicitly repudiates violence.[102] Rather than invoking revolution at this moment, Antonio is more concerned with shifting sympathy from the *patria* to the emergent nation. What he cultivates instead is a sentiment of separation, of growth, adolescence; not necessarily a break with the *patria,* but a coming into one's own.

In his syntactically convoluted sentence, Antonio begins by addressing his townspeople as *Americanos,* united by religion, king, and *patria.* At the other end of his verbose sentences, he concludes by taking a stance and declaring himself along with his *pueblo Americano* against "European traitors." He begins by reconfiguring the *pueblos* and calling into being a new people, and concludes by awkwardly naming the "other" of *Americanos.* But these traitors could be of two kinds; it certainly references those Spaniards who had sided with Napoleon and sought to bring Spanish America under his dominion. But it could also refer to the monarch-appointed peninsular administrators who had arrived with the Bourbon reforms. To the people in the town square, Antonio was declaring loyalty to Catholicism and the Spanish monarch against those European traitors. To more discerning ears, Antonio was already invoking the dream of America's coming into being, that long-awaited moment where national sentiments ("our nation's interesting matters") could finally flourish. He has already begun to cleave the monarch's subjects in two: Americans and Europeans, ambivalent though that distinction may be.

But the performative, emotional work of an emergent nationalism will not be enough. It must also transform into a political project, what Monica Quijada describes as the institutional dimension of *nación,* one where the ideological work of representation is worked out utilizing political language.[103] The proclamation explicitly invokes the language of natural law and the right to overthrow tyrants. The "horrorosas tramas que han urdido contra lo más sagrado de las leyes preciosas de la naturaleza, los acrimina tánto cuanto es necesario exitar en nosotros, la más justa indignación y venganza They (European traitors) have woven the most horrific plots that go against the most sacred of natural laws. Thus, they are incriminated so much that it should provoke in us the most just indignation and desire for revenge]."[104] Yet Antonio explicitly directs his fury not toward the monarch but to both those who had sided with Napoleon and Spanish peninsular bureaucrats.

Throughout, Antonio treads a fine line between lambasting the Spanish administrators alongside his inauguration of the birth of a new nation and his emphasis on an optimistic future:

> En fin, lo que no está por nosotros, con impaciencia desea estarlo. La conquista camina a pasos muy veloces. Poco tardará México en ser de nosotros, y lo mismo toda la América, según nos proteje el Dios de los ejércitos y nuestra divina patrona María Santísima de Guadalupe.
>
> [In the end, those who are not on our side with impatience desire to be so. Conquest travels with fast steps. Soon, Mexico will be ours, as will all of America, as long as we remain protected by the God of the armies and our divine patron the most holy Mary of Guadalupe.][105]

Antonio gives voice to what the historian David A. Brading has described as "creole patriotism," that history, as discussed earlier, that resented the peninsular denigration of Spanish-American creoles.[106] But creole patriotism, and its resolute connection to *patria,* sought recognition from the fatherland, the *patria,* rather than the inauguration of some new community of belonging. In Antonio's hands, however, this patriotism was rapidly disappearing under Bourbon restrictions, and morphing into an emerging nationalism.

How this optimistic rhetoric would do more than bring people together and construct the basis of a new nation had yet to be worked out. Even here, in closing, Antonio, much like his fellow revolutionary Spanish Americans, is at pains to demonstrate allegiance to King Fernando: "¡Viva nuestra católica religion! ¡Viva Nuestra Patrona María Santísima de Guadalupe! ¡Viva nuestro amado Fernando VII! ¡Viva nuestra noble nación Americana! ¡Viva nuestra patria y muera el vicio y mal gobierno! [Long live our Catholic religion! Long live Our Most Holy Patron (Virgin) Mary of Guadalupe! Long live our beloved King Fernando VII! Long live our noble *Americana* nation! Long live our *patria* and death to vice and bad government!]"[107] Antonio's ambivalence is less a rational equivocation regarding what path to pursue than it is an emotional, existential disquiet regarding the world-changing events of the king's deposition. That is, as much as he wants to create a unified world of *Americanos,* he still longs for the security offered by the king, both real and metaphysical.

Unlike their American neighbors to the north, these *Americanos* develop a nationalism not by rejecting Europe, king, and God; nor does it develop through the circulation of print culture. Rather, Spanish-American nationalism begins in communal, public forums, through proclamations and festivals. These, in turn, work to reconfigure the enduring symbols that had served as the foundation of the Hispanic world as foundations for the new nation: God, king, law, language, and, what Antonio described as "the other arts that we practice for our happiness, government, and utility." Still, the path was uncertain, frightening, for sure. For many of these *Americanos,* their connection to the past is not one to be rejected but corrected, allowing them to proclaim that "nostros somos ahora los verdaderos Españoles [we are now the true Spaniards]."[108] For those Americans to the north, the past is something to be excised and forgotten. And believing that they have cut themselves off from the past, Anglo-Americans can imagine their present and future as a tabula rasa emerging from the American soil itself.[109] But what exactly had emerged from this other America in the north, and what could this newly independent nation offer to their brethren in the south? While Antonio remained along the Nuevo Santander-Texas border, his brother Bernardo prepared to embark upon a journey to the United States, where he would encounter new ways of imagining the world.

CHAPTER TWO

"Oh! How Much I Could Say!"

Imagining What a Nation Could Do

Voyage to the United States

On March 16, 1811, only a week before Father Miguel Hidalgo's capture, José Bernardo Gutiérrez de Lara presented himself to Hidalgo's forces in Santa María, on the outskirts of Saltillo, some 160 miles southeast of his birthplace, and there offered his services to the cause. The royal forces were not far behind, and Hidalgo's most recently deputized envoys to the United States had already been captured by royalists weeks earlier in San Antonio de Béxar, the capital of Texas. Fearing the worst, Hidalgo's men immediately deputized Bernardo with the ostentatious title of "Lieutenant Colonel and Commanding General of the Northern Provinces," and named him ambassador to the United States, hoping that he at last would be able to complete the mission of traveling there and requesting military support. And succeed he did.[1]

Immediately upon Hidalgo's capture in March 1811 the Gutiérrez de Lara brothers, like insurgents throughout Texas and the rest of the Eastern Interior Provinces, went into hiding. As the royal forces moved in on Bernardo and others, he finally set out to the United States on the first of August, 1811, taking with him twelve men, munitions, all of what remained of dispatches and letters of introduction from Hidalgo, and a treasure of gold and silver to be used to purchase supplies in the United States (see Figure 12). Bernardo's brother and political mentor Father José Antonio

Figure 11. Ramón García Zurita, *José Bernardo Gutiérrez de Lara* (1950s).

Oil on canvas. Courtesy of the Colección Gobernadores, Instituto de Investigaciones Históricas de la Universidad Autónoma de Tamaulipas, México. An exhaustive archival search did not yield the 1812 portrait of Bernardo painted in Washington, D.C. According to the historian Juan Díaz Rodríguez (personal communication via e-mail), García Zurita based this portrait on a photograph of a portrait of Bernardo. It may be that the photograph was of the 1812 portrait.

would stay behind, evading persecution by wandering, in rather striking Christian imagery, in the mountainous deserts for several years.

A gulf separates the arguments made during this revolutionary period and the ways those arguments would come to be described by later generations. Indeed, historians now agree that the initial insurgency lacked any coherent political program. Strict political severance with Spain certainly was not part of the equation in the early phase of insurrections that began after Napoleon Bonaparte's invasion in 1808, but with time and the expansion of revolt against peninsular domination, insurrectionists began to demand the independence of Spanish America. The shifting political terrain, as well as the nationalist interests of several generations of historians who have sought to trace the origins of the Mexican nation during this period, makes it difficult to delineate a clear political program in the early period of the insurrection.[2]

How these ideas developed, whether the goals were reform or a complete break with Spain, would vary throughout the early nineteenth century. So much did they vary that three years after Antonio advocated insurrection in 1811, he would deny any affiliation with his brother Bernardo's political thinking. It was in the United States, Antonio would write, "donde sobre mesa tendida y ya preparada crió y abrazó ideas bélicas que fomenta: no, no fuí yo el que se las sugirió [with the table set and well prepared, that he developed and embraced those militaristic ideas that he foments: no, it was not me that suggested them to him]."[3]

Indeed, his voyage to the east coast of the United States and his encounters there greatly affected Bernardo. Despite losing his official papers, he did his utmost to be received as an official representative of the insurgent forces. And in Louisiana he found willing hosts. Anglo-American officials had followed closely the various uprisings throughout Spanish America including New Spain; now, an actual Spanish-American insurgent had arrived at their door.[4] The Natchitoches-based U.S. Indian agent[5] John Sibley, governor of the Orleans Territory William Claiborne, and other judges and officials corresponded with one another and "expressed the need of 'the revolution's assuming a proper direction'. . . . since it was important to the interests of the United States 'that the secretary of state receive early and correct information.' "[6] Shortly after meeting Bernardo, Sibley wrote to the secretary of state, exaggerating the strength of the insurgents in New Spain.[7] Sibley was particularly well connected with the nascent federal government, having been appointed to various positions by Thomas Jefferson. Indeed, he worked steadfastly for U.S. imperial interests along the Louisiana-New Spain frontier, supplying Jefferson with much needed information on the Louisiana territory, Native Americans, and New Spain. According to the historian Julia Garrett, he was a "purveyor of news, as well as a manipulator of diplomacy and statecraft," during a period when the United States sought to extend the Louisiana Purchase territory down to the Rio Grande.[8] While in the Orleans Territory, Bernardo procured letters of introduction from Sibley to U.S. secretary of war William Eustis, and from Captain John Overton to his brother, General Thomas Overton, of Nashville, Tennessee, in which they requested that they do everything in their powers to aid Bernardo.[9] He wrote letters of his own as well, initiating correspondence with Secretary of War Eustis and Secretary of State James Monroe.[10]

By mid-September 1811 Bernardo had arrived in Nacogdoches, traveling some 500 miles through, at times, unfriendly Native American territory near the Texas Gulf Coast, along the way surviving various skirmishes with royal forces, and befriending some Native American communities while convincing them to support the revolutionary cause. But there in Nacogdoches, at the periphery of the Spanish empire and at the border of what had been officially declared "Neutral Ground" between New Spain and the United States, Bernardo and his men were ambushed by royalists. Losing all of the money and all the documents proving his commission, Bernardo barely escaped to the Orleans Territory of the United States. He spent the rest of the month in the town of Natchitoches planning his trip to the northeast.[11]

Bernardo finally set out again in mid-October, accompanied only by a young interpreter; he sent the few remaining insurgents to foment insurrection in Béxar. Bernardo and his interpreter spent the bitterly cold months of November and December traveling up the Mississippi and Tennessee rivers, through what was then known as the Old Southwest, collecting more letters of introduction from various officials before arriving in Washington, D.C. But in Knoxville his interpreter would abandon him, and he traveled on his own for most of the trip.[12] Bernardo, however, had managed to keep a small notebook that he used as a diary. These well-traveled pages are a crucial, and underappreciated, complement to Antonio's emergent nationalism.[13]

The first part of the journey, from Louisiana to northeastern Mississippi, is missing along with a crucial period of about three weeks in early 1812 when Bernardo was in Philadelphia. Bernardo was meticulous in writing his entries (see Figure 13). He carefully entered each date flushed left, never missing a date, even if there was no entry, followed by careful indention of the text throughout. The handwriting is incredibly legible, the lines are perfectly parallel to one another, there is no marginalia, and there are only a handful of crossed out words. The only other breaks in the packed, sixty-two-page document occur at the end of a month, at which he would center the name of the next month in slightly larger script. Except for the missing pages, the diary is in impeccable condition, with nary a water stain. In other words, it is almost certainly in too-perfect condition for it to have been the original.

However, the level of detail (such as how much money he spent on specific meals or the amount he received for his mules) and the consistent usage of the present tense signal that Bernardo wrote his diary as he was traveling and not in retrospect. Given the near-perfect condition of the diary and the circumstances of his trip—being pursued by the royal forces

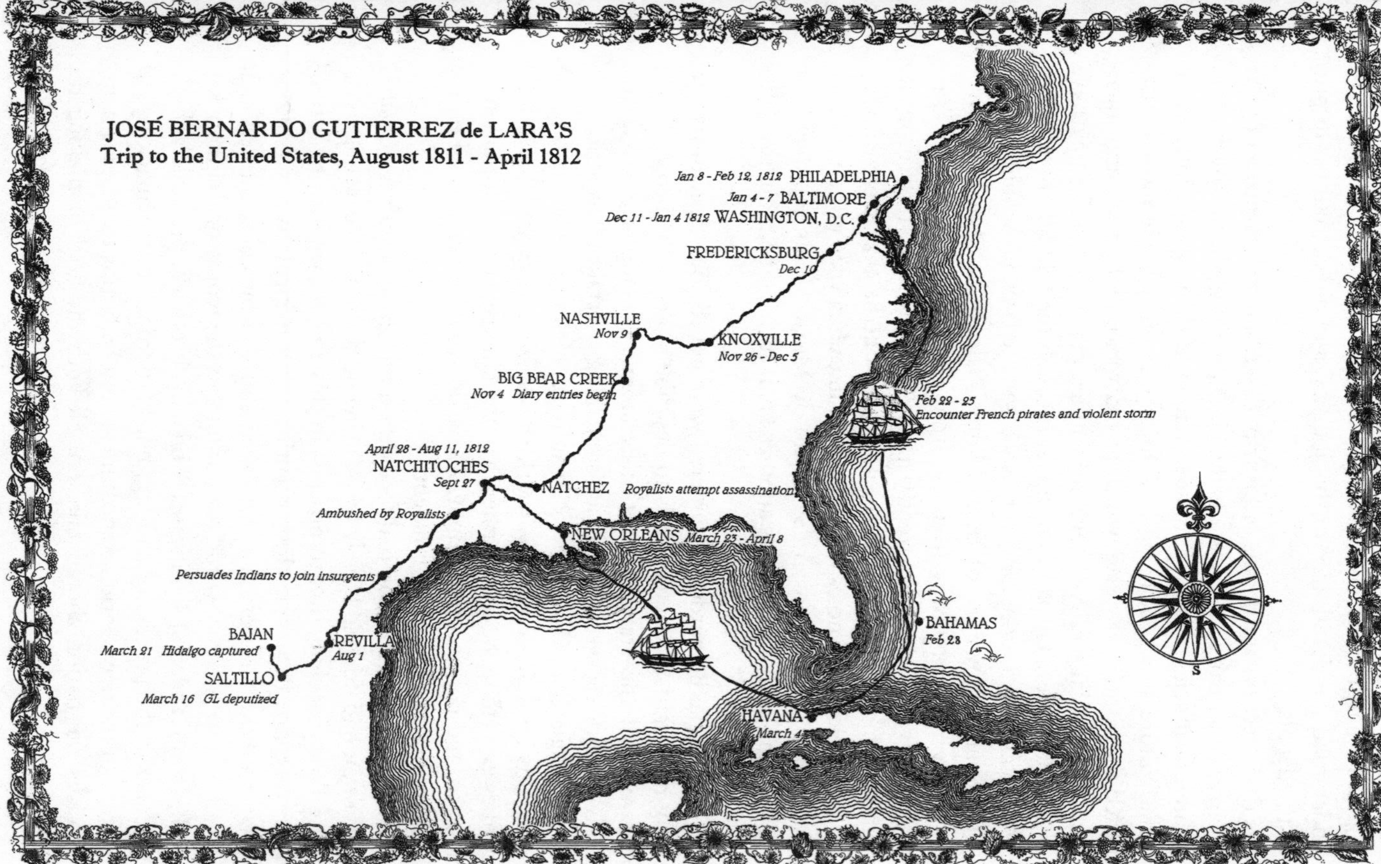

Figure 12. Route of José Bernardo Gutiérrez de Lara's trip to the United States, August 1811–April 1812.

Map designed by Anna Theresa Coronado de Rueda.

and traveling through unfamiliar territory through rain and snow—it is clear that Bernardo must have recopied his journal at a later date. Clearly, he understood the significance of this journey, and did the utmost to preserve the details.

The diary records the details of his trip, describing his voyage along the old Native American trail known as the Natchez Trace, the inconveniences of winter, insufficient funds, an inadequate (and then absent) interpreter, and the culture shock of being in a foreign country.[14] He meticulously recorded the distance traveled, which he did variously by mule and stagecoach at an average rate of seventeen miles per day, and he may have been one of the few Hispanics to travel through the Old Southwest since the American Revolution; however, as we will see later, his would-be nemesis, the Spanish governor of Texas Manuel Salcedo had traced this very route in reverse on his way to Texas from Philadelphia in 1808.[15] Still, Hispanic travelers were apparently a rare phenomenon. Indeed, in describing his encounter in Tennessee with someone he characterized as an Englishman, Bernardo notes that "disen q^e^ nunca han visto por estos Paises tan lejos otro hom^e^ como yó del Reyno de Mexico [they say they have never seen in these distant lands another man, such as me, from the Kingdom of Mexico]."[16]

But the people Bernardo encountered were not the only spectators witnessing new sights. As he proceeds to describe in detail the people he encountered and the state of political-economic development along this quickly developing western frontier, something overtakes Bernardo's narrative. A language of visuality slips in and begins to suffuse his writing. He becomes awestruck by the new world he is witnessing, and obsessively describes everything he sees. Rather than the language of revolution, independence, and political philosophy, Bernardo would focus instead on the visual aesthetics of good government.

If Antonio's proclamation had focused on the anxious shift from *patria* to *nación,* it had done so largely by focusing on the form, the feeling of the nation. From proclamation to process, in this chapter we turn to Bernardo's travel diary. By paying close attention to his meticulous observations, we witness how one person experienced shifts in his consciousness that allowed him to give the word "revolution," in the words of Reinhart Koselleck, "transcendental significance." Like his brother's, Bernardo's thinking is also in the process of shifting, but Bernardo is taken aback by the sublimity of the new world he encounters, and he begins to imagine many new tasks the nation should take on, all with the goal of making the *pueblo* happy. In arriving at these insights, he becomes even more wedded to self-determination and independence. He would then return to Spanish Texas yearning to usher in a whole new world.

Seeing a New Country

Bernardo must have been relieved to have arrived in Knoxville, then the capital of Tennessee, on the morning of November 26, 1811. Prior to Knoxville, he had had little flattering to say about either climate or inhabitants. He had encountered very cold snowy weather, something he had apparently never experienced before, and he writes of having met with various ruffians who attempted to cheat him of his money and belongings. Indeed, not only was he fortunate to not have been robbed, but he was also lucky enough to have escaped with his life. His journey through the Old Southwest—stretching from the Louisiana territory up through the Mississippi territory—was through an entirely undeveloped frontier, known for harboring outlaws and encouraging anarchy. But finally he entered Tennessee, the home of the mythic Davy Crockett; and, in fact, passed near Crockett's residence in Jefferson County. With a population near 800, Knoxville was the first developed town Bernardo had come across since leaving Natchitoches.[17]

Once arrived, he presented the various letters of introduction he had amassed and was quickly greeted by the governor of Tennessee. He was wined and dined, and slept quite comfortably.[18] The following day, he writes, "me hisieron q$^{e.}$ fuera a la casa en donde esplican los abogados las Leyes del Govierno, y me divertí mucho con *ver* cosas nuebas [they had me go to the house where the lawyers interpret the laws of the government, and I was much entertained at *seeing* new things]."[19] The language is matter of fact. Yet, Bernardo had begun his journey down the path of imagining vibrant new sociopolitical content—that is, new kinds of governments—for the new nation.

Like nearly all contemporary Spanish-American writing, Bernardo's references to matters of state continue to be made in the idiom of monarchical government. In his encounter with the Englishman described above, he refers to himself as being "from New Spain" and, more specifically, from the "Kingdom of Mexico."[20] And like his brother, Bernardo's thinking is also in the process of shifting, from identifying with the kingdom of New Spain to the nation of Mexico, albeit a monarchical Mexico. Yet, Elizabeth West mistranslates this and other significant terms. Where he writes "Reyno de Mexico," West translates it as the "realm of Mexico" instead of as the "Kingdom of Mexico." But Bernardo consistently capitalized "Reyno," making it clear that he meant "kingdom" and not "realm." Even then, the *Diccionario de la lengua española de la Real Academia Española* (*Dictionary of the Spanish Language of the Royal Spanish Academy* [*DRAE*]) does not find "realm" as a denotation of "Reyno" until 1851. Paying closer attention to Bernardo's original language allows us to trace the gradual shifts in his political thinking.

As he begins his approach to Washington, D.C, he reveals a political lexicon that is familiar only with a monarchy. "[M]e marcharè para la Corte de este Reyno [I shall go forward to this Kingdom's Court]," he writes, not realizing the incongruity of his language with a decidedly anti-monarchical, if not anti-aristocratic, Anglo-American community.[21] But across the next four months, as he journeyed from his native Revilla to Washington, D.C, Baltimore, Philadelphia, and back to New Orleans via the Bahamas and the Gulf, Bernardo would transform his political language, from monarchical to republican.

Bernardo's voyage should not be understood as some teleological metaphor for the shift in his political thinking, with his departure from New Spain representing some break with a premodern, semi-feudal way of thinking and his arrival in the United States signifying the development of modern political thought. Such a metaphor would merely replicate our clichéd notion of the United States as the normative agent, positing it as the teleological end of the modern political world; at the other end of the spectrum, of course, would be Spanish America, hurriedly attempting to follow the United States' path to modernity. This is the conundrum of comparative work, the inescapability of positing norms and standards to which some fail to live up. The task requires us to decenter the normative history that has set up the Protestant Atlantic's path to modernity as the ideal.

That Spanish Americans had become frustrated with Spanish imperial rule is true, but many at first, as we have seen, sought reform. Even later, with independence in the 1820s, Spanish Americans vociferously debated whether to establish monarchical or republican rule. As the social geographers Allan Pred and Michael Watts remind us, "how things develop depends in part on *where* they develop, on what has been historically sedimented there, on the social and spatial structures that are already in place there."[22] Instead of viewing Bernardo's thought as a tabula rasa, we should see him as emerging from a Hispanic world where the Spanish monarchy was in the process of being redefined, just as Antonio did in his rethinking of *patria* and *nación*.

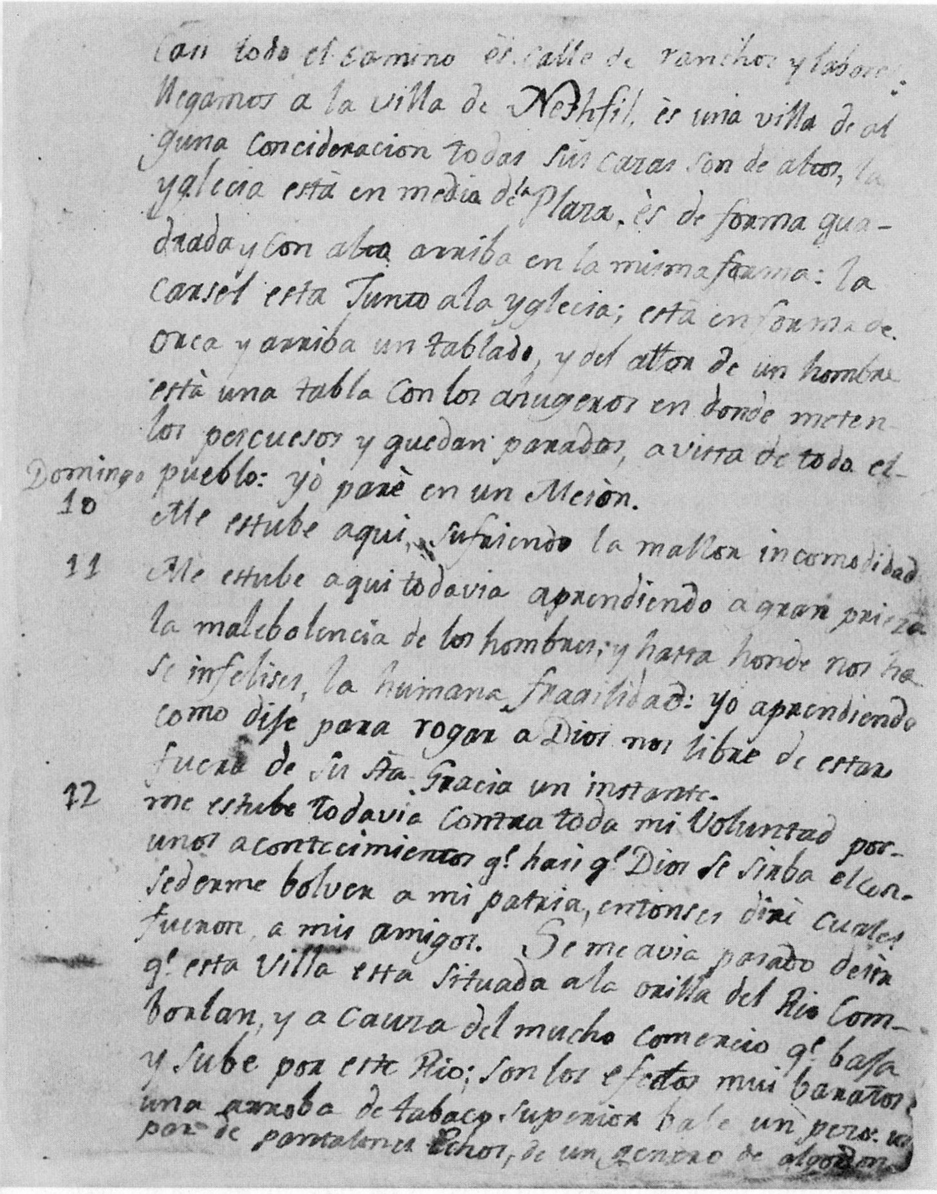
Casi todo el camino es calle de ranchos y labores;
llegamos a la villa de Nethfil, es una villa de alguna consideracion todas sus casas son de adobes, la
yglecia esta en medio de la Plaza, es de forma qua-
drada y con adoa arriba en la misma forma: la
carsel esta junto a la yglecia; esta en forma de
orca y arriba un tablado, y del altor de un hombre
esta una tabla con los arugeros en donde meten
los percuesos y quedan pasados, a vista de todo el
Domingo pueblo: yo pase en un Meson.
10 Me estube aqui sufriendo la mallor incomodidad
11 Me estube aqui todavia aprendiendo a gran prieza
la malebolencia de los hombres; y hasta donde nos ha
se infelises, la humana fragilidad: yo aprendiendo
como dise para rogar a Dios nos libre de estar
fuera de su Sta. Gracia un instante.
12 me estube todavia contra toda mi Voluntad por-
unos acontecimientos q.e hai q.e Dios se sirba el con-
sederme bolver a mi patria, entonses dire cuales
fueron a mis amigos. Se me avia pasado decir
q.e esta Villa esta situada a la orilla del Rio Com-
bolan, y a causa del mucho comercio q.e baja
y sube por este Rio; son los efectos mui baratos;
una arroba de tabaco superior bale un peso: un
par de pantalones echos, de un genero de algodon

Figure 13. Representative page from José Bernardo Gutiérrez de Lara's diary (1811–1812). 4E-2b. Manuscripts Collections. Archives and Information Services Division, Texas State Library and Archives Commission, Austin.

Bernardo, like other Spanish Americans, would adapt the language of republican political philosophy, melding it with the language of more familiar traditions. But it is not the language or content of republican political thought that initiated these changes. Rather, it was the aesthetics or the form of republican development—that is, the visual, physical transformations that Bernardo came to associate with republican government—that first attracted him. And this is precisely what he struggles to put into words.

The shift is almost imperceptible. A day after he arrived in Knoxville, Bernardo elected not to go to the capitol; rather, he writes, "they had me go." It is as if his guests were aware of the effect this visit might have on Bernardo; but surely they understood that the effect would not be conveyed discursively, given that his translator had since abandoned him. After the legislative proceedings, he confesses that "I enjoyed myself immensely at *seeing* new things." From this moment forward, and especially so because he was without a translator, he becomes obsessed with vision.

The irony is that in this impeccably written diary, in which the ocular dominates the page, there are no images. Bernardo included no sketches or diagrams, no emblems or illustrations. Instead, we have perfectly indented lines, and impeccably legible handwriting with only the slightest of flourishes. From his first experience of republican government, at Knoxville's capitol, he may have been impressed by the image of the building, but he only put down words. It is the visuality, indeed the spectacle, of legislative proceedings that produces pleasure; and given his father's role as a prominent leader and alderman in Revilla, Bernardo, too, may have imagined new ways of conducting affairs that went beyond mere reform. Hence, it is his having "seen new things" versus his having learned some new political precept, having read some piece of political philosophy or history of the United States, or having understood the discursive processes of state formation, that is, of legislation, that enables him to "enjoy himself." In an ironic way, words, at this particular moment, are of no consequence.

What was said during the proceedings is not noted at all, since he could not understand them without a translator. Still, the pleasure derived from viewing the proceedings was something he had to transcribe into words. Democratic deliberation, as represented by the proceedings, is a spectacle for Bernardo. It is an untranslated performance one can see and hear without comprehending its verbal content. He must, then, "translate" what he sees into words. In this sense, his inability to aurally comprehend the deliberations is not merely supplemented but almost entirely replaced by visual comprehension. It would only be later, in Philadelphia and upon his return to Texas, that the language of political philosophy would take over. Only then will he be able to put into precise words his and his fellow revolutionaries' vision of a new world. Here, for the moment, Bernardo is enthralled more by the visual world of republican rule than by the specificities of republican thought.

Admiring the Well-Being of the Nation

It is no wonder that upon Napoleon's deposition of King Fernando VII, the performances, parades, and sculpture in support of the deposed king that proliferated throughout Spanish America far outnumbered the publication of tracts against Napoleon (though these, too, existed).[23] This abundance of physical, visual tributes helps us better understand how the public reading of Antonio's proclamation would have had a much more powerful impact among the communities of the Eastern Interior Provinces in northern New Spain, rather than its circulation in print form. His words were meant to be heard; the emotional rhetoric was meant to be felt, and all by a community of listeners and viewers who had learned to make sense of the world by seeing and hearing, all the while being guided by the Church in how to interpret these things.[24]

But Bernardo traveled on his own. Even when in the company of others, he could not talk with them because there were no translators, at least until he arrived in Washington, D.C. There was no one with whom he could share the experience, and he had to turn instead to his journal as a delayed substitute for community. He attempts to put into words the experience of meaning. "[D]e solo el ver tantas y admirables cosas, si me pusiera a escribir todas las cosas . . . seria nesesario mucho tiempo y papel [Just in seeing so many admirable things, if I should set myself to write about all the things . . . a great deal of time and paper would be required]."[25] Indeed, he would never be able to finish. Seeing becomes a trope for deferred meanings. It is a signpost for thought-in-formation, of the political content that would decidedly shift us from the *patria* in Antonio's proclamation to the rationale for declaring independence and the founding of the *nación*.

The day after viewing the legislative proceedings, Bernardo strolled through the town of Knoxville, and toured "una gran fabrica de cotense grueso q^{e}. hasen de canamo [a large factory where coarse, thick fabric is made out of hemp]." Pleasure emerges again—"me divertí mucho mirando moverse tantas maquinas [I enjoyed myself immensely watching so many machines move]"—yet this time it is a machine, a factory that becomes the source of joy.[26] Bernardo derives pleasure from visual stimulation and, more specifically, from the machines surrounding him, from the beauty of legislative proceedings to the power of textile factories (only just beginning to spread throughout the United States).

Bernardo is an eyewitness to the early industrialization of the United States, and he marvels at humanity's capacity not only to produce the massive abstract projects of state formation, but also to materialize these efforts in the shape of textile factories. In this respect, Bernardo is not far from his contemporary Anglo-Americans and their fetishization of the machine. They, too, were mesmerized by the aesthetics of the machine, and would spend hours admiring its sublime complexity. Leo Marx, for example, argues that this sentiment emerged among Anglo-Americans in the late eighteenth century and became deeply sedimented by the early nineteenth century. "Running through much of what they had to say is an inchoate sense of the transformation of life to be accomplished through what we should call economic development or industrialization. . . . [But their] vocabulary . . . was inadequate to express their full sense of the power to be released through the combined agencies of commerce, science, technology, and republican institutions."[27]

That relationship begins to form at this moment. In Bernardo's eyes there is an intimate connection between the making of governments (what he describes as "explaining laws") and the making of industry. These are the ideas that begin to gestate; Bernardo begins to imagine the nation-state as a machine that should work toward making the people happy. Two weeks later, as he passes through the Virginian towns of Fredericksburg and Alexandria on his way to Washington, D.C, Bernardo is taken aback by the spectacle of the industrializing city. Detailing the urban layout of these towns, he writes:

> Este pueblo està en la orilla de un caudaloso rio y en la orilla estan las casas metidas dentro del rio sus simientos, todas estas casas q^{e} estan en la orilla son de 4 altos y todas estan llenas de diferentes maquinas q^{e} todas se handan con la agua, y son tantas q^{e} casi toda la agua se ocupa.
>
> [This town is located on the bank of a broad, fast-flowing river, and the homes' foundations are set at the edge of the river. All the homes along the bank are four stories tall, and they are all full of different machines that are operated by water; and they are so numerous that nearly all the water is used.][28]

He became fascinated with machines, and would write about them throughout his journey. But the legislature was also a kind of machine, a figurative one that helped produce the world he was observing.

This mechanistic metaphor also captured Anglo-Americans' imagination. Prior to the 1787 Constitutional Convention, agrarian nationalism—the return to the idea, celebrated by Franco-American J. Hector St. John de Crèvecoeur, of "salubrious effluvia"—was seen as capable of curbing human vice and love of luxury. But already by 1787 U.S. republicanism was being reoriented away from agrarianism and toward the machine age. Indeed, the historian John F. Kasson argues that "the overriding metaphor for the structure of government within the Constitution itself was a machine, which through a system of 'checks and balances' harmoniously regulated itself and channeled the energies of the people. The image undoubtedly reflected the delegates' and the age's conception of an orderly universe, but it suggested even more particularly the common purpose of technology and republican government."[29] Republican government and machines, in other words, were inseparable at the turn of the nineteenth century.

Yet Bernardo witnessed this legislative machine *after* it was invented. What is attractive to him, then, is the state as a machine, a machine that *produces* and *directs* society rather than the state as a *product* of society (of a particular political philosophy or of a will of society). At this point, given his inability to understand English, he is fascinated by the aesthetics of the form and less by the complexity of the content. The legislative machine as the end product is ultimately, at this juncture, of more interest than how it came into being; hence, the particular political language—whether it be monarchical or republican—is yet of little significance.

Bernardo is mesmerized by the development of the towns. In writing about the mills at the bank of the river, he confesses:

> Admiro ber como trabajan estos hombres, y el alivio qᵉ tienen en un todo por tener facilitadas todas las artes, y todo este vien le resulta a esta Nacion por el buen Govierno que tiene. !O¡ cuanto dijera. . . .

> [I admire seeing how these men work and the relief that they have due to their having progressed so well in all of the arts. All this well-being comes to this nation as the result of having a good government. Oh! How much I could say . . . !][30]

The "arts" in this instance, according to the 1817 edition of the *DRAE*, includes "all that is related to man's industry and ability."[31] But the thought remains incomplete. The sentence is cut short and ends with an ellipsis; the sublimity of the well-ordered industrializing city overpowers Bernardo.[32] Language overwhelms Bernardo in this instance. The new machines induce new pleasures, yet these pleasures emerge through the visual and are then translated into new thoughts. These thoughts, then, are what produce pleasure. But pleasure does not emerge as something private, as a thing that he enjoys for himself. Rather, emphasis is placed on "relief" and "well-being" for the community that his journal metaphorically represents. But he is overtaken by the power of these images once he attempts to translate these pleasures ("relief" and "well-being") into written language.

Viewing the newly sprouted textile mills, Bernardo is taken by their ability to harness nature's power in a controlled fashion (see Figure 14). But this harnessing has a specific purpose. The mills convert nature's power into social energy: these factories provide "relief" for mankind, allowing them to focus their energies less on the material reproduction of their lives. Yet still, if Bernardo is able to translate the visual into language (from the description of the homes on the river to textile mills, mills to social relief, and relief to nation), this translation is cut short.

The beauty of the textile factories overwhelms him precisely at the moment that his amazement releases its signification: "todo este vien le resulta a esta Nacion por el buen Govierno que tiene [all this well-being comes to this nation as the result of having a good government]." Amazement yields to "relief," "relief" to "well-being," and here, finally, well-being unfolds and releases the concepts of "Nacion" and "buen Govierno." At last, Bernardo has bridged his thinking with that of Antonio, arriving at the concept of *nación,* yet he pushes further still by declaring that the well-being of a nation is based on good government. But he finishes with the elliptic, "Oh! How much I could say . . . !" overwhelmed by the sublimity of his thought-associations that can not, at the moment, go beyond associating the well-being of the nation with good government.

The textile mills become sublime, causing consternation because to associate the "arts" of machinery with social relief leads Bernardo to desire such relief, and such relief is possible only through the means of "good government." But "good government" requires that he begin to imagine alternative modes of being in the world, different social relations, different governments. He thus appears to move closer to developing yet another reason for pursuing independence. The creole complaint of being marginalized by Spain in matters of state and economy may have initially spurred him to support insurrection and reform, but now he has witnessed the relationship between industrial development, social relief, and good government. And it is this combination that overwhelms him, filling him with innumerable ideas that would take innumerable sheets of paper to describe. The ellipsis serves as a placeholder for what is not there but is to come. Given the political purpose of his journey we can imagine what fills

Figure 14. Anonymous, *Lincoln Cotton Mills, Lincolnton, 1813.*
In E. Everton Foster, ed., *Lamb's Textile Industries of the United States,* vol. 2 (Boston: James H. Lamb, 1916), 330.

the space of the ellipsis: the desire for his kingdom of Mexico to have a good government so as to foster the development of the "arts." "Good government" is profound not so much because it secures an individual's rights to property and the pursuit of happiness, but rather because it seeks to provide "relief" for its citizens and "well-being" for the nation.

This becomes the ocular-intellectual knot for Bernardo: the tetrad of industrial arts, social relief, good government, and nation, and the simultaneous melding and explosion of this syntagm into a proliferation of sheets of paper filled with arguments will yield to the concept of "independence." But at this moment, the initiation of this line of thought (that is, the rationale for insurrection), originates not through a language of individual rights but through the language of social relief. Indeed, not once does Bernardo make reference to the concept of natural rights or any specific kind of rights of man. Nor could he, really, given that the language of individual rights over the rights of the social corporate body, that is, of the *pueblo,* was far from dominant in the Hispanic world.[33] Rather, his emphasis throughout is the association between good government and its effects on the social body.

What amazes Bernardo about the factory mills is not the possible accumulation of capital, nor their benefits to individuals, but rather "the relief that *men* have due to their having developed well all of the arts" (emphasis added). It is the sociopolitical body, the collective "they," that shall reap the benefits of good government. The "well-being" of the social body trumps the well-being of the individual. Which means, then, that the concept of democracy in which each *individual* has his or her *particular* right to equally participate in the making of a government will be unintelligible as well. In this sense, Bernardo differs radically from his Anglo-Americans in that, by the early nineteenth century, liberalism—with its emphasis on individual rights and prosperity—had come to replace republican virtues of the common good.[34]

Struggling to Articulate the Sublime

Bernardo was welcomed with open arms in Washington, D.C. Immediately upon his arrival on the morning of December 11, 1811, he was rushed to make an appointment with the secretary of war, William Eustis.[35] Bernardo's foray into international diplomacy began in earnest the following morning. Bernardo declared to Eustis that he wanted military and financial support for independence; Eustis, in turn, wanted to "take possession" of Texas down to the Rio Grande. Eustis imperially persisted, and Bernardo diplomatically stated that "los auxilios q[e] yo pedia hera que se ministraran de tal modo q[e] resultara beneficio à ambas Americas [the aid that I requested should be administered in such a way that the results should benefit both Americas]."[36]

Bernardo expresses an ambivalence toward, if not a complete absence of, Mexican nationalism. He does not refer to his homeland as Mexico, but here, in his initial interactions with official U.S. representatives, he refers to it as one of *two* Americas in the hemisphere. This emergent nationalism, one that is beginning to take shape—does not only emerge dialectically, that is, in contradistinction to the *patria,* to that of Spain, as we saw in Antonio's proclamation. Here, Bernardo would appear to have articulated a third contrapuntal reference, that of the United States. This emergent nationalism would begin to take shape in distinction to *both* that of Spain and the other America, the United States of *Norte América,* as Latin Americans to this day refer to it.

Nonetheless, yet another productive tension had already emerged: the relationship between what Bernardo had referred to previously as the "Kingdom of Mexico" and *América.* But it is a constraint only from our modern vantage point from which nationalism requires loyalty to one nation. Bernardo's Hispanic world, however, as discussed earlier, was one that had nurtured concentric senses of loyalty. In keeping with a Catholic (in both the religious and secular senses of the word) vision of the cosmos, the Hispanic world began, not unlike the sixteenth-century Spanish theory of the great chain of being, with God and descended to the Spanish monarch; it then branched out to the various kingdoms of Spain and the Americas that comprised the Spanish composite monarchy, and, finally, ended with *pueblos* and their loyalty to their local *patria chica.* Throughout the nineteenth century, and in different ways, Spanish Americans, from Simón Bolívar to José Martí, would toil with competing senses of loyalty: one that tenaciously reverberated the Catholic concentric tradition and another that was becoming the dominant, modern nationalism.[37]

For now, Bernardo was in Washington, D.C, thinking of Mexico, advocating for both Americas, and about to meet, for the first time, actual *Americanos* from the rest of *América.* Unbeknownst to him, however, many Spanish Americans had already arrived in Washington, D.C., seeking recognition for their independent nations, along with material support to help make this dream a reality. The United States was now faced, for the third time in its youthful history, with the question of how to recognize newly independent nations.[38] Historians have addressed the political negotiations between these Spanish-American representatives and the subsequent rise of the Monroe Doctrine; while these are crucial to understanding the emergence of U.S.–Latin American relations and of U.S. imperialism, what is also of interest here—if not simply by sheer page numbers—is Bernardo's account of the United States.[39] To put it simply, he was taken aback by the sublimity of the city and its impact on its people; it is the sublime that forces him to imagine how a nation could help produce a happy people. Only after doing so could he then turn to how his nation would engage with others.

During the three weeks that he was in Washington, D.C., Bernardo met with Secretary of War Eustis, Secretary of State James Monroe, President James Madison, and congressional representatives. Yet based on what he chose to write about in his journal, Bernardo was concerned less with recording the intricacies of international diplomacy as he was with documenting what he saw in the United States. After delicately dealing with the insistent Eustis and the question of the United States' occupation of the "Mexican Kingdom" down to the Rio Grande, Bernardo deftly leaves the meeting without compromising himself, and remarks, "Maria Sma. sea en mi alluda, y me saque de entre estos [Holy Mary, help me and rescue me from these men]." Indeed, Elizabeth West, translator of the diary, remarks that "Lazáro Gutiérrez de Lara tells of a family tradition that his great-

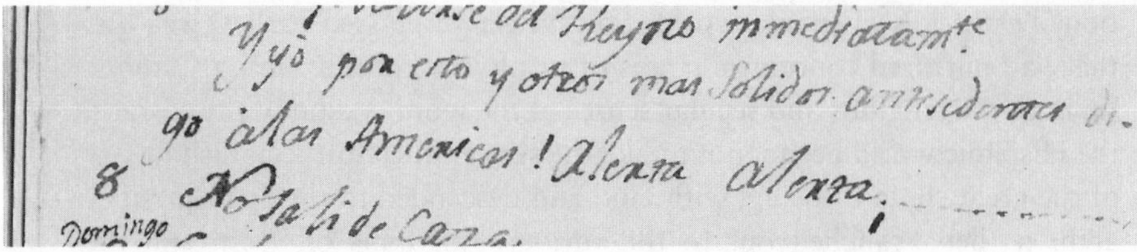
Y yo por esto y otros mas Solidos antesedentes di-
go alas Americas! Alerta alerta;

Figure 15. Bernardo, exasperated after his first meeting with Secretary of War Eustis, who wanted to "occupy" Mexico down to the Rio Grande, offers a prescient warning: "digo a las Américas! ¡Alerta!" José Bernardo Gutiérrez de Lara's diary (1811–1812).

4E-21b. Manuscripts Collections. Archives and Information Services Division, Texas State Library and Archives Commission, Austin.

grandfather learned to swear in English under the stress of his difficulties with the men in power at Washington!"[40] Still later, even deeper into negotiations, he exclaims, "Y yo por esto y otros mas solidos antesedentes digo alas Americas ¡Alerta alerta . . . ! [And for this and other more solid antecedents, I say to the *Américas,* 'Beware! Beware . . . !]"[41]

Stressful as these negotiations may have been, Bernardo fills most of his journal with his impressions of the United States, where, at last, his political idiom subtly begins to shift. After meeting with Eustis, he strolls through the Capitol, what he refers to as the "palace." "¡O! que obra tan admirable! [Oh, how admirable an edifice!]" he writes. "[D]e solo el ver tantas y admirables cosas, si me pusiera a escribir todas las cosas, y el admirable orden de todo cuanto hai echo por estos hombres, seria nesesario mucho tiempo y papel: Pero me contentaré con desir que un buen Govierno hase a un Reyno feliz. [If I should set myself to write about all that I see and the admirable order of everything in which these men have organized them, a great deal of time and paper would be required: But I shall be content in saying that a good Government makes a happy Kingdom.]"[42] Bernardo continues developing his political thinking: a good government should produce a happy social body comprised ostensibly of the monarch and his subjects, or what he refers to as "a happy Kingdom." But he has made his first slip in political thought. Now, in Washington, D.C., he begins to refer to Mexico as "la Republica del Reyno de Mexico."[43] He does not elaborate on his political terminology, and never defines a kingdom's proper form of government as that of a monarchy or republic. Rather, he creatively utilizes the political language available to him at the time, and he does so while allowing the meaning of these terms to slip. Rather than expounding on political terminology, Bernardo instead cultivates a language of urban aesthetics, one in which the beauty of the city, its architecture, and "the admirable order of everything" is a product of good government.

On one of his Sunday afternoon strolls, he comes upon the "arzenal en donde se estan haciendo los barcos, lanchas, cañoneras, y otros basos [the arsenal where they are making gunboats, launches, and other vessels]" that the United States was building in preparing for war with the British:

> Es cosa digna de verse, tantas admirables manicas [*sic*] q^e estan andando unas por fuego, y otras de otros modos. . . . tengo que bolver a exsaminarlas para hacerme cargo un algo [*sic*]. Admiracion me causò bastante [la] cañonería y monteros.
>
> [It is worth seeing—such admirable machines, some operated by steam, others in other ways. . . . I must come back to examine these machines in order to understand them somewhat. I greatly admired the cannon and mortars.][44]

Beauty is that which humans have constructed. It is found wherever humans are able to carefully redirect the power of nature, whether it be converting human-social energy into a machine-state (the legislative hall), dominating rivers and channeling their power into textile mills, or challenging nature's beauty by constructing edifying edifices.

Bernardo encounters a world in which humans radically transform their surroundings and produce the world they desire to inhabit. In the end, that which is beautiful is that which can be restrained carefully, organized properly. The sublime is that which leads to imagining alternative forms of government that have as yet, for Bernardo, not been contemplated. The sublime is what prevents him from fully spelling out his elliptical exclamation, "Oh! How much I could say . . . !" It is the unknown that must be converted into language, and to do so—to finish his sentence and put what he wanted to say into words—will lead to the syntagm of revolution and independence.

Beyond negotiating, walking, and writing, he socialized a great deal; met the renowned scientist, Hispanophile, and U.S. representative Samuel Latham Mitchill; had his portrait painted; and, on Christmas Eve, had a rather distressing experience—the only one he noted—when several friends put him in their carriage and took him to a place "en donde he visto cosas q.^e en toda mi vida [no] havia visto: ¡O! q.^e formidables espejos hai aqui para ver en ellos la monstruosidad del mundo! [where I have seen things which in all my life I had (never) seen before. Oh! what formidable mirrors there are here in which to see the monstrosity of the world!]."[45] One can imagine, perhaps, that being in the company of men he may have been taken to a brothel. But even here, we can see already that the dream of modernity—urbanization, industrialization, and prosperity—too, has its underbelly.

With financial support and letters of introduction from the U.S. government, he made plans to return to New Spain in order to collect the official documents that would enable him to purchase arms from the United States.[46] After five days of travel, Bernardo finally arrived in the City of Brotherly Love on January 8, 1812. He was fitted for a suit, and visited a wax museum, Charles Willson Peale's famous museum (what became the Philadelphia Museum), and the University of Pennsylvania. Of the university, he wrote:

> me llevo uno de los mallordomos a un cuarto en donde hai cosas admirables vide la maquina electrica, vi el firmamento con las estrellas, cometas, y signos, vi el globo terrestre con todos los paises del mundo, y los mares, è islas y sus ismos, todo colorado, vide una infinidad de Baròmetros, y termometros de todas formas y tamaños, vi una infinidad de maquinas chicas y grandes para toda clase de esperimentos, vi tambien la ciudad de Londres, Roma, Paris, y otras ciudades grandes de Europa con tanta propiedad y naturalidad como son en realidad, sus templos, calles y edificios del mismo tamaño q$^{e.}$ son, y con su grande y admirable arquitectura, los coches, los hombres y mugeres andando por las calles como si en realidad fueran vivos.
>
> [one of the caretakers took me to a room in which there are wonderful things; I saw the electric machine; I saw the firmament with the stars, comets and signs (of the Zodiac); I saw the terrestrial globe with all the countries of the world, and the seas, islands, and isthmuses, all colored; I saw an infinitude of barometers and thermometers of all shapes and sizes; I saw a world of apparatuses, great and small, for all manner of experiments; I saw also the cities of London, Rome, Paris, and other great cities of Europe, with as great accuracy and naturalness as they are in reality, their temples, streets, and buildings of the same form as they are, with their great and admirable architecture, the carriages, the men and women going about the streets as if in reality they were alive.][47]

The torrential prose of his journal is testimony to the impact of everything Bernardo witnessed. Not ceasing to pause for even more than a comma, he instead attempts to detail everything he saw.

His visit was a moment of perfect symbiosis. The alienating aspects of industrial labor, the grimy detritus of industrialization have yet to cake over the landscape. Instead, in 1812, Bernardo embraces reification and marvels at the perfect marriage between industry and government and wonders at the possibilities for the Americas. The dioramas and objects of scientific experiment are a testament to humanity's power to harness—though not to duplicate—nature's beauty. And if this could be done, could not humans likewise parallel nature in creating as beautiful and as orderly a government and a "happy Kingdom"? As a result, he shifts closer to imagining the world as something that is not merely inherited from God but one that humans can actively transform.

This indeed is what many Spanish Americans thought, and this notion is what had been reinforced upon their arrival in the United States. In Washington, D.C. and Philadelphia, Bernardo met for the first time on his journey other *Americanos* who sought to flesh out the phrase "revolution and independence," and he briefly mentions four of these individuals in his journal.[48] Only six months prior to Bernardo's arrival in the capital, in July 1811, an agent sent from Venezuela, Telesforo de Orea, had arrived seeking U.S. support of Venezuelan independence. Bernardo thought he had an "arrogant and haughty spirit," and says little more of him.[49] He also met a José García de Cadíz, "a Creole of Caracas," and "Licenciado Revengos," of whom Bernardo says little else but whom Elizabeth West identifies as another Venezuelan revolutionary, José Rafael Revenga.[50] A fourth, José Álvarez de Toledo, had been the Santo Domingo deputy sent to the Spanish Cortes after Napoleon's invasion. But he fled Cádiz in exile, after he was accused of sedition for advocating the independence of Spanish America.

Álvarez de Toledo arrived in Philadelphia in September 1811, three months before Bernardo, and had engaged, as we will see later, in a pamphlet-publishing frenzy defending his honor against Spanish charges of treason. Bernardo learned that Álvarez de Toledo was in Philadelphia after reading a letter Álvarez de Toledo published in the Philadelphia *Aurora* on December 17, 1811. Bernardo transcribed the letter in his journal without comment, but ten days later they met in Washington, D.C.:

> Hoi he tenido el grandisimo gusto por haver venido de Filadelfhia el Sor Albares de Toledo, es un hom.^{e} de grandes talentos, y mui apacionado por la livertad del Reyno de Mexico; y para ahora tiene trabajado mucho en esto; y su merito en esto ya es grande, y digno de recompensa, y ampliasionar en dicha causa, por aquella Nacion: los discursos de este cavallero son grandes y justos.
>
> [Today I had the greatest pleasure because Señor Alvares de Toledo has come from Philadelphia; he is a man of great talents, and passionately devoted to the liberty of the Kingdom of Mexico; up to the present time he has worked much to this end; his merit therein is great and he is worthy of recompense and advancement in the cause, by that Nation: the discourses of this gentleman are admirably great and just.][51]

Oddly enough, Bernardo does not elaborate on these first, initial encounters with Spanish-American revolutionaries. This silence seems even more strange when compared to the flourishing Hispanophone print culture that had trickled down to the capital from Philadelphia. Bernardo had finally met Spanish-American revolutionaries and encountered a vast literature on Spanish-American history and politics, yet he says nothing of this in his journal.[52] Or rather, to be more precise, what *remains* of his journal contains very little of this new world. He was a meticulous journal-keeper: he submitted an entry for every day of his trip (except for six days at the end of his journey); and on days when he recorded nothing, as mentioned, he would still enter the date and leave a blank space. Unfortunately, his journal is missing the crucial pages of his three weeks in Philadelphia.

We can't help but wonder about this excision. A mere two days after his arrival in Philadelphia, the journal cuts off abruptly in mid-sentence as he begins to describe his visit to Peale's museum on January 10, 1812. The journal picks up again, also in mid-sentence, on February 1 as he recounts a conversation he had with a Philadelphia prisoner who was from the Spanish island of Mallorca. Bernardo provides extensive detail of this rather philosophical conversation. "Friend," says the prisoner to Bernardo,

> en el mundo q.^e tengo andado, no he visto govierno mas savio q^e este y q^e mas contribulla a la felicidad general, todos los mas de estos presos q^e viven aqui tienen delitos q.^e en España fueran reos de muerte; pero la piedad de este Govierno no sentencia a la muerte a ningun hom.^e lo q.^e hase ès q.^e segun sus delitos asì los condena a estar en esta pricion mas ò menos tiempo.
>
> [in the world over which I have travelled I have not seen a government which is wiser than this and which contributes more to the general happiness. Most of the prisoners who live here are guilty of crimes which in Spain would be capital offences; but this government in its mercy sentences no man to death; what it does is to sentence criminals to remain in this prison more or less time in proportion to their crimes.]

After learning that prisoners are allowed to work and earn a salary that is given to them upon their release, Bernardo remarks, "Bendito y dichoso ès el Pais q.^e tiene un Govierno Savio [Blessed and happy is the country that has a wise government]."[53] What is remarkable here is that this conversation, five weeks after his arrival in Washington, D.C., marks the first time Bernardo provides any detail on a conversation he had with another Spanish-speaker. Nonetheless, the conversation, in which a prisoner sings praises to the very judicial system that has imprisoned him, seems rather embellished and suggests, perhaps, that Bernardo may have elaborated (and exaggerated) it. Still, more to the point, he has embarked on his first extensive comparative evaluation of the U.S. government with another country's, that of Spain. But Bernardo would have had many occasions to engage in conversation with other Hispanics in Philadelphia, and he most definitely would have encountered the Hispanophone publications that were coming off the press. Between 1810 and February 1812, at least twelve Hispanophone publications were printed in Philadelphia alone, not to mention the various imprints circulating in Philadelphia from throughout the Atlantic world, from broadsides, to pamphlets, and books. The journal only captures his first three and final six days in Philadelphia.

Could it be that these missing three weeks contain those lost conversations? The travel narrative had been recopied, as was noted above; a comparison of the handwriting with that of Bernardo's correspondence to U.S. officials confirms that the existing narrative was indeed written by him. For some unknown reason, he or someone else tore out these pages after he had transcribed them. Perhaps they revealed too much detail about the kinds of conversations he had or the documents he read, and were torn out for political reasons? Or perhaps less dramatically, were they torn out by someone who, for one reason or another, wanted to keep a list of what he read and who he met? Historians have cited this journal since at least the late nineteenth century, yet no one has mentioned any events that occurred during this missing period, suggesting perhaps that the pages were expunged at some point during the nineteenth century.[54]

If Bernardo lacked the discursive space to put into language the full impact of the sensual world, his interaction with other Spanish Americans and Spaniards upon his arrival in Washington, D.C., and Philadelphia would supply him with that discursive space. Only after he had returned to the Hispanophone world did he have the opportunity to process the visuality of political-economic modernity with the political philosophy undergirding that modernity. Here, at last, would "theory," in its original, closer-to-Greek sense of "sight, spectacle, or mental view," and *logos,* "word, speech, reason," come together.[55] They would help him congeal a political philosophy that would match the growing imaginative power of the *nación.*

For the moment, Bernardo's political education, his commitment to an independent, reformed (if not explicitly republican, and definitely not democratic) nation, gradually emerges from his attempt to code visuality into language. The visual becomes sublime—incapable of translation, causing consternation and excitement—immediately after his thinking expands to incorporate the concepts of nation and good government. His education is based on his having witnessed and, in his mind, having paired economic industry with political industry. Just as significant, the sociopolitical body that he becomes increasingly concerned with has now become "the republic of the kingdom of Mexico." His commitment would not originate through debate, discussion, or the reading of political philosophy. Rather, through its ceaseless repetition, his narrative strives to give linguistic shape to the ocular. These new technological machines, of state and of industry, overwhelm the senses.

What seizes Bernardo's wonder are not natural landscapes, as the sublime power of Niagara Falls would transfix a later generation of poets from the Americas, North and South; rather, it is an abstracted world, an artificial one at that, produced by legislatures, factories, buildings, and dioramas, that takes control of his imagination.[56] In effect, the spectacularness of the modern city and the conjoining of industrial power with political might become part of the reason to support revolution. The abstraction of human labor into industrial machines and the well-planned-out beautiful city come to represent all that is good about government. Form and output dominate at this point over content and history. Bernardo was seduced by and came to desire the aesthetic abstract world of production, seeing the world as a produced order, a malleable order that humans actively shape. Rather than celebrate the rights of Man, he latched onto industrial development, the urban city, and its government. These became his touchstones, and all in the service of producing a happy social body. Already, even before delving into the heady world of Hispanophone politics, Bernardo has shifted even more than his brother Antonio from the *patria* to the *nación;* he has begun to imagine the rationale for cultivating a type of *nación* that will become equated solely with the social body, that of the *pueblo*.

II

PURSUING REFORM AND REVOLUTION

CHAPTER THREE

Seeking the *Pueblo*'s Happiness

Reform and the Discourse of Political Economy

The Need to Reform the Monarchy

José Bernardo Gutiérrez de Lara was the first insurgent from New Spain to arrive in the United States. During his month in Washington, D.C., from December 11, 1811 to January 4, 1812, he tells us of countless meetings with political dignitaries and Spanish-American revolutionaries, and endless support for the independence of Spanish America (which also translated into generous financial support of Bernardo's travels). Yet if Washington was the political capital of the United States, it was far from being the cultural capital. The seat of federal government had only relocated to Washington from Philadelphia a mere eleven years earlier, in 1800. "Washington," writes Elizabeth Howard West, translator of Bernardo's diary, "was commonly described at this time and for more than a century afterward in some such terms as a 'straggling village.'"[1] Indeed, with barely 5,000 inhabitants, others referred to it as the "City of Magnificent Distances," "the wilderness city," or "the Capital of Miserable Huts."[2]

Philadelphia, in contrast, was by far the most cosmopolitan city of the United States. It had one of the country's most robust economies; it was the largest city at the time, with some 111,000 residents (New York came in second at 96,000); it was the center of the country's intellectual activity; and it served as a refuge to republicans fleeing the faltering revolutions of the Atlantic, especially those of France (1789–1799) and Haiti (1791–1804).[3]

Figure 16. Christopher P. Cranch, *The Capitol* (1841).
Architect of the Capitol, Washington, D.C.

Philadelphia was, as a contemporary noted, "one great hotel, or place of shelter, for strangers hastily collected together from a raging tempest."[4] By the time of Bernardo's arrival, revolutionary Hispanics in Philadelphia, like radicals from multiple corners of the world, had started to develop a vibrant print culture. Hispanophone publications had emerged as early as the 1790s, but the number increased significantly with the arrival of revolutionaries after 1808.[5]

Historians had long been fascinated with teasing out the particular American, British, and French intellectual influences in the writings of Spanish-American revolutionaries, hoping to identify the moment that Spanish Americans fully embraced the political language of rights, self-determination, and liberty. But the quickly proliferating Hispanophone print culture in Philadelphia and rest of the United States was not initially suffused with the language of the rights of man and the need for revolution. Rather, their criticism of the Hispanic monarchy was often couched within the language of reform, and, in particular, the desperate need for commerce (in the much more expansive sense of the term as it was used then, as in social, intellectual, and economic commerce). Commerce, they argued, led to a much more capacious sense of the world, allowing for an increase in what they described as *la felicidad pública* or public happiness. To secure this happiness, they argued, required a fundamental shift in their understanding of economic commerce.

To fully capture the nuances of this intellectual tradition and, thus, to grasp the polemical claims made in the Spanish-language publications from the United States, the ones that Bernardo most certainly had read, requires our tracing this lineage to the larger Hispanic world itself. Here, in Part II, our narrative focus takes us both out and away from Bernardo, his activities in Philadelphia, and the unfolding insurrection in Texas and the rest of the Eastern Interior Provinces. And it also takes us back to the late eighteenth-century world of Hispanic reform. That is, rather than moving forward in linear chronological style, our story unfolds more like a spiral-like orbit, tracing the broader discursive history of Hispanic reform in order to come back around, with more gravitational force, in Chapter 4, to the world of revolutionary Hispanic print culture in Philadelphia.

If the Napoleonic invasion of 1808 marked a radical turning point, the initial responses of the emerging group of revolutionaries were not out of line with how Hispanic *letrados* had sought to improve their world. The mid-eighteenth-century Bourbon reforms may have attempted to stifle Spanish-American sovereignty in order to streamline the Spanish monarchy, but they had also reenergized Hispanic *letrados,* that class of elite men of letters who served as statesmen and administrators. During the late eighteenth century, these *letrados* generated innumerable essays, reports, and projects on ways that the Hispanic monarchy could be reformed. By delving deep into this intellectual past, one that has long been obscured by focusing solely on external influences, we will arrive at a richer, more nuanced understanding of the revolutionary Spanish-American world at the turn of the nineteenth century.

To care for this social body, *letrados* turned to emerging theories that addressed the social body's needs and its wants. The theories of choice were those related to political economy, as the field of study was being reconfigured into its modern, recognizable variant. The field transformed during the eighteenth century, emerging as a way to better understand the relationship between the circulation of wealth and what had become the modern nation-state. But even as *letrados* turned to these developing ideas, they subtly though significantly altered the connotation of the social body, one that shifted from the monarch proper to a much more expansive sense of the term. In doing so, Hispanics may have been seeking ways to ameliorate socioeconomic conditions, but they were also involved in a larger epistemic shift, one that over the course of the eighteenth century they began to describe as "modern."[6] This shift was on the surface one from mercantile capitalism to free-trade capitalism, but it was embedded in a much larger systemic transformation, one where people were slowly no longer viewing the world as a received order but, rather, as a produced order.

The Discourse of Political Economy as the Vehicle for Greater Happiness

Spain's fortunes had changed drastically since its golden age, that period stretching across the sixteenth and seventeenth centuries which coincided with the rise of Habsburg rule (1516–1700). It was during this period that Catholic Spain emerged as a religiously-politically consolidated unit, accomplished, in part, via the expulsions of Moors and Jews from the Peninsula, the colonization of the Americas, and the wholesale transfer of bullion from the Americas to European coffers. It also produced a wealth of artistic and literary treasures, reflecting a burgeoning religious and nationalist fervor. But Spain began a precipitous decline in the late seventeenth century. By the late 1700s, shifting European alliances placed Spain on the defensive and made it reliant on France, while the stream of American silver seemed to pour through the sieve of the Spanish economy into the treasuries of other European states. It was plagued by expensive and endless wars, while its grip on North America slowly began to slip. It was more than clear that Spain's global status had diminished, and *letrados* focused their energies on reforming the Hispanic monarchy by turning to new philosophies that sought to improve both the grandeur of Spain and the happiness of the people—projects, not coincidentally, that were seen as inextricably linked.[7]

Spain had long lost its grandeur; the great Spanish eighteenth-century *letrado* Gaspar Melchor de Jovellanos knew this only too well. "No nos engañemos [Let us not deceive ourselves]," he wrote in 1785:

> La grandeza de las naciones ya no se apoyará, como en otro tiempo, en el esplendor de sus triunfos, en el espíritu marcial de sus hijos, en la extension de sus límites ni en el crédito de su Gloria, de su probidad ó de su sabiduría. Estas dotes bastaron á levantar grandes imperios cuando los hombres estaban poseidos de otras ideas, de otras máximas, de otras virtudes y de otros vicios.

> *Todo es ya diferente en el actual sistema de la Europa. El comercio, la industria, y la opulencia, que nace de entrambos, son, y probablemente seran por largo tiempo, los únicos apoyos de la preponderancia de un estado,* y es preciso volver á estos el objeto de nuestras miras, ó condenarnos á una eternal y vergonzosa dependencia, mientras que nuestros vecinos libran su prosperidad sobre nuestro descuido.
>
> [The greatness of nations is no longer based, as it was formerly, on the splendor of its triumphs, in the militaristic spirit of its sons, in the expansion of its borders, nor on the fame of its Glory, of its probity, or its wisdom. These qualities were sufficient to raise grand empires when men held other ideas, other maxims, other virtues, and other vices. *But everything is now different in the present state of Europe. Commerce, industry, and wealth, which are born among one another, are and probably will be for a long time the only bases for the superiority of a state,* and it is incumbent upon us that we make these the object of our goals, or we shall condemn ourselves to an eternal and shameful dependency, while our neighbors wage their prosperity over our neglect.][8]

Jovellanos was not alone in his sentiment; many others, including the great Spanish statesman Pedro Rodríguez de Campomanes, also lamented Spain's economic decline.[9]

It was well known that Spain had no industry, no public works, no transportation network of roads, and no navigable rivers; it had suffered a series of incompetent monarchs; in turn, its population, which was only beginning to grow after shrinking in the seventeenth century, was immersed in poverty and steeped in superstition. Spain's economy was primarily a manorial one, where the vast majority of the productive land was locked in the hands of the nobility and clergy and where more than half of the population was rural. In short, "the Spanish economy was an archipelago, islands of local production and consumption, isolated from each other by centuries of internal tariffs, self-sufficiency, poor roads and meager transport." The situation in Spanish America was far worse.[10]

Yet, if there were small pockets of merchants in the port cities of Cádiz and Barcelona, they certainly were not evidence of an emergent bourgeoisie. As a result of the absence of this social class, as José Antonio Maravall has astutely observed, there were no bourgeois politics or interests as there had been in France and the United States. Rather, the upper classes continued to consist of the nobility and clergy. Still, Maravall's subtle analyses demonstrate that though a bourgeois class may not have existed, many of the royal reformers, *letrados* par excellence, certainly embraced the thought affiliated with that class.[11]

From the 1760s to 1790s, Campomanes, like Jovellanos, served as powerful statesmen within the monarchy. As such, they developed several far-reaching, prescient proposals to aid the deteriorating trans-Atlantic monarchy by stimulating agriculture, commerce, and industry.[12] More than anything, they latched onto the concept of *felicidad* ("happiness") and *amor a la patria* ("love of country"), and sought ways to improve the well-being of the *patria*. Their growing attention to happiness, and to the desire to change the material conditions so as to make it accessible to all, was but part of a larger European symptom, as Vivasvan Soni has demonstrated. Eighteenth-century European intellectuals revivified the classical concept of happiness, and used it as the rationale for the consolidating state. And this is what Jovellanos had intuited. He sensed a shift in values, but, more than that, the concepts of *felicidad* and *patria* began to reorient themselves.

Both Soni and Maravall reveal how the idea of happiness or *felicidad* underwent a far-reaching shift in the eighteenth century. Where it had long denoted the Christian concept of happiness in the eternal afterlife, it increasingly connoted happiness in the present, temporal world of the now. And that happiness was understood not as an abstract, sentimental emotion as we do today but as something that could be acquired through the quite material means of economic prosperity, something that would be secured by good government.[13] By century's end, Soni finds that in northern Europe the political connotation of happiness had been bracketed, reduced to a privatized, sentimentalized, trivial concept.[14] But Spain appears to part with that of more Protestant northern Europe. In the Hispanic world, *felicidad* does not completely undergo this process of interiorization, as something that is understood as an individual's desire for happiness. Even though *letrados* such as Jovellanos understood that the happiness of the individual is the basis of the common good, *letrados* continued to place greater emphasis on sociality, on "the sum or result of all individuals' happiness," as Jovellanos expressed it.[15]

By the late eighteenth century, the concept develops into the syntagm *felicidad pública* or public happiness, producing an elaborate discourse on the need to secure the happiness of the social body, the collectivity. Granted, the republican spirit of the American and French revolutions had certainly placed emphasis on the common good, but these, especially that of the United States, quickly gave way, by the late eighteenth century, to liberalism's greater emphasis on the individual's well-being as the rationale for the state. The Hispanic world, on the other hand, continued to emphasize the well-being of the social body. As Maravall notes, few eras have experienced that profound sense of *comunitas* that Hispanics felt during the eighteenth century, something that they described as beneficence. For *letra-*

dos, this meant nothing less than "dedicating one's self to improving the well-being of each one of one's compatriots, at the level of the nation and for all of humanity in general."[16]

Patria, too, alters, placing greater emphasis on an expanded imagined community that is no longer limited to the monarch (patriarch), nobility, and clergy, but also begins to include the *pueblo* ("the people"). The shift from *patria* to the modern concept of the *nación,* as we saw in Chapter 1, will be a longer, circuitous process. For now, the imagined community of the *patria* will continue to resound Catholic political thought that theorized the monarchy as composite, a series of concentric circles of belonging beginning with God and descending down from the monarch, to the various kingdoms that comprised the monarchy, to the *patria chica* or the region of one's origin. By the late eighteenth century, *la felicidad pública* becomes celebrated as the supreme political virtue, explicitly related to the monarch's caring for the well-being of his vassals, increasingly described (nonderisively) as the *pueblo.* As one proponent declared, a good prince's duty was "proporcionando al pueblo toda la comodidad, ventajas y bien que le sea dable [providing the people with all the possible comfort, benefit and well-being]."[17] It is in this way that the reconfiguring economic discourses, as a means to achieve the well-being of the people, enter the Hispanic world.

Alessandro Roncaglia's magisterial historical account of the rise of political economy as a field of study traces the nuanced shifting discourses, from Antiquity to the present, related to economic thought. These, he argues, centered around two broad questions, one moral, the other scientific. First, what ethical rules should humans follow in the realm of economic activities; and, second, how can we accurately describe the way society functions, especially in regard to the division of labor and the means used to satisfy humans' needs through the production of commodities? These questions came to the fore in the seventeenth century just as the modern European nation-states began to crystalize, leading monarchs to cultivate advisers whose objective was to concentrate wealth and power in the hands of monarchs. "Political economy began to be recognised as an autonomous discipline, distinct from other social sciences, very gradually, beginning in the seventeenth century. Only in the nineteenth century, with the creation of the first economics chairs in universities, was the economist recognised as an autonomous professional figure."[18] Spain, in this regard, was not unlike the rest of Europe. The term "political economy" is used in print in Spain for the first time in 1769; the first Spanish manual on studying political economy was published in 1779; and the first academic chairs in political economy were established beginning as early as 1784. But the study of political economy during this period focused just as much on the moral aspects as on the scientific. And those working within the field did not see their work as disconnected from political-philosophical questions related to society or, more specifically, to the best means of securing the common good or public happiness.[19]

Campomanes sought economic reform by shifting the agricultural-based economy to an industrial-based one, though for Campomanes this meant handicraft industry rather than the incipient industrial factories in Barcelona, for example, which were only beginning to develop on the same scale as the ones in Britain and the United States. As a means to employ the impoverished, rural masses, he supported cottage industries over the few urban factories that did exist. More significantly, influenced by Adam Smith's *The Wealth of Nations,* he sought ways to cultivate self-interest among the peasants in order to promote industry, and he struggled with ending the manorial system. In effect, he attempted to restrict the power of the nobility and the clergy. His widely disseminated 1774 *Discurso sobre el fomento de la industria popular* served as a declaration for economic development. Written as an official statement to the crown, it offered a detailed twenty-one bulleted program. Jovellanos, too, offered his proposal in *Informe sobre la ley Agraria* (1795), which sought to continue Campomanes's efforts at ending mortmain. "Above all, the aim of these far reaching reforms was to lift all constraints on individual interest and create a nation of peasant proprietors, entrepreneurial citizen-farmers, from whose labours and production would stem the wealth, freedom and increase of Spain."[20] But their efforts largely failed, victims of the entrenched nobility and clergy along with local, immediate interests that resisted change.[21] Still, in the lines above, we see Jovellanos actually intuiting a much larger, epistemic transformation, one that he clearly saw related to the economy and one that was replacing the previous order of things.

The period leading up to the French Revolution and execution of Louis XVI in 1793 was a moment of great intellectual transformation in Spain. The Spanish monarch freely adopted models and ideas from his French cousin. Desperate to foment industry within Spain, King Charles IV's ministers embraced aspects of the Enlightenment, focusing on theories of economic development and the consolidation of the nation-state.[22] This loosened, especially, restrictions on the circulation of thought. Campomanes, as minister of finance, for example, set out to create formal salons dedicated to the study of economic development, and received royal endorsement to establish the Sociedades Económicas de Amigos del País (Economic Societies of Friends of the Country) which were sometimes referred to as *socie-*

dades patrióticas (patriotic societies). Influenced by the emerging comparable royal academies throughout Europe, he argued that the Economic Societies should be considered the "guiding lights of political economy," where the children of the nobility would be educated in the hope that they would go out into the world and transform the massive, impoverished Spanish population.[23] The Economic Societies were first created in the Basque Country in 1765, increasing to more than seventy in number throughout Spain, America, and the Philippines. As a buffer zone between France and central Spain, the Basque Country served as a crucial intellectual melting pot, a place where people, goods, books, and ideas circulated with much more ease than in other parts of Spain, and this was the place that generated some of the most innovative work in socioeconomic thought.[24]

The Economic Societies focused their efforts on stimulating the economy and decreasing poverty, and sought to circulate ideas from throughout Europe that could aid in developing the Hispanic world. Yet if there was no bourgeoisie leading the vanguard for free-trade capitalism, from whom did the Economic Societies receive so much enthusiastic support? Strangely enough, during the eighteenth century there were no Economic Societies in the cities that had small yet growing numbers of bourgeoisie, such as Barcelona, Bilbao, and Cádiz. This was precisely because the bourgeoisie were not the supporters of the Economic Societies; rather, the work of the Economic Societies fell to the *letrados*. As such the members of the Economic Societies consisted of clerics, magistrates, civil or military functionaries, educators, and, to be sure, some representatives of the fledgling manufacturing interests. In many cases, in fact, bishops and even members of the nobility were key sponsors. The case was quite similar in the Americas, where the Economic Societies were sponsored by viceroys, other royal administrators, and members of the landed elite; and where, given the restrictions placed on commercial trade, there certainly was much less of a sense of a bourgeoisie.[25]

The Economic Societies sought to reduce poverty and increase the prosperity of the *pueblo* by focusing on political economy and "useful" scientific knowledge that would help improve agriculture and mining. As a means to do so, they held weekly meetings, produced the first immense scientific reports that gathered data on agriculture and mining, and sponsored schools where spirited, vigorous debate was held. They helped establish the first university chairs in political economy, where both theory and practice regarding industrial development were taught. But if the American Economic Societies worked in isolation for the most part, with virtually no correspondence between one another, their work helped create the material basis for networks of communication that would later foster a sense of belonging in the Americas. Their efforts too often failed to translate into policy, but they contributed to the diffusion of basic statistical knowledge of the Americas—its agriculture, production, landscape—along with the new philosophy of political economy. Here, we can begin to see the shifts in how Spanish Americans had already started to imagine a world that they could actively shape and, eventually, transform.[26]

Along with the establishment of the prominent Economic Societies, the monarchy supported the *letrados'* desire to circulate the new wave of ideas by supporting over a dozen periodicals, though these were all based in Madrid. Among these was the first daily newspaper published in all of Europe, the *Diario de Madrid* (1758–1808). But the two that had such a broad influence and wide readership in America were the *Correo literario de la Europa (Literary Messenger of Europe),* published first in 1780–1781, and then briefly revived between 1786 and 1787, and the *Espíritu de los mejores diarios literarios que se publican en Europa (The Spirit of the Best Literary Dailies Published in Europe),* published between 1787 and 1791. In these periodicals, one could find translations and significantly edited adaptations—carefully removing critiques of Catholicism—of important Enlightenment authors even as the editors often fiercely disagreed with them, such as l'abbé Raynal, Edward Gibbon, Jean-Jacques Rousseau, Voltaire, Denis Diderot, Benjamin Franklin, John Locke, Jean-Baptiste Racine, John Milton, and other mainstays of what had emerged from the Protestant-now-becoming-secularized Enlightenment world.[27] Similar periodicals were established in the Americas, though religious and civil authorities—inspired by the Bourbon reforms to convert Spanish America into colonies—wielded significantly more authority and were much more conservative in what was permissible for publication. These emphasized much more the quantitative knowledge regarding agriculture and natural history of Spanish America along with ecclesiastical reports.[28] Still, the periodicals served as a model of rational discussion and helped disseminate the principles of scientific thought, such as that of the Franciscan Scholastic, François Jacquier, as we saw in Chapter 1. In doing so, they continued to undo the dominance of Late Scholastic thought.

The Shifting Ideologies of Mercantilism to Free-Trade Capitalism

At the heart of reform, as Jovellanos, Campomanes, and their *letrado* allies knew so well, was a need to shift from mercantilism to free-trade capitalism. Mercantilism, an early nationalist form of capitalism, had been the dominant European economic mode of production since the fifteenth century, and began to give way to free-trade capitalism in the late eighteenth century. Historians of economic thought now recognize that there was no uniform theory of mercantilism and acknowledge that it was wide-ranging in thought. Still, for our purposes, they have sketched out in general terms the significant difference between mercantilism and the laissez-faire capitalism that Smith would champion in the late eighteenth century.[29]

According to this early modern economic theory, wealth was measured by how much bullion, or gold and silver, a nation held in its coffers, not by what it produced. In this instance, wealth was embodied in the object traded itself, in gold or silver. Bullion was not a symbol standing in for the possibility of the exchange of wealth; it was wealth itself. From the fifteenth to eighteenth centuries, that is, the period that saw the development of the modern nation-state, European states set for themselves the goal of controlling trade in order to retain as much bullion as possible. They chartered national companies with the exclusive right to engage in trade, established protectionist statutes, created colonies in order to exploit their raw goods, and encouraged exports while discouraging imports. Exports meant a nation would receive more bullion while importing meant the nation would have to release bullion in exchange for goods. In this world, the economy works hierarchically, decisions made by the prince's ministers are thought to benefit the nation-state.[30]

This is to say, under mercantilism, the conceptualization that surplus value can be produced through exchange does not exist. The production of wealth can only come about through the hoarding of bullion. For Foucault, this particular understanding of wealth is related to what he describes as the Classical episteme that began to supplant the Scholastic episteme in the sixteenth century. If under the Scholastic episteme, one could never know the cosmos because it was God's world, then all we could aspire to know about God's cosmos was accomplished by comparing the resemblances of his fingerprints, the traces he had left imprinted on every object, all "in order to stir the language that lay dormant within them and to make it speak at last."[31] It was a poetic understanding of the world where similitude was the operating form of producing knowledge, where everything was connected through the great chain of being. But in the Classical episteme, with the modern philosophy of the Renaissance and the Reformation, knowledge was now made accessible and immediate, opening at last God's book of knowledge. Rather than being a poetic approximate of *logos,* language now represented reality: "just as words had the same reality as what they said, just as the marks of living beings were inscribed upon their bodies in the manner of visible and positive marks, similarly, the signs that indicated wealth and measured it were bound to carry the real mark in themselves."[32] Everything there was to know was already laid out on the table of the universe waiting to be tabulated and taxonomized. It could not grow nor depreciate. Thus, in the world of mercantilism, the monarch's ministers saw themselves as merely moving pawns on the table of the economy, confident that their strategies would ensure the *felicidad* of their *patria*.

But in 1776 Smith revolutionized economic thinking. Wealth, he argued, was not measured by the amount of gold or silver a nation held, but rather by how much a nation produced and traded. He inverted the hierarchical system of thinking by placing individual producers, not the prince's ministers, at the top of the economic system, and argued against mercantilism's nationalist policies. Rather than trade restrictions, free trade, where individuals could pursue their self-interest, would ultimately work toward creating a better society precisely because their individual economic choices would help cultivate a balance between buyers and sellers.[33] Indeed, Jovellanos himself, like Campomanes, was taken by Smith's radical ideas. Jovellanos read Smith in English and French, and frequently noted in his diary that at the end of the day he had "read Smith."[34]

The goal of economic reform, for Smith as for Jovellanos and Campomanes, was not only wealth and power for the monarch but, increasingly, as we have seen, the material happiness of the people. Wealth was but a means to an end, where the goal was the well-being of the nation, of the people. At this moment, in the late eighteenth century as the modern discourse of political economy consolidates, there is a clear relationship between economic reform and what we may now describe as the social contract.[35] Social contract theory flourished during the Reformation when Protestant and Catholic philosophers debated the origin of society as a way to rationalize the legitimacy of political authority, and had led to the formulations, beginning in the seventeenth century, by Francisco Suárez (whom we will hear more from later), Thomas Hobbes, Locke, and Rousseau. The premises of social contract theory begin with the idea of people coming together and giving up certain rights in order to ensure tranquility and stability. But in the course of the Hispanic eighteenth century, the social contract, at this moment that of monarchical government, becomes associated with the well-being of the people.

The depth of that connection may have been obscured by our contemporary parlance. At best, we tend to see political economic discourse as inherently asocial, concerned primarily with quantitative scientific analysis, and at worst, we assume it is disconnected from anything having to do with social justice or human rights. But as the economic historian Emma Rothschild demonstrates, for Smith and eighteenth-century economic philosophers free trade—which they called freedom of commerce—"is an emancipation from personal, political, and sometimes physical oppression. The poor are oppressed by the laws of settlement . . . ; the Germans are oppressed by having to feed sovereigns' horses; people who try to export sheep are oppressed by laws 'written in blood'; apprentices are oppressed by corporations. . . . The personal and the commercial, the economic and the political, the rational (or calculable) and the emotional (or intuitive) are here intimately interrelated."[36] Economic reform leads to the end of an oppressive, difficult life; it seeks to improve the quality of the individual's life chances. Indeed, this is also one of the original definitions of political economy. In his 1755–1756 essay, "Discourse on Political Economy," Rousseau argues that it "originally merely means the wise and legitimate government of the household, for the *common good of the entire family.* The meaning of the term was subsequently extended to the government of the large family which is the state."[37] Political economy in this period is grounded in the concern for the well-being of the nation-state, one whose symbolic representation vacillated between that of the monarch and, increasingly, the monarch's vassals. In the words of the economic historian Karl Polanyi, it is as if eighteenth-century statesmen and intellectuals have "discovered society."[38]

As historians and theorists have demonstrated, the rise of Smith's revolutionary vision of economics was inseparable from the formation of liberal republican nation-states in the Protestant Atlantic world. The ideology of one ineluctably built on that of the other; in both, the concept of the rights of the *individual* as the locus of economic and political sovereignty was crucial.[39] If one generalization may be made of liberalism, that vastly broad school of thinking inaugurated by Hobbes and one that developed in the more Protestant segments of the Atlantic world, it is that it takes as its foundation the freedom of the autonomous individual as the highest economic and political virtue.[40] This foundational autonomous subject is driven by his "personal interests" in helping to shape the world he seeks to inhabit; and, peeling the discursive layers of history further still, the emergence of this sense of autonomy (of having "personal interests") has, too, its particular history. Indeed, these seeds of personal interest—beginning with the Protestant notion of individual salvation, the Cartesian and Lockean theories of subjectivity as the source of all knowledge, the Smithian claim that pursuing individual interest would lead to a more productive, fuller life—had already been so deeply implanted by this time as to be the norm in Anglo-Protestant countries.[41]

This Anglo-Protestant theory of subjectivity was shaped in the political cauldron of the social contract: from absolutist monarchies, constitutional monarchies, to, in the United States, liberal republican government. In the eighteenth century, Anglo-Americans developed their critique of monarchical rule through the language of corruption. If the 1688 Glorious Revolution in England had resulted in a virtuous constitutional monarchy, by the eighteenth century, Anglo-Americans firmly believed that British monarchical virtue had become corrupted through royal bureaucrats' pursuit of self-interest. As a result, Anglo-Americans turned to various intellectual traditions, and "fashioned their vision of a republic grounded in the virtue of citizens who placed the common good [i.e., happiness] above the pursuit of mere self-interest."[42] The tension between self-interest and the common good was a fine line to tread. After all, already built into their critique was the concept of possessive individualism, the idea that the individual alone owns and is responsible for their own skills and can thus use them to their own ends, toward their own self-interest. The historian J. G. A. Pocock argues that this republican rhetoric predominated in the United States *prior* to the 1787 Constitutional Convention. By the end of the convention, however, republicanism had begun to give way to liberalism, a shift that many historians have described as the "end of classical politics." If the ideal republican citizen had worked toward achieving the common good, the liberal citizen "appears as conscious chiefly of his interest and takes part in government in order to press for its realization."[43] But this balancing game, between pursuing one's self-interest while creating the sociopolitical conditions that would allow for others to flourish would, by the early nineteenth century in the United States, yield to the pursuit of self-interest characteristic of liberalism.[44]

The situation was rather different in the Hispanic world. Where Jovellanos and Campomanes, among others, advanced anti-mercantilism and limited free trade in order to reform the Hispanic monarchy, few had fully embraced the language of possessive individualism and of rights. They sought reform as members of the aristocracy *becoming* bourgeoisie (many *letrados* were involved in extensive private business ventures that suffered because of the lack of free trade) who had witnessed the impoverished living conditions of vast numbers of Spaniards. It is in this regard that a small group of *letrados,* so inspired and influenced by French and English Enlightenment thought, "tried the double impossibility of forcing Spain to make a great historic leap in the realm of economic and social development and, then, to stop it in its evolution: a double and contradictory effort to accelerate and then paralyze the flow of history." That is, they sought free trade and desired to cultivate self-interest among the masses, but they halted at the threshold of liberal, individual, political freedom, of embracing fully the concept of the "rights of man" for the masses. In many ways, this was because these *letrados* were not bourgeois, notwithstanding their bourgeois mentality. The ultimate goal of economic reform was not the cultivation of a language of *individual* rights, but rather the well-being of the *pueblo*. But this "well-being" continued to be understood patriarchically as something that the elite knew how best to arrive at.[45]

Here, we are at a clear crossroads between the Protestant-now-becoming-secular north Atlantic world (as theorized by Max Weber) and the adamantly Catholic Hispanic south (as theorized by Maravall). Where the Protestant Reformation served as a means to internalize rationalization, it also helped cultivate a sense of self-sufficiency, autonomy, or what Charles Taylor has described as a "buffered self."[46] This sense of isolation, of the emergence of individuation, was an unintended consequence of the Protestant Reformation, where, as Weber puts it, Protestants were faced with an "unprecedented inner loneliness of the single individual. . . . [H]e was forced to follow his path alone to meet a destiny which had been decreed for him from eternity. No one could help him. No priest, for the chosen one can understand the word of God only in his own heart."[47] But the Catholic Hispanic world refused this path. Thus, while Protestant Europe cultivated—at an unconscious level via detours and dead ends, to be sure—the political theory of possessive individualism as the basis of the new political economy of free trade, the Hispanic world turned instead to the well-being of the *pueblo*. For example, even as Campomanes championed land reform, opening up the manorial system that benefitted the nobility and clergy to the detriment of the masses, he held strong to the idea that Spain needed an absolutist monarch guided by his ministers to ensure that these changes took place; there certainly was no need for a language of individual rights.[48]

At last, reformers were able to convince vested interests to lift at least some of the mercantilist trade restrictions placed on Spanish America. As part of the Bourbon reforms, from the 1760s forward several experimentations with free trade were implemented in Spanish America. But these were quite restricted efforts that, in the end, would only serve to embolden Spanish-American demands. The misnamed program of *comercio libre* (free trade) "abolished the monopoly of Cádiz but reaffirmed the monopoly of Spain; it opened Spanish America to all Spaniards but closed it more firmly to the rest of the world. The colonies were given more avenues into the Spanish market but denied access to the world market. They were flooded with imports from Spain but protected more closely against foreign interlopers." The reforms, however, were aimed at benefitting Spain first. The Americas remained mere objects to be used. Thus, even while other European countries began to shift economic priorities, the Spanish monarchy held fast to the hierarchical logic of mercantilism. Spain refused to abandon the mercantile system, and instead instituted even stricter mercantilist policies. It actively sought to convert the Americas into colonies whose sole purpose was to produce raw materials and consume goods sold to them only by Spain.[49]

This shift in capitalism, from nationalist-mercantilist policies to free trade, required a larger epistemic shift. It required individuals to begin to see the world as one that was no longer hierarchical and relatively fixed, where economic decisions were best made not by ministers. Rather, economic agency was relocated to the level of the individual. In doing so, individuals, no longer merely statesmen and merchants but increasingly the masses, began to see themselves and are themselves interpellated as sovereign subjects. But such was not the case in the Hispanic world. It may have embraced the new thinking of the economy, but it continued to place more emphasis on corporate entities, where the rights of the *pueblo* (an indivisible entity, as we saw earlier) would continue to reverberate slightly stronger than the rights of the nobility and clergy.

If Spain had started to liberalize in the 1760s by allowing the circulation of Enlightenment political economic thought and instituting limited economic reforms, the Atlantic Revolutions (American [1775–1783], French [1789–1799], Haitian [1791–1804]) brought an abrupt halt to that. Even more personally devastating to the Spanish king, his cousin, the French Bourbon King Louis XVI, was beheaded by the French revolutionaries in 1793. As a result and in a desperate attempt to prevent the contagion of revolution, Spain sought to lock down the press and suppressed much of the work of the Economic Societies. The Spanish minister, the Conde de Floridablanca, who had previously been an ardent supporter of the Economic Societies and dissemination of Enlightenment thought, became not unnecessarily paranoid, fearing that the French Revolution would spill over into Spain. Repressive restrictions of all kinds were instituted where a modicum of freedom had existed before; and in America, where freedom of thought had never existed to the extent it had in Spain, repression became more severe.[50] Still, the Hispanic *letrados* continued to struggle to find ways to imagine new methods of improving the well-being of their *patria* without raising the suspicion of the anti-French censors. From what had been a vibrant intellectual world would emerge prominent Hispanics who would serve as unofficial observers and diplomats in the United States and all of whom were enmeshed in the world of commerce.

The Commercial Interests of Philadelphia's Early Spanish Diplomats

The Cuban creole Juan de Miralles y Trajan was the first to arrive and make a lasting impression when he secretly arrived in Charleston, South Carolina, on December 12, 1777. Miralles had entered the United States surreptitiously as an "observer" of the Constitutional Congress.[51] Embittered by the recent defeat at the hands of the British, Spain had sought ways to undo the British Empire, and saw the turmoil in the British-American colonies as a perfect opportunity to regain prestige along with some of the American territory it had lost.[52] Yet Spain was apprehensive and did not want to provoke any similar unrest among its Spanish-American colonies. Thus, it preferred its official policy of neutrality while clandestinely supporting the Continental Congress by sending supplies through New Orleans and military forces from Spanish Texas; and rather than sending official diplomats, Spain preferred to gauge its interests by sending unofficial observers.[53]

If the early Hispanic diplomats all have one thing in common, it is their profound investment in commercial trade. Miralles, for example, came

> [f]rom one of the most powerful commercial families in Cuba. . . . His father, Manuel de Miralles, had secured official approval to trade with the English in the early 1700s and had earned a substantial fortune. Juan continued the family tradition of successful commercial operations. He had a network of contacts that extended through the Caribbean to the Atlantic Coast of North America. Fluent in English, he had numerous business dealings with Philadelphia merchants. . . . And [he] was "one of the Havana traders most active with the thirteen colonies."

Spain came to rely on commercial interest as the subterfuge for espionage. So much did Spain not want to alert the British to Miralles's presence that it created a great, elaborate plan involving schemes to establish a trading firm, all endorsed with various official Spanish documents, and, to top it all off, an unfortunate "emergency" at sea that required Miralles to land in Charleston. By June 1778 he had installed himself in Philadelphia and befriended almost everyone he met. He was a consummate host and was considered by everyone a quasi-diplomat, notwithstanding his repeated denials.[54]

Other diplomats built upon Miralles's expertise in economic trade, expanding their repertoire from practice to theory. Diego María de Gardoqui Arriquibar (1735–1798) was the first official Spanish diplomat to the United States; yet rather than being appointed minister, he was assigned the lesser rank of chargé d'affaires due to Spain's refusal to acknowledge U.S. independence. Like Miralles, Gardoqui was appointed because of his extensive commercial networks. But Gardoqui's interests shifted from Miralles's north-south networks (between the United States and the Caribbean) to a trans-Atlantic east-west network (among Spain, England, and the United States).

Along with material interests, Gardoqui was just as invested in the new wave of thinking regarding commercial trade. He supported the publication of the crucial *Correo Mercantil de España y sus Indias,* one of the earliest periodicals designed to publish data on trade in the Hispanic Atlantic in order to promote it.[55] Born in the Basque city of Bilbao, Spain—something he would have in common with many other politically and economically inclined Spaniards—he was educated in England, and established a banking and trading firm. Through this firm, Gardoqui, on behalf of Spain, had clandestinely supplied Anglo-American revolutionaries with much-needed supplies at the outset of the American Revolutionary War. He arrived in the United States in 1785 to negotiate the boundaries of Spanish America with the United States and, more importantly, the terms of the navigation of the Mississippi River. He would ultimately fail in developing a treaty and would return to Spain frustrated and exhausted in October 1789.[56]

In 1795 Spain finally capitulated to U.S. demands and signed the Treaty of San Lorenzo, known as the Pinckney Treaty in the United States, and at last recognized the United States as an independent nation. Spain had been immersed in several turbulent crises in the 1790s: the French Revolution and fear of contagion, uprisings throughout Spanish America, escalating tensions with Britain, and internal dissension among Spaniards who had become frustrated with an increasingly bureaucratic and corrupt regime. As a result, Spain sought to establish amicable relations with the United States and signed the treaty, giving the latter full navigation rights to the Mississippi River and the right of deposit at the port of New Orleans for three years and establishing the boundary between the United States and Spanish Florida.[57] The king's legation in Philadelphia was upgraded; the number of diplomats sent from Madrid began to grow, and the chargé d'affaires was replaced with the new, official diplomatic position of minister plenipotentiary.[58]

Figure 17. Artist unknown. *Don Diego María Gardoqui* (ca. 1785).
Courtesy of the Palace of the Governors Photo Archive (NMHM/DCA), Negative #191935.

Miralles and Gardoqui established an early pattern in U.S.-Spanish relations, one that would continue to develop. If diplomacy was the primary reason for their being in the United States, it was because free-trade capitalism was central to the shifting world of international relations. The modern usage of the word "diplomat," as relating to a person engaged in international affairs, became established in the period leading to the French Revolution, the bourgeois revolution par excellence.[59] The expansion of commercial networks, in other words, was crucial to diplomacy especially because, as Smith had declared so radically in his 1776 *Wealth of Nations,* free trade was the foundation to a truly lasting peaceful international order. As an emerging discourse, the field of political economy, at this moment, is intimately intertwined with the philosophies of justice and desire for peace.

Markets, trade, and the desire to tie the economic future of the Hispanic world with that of the United States became the practical goal of these early diplomats. Both Miralles and Gardoqui came from prominent families with long-established roots in banking and trade, and their efforts resulted in suturing the markets of Philadelphia and Havana along with other trans-Atlantic ports. The new official legation continued in the steps of their predecessors who, during the American Revolutionary War, had tightened what was already by then an extensive trade network between Philadelphia, England, Spain, and Spanish America, in particular Cuba.[60] But the next generation of Spanish diplomats would not only bring practical experience in markets; they would also be steeped in theory. Fascinated by the philosophy of political economy, they would help integrate Philadelphia into a trans-Atlantic Hispanophone print culture.

Early U.S. Hispanic Publications, the Critique of Mercantilism, and the Common Good

If early Spanish diplomats to the United States had been ensconced in the commercial world more so than in the life of the mind, the first official Spanish diplomats to the United States were emphatically involved in both. Carlos Martínez de Irujo (1763–1824), the Marquis de Casa Irujo after 1802, served as the first official Spanish diplomat to the United States and minister plenipotentiary, arriving in July 1796.[61] He had quickly risen up the diplomatic ranks, having served the Spanish embassies in The Hague and London, and had, like his predecessors, developed extensive commercial enterprises. But unlike his predecessors, Casa Irujo had to contend with a contentious U.S. administration, one that had set its eyes on the Spanish possessions of Florida, the Mississippi Valley, and parts of New Spain, and his cantankerous personality certainly did not ease diplomatic relations. Along with his diplomatic interests, Casa Irujo likewise cultivated his interests in letters. In the United States, he became one of the first Hispanic members of the American Philosophical Society as Benjamin Franklin published his *Letters of Verus* in 1797, a strident defense of the Treaty of San Lorenzo that secured the Americans' right to navigate the

Mississippi.[62] While in London, he prepared a partial translation of the Marquis de Condorcet's compendium of Smith's *Wealth of Nations.*

Casa Irujo's interest in political economy and Smith, mediated by Condorcet's summary in French, was quite representative of the particular stream of Enlightenment philosophy that entered and flourished in Spain. The Inquisition had banned *The Wealth of Nations* in 1792, the same year that Casa Irujo published his version of Condorcet's summary of Smith. In fact, Casa Irujo relied on the goodwill of the Spanish prime minister Manuel de Godoy, who facilitated publication. But the censors were far from uniform in their persecution, and merely excluding the targeted author or book's name was enough to evade censure. Thus, while Casa Irujo's translation includes the title of Smith's work, it never mentions him by name, and deceitfully claimed that the author was Condorcet.[63] "Háganse

Figure 18. *Carlos María Martínez, Marqués de Casa D'Yrujo.* Attributed to a member of the Sharples family, after James Sharples Sr., ca. 1796–1810.
Independence National Historical Park, Philadelphia.

familiares sus conocimientos [Let its knowledge become well-known]," Casa Irujo wrote in the preface to his translation:

> Cundan, y esparzanse las buenas ideas, y destierre al fin la verdad al error de un Imperio que por nuestra desgracia ha tenido muchos años. Este ha sido el objeto que me he propuesto en la traduccion del compendio de la mejor obra de economía política que se ha escrito hasta ahora. *La Riqueza de las Naciones* es ya obra muy conocida, y acreditada para detenerme en hacer su elogio: el nombre del Marques de Condorcet que ha hecho el analisis que presentamos, es un testimonio del aprecio que debe merecer esta obra.
>
> [Let good ideas spread and grow, and let them at long last banish the truth of an Empire's mistake, which to our misfortune it has held for many years. This has been my goal in translating the compendium of the most important work of political economy that has been published to this day. *The Wealth of Nations* is a very well-known and reputable work, and here let me make tribute: the name of the Marquis of Condorcet, who produced the analysis that we present here, is a testament of the esteem that this work deserves.][64]

Publishing required permission from the Inquisition, but even when they denied permission, censure could serve as positive publicity for proscribed works. Indeed, according to the literary historian Jefferson Rea Spell, "The publicity involved in the [Inquisition's] prohibition was to be desired by an author rather than dreaded."[65] The Inquisition's edict notwithstanding, *The Wealth of Nations* had circulated among literate Spaniards, small though the community of readers may have been, and was read in English or, as was more likely the case, in the abridged French translation, given that "before 1788 the person who could read English was a rarity in Spain." French, instead, had by far a much larger influence on Spaniards both because of its proximity to Spain and because of the shared Bourbon dynasty. English was hardly known in France in the early eighteenth century. Even then, British philosophers had only started to produce their work in English at the end of the seventeenth. Indeed, English remained a minority language in Europe, where Latin and French were considered the lingua francas.[66]

When British philosophers were introduced into Spain they were often mediated via French translations—as in the case of Casa Irujo's translation of Condorcet's compendium of Smith or, as we will see later, Valentín de Foronda's version of Étienne Bonnot de Condillac's summary of Locke, and these were abridged, adapted, and appended by both French and Spanish translators, resulting in the production of a completely new work. Indeed, French translations of Locke "remained the most important vehicle for the European diffusion of the *Essay* [*concerning Human Understanding*],"

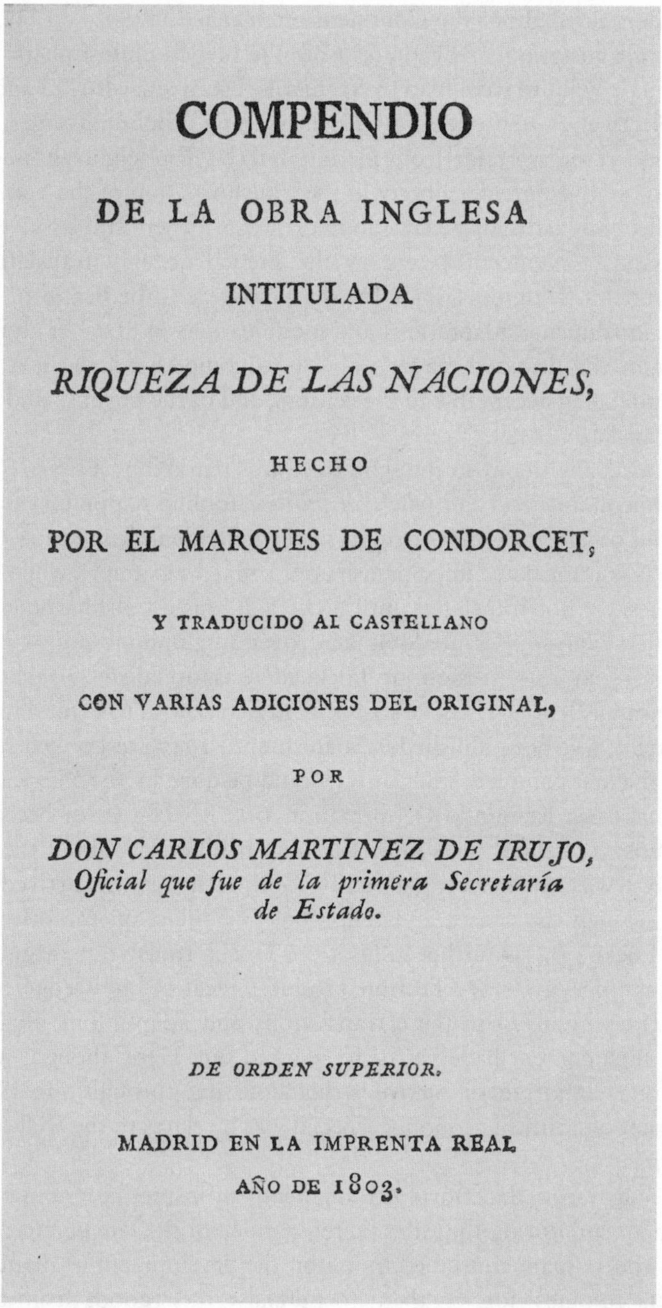

COMPENDIO

DE LA OBRA INGLESA

INTITULADA

RIQUEZA DE LAS NACIONES,

HECHO

POR EL MARQUES DE CONDORCET,

Y TRADUCIDO AL CASTELLANO

CON VARIAS ADICIONES DEL ORIGINAL,

POR

DON CARLOS MARTINEZ DE IRUJO,
Oficial que fue de la primera Secretaría de Estado.

DE ORDEN SUPERIOR.

MADRID EN LA IMPRENTA REAL

AÑO DE 1803.

Figure 19. Carlos Martínez de Irujo, *Compendio de la obra inglesa intitulada Riqueza de las Naciones, hecho por el Marqués de Condorcet* (Madrid, 1803; orig. 1792).

University of Seville.

and readers throughout the Continent often relied initially on French reviews and translations.[67] Even anti-Catholic French philosophers such as Rousseau or Voltaire were read by Spaniards, but Spaniards read and translated selectively, often excising virulently anti-Catholic passages. Translations, however, were far from mere mimicry. "The [eighteenth-century] translator enjoyed greater liberty in the transformation of the text," notes the intellectual historian Vicent Llombart Rosa, "There still survived from the previous [seventeenth] century the French taste in translating: las belles infidèles (Mounin 1955). Translations were to be beautiful yet unfaithful, introducing adaptations and modifications in favor of good taste, in favor of the destined reader's ability to comprehend the text, of the translation being acceptable to the censors, and of the purpose and quality of the translation itself."[68]

Hispanic Enlightenment thought, then, was marked by a sharp focus on political economy and the *felicidad pública* (public happiness) over any discussion of natural rights or rights of the individual. Rousseau's *Contrat social* was not translated into Spanish until 1799, for example, while Locke's *Treatises* were not translated until 1821.[69] It was a world where French and Italian *philosophes* predominated over Anglophone authors, where Condillac's extreme version of Lockean sensationalism overshadowed Locke himself.[70] In fact, Locke's 1690 *Essay,* so central to Protestant Western thought, was not published in Spanish until 1940 (and only a selection at that; the first complete translation would be done by the Mexican intellectual historian Edmundo O'Gorman in 1956).[71] The *Essay* became one of the most influential texts in establishing truth claims about the world: knowledge was not innate, planted by God; rather, it was arrived at primarily through the senses and reflection. Condillac, on the other hand, pushed Locke's thesis further in his 1746 French translation, arguing that the senses alone, and not reflection, produced ideas or knowledge. Still, the complexities involved in these translations and adaptations in the Hispanic Enlightenment have yet to be worked out. Here, though, we have traced one elaborate discursive string coursing through the Hispanic world, that of political economy especially as it relates to the well-being of the people.

As we have seen, the efforts at Enlightenment-inspired economic reform came to an end during the Atlantic revolutions of the late eighteenth century. In effect, Spain continued to inhibit the development of manufacturing in its colonies, forcing them to purchase their goods from Spanish monopolies, and even restricted trade between Spanish American colonies. What had been the consequences? Three years after Casa Irujo arrived in

Philadelphia, a ninety-page pamphlet attempted to answer this question. Published in Philadelphia in 1799, *Reflexiones sobre el comercio de España con sus colonias en America, en tiempo de guerra (Observations on the Commerce of Spain, with Her Colonies, in Time of War)* is the third known Hispanophone imprint in what is today the United States.[72]

The unsigned work has been attributed, variously, to Casa Irujo, his consul general, Foronda, and an expatriate from New Granada, Manuel Torres (whom we will see again). Barbara and Stanley Stein suggest Foronda was the author. However, the pamphlet was published in Philadelphia two years prior to his arrival. Secondly, in the 1801 English translation, the author claims to have written the pamphlet in October 1799. However, the following month, in November 1799, Foronda would write a letter while in Spain to the prime minister pleading for financial support because he was on the verge of bankruptcy; it is thus unlikely that Foronda could be the author. Charles H. Bowman Jr. makes the case for Torres's authorship, but his source is not clear. However, in an 1800 review of the English translation, the New York *Monthly Magazine and American Review* (edited by Charles Brockden Brown) states, "The Chevalier de Yrujo . . . is said to be the author." Other internal evidence also points to Casa Irujo. He had already exhibited a keen interest in political economy; he had translated Condorcet's compendium of the *Wealth of Nations;* and had gathered firsthand knowledge and experience of diplomacy and trade in The Hague and London. The pamphlet cites sources that Casa Irujo, as minister plenipotentiary, would have had more access to than would have Torres: detailed reports on trade, including tonnage and dollar amounts, from the port of Cádiz and other regions of Spain; reports on trade throughout Spanish America; citation from a French book the author had read ten years prior (that is, in 1789, while Torres was in Bogotá); and quotes from a letter sent to the "Spanish Minister in Philadelphia," that is, Casa Irujo himself. Given the sources, the documentation, and anti-mercantile argument, clearly Casa Irujo must be the author and not Foronda or Torres.[73]

Regardless of who the author is, the pamphlet begins with an unyielding critique of Spain's mercantile policies, and is adamantly pro-Spanish American in its views. Indeed, after beginning with an epigraph from *The Wealth of Nations,* the author begins by listing the effects of Spain's mercantilist policy on Spanish America: "Una estagnacion generál de Comercio, una falta absoluta de todo, los frutos preciosos del Pays sin salida, y como suele decirse por los suelos, los articulos de Europa los mas necesarios, como las ropas, lenzeria, zapatos, caldos, y otros de esta naturaleza, à precios exorbitantes. La Agricultura de resultas en decadencia, todo

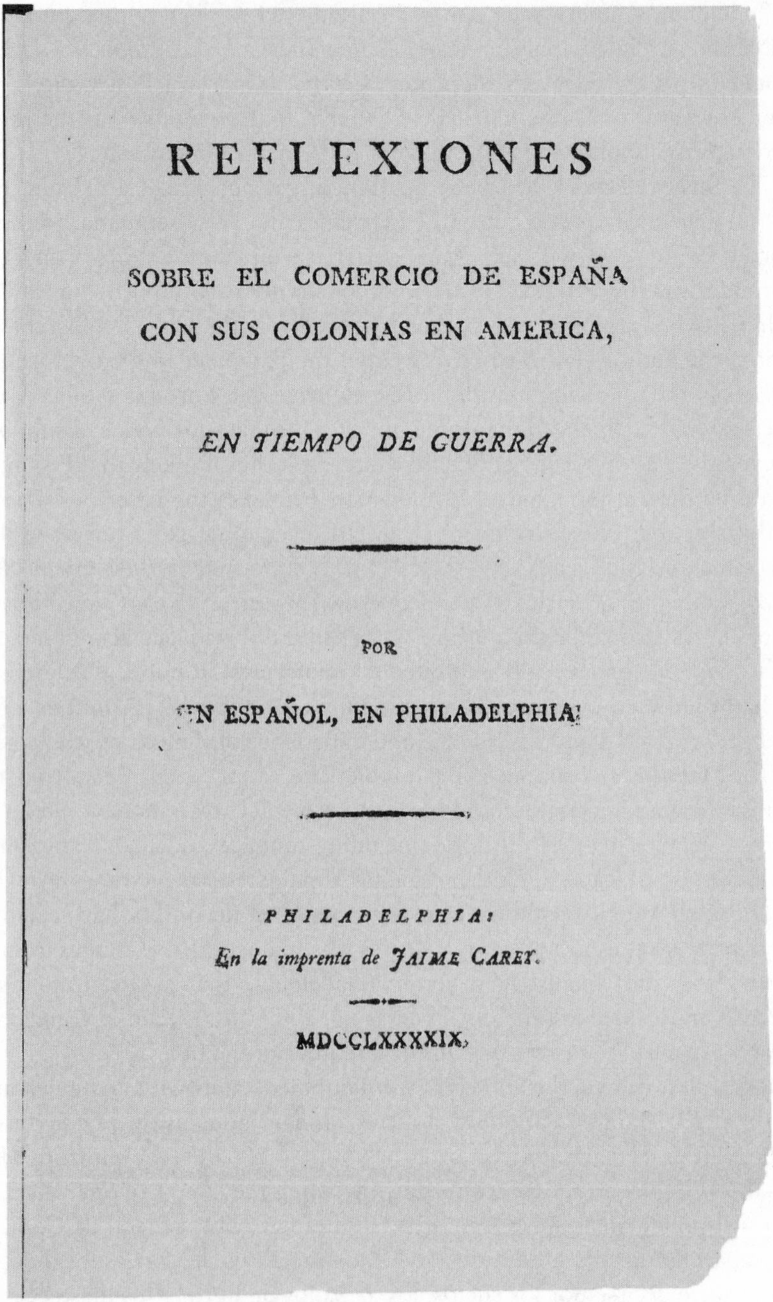

REFLEXIONES

SOBRE EL COMERCIO DE ESPAÑA

CON SUS COLONIAS EN AMERICA,

EN TIEMPO DE GUERRA.

POR

UN ESPAÑOL, EN PHILADELPHIA.

PHILADELPHIA:

En la imprenta de JAIME CAREY.

MDCCLXXXXIX.

Figure 20. Anonymous, *Reflexiones sobre el comercio de España, con sus colonias en America, en tiempo de guerra* (Philadelphia, 1799).

Courtesy of the John Carter Brown Library at Brown University.

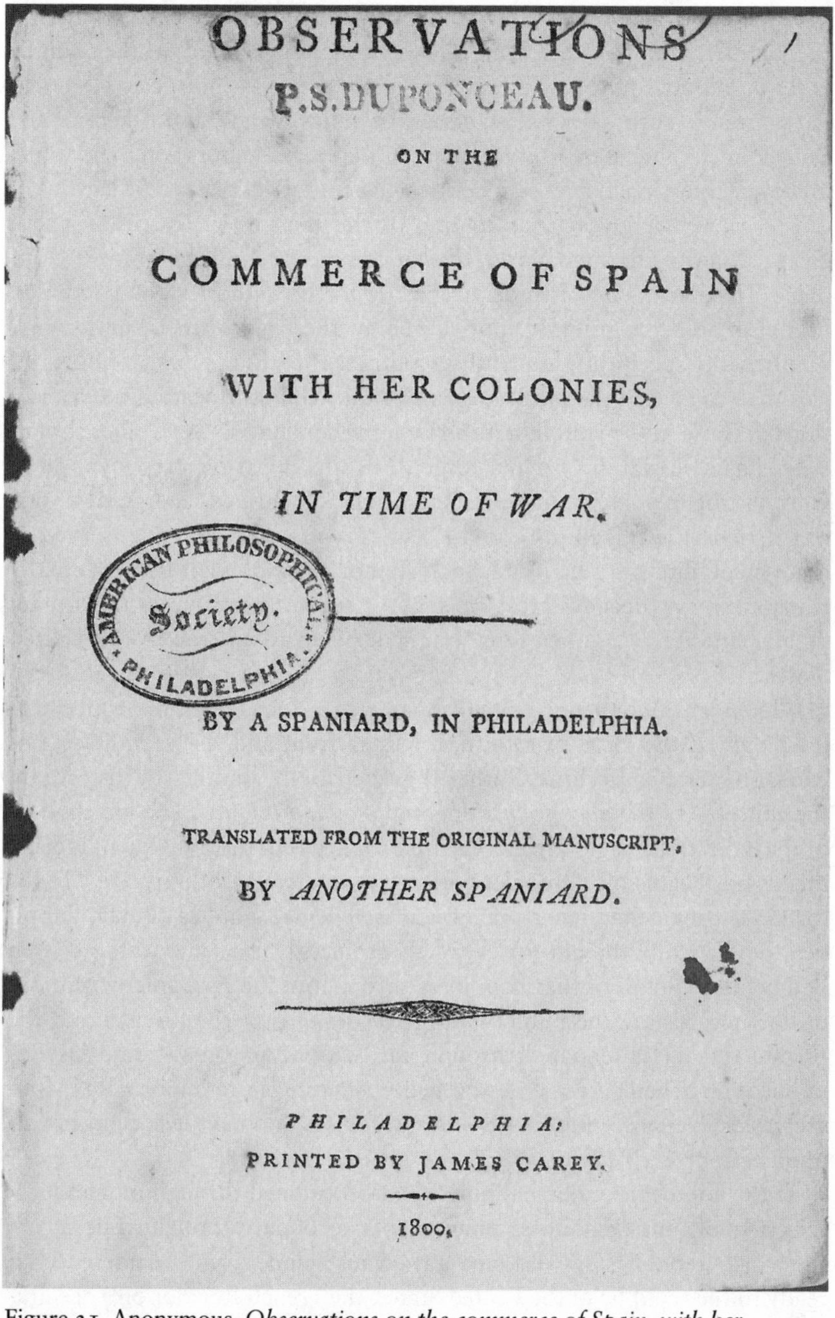
OBSERVATIONS

P.S.DUPONCEAU.

ON THE

COMMERCE OF SPAIN

WITH HER COLONIES,

IN TIME OF WAR.

BY A SPANIARD, IN PHILADELPHIA.

TRANSLATED FROM THE ORIGINAL MANUSCRIPT,

BY *ANOTHER SPANIARD.*

PHILADELPHIA:

PRINTED BY JAMES CAREY.

1800.

Figure 21. Anonymous, *Observations on the commerce of Spain, with her colonies, in time of war.* Philadelphia, 1800.

American Philosophical Society.

parado, y solo activo el Comercio de Contrabando [A general stagnation of Commerce, an absolute want of everything, the produce of the country without export, and consequently very low; the most indispensable European articles, such as woolens, shoes, brandies, wines, and others of the same kind, at a most exorbitant price. Agriculture of course on the decline, and everything inactive except contraband trade]" (42–43; 30).

The pamphlet gives voice to one of the most volatile critiques that emerged in the Hispanic world, that of commerce and economic development. This very issue of trade, according to the author of the pamphlet, had also been the primary motive behind the Anglo-American colonial revolt. More specifically, the author continues, it was the mercantilist policies that benefitted the merchants in Britain while suffocating the aspirations of those in the colonies. As a result, he concludes, "los Comerciantes, y Artistas de Inglaterra privó á Jorge III de una de las mejores Joyas de su Corona [the merchants and artists of England deprived George III of one of the richest jewels of his crown]" (31–32; 22). The pamphlet served as a prescient, dire warning to the Spanish monarchy of what would actually transpire a few decades later. As such, it is representative of the stream of Hispanophone publications that will begin to emerge in the United States.

If late eighteenth-century Spanish statesmen focused on the concept of the *patria* as the locus of reform, for Casa Irujo and, as we will see, Foronda, the emphasis shifts. Rather than *patria,* they both rely, instead, on the concepts of the *nación, pueblo,* and *felicidad pública.* The life chances of the collective *pueblo* are emphasized over that of the individual. Indeed, the author begins his pamphlet with a clear statement of purpose: "Todos los Goviernos deben tener por objeto la felicidad publica [Public happiness ought to be the aim of every government]." The mercantile system had helped ruin all of that happiness throughout the Hispanic world. But in this new vision, the public takes precedence over the private, and the private remains attenuated throughout. "Las Monarquias como las Republicas no deben perder un instante de vista este punto importante [Monarchies, as well as republics, should not for one moment lose sight of this important object]" (13).

At this moment, public happiness can be attained through monarchical government, but "republics" emerge as a secondary thought. But surely, the word "republics" would have raised suspicion, given the reference already to the republic of the United States, the French Revolution's declaration of a republic, and the Haitian declaration of independence. In this sense, the casual, innocent insertion of "republic" serves as a sign, ostensibly empty of political weight, much as it had with Bernardo's initial uses of the word. Still, the author does not pursue this line, but he does elaborate on the reciprocal relationship between the monarch and the people.

> Los pueblos como los individuos bendicen la mano que les hace felices, y es indubitable, que el amòr de los Vasallos es la basa mas solida del Trono. De esta reciprocidad de intereses debe resultar el esmero de parte de los que govi-ernan en fomentar la prosperidad generál: su poder se consolidará por la grati-tud publica, y las Naciones cogerán el fruto de su cuidado y vigilancia. (13)

> [Nations, as well as individuals, bless the hand that makes them happy; and surely the love of the subject is the most solid basis of the throne. From this reciprocity of interests must arise, on the part of those who govern, every endeavor toward the general prosperity; their power will consolidate itself by public gratitude, and nations will reap the fruit of their care and vigilance.] (9)

The common good, in this account, is a product of the dialectical relationship between "those who govern" (here the monarch and his advisers) and the nation. It is in the space between the nation and the sovereign that a "reciprocity of interests" emerges. But in the last instance, the preponderance of responsibility for the common good, "general prosperity," and "public happiness" comes to rest "on the part of those who govern." On them rests the responsibility to cultivate commerce and free trade in order to satisfy "all the wants of the infant Colonies" (13; 9).

If the author of the pamphlet focused his attention on ameliorating the socioeconomic conditions in Spanish America, the next diplomat to arrive would make an even more radical proposal. He would be the first Spanish official to declare that Spain should rid itself of its American colonies. Valentín de Foronda (1751–1821) has emerged as one of the most significant writers of the Spanish Enlightenment. Born in the Basque city of Vitoria, he was one of the most liberal of the Spanish ministers of this period, serving first as consul general (1801–1807) under Casa Irujo and then as acting minister after Casa Irujo's departure (1807–1809). A true representative of the full spectrum of Enlightenment thought, more so than any other Spaniard, Foronda appears to have been more mild-mannered than Casa Irujo, who chafed both U.S. diplomats and Foronda himself.[74] In keeping with his predecessors, he, too, was involved in several entrepreneurial ventures, many of which suffered because of Spanish mercantile policy.

Foronda was a man of letters who preferred to devote his energy to aiding the Spanish monarchy by producing and disseminating useful knowledge rather than rising through the diplomatic corps. He managed to combine his role as diplomat with that of a travel writer, moving about Europe reading and imbibing from texts that had been difficult—though not impossible—to acquire in Spain. He became a professor at the prestigious Seminario Patriótico of the Basque Economic Society in Vergara, Spain. He contributed regularly to Spanish periodicals and wrote widely on a variety of topics: penal reform, political economy, freedom of the press, public health, poverty and social reform programs, Locke's treatise on education, Miguel de Cervantes' *Don Quixote,* and Rousseau's *Social Contract.* He also translated Condillac's *Logique.* And though he became one of the most liberal Spanish reformers, he later (after the French Revolution shut down the wave of freedom of thought in Spain) suffered bitterly at

Figure 22. Anonymous, *Valentín de Foronda y González de Echavarri* (1751–1821).

Euskomedia. Public domain.

the hands of the Inquisition, was eventually imprisoned because of them, and many of his writings were censored and left unpublished.[75]

Philadelphia, by contrast, was a different experience; here, Foronda published widely and freely, enjoying the company of other intellectuals, and in 1804 became an official member of the American Philosophical Society. There he established a long friendship with Thomas Jefferson. After Napoleon's invasion and the creation of the Cortes of Cádiz, Foronda solicited Jefferson's opinion while drafting a constitution for Spain.[76] Yet he was not without his criticisms of the United States. He was flabbergasted when the government apparently did little more than shrug its shoulders as Anglo-Americans flagrantly disobeyed Spanish law and sent their goods down the Mississippi to New Orleans. In an analytical essay in which he explored U.S. sociopolitical culture and its economy, he bitingly wrote:

> algunos creerán que, aqui hay un verdadero espiritu Republicano: que todas las miras se dirigen á este objeto, pero se equivocaran. De nada se cuida menos que de infundir semejantes principios que son risibles, que son objetos de sarcarmos [*sic*], de mofas, de burlas en la parte rica de sus Naturales. Esto és muy natural; el Peluquero, el Zapratero [*sic*], el Panadero, el Cocinero ca ca. hacen dinero, al momento quieren convertirse en Señores; asi se desdeñan de llamarse iguales, y solicitan preeminencias, y como aqui no las hay creen que las consiguen riendose de todo lo que huela a Democracia.
>
> [Some may think there is a true Republican spirit here: that everyone has their eyes set on this goal, but they would be wrong. They care nothing less than instilling the most risible principles, which are the object of sarcasm, scorn, and ridicule on the part of the wealthy here. This is only natural: as soon as the barber, the cobbler, the baker, the cook, etc. etc., earn money, they immediately want to be recognized as Gentlemen. This is how they disdain themselves in calling themselves equals. They solicit titles of preeminence, and since none exist here, they believe they can obtain them by laughing at everything that smells like Democracy.][77]

Here, Foronda appears to pierce through the façade of the United States' ostensibly anti-aristocratic, democratic culture; the U.S. rhetoric of republican-democratic rule was just that. Rather than sing accolades to U.S. political culture, Foronda spent his years in the United States developing various means to help his country. And it was through the means of the commerce in ideas that Foronda thought he could best achieve this. He committed himself to the spread of knowledge, and he modeled this behavior for his Hispanic readers. In the preface to his *Letters on Political Economy,* he wrote:

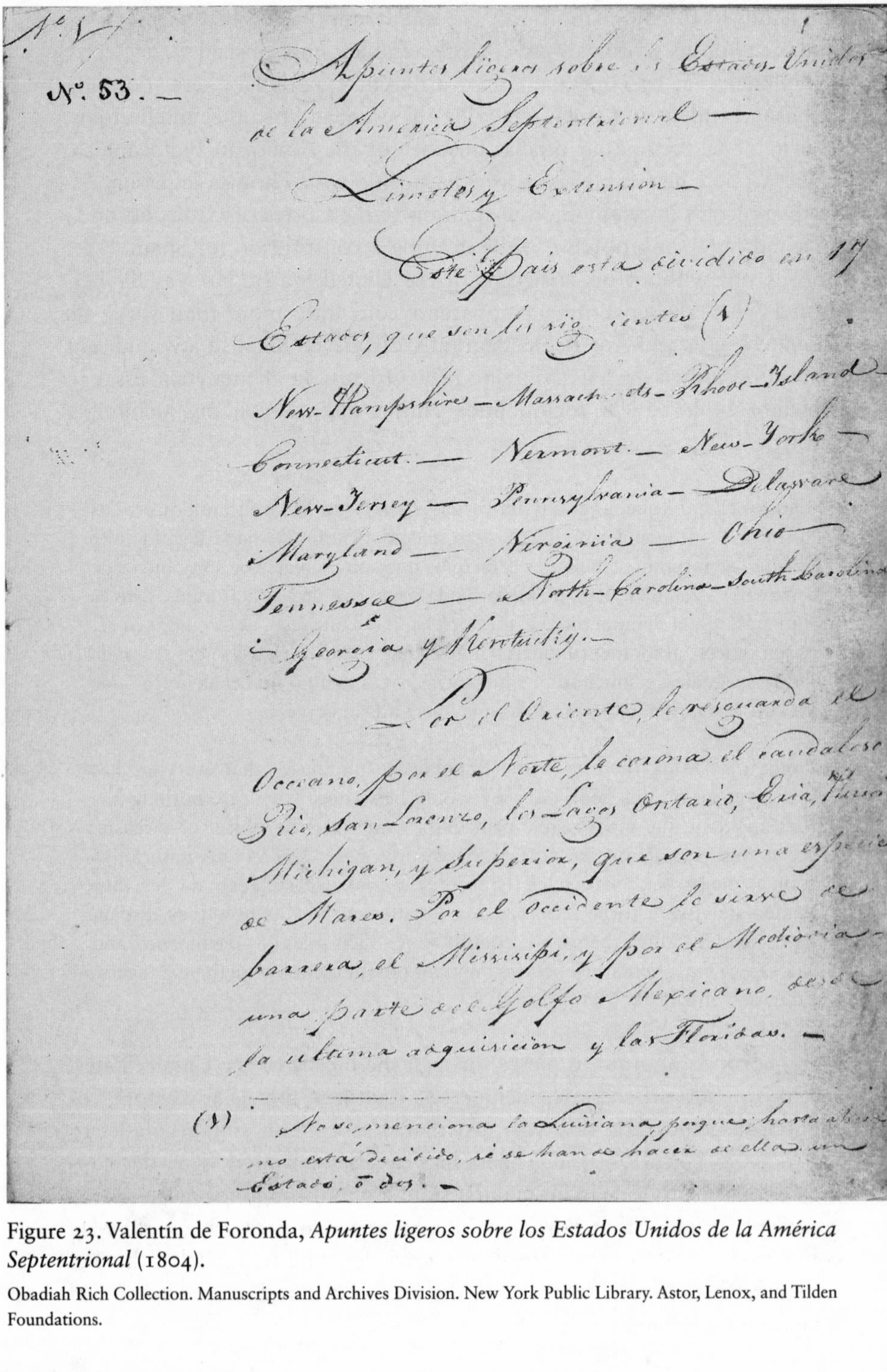

Figure 23. Valentín de Foronda, *Apuntes ligeros sobre los Estados Unidos de la América Septentrional* (1804).

Obadiah Rich Collection. Manuscripts and Archives Division. New York Public Library. Astor, Lenox, and Tilden Foundations.

> La lectura de libros me ha hecho desnudar de algunos de los muchos errores de que tenia revestida mi cabeza: los demas deseo estirparlos, y espero conseguirlo á favor de las luces que me prestarán los libros y la meditacion. Me persuade que conseguirán lo mismo todos mis compatriotas que se hallen en las mismas circunstancias que yo.
>
> [Reading has helped me get rid of many of the misconceptions with which my head was covered. Of the rest, I hope to extirpate them, and replace them with the enlightened thoughts borrowed from books and contemplation. I am persuaded that my compatriots, who find themselves in similar circumstances, will do the same.][78]

Foronda explored in his writings the many ways that knowledge could be used to ameliorate Spain's conditions. Two years prior to arriving in Philadelphia he wrote a prospectus for a newspaper entitled *Humanidad*. Among its aims were the following:

> Minorar los males que aflixen a los Españoles, suabizar sus penas, socorrer a los indigentes, destruir la mendicidad, mejorar las prisiones, perfeccionar los Hospitales, encadenar muchas enfermedades y extinguir otras, promober las casas de Misericordia y todos los albergües piadosos, ofrecer a los infelices Artesanos medios baratos de mantenerse, proporcionarles comodidades y ocupaciones lucrosas, aniquilar los germenes de los crímines, ahogando el espíritu de olgazanería e inspirando el amor al trabajo: en una palabra mejorar la suerte de sus vasallos y enriquecer la Nación.
>
> [To lessen the evils that afflict Spaniards, soothe their sorrows, help the poor, destroy mendicancy, improve prisons, expand hospitals, stop the spread of many diseases and exterminate others, support charity homes and all religious shelters, offer the poor, wretched artisans inexpensive goods to support themselves along with homes and lucrative occupations, annihilate the roots of criminality, stifle the spirit of idleness and inspire the love of work: in a word, enrich the Nation and improve the good fortune of its vassals.][79]

Throughout, the rhetoric of multiplicity dominates that of singularity; the care of the social body is prioritized over the care of the individual; thus, if one concentrates one's efforts on the undifferentiated nation, the well-being of its "vassals" will be secured. Throughout his work, Foronda elaborates various plans that would improve the well-being of his nation, particularly via political economy.

It is no surprise then that when Foronda turned to social contract philosophy he was drawn to Rousseau over Locke. In Rousseau's account, he sublimates the individual and focuses on the social body while Locke holds fast to the individual. Like Casa Irujo's translation of Condorcet's compendium of Smith, Foronda translated Condillac's compendium of

Rousseau's *Contrat Social* ("suppressing," as the subtitle explains, "that which can injure the Apostolic Roman Catholic Religion").[80] Foronda may have utilized the language of natural law—including its modern derivative, that of natural rights or what would become human rights—but his vision of the social contract emphasized sociality over individuality: "El hombre, cuando entra en sociedad, debe hacer aquellos sacrificios que obligan a todos indistintamente para la felicidad general, que es lo que aspira todo individuo [Man, when entering society, should make those sacrifices—of which everyone is obligated to make without distinction—for the happiness of all]."[81]

Toward the end of 1803 he delivered a fascinating thought experiment to the American Philosophical Society in Philadelphia in which he contemplated ways that Spain might improve its economic standing among nations. Written while he was a professor in Vergara, the fifteen-page document is titled *Carta sobre lo que debe hacer un príncipe que tenga colonias a gran distancia (Letter concerning what a prince should do with his colonies held at a great distance)*. The letter is a curious document, written in the style of a minister's advice to a monarch, though verging on the fantastic. Using a variety of rhetorical subterfuges, in order to avoid censure, Foronda barely disguises the fact that he writes about Spain and Spanish America. The letter begins by dismissing the many spurious mercantilist policies that insisted on treating the "Colonias como una oveja que debe conserver su ámo para cortarle la lána y chuparle la lèche [Colonies like sheep to be kept by their owner in order to cut their wool and drink their milk]." Spain needed commerce, not colonies, those "Bampiro[s] chupador[es] de los bolsillos [vampires always sucking from the treasury." Likewise, preventing free trade and cutting Spain and Spanish America off from the world of commerce only embroiled the monarchy in expensive wars, since, after all, these mercantilist policies required the expenditure of so much wealth on defense. But by ridding itself of the colonies, Spain would become so enriched; and Foronda provides a beautiful litany of great possibilities for Spain, from bridges and roads to hospitals and houses of mercy. In the process, however, Foronda has subtly though powerfully shifted the connotation of wealth. The examples he provides say little about increasing the monarch's specific wealth; rather, the changes would benefit the nation as a whole, the people directly.[82]

Mercantilist policy had diverted the monarch's vision. Wealth was not measured by the amount of bullion in his coffers. Rather, Foronda continues by recalling a French author's analysis (Condorcet's compendium of *The Wealth of Nations*) in which he delineated how "el verdadero comerciante (no es el traficante), és el Labrador, el manufacturero [the real

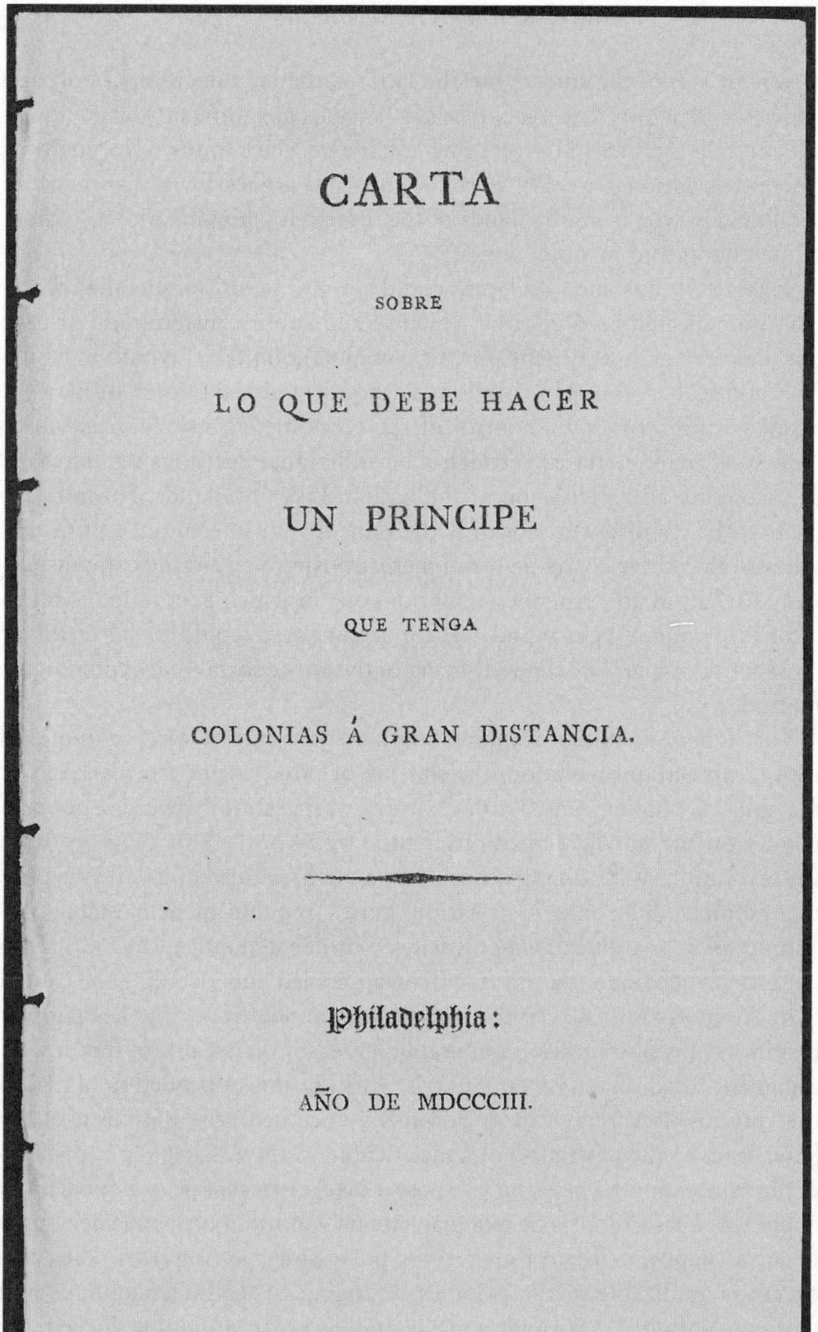

CARTA

SOBRE

LO QUE DEBE HACER

UN PRINCIPE

QUE TENGA

COLONIAS Á GRAN DISTANCIA.

Philadelphia:

AÑO DE MDCCCIII.

Figure 24. Valentín de Foronda, *Carta sobre lo que debe hacer un príncipe que tenga colonias a gran distancia*. American Philosophical Society, 1803.

American Philosophical Society.

merchant is (not the trader) but the laborer, the manufacturer]." Foronda realizes how wrong "varios Gobiernos [various governments]" were in understanding their role in promoting commerce, since to them the goal was to control national wealth. Foronda, instead, argues for a dispersion of economic power, from the hands of the monarch's administrators to those of merchants and manufacturers.[83]

Such a shift, Foronda declares, would amount to an "inesperada revolucion [unexpected revolution]," which would cause consternation at first, but then tremendous benefits for the common good. The revolution would be a political-economic revolution, a wholesale abandonment of mercantilism with its top-down control of the economy, an inversion in which individual manufacturers through their individual decisions would shape the economy and well-being of the nation. Like Jovellanos, Foronda appears to be cognizant of not only the radical shift in economic priorities, but also that these changes—from mercantilism to free-trade capitalism—would result in an epistemic revolution, one in which Spain's long-valued virtues of military glory and territorial conquest would be replaced by more modern ones like the well-being of the entire social body and not just its elite.

This economic line of thinking contains the germ of what would later lead to an actual revolution, the shifting of power from the sovereign to the subjects-cum-citizens. Foronda in no way gestures toward a *political* revolution and nowhere mentions natural rights or the bourgeois rationale for revolution. With that absence of an actual revolution, it is no surprise that political philosophy in its various guises (republican, democratic, constitutional, monarchical) is not discussed or debated at length.

Foronda concludes the letter with an appended note detailing the United States' exports for 1801 as evidence that commerce not only leads to the cessation of wars but also indubitably increases the wealth of nations, an argument lifted directly from Smith's work. In this appended note and in the very last two sentences of Foronda's document, the optimism of the letter leads to the pessimism of a melancholic reality: "Luego la España no es tan felíz, como yo pensaba por poseer las Americas. Luego este sueño es applicable á las Colonias de esta magnanima y gloriosa Nacíon [Then Spain is not as happy, as I had thought, for possessing the Americas. Then this dream is applicable to the colonies belonging to this magnanimous and glorious Nation]."[84] Foronda's melancholy is far from unique. Indeed, the trope was a dominant one in eighteenth-century Hispanic culture, and may be understood as related to the epistemic shift from viewing the world as a fixed, received order—from God—to a world in which humans come to see themselves as actively producing their world.[85] Pessimism, then, becomes the affective manifestation of the disenchantment of the world, with the withering away of God. Foronda says little as to how Spain would go about "ridding" itself of its colonies. He mentions, in passing, the king "selling" and later "exchanging" the colonies for other territory, but the majority of the essay preoccupies itself with explaining the benefits of free trade over mercantilism. His emphasis throughout, nonetheless, is the development of Spain and humanity's happiness. It would not be long, however, before his compatriots would arrive in Philadelphia with plans of their own.

Epistemic Shift

Jovellanos, Campomanes, Casa Irujo, Foronda, and other Hispanic Enlightenment thinkers yearned for reforms that would raise the prestige of their *patria.* But *patria* no longer only signified the monarch, nobility, and clergy; it also meant the *nación,* the *pueblo,* the social body, and the state. The concept of the nation had been given flesh. If, prior to the late eighteenth century, *nación* had connoted an ethnic group (such as Castilians, Moors, Indians, or Jews), now it had expanded. It now connoted the social body of the vassals along with the modern concept of the bureaucratic state.[86] As such, the *nación* becomes vivified. Not only is it an imagined community, but this abstract entity now has an administrative structure—the state—designed to insure its well-being. Likewise, prestige, honor, and valor had been reconfigured. These are now measured, not, as Jovellanos noted above, by the monarchy's territorial domain, the ostentatious performance of chivalry, or the cultural refinement of the aristocracy but rather by the well-being of the social body. These desired traits, in turn, are secured through commerce, industry, and the production of wealth. Foronda's letter in effect dreams of a bourgeois economic revolution (not unlike the American and French Revolutions), but it is a dream that has no place in reality. There are few bourgeois institutions in the Hispanic world at this time; there is no dominant bourgeoisie; and, thus, there is no attendant dominant bourgeois ideology of liberalism.

Some of these ideas had only begun to sprout in late eighteenth-century Spain. Casa Irujo's pamphlet and Foronda's dream are bourgeois manifestos that sought to replace an outdated, aristocratic mercantile system. As Jovellanos and Foronda intuited, the shift from mercantilism to laissez-faire capitalism involved a whole-scale epistemic shift. But if in the United States republican virtue was replaced with an attendant liberalism and its emphasis on self-interest, the path in the Hispanic world would continue, well into the nineteenth century, to emphasize instead sociability. The late eighteenth-century Atlantic world struggled with these shifting epistemes, between a world demarcated by mercantilism and its attendant ideologies on the one side, and free-trade capitalism on the other. There is a moment of transition here where "commerce and economic activity is [seen as] the path to peace and orderly existence."[87] But where the turn of the nineteenth-century Anglo-Protestant world shifted from this republican ideology of the common good to liberalism's emphasis on self-fulfillment, the Hispanic world would not.

For Hispanics, the language of political economy emerged not solely out of a desire to increase individual wealth but rather as a means to increase the happiness of the nation, a nation comprised of constituent groups rather than self-interested individuals. "In these societies," writes François-Xavier Guerra, "the group has priority over the individual not because men are not conscious of their individuality, but because they consider themselves and act as part of a whole, inextricably bound to one other through permanent links." As a result, this Hispanic modernity places more emphasis on the social body over the individual with his (*sic*) rights, resulting in the ideal of eschewing pecuniary self-interest over the public good.[88]

Hispanics, therefore, emphasized the other more communitarian spectrum of the new political economic language of "commerce." But they did so by drawing out both of its contemporary connotations, those of trade and sociability, of enriching the interaction between individuals through social and intellectual commerce by meeting their needs. What emerges in these texts is an emphasis on political economy as the "grammar" of social contract, as the method for ensuring the well-being of the nation. It is in this sense that Maravall characterizes this period as "marked not by egotistical individualism but instead by a *sociability* that acquires a moral character," a sociability, nonetheless, prefaced on the idea that the patriarchal elite knew best what was in the social body's interest.[89] Turn-of-the-century Hispanics had sought various ways to reform their world. But if these elites yearned to propagate and implement these ideas, others did as well, and were willing to use more radical means.

CHAPTER FOUR

From Reform to Revolution

Print Culture and Expanding Social Imaginaries

Communication Networks

If trade had sutured the Atlantic economies, it had also facilitated the circulation of revolutionary ideas. London and Philadelphia were crucial markets for Spanish America, and both competed heavily for Spanish-American trade. By the 1780s—as the Spanish monarchy was experimenting with limited free trade and the circulation of Enlightenment thought—more and more liberal-minded Hispanics were following these same routes and ending up in London and Philadelphia. The French Revolution and the beheading of the Spanish king's cousin, however, put an abrupt end to that practice. The screw was tightened once again. The Spanish monarchy instituted more extensive efforts to control commerce, both in goods and ideas. Rebellions against Spanish administrative rule, as we now well know, began to percolate soon thereafter, both in the Americas and in Spain.[1]

Revolts had long taken place throughout Spanish America, but they had been led by the more exploited, subaltern classes—the conquered Native Americans, enslaved Africans, and impoverished peasants—as opposed to the aristocratic elite.[2] By the 1780s, however, the despised Bourbon reforms had so infuriated elite Spanish Americans that they were seeking other means of protesting besides lodging complaints.[3] Meek attempts at reform emboldened more daring demands for more extensive change.

Along with temporarily loosening trade restrictions, the reforms had inadvertently stimulated new forms of sociability among the elite that allowed for the diffusion of ideas and distilling the opinions of various publics: reading groups; religious confraternities; scientific organizations; and most significantly, as we have seen, chapters of the Sociedades Económicas de Amigos del País (Economic Societies of Friends of the Country); along with other formal and informal groups were all established during this period, though these were primarily restricted to the regional capitals and trading centers. There had been no developed culture of public literary salons or cafés where ideas could be discussed in the open since, in effect, such organizations had required legal sanctioning.[4] Instead, there had long been informal *tertulias,* private gatherings held in the privacy of one's home where men and women, often members of an extended family and their friends, would come together and discuss literary, scientific, and political ideas, such as the celebrated *tertulia* that Antonio Nariño organized in Bogotá, New Granada.

But with the sanctioning of the Economic Societies in the 1780s, some of these groups became public, meeting in schools, government buildings, or homes, where, for the first time, meetings were open, as one contemporary pronounced, to all "who were 'honorable, decent, of good conduct,' either religious or secular, capable of being 'useful by reason of their enlightenment, knowledge, or talents.' " From here, the organizations began to model for a much larger segment of the public various styles of debate while facilitating the diffusion of ideas. By the turn of the nineteenth century, many of these organizations would produce offshoot groups that became underground hotbeds of radical thought, and only during that period did these new forms of sociability begin to diffuse among the more popular classes.[5]

So, too, were there new print culture mediums to facilitate the circulation of ideas. While irregularly published newspapers had emerged as early as 1722, from 1790 forward the first weekly newspapers in Spanish America appeared, in many cases edited by the very same members of these organizations. If Madrid had served as Spain's capital of periodicals, with very few newspapers appearing outside of Madrid, then the same could be said of Mexico City. The first printing press in all of the Americas had arrived in Mexico City in 1539, and the first Spanish-American newspaper, the *Gazeta de México,* appeared there in 1722, issued semiweekly. The first daily in Spanish America also emerged in Mexico City in 1805. Throughout the rest of Spanish America, the first newspapers also began to appear as early as the 1720s, in Guatemala in 1729 and Lima in 1743. The relatively low literacy rates across Spanish America (at best 10 percent in the early nineteenth century) would make it easy to dismiss these manifestations of print culture as unimportant. But as we will see, these papers were embedded in a culture where public reading had long been established, making the ideas contained in the papers accessible to a much larger audience.[6]

Nonetheless, much of this officially sanctioned commerce came to a screeching halt during the French Revolution as censorship was renewed, driving public discussion of dissent underground.[7] Meanwhile, in Spain, the unfulfilled efforts at reform had produced a growing, politically volatile group of people comprised of intellectuals (particularly lawyers, doctors, educators, and clerics), alienated members of the nobility, and the small, nascent clumps of bourgeoisie. As the first Spanish ambassador to the United States, Carlos Martínez de Irujo wrote, the American and French Revolutions had emboldened radical spirits so much that "Republican ideas were fermenting in many peninsular heads and hearts, full of fire and energy on one hand and on the other irritated by the weakness of the monarch." The Spanish monarchy did its best to prevent the circulation of news regarding the French Revolution, and it certainly did an admirable job at stymieing news regarding the American Revolution within Spanish America. Indeed, even into the 1830s Spanish Americans would complain that they knew far more about European events than they did about U.S. ones—so great was Spain's fear that the contagion of revolution would filter through the Hispanic world.[8] Their fear was well founded.

The paucity of Spanish Americans in Philadelphia had not dissuaded Hispanics from publishing their work there. The families of the Spanish legation had been the backbone of the Hispanic community in Philadelphia, producing a fluid, fleeting community. Spanish diplomats to the United States had sought with desperation since the 1790s to repair the ailing monarchy. Clearly, both Casa Irujo and Valentín de Foronda had taken advantage of the Philadelphia press to make their ideas known to their compatriots back home. Indeed, as Foronda later noted, it was much cheaper to print 200 copies of his pamphlet in Philadelphia than to have paid for four manuscript duplicates, all so that they could be circulated in Spain.[9] But they were not alone.

Philadelphia had also served as a crucial node in the trans-Atlantic circulation of Hispanic revolutionary thought and its arguments for ending Spanish rule in favor of American independence.[10] As we have seen, Nariño's 1794 translation and printing of the French Declaration of the Rights of Man and of the Citizen in Bogotá may have been the first in Spanish America, but it definitely was not the earliest example of the circulation of clandestine revolutionary thought. Certainly, attempts at ending Spanish monarchical rule had occurred throughout Spanish America, but, again, these had been led by Native Americans and Africans, leading in some cases to the creation of their own autonomous communities.

The creole Spanish Americans had their own intellectual sources from which they could have developed alternative theories of sovereignty. Among these were the classics, such as Plato's *Republic* and Marcus Aurelius's *Meditations* which held as an ideal a written constitution based on equality before the law, and the early Church fathers, such as St. Augustine's revolutionary theories in *City of God* and Aquinas's concept of distributive justice. All these had been synthesized during the medieval period and, influenced by Arabic political thought, had led to the Scholastic tradition. Scholasticism, in turn, offered the seeds for thinking of the social contract and the origin of sovereignty as emerging from the *pueblo* (people), and this line of thinking could have and, indeed, later did influence revolutionary thought. But this line of thinking had not theorized as much the possibility of *transforming* the already existing social contract of monarchical rule. It is not until the Renaissance-inspired method of skepticism was incorporated into the Hispanic eighteenth century that we begin to see rifts in the social imaginary, the imagining of different possibilities for constructing the world.

Tracing the circulation of revolutionary thought between the United States and Spanish America has proven difficult in large part because the censorship of the period made it illegal to traffic in revolutionary literature. As a result, the documents were often ephemeral and not carefully archived. Still, we can identify at least three undulating waves of revolutionary thought from the late eighteenth century through 1810, waves that with greater intensity brought Philadelphia and Spanish America closer together. The first consisted of underground, private circulation of revolutionary thought. By its nature, it is a difficult history to document, but one that percolates in the archive especially when royal authorities recorded the capture of illicit documents or persecuted individuals for their beliefs. In the pages that follow, we will have occasion to witness some of these cases. Beginning in the 1790s, this initial wave expands, becoming much more visible as revolutionary publications in the United States increase significantly. In the years leading up to the 1790s, only one Hispanophone publication had been published in what is now the United States, and that had been Cotton Mather's feeble attempt in 1699 to proselytize.[11] But in the 1790s at least ten more were published, most if not all in Philadelphia. These revolutionary documents begin to compete with the social imaginary of the more official publications of those reform-minded Hispanics that we saw in Chapter 3. But more often than not revolutionaries disperse their publications into the anonymous universe of the public sphere, unsure of where they will land.

With Napoleon Bonaparte's invasion of Spain in 1808, the U.S.-based Hispanophone public sphere exploded with a third quickly proliferating and increasingly complex wave. In the first two decades of the nineteenth century, more than thirty Hispanophone documents were published, and again most emerged from Philadelphia. Authors now became self-aware of their public sphere's temporal cycle and their audience, and they began to write fully aware of the lag in time and the need for documents to circulate in order to produce an imagined community. For two short years, from 1808 to 1810, this print culture was suffused with the rhetoric of reform that we traced in the previous chapters. But even here there are already sources of dissension, as competing visions appear to push toward civil war. Matters changed dramatically after 1810, when the Spanish Cortes of Cádiz called for elections throughout the Hispanic world. Then, at last, civil war began to morph, in many parts of the Hispanic world, into revolution. If the public sphere exploded in 1808, producing a plethora of documents in the ports on either side of the Atlantic, then by 1810 print culture, too, proliferated in the metropolitan cities of Spanish America. Thus, the once trans-Atlantic imagined community of revolutionary interlocutors began to give way to more localized regional—and soon to become national—revolutionary print cultures. Just as we previously explored the shifts in economic thinking that led to an invigorated desire to reform the Hispanic monarchy, here, let us flesh out these threads of trans-Atlantic Hispanic revolutionary thought, focusing particularly on Philadelphia as a node. But, given the profundity of the Hispanic archive, that Borgesian library of Babel, let us do so fully aware that these examples represent the mere tip of the trans-Atlantic revolutionary iceberg.

Initial Ruptures

The first wave of ideas that advocated ending the old regime of Spanish monarchical rule circulated clandestinely. Surely such ideas had been aired from the very initial moment of Spanish colonization, but starting in the mid-eighteenth century they became more and more abundant. This was the moment of commercial expansion in the Atlantic world when Spanish-American sailors and merchants began to have much more interaction with the non-Hispanic world and when the much-maligned Bourbon reforms were instituted. Besides what was spread by word of mouth, the first revolutionary ideas to materialize in writing were in

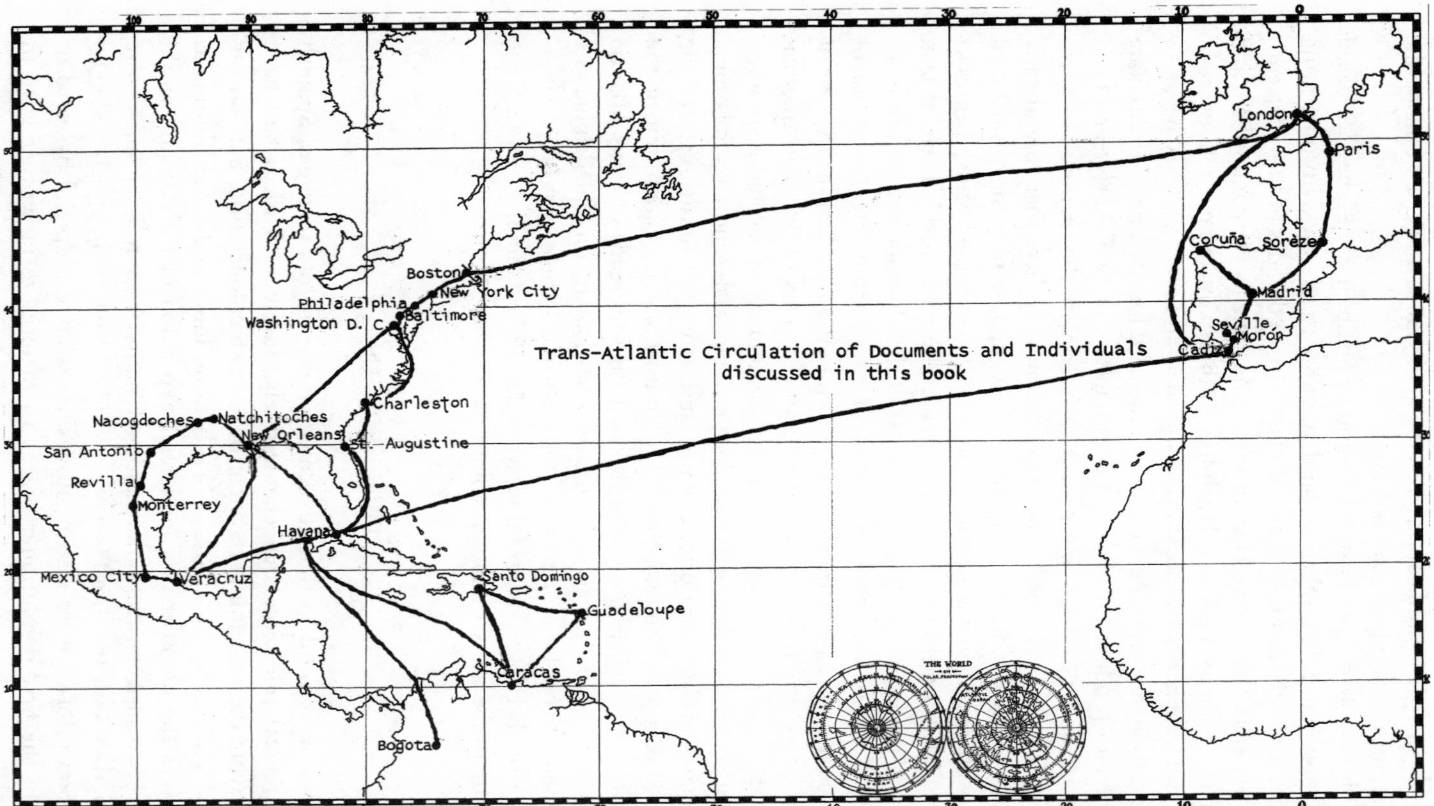

Figure 25. Origin of documents discussed in this book.

Map designed by Anna Theresa Coronado de Rueda.

manuscript form, given that the printing press was under the control of local authorities.[12]

The earliest evidence found as of yet is the curiously fascinating case of José Ignacio Moreno, rector of the University of Caracas from 1787 to 1789. In the 1970s, historians discovered a handsomely bound commonplace book, a type of scrapbook used to collect useful information, aphorisms, letters, and the like. In it, they found immaculately hand-written translations of two proclamations, from 1774 and 1775, made by the Continental Congress in Philadelphia. The proclamations, which Moreno had translated in 1777, boldly declared their right to defend their liberties at the hand of English despotism. While they certainly were not printed, the proclamations more than likely circulated clandestinely among the Caracas *tertulias*. Little is known of the owner of this commonplace book, but he, like José Antonio Gutiérrez de Lara from Chapter 1, was also a professor of philosophy and theology, having received his degrees the very same year he translated the Philadelphia proclamations. And, like Antonio, Moreno had been shaped by François Jacquier's eclectic modern philosophy, since among Moreno's belongings was a 1784 Latin edition of Jacquier. Historians have yet to discover how Moreno, a wealthy man of means, was able to get his hands on the Philadelphia proclamations. Nonetheless, Moreno clearly was sympathetic to imagining new political possibilities. Two decades later, in 1797, he would become associated with the ultimately unsuccessful Gual y España conspiracy that sought to gain Venezuelan independence, a conspiracy that would produce more protagonists in our story.[13]

The connection between Caracas and Philadelphia did not end with Moreno. In June 1779, Spain declared war on Britain, and focused its energies on driving the British from what had been, until 1763, the Spanish Floridas and from Spanish Louisiana, the former having become a haven for British loyalists. The talented Spanish governor of Louisiana, Bernardo de Gálvez, made preparations, and by 1781 he commandeered forces that had arrived from Havana via Galveston, Texas. In order to finance the war, Spain ordered all residents of New Spain's Interior Provinces to pay a tax; many soldiers from Spanish Texas participated in the war as well. The war, too, generated much needed commerce for Spanish Texas. In order to feed the Spanish army in Louisiana, Hispanic Texans organized one of the earliest cattle drives, sending some 9,000 head. As part of all these mobilizations, the famous Spanish-American captain from Caracas, Francisco de Miranda, arrived in Pensacola, Florida, and participated in the American Revolutionary War.[14]

Considered one of the precursors of Spanish-American independence, Miranda would later become an active participant in the French Revolution, travel throughout Europe, Asia, and Russia, and attempt to persuade the British to help Spanish America gain independence. Like Simón Bolívar, Miranda, too, was famous for the many cases of books he collected and took with him on his travels. He was born and received a premiere education in Caracas, joined the military, and successfully petitioned to serve in the royal forces in Spain, hoping to gain glory. During these years, Miranda read widely, and it would appear that he began to embrace revolutionary ideas prior to Pensacola. But, upon his return to Havana, Miranda found himself accused of being a spy and smuggling contraband. He escaped into the hills of Havana, sending letters to the newspaper in the hope of clearing his name. At the age of thirty-three, Miranda had dedicated himself to Spain. But now, along with being accused of criminal activities, he had also received depressing news from his home of Caracas. Juan Vicente Bolívar (father of Simón Bolívar) and several other prominent men of Caracas had written to Miranda, declaring that "'the lamentable state of this province today, and the general desperation and tyrannical measures of this Intendant (who seems to have come here for no other reason but to torment us, like a new Lucifer)' had brought Caracas to the brink of revolution." He made up his mind. He would flee to the United States, travel through Europe, and arrive in Spain where he hoped to clear his name. He arrived in New Bern, North Carolina on June 10, 1783.[15]

For the next eighteen months, Miranda would travel from Charleston, South Carolina, to Philadelphia, New York, New Haven, and Boston, and would befriend George Washington, Thomas Paine, Alexander Hamilton, and Thomas Jefferson, among others. Through this all, Miranda kept a detailed diary, noting the university libraries he visited (he was not impressed by Yale's collection), books he read (Cotton Mather's *Magnalia Christi Americana,* for example), and debates he had (Samuel Adams ultimately agreed with Miranda on how, in a democracy, all prestige was unfortunately placed in property and not in virtue). For the rest of his life, Miranda would struggle to gain the independence of Spanish America; he spent the next decades traveling the world and refining his political ideals.[16]

Missing Miranda by a mere four months, the Spanish priest Antonio José Ruiz de Padrón arrived in Philadelphia in May 1785. It had all been an accident. He had set out from his native Canary Islands for Cuba, but his ship got lost at sea during a terrifying storm and landed off the coast of Pennsylvania. The twenty-eight-year-old Franciscan had been a member of the Economic Societies, and had already developed liberal ideas. In Philadelphia, he became a sensation, apparently because liberal thought and

Catholic priests had seemed antithetical. He attended Benjamin Franklin's and Washington's literary salons, participated in debates on religious freedom, and delivered a sermon against the Spanish Inquisition. This sermon alone, he declared, had served to convert several Protestant families to Catholicism. It is not clear when he made his way to Havana, but he stayed for a remarkable three years, since the date of his sermon was given as 1788. Later, after Napoleon's invasion and the installment of the Cortes of Cádiz, he would serve as one of its distinguished liberal representatives.[17]

These few remarkable individuals may not all have embraced the overthrow of the monarchy, but they certainly sought radical reform. But in all cases, though the individuals may have encountered the Anglo-Protestant world, the seeds of their revolutionary thinking, as we will see later, ultimately emerged from Catholic political thought. Indeed, Father Ruiz de Padrón thought that his radical critique of the Inquisition had served to convert Protestants to Catholicism, not repel them. By the 1790s, the circulation of ideas began to manifest itself in print as well, expanding to the second wave of revolutionary ideas.

The first published threat to the Spanish monarchy appeared as a specter in December 1793. In Bogotá Nariño translated and published 100 copies of the French Revolution's "Declaration of the Rights of Man and of the Citizen."[18] But even before the ink had dried on this first Spanish translation of the world-shattering French document, Nariño burned them all. He heard rumors that the authorities were searching for the culprit who had had the audacity to publish such a seditious document. But Nariño had not acted alone. For well over a decade, rebellions against Spanish rule in New Granada had been savagely defeated by the royal authorities. Now, however, authorities feared that the press would be used to marshal revolutionary aspirations.

A second threat quickly followed upon the heels of Nariño's printing of the declaration. But this time it emerged at the other end of the Americas, in Philadelphia. Less than two months later, in early February 1794, the first known publication from the Hispanophone world that explicitly called for an end to Spanish monarchical rule and the establishment of a republican government had emerged.[19] For well over a year, the eccentric Santiago F. Puglia had struggled to find subscribers for his publication. Born in Geneva, Puglia was educated in Genoa, and, very briefly, was a merchant in Cádiz, Spain. After going bankrupt at the age of twenty-seven, he was imprisoned in Spain, spent two bitter years in prison, and upon his release in 1790 quickly made his way to Philadelphia. Once installed there, Puglia turned his pen into a weapon, publishing various tracts against the

Spanish monarchy. At 113 pages, divided into four chapters, *El desengaño del hombre* [*Man Undeceived*] is the second known Hispanophone publication from the United States (following the 1699 publication of Cotton Mather's *La fe del Cristiano*). Puglia's work is packed with satire, ironic wit, diatribes against monarchical government, and several translated pages of Paine's *The Rights of Man*.[20]

Royal political administrators throughout the Americas panicked. In July 1794, five months after the publication of the book, a Spanish sailor in Philadelphia became concerned upon seeing it, and took with him two copies to Spanish Florida. The Spanish governor in Florida promptly forwarded the copies to the Spanish governor in Cuba, who forwarded them to the viceroy in New Spain, who then finally forwarded them to the prime minister in Madrid. By October 1794, ten months after its publication, broadsides were posted on the church doors in Mexico City warning of the book and announcing that it had been placed on the Inquisition's *Index*. Letters were sent to the viceroy in Bogotá and to the captain governing the Eastern Interior Provinces of northern New Spain (what were, as we have seen, today's Texas and northeastern Mexico), warning them of the book. The viceroy in New Spain was particularly concerned that the French residents of Spanish New Orleans, inspired by the unfolding French Revolution, would attempt to smuggle the book into New Spain through Texas. Yet there was no need for such panic. The only copies to have made it into Spanish America, as far as we know, were the very same ones that circulated among the Spanish governors.[21]

The Spanish diplomats based in Philadelphia along with royal commanders in New Granada, Cuba, and New Spain feared that these documents would spread throughout the Caribbean and Gulf of Mexico. Some even thought that Nariño's and Puglia's texts were but versions of the same document, imagining some kind of trans-American web of conspirators, linking Philadelphia and Bogotá through New Orleans, Mexico, and the Caribbean.[22] But such books, spectral and otherwise, did more than haunt Spanish administrators. They gathered military forces, put the Inquisition into motion, caused broadsides to be produced warning of their impending arrival, and as a result developed a deep curiosity among people as to what these objects were. What could these books contain that would cause the marshaling of so much energy?

The revolutionary energy finally hit home in Madrid in 1796. Another literary group, not unlike Nariño's, comprised of disenchanted intellectuals—professors, lawyers, doctors, and other professionals—had decided to put words into action and orchestrated a revolutionary plot to overthrow the monarchy and establish a republic. But they, as Iris M. Zavala has re-

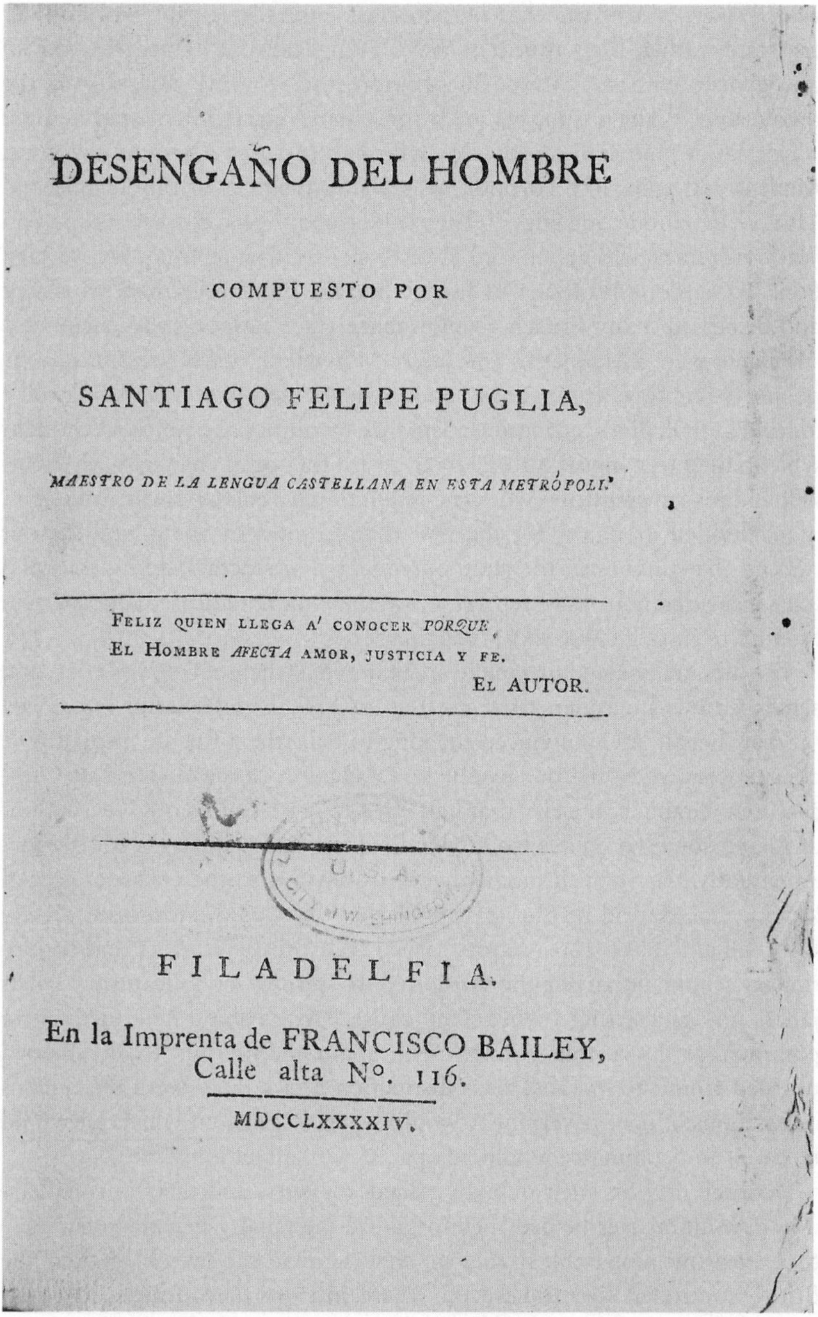

DESENGAÑO DEL HOMBRE

COMPUESTO POR

SANTIAGO FELIPE PUGLIA,

MAESTRO DE LA LENGUA CASTELLANA EN ESTA METRÓPOLI.

Feliz quien llega á conocer *porque*
El Hombre *afecta* amor, justicia y fe.
El AUTOR.

FILADELFIA.

En la Imprenta de FRANCISCO BAILEY,
Calle alta No. 116.

MDCCLXXXXIV.

Figure 26. Santiago Felipe Puglia, *El Desengaño del Hombre* (Philadelphia, 1794).
Rare Book and Special Collections Division, Library of Congress.

vealed, were not of the elite *letrado* class enmeshed in the workings of the state; rather, they appear to have been part of an emergent radical bourgeoisie who sought to "incorporate the working classes into the revolution."[23] The group was led by one Juan Mariano Bautista Picornell y Gomila, a philosophy professor who had founded a private school in Madrid and who, like Foronda, was also a member of the Basque and Madrid Economic Societies.[24] The revolutionary plot, known as the San Blas conspiracy, was denounced prior to its execution, but not before Juan Pons Izquierdo, a professor of French and the humanities, had translated and dispersed many French revolutionary tracts. Among the documents circulated were a *Manifiesto* and *Instrucción* which "gave directions to the people for uniting, arming, and serving the revolutionary cause."[25] Unlike Nariño's or Puglia's pronouncements of revolutionary political thought which failed to congeal into a larger desire for social change, with Picornell and his conspirators' work the revolutionary energy of the Enlightenment flooded its banks for the first time in modern Spain, spilling out beyond the confines of the state bureaucrats, aristocrats, and clerics and their measured policies of reform. Now, these more radical *letrados* would attempt to install a new social imaginary.

The monarchy sought to make an example of these revolutionaries, and sentenced the ringleaders to death. But the French ambassador interceded on their behalf, and convinced the king to exile them for life instead. The conspirators were sent, one by one, to La Guaira, on the outskirts of Caracas, New Granada, the city that had already produced its own revolutionaries and some 700 miles from where Nariño had printed his translation. Apparently, the Spanish monarchy was oblivious to the consequences of sending the Madrid revolutionaries to the Americas. Almost immediately Picornell and his co-conspirators turned their prison into a virtual revolutionary school, imparting the revolutionary spirit of republicanism to their jailers and converting them to the cause. "Astonishing new ideas were presented to the curious young [men]: Spain had no right to an America usurped from the Indians; class distinction and slavery were outrageous impositions; a new government would be established 'in which all would be equal and commerce would be opened with all nations.' "[26]

Picornell and his men quickly gained converts, and their once-jailers-now-revolutionaries helped them organize the Gual y España conspiracy to overthrow monarchical rule in New Granada. They escaped to the British-controlled West Indies from where, in 1797, they printed and circulated more revolutionary propaganda, including 729 copies of *Derechos del hombre y del ciudadano con varias máximas republicanas y un dis-*

Figure 27. Anonymous drawing of Juan Mariano Picornell.

Reprinted from Casto Fulgencio López, *Juan Picornell y la conspiración de Gual en España,* 2nd ed. (Caracas, Venezuela: Biblioteca Nacional de la Historia, 1997).

curso preliminario dirigido á los americanos (The Rights of Man and of the Citizen with Various Republican Maxims and a Preliminary Discourse Directed to the Americans). Following a standard means to evade authorities, Picornell used the false imprint of Madrid for this pamphlet; historians argue that it was printed in either Guadeloupe or Santo Domingo, both under French control at the time.[27] Authorities quickly responded and arrested the Gual y España conspirators in New Granada, but it was too late: the ideas of revolution had already begun to spread throughout the region. In the next year, nearly 10,000 copies of Picornell's translation would be reprinted, circulating from the Caribbean to Spain, back to Santo Domingo, and dispersed throughout.[28] Having escaped Spanish-controlled territory, Picornell eventually left the English and French Caribbean and made his way to the United States, where he lived in Baltimore and Philadelphia sometime between 1801 and 1806; later, he would participate in the revolutionary events in Texas.[29]

While most Hispanics resided only temporarily in Philadelphia or the East Coast, one in particular made Philadelphia his home. Manuel de Trujillo y Torres established the longest and deepest roots, having arrived in 1796 (the same year that Casa Irujo arrived as minister plenipotentiary and Picornell's plans were discovered) and residing in Philadelphia until his death in 1822. Torres therefore bridges the agitation of Picornell and Nariño in South America and the established Hispanic presence on the U.S. East Coast of the early nineteenth century. A native of Spain (like Picornell), Torres had immigrated to Bogotá in 1778 with his uncle the Archbishop (later Viceroy) Antonio Caballero y Góngora, who transformed the local university into a beacon of the new, eclectic Hispanic Enlightenment thought. Torres had access to his uncle's vast library, and was also educated for a period in Sorèze, in southern France.[30]

Upon his return to Bogotá in 1787, Torres participated in several literary salons created by none other than Nariño. After participating in a failed 1794 uprising with Nariño, Torres fled two years later to Philadelphia.[31] Once installed there, his aristocratic background and funds remitted to him from New Granada "enabled him to hold intercourse with the most fashionable circles."[32] He established a lifelong friendship with the Irish-born William Duane, a prominent Pennsylvanian politician and editor of the Philadelphia *Aurora,* to which Torres became a regular contributor.[33] This mutual friendship would be cemented over decades, as both worked toward the common cause of free trade and independence in the Americas.[34] Like Puglia, Torres eventually became a teacher of Spanish, and co-translated and adapted Nicholas Gouin Dufief's foreign-language textbook in 1811.[35] He also pursued various business ventures and, in the bourgeois spirit of his compatriots Casa Irujo and Foronda, was a fierce critic of mercantilism, an ardent promoter of free trade with Spanish America, and a prodigious student of the U.S. economy. The latter was "a matter to which he devoted considerable energy from his arrival in Philadelphia in 1796. Among his sources of information on federal coinage, income, and expenditures were Secretary of the Treasury Albert Gallatin and his Philadelphia confidants Robert Patterson, director of the second Bank of the United States."[36]

On November 30, 1805, Miranda returned to Philadelphia from London, where he had failed to enlist British support for Spanish-American independence and was hoping, once again, to gain aid from the United States. Miranda noted that Torres was one of "some distinguished persons" residing in Philadelphia.[37] By then, Torres had cultivated an extensive network of political and financial supporters of Spanish America. He had done so through promotion of trade with Spanish America, especially considering his own private ventures there, and his ardent editorial work on behalf of Spanish-American independence. In 1816 he published a business manual for those wishing to establish trade with Spanish America, describing in detail the monetary system, units of measurement, and their equivalents in the United States. Torres was so well connected that both the director of the U.S. Mint and the vice provost of the University of Pennsylvania wrote a forward to the manual.[38] Given Torres's connections and inclinations, it is likely that he helped Miranda secure arms and financial support for an insurrection in New Granada. For, on the latter's second attempt to garner financial backing, he was finally successful. Miranda procured guns, ammunition, and 200 volunteers in support of Venezuela's independence and departed Philadelphia on February 2, 1806. The venture, however, would prove a disastrous failure.[39] Yet Torres's most important role would be that of unofficial ambassador to Spanish-American revolutionaries as they began to arrive in 1808.[40]

In the decade bracketing the turn of the century, revolutionary publications begin to catch up with the energetic rebellions that had begun to bubble up throughout the Hispanic world. Commercial trade had cemented shipping routes, and liberal Hispanics used these as a means to pursue their goals. These emergent revolutionaries create personal networks that traversed the Atlantic world: Miranda, Picornell, Torres, Nariño, and many others all traveled in the same circles. They created a web that linked Spain to New Granada, to the British and French Indies, Cuba, New Spain, and Philadelphia.[41]

But the sparse publications that this web produced were unable to fully live up to their potential. Some, like Puglia's, never reached their intended targets. A few, like Picornell's broadside, spread like wildfire only to be suffocated by royal forces. The royal commanders had already sensed and feared the power of print culture: it could unleash innumerable imaginative possibilities for the world, producing competing visions of sovereignty. Still, the authors who published during the turn of the century, those belonging to the second wave of revolutionary thought, did so for a larger, imagined, anonymous world of Spanish-speakers whom they sought to engage in conversation.

The Demise of the Hispanic Monarchy and the Birth of the Modern World

The wheels of revolution would find unimaginable traction after 1808. In the absence of King Fernando VII—"the desired one"—Hispanics immediately responded with overwhelming patriotism, stifling, but only for a moment, those revolutionary energies that had been building up. But the launching of the Hispanic world's first modern parliament in 1809 served as a means to reorganize revolutionary aspirations.

Upon Napoleon's invasion, as we have seen, representatives from the peninsular kingdoms had created the Supreme Central Junta, or governing council, as a way to govern Spain and protect it from the quickly advancing French. After its creation in September 1808, the Supreme Central Junta was chased south to Seville. In a hastily convened meeting and in desperate need of American support, on January 22, 1809, it called for one representative to be elected from the viceroyalties in America and the Philippines, while the Peninsula kingdoms each had two. The Supreme Central Junta offered detailed instructions on how to go about holding elections: *vecinos* (literally "neighbors" but also a Hispanic legal category for reputable inhabitants of a province) would cast their votes at their local *ayuntamiento* or municipal council, which would forward a nominee to the head of the viceroyalty, and from all these, after a complex process, one representative would be chosen. What is even more remarkable is that elections were held only in Spanish America; the peninsular juntas had chosen their delegates. The news regarding the elections arrived in New Spain by April 1809, and was immediately forwarded to the Interior Provinces in northern New Spain. While limited, local elections had been held before in the Americas, the Supreme Central Junta now boldly declared that sovereignty rested in the people as represented by their *pueblo*'s *ayuntamiento*. In doing so, it reverted to the traditional Catholic political concepts of sovereignty as resting in the *pueblo*—a tradition the Bourbon monarchy had desperately sought to undo. But in reembracing these long-held political concepts, the Supreme Central Junta revised them as well, adding to this imaginary the modern concept of popular elections and unleashing and authorizing new ways of thinking of sovereignty and government.[42]

While the elections unfolded unevenly across the Americas, the French took over most of the Peninsula, terrifying most Spanish Americans who were convinced the French would win. The members of the Supreme Central Junta, still awaiting their American counterparts, had by January 1810 retreated from Seville to the furthest point in the south, to the port of Cádiz. Exhausted, the members did the unimaginable. They invoked the

Spanish medieval tradition of Cortes or parliament which had served in varying degrees as an advisor or, in some cases, as an authority equal to that of the monarch. In doing so, the Supreme Central Junta called for the reinstatement of the Cortes, an institution the Spanish monarchy had abolished, after protracted struggle, by the sixteenth century. The members dissolved their Supreme Central Junta on January 13, 1810, and called for the creation of the Cortes. Now, rather than a twenty-four-member Supreme Central Junta, the Cortes—with over one hundred elected representatives from throughout the Hispanic world—would govern. New elections would be held. Even more radical than before, the franchise was extended to Indians and mestizos (though it said nothing about those of African ancestry). Still, peninsular Spain maintained its numerical superiority by proclaiming that the *ayuntamiento* of each district would have a representative along with one representative for every 50,000 inhabitants. The Americas and the Philippines, on the other hand, would be restricted to one representative per province instead of one per district (a province was comprised of several districts). The Cortes was to meet as one unified national body, with no distinction as to rank or standing as a member of the military, nobility, or clergy.[43]

One by one—from the Peninsula, up and down the Americas, and as far as the Philippines—the representatives rushed to the economically crucial city of Cádiz. The choice of the capitalist port was quite appropriate for what would become the Hispanic world's fledgling liberal project of representative government. Not only did 90 percent of American trade pass through Cádiz, but it had also been the merchants of Cádiz who encouraged the Supreme Central Junta to call for the creation of the Cortes. The Cortes finally convened on September 24, 1810. In the end, 300 representatives, 86 of these Americans, would participate in the Cortes, though the vote tallies would rarely exceed 150. As for their background, the clergy represented one-third, the nobility comprised one-sixth, while the rest came from the third estate or professional classes. The members quickly fell along liberal and conservative lines, with the liberals in the majority and, with one major exception, no clear distinction between peninsular Spaniards and Americans. Only on the question of equal representation did peninsular and American representatives vehemently disagree. For a moment, it seemed as if liberals would finally be able to implement fully all of their reforms. American representatives, for their part, saw this as an opportunity to address their grievances. But they were not alone. Liberal Hispanics from Spain and the Philippines, too, joined the chorus, seeking to reform the Hispanic monarchy in order to improve the well-being of their constituencies.[44]

Figure 28. Salvador Viniegra, *La Promulgación de la Constitución de 1812* (1912). Museo de las Cortes de Cádiz. Courtesy of the Ayuntamiento de Cádiz, Spain.

Just two months after its first convening, the Cortes did the unthinkable: in November 1810 it declared freedom of the press, unleashing an unrestrained public sphere where books and pamphlets at last circulated and were printed freely throughout the Hispanic world. Censorship did not end immediately or evenly, given that royal administrators in America did their best to slow down the pace of change.[45] The Cortes then declared America equal to Spain in status if not in representation. By 1812 the Cortes had produced Spain's first written constitution, that foundational document that would become the basis of liberalism throughout the Hispanic world. The constitution declared Spain a constitutional monarchy with sovereignty resting in the monarch and parliament, and it reduced the powers of the Church and nobility. This was all to the consternation of royal bureaucrats in the Americas who had desperately sought to calm local disturbances (as the Constitution had perturbed conservatives in Spain). Still, there were internal contradictions. Many peninsular Spaniards realized that equal representation meant that *Americanos* would outnumber peninsular Hispanics, and they quickly moved to deny them equal representation.[46] The Hispanic world soon teetered on the verge of civil war as long-simmering tensions boiled over and competing social imaginaries, especially those unleashed by the Cortes, clashed with preciously held notions of monarchical rule. While their representatives sought reform, Spanish Americans in the Americas sought even faster, more decisive change. The Cortes's experiment would soon be overshadowed by far more radical efforts.[47]

The spring of 1810 was the turning point. Disgruntled creole-led rebellions began to erupt throughout Spanish America, in what would become Venezuela, Colombia, Argentina, Chile, and Mexico. They began initially as the *ayuntamientos* made bold declarations of autonomy. Matters had become terribly confusing, especially in a world where it took two to four months for news to reach the Americas.[48] The ascendance of the French-based Bourbon dynasty in the early eighteenth century had produced many pro-French Spaniards, referred to derisively as *afrancesados,* and many of them had supported Napoleon's invasion. Upon invading Spain, Napoleon had quickly dispatched his representatives to America, with publications in hand, declaring with guile that he only sought to "rejuvenate" an "old monarchy" that had been full of "friction, disorders, and convulsions." "I shall improve your institutions," he proclaimed, as he informed them that the Spanish monarch had merely transferred powers to Napoleon's brother, Joseph Bonaparte.[49] As a result, even greater uncertainty spread. With news that the Supreme Central Junta had been forced to abandon Seville for Cádiz and then that it had dissolved itself in favor of the Cortes, Spanish Americans sought to create local political stability. Beginning in Caracas and Buenos Aires, the *ayuntamientos* declared themselves in favor of the king and against Napoleon and anything hinting of French influence. But soon other *ayuntamientos* reacted against the Cortes' insults in denying America equal representation, and they also yearned to reconfigure the monarchy in order to address economic and political grievances. Over the next decade, civil war would become wars of independence.[50]

Hoping to gain support for their cause, the *ayuntamientos* sent representatives to the United States. Some were lawyers and merchants while others were educated landed elites, but all sought to radically reform their world, if not build it from scratch.[51] For most if not all, the search for an audience meant they came to Philadelphia. One by one, they descended upon Manuel Torres's home. As his dear friend would later note:

> To him all the agents from all sections of South America resorted, as the Franklin of the southern world; and in his experience and sagacity, they found the counsels and the resources by which the revolution was consummated; divisions quietted [*sic*] or averted; enmities subdued; the jealousies incident to revolutions frustrated; and a common sentiment; and a due knowledge of their common interests spread over South America.[52]

Torres's home became a veritable salon where revolutionary agents gathered, and he introduced them to one another along with U.S. politicians and financiers. He quickly became the object of the Spanish legation's scrutiny. Not only did Spanish minister Luis de Onís begin to provide detailed reports of Torres's and the recently arrived insurgents' activities, producing fascinating cloak-and-dagger tales of intrigue, but Onís, in fact, also attempted to have Torres assassinated a few years later.[53]

The first agents arrived in June of 1810 from Venezuela. The insurgent representatives from Caracas Juan Vicente Bolívar (brother of Simón Bolívar) and Telésforo de Orea made their way to Philadelphia. Once there, Torres quickly joined their efforts and helped them secure arms for the rebellion. By April 1811 another Venezuelan by the name of José Rafael Revenga had arrived. Agents began to trickle in from all parts of Spanish America, including Argentina, Colombia, Cuba, and Chile, all desiring to acquire arms and U.S. support.[54]

By the time the Mexican insurgent José Bernardo Gutiérrez de Lara arrived in Philadelphia in January 1812, the city was awash with schemes to send armed forces to Spanish America. In his diary Bernardo notes having met with de Orea and Revenga in Washington, D.C., on December 14 and 29, 1811, respectively.[55] While the Spanish-American press was in the midst of radical transformation, the U.S. press reported extensively on the unfolding rebellion, and Bernardo writes that "estoi admirado de los deseos q^e^. todos tienen q^e^. los ynsurgentes ganen, y disen q^e^. defienden la mas Justa causa q^e^. seha defendido Jamas en todas las edades [I admire everyone's desire that the insurgents win, and they say that they champion the most Just cause that has ever been defended]." The enthusiasm was so overwhelming in fact that "muchos se han puesto en escuela con maestro q^e^. han pagado para q^e^. les enseñen la lengua española [many (Anglo-Americans) have placed themselves in a school with a teacher whom they have paid to teach them the Spanish language]" in order to travel and fight in the revolutions.[56] This teacher was more than likely Torres himself, who had published a Spanish grammar book in the year of Bernardo's arrival.[57] It is not difficult to imagine that Bernardo also met with these insurgents and participated in conversations regarding commerce, free trade, and the overall goal of the Spanish-American uprisings.

With the arrival of the insurgents an outpouring of Hispanophone publications began to come off of the Philadelphia presses, giving way to the third—and most explosive—wave of revolutionary thought to emanate from the city.[58] If the earlier U.S. Hispanophone publications concentrated on economic development as a mode of social contract—that is, as a means to achieve the common good—Hispanophone imprints after 1810 expanded their political repertoire, from the language of reform to the language of revolution. They experiment with different idioms of political philosophy, drawing from various models of sovereignty in order to imagine new ways of reconfiguring their social bodies.

Print Culture and the Eruption of the Public Sphere

With the decree of freedom of the press in both Spanish America and Spain, these publications now circulated freely (though still unevenly) throughout Spanish America in the post-1810 period, including, at long last, Puglia's 1794 *Desengaño del hombre.* Other publications appeared, including translations of Paine, histories of the United States, and various political manuals on republican forms of government, all with an eye to translate and adapt these political ideas into the language they were much more familiar with, one founded in Catholic Scholastic thought.[59] New Orleans, too, had a small community of revolutionary expatriates. Minister Onís noted in November 1809 that there was a group who sought to foment insurrection; the group was probably comprised of French and Anglo-American filibusters and Spanish Americans. The few Spanish imprints of Louisiana from the turn of the century had been government broadsides, but beginning in 1808 we see at least two pamphlets published against Napoleon's invasion and in favor of the Cortes of Cádiz. The Spanish-language print culture that emerges during this period was small compared to Philadelphia's, but it did manage to produce the first known newspaper that contained Spanish-language material. *El Misisipi* was published irregularly from 1808 to 1810 in bilingual format by Anglo-Americans. By the 1820s, New Orleans would rival Philadelphia for Hispanic revolutionaries.[60] But, for now, Philadelphia was the base for this flourishing print culture.

In April 1810, the Colombian Juan Manuel Villavicencio translated and published the first Spanish translation of the U.S. Constitution.[61] The historian Pedro Grases claims Villavicencio's translation "must have been published and dispersed quickly," since on April 27, 1810, Onís, based in Philadelphia, warned administrators in South America that copies were being distributed. Much like his compatriot José Ignacio Moreno, very little is known of Villavicencio or of his activities in Philadelphia. Born in 1778 in Coro, Venezuela (located between Maracaibo and Caracas), Villavicencio came from humble origins. He studied philosophy and canon and civil law at the University of Caracas from 1798 to 1802, beginning his studies in Caracas only two years after the Gual y España uprisings in which Picornell had been implicated. By 1807 he was practicing law and was a professor at the University of Caracas. The first sign of his being in Philadelphia is the publication of the translated U.S. Constitution in April 1810.[62]

Just as the revolutionary representatives were starting to arrive in Philadelphia, their counterparts at the Cortes of Cádiz in Spain quickly became disillusioned at the prospect of reform. Very little was known about the Americas, even by the educated classes in Spain. Among the American representatives, peninsular ignorance of the vastness of America quickly became a running joke; peninsular Spaniards regularly asked the representatives from Mexico, Colombia, and Venezuela if they knew their relatives. Other peninsulars, with complete sincerity, asked the American deputies "if the Americans were like us; if they spoke the same language; if they professed the same religion." But ignorance also led to arrogance, leading one peninsular representative to the Cortes to proclaim that "it was still unknown to what class of animals Americans belonged."[63] Here, peninsulars clearly echoed the contentious debate between eighteenth-century Americans—Spanish and British—and European philosophers who denigrated all things American.[64]

American representatives tried to educate their peninsular counterparts, publishing extensive reports on their provinces, detailing the history, geography, economy, and social structure of these far-off lands. In November 1811, for example, the representative from Coahuila, one of the northern provinces of the "Kingdom of Mexico," Miguel Ramos Arizpe, wrote a report on the provinces of Coahuila, Nuevo Leon, Nuevo Santander, and Texas.[65] Like Bernardo's brother Antonio, Ramos Arizpe had also been educated at the Franciscan college in Monterrey in the 1790s, where Jacquier's new modern philosophy had been taught; he would later receive his doctoral degree in canon and civil law from the University of Guadalajara. And like Antonio he, too, would be ordained as a priest and would teach at the same seminary. His experience at the Cortes would prove to be productive.[66]

The first forty pages of Ramos Arizpe's sixty-page pamphlet document the sheer poverty and dire conditions in which the region's "miserable Spaniards" live (26, 27). It paints a wretched portrait: rich, opulent, fertile lands remain undeveloped because of tyrannical rulers and laws that inhibit the development of industry. If the first forty pages offer a diagnosis of the provinces, the final twenty pages offer a "cure":

> Para curar, segun ha prometido V.M. unos males tan generales como graves, es necesario establecer en cada provincia una *Junta gubernativa* ó llámese *Diputacion de provincia,* á cuyo cargo esté la parte gubernativa de toda ella,

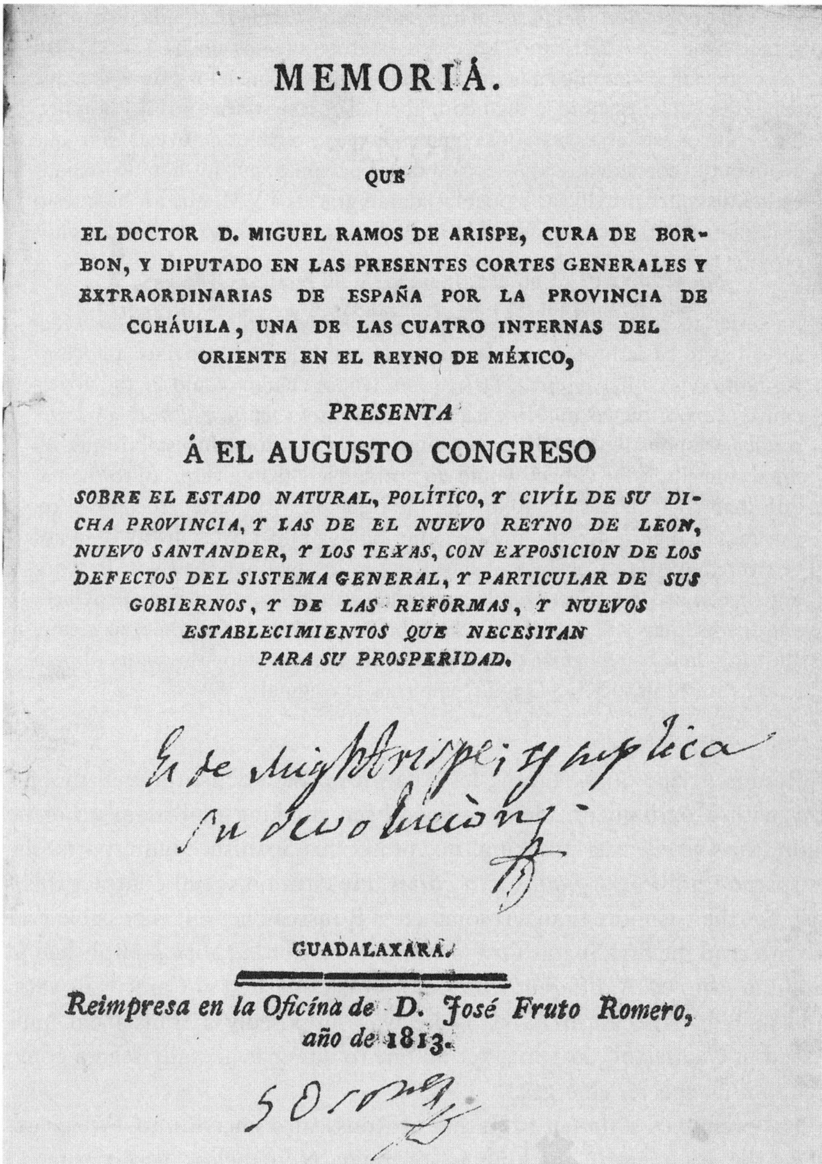

MEMORIÁ.

QUE

EL DOCTOR D. MIGUEL RAMOS DE ARISPE, CURA DE BORBON, Y DIPUTADO EN LAS PRESENTES CORTES GENERALES Y EXTRAORDINARIAS DE ESPAÑA POR LA PROVINCIA DE COHÁUILA, UNA DE LAS CUATRO INTERNAS DEL ORIENTE EN EL REYNO DE MÉXICO,

PRESENTA

Á EL AUGUSTO CONGRESO

SOBRE EL ESTADO NATURAL, POLÍTICO, Y CIVÍL DE SU DICHA PROVINCIA, Y LAS DE EL NUEVO REYNO DE LEON, NUEVO SANTANDER, Y LOS TEXAS, CON EXPOSICION DE LOS DEFECTOS DEL SISTEMA GENERAL, Y PARTICULAR DE SUS GOBIERNOS, Y DE LAS REFÓRMAS, Y NUEVOS ESTABLECIMIENTOS QUE NECESITAN PARA SU PROSPERIDAD.

GUADALAXARA.

Reimpresa en la Oficina de D. José Fruto Romero, año de 1813.

Figure 29. Miguel Ramos Arizpe, *Memoria que el Doctor D. Miguel Ramos de Arispe . . . presenta á el Augusto Congreso* (1813).

Nettie Lee Benson Latin American Collection, University of Texas Libraries, University of Texas at Austin.

y en cada poblacion un *cuerpo municipal ó cabildo* que responda de todo el gobierno de aquel territorio. En todos establecimientos no hará V.M. otra cosa, que dar testimonios á la nacion de ser consiguiente á los principios, que tiene proclamados sobre la dignidad, libertad, y demas derechos del hombre. No seran los españoles tratados como esclavos, ó rebaños de ovejas, sino que cooperando con su voto á la eleccion de las personas, que los han de mandar en tan distantes provincias y pueblos, darán gracias á V.M. que los ha puesto en estado de conocer su dignidad, y gozar tranquilamente de los derechos propios de un hombre constituido en sociedad.

[In order to cure, as Your Graces have promised, some ailments so widespread as to be serious, it is necessary to establish in each province a *governing junta* or call it a *regional Delegation,* whose charge would be the governance of its province, and in each town establish a *municipal body* or *town council,* responsible for the governing of said territory. In establishing all these councils, Your Graces would do nothing less than give proof to the nation that Your Graces are following the principles you have proclaimed regarding the dignity, liberty, and the other rights of man. Spaniards would not be treated like slaves or flock of sheep, but rather by using their vote to work together in order to elect people, who shall be sent from far away provinces and towns, they will give thanks to Your Graces for placing them in a state allowing them to recognize their dignity and serenely enjoy the rights of man as constituted in society.] (43–44, emphasis in original)

Ramos Arizpe does nothing less than propose a constitutional monarchy with a parliament. He may have been thinking of Britain's, but he more than likely was invoking, not unlike his Spanish counterparts, the Hispanic tradition of *juntas* and *cortes.* He cites no social contract theorist, but there is more than a resonance of Rousseau here. It is possible that he had read the first Spanish translation of the *Contrat social,* published in London in 1799. A different translation was published in Caracas in 1809 and in Buenos Aires in 1810. There was supposedly a translation published in Charleston, in 1803, yet no one to date has actually seen a copy; yet another specter emerges.[67]

His premise is different from that of Rousseau's since Ramos Arizpe accepts the argument of the king as sovereign. Nonetheless, he pronounces the "rights of man," or rather, hoping to avoid the politically fraught terrain he has entered by daring to use this very French phrase, he merely affirms that it was "Your Graces"—not Ramos Arizpe—who had already "proclaimed the . . . rights of man." Yet "Your Graces" is a simulacrum for the deposed king for, in effect, Ramos Arizpe's audience is the representatives at the Spanish Cortes of Cádiz. More significantly, if cryptically, he declares that Spaniards would no longer be treated like "slaves or flock of sheep." In doing so, Ramos Arizpe uses the same examples and in the same order that Rousseau did in theorizing the origin of society at the beginning of the *Contrat social.*[68]

Some Spanish-American representatives, like Ramos Arizpe, chose to negotiate with their peninsular counterparts (but, as in the case with countless other politicians, Ramos Arizpe was nevertheless eventually imprisoned for many years because of his views). Others, like the representative from the Spanish-American island of Santo Domingo, José Álvarez de Toledo y Dubois, who would come to play a crucial role in Texas, became irritated with peninsular condescension. Álvarez de Toledo expressed his frustration in a letter he attempted to send from Cádiz to the captain general of Santo Domingo. The letter was intercepted by peninsular authorities who promptly sought to arrest Álvarez de Toledo on the grounds of sedition. He managed to escape to Philadelphia with assistance from the U.S. Consul in Cádiz, but not before consulting with Ramos Arizpe. Álvarez de Toledo sought to return to the Caribbean and fight for the independence of Cuba, but Ramos Arizpe and other Spanish Americans convinced him to shift his focus to Mexico instead because "emancipation of New Spain would inevitably lead to that of Cuba." He received a written commission from these Spanish-American representatives authorizing him to liberate the Interior Provinces of Northern Mexico.[69] Thus, Álvarez de Toledo arrived in Philadelphia in September 1811 prepared to engage in political battle.

His biography, not unlike those of many of his contemporaries such as the Mexican Fray Servando de Mier, reads like a soap opera. An elite creole born in 1779 Havana to an influential peninsular family involved in the military and trade, Álvarez de Toledo was educated at the eminent Escuela Naval de Cádiz (Naval Military School), a school dedicated to educating the nobility. He rose to lieutenant in the navy, and devised an ultimately abandoned plan to rescue the deposed King Fernando after Napoleon's invasion in 1808. He was elected representative to the Cortes of Cádiz from Santo Domingo. But he quickly became disillusioned at the prospects for American sovereignty when American representation was severely undercut in proportion to peninsular representation. In December 1810, he wrote to the Santo Domingo captain general, the equivalent of a governor, expressing his concerns. The letter, however, was intercepted by peninsular royalists, and used as the basis for charges of sedition. With the help of the U.S. consul, he escaped to the United States on June 25, 1811, arrived in Philadelphia by September, and made his way to Washington, D.C., in December 1811.[70]

But Álvarez de Toledo, like many revolutionaries of the period, betrayed both the Spanish monarchy and, eventually, the insurgents on several occasions. He ultimately served as a spy for Spain, revealing various plots for independence. He attempted to persuade Americans to forgo independence, and he returned to Spain in 1817 where he remained loyal to the monarchy.[71] For now, however, he used his rhetorical prowess to call his fellow Americans to arms. And, as we will see later, he authored some of the most influential broadsides that moved *Americanos* in Texas to revolt against Spain.

The battle began with the publication in Philadelphia of an eighty-three-page pamphlet entitled *Manifiesto ó satisfaccion pundonorosa, á todos los buenos Españoles Europeos, y á todos los pueblos de la America, por un diputado de las Cortes reunidas en Cádiz (Manifesto or Punctilious Satisfaction, to All the Good European Spaniards, and to All Peoples of America, by a Deputy to the Cortes Gathered at Cádiz).*[72] Published sometime between late October and early December 1811, *Manifiesto* sets out to correct all of the calumnious gossip regarding Álvarez de Toledo's actions:

> Yo no me hubiera detenido en bosquejar este sombrio quadro, si los mismos que figuran en él con la mas horrorosa deformidad, no hubiesen expedido circulares a todos los dominios de la vacilante monarquia para difamar alevosamente mi nombre y urdir tramas execrables contra la seguridad de mi persona.
>
> [I would not have sketched such a gloomy portrait had the very people who, due to their actions, emerge herein with the most horrible deformity not issued circulars throughout the faltering monarchy's dominions in order to treacherously defame my name and weave heinous plots against my person]. (73)

In an effort to persuade peninsular Spaniards to work toward the reform of the Hispanic monarchy so as to improve the conditions of the Americas, he works hard to not pit peninsular Spaniards and American Spaniards against one another. Rather, he claims, the struggle was against "the Ministerial intrigues" that sought to undo the work of the representatives of the Cortes. However, he quickly realized that the Cortes "sería dominado por los enemigos ocultos de la España y de la America, que no llevaban en la ostentosa alianza otro objeto mas que el de sus intereses propios, y el de arruinar para siempre al Imperio Español en Ambos Mundos [would be dominated by Spain and America's covert enemies, whose ostentatious alliance held no other object than their own private interests and that of ruining forever the Spanish Empire in Both Worlds]" (34). Authoritarianism and intrigue, alongside solipsism, are all at the root of imperial decay. Only their opposites—the representative Cortes, and its spirit of openness, collaboration, and a concern for the nation (both its people and the state)—could save the Spanish empire. When it becomes clear to Álvarez de Toledo that this would not be possible, he writes that "cada dia encontraba nuevos motivos que me hacian créer como irremediable la perdida de España [each day I found new reasons that made me believe how irremediably lost Spain was]." He and his fellow American representatives also realized "de absoluta necesidad el que los Pueblos de America se pusiesen en tiempo oportuno á cubierto de las tentativas ambiciosas . . . contra ella las dos Naciones rivales que se disputan el Imperio del mundo [how absolutely necessary it was that the People of America prepare and protect themselves from any possible ambitious attempts . . . against her on the part of the two rival Nations (France and Britain) fighting for global Empire]" (35).

Both Ramos Arizpe and Álvarez de Toledo's writings agree on an emerging set of political virtues: representative government (via a constitutional monarchy and parliament), public deliberation, and economic development. Like so many of their compatriots, they struggled to reform, not overthrow, the Hispanic monarchy. But if the monarchy was to fall, they reasoned, then these political virtues had to be preserved at all costs in America. It is in this sense, then, that the title of Jaime E. Rodríguez O.'s book eloquently captures the sentiment of the global Hispanic civil war during this period: *Nosotros somos ahora los verdaderos Españoles (We Are Now the True Spaniards)*.[73]

In rather grandiose fashion, Álvarez de Toledo emerges in this document as an allegorical figure for Spanish America. "Miéntras he podido ser util en medio de vosotros [While I could be useful among you]" in Spain, he writes:

> mis facultades, mi reposo, mi vida, todo lo he arriesdago con dulce entusiasmo para contribuir á la Gloria y al buen exîto de vuestra lucha. Llegó el momento en que debi separarme de vosotros para evitar la persecucion mas atroz; y mi ultimo á Dios á ese suelo desgraciado, fué interrumpido por las emociones patéticas de la ternura y del dolor. La memoria de los Buenos estará siempre gravada en mi alma con afectuosa estimacion y respeto; y la de los malos me servirá en todos tiempos de leccion y de escandolo.
>
> [my abilities, my serenity, my life, all of it I risked with sweet enthusiasm in the hope of contributing to the glory and success of your struggle. But the time arrived in which I should separate myself from you in order to avoid the most atrocious persecution. However, my final adieu to that wretched land was interrupted by the most pitiful emotions of tenderness and pain. The memories of the Good (Spaniards) will forever be imprinted on my soul with

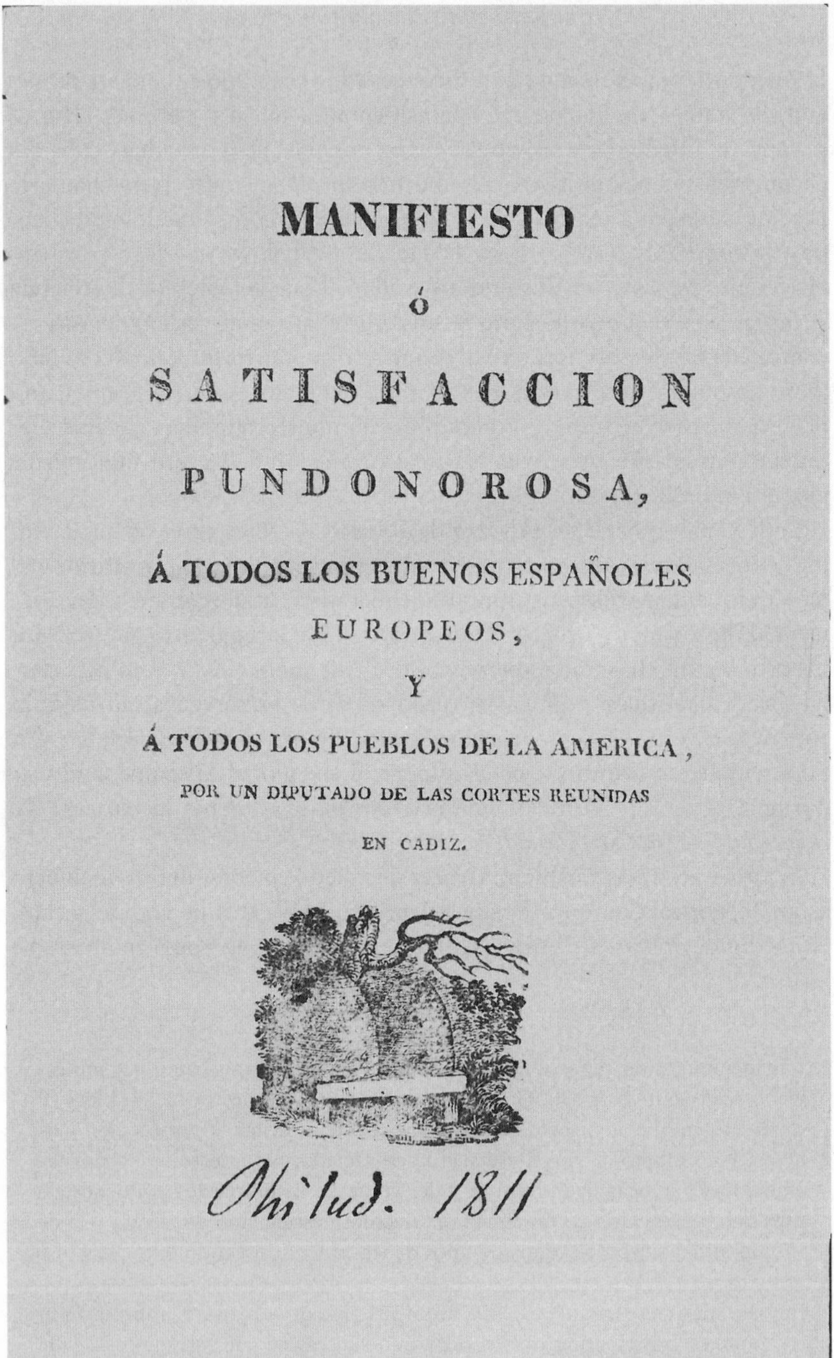

MANIFIESTO

Ó

SATISFACCION

PUNDONOROSA,

Á TODOS LOS BUENOS ESPAÑOLES

EUROPEOS,

Y

Á TODOS LOS PUEBLOS DE LA AMERICA,

POR UN DIPUTADO DE LAS CORTES REUNIDAS

EN CADIZ.

Philad. 1811

Figure 30. José Álvarez de Toledo, *Manifiesto o satisfacción pundonorosa.* Philadelphia, 1811.

American Philosophical Society.

> affectionate esteem and respect, and the memories of the bad will forever serve me as a lesson and as a scandal.] (74)

He dedicates over seventy of the eighty-three pages to documenting the wrongs committed by treacherous Spaniards against himself and, allegorically, against the Americas. Only in the final pages, and rather tenuously at that, does he arrive at the heartrending conclusion that he, like America, must separate himself from the past, from the collectivity of the Hispanic monarchy.

Álvarez de Toledo's decision is a bitter, melancholic one. He remains stuck in what Harry Harootunian has described as the "historical present," incapable of moving forward, unable to propose an optimistic future for the Americas, but knowing fully well that he can not return to the previous order of things. Citing Hannah Arendt, Harootunian describes the historical present as a liminal moment of stagnation, an "odd in-between period which sometimes inserts itself into historical time when not only the later historians but the actors and witnesses, the living themselves, become aware of an interval in time which is altogether determined by things that are no longer and by things that are not yet."[74] It is a moment of great uncertainty for these American representatives, separated by an ocean from the events unfolding in the Americas and united, for the moment, with their Hispanic brethren in an attempt to not merely save but produce an even more virtuous Hispanic monarchy.

Gloom and despair mark the writings of Ramos Arizpe and Álvarez de Toledo, as they did Foronda's essay. Ramos Arizpe's and Álvarez de Toledo's is a desolation regarding the past, a past that nonetheless manages to seep into the present, trapping them and rendering them unable to move into the optimism of the future. Yet melancholy had already emerged as a powerful if overpowering trope in the late eighteenth century, as we have seen with Gaspar Melchor de Jovellanos, Foronda, and other writers who sought to ameliorate the living conditions of their fellow Hispanics. This trope, in fact, has been long debated, one that has been associated with the seventeenth-century emergence of the Hispanic Baroque, as a response to the Reformation, the Renaissance, and the demise of Catholic hegemony in the West.[75]

But where peninsular writers despaired at the present conditions of Spain, Spanish-American writers could not disconnect the present from the past. Ramos Arizpe, Álvarez de Toledo, and even earlier Spanish-American writers saw the present as an effect of the history of American denigration that by necessity had to be documented. When the entire Jesuit order was summarily expelled from Spain's dominions in 1767, they

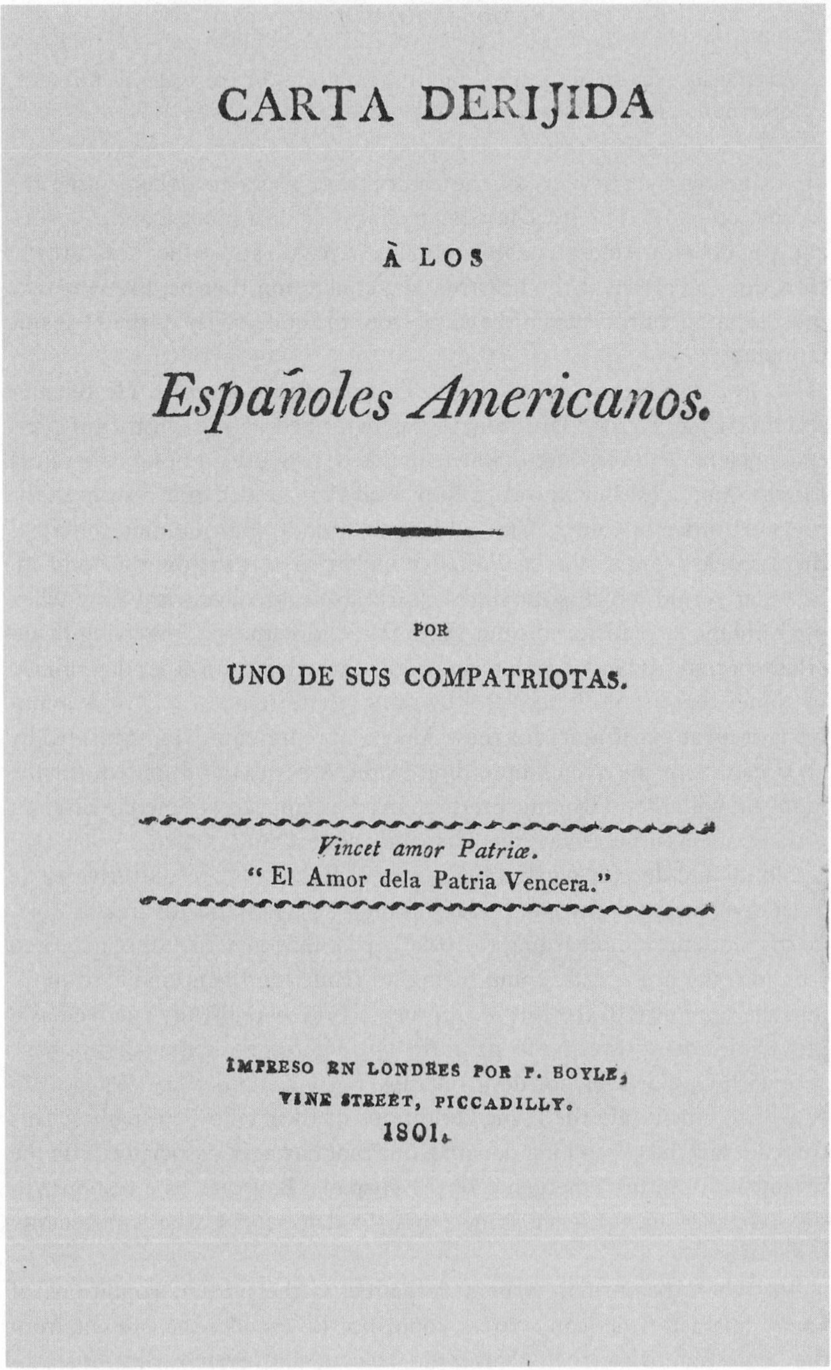

CARTA DERIJIDA

À LOS

Españoles Americanos.

POR

UNO DE SUS COMPATRIOTAS.

Vincet amor Patriæ.
" El Amor dela Patria Vencera."

IMPRESO EN LONDRES POR P. BOYLE,
VINE STREET, PICCADILLY.
1801.

Figure 31. Juan Pablo Viscardo y Guzmán, *Carta a los españoles americanos* (1801).

Foyle Special Collections, King's College, London.

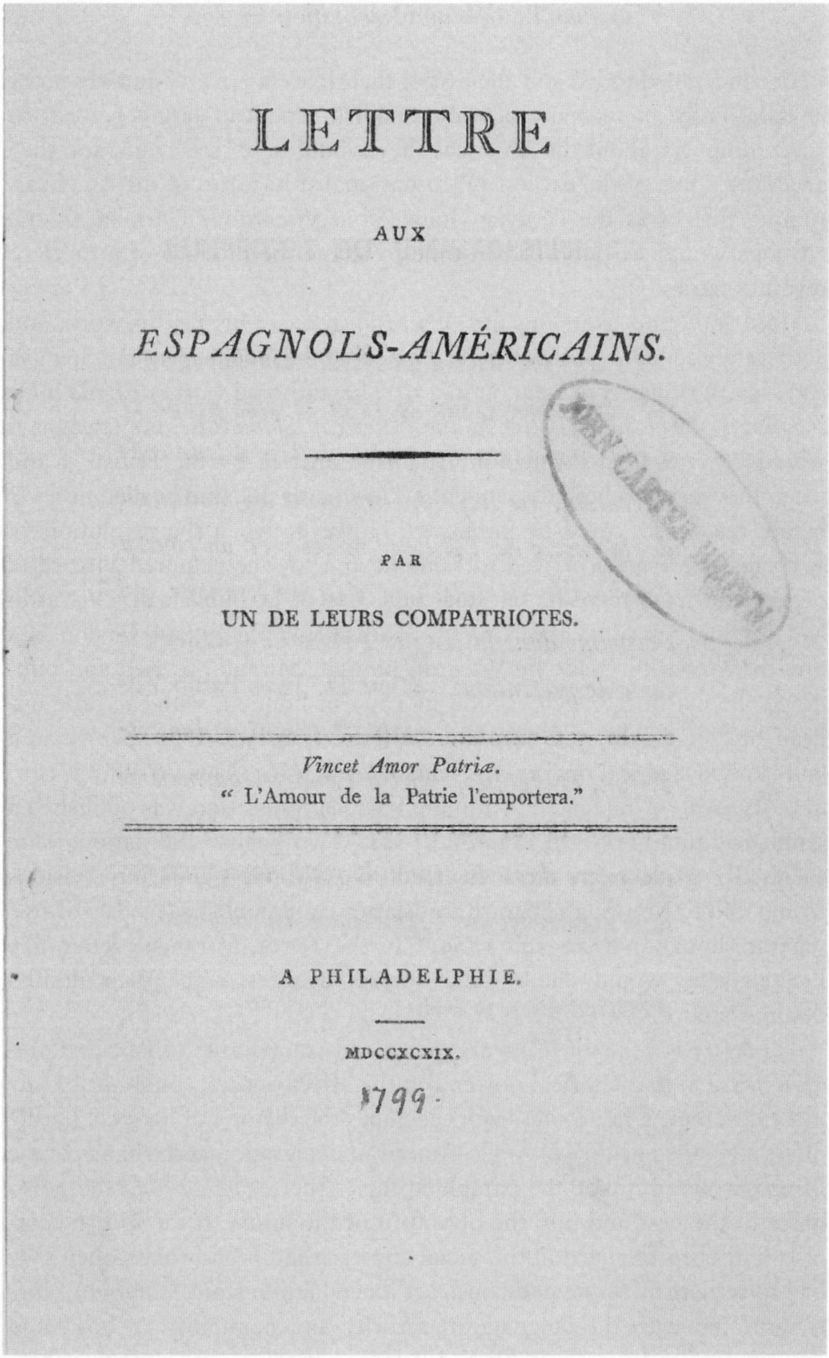

LETTRE

AUX

ESPAGNOLS-AMÉRICAINS.

PAR

UN DE LEURS COMPATRIOTES.

Vincet Amor Patriæ.
" L'Amour de la Patrie l'emportera."

A PHILADELPHIE.

MDCCXCIX.

1799.

Figure 32. Juan Pablo Viscardo y Guzmán, *Lettre aux espagnols-americains* (London [false imprint], 1799).

were condemned to live out the rest of their lives in poverty and obscurity in Italy. From there many of these Spanish-American Jesuits set out to write longingly about the Americas they would never see again, and they produced some of the earliest proto-nationalist histories of the Americas. Among them was the Peruvian Juan Pablo Viscardo y Guzmán, whose writings would be published in time to shape the thought of post-1810 revolutionaries.[76]

From Italy and later England, Viscardo, too, set his pen to work, and desperately sought to enlist British support in the independence of Spanish America. Writing from London in 1791, he authored *Carta dirigida a los españoles americanos (Letter to the American Spaniards),* hoping that it would be circulated throughout Spanish America by the British if and when they aided in her independence. They never did, and he died in 1798 before his works could be published. However, when the revolutionary Venezuelan Miranda arrived in London in 1799, he acquired Viscardo's papers and from these he selected the *Carta* to be published.[77] Viscardo had originally written the letter in Spanish, but the extant version is a French translation made by Viscardo himself. Miranda revised and published the existing French version in 1799 in London, with the false imprint of Philadelphia; he then had the letter translated into Spanish, and had it published in London two years later in 1801. This version "was to have its greatest influence . . . and the Spanish translation was published a number of times between 1810 and 1822." Two English translations were eventually made from the French edition without significant revisions (compared to Miranda's Spanish translation) and published as part of two separate books in 1808 and 1809.[78] In the 1810s, Miranda's letter, like Puglia's text, would finally, after several decades, reach their desired destinations.

The letter is brilliant in its argument and comparable to Paine's *Common Sense* in its rhetorical power. But the affect of each could not be any more different. While Paine's work includes the rhetoric of injury, it hardly offers a detailed history of Anglo-American denigration at the hands of the British crown. Instead, the pamphlet moves the reader *beyond* the pessimism of the past and into the optimism of the future. If the British colonists had been wronged, if the social contract had been broken, then they had to seize their future and construct a new nation-state. *Common Sense* is saturated with the language of futurity and possibility, of hope and dreams. Given the well-established British-American public sphere where political ideas had been debated and discussed in print, pubs, and town halls, *Common Sense* affirms a future that had, by the early 1760s, already begun to be imagined.[79] While Paine's prose offers a resolve that had never been printed before, its conclusion had already been murmured, deduced, and discussed by many Anglo-American colonists.

This is not to say that pessimism was not an affect among late eighteenth-century Anglo-American writers; one need only remember the anxieties surrounding the possibility of creating a united federalist nation or the demise of republicanism and advent of liberalism.[80] Even those who were more neutral during the American Revolution left a somber, melancholic account of this traumatic transformation to modernity, as J. Hector St. John de Crèvecoeur's twelfth letter "Distresses of a Frontier Man" attests.[81] But the fact that these accounts have been excised from nationalist memory is precisely the point. Benedict Anderson has argued that in creating a nationally imagined community, the people must be forced to remember certain events that have already been *forgotten*. Anderson is referring to acts of violence perpetrated in the distant past by people who may have inhabited the same geographic space of the emergent nation but who, during that period, had no conception of themselves as even being of the same nation. That is, the nation-state must construct an imagined genealogy of fratricide in order to offer an emotional suturing of the people in the present. The people of the emergent nation come together through an imagined, constructed past of pain and mourning. From that emotionally stagnant past recounted in nationalist historical narratives, those in the present emerge invigorated to act in the future.[82] But what about the inevitable eighteenth-century anxieties regarding the failure of the nation to come together? What about late eighteenth-century Anglo-American fears that the solipsism of liberalism will prevent the nation from cohering? In this regard, Anglo-American nationalism sublimated (and in many ways continues to do so) the pessimism of the past to the optimism of the future, and this is what has made it so powerful.[83]

Viscardo's *Letter,* in contrast, was written in a discursive vacuum; there was no uncensored Hispanophone public sphere in which the *Letter* could have been published and debated. Only after his death would it be dispersed throughout Spanish America, influencing insurgents from London, to Philadelphia, New Orleans, Mexico City, down to Buenos Aires.[84] Yet, in contrast to Paine's optimistic affect of futurity, Viscardo's is a pessimistic longing, a yearning for an entity that has not been dreamt of yet, not even by him. Indeed, not once does he refer to the inhabitants of Spanish America as "Americans" but rather calls them "American Spaniards."[85] Thus, his letter lingers and remains immersed in the past, painstakingly documenting 300 years of grievances.

A sense of collective affect, a community forged through suffering marks the entirety of the *Letter:* "El Nuevo Mundo es nuestra patria, su historia es la nuestra. . . . [y] se podría reducir a estas cuatro palabras, *ingratitud, injusticia, servidumbre y desolación* [the New World is our country; its history is ours. . . . (and) one might abridge it into these four words—*ingratitude, injustice, slavery, and desolation*]" (73, 63, emphasis in original). Viscardo writes to an imagined community that does not yet exist, to members of a community that can not communicate easily with one another, and for these reasons he creates a shared affective history of denigration: "Si corremos nuestra desventurada patria de un cabo al otro hallaremos donde quiera la misma desolación [Let us survey our unhappy country all over, and we shall every where find the same desolation]" (79, 69). What he finds after "consult[ando] nuestros anales de tres siglos [consult(ing) our three centuries of archives]" is a broken contract wherever the Spanish monarchy has tread (79, my translation). But Viscardo's contract is an amalgam of what had become an established contract between the monarchy and the Americas since their colonization and the social contract theories that Viscardo had encountered in Europe.[86] Rather than emerging as a social body comprised of individuals who, in order to move away from an anarchic state of nature, have transferred some of their natural rights in order to establish civil society, his contract emerges as it did in other Hispanophone writers, as a mode of political economy whose goal is the commerce of ideas, peoples, and goods.

Viscardo begins his account clearly echoing social contract theorists: "Desde que los hombres comenzaron a unirse en sociedad para su más grande bien [Since men began to unite in society for their mutual interest]" (75, 65). Yet what follows this clause is not an elaboration on how and why individuals must alienate their natural rights in order to protect their interests; rather, he continues, "nosotros somos los únicos a quienes el gobierno obliga a comprar lo que necesitamos a los precios más altos, y a vender nuestras producciones a los precios más bajos [we are the only people whom government has compelled to provide for our wants at the highest price possible; and to part with our productions at the lowest price]" (75, 65). "Mutual interest" or, as the original Spanish would be translated, "the greater good," is defined here as a satisfaction of wants or, as Rousseau had it, as the government's wise management of and fulfillment of the "common good." But Spain had broken this compact and imposed its "mercantile tyranny" (76, 65). When the language of rights ("the rights of man") does emerge, Viscardo does not resort to his contemporary political philosophers (to whom he had recourse while living in Italy and London). Unlike his adaptation of Adam Smith's political economic philosophy, Viscardo turns instead to the medieval history of the Spanish Cortes and its tradition of political representation. But the Cortes, especially by the 1790s, had long been abandoned, and he laments its demise.

By insisting on the Spanish tradition of rights via the medieval Cortes, Viscardo in effect offers a placeholder for the future. He plants the seed for a different genealogy of rights originating in Spanish tradition but onto which would be grafted what was becoming already the dominant Anglo-Protestant tradition of possessive individual rights. His task was great. But ultimately, the *Letter* says less about this genealogy of rights, and focuses instead its affective energies in ensuring that its potential readers could begin to imagine themselves belonging to one another via a painful history that, by necessity, had to be transcended. How it would be transcended and what would replace Spanish rule would have to wait until they had "examina[do] nuestra situación presente para determinarnos, por ella, y tomar el partido necesario a la conservación de nuestros derechos propios, y de nuestros sucesores [examine(d) our present situation with its causes, in order to determine us, after mature deliberation, to espouse with courage, the part dictated by the most indispensable of duties towards [them] selves and [their] succesors]" (73, 63).

His letter, as noted above, was finally published in Spanish in 1801; it is this version that had the widest circulation, especially throughout the Gulf of Mexico and Caribbean. Many more Spanish editions emerge after 1810: a second in London in 1810, which circulated in Mexico, a third in Bogotá also in 1810, a fourth in 1816 Buenos Aires, a fifth in 1822 Lima, and innumerable ones after.[87] We can imagine, then, that decades later, once the letter was received by its proper recipients, Viscardo's pessimism would form part of a larger sphere of dialogue with competing affects and visions. Viscardo had written from the past in 1791 to his future fellow "American Spaniards" in 1810. Through this imagined, discontinuous, enriched dialogue, and all enacted through print culture and the circulation of ideas, we can imagine that they collectively worked to make productive use of Viscardo's pessimism in order to produce a new way of imagining their emergent *nación*, an *Americano* one as we saw with Antonio earlier.

Even among hopeful revolutionaries the melancholic trope could not be avoided. Like Viscardo's, Álvarez de Toledo's tone throughout *Manifiesto* is marked by historicity: for seventy pages he details the events that had led to his arrival in Philadelphia and the history of American denigration. Only in the final pages does he offer a salve that could soothe Americans' pains:

> Trabajad por hacer felices á los Pueblos del Nuevo Mundo, y por ser la admiracion y la dulce envidia de la orgullosa y tiranizada Europa. . . . Es preciso sacrificarlo todo al bien general; y sobre las bases mas puras y solidas construir la obra que debe hacer inmortal y admirable á la America en las edades venideras. Aprovechaos de las luces y de los errores del genero humano: estudiad las constituciones de todos los Pueblos antiguos y modernos; y calculad á la luz de la historia y de la filosofia, qual puede ser la forma de Gobierno mas adaptada á las distantes, inmensas, y ricas provincias del hemisferio Indiano.
>
> [Work to make the peoples of the New World happy. Strive to become the cause of admiration and sweet envy of a proud, tyrannized Europe. . . . You must sacrifice everything for the common good; and construct on the purest and solid ground an oeuvre that will make America immortal and admirable for ages to come. Take advantage of humanity's knowledge and errors: study the constitutions of both ancient and modern peoples; and using history and philosophy as your guide, decide which form of government can best be adapted for the distant, immense, and rich provinces of the Spanish Indies.] (74–75)

But here, as he closes, Álvarez de Toledo does not immediately use the word "independence," nor does he offer elaborate plans for the future. Indeed, futurity is cut short. Rather than declaring a republican form of government, a constitutional monarchy, or insisting that we dream of future possibilities, Álvarez de Toledo appears to equivocate: study, he says. He offers various models of inspiration: federalism, the U.S. Constitution, civil liberty, equality before the law, among others. But these, he argues, must be filtered through the history and experience of the Hispanic world—both peninsular and American.

After appealing to the collective love of country, of America, he, like Viscardo before him, encourages his compatriots to study the past. But "study" invokes that other connotation of commerce as an exchange of ideas. He means that the American *pueblo* should publish, debate, discuss, in print and face to face, the various forms of government, both ancient and modern, and adapting from these construct the best-suited government for Spanish America. In the decade to come, in the midst of the full-blown wars of independence from Spain, Álvarez de Toledo as well as many other Hispanophone writers would participate in this developing trans-Atlantic public sphere by engaging in heated debates with peninsular Spaniards writing from London and Spain.[88] But for now, in 1811, he argues that by creating a public sphere the future of the nation will be constructed. In the absence of one, Álvarez de Toledo and other Spanish Americans can only begin to theorize and wait.

Reconfiguring Time and Space

Most of the authors discussed here may have published their work in Philadelphia, but they did so imagining a community of readers that was located elsewhere in the Atlantic world. They imagined themselves participating in a developing, uncensored public sphere that transcended Philadelphia, the United States, and even the Americas—a public sphere that encompassed the Hispanic globe. At the turn of the nineteenth century, Hispanics everywhere desperately sought ways to improve the living conditions of the Hispanic world. Some sought reform, others outright revolution. But Napoleon's 1808 invasion made the world topsy-turvy as the majority of Hispanics reacted with patriotism, squashing for a moment rebellious movements. Overnight, the Cortes of Cádiz immediately declared themselves—precisely because they were comprised of representatives of the people—the legitimate source of the nation's sovereignty, arresting anyone who questioned their authority. The Cortes released the absolutist regime's stranglehold on the press and society. But they also demanded that the people, via their representatives, see themselves as the authors of their new nation. As a result, Hispanics engaged in a battle of competing social imaginaries: while most advocated for a constitutional monarchy, the more radical yearned for a republic, and many sought to hold on to what remained of the *ancien régime*. Overnight, the Cortes had unleashed the forces of modernity.

The print culture component of the trans-Atlantic Hispanophone public sphere explodes amidst this expressive freedom, producing works that circulated throughout the ports of the Atlantic. The numbers are staggering. In the first eight years of the nineteenth century, Mexico had one newspaper consisting of 26 issues a year. By 1809, that number had increased to six newspapers, which produced a total of more than 600 issues. Even more dramatic, between 1810 and 1811 the number of newspapers jumped from ten to sixteen with over 754 issues per year. The number of books published in Mexico is just as revealing. From 1804 to 1808, the number varied from 68 to 153. But it skyrocketed in 1809 to 244 and then 275 in 1810. More importantly, before 1808 less than 1 percent of the books were of a political nature; that percentage increases to 45 percent in 1808.[89] Philadelphia too, though far from the center of Spanish America, participated in this expanding print culture. Prior to 1800, there were less than ten Spanish-language imprints. But from 1800 to 1813, the number increased to more than thirty, which then circulated across the Atlantic to London and Spain, and south and west throughout Spanish America. Still, while the Spanish Cortes had decreed freedom of the press, royal administrators in the Americas refused or delayed implementation of that freedom. Regardless of these continuing restrictions, the practice of printing, publishing, and debating only grew, and from these growing efforts the concept of the public continues to morph, as we saw in Chapter 3. Through print, these arguments become abstracted and ascribed onto an amorphous, quasi-anonymous body of people.[90]

The Spanish-language print culture in Philadelphia emerged quite differently from those of the metropolitan centers of Spanish America. As part of a trans-Atlantic network of communication, the authors paid less attention to the particular affairs unfolding in the centers of Spanish America. Instead, they focused more on the Hispanic universe as a whole, on Napoleon, the future of the monarchy, the need to attend to American concerns. The distance—both in time and space—between the immediate, material location of publication (Philadelphia) and the reading public the author sought to impact often took two to four months to cover and spanned thousands of miles. In this regard, the origins of a trans-Atlantic Hispanic public sphere are an abstracted ideal. These initial publications were published at great distances from the place of desired impact; they were separated and divorced from the immediate, material interests of local politics. But they were also separated from the explosion in local print cultures, such as that of Mexico City, for example.

The temporality of the communication network—the length in time it took for imprints to circulate across the Atlantic—appears to have varied between two to four months, as noted above. For example, after Álvarez de Toledo's *Manifiesto* was published sometime between late October and early December 1811 in Philadelphia, an equally cantankerous though royalist pamphlet was published in early 1812 responding vociferously to it. The royalist published a biting, eviscerating annotated edition of *Manifiesto* in Charleston, ridiculing what he saw as Álvarez de Toledo's ostensible self-aggrandizement and false humility.[91]

The debate continued in Washington, D.C., with the February 15, 1812, publication of *Dedicada a los nuevos refutadores del Manifiesto de Don José Alvarez de Toledo, aparecidos en las margenes del Delaware, por un Indio patriota (Dedicated to the Refuters of Don José Alvarez de Toledo's Manifesto, Having Appeared at the Edges of the Delaware, by a Patriotic Indian).* This anonymous defense of *Manifiesto* then prompted Álvarez de Toledo himself to respond in gratitude with his own pamphlet, *Contestación á la carta del Indio Patriota,* just two weeks later on February 28.[92] Though the debate that unfolds through these sources is fascinating, what is of greater interest to us is the rapid circulation of these Hispanophone documents. The frequency of their creation, and the speed of their

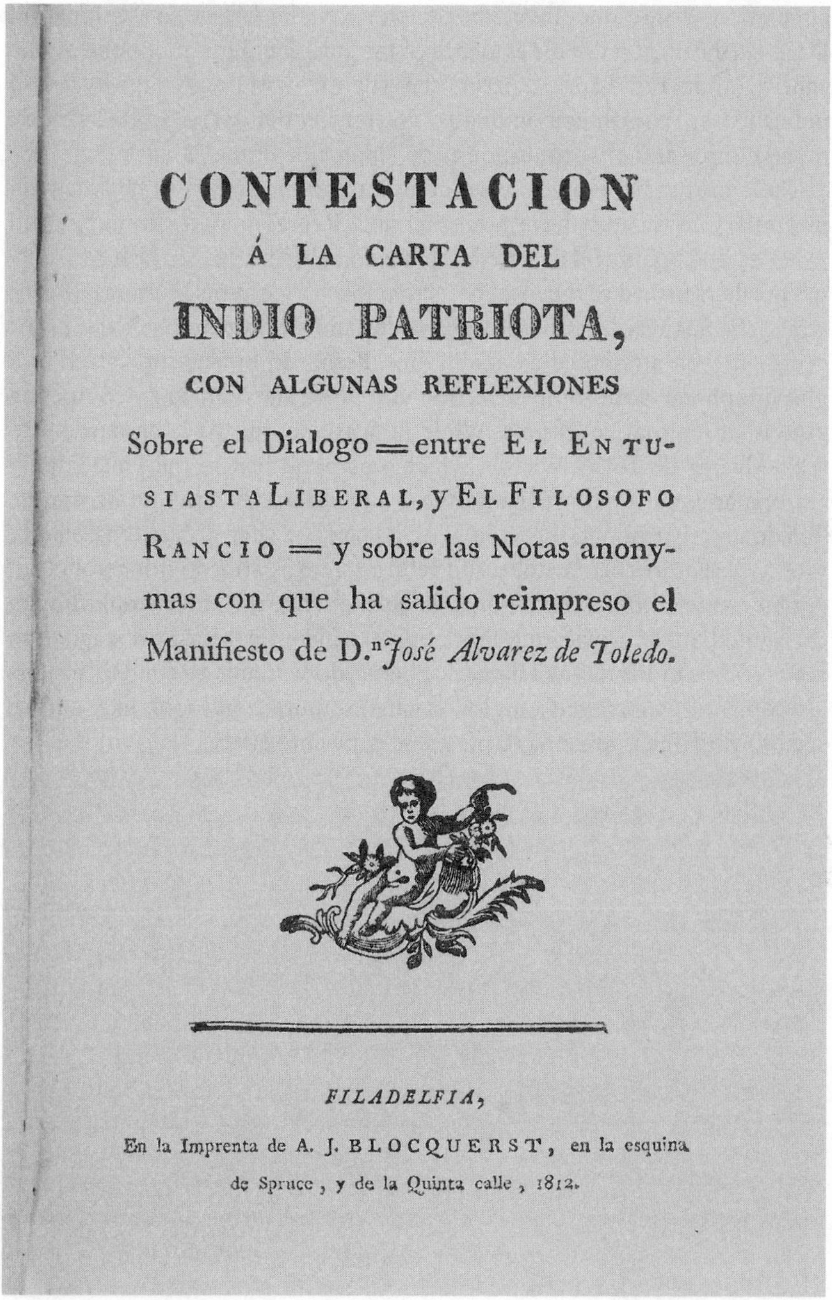

CONTESTACION

Á LA CARTA DEL

INDIO PATRIOTA,

CON ALGUNAS REFLEXIONES

Sobre el Dialogo = entre El Entusiasta Liberal, y El Filosofo Rancio = y sobre las Notas anonymas con que ha salido reimpreso el Manifiesto de D.n *José Alvarez de Toledo.*

FILADELFIA,

En la Imprenta de A. J. BLOCQUERST, en la esquina de Spruce, y de la Quinta calle, 1812.

Figure 33. José Álvarez de Toledo, *Contestación á la carta del Indio Patriota* (Philadelphia, 1812).

Beinecke Rare Book and Manuscript Library, Yale University.

circulation, from London, to Philadelphia, to Charleston, to Washington, D.C.—is the most palpable evidence of the emergent Hispanophone public sphere and its rapid spread across the Atlantic world. Authors wrote and published in Spanish responding to documents that were printed not six months prior and at various points on either side of the Atlantic.

The world that Bernardo encountered upon his arrival in Philadelphia in January 1812 must have been dizzying. Representatives from Spanish America and Spain collaborated in plans to help liberate Spanish America, while others turned to the local press to publish their proclamations. Meanwhile, the Spanish legation did everything in its power to deter the insurgents—it even attempted assassinations. Bernardo became immersed in a Hispanophone world of insurrection and print, surrounded by competing visions of alternative futures. While in Washington, D.C., Bernardo had read Álvarez de Toledo's letter, which was published in the Philadelphia *Aurora*, and they finally met a few days later. Bernardo admired Álvarez de Toledo greatly (though that, too, would change). They decided to collaborate on a venture: Bernardo would return to Texas armed with revolutionary literature authored by Álvarez de Toledo while the latter would stay in the United States advocating for support. Unlike the historical stagnation among some of his fellow Hispanics, Bernardo was able to connect his disaffection with concrete examples of what a future could look like, and he sped toward Texas anxious to put these plans into effect.

III

REVOLUTIONIZING THE CATHOLIC PAST

CHAPTER FIVE

Seduced by Papers

Revolution (as Reformation) in Spanish Texas

Modern Tempests

After spending the rest of the icy winter of 1812 in Philadelphia, José Bernardo Gutiérrez de Lara made plans to return to Texas via sea. Notwithstanding his ostentatious title of Lieutenant Colonel and Commanding General of the Northern Provinces of Mexico, our Mexican insurgent had lost all of his official documentation during an ambush in Texas; and, thus, could not verify the mission he had been given to secure any means of support from the United States. The United States was reluctant to become directly involved, though he had received personal financial support from the government and enthusiastic support from the public. Thus, after plotting with other Spanish-American revolutionaries, including José Álvarez de Toledo, the former Santo Domingo representative to the Cortes of Cádiz, it had been decided that Bernardo would return to Spanish Texas with only a few filibuster volunteers and no military support, hoping he would gather more volunteers along the way. Meanwhile, Álvarez de Toledo would stay near the seat of U.S. government in order to advocate for the independence of Spanish America.[1]

Twice Bernardo's departure was delayed because of "mountains" of ice floating off of Baltimore's port. Finally, on February 19, 1812, he was able to depart, and he quickly resumed his journal writing. A few days later, he notes, his ship's captain sighted a French pirate corvette quickly making its way toward them. They managed to escape the pirates by sailing into a storm. "Nos comensò à seguir [They began to follow us]," he writes, "pero asi q^{e}. vido q^{e}. ntro. buque era mui velero y que un formidable temporal nos acometia, desistio de la empresa y boltiò velas [but as soon as they saw that our vessel was very swift and that a formidable gale was coming down upon us, they desisted from their pursuit and struck sail]."[2]

Now the tempest, rather than the pirates, overtook them. After several days embroiled in a horrifying storm, he describes the experience in his journal:

> q^{e}. conflictos, y congojas teniamos cuando veiamos lebantarse el buque—tan alto que parese q^{e}. llegaba alas nubes, y de alli verlo bajar con tanta velocidad, y sepultarse en lo profundo del mar, y ver caerse por encima las sovervias montañas de agua, y todo esto con tanto estrepito que aturdia!
>
> [What inner conflict and anguish we suffered when we saw the ship rise so high that it seemed to reach the clouds, and from there see it drop down with such swiftness and bury itself in the depths of the sea, and then watch the proud, arrogant, mountain-high waves crash down upon us; and all this with such a deafening noise that left us dumbfounded!]

He says little else; on this voyage where he alternates between seasickness, fear, awe at seeing the distant hills on the islands of the Bahamas and Cuba and new animals (porpoises), his entries are unsurprisingly brief. Still, this tumultuous voyage serves as an apt, if ironic, allegory for the events that were unfolding in the Atlantic world.[3]

Napoleon Bonaparte, the French pirate, had invaded Spain, pursuing the Spanish political elite down south to the port city of Cádiz. Located on a peninsula, barricaded by ancient walls, and protected by the British fleet, Cádiz was also home to Spain's merchants and the country's budding bourgeoisie. Cádiz, the sequestered Cortes representatives thought, would succor them. The Cortes and their reimagined brand of representative government, one founded on ancient tradition and retooled for modern purposes, thrashed what remained of the *ancien régime.* As they set out to create the Hispanic monarchy's first written constitution, thinking they had escaped the grips of the French pirate, they instead created the conditions for a different fate. Cádiz enmeshed them in a modern political maelstrom as liberals and conservatives sought to shape the future of their world.[4] As actions were unfolding across the Atlantic in Europe, altering the future of the Americas, Bernardo found himself on a political ship heading into unknown waters.

Like Juan Pablo Viscardo y Guzmán passionately writing an open letter to an anonymous community of "American Spaniards"—one he would never see—or Santiago F. Puglia attempting to reach an unknown but much-desired Spanish-American audience, Bernardo spent months writing about experiences that had transformed his way of thinking. But he had been unable to share these thoughts and feelings with his *pueblo,* the people of the Eastern Interior Provinces or what is now the southern Texas-Mexico border. Like these predecessors, Bernardo writes for a public that does not yet exist.

By 1810, rebellions had detonated throughout South America. Then, in September of 1811, the monarchy's crown jewel, New Spain—that bastion of immense mineral wealth and far more politically conservative than other parts of Spanish America—did the inconceivable and declared an end to peninsular rule with Father Miguel Hidalgo's famous "Grito de Hidalgo [Cry of Hidalgo]." Some parts of Spanish America may have declared independence, but most did not seek a break with the Hispanic monarchy and certainly not with the Church. Rather, their aim was to reform the government and to oust the corrupt peninsular Spaniards at the helm of the Bourbon reforms in America. They had set out to act in the world in order to actively produce the world they wanted to inhabit. By actively taking part in the world, they thought their actions would translate into the fruition of their dreams. But like Bernardo's ship and like the inauguration of the Cortes, they soon came to understand that their actions had unforeseen and unknowable consequences. To paraphrase Foucault's well-known phrase, they knew what they did, but they quickly realized that they did not know what they did did.[5]

Our story now spirals back to our origin, to the 1812 revolt in Texas. In Parts I and II we moved helically forward, out, and back in time to the Reformation and late eighteenth-century Hispanic world to trace the genealogy of reform, revolution, and shifting affects of belonging. Now, our narrative comes back around, not to the same moment with which we began, but to one informed by the past in order to appreciate the complexity of the present. But here, too, our narrative will orbit out and back once again, having occasion to revisit the deep intellectual past of the Catholic Hispanic world in order to comprehend the passion with which Bernardo and his fellow Spanish Americans sought so desperately to produce a new world.

The Spanish commanders left a wealth of written documentation that detailed their attitudes toward the insurrection and the revolutionary literature. What did revolution mean to these royal officers? How did these Spanish loyalists view their world and their subjects? As we pursue the archival trail in order to better understand the social imaginary of these royal officers, we will see that revolution was not simply a matter of replacing one form of government with another. It was, in their eyes, the very end of the world. For this reason, they desperately did everything in their power to prevent the entrance of these revolutionary documents.

On the Spanish Texas–Louisiana Border

By March 23, 1812, Bernardo was dining with Louisiana politicians in New Orleans, as he slowly made his way back to the Louisiana-Texas frontier (see Figures 5 and 7). Everywhere, he encountered Anglo-Americans, French, and Spaniards seeking to influence him. Among them was U.S. special agent William Shaler, who would accompany Bernardo to Natchitoches. Shaler, along with two other U.S. officers—Natchitoches-based Indian agent John Sibley and Orleans Territory governor William Claiborne—all sought to "guide" Bernardo in order to ensure that the revolution assumed a "proper direction" that would benefit U.S. interests.[6] After traveling some 250 miles north-northwest up the swampy rivers of Louisiana, and after surviving an abundance of mosquitoes and near-attacks by alligators and panthers, Bernardo arrived in Natchitoches ready to enter Texas.[7] However, unlike Hidalgo's forces who attempted to make their way into Texas using military strength, Bernardo returned to strew the revolutionary path, as it were, with pamphlets, broadsheets, and other documents. It would be several more months before he would march into Texas with military forces.[8]

He arrived in Natchitoches at 10 a.m. on April 28, 1812, and was promptly met by "todos los principales con la mayor ovediencia, como se obserba haserlo en las colonias de España con los que vienen de la corte [all the leading men with the greatest deference, as is the custom in the colonies of Spain of those who come from the court]."[9] Established by French traders in 1714, Natchitoches was one of the crucial trading posts situated at the intersection of expanding Spanish, French, and British-American empires (the other crucial posts were St. Louis and the Arkansas Post).[10] By the turn of the nineteenth century, the Natchitoches area had developed a unique, creole culture, blending Spanish, French, Anglo-American, Native American, and African (both slave and free) peoples. The relative absence of European women also meant that intermarriage between Europeans and Indians was common, as was the practice of holding Indians as domestic slaves.[11] In 1810, the population stood at 2,870, with 1,213 whites, 181 free people of color, and 1,476 slaves, but the number would have swelled significantly if one included the traders—Native American, African, and European alike—that moved perpetually through the entire region.[12] Bernardo enjoyed his stay in Natchitoches, receiving invitations everyday, which "los tendremos hasta q^{e}. seles olvide que vengo del Govierno [we shall have . . . until it is forgotten that I come from the Government]."[13] He also met with the prominent Native American chief Dehahuit, the head of the Caddo Nation. Dehahuit had served as chief of the Caddos since 1800 and would continue doing so until 1833. He was a well-respected, powerful, persuasive politician to whom other Native nations went to for advice, and was likewise keenly aware of shifting imperial interests between Spain and the United States. According to the historian F. Todd Smith, Dehahuit "expertly played the two powers against one another."[14]

Insurrection in New Spain and Texas, however, had destroyed the tenuous balance of power between the Spanish political administrators and various Native American peoples in Texas. The Caddos had inhabited the western boundary of the Eastern Woodlands (encompassing the territory located at the intersection of what is today Texas, Oklahoma, Arkansas, and Louisiana) since at least the eighth century, and had developed large cities based on the farming of corn. Though their cities had diminished due to European disease, they continued to hold considerable political power. Throughout the eighteenth century the Caddos had been able to broker treaties between Europeans, Tonkawas, and Comanches both in Texas and Louisiana. But the rapidly expanding United States had forced other Native peoples (among them the Choctaws, Cherokees, Chickasaws, and Creeks) west into Caddo territory; and Spain, realizing it needed a buffer with the United States, welcomed these new Native peoples into the region. Needless to say, the demand for land created animosity as well as vulnerable, quick-to-change alliances between all these peoples.[15]

Meanwhile, in central Texas, the great Comanche empire was at its peak, expanding from the southern Great Plains down into central Texas and benefitting from trade in livestock with Anglo-Americans. It renewed its encroachment on San Antonio de Béxar, pushing as well the once-dominant Lipan Apaches further south, where they conducted extensive raids as far as central Mexico.[16] Bernardo notes, during his stay in Natchitoches:

> saviendò yò que las Naciones indias handan haciendo daño alos soldados y vecinos de San Antonio; mande llamar al Gefe de los Cadò, como supremo Gefe de las Naciones Indias y le reprendi sobre esto, y le mandè inmediatamt^{e} fuera a intimar de mi parte a las dichas naciones que luego sesen de ostilar

alos españoles y se esten esperando ordenes mias de lo q^{e}. se deva hasèr en adelante. El dicho Gefe mehà reconocido por Supremo Gefe, y se partiò a cumplir con lo mandado.

[knowing that the Indian Nations are doing damage to the soldiers and citizens of San Antonio; I summoned the Chief of the Caddoes, as supreme Chief of the Indian Nations, and I rebuked him for this; and I ordered him to go immediately to tell the said nations in my name to cease all hostilities against the Spaniards, and to await my orders as to what they should do in the future. The said chief has recognized me as Supreme Chief, and he left to comply with my orders.][17]

Clearly, Bernardo's ignorance and ethnic arrogance emerges here as he assumes that the Comanche Nation would obey the Caddos, or that the powerful chief Dehahuit would recognize the recently arrived Bernardo as "supreme chief." Indeed, Bernardo was wrong. Sensing the changing political tide, Dehahuit had already shifted his alliance to the United States, especially since Spain had done virtually nothing to protect the Caddos from the encroachment of other Native Americans. In the end, the Caddos would not join Bernardo's forces, while members of the Tonkawas, Lipan Apaches, and the recently arrived Choctaws would.[18]

Positioned in Natchitoches, Bernardo prepared to pounce on what was left of an ever-weakening Spanish colony. The documents he brought with him had been produced in Philadelphia by revolutionary Hispanics who had come from throughout the Atlantic world, and the documents would eventually continue their voyage into Texas and down along the Rio Grande Valley deeper into Mexico. There were three specific documents that were dispersed widely: a handwritten manuscript proclamation by Bernardo, a sixteen-page pamphlet titled *El Amigo de los hombres,* and a double-sided broadsheet with three broad crosses at the top, all wrapped up in sheets of the New Orleans–based newspaper *Le Moniteur de la Louisiane.* These documents, as we will see, facilitated the circulation of a new affective, political feeling, one that certainly built upon the new ideas that had arrived with Hidalgo's forces in 1811. It was a feeling so powerful that it led entire communities to abandon the world they had long known.

The documents certainly were not without their detractors. Spanish royal officers in Texas did their utmost to defend the world they inhabited, and clashed head-on with the ideas promulgated in these revolutionary texts. Royalists had responded similarly in the capital of Mexico City. Upon the public announcement in June 1808 of the fall of the Bourbon monarch, pro-independence broadsides were quickly printed and posted in public venues. The peninsular-dominated *audiencia* ("court") had no qualms in immediately sentencing one of the authors, Fray Melchor de Talamantes, to death.[19] Royal officers had a very well-established line of communication throughout the Americas that allowed them to alert one another of any threats. In Texas, the Spanish governor was required to retain copies and send duplicates of all correspondence to his superior in Chihuahua, most of which would then be recopied, annotated by his superior, and forwarded to Mexico City, or, the governor's superior would reply in the well-spaced margins and return the commented-on copy with instructions to the governor.

The northeastern Spanish frontier of Texas with Louisiana had long been the bane of royal officers in the Americas, and for good reason. It was the weakest link in the entire Spanish domain, the stretch of land most susceptible to foreign intrusion.[20] As the Spanish governor of Texas wrote—and would repeat on many occasions to as many authorities as he could—"[E]sta Prov.ª . . . debe conciderarse sin duda alguna el antemural de este Reino [Without a doubt, this province should be considered this Kingdom's frontline of defense]."[21] By the late eighteenth century, fear of imperial invasion had also cultivated a fear of a literary invasion. As we have seen, the 1794 publication in Philadelphia of Puglia's *El desengaño del hombre,* the first known revolutionary anti-monarchical Hispanophone imprint, warranted an all points bulletin throughout Spanish America. Within months, broadsides were posted in Mexico City, letters were couriered to New Granada, and orders were sent to royal officers in Texas, warning them all of this seditious entity. Officers became paranoid and fixated on the movement of revolutionary literature from New Orleans into Texas. From Texas, they imagined a domino effect where the ideas contained in the documents would trickle down and corrupt the gem of the Spanish monarchy, New Spain.

Indeed, the Spanish royal governor of Texas, Manuel Salcedo, never ceased reminding his superiors of his region's frontline status, pleading with them to send the requisite military support to protect Texas. Born on April 3, 1776, just weeks before the U.S. Declaration of Independence, Salcedo had been educated at the Royal Seminary of Nobles in Madrid in the 1790s. Having then served in the military with distinction, Salcedo lived in Spanish Louisiana from 1801 until 1804, where his father served as governor of Spanish Louisiana first and, after the Louisiana Purchase, as governor of West Florida, and where the younger Salcedo also became involved in negotiating the boundaries between former French Louisiana and Spanish West Florida. Three years after his return to Spain, Salcedo was appointed governor of Texas in 1807 at the young age of thirty-one, and is to date the youngest person to ever serve as governor of Texas. Upon his appointment, according to the historian Nettie Lee Benson, "he made a leisurely trip to Texas during which he spent a while in Philadelphia with the Spanish Consul-General, Valentín de Foronda, toured the central part of the United States, visited with the governor of Kentucky, and stopped for some time in both Natchez, and Natchitoches, Louisiana before proceeding to Nacogdoches [the border Spanish Texan town located one hundred twenty miles west of Natchitoches] in October, 1808."[22] In effect, Salcedo had poetically traced the route that Bernardo would embark on, in reverse, some three years later. What's more, the historical narrative unfolding here tightens even further, reducing the vast space across the Americas and Atlantic: Salcedo and Valentín de Foronda (whose writings we explored in Chapter 3) had met in Philadelphia. One only wonders what conversations these aristocratic men—one a soldier-commander, the other a bourgeois-diplomat—may have had regarding the future of the Hispanic world.

From the beginning Governor Salcedo, like many other Hispanic *letrados,* dedicated himself to improving the conditions in Texas. But each of his proposals would be met by rejection, an unfortunate outcome given that Texas had been plagued by ineffectual governors since the 1780s.[23] Certainly the local residents recognized his efforts. Upon the call for elections for a Texas representative to the Cortes of Cádiz, they twice elected Salcedo as their representative, and twice he was disqualified by the *audiencia* in Guadalajara because he was not a native of Texas.[24] Though he never served as deputy to the Cortes, he did pen a detailed report describing the need for development in Texas, and he hoped it would be useful to the Cortes. His report is a prescient analysis of the "ambitious" United States and a moving call to aid the residents of Texas. Clearly, Salcedo had learned a significant amount regarding the expanding United States while he was in Louisiana and West Florida. The report was similar to others produced by the various provinces of the Americas, such as the one we have seen by Miguel Ramos Arizpe. Salcedo's report offered detailed information on socioeconomic conditions and made specific policy recommendations.

With his characteristic poetic flair, Salcedo wrote of Texas: "nada hay y de todo se necesita [there is nothing and everything is needed]."[25] Even on the eve of Bernardo's arrival, Salcedo insisted that Spain allow Texas to develop the requisite infrastructure in order for the province to flourish. Texas, he wrote, "es la llave del Reino [de Nueva España], y es la mas despoblada, y exhausta de quanto es necesario para su defenza y fomento [is the key to the Kingdom (of New Spain). Yet it is the most depopulated (province), impoverished of all that is necessary for its defense and development]." Echoing the familiar melancholic refrain discussed previously, Salcedo continued by making the case for the economic development of Texas: by allowing more people to migrate there, sending more money and artillery, and building a much needed port at Matagorda Bay (some 100 miles southwest of present-day Galveston), Texas "pudie[ra] ser la mas rica y el antemural respetable de las ambiciosas Miras de Nuestros Vecinos [could be the wealthiest and most respectable fortification against the ambitious Desires of Our Neighbors]."

He had already been overwhelmed by a confused insurrection in 1811. As we have seen, upon Hidalgo's advance, many believed that Salcedo was preparing to abandon Texas and flee to Louisiana. As a result, Juan Bautista de las Casas led an uprising, and arrested Salcedo on January 22, 1811. The revolt was soon suppressed. Casas was sent to Monclova where he was promptly beheaded, his head shipped in salt to Béxar and placed on a pike in the town square as a reminder to Bexareños of the cost of insurrection. Salcedo returned to power by the end of the year. But he would never forget the humiliating experience of being placed in chains, and, as a result, he begged his superiors for support against the insurgents. If Texas was lost to the revolutionaries, he proclaimed, "[su] perdida [sería] transcendental al continente y de dificil reparacion si se malogra [its loss would be transcendental to the continent and difficult to repair if it were to unfortunately come to fruition]." His groveling notwithstanding, Salcedo would never receive the support he desired.[26]

Only a little more than a year later, Bernardo, Salcedo's senior by two years, had arrived in Natchitoches on April 28, 1812, with plans of his own. But he had not arrived alone. A week later on May 5 the Spanish agent in Natchitoches, Marcelo de Soto, reported that "que se dice q.^{e} en poco habrá aqui una imprenta y se supone que no sera q.^{e} para hacer proclamas y mentiras aprovocar una ynsurreccion. Son dos impresores el uno Español y el otro Portugues [it is said that a printing press will soon arrive and it is assumed that it will be for no other reason than to make proclamations and lies in order to provoke an insurrection. There are two printers, one Spaniard the other Portuguese]."[27] Finally, Salcedo was able to confirm that two printers had set up in Natchitoches. Indeed, Bernardo had insisted that his Anglo-American patrons in Louisiana pay for printers to travel with him to Natchitoches.

Very little is known regarding the press's origin or its destiny or the names of the printers, but it was the first to arrive in western Louisiana and the closest a printing press had ever been to Texas.[28] The wooden printing press technology had changed very little since 1500, and would

Figure 34. The Natchitoches wooden printing press was similar to Isaiah Thomas's press, shown here.

Courtesy of the American Antiquarian Society.

not do so until well after the invention of the first cast-iron Stanhope press in 1800. Even then, the wooden press, because it was lighter and less expensive than the iron or steel press, would continue to be used well into the late nineteenth century. The Natchitoches press would have stood at about six feet.[29]

By month's end, Bernardo, too, wrote about the printers and, more importantly, the work they had set out to do. On May 25 he noted in his journal that: "fui a la imprenta a ver imprimir un mil de exemplares de la proclama q.^{e} ba para el Reyno de Mexico: me diverti mucho en ver la destreza de los impresores [I went to the printing press to see printed a thousand copies of the proclamation that goes to the Kingdom of Mexico: I enjoyed myself very much seeing the dexterity of the printers]" (see Figure 35).[30] Two men were required to operate the cumbersome press efficiently. And at a rate of 240 sheets per hour, they spent a day putting out 1,000 double-sided proclamations. It was the language in these documents that was intended to salve the path to independence, preventing, as Bernardo would claim several times, the unnecessary shedding of blood.[31] Like Viscardo, Bernardo knew he had to cultivate a new political affect of belonging, and, thus, used the printing press to help disseminate these new ideas. With the appearance of the press, it now seemed that destiny had finally arrived. Revolution sat poised on the Louisiana-Texas border. But revolution had not arrived in boots armed with guns. It had arrived on paper. Salcedo and the other royal officers had nothing to say regarding the lofty political ideas that permeated these tracts, deeming them unworthy of commentary. What they feared, however, and could not control was the effect these seductive ideas were having on their subjects.

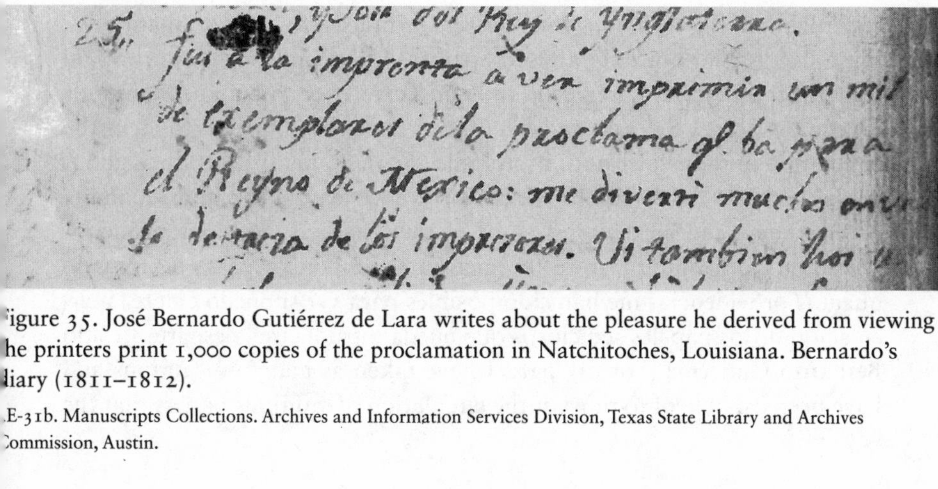
25. fui a la imprenta a ver imprimir un mil
de exemplares de la proclama q. ba para
el Reyno de Mexico: me diverti mucho en
la destreza de los impresores. Vi tambien hoi

Figure 35. José Bernardo Gutiérrez de Lara writes about the pleasure he derived from viewing the printers print 1,000 copies of the proclamation in Natchitoches, Louisiana. Bernardo's diary (1811–1812).

E-31b. Manuscripts Collections. Archives and Information Services Division, Texas State Library and Archives Commission, Austin.

Revolution as End of the World

The revolution was not led by invading barbarians or a military leader. Instead, revolution had come in the form of manuscripts, pamphlets, and broadsheets, fulfilling at long last the fear officers from throughout the Americas had expressed regarding the movement of revolutionary documents into Texas from Louisiana. As Salcedo proclaimed, "el genero de guerra que estos nos han de hacer [es] por medio dela seduccion [the type of war they want to engage us in is through the means of seduction]."[32] As another officer wrote, "Estos Pueblos incautos por una parte y alucinados por ótra, ábrazan facilmente la seduccion [These Towns, at once naïve and prone to deception, easily embrace seduction]."[33] It was for this reason that in May 1812 Salcedo gave no second thought to sending out troops to east Texas, some 300 miles northeast of the capital of Béxar, in search of those malevolent political tracts that had converted his subjects into "adictos [de] la rebolucion [addicts of the revolution]."[34] And yet, even before expending the little resources and energy that his forces had left—indeed, even before a drop of blood had been shed—Salcedo was aware that he had already been routed. The life and minds of his subjects had already been seduced by what appeared to be, as we will see in Chapter 6, a new political language of community.[35]

Even prior to the printing of the proclamations, the Spanish captain Bernardino Montero of Nacogdoches reported to Salcedo his varied attempts to prevent the entrance of those malicious tracts. So seductive were these ideas and so varied were the final goals of rebellion that soldiers and officers had also been swayed, abandoning the royal cause in favor of revolution. But insurrection to many of these people had not meant an end of monarchical rule. Rather, many thought that the royal officers, those recently arrived *gachupines* (the derisive term used to refer to Spaniards), like Salcedo, had not only abused Spanish Americans, but now, as Spain was falling, they were preparing to hand Texas over to Napoleon and his French.[36] Clearly, Salcedo and his officers thought, they had to stem the circulation of these false notions. As Salcedo and other officers throughout Texas and the bordering provinces of Nuevo Santander and Coahuila noted, they could hardly trust some of their soldiers, let alone residents. On May 12, Montero wrote to Salcedo: "que por mi parte he tomado quantas providencias me han sido posibles para ver si puedo evitar la circulacion de los papeles sediciosos que pueda introducir el desnaturalizado Bernardo Gutierrez [For my part, I have taken as many precautions as I have been capable of to prevent the circulation of seditious papers that the degenerate Bernardo Gutierrez may introduce]." One can note here, in the first official report to Salcedo regarding Bernardo's arrival, how Montero places emphasis on those "seditious papers"—even before they were ever printed—over the person of Bernardo. Montero's first mention of Bernardo reduces him to a mere modifier of the truly important subject matter here: the direct object "circulation of seditious papers."[37]

Montero's letter reveals a common thread among the Spanish royal officers' correspondence during this period. As in the case of the circulation of the French Declaration of the Rights of Man and of the Citizen in New Granada, the revolutionary literature itself becomes the primary focus of attention, even prior to the arrival of the actual insurgents themselves. Montero's explanation is telling: he claims that the documents "intentan perturbar nuestro reposo con el depravado fin de ponernos en rebolucion [intend to disturb our repose with the depraved goal of placing us in a state of revolution]."[38] Montero, in other words, attributes agency to these documents. In doing so he also reveals a distinctly Catholic Hispanic view of the world, one where agency did not rest in the rights-bearing individual, but remained dispersed throughout the universe.

The language evokes a world of tranquility, "nuestro reposo," that will not be revolutionized through its own will. Instead, the agency is displaced from the inhabitants of Spanish America to the documents themselves (despite the fact that they were authored by those very inhabitants in the first place). By divorcing human agency in the production of the documents, the royal officers rhetorically dehumanize the language in them; they effectively remove human *author*ity, allowing them to demonize the new ideas articulated in them. Thus, Montero can conclude that not only will the documents "disturb our repose" and "place us in a state of revolution," but having accomplished that, they will cause the inhabitants to become "destituidos unos con otros . . . [y seremos] esclavit[izados a] una Nacion sin govierno ni Religion como la Americana [deposed and displaced, we will all, one with others, become enslaved to a nation without government or religion like that of America]."[39]

For the Spanish officers, revolution was far from a mere political event; it was, at root, an epistemic rupture, a complete reshaping of the social world that would return them to a state of nature, one where neither God, King, or *patria* (country) existed. These Spanish officers had arrived in Texas as part of the Spanish Bourbon reforms, and they adhered to the Bourbon theory of divine right. In an effort to diminish local autonomy, the Bourbon monarch ended the policy of appointing American-born Spaniards to administrative posts, ending, in effect, the relative self-rule that American Spaniards had known since they had colonized the New World. Now, the most coveted administrative positions in America were given to Peninsula-born Spaniards, and these new officers were, according to historians, often, "second class despotic administrators . . . anxious to fill their own pockets."[40] As we have seen, the reforms created deep animosity among Spanish Americans who continued to imagine their social world under the Habsburg monarchical principle of a quasi-federation of kingdoms.[41] But to these new peninsular officers and the Hispanic world they inhabited, ontological and transcendental truth resided in a Catholic God and a Catholic king. God, king, and *patria* (fatherland or country), in this precise order, defined the means of achieving *la felicidad pública* (public happiness) or the common good.[42] In this, they were not unlike Pedro Rodríguez de Campomanes, Gaspar Melchor de Jovellanos, and other late eighteenth-century Spanish statesmen who also sought to reform the Hispanic world. But they did so, as we saw in Chapter 3, imagining the world hierarchically, where they, as the aristocratic elite knew best how to achieve happiness for all.

The basis of meaning, of authority, of interpreting the world unfolds from this premise. Without the infallible link between God and king, as the preordained giver of meaning, the epistemic basis of the social order would evaporate. The world that the royal officers embraced was a fixed, aristocratic world, shaped very much by St. Thomas Aquinas's political philosophy, elaborated in the thirteenth century and reaffirmed by the Catholic Church during the Reformation. It served as the very foundation of the Hispanic world. The Thomist world, where individuals were born into stations assigned to them by God and secured by divine law, was fixed and hierarchical; but it was also, the royal officers believed, a delicately woven tapestry in which each relied on the other to secure their place. It was the officers' responsibility to care for the monarch's community. The dominant Hispanic worldview imagined the community as "un conjunto de individuos sumergidos en un tejido social desigual compuesto de estamentos y distribuido en heterofórmicos territorios o reinos [a group of individuals immersed in an unequal social fabric comprised of estates and distributed in heteroformic territories or kingdoms]." This Thomist account of the world permeated the Hispanic social imaginary.[43] It was, to invoke Max Weber, an enchanted world, one that was inherited from God. Yet even Weber's description fails to capture the complexity of this Hispanic social imaginary. Ultimately, it is a world so foreign to us, built on concepts so far from our own, that it is difficult for us to comprehend its logic.

Charles Taylor, as we saw earlier, has described this enchanted worldview most succinctly as one in which the modern concept of subjectivity and agency did not exist. Instead, power was mediated by good and evil forces, by an elaborate spectrum of angels and saints, one where objects and invisible forces had power over the living. Certainly people believe this today. But in our modern world this is merely one option of many, and most definitely not the hegemonic point of view defining the way we relate to the world in the West. In the enchanted world, on the other hand, this was the dominant view.[44] It is in this sense, then, that Spanish officers could ascribe agency to these documents, as parchments that wielded destructive power.

In the writings and speeches of royal officers, the documents of revolution come to be seen as agents of an evil, corrupting, non-human force. By contrast, the royalists portray the region's inhabitants as lacking the agency or wherewithal to transform their consciousness. The documents become active, and the inhabitants remain passive. The contrast here may be interpreted in at least two ways. A more generous reading is that Montero and his cohorts rejected the possibility that their loyal inhabitants would even desire to put an end to their world by supporting a revolution. Hence, the documents themselves instigate a revolt. But a more cynical reading is that Montero believed his inhabitants literally had no agency, knowledge, or power to even consider throwing their world into revolt. They, as mere subjects, were simply not endowed with the capacity to actively choose to transform their world; they were very unlike the officers, those selected few chosen to govern the world.

The residents of Texas were, from this second perspective, "seduced" by these seditious ideas. Montero and his fellow officers, in turn, were among the chosen ones to be forcibly stockpiled, placed in the same collective, homogenous, mass of unthinking residents. The Spanish officers did not view their subjects as autonomous, individual beings capable of reason; such agency was simply not in the realm of possibility.

In either reading, the end result is the same. Whether their sentimental view denied the possibility that residents would want to bring revolution, or whether a patriarchal view rejected the very existence of their agency, Montero and the other Spanish officers unequivocally attributed revolutionary power to what they described as, "incendiary, heretical, and revolutionary" documents. Thus everything, they insist, must be done to "prevent the circulation of the seditious papers."[45] But this they could not achieve.

Revolution becomes in effect a second Reformation for the officers, an attempt to end the very basis of their existence. Governor Salcedo says as much when, after the insurgents finally invaded Nacogdoches, he wrote and read aloud a proclamation to the "Fieles Habitantes de esta Cap.[l] [Faithful Inhabitants of this Capital]," where he informs his audience that he has requested military aid from the neighboring provinces in order to "defend our Holy Religion" (see Figure 36). The proclamation essentially becomes a declaration of faith:

> Protesto, ante el todo poderoso morir antes q.[e] consentir q.[e] sus sagrados templos y Divinas imagines—sean la mofa y el escarnio de los Luteranos, Sacramentarios, y demas Hereges y Protestantes, que trataron de seducir vuestra fidelidad y Catholicismo. Esta misma protesta debeis hacer conmigo todos los q.[e] sean Catholicos y vasallos de Fern.[do] 7.[o] Huya, pues de entre nosotros el cobarde, el traidor, y vayase a reunir con la turba de Hereges q.[e] solo viene para saciar la ambicion de la plata y oro de este Reino: vivan entre ellos sin Ley, ni temor de Dios, y entreguense a todo genero de vicios; pero espere despues el inexorable asote del Altisimo para morir llenos de miseria, desesperacion, y desprecio del cielo de la tierra. Preparemonos, pues fieles Habitantes de esta Cap.[l] para pelear y cubrirnos de Gloria.
>
> [I profess before the Almighty Lord, to die before allowing the Lutherans, Sacramentarians, and the rest of the Heretics and Protestants to reduce your sacred temples and divine images to mockery and derision. These very same tried to shake your faith and belief in Catholicism. All of you who are Catholics and vassals of King Fernando VII should join me in making this same profession of faith. Let them flee then, those cowards and traitors among us, and go and join the heretical mob who only come to satisfy their desire for this Kingdom's silver and gold: let them live among those without Law nor fear of God, and surrender themselves to all forms of vice; but then expect afterward the Almighty's inexorable whip as the Kingdom on earth watches them die in misery, despair, and contempt. Let us prepare then, faithful Inhabitants of this Capital, to fight and to cover ourselves with glory.][46]

Salcedo's turn to the rhetoric of religion is not cynical; rather, religion was the natural, perhaps inevitable, means to rally the residents of Béxar (to have used religion cynically, on the other hand, would have been, ironically enough, a rather Machiavellian gesture). Other officers responded similarly.

Bernardo, for example, sought revolutionary support from certain vulnerable royal officers who had equivocated before and had momentarily supported Hidalgo's movement in 1810. Thus, he wrote a most formal, moving letter to royal officer Ignacio Elizondo, using the formal second-person *usted* instead of the informal *tú*, asking him to help prevent "la sangre derramada de nuestros hermanos [spilling of our brothers' blood]" by uniting with "nuestra santa causa [our holy cause]" against "el nombre

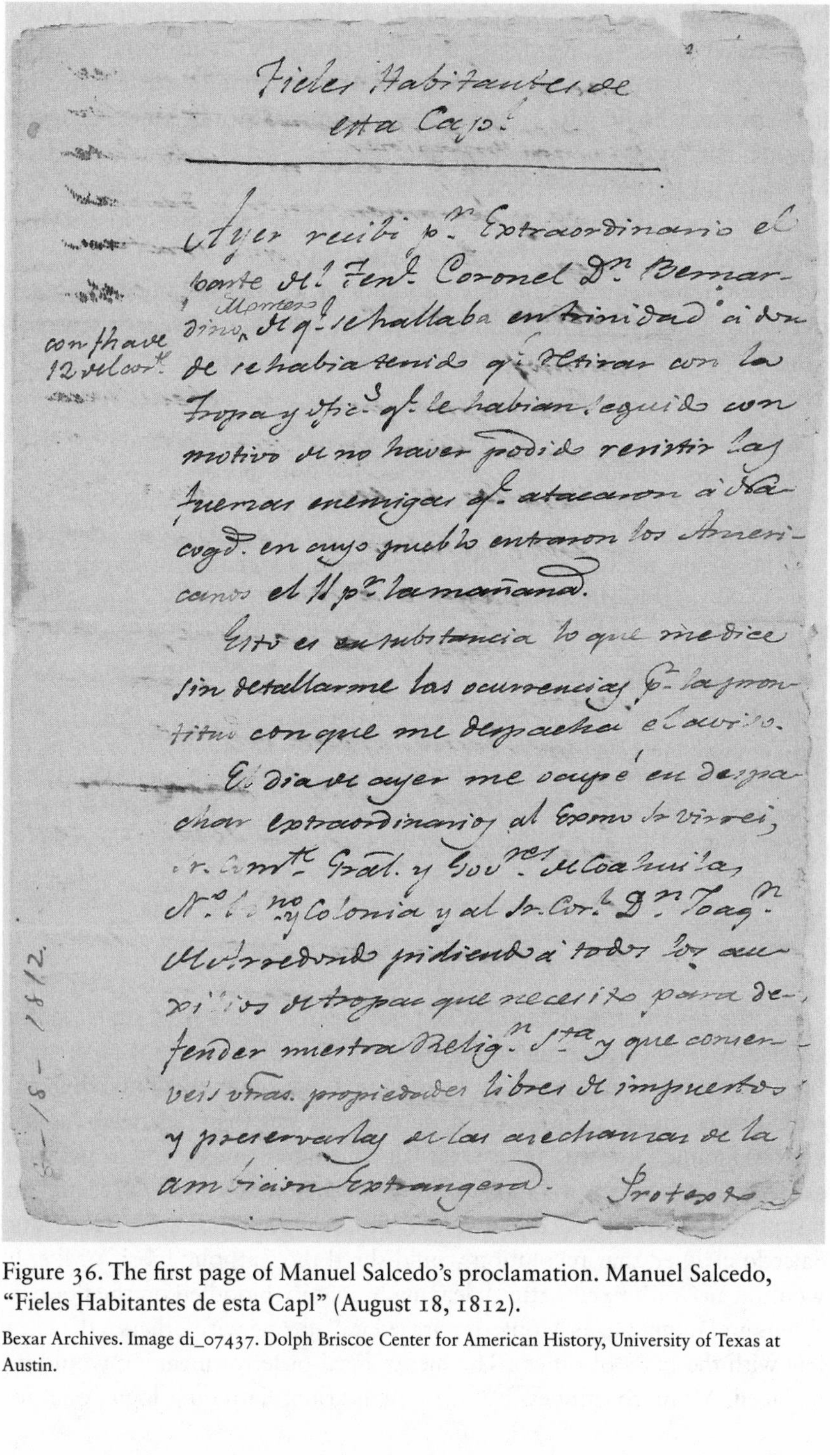

Figure 36. The first page of Manuel Salcedo's proclamation. Manuel Salcedo, "Fieles Habitantes de esta Capl" (August 18, 1812).

Bexar Archives. Image di_07437. Dolph Briscoe Center for American History, University of Texas at Austin.

imaginario de un rey que ni existe ni lo hay [the imaginary name of a king that neither exists nor ever has]." Bernardo closed by saying, "Quede usted seguro de mi buen afecto hacia a su persona ofreciéndome ser de usted un fiel hermano y no un jefe . . . como un verdadero patriota y amigo de usted que lo ama y atento su mano besa [Please be assured of my great affection for you, and I offer myself as a loyal brother and not a commander . . . as a true patriot and friend of yours that loves you and attentively kisses your hand]."

Elizondo, however, would have nothing of it. He responded vituperatively in the most condescending of terms, rebuffing Bernardo's use of *usted* with his own very informal *tú*. Bernardo, he writes,

> Con el mayor desprecio he visto tu carta seductiva. . . . Tú con tus protestantes y herejes defiendes la causa del demonio, y yo con mi ejército de católicos la del dios de los ejércitos, tú estás descomulgado con todos los tuyos por la Santa Inquisición y por el señor obispo de esta diócesis, y yo soy un defensor de la religión, tú homicida y traidor de tu patria, y yo un realista y patriota decidido. . . . [E]stoy resuelto a que si en los infiernos te metes que será tu último refugio, sacarte de las greñas, quemar tu cuerpo y desparramar tus inmundas cenizas.
>
> [With the utmost contempt have I received your seductive letter. . . . You, with your protestants and heretics, defend the devil's cause, while I, with my Catholic army, defend that of God of the Armies. You and all your men have been excommunicated by the Holy Inquisition and by the Bishop of this diocese. I am a defender of religion, you a murderer and traitor to your country. . . . And I am determined that even if you go to hell, it will be your last refuge, because I will drag you out by your matted hair, burn your body, and scatter your filthy ashes.][47]

For the royalists, revolution was a holy war, not a war of rights, not a conflict over self-determination.[48] Even for those more liberal Hispanics, such as the eighteenth-century statesman Campomanes, monarchy and religion were not to be questioned, notwithstanding their desire for radical socioeconomic reform. The case was similar with Spanish Americans who saw Anglo-Americans as "guilty of religious heterodoxy which created an insuperable obstacle to direct and definite understanding."[49] Governor Salcedo claimed that revolution would shred the Catholic fabric of life. It would tear God's fixed pattern, leaving humanity bloodied on the floor, in shreds and mingling, as Montero phrased it, "all, one with others," the elect few with the mass of others. The hierarchical order of meaning would be replaced, Montero implies, by some egalitarian, flattening logic, one devoid of structure, the divine, and meaning. Instead of fixity, structure, and order, the new world would be governed by anarchic fluidity, movement, and disorder.[50]

The fears of these Spanish royal officers are the logical, seemingly inevitable, conclusion of the Scholastic worldview. Writing about the Spanish-American Scholastic intellectual world, the historian Mariano Picón-Salas claims that "from this philosophic intellectualism another characteristic of the colonial mentality may be deduced, namely, the denial of progress because the divine order is regarded as immutable. The colonial wished to live in a world unaffected by things temporal and accidental and it therefore lacked the historical spirit, that is, a consciousness of change."[51] Yet in claiming that they "denied" the concept of progress, Picón-Salas mistakenly claims that Spanish-American society had a "choice," had the capacity to choose an alternative sense of temporality when, in fact, this was not in the epistemic realm of possibilities.

The revolutionaries' call to remake the world must have, in some very basic way, baffled the royal commanders, because for them it was not possible to alter the world as it existed. In many ways, this was the physical manifestation of the intellectual debates that José Antonio de Alzate had reported on in 1788, between Scholasticism and modern philosophy. As we have seen, Bernardo's brother, Father José Antonio, had embraced this new way of thinking. But more than a new way of thinking, it was an epistemic shift. For the royal commanders, agency in the modern sense was unfathomable because God had produced the world. Agency did not rest in the monist individual but was bestrewn in the tissue of sociality, among animate and inanimate objects alike. It was a world where temporality was aligned with God, not with mundane humans, and it was a world where ontological meaning, a sense of presence and belonging in the world, was not rooted solely in the self but rested in social relations, with the beings and objects of God's universe.[52] How profoundly distressing it must have been, then, when this episteme began to morph with the various transformations of the eighteenth century: the alienating Bourbon reforms, the seeping of rational science and philosophy into Hispanic culture, and, finally, Napoleon's deposing of the Spanish king. If we consider the abject terror that these royalists must have felt, Elizondo's furious rebuttal to Bernardo and Salcedo's dire proclamations starts to make more and more sense.

Picón-Salas is indeed accurate in identifying a shift to a new sense of historical awareness, one that is undeniably modern, secular, outside of God's time, and thus very troubling for the royalists. With the disruptions of the late eighteenth and early nineteenth centuries, the debates between

Scholastics and moderns, the penetration of skepticism into the social fabric, the sociopolitical reforms, and Napoleon's deposing of the king, the sense of time, too, begins to reconfigure. The dominant version of time had been that of God's universal time, one where humans were mere pawns in God's larger plan, where religious holidays were central because they allowed humans, for a fleeting moment, to connect with the divine, where the religious nativity procession during the Christmas holidays—one where the participants could actually sense the Holy Family's presence—was temporally much closer to the actual birth of Christ than it was to November or January. Time was messianic, vertical, aligned with God. Now, the emergent-becoming-dominant sense of time placed humans at the center of the universe. Certainly, as Taylor observes, there had been other senses of time, such as that of linear progress. But this version had had little relative importance. Now, it comes to take center stage. Time comes to be seen as a movement forward, a progression, in what Walter Benjamin describes as "homogenous, empty time."[53] Again we see that the Spanish American uprisings were not merely revolutionary battles. They were an irreconcilable epistemic war between a world of permanence and a world of change.

Revolution as Seduction

Only a few weeks after the documents had been printed on May 25, the territory was awash with pamphlets, broadsheets, and other documents.[54] The Spanish officers had sent spies along the 300-mile courier route between Nacogdoches and Béxar to intercept insurgent propaganda. Yet they did not need to roam far from Nacogdoches. On June 8, 1812, one of Captain Montero's loyal soldiers handed over documents given to him by one of Montero's own defected soldiers, José Francisco Vanegas, to circulate among the soldiers. With painstaking detail, Montero described in a letter to Salcedo the documents that Bernardo had produced, waiting until the very end, after some five pages, and almost as an afterthought, to name the individual who had introduced them, Vanegas (much as had been the case in the reporting of Bernardo's arrival where his name had been mentioned after commenting on the documents). The documents consisted of

> un quaderno que contiene 9 foxas con la caratula yntitulada el Amigo de los Hombres, un pliego que empiesa con Jesus, M$^{a.}$ y José, ótro firmado de Espalier con una llana escrita y una Blanca, y una Gazeta escrita en frances que no

se sabe su contenido por no entender este ydioma en que venian embueltos dichos papeles.

[a pamphlet of nine sheets of paper with a title page entitled Amigo de los Hombres, one document that starts with Jesús, María, y José, another written on one side and the other side left blank and signed by Espalier, and one gazette written in French (the New Orleans *Moniteur de la Louisiane*), whose contents are unknown since I do not understand the language, in which all of the documents were wrapped.][55]

Montero scoured east Texas searching for Vanegas, but found instead these same pamphlets and broadsheets scattered by the insurgents and their Indian allies. As Montero reported to Salcedo: "Acabo de tener noticias probables que el dia 24 de este han pasado por el Pueblo de Alibamó los Desertores Juan Galvan y Feliz Arispe guiados por vn Yndio de los Chatós con direccion a Revilla conduciendo cantidad de Papeles Ynsendarios, ereticos, y rebolucionarios, para de alli circularlos alos demas Pueblos incautos [I have just received the probable news that on the 24th of this month (June) the defectors Juan Galván and Feliz Arispe passed through the (Indian) town of the Alabamas, guided by a Choctaw Indian, en route to Revilla (Bernardo's hometown) taking with them great quantities of incendiary, heretical, and revolutionary papers, in order to circulate them from there to the rest of the unsuspecting towns]." Revolution and seduction, in the minds of the officers, spread itself thick and heavy, absorbing the inhabitants as it made its way south.

Three days later, on June 27, Montero's wish was fulfilled; his men captured Vanegas. The insurgent carried "un costalito de cotense sumamente bien cocido y marcado con la marca de margen [a small burlap sack, sewn tightly closed, and stamped with a reference mark]." It was inside this pouch that they discovered the same documents that had been captured several weeks before: "quarenta y tres exemplares en un pliego marcados con dos cruzes, y quatro quadernos titulados el Amigo de los hombres; todos firmados del traidor Bernardo Gutierrez [forty-three copies of a broadsheet marked with two crosses and four pamphlets titled Amigo de los Hombres; all signed by the traitor Bernardo Gutierrez]." Vanegas was promptly tried and executed. But two others had escaped, and they were well on their way to Revilla and adjacent towns.[56]

The incendiary material produced miracles. But if Montero prevaricated on the question of agency, Salcedo most emphatically did not. The revolutionary material began to unfold its machinations, and the governor insisted that it was through the arts of seduction that it intended to bring revolt. Wrote Salcedo, "siendo la gente sencilla é inexperta la menor seduccion la trastorna [being a simple, inexperienced people, even the most minor of seductions easily disturbs them]."[57] Royalist commentators throughout the Hispanic world, from Texas down to South America and across to Spain, latched onto the word *seducir* to describe the insurrections. Salcedo's position was crystal clear: the inhabitants of Texas were a simple, uneducated lot, easily swayed by even the most minor of "seductions." Whereas Montero attributed full agency to the documents, Salcedo here acknowledges the inhabitants' ability to act in the world and to make decisions based on these new ideas. But he likewise implies that they also lacked the requisite rational skills to critically interpret this new philosophy.[58] To Salcedo the inhabitants were far from being autonomous individuals endowed with the ability to use reason. Likewise, he implies that he and his fellow officers could easily penetrate the false logic in these ideas and thus dismiss them. But this was not the case for others. His is an aristocratic, patriarchal, condescending view of his vassals.

The connotation of the repeated keyword of *seducir* and its derivatives, in fact, contains this idea of change, of movement away from place and stillness to something unfamiliar. Its more common sexual connotation, as in "induc[ing] (a woman) to surrender her chastity," does not enter the *Diccionario de la lengua española de la Real Academia Española* (*Dictionary of the Spanish Language of the Royal Spanish Academy* [*DRAE*]) until 1884, though the *Oxford English Dictionary (OED)* finds it in the latter eighteenth century. The Spanish verb *seducir* and the English "seduce" are both derived from the Latin "sēdūcere," meaning "to lead astray." More specifically, the Latin prefixes "sē" and "sēd" carry with them the connotation of movement: in verbs, they have the adverbial sense of force, as in "without" or "apart"—as seen in the English verbs "secede," "seclude," "seduce," "segregate." The *DRAE* defines "seducir" as "engañar con arte y maña, persuadir suavemente al mal [to deceive with artful cunning; to gently persuade toward wrong]"; the English "seduce" has, according to the *OED,* as its primary connotation "to persuade (a vassal, servant, soldier, etc.) to desert his allegiance or service."[59] But the prefix "sē" is also ontologically related to a sense of self; according to the *OED,* "sē" also serves as the Latin pronoun "oneself." We may think of this Spanish royal emphasis on "seduction" as a movement away from fixity and stability, from the known, from oneself, and thus as a movement toward the foreign, the unknown and unthought. Yet, if it also connotes this movement away from the self ("to be led astray from oneself," in a sense), it also carries with it a version of the modern psychoanalytic concept of a splitting of the self, of, in contemporary parlance, "losing one's mind."[60]

"Seduction," in effect, becomes the trope for describing the people's shifting consciousness, and appears almost obsessively, since at least the appearance of Puglia's book in 1794, through the correspondence of Spanish officers. It serves as a trope to describe the reconfiguration of their episteme, of the people's movement away from thinking of themselves as subjects of the king and toward the new modern way of imagining oneself as a sovereign by actively taking part in the world and its governance. To Salcedo, Montero, and other Spanish officers, however, this shift was not so teleological. To them, it was a shift from a Catholic world and monarchical rule to a world ruled by madness, a world in which people have literally lost their minds. Yet, notwithstanding Salcedo's ability to dismiss this wave of seduction, the new ideas were transmitted across Texas like seeds, dispersed on the wind and germinating wherever they landed. The ideas were disseminated, and now, formerly allied Native Americans turned against the Spanish forces. Even soldiers began to defect en masse, easily replacing the executed Vanegas, further aiding the insurgent cause by spreading the literature deeper into New Spain.

A mere two months after the documents began circulating, the insurgents crossed the Louisiana-Texas border from Natchitoches and attacked Nacogdoches on August 11, 1812. Captain Montero suddenly found himself alone and had to abandon the town. As Governor Salcedo later reported to the viceroy: "Muy pocos . . . le siguieron, quando al Ver que ni al toque de Generala ni de llamada se reunia aq.[l] vecindario por estar todo seducido por los enemigos, ni la tropa que no obedecia mas que su capricho, se retiró [Montero] para la Villa de Trinidad presipitadamente por que acestaban contra su vida [Only a very few (soldiers and residents) followed him when he saw that no one gathered after sounding the call to arms, the whole town having been seduced by the enemy, not even the soldiers who now obeyed no orders except their own whim. Montero swiftly retreated to the village of Trinidad (seventy miles southwest of Nacogdoches; see Figure 7) because the insurgents threatened to kill him]."[61]

What precisely were these ideas that went along seducing inhabitants and soldiers alike? What enticing alternative vision of sovereignty and belonging could they offer the inhabitants of Texas, so enticing that they would be willing to reject the order of things and the world of authority they and their forebears had long known? Pursuing this line of inquiry will allow us to better understand the epistemic transformations by focusing on the alternative language of belonging that was unfolding in this province. By contrasting the Spanish royal officers' hierarchical view of the world with that of the documents, we can begin to see what revolution meant to the inhabitants of what was not even then the U.S.-Mexico border.

From Patriarchal Respect to Reciprocal Love

A certain body of mutinous literature found itself traveling throughout east Texas in June 1812. Smuggled into Texas by seditious soldiers or dispersed by Choctaws and other Native American nations to Béxar and the Nuevo Santander towns along the Rio Grande, these texts become, in effect, carnal. They did not merely convey ideas so much as instigate revolt, marching both metaphorically and quite literally at the head of the revolutionary forces, sowing the seeds of sedition, and preparing the field for battle. Thus, it is no surprise that the royal forces set out to capture this "being," describing it in detail: its clothing (made of coarse hemp cloth) along with the company it kept (Francisco Vanegas, Juan Galvan, Feliz Arispe, several unnamed Indians), and its movements (from Nacogdoches, through an Alabama Indian community in east Texas, en route to Revilla).[62] Let us begin with the genealogy of this corpus.

If the royal officers understood revolution as an epistemic shift, then certainly it would have appeared as such to most of the inhabitants. It is in this sense, then, that the literature that circulated in Spanish Texas served as a salve, offering both affective and political rationales for ending Spanish rule. According to the Spanish commanders, at least three different documents made their way into Texas: one single-sided folio handwritten manuscript signed by "Despallier," a printed pamphlet entitled *Amigo de los hombres,* and a double-sided, printed broadsheet. Captain Montero forwarded copies of all three documents to Governor Salcedo on June 8, who then forwarded them to the viceroy in Mexico City on June 25.[63] This official correspondence and the documents themselves are now part of Mexico's National Archives, many of which were transcribed in the early twentieth century by historians in the United States. The three documents do quite different work. The first two, discussed here, may be seen as paving the way to the explicit political language of rupture, of separating from the Hispanic *patria* in order to create the nation. The third document, discussed in Chapter 6, may have only been a double-sided broadsheet, but it offered a brilliant analysis of the world to come. It is no surprise, then, that Bernardo took great pleasure in watching his two printers, "the one Spaniard and the other Portuguese" print 1,000 copies of it in Natchitoches.[64]

The first captured document was signed by Bernardo Martín Despallier, a Frenchman living in the diverse, multicultural, border town of Nacogdoches. He had served in New Orleans under French Louisiana governor Carondelet in 1794, and arrived in Nacogdoches in 1804 where he married the Spanish-American María Candida Grande, whose relatives had also helped courier Bernardo's literature. Two years later, they moved to Spanish Texas, but Despallier was expelled for engaging in illegal trade, and he developed deep animosity toward Spanish rule. Thus, upon Bernardo's arrival, he enlisted in the insurgent cause, and used his extensive contacts to help distribute the literature to other Spanish Americans and Native Americans.[65] The manuscript was dated Natchitoches, June 1, 1812, and began: Coronel Don José Bernardo Gutiérrez "desea que todos los Criollos avitantes en las Provincias de Mexico sepan lo siguente [desires that all the creole inhabitants of Mexico's Provinces know the following]." The document contained eleven brief points that summarized Bernardo's intentions to liberate his "Hermanos los Criollos [Brothers the Creoles]."[66] Despallier, then, helped disseminate the literature deeper into Texas and, finally, into the capital of Béxar.

The pamphlet, *Amigo de los hombres,* was published in Philadelphia, and may be found in the Early American Imprints (Second Series) collection of the Readex Archive of Americana, which is available online. Comparing the pamphlet from Mexico's National Archives with the Early American Imprints version, it is clear that they are the same pamphlet, except that the Early American Imprint version contains a nine-page appendix. Excluding the appendix, the pamphlet is sixteen pages long, and the full title is: *El Amigo de los hombres: á todos los que habitan las islas, y el vasto continente de la America Española: Obrita curiosa, interesante, y agradable, seguida de un discurso "Sobre la intolerancia religiosa" (The Friend of Man: To All Those Who Inhabit the Islands, and the Vast Continent of Spanish America: A Curious, Interesting, and Pleasant Work, Followed by a Discourse "On Religious Tolerance").* The appendix itself has a different title: "La voz de la verdad. Sobre uno de los puntos que mas interesan á la felicidad de los Hombres" ("The Voice of Truth: On One of the Subjects That Is of Most Interest to the Happiness of Mankind"), and does not appear to have circulated in Texas, since it is not mentioned in any of the commanders' correspondence. Indeed, given its subject matter—religious tolerance—and given that religion was never called into question by the insurrectionists throughout Spanish America, it is no surprise that it was not chosen to be distributed.

The author's name is not printed anywhere, but historians attribute the pamphlet to none other than José Álvarez de Toledo.[67] The title page reveals that the pamphlet was published in Philadelphia by Andrés Josef Blocquerst, a Frenchman known for being the first printer on the Spanish-American island of Santo Domingo—the very island that Álvarez de Toledo had represented at the Spanish Cortes de Cádiz—and he may very well have known Álvarez de Toledo then. Blocquerst arrived in Santo Domingo

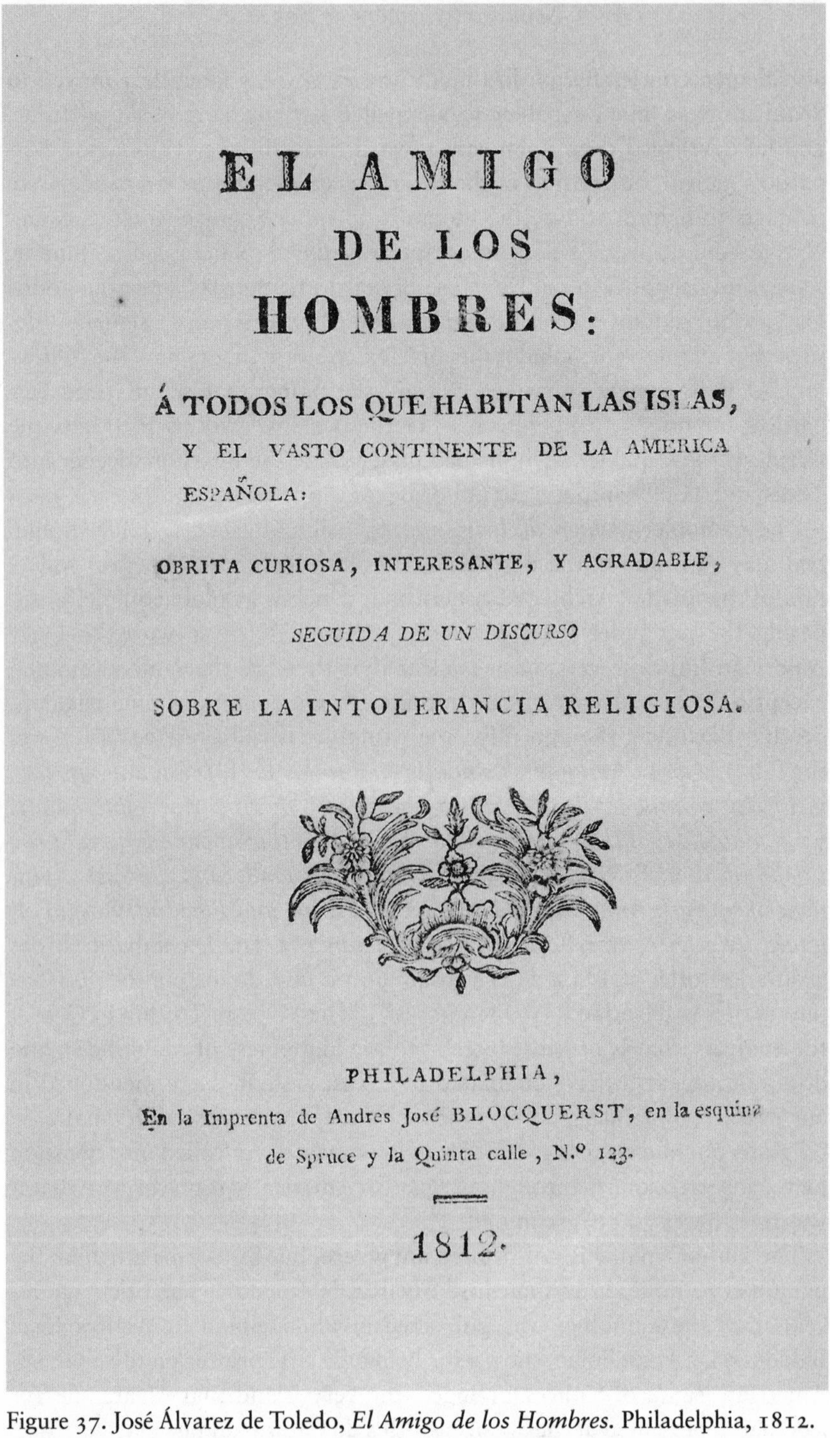

EL AMIGO
DE LOS
HOMBRES:

Á TODOS LOS QUE HABITAN LAS ISLAS,
Y EL VASTO CONTINENTE DE LA AMERICA
ESPAÑOLA:

OBRITA CURIOSA, INTERESANTE, Y AGRADABLE,

SEGUIDA DE UN DISCURSO

SOBRE LA INTOLERANCIA RELIGIOSA.

PHILADELPHIA,
En la Imprenta de Andres José BLOCQUERST, en la esquina
de Spruce y la Quinta calle, N.º 123.

1812.

Figure 37. José Álvarez de Toledo, *El Amigo de los Hombres*. Philadelphia, 1812.
American Philosophical Society.

in 1782, and published the first known imprint there, a religious pamphlet, in 1800, and several years later published the first newspaper, *Boletín de Santo Domingo* (1807–1809). He, along with the other French, was expelled from the island in 1809. From 1811 to 1820, he appears as a printer in several Philadelphia directories. His name, like those of other Philadelphia publishers of the period, appeared variously in imprints—in its Anglicized, Hispanicized, or Frenchified versions.[68] More evidence for Álvarez de Toledo's authorship is the dedication "to those who inhabit the [Caribbean] Islands," a reference to Álvarez de Toledo's Cuba and Santo Domingo. The title page is dated 1812, but at the end of the pamphlet, the author dates it "Washington, December 10, 1811." On this same day and with the same publisher, Álvarez de Toledo published the pamphlet discussed in the previous chapter, this time not anonymously, *Manifiesto ó satisfaccion pundonorosa, todos los buenos españoles europeos, y todos los pueblos de la America, por un diputado de las Cortes reunidas en Cadiz (Manifesto or Honorable Satisfaction, All the Good European Spaniards, and All the People of America, by a Deputy to the Cortes meeting at Cádiz),* in which he defended himself against charges of sedition (see Figure 30).[69]

The pamphlet is written in the style of a letter, in the second person, and addressed to the "Americanos." But the pamphlet's title itself, *The Friend of Man,* invokes a familiar Enlightenment-era trope of universal brotherhood or of philanthropy (in its original denotation of love of mankind). It was a term widely studied by philosophers who were in the process of rethinking fundamental social relations in a world of transformation.[70] If, as we have seen, the eighteenth century saw the shift from mercantilism with its top-down economics to free trade with its emphasis on individual free choice, then moral philosophers developed a new ethics of moral obligation and friendship in a world that was emphasizing more and more a sense of homogeneity over hierarchy.

The famed French economic philosopher Victor Riqueti, the Marquis de Mirabeau, perhaps made most explicit the link between the shifting modes of production and social relations. In 1757 he published the bestseller *L'ami des hommes, ou traité de la population,* "a project of [socioeconomic] reform based upon a philosophy of society that regarded 'the feudal system, renewed and adapted to the needs of the society of his time, as a natural transition from the economic *régime* of the Middle Ages to the modern *régime.*' "[71] Decades later, Immanuel Kant had intricately worked out the new ethics of amity, that is, of the responsibilities and duties that held between individuals. In Jacques Derrida's reading of Kant, "friendship supposes both *love* and *respect.* It must be equal and reciprocal: reciprocal love, equal respect. One has the duty to tend toward and to nurture this ideal of 'sympathy' and 'communication' *(Mitteilung)*. For though friendship does not produce happiness, the two feelings composing it envelop a dignity; they render mankind *worthy* of being happy."[72] Kant helps construct an intellectual edifice where morality is no longer something to be dictated—by religion, monarchy, or some other individual authority—but is something that emerges collectively, as an ethics of love and respect for one another, as friends to one another.[73] This, too, was the spirit of the influential late eighteenth-century Sociedades Económicas de Amigos del País (Economic Societies of Friends of the Country), whose goal, as we have seen, was socioeconomic reform in order to secure the *pueblo*'s happiness. In effect, there is a synergy among these discourses. The emerging field of political economy, the desire to secure people's happiness, and the new language of ethics and amity (which was also being played out in the new literary genre of the novel and its rhetoric of sympathy): these come together and invigorate the concept of equality. They begin to create the conditions of possibility that allow the modern subject, with his (*sic*) individuality and rights, to flourish.[74]

Álvarez de Toledo embedded his polemic within these shifting discourses in order to make more emphatic his claim that while Spanish America desired to remain part of the Hispanic monarchical family, it would only do so on the basis of Spanish-American equality to Spain. The pamphlet is a fiery, trans-Atlantic volley aimed directly at two Spanish-language documents published in London: issue number sixteen of the exiled liberal Spanish journalist José Blanco White's newspaper *El Español* and the political economist Álvaro Flórez Estrada's *Exámen imparcial de las disensiones de la America con la España, de los medios de su reconciliacion, y de la prosperidad de todas las naciones (An Impartial Study of America's Dissension with Spain, the Means of Reconciliation, and the Prosperity of all Nations)*.[75] Issue sixteen of *El Español* was published on July 30, 1811, and *Exámen imparcial* was first published in 1811 and translated into English in 1812. Álvarez de Toledo, then, had finished writing his pamphlet on December 10, 1811, four months after *El Español* had been published.

Ironically enough, Blanco White and Flórez Estrada were two of the most liberal peninsular Spaniards, and had to flee, in part, because of their liberal views. Still, though in favor of major political-economic reforms for Spanish America, they implored Spanish America to remain a part of the Spanish nation, especially during the crisis of Napoleon's invasion. Spain had lost her monarch and was under the control of France, they argued, and now the Americans were trying "de separaros de nosotros en la única occasion, en que todos debiamos trabajar unidos para conseguir nuestra libertad! ¡En el momento en que ibais á ser Nacion con nosotros; en el momento en que el Gobierno espontaneamente os habia concedido ya derechos [to separate yourselves from us during the extraordinary occasion in which we should all unite in order to secure our liberty! At the moment in which you were to become a part of the Nation with us; at the moment in which the Government spontaneously conceded you rights]."[76]

Expressing his dismay at their judgment against the Spanish-American desire for independence, Álvarez de Toledo writes: "Estoy escandilisado de ver á estos dos hombres, dotados de bastantes luces, y de firmeza de caracter, prostituirse á las miras interesadas y tortuosas de la politica ministerial; y . . . insultar á los derechos, y á la alta, dignidad de todos los pueblos del nuevo mundo [I am scandalized to see these men, endowed with intelligence and of firm character, prostitute themselves to the biased and torturous schemes of ministerial politics . . . and insult the rights and dignity of all the new world's *pueblos*]."[77] The rest of the pamphlet is structured as a pointed rebuttal against six specific claims made by Blanco White and Flórez Estrada. But Álvarez de Toledo's response is less an original, visionary statement of independence as a reaction against royalist pretensions. Of interest here, however, in regards to the pamphlet's circulation in Texas, are the ideas related to sovereignty.

Countering the claim that America lacks sovereignty to declare itself independent, the pamphlet demonstrates that, in fact, the town councils known as *cabildos* or *ayuntamientos* and established since the colonization of America

> han convocado al pueblo de sus provincias para comunicarle el estado de las cosas, y remitir á su exâmen y deliberacion . . . las medidas que juzgase necesario tomar. El pueblo eligió con toda libertad sus representantes, y delegó en ellos todas sus acciones y derechos para que acordasen y estableciesen lo que fuera mas conveniente á su felicidad.
>
> [have convocated the people from their provinces in order to communicate to them the state of things, and submit to their examination and deliberation . . . the necessary steps that should be taken. The people elected with all their liberty their representatives, and delegated to them all of their actions and rights so that they may resolve and establish what may be most appropriate for their happiness.] (3)

By his logic, sovereignty rests in the people as represented by the *ayuntamiento*. Indeed, Álvarez de Toledo was quite accurate historically in proclaiming the *ayuntamiento* as embodying sovereignty. The *ayuntamiento* had been the Spanish Habsburg method of instituting political rule in the process of colonizing the Americas; members were either appointed or elected, and represented the interests of the landed elite. But though based in a specific town, *ayuntamientos* also represented the smaller municipalities surrounding that town, cultivating, in a sense, a sense of belonging to that particular province. Sharing sovereignty with *ayuntamientos* were *audiencias,* the courts also established during Spanish colonization as a means to establish royal authority over its subjects. Thus, *audiencias,* representing the interests of the Church and the monarchy, often wielded more authority than *ayuntamientos.* In practice, however, the *ayuntamiento*'s power had always been seriously undermined and manipulated by monarchical interests; but in theory the *ayuntamiento* had indeed been structured to represent the will of *vecinos* (literally, "neighbors"), a political category established during the medieval period in Spain that guaranteed individuals rights as residents of a town.[78] Álvarez de Toledo's language reveals how carefully schooled he was in the history of Hispanic political thought.

Yet even if sovereignty resided in the *ayuntamiento,* the pamphlet reveals a deep suspicion toward the concept of direct democracy: "La reaccion para combatir y derrocar á la tirania, no puede ser emprendida jamas por el consejo de la multitud: es indispensable, que sea siempre el resultado de los calculus, y exfuerzos generosos de algunos individuos, que todo lo posponen al buen de sus hermanos, y á la Gloria de su pais. [The strategy in fighting and defeating (peninsular) tyranny can never be brought about by consulting the multitude: it is indispensable that (the strategies) be the result of the calculation and generous effort on the part of a few individuals who postpone everything in the name of their brothers and the glory of their country]" (4–5). Álvarez de Toledo appears more aristocratic than democratic, believing that only a select few could best organize a strategy against Spanish "tyranny." But Álvarez de Toledo was not unlike his liberal Anglo-American and European counterparts who had embraced a mixed government rather than a pure democracy. Even then, written into the Anglo-American social imaginary had been foundational exclusions as to who counted as a citizen, such as educated, propertied, white men.[79]

Álvarez de Toledo's language reveals the melding of various political idioms, that of a Catholic-Thomist view, like those of the Spanish commanders who saw the world as hierarchically ordered where some were born to rule and care for others. (Likewise, his use of the word "multitude" signals, as will be seen in Chapter 6, a longer tradition of Catholic political thought.) But he was influenced by U.S. and French revolutionary thought as well, as his insistence on political representation suggests. So, too, does his focus on tyranny as a rationale for seeking independence reflect eighteenth-century Anglo-American claims against the British monarchy.

The pamphlet, however, does not spell out what this plan should consist of, or, for that matter, how these "few individuals" would be selected. Nor does it address the question of the origin of sovereignty. How does one adjudicate between various forms of government? The pamphlet never answers these questions. Instead, the argument emerges just as the pamphlet is organized: as a reaction against an idea rather than as a creative, original attempt to offer a new vision of the world, a new social imaginary that could replace centuries of Spanish rule.

What the pamphlet does brilliantly achieve is another much-needed, important goal. It offers the premise that had to be established in order to make that next step, that of declaring the creation of a new independent government. Álvarez de Toledo's pamphlet embraces (and models for his readership) the new language of amity and equality, of mutual love and respect. In doing so, he works to replace the hierarchical, servile, affective language of belonging based on a patriarchal monarchy, that of the *patria*. Here, however, he differs from his fellow Spanish American, Father José Antonio Gutiérrez de Lara who, as we have seen, focused on shifting the emotionally charged language of belonging to the *patria* to belonging to the new *nación*. Álvarez de Toledo, instead, turns less to an emotional language and more toward the rational, historical claims of political sovereignty. Combined, however, their works produce the conditions that will allow their fellow Spanish Americans to embrace more and more the possibility of independence. In fact, it is for this precise reason that the Spanish minister to the United States, Luis de Onís, found *Amigo de los hombres* "to be more inflammatory than [Álvarez de Toledo's] *Manifiesto* in furthering rebellion in Spain's American colonies," and did his utmost to prevent its circulation.[80] But it had already entered Texas.

Alone with the Hurricane

Revolution forces the Catholic Hispanic world to face once again the threat of the secular, that is, the sequestering of the divine away from the temporal world. Modernity, then, manifests itself here as the end of the *ancien régime*. But it is, at this moment, stuck in the historical present, working toward an unknown future. Modernity is not a trope signaling the birth of freedom, of rights, independence, and the nation, a teleological story we tell ourselves. Rather, it signifies *first* a historical trauma, the end of a Catholic vision of the world, one where fixity, the security of knowing that everything had its perfect place as in a perfectly woven tapestry, was coming to an end. Modernity becomes, first, the disenchantment of the world, as the well-known Cuban poet José María Heredia's poem "En una tempestad" ("In a Tempest") would describe it a few years later, in the immediate aftermath of the independence of most of Spanish America. Facing the storm of modernity, the narrator bids adieu to the world before it is reconfigured by the hurricane: "Al fin, *mundo fatal,* nos separamos: / el huracán y yo solos estamos [At long last, *terrible world,* we separate: / the hurricane and I remain alone]" (emphasis added). The devastating effects of modernity force us to face the fact that we, in the end, are left all alone with ourselves. Humanity will increasingly come to take God's metaphysical place, as the place of certainty, of meaning, of belonging in the profane world. The trope of progress and production, no matter how awe-inspiring, brings with it disenchantment. No longer is it a world produced by God where one found everywhere the trace of God's finger. For now, humanity is left alone, without God, and with the hurricane.[81]

Indeed, Bernardo and other revolutionaries in Texas and the rest of New Spain, just like their counterparts in France, knew the consequences of their efforts all too well: they had birthed a new world, and with it would have to come a new understanding of how the world worked. It explains in part why they felt the need, in their correspondence, to restart the calendar with year one of Independence.[82] The revolutionaries would have to create a new basis on which to make truth claims, an ontological basis from which to ascribe meaning to the unfolding of events. Gone (or at least decentered) would be God as the author of the social world. Lost, abandoned, and without transcendental meaning, they, according to Captain Montero, would become slaves to the governmentless and godless United States.[83]

As we have seen, the comparisons to the experience of Anglo-Americans during the American Revolution abound, especially to those more supportive of the royal cause. Nonetheless, the difference is that the Anglo-American trauma of modernity was brought about over centuries, beginning with the sixteenth-century Reformation, extending through the seventeenth-century demise of divine right, particularly after the 1688 Glorious Revolution, and continuing with the eighteenth-century Enlightenment and revolutions. The disenchantment of the Anglo world was a gradual process, while the trauma of modernity occurred in the Hispanic world literally over night when Napoleon deposed the Spanish monarch. And now, not five years later, the agency-wielding documents—those carnal soldiers of insurgency—marched in and implanted this godless revolution in Texas. If Álvarez de Toledo's pamphlet cultivated the language of equality, one of the other documents that circulated throughout Texas, the double-sided broadsheet, offered a brief but brilliant account of the origin of sovereignty.

CHAPTER SIX

"We the *Pueblo* of the Province of Texas"

The Philosophy and Brute Reality of Independence

Reading Revolutionary Broadsheets Aloud

José Bernardo Gutiérrez de Lara must have relished watching the typesetting of the broadsheet. As we saw in Chapter 5, while he was in Natchitoches, Louisiana, Bernardo had taken care to personally witness the printing of 1,000 copies that were to be sent into the "Kingdom of Mexico." This was the document that boldly offered a new political vision for Spanish Texas.[1] If the handwritten Despallier document quickly summarized Bernardo's goals and if *Amigo de los hombres* offered a new model of fraternal love and mutual respect that could replace the patriarchal language of the *patria,* then the broadsheet spelled out the details of a new world. The broadsheet not only "seduced" the Spanish-American soldiers and inhabitants like a wave spreading diagonally from east Texas, over to central Texas, and down to the towns in south Texas and the province of Nuevo Santander (see Figures 5 and 7), the broadsheet's language also appealed to a much more expansive social imaginary, one that Hispanicized Native Americans also embraced. Indeed, it would lead Texas to boldly declare itself independent as a republic, the first province in all of New Spain to do so. But embracing this powerful social imaginary would come at a great price. From the very beginning to the end, virtually anyone seen affiliated with this entity—this broadsheet and its companions—met violent deaths at the hands of Spanish officers. And these officers, inevitably, would likewise meet similar fates. Let us turn to this unusual revolutionary soldier, and examine its form and content.

The double-sided broadsheet does not begin with words; instead, it offers images (see Figure 38). Laid out evenly across the top of the sheet are the images of three crucifixes of the same size. Below each cross are the names "JESÚS," "MARÍA," and "JOSÉ" in bold capitals and in a larger font than the rest of the text (see Appendix 2 for the translation). Placed slightly below the names and centered across the page in a slightly smaller font but still larger than the rest of the text is the opening line: "En el nombre de DIOS, y de Nuestra SEÑORA de Guadalupe [In the name of GOD, and of Our LADY of Guadalupe]." After this line, the broadsheet offers four paragraphs and slightly over 2,000 words. The text is densely packed onto a single double-sided 16.5 by 11 inch sheet of paper.

Bernardo signed the proclamation at the end, on the backside. Printed flush-right of the date, however, are the initials "J.A.T." These initials are none other than those of José Álvarez de Toledo, the same author of the pamphlets *Amigo de los hombres* and *Manifiesto,* with whom Bernardo had decided to collaborate during his stay in Washington, D.C. Yet, the broadsheet is dated Philadelphia, October 1, 1811, where it was originally printed, rather than Natchitoches. Bernardo had carried it with him on his voyage back, and, once in Natchitoches, used it as the basis for a new printing. The Natchitoches printers must have seen themselves as reproducing the broadsheet, which explains why they retained "Philadelphia." In this sense, the printers saw themselves serving more as reproducers or copiers of the document rather than printing an original document.

If the explicit Catholic invocation in the title, "*JESÚS, MARÍA, Y JOSÉ*"—accompanied by an image of a crucifix above each of the names—was not enough, the broadsheet continues by invoking God and the Virgin of Guadalupe. From the outset, the proclamation adamantly declares its religiosity, integrating a Catholic outlook with revolutionary political language. The language is saturated with political philosophical pronouncements as it bitterly critiques the Spanish monarchy. For some the Catholic invocation of God accompanied by revolutionary political language may seem incongruous.

Historians have long dismissed this and the other documents that circulated in Texas as mere "pompous disquisitions," "pretentious tract[s]," and "tirades" "with superficial knowledge of revolutionary philosophy," while attributing the documents' more modern, republican elements to the influence of Anglo-American and French thought.[2] Indeed, based on rather ethnocentric (if not outright racist) Anglo-American sources, some historians even doubted Bernardo's dedication and ability to organize an insurrection, arguing that he was a mere puppet for the true commanders of the expedition, who happened to be Anglo-Americans. Writing in 1901, Walter F. M'Caleb makes the following unsubstantiated, arrogant claim, a version that would be repeated for decades: "These manifestoes exhibit the full code of the revolution. They were not, however, the creations of Gutierrez; he was an ordinary mortal, and proved utterly inefficient. The handiwork of the [Anglo-]Americans is everywhere manifest." But Virginia Guedea and David Narrett have found clear evidence that Bernardo indeed was the commander of the forces.[3]

Even more to the point, individuals were willing to sacrifice their lives, and as the famous nineteenth-century Tejano José Antonio Navarro later described in gruesome detail, many were executed, their heads "caged and placed on the point of a pike at the same place where the American banner now proudly waves." And they did this in order to ensure that the ideas conveyed in these documents made their way into San Antonio de Béxar and other towns along the Rio Grande. If these documents, especially the broadsheet, were worth dying for, it would seem that they merit closer attention.[4]

The broadsheet may have been shorter than the sixteen-page pamphlet *Amigo de los hombres* that accompanied it, but it was no less effective. Indeed, royalists found the broadsheet so disconcerting that they published a response to it in Philadelphia, pleading with those influenced by it to remain faithful to the Spanish king.[5] The documents, and especially so the broadsheet, provide textual evidence of the world that Spanish Americans sought to bring into being. They offer a concrete vision of new sociopolitical relations, and utilize quite sophisticated political philosophy.

In contrast to *Amigo de los hombres,* the broadsheet was meant to be heard, pronounced aloud to a community of listeners, and experienced communally. Such were Bernardo's specific instructions. By June 16, 1812, the proclamation had made its way south to various towns in Texas and the Rio Grande Valley, but it had been difficult to smuggle them into the capital of Béxar.[6] Spies had been dispersed throughout the old Camino Real road from Nacogdoches to Béxar, prepared to intercept any and all literature that attempted to make its way in (see Figure 5). Thus, Bernardo ordered the literature be sent "por conducto de indios capases de desempeñar tan importante comicion [by Indians capable of taking on such an important commission]"; once in Béxar, he wanted the proclamation "tir[adas] en barias puertas de las casas de los de mas confianza, y de este modo lograremos que se communique la verdad de unos à otros y se

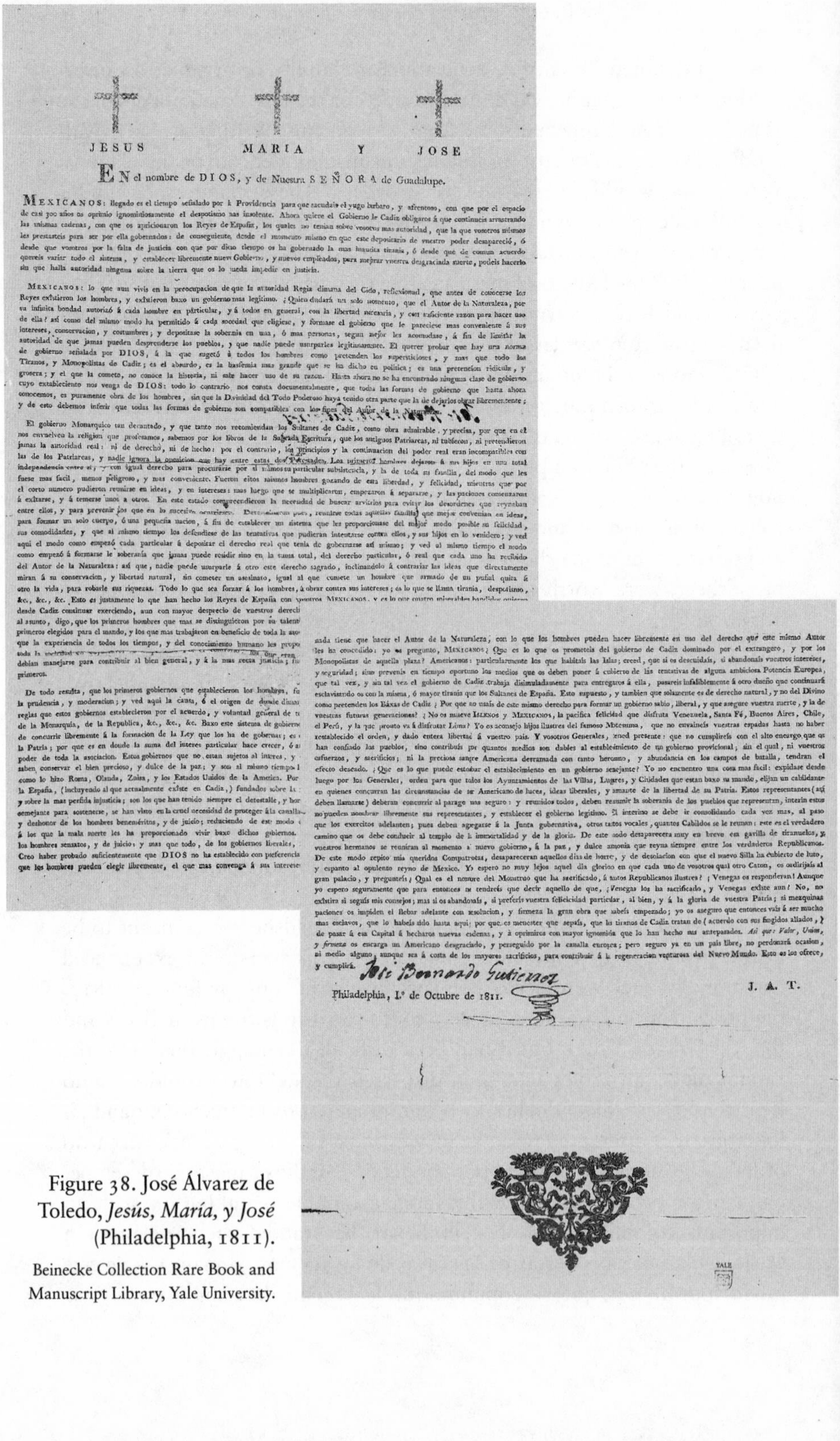

JESUS MARIA Y JOSE

EN el nombre de DIOS, y de Nuestra SEÑORA de Guadalupe.

MEXICANOS: llegado es el tiempo señalado por la Providencia para que sacudais el yugo barbaro, y afrentoso, con que por el espacio de casi 300 años os oprimio ignominiosamente el despotismo mas insolente. Ahora quiere el Gobierno de Cadiz obligaros á que continueis arrastrando las mismas cadenas, con que os aprisionaron los Reyes de España, los quales no tenian sobre vosotros mas autoridad, que la que vosotros mismos les prestasteis para ser por ella gobernados: de conseguiente, desde el momento mismo en que este depositario de vuestro poder desapareció, ó desde que vosotros por la falta de justicia con que por dicho tiempo os ha gobernado la mas inaudita tirania, ó desde que de comun acuerdo quereis variar todo el sistema, y establecer libremente nuevo Gobierno, y nuevos empleados, para mejorar vuestra desgraciada suerte, podeis hacerlo sin que halla autoridad ninguna sobre la tierra que os lo pueda impedir en justicia.

MEXICANOS: lo que aun vivis en la preocupacion de que la autoridad Regia dimana del Cielo, reflexionad, que antes de conocerse los Reyes exîstieron los hombres, y exîstieron baxo un gobierno mas legitimo. ¿Quien dudará un solo momento, que el Autor de la Naturaleza, por su infinita bondad autorizó á cada hombre en particular, y á todos en general, con la libertad necesaria, y con suficiente razon para hacer uso de ella? así como del mismo modo ha permitido á cada socedad que eligiese, y formase el gobierno que le pareciese mas conveniente á sus intereses, conservacion, y costumbres; y depositase la soberania en una, ó mas personas, segun mejor les acomodase, á fin de limitar la autoridad de que jamas pueden desprenderse los pueblos, y que nadie puede usurparles legitimamente. El querer probar que hay una norma de gobierno señalada por DIOS, á la que sugetó á todos los hombres como pretenden los supersticiosos, y mas que todo los Tiranos, y Monopolistas de Cadiz; es el absurdo, es la blasfemia mas grande que se ha dicho en politica; es una pretencion ridicula, y grosera; y el que la cometo, no conoce la historia, ni sabe hacer uso de su razon. Hasta ahora no se ha encontrado ninguna clase de gobierno cuyo extablecimiento nos venga de DIOS: todo lo contrario nos consta documentalmente, que todas las formas de gobierno que hasta ahora conocemos, es puramente obra de los hombres, sin que la Divinidad del Todo Poderoso haya tenido otra parte que la de dejarlos obrar libremententе; y de esto debemos inferir que todas las formas de gobierno son compatibles con los fines del Autor de la Naturaleza.

El gobierno Monarquico tan decantado, y que tanto nos recomiendan los Sultanes de Cadiz, como obra admirable, y precisa, por que en el nos envuelven la religion que profesamos, sabemos por los libros de la Sagrada Escritura, que los antiguos Patriarcas, ni tubieron, ni pretendieron jamas la autoridad real: ni de derecho, ni de hecho: por el contrario, los principios y la continuacion del poder real eran incompatibles con las de los Patriarcas, y nadie ignora la oposicion que hay entre estas dos Potestades. Los primeros hombres dejaron á sus hijos en una total independencia entre si, y con igual derecho para procurarse por si mismos su particular subsistencia, y la de toda su familia, del modo que les fuese mas facil, menos peligroso, y mas conveniente. Fueron estos mismos hombres gozando de esta liberdad, y felicidad, mientras que por el corto numero pudieron reunirse en ideas, y en intereses: mas luego que se multiplicaron, empezaron á separarse, y las paciones comenzaron á exîtarse, y á temerse unos a otros. En este estado comprendieron la necesidad de buscar arvitrios para evitar los desordenes que reynaban entre ellos, y para prevenir los que en lo sucesivo ocurriesen. Determinaron pues, reunirse todas aquellas familias que mejor convenian en ideas, para formar un solo cuerpo, ó una pequeña nacion, á fin de establecer un sistema que les proporcionase del mejor modo posible su felicidad, sus comodidades, y que al mismo tiempo los defendiese de las tentativas que pudieran intentarse contra ellos, y sus hijos en lo venidero; y ved aqui el modo como empezó cada particular á depositar el derecho real que tenia de gobernarse así mismo; y ved al mismo tiempo el modo como empezó á formarse le soberanía que jamas puede residir sino en la suma total, del derecho particular, ó real que cada uno ha recibido del Autor de la Naturaleza: así que, nadie puede usurparle á otro este derecho sagrado, inclinandolo á contrariar las ideas que directamente miran á su conservacion, y libertad natural, sin cometer un asesinato, igual al que comete un hombre que armado de un puñal quita á otro la vida, para robarle sus riquezas. Todo lo que sea forzar á los hombres, á obrar contra sus intereses; és lo que se llama tirania, despotismo, &c., &c., &c. Esto es justamente lo que han hecho los Reyes de España con vuestros MEXICANOS, y es lo que quatro miserables bandidos quieren desde Cadiz continuar exerciendo, aun con mayor desprecio de vuestros derech

al asunto, digo, que los primeros hombres que mas se distinguieron por su talent

primeros elegidos para el mando, y los que mas trabajaron en beneficio de toda la aso

que la experiencia de todos los tiempos, y del conocimiento humano les propo

toda la sociedad ... los que eran

debian manejarse para contribuir al bien general, y á la mas recta justicia; fu

primeros.

De todo resulta, que los primeros gobiernos que establecieron los hombres, fu

la prudencia, y moderacion; y ved aqui la causa, ó el origen de donde dima

reglas que estos gobiernos establecieron por el acuerdo, y voluntad general de t

de la Monarquía, de la Republica, &c., &c., &c. Baxo este sistema de gobiern

de concurrir libremente á la formacion de la Ley que los ha de gobernar; es

la Patria; por que es en donde la suma del interes particular hace crecer, ó a

poder de toda la asociacion. Estos gobiernos que no estan sujetos al interes, y

saben conservar el bien precioso, y dulce de la paz; y son al mismo tiempo l

como lo hizo Roma, Olanda, Zuisa, y los Estados Unidos de la America. Por

la España, (incluyendo al que actualmente exîste en Cadiz,) fundados sobre l

y sobre la mas perfida injusticia; son los que han tenido siempre el detestable, y hor

semejante para sostenerse, se han visto en la cruel necesidad de proteger á la canalla

y deshonor de los hombres beneméritos, y de juicio; reduciendo de este modo

á los que la mala suerte les ha proporcionado vivir baxo dichos gobiernos.

los hombres sensatos, y de juicio; y mas que todo, de los gobiernos liberales,

Creo haber probado suficientemente que DIOS no ha establecido con preferencia

que los hombres pueden elegir libremente, el que mas convenga á sus interese

nada tiene que hacer el Autor de la Naturaleza, con lo que los hombres pueden hacer libremente en uso del derecho que este mismo Autor les ha concedido: yo os pregunto, MEXICANOS; ¿Que es lo que os prometeis del gobierno de Cadiz dominado por el extrangero, y por los Monopolistas de aquella plaza? Americanos: particularmente los que habitais las Islas; creed, que si os descuidaís, si abandonaís vuestros intereses, y seguridad; sino prevenis en tiempo oportuno los medios que os deben poner á cubierto de las tentativas de alguna ambiciosa Potencia Europea, que tal vez, y sin tal vez el gobierno de Cadiz trabaja disimuladamente para entregaros á ella, pasareis infaliblemente á otro dueño que continuará esclavisando os con la misma, ó mayor tirania que los Sultanes de España. Esto supuesto, y tambien que solamente es de derecho natural, y no del Divino como pretenden los Báxas de Cadiz; ¿Por que no usaís de este mismo derecho para formar un gobierno sabio, liberal, y que asegure vuestra suerte, y la de vuestras futuras generaciones? ¿No os mueve ISLEÑOS y MEXICANOS, la pacifica felicidad que disfruta Venezuela, Santa Fé, Buenos Aires, Chile, el Perú, y la que pronto va á disfrutar Lima? Yo os aconsejo hijos ilustres del famoso Motezuma, que no envaineís vuestras espadas hasta no haber restablecido el orden, y dado entera libertad á vuestro pais. Y vosotros Generales, tened presente: que no cumplireís con el alto encargo que os han confiado los pueblos, sino contribuís por quantos medios son dables al establecimiento de un gobierno provicional; sin el qual, ni vuestros esfuerzos, y sacrificios; ni la preciosa sangre Americana derramada con tanto heroismo, y abundancia en los campos de batalla, tendran el efecto deseado. ¿Que es lo que puede estorbar el establecimiento en un gobierno semejante? Yo no encuentro una cosa mas facil: expidase desde luego por los Generales, orden para que todos los Ayuntamientos de las Villas, Lugares, y Ciudades que estan baxo su mando, elijan un cabildante en quienes concurran las circunstancias de ser Americano de luces, ideas liberales, y amante de la libertad de su Patria. Estos representantes (así deben llamarse) deberan concurrir al parage mas seguro: y reunidos todos, deben resumir la soberania de los pueblos que representan, interin estos no pueden nombrar libremente sus representantes, y establecer el gobierno legitimo. El interino se debe ir consolidando cada vez mas, al paso que los exercitos adelanten; pues deben agregarse á la Junta gubernativa, otros tantos vocales, quantos Cabildos se le reunan: este es el verdadero camino que os debe conducir al templo de la immortalidad y de la gloria. De este modo desaparecera muy en breve esa gavilla de tiranuelos, y vuestros hermanos se reuniran al momento al nuevo gobierno, á la paz, y dulce amonia que reyna siempre entre los verdaderos Republicanos. De este modo repito mis queridos Compatriotas, desapareceran aquellos dias de horror, y de desolacion con que el nuevo Silla ha cubierto de luto, y espanto al opulento reyno de Mexico. Yo espero no muy lejos aquel dia glorioso en que cada uno de vosotros qual otro Caton, os ordirijaís al gran palacio, y pregunteís ¿Qual es el nombre del Monstruo que ha sacrificado, á tantos Republicanos ilustres? ¡Venegas os responderan! Aunque yo espero seguramente que para entonces no tendreís que decir aquello de que, ¿Venegas los ha sacrificado, y Venegas exîste aun? No, no exîstira si seguís mis consejos; mas si os abandonaís, si preferís vuestra felicicidad particular, al bien, y á la gloria de vuestra Patria; si mezquinas paciones os impiden el llebar adelante con resolucion, y firmeza la gran obra que sabeís empezado; yo os aseguro que entonces vaís á ser mucho mas esclavos, que lo habeís sido hasta aqui; por que es menester que sepaís, que los tiranos de Cadiz tratan de (acuerdo con sus fingidos aliados,) de pasar á esa Capital á hecharos nuevas cadenas, y á oprimiros con mayor ignomiñia que lo han hecho sus antepasados. *Así que: Valor, Union, y firmeza* os encarga un Americano desgraciado, y perseguido por la canalla europea; pero seguro ya en un pais libre, no perdonará ocasion, ni medio alguno, aunque sea á costa de los mayores sacrificios, para contribuir á la regeneracion venturosa del Nuevo Mundo. Esto os los ofrece, y cumplirá.

J. A. T.

Philadelphia, 1.° de Octubre de 1811.

Figure 38. José Álvarez de Toledo, *Jesús, María, y José* (Philadelphia, 1811).

Beinecke Collection Rare Book and Manuscript Library, Yale University.

evitarán muchas desgracias [posted on the doors of the homes of those who can be trusted the most. In this way we'll be able to spread the truth, from one to many, and thus avoid many misfortunes]."[7]

"Reading," for these men and women, meant something radically different from our own concept of the silent, often solitary, comprehending of a printed page. Rather, for the vast majority of Texas, as it was for the rest of the Hispanic world, it meant comprehending a text aurally and communally, as it was declaimed; the script itself was not often seen, and it certainly was not meant to have been read silently to oneself. As Angel Rama notes, throughout the Hispanic world writing "took on an almost sacred aura and doubly so in American territories where it remained so rare and so closely linked to royal authority." It was part of a larger, far more expansive universe of signs that were all meant to be interpreted, from religious rituals, to ceremonial processions, theatrical displays, music, and dance. "The best examples of this discourse," continues Rama, "are obviously not the mute texts that we have conserved but in these ephemeral festivals of the arts."[8] The oral tradition was by the seventeenth century firmly set in Spain. Not just monarchical dictates, but everything from poetry, to romances, to histories were designed to be read aloud to a community of listeners. Miguel de Cervantes made this explicit in the title of one of the chapters of *Don Quixote,* writing that the chapter "trata de lo que vera el que lo leyere o lo oira el que lo escuchare leer [deals with what any reader of these pages will see for himself or what anyone who has this read to him will hear]." So, too, did Bernal Díaz del Castillo emphasize the orality of his text in the prologue to his famed 1632 *Historia verdadera de la conquista de la Nueva España (The True History of the Conquest of New Spain):* "Mi historia, si se imprime, cuando la vean e oyan, la daran fe verdadera [If my history is printed, people will really believe it when they see or hear it]."[9]

This actually puts the literacy rates of the period into perspective. For Spanish America, roughly 10 percent of the population were literate during the early nineteenth century. In Texas, by 1850, this had increased to 25 percent.[10] But the ability to read the world and engage with ideas must be expanded beyond mere literacy statistics, as if these low numbers reflected people's level of intelligence. "Oral language," as Jacques Derrida famously noted, "already belongs to this [larger symbolic system of] writing. . . . If writing is no longer understood in the narrow sense of linear and phonetic notation, it should be possible to say that all societies capable of producing [the linguistic classification of the world] . . . and of bringing classificatory difference into play, practice writing in general."[11] This is not unlike the claim put forward by the literary historian Margit

Frenk in regards to reading during the Spanish Golden Age period of the sixteenth and seventeenth centuries.

> Given the continued importance of the voice in the transmission of texts, the public for written literature was not limited to its "readers," in the modern sense of the term, but also included a large number of auditors. Every print piece or manuscript was like a hub from which innumerable receptions might emanate, either when the text was read orally or when it served as a basis for memorization or free repetition. The high illiteracy rate was not in itself an obstacle to the existence of a very large audience. If in a given family or community one person knew how to read, that was sufficient for virtually any text to be widely enjoyed.[12]

From this perspective, the rather low literacy rates among Spanish Americans in Texas elides the complex manner in which they engaged with texts: the written word was something to be heard, seen, felt, and, above all, to be experienced communally.

This practice of engaging with textuality had developed since the Catholic Reformation. The historian of religion Dominique Julia argues that the Catholic Church insisted that listening to the spoken word was key to catechism. In 1546, the Council of Trent responded to the Protestant claim of *sola scriptura,* the Reformation's doctrine that only scripture and an individual's personal, unmediated relationship to it—that is, by reading—could lead to salvation. Instead, the Council insisted that spiritual knowledge be conveyed orally. As Julia notes:

> At the same time, the Council reinforced the distinction between the respective roles of the clergy . . . and the laity: priests were responsible for preaching to the assembled faithful, for individual spiritual guidance, and for reminding their parishioners, during auricular confession, to heed the demands of the divine Word; *the laity's role was to listen, absorb and appropriate the message that an authorized voice had delivered to them.* One did not need direct access to the sacred texts to advance on the road to holiness. Thus Catholic reservations concerning solitary reading of print matter had a carefully argued theological and ecclesiological basis.[13]

Textuality was accessed, then, via sight and hearing, and the broadsheet was intended to be read as well as heard. But the document, as a whole, was to be viewed as well, and it held visual cues that did not require the ability to read script. Let us turn, first, to the words on the page. But we will see that in order to fully grasp the power of this new vision, our narrative will need to swing back in time, as if in a helical orbit, returning to the moment of the Catholic Reformation and its earth-shattering theories of sovereignty. In doing so, we can then return to the revolution in Texas—including the many other documents they produced, such as its declaration of independence—and appreciate why the inhabitants chose to give up the order of things for a new vision. They would, however, come to find that not only their vision but also many of their lives would be cut short.

The Broadsheet's Content

The broadsheet is a string of long sentences, dependent clause building upon dependent clause. The document itself is dizzying, packed as it is with text. But hearing it, one feels the cadence, the measured beat as the litany of wrongs and rationales for independence build up, leading to the declamatory, fierce but logical conclusions made at the end of sentences. In contrast to the derivative pamphlet *Amigo de los hombres,* the broadsheet rings fresh, proclaiming an original vision of the universe.

The first two paragraphs begin with bold pronouncements. In capitalized letters, they directly address the broadsheet's audience with the word "MEXICANOS." Álvarez de Toledo capitalized "Mexicanos" precisely because he knew how utterly radical it was to refer to the inhabitants as such. The term had yet to congeal as a term of self-identification for the Spanish Americans of New Spain, and would not do so until much later in the nineteenth century. In fact, this is one of the first, if not *the* first, use of the term to refer to the residents of all of New Spain. "Mexicano," throughout the colonial period and well into the nineteenth century, had connoted either the Meso-American inhabitants of central Mexico or the urban residents of Mexico City itself. During the early years of the insurgency, the revolutionaries themselves would more often use "Mexico" or "Mexicano" to refer to the Spanish-controlled government of Mexico City. Instead, like Father José Antonio Gutiérrez de Lara in his own proclamation, they used the more hemispheric "Americano" in referring to themselves.[14] In using "Mexicano," Álvarez de Toledo calls into being an imagined community of "Mexicanos" that had not existed before. Indeed, for Spanish Americans in Texas even the term "Tejano" would have sounded odd to their ears. For the residents of Béxar, the more familiar appellation would have been "Bexareño," a sense of identification that had developed by the 1780s. So, too, would "Isleño" have been familiar. But this term, referring to the 1718 Canary Islander founders of Béxar, was used then, as it is to this day, more as a marker of elite status.[15]

Besides the nationalist invocation of "Mexicanos," the broadsheet is unlike the moving proclamations and letters discussed in previous chapters, which offered powerful rhetoric but little in terms of concrete arguments for a new government that would replace monarchical rule. By contrast, this broadsheet offers a clearly delineated political argument for independence. The first paragraph makes the provocative claim that sovereignty or political authority rests in the people of Mexico and not the king or the Cortes of Cádiz; the second paragraph provides the rationale by elaborating on how sovereignty rests in the people. The next paragraph makes the theory concrete by turning to history in order to explain how governments arose. The final paragraph, as long as the first three combined, transitions from the past into the present in order to begin to think about the future.

The proclamation begins by announcing the birth of a new temporal regime, one that breaks with the past and introduces a new way of thinking: "MEXICANOS: llegado es el tiempo señalado por la Providencia para que sacudais el yugo barbaro, y afrentoso, con que por el espacio de casi 300 años os oprimio ignominiosamente el despotismo mas insolente [MEXICANOS: come is the time appointed by Providence to shake off the barbarous and offensive yoke with which for the space of almost 300 years the most insolent despotism has ignominiously oppressed you]." Yet the pronounced rupture is not so much a temporal movement forward. Rather, by signaling to Mexicans that they break the "offensive yoke," the broadsheet implies that at some unstated moment, prior to the mentioned 300 years, Mexicans had somehow not been enslaved. Thus, the rupture in time is actually a return to the past, a period in time when Mexicans had lived in a different state where they ostensibly had more freedom. Revolution arrives in Texas, but not in the modern sense of the word as something rebellious, transformative. Instead, revolution is a complete rotation, a return, in the original connotation of the word, to a previous order.[16]

The broadsheet's vision of a more perfect past is based on the political principles of the Habsburg dynasty. As we have seen, under the Habsburgs, Spain emerged as a consolidated monarchy, a quasi-federation of kingdoms, governed by viceroys and an entire political structure that included *ayuntamientos* (town councils) and *audiencias* (high courts). Granted, the monarchy gradually seized power over these entities, but they continued to exist, especially in the Americas. The concept of divine right (that monarchs derived their right to rule directly from God and were not subject to any other authority) was not the governing principle under the Habsburgs, and the highly influential seventeenth-century Catholic University of Salamanca developed a political philosophy that likewise denied the claim of divine right. But when the Bourbon dynasty replaced the Habsburgs in the eighteenth century, they attempted to wipe the slate clean, and initiated a massive effort to create a hierarchical state where divine right was the ruling principle. The reforms created deep animosity among *Americanos* who continued to imagine their social world under Habsburg principles. And this is the world to which the broadsheet sought to return.

If the broadsheet wanted to persuade its audience that they had the power to create a new government, then it had to offer a convincing explanation as to how sovereignty rested in the people. What gave them the authority to end nearly 300 years of Spanish rule? Indeed, the broadsheet addresses this dilemma head on at the beginning of the second paragraph: "MEXICANOS: lo[s] que aun vivis en la preocupacion de que la autoridad Regia dimana del Cielo, reflexionad, que antes de conocerse los Reyes exîstieron los hombres, y exîstieron baxo un gobierno mas legitimo. [MEXICANOS: those of you who worry whether divine rule is ordained by Heaven should contemplate the fact that man existed before Kings came into being, and they existed under a more legitimate government]."

Divine right is first questioned on historical grounds: there had been other legitimate forms of government prior to monarchical rule. But if monarchical government is not ordained by God, then who decides how best to organize society? From where does sovereignty emerge? And what was the "more legitimate government" that had existed prior to kings?

Here, the broadsheet turns to one of the classic premises of natural law as it had been developed by Scholastic philosophers since St. Thomas Aquinas in the thirteenth century: "¿Quien dudará un solo momento, que el Autor de la Naturaleza, por su infinita bondad autorizó á cada hombre en particular, y á todos en general, con la libertad necesaria, y con suficiente razon para hacer uso de ella? [Who would deny for a single moment that the Author of Nature through his infinite goodness granted each individual man and to everyone in general the necessary liberty and enough reason in order to use it?]" The proclamation effectively rejects the concept of divine right, proclaims the sovereignty of the people, and provides the basis for regime change. In doing so, it appears to rehearse familiar refrains from Anglo-American, British, and French political thought. Closer examination, however, reveals an alternative tradition of modern thought. The broadsheet engages with the key conceptual political philosophical arguments at the turn of the century, the very ideas that have given shape to the terms in which we discuss modern political life, but it uses an idiom emerging from the Catholic Hispanic world.

If political economy, as a modern distinct field of study, had started to emerge in the seventeenth century as a way to understand the economies of the recently consolidated European states, then political philosophy—as a mode of thought that helped configure the modern state by elaborating theories of the legitimacy and origin of sovereign power—had emerged slightly earlier. Like economic discourses, political philosophy, too, had its roots in antiquity. But political theories reached a radical bifurcation during the sixteenth- and seventeenth-century Protestant and Catholic Reformations. The broadsheet fully engages with this intellectual history. It begins with the claims of natural law in order to describe the origin of sovereignty, and continues by offering a theory of the social contract, that is, the emergence and legitimacy of political authority as a pact made by a group of people in order to constitute a government. In drawing from a particularly Catholic variant of natural law, the broadsheet takes a different path of modernity than the one more familiar in the Anglophone Protestant world. Let's delve into this under-studied history. In doing so, we will emerge with a richer political conception of the *pueblo* and its rights.

Francisco Suárez and the Catholic *Corpus Mysticum*

Natural law emerged, by the thirteenth century, as a synthesis of classical, Christian, Jewish, and Islamic thought. Aquinas produced an elaborate account of natural law that continues to serve as the epistemological foundation for the Catholic Church to this day, and it also remains as the foundation of natural law philosophy. Its purpose is to arrive at universal moral truths as they are "written in men's hearts." It begins with the premise that humans are endowed with reason, and using the method of deduction, develops a moral and political philosophy for acting in the world. Thus, natural law becomes an examination of human behavior, in order to assure it concords with Christian teaching, and is inspired by revelation. It serves as a foundation for the exploration of all moral and political questions. For Aquinas, the law of nature was part of a highly complex, hierarchical relation of power. At its simplest, Aquinas argued that there were various kinds of laws that were organized hierarchically beginning with God's or eternal law, which was expressed as divine law as recorded in scripture and Church tradition. This, in turn, led to natural law (though Aquinas made various exceptions that resulted in a highly intricate theory).[17] With the rise of humanism in the fourteenth century, however, his philosophy was critiqued and cast aside, especially in northern Europe.

Aquinas's philosophy, referred to as Thomism, experienced a revival two centuries later during the Reformation as the heart of the Catholic response to Protestants. The Catholic Reformation offered a strident political defense of its worldview against that of the Protestant reformers: against the Protestant concept of *sola scriptura* (that scripture alone contained the source for salvation), they insisted that the divine power of scripture was too overwhelmingly powerful and baffling for the masses and, thus, required spiritual guides who could transmit its message via ritual and the spoken word; against the Protestant concept of a universal Church, in which all Christians were nominal equals, they emphasized the hierarchical apostolic church and the need for a jurisdictional head to guide the people. The Protestant Reformation had postulated that human beings were fallen creatures, living in a postlapsarian world ruled by anarchy and fear. Only through God's divine grace had they been granted political society, and he had endowed a chosen, select few with the power to rule society. Indeed, Protestant political philosophers had sought ingenious ways to divest the Church of its political power, and argued that there were two polities, temporal and spiritual. God had made the pope the sovereign over the spiritual realm while currently existing princes, on the other hand, had been ordained by God to rule over the temporal world. In effect, they had posited divine right.[18]

Sixteenth-century Catholic Reformation theologians, in turn, resoundingly rejected the Protestant theory that God ordained political society and, thus, had ordained certain individuals as monarchs. But in rejecting these claims, Catholic theologians offered their own politically and philosophically complex version of the origin of political society, and the Spanish School of Salamanca served as a vigorous source of innovative Catholic thought. As Quentin Skinner notes, the Catholic Scholastics (referred to as Thomists because of their adherence to Aquinas) created "a vocabulary of concepts and an accompanying pattern of political argument" to be taken up, absorbed, and used by Protestant philosophers as the foundation for modern political thought.[19]

Against the Protestant (and thoroughly Augustinian) claim of humanity's depraved nature, the Catholic scholars offered a thoroughly Aristotelian-Thomist counterclaim: humans had always been sociopolitical animals and, as Christians, had been saved.[20] Humans, then, had always lived *within* society, and had been governed by natural law. Over the next centuries and in contentious debate with Protestant philosophers, the Thomists refined and extended Aquinas's views on natural law, and used it as a premise for the rationale of political society.[21]

But these Scholastic philosophers have long been marginalized in contemporary accounts of political thought, studied primarily by specialists and seen as antecedents to *modern* political thought. Only recently has their significant role in Spanish-American intellectual history been acknowledged.[22] The Thomist School of Salamanca flourished under the patronage of the Spanish Habsburgs. As Skinner notes, the Thomist philosophers "have often been portrayed as the main founders of modern constitutionalist and even democratic thought," where its members "have been credited with 'inventing' the concept of the social contract and exploring for the first time its implications for the theory of justice."[23] The members of this school of thought, of course, were far from homogeneous. Both the Dominican and Jesuit orders engaged in vigorous debate not just with Protestant philosophers but also with one another. Signaling even more clearly the complexity of Scholastic thought, this period is known, in fact, as Late Scholasticism. If we put aside the intricacies of their debates, however, we can still appreciate the broad structure of Thomism, and thus arrive at a better understanding of early nineteenth-century Spanish-American political thought.

Of these philosophers, Francisco Suárez (1548–1617) "provide[s] the clearest summary of . . . the whole school of Thomist political philosophers in the course of the sixteenth century."[24] He offered a relentless, brilliant argument against the Protestant theory that God had ordained divine rule. God, he claimed, "conferred immediately the sovereign civil power, as such, on men assembled in a State or perfect political community, . . . and therefore by virtue of such a donation this power is not vested in any single person or limited group of men, but in the entire perfect people, i.e. the body of the community."[25] His thought immediately became anathema in Protestant northern European countries; indeed, in England and France his official response to the absolutist claims made by King James I was publicly burnt.[26] Still, despite his tremendous influence on both Protestant and Hispanic thought, only some of his texts have been translated from the original Latin into Spanish, and even fewer into English.[27]

Considered one of the greatest Scholastics after Aquinas, by the eighteenth century Suárez became a leading figure in Hispanic universities, both in Spain and the Americas. His teachings became doctrine, and predominated over that of any other philosopher. More significant yet, Suárez had an "irrefutable intellectual influence in Spanish America," where all university teachings had to accord with his philosophy.[28] Indeed, the historian of Hispanic political philosophy, Joaquín Varela Suanzes-Carpegna, has demonstrated that Suárez's political theories had by far the largest influence on the writings of Spanish-American representatives at the Cortes of Cádiz in the early nineteenth century, the very Cortes at which Álvarez de Toledo served as a representative.[29] Nonetheless, historians have long exaggerated the French, English, or U.S. influences on Spanish-American revolutionary thought over that of Scholastic political philosophy.[30] Suárez, as we will see, turns out to be central to understanding the broadsheet's vision of the world.

Suárez found Aquinas's theory of law to be imprecise, and set out to revise it. In doing so, he offered what we may describe as a blueprint for this Catholic worldview. In *De Legibus* from 1612, Suárez argues that political authority originates with God, and describes this as eternal law, which is difficult to discern and comprehend precisely because it is in God's realm, and had led to the development, in descending order, of divine, natural, and, finally, civil or positive law. Eternal law was expressed in two ways. It was revealed to a select few, thus becoming divine law, as in the example of the Bible. But it was also imprinted in nature, observed in the natural order of the universe; and, when interpreted correctly—using reason while inspired by revelation—would give rise to natural law, universal truths that applied to all beings. Natural law was finally codified by humans into civil law or positive law, the laws created by society in order to insure stability, order, and authority (see Figure 39).

Each realm of law had to accord with God's plan, which was ultimately happiness, defined as the common good (that concept that would become reconfigured in the eighteenth-century discourse of political economy),

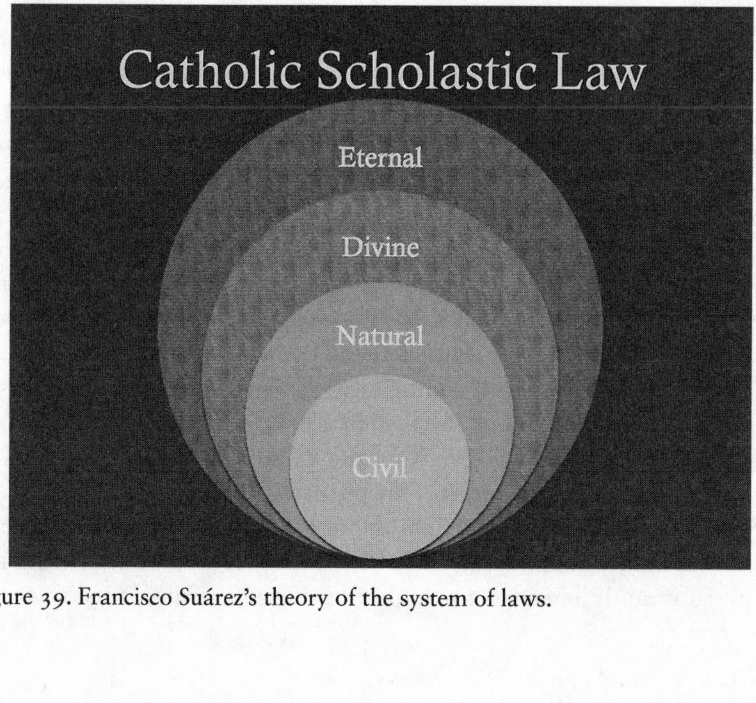

Figure 39. Francisco Suárez's theory of the system of laws.

achieved by becoming one with God; thus, civil law could be adjudicated against natural law, which in turn could be judged against divine law. Yet while each level emerged from the one preceding and had to accord with it, each functioned independently. God had created the entire structure, but he had endowed humans with reason and free will; and using free will and reason, they could study the world in order to deduce the laws of nature, and from there create society (civil law).[31]

For the Thomists, merely countering the Protestant claim of divine right was not enough; they had to offer a theory of the origin of sovereignty. They claimed instead that political society had emerged from the law of nature, which though related to divine law was separate from it. Thus, it was impossible for God to have ordained monarchs as divine. But to get to this claim, Thomists had to clarify how sovereignty emerged, and they did so by developing the concept of the state of nature, a proto-anthropological theory that imagined the original condition in which humans found themselves living in nature under natural law, before the establishment of civil law.[32] This concept of the "state of nature" has become one of the cornerstones of modern Western political thought. It was adopted by the Protestant political philosopher Thomas Hobbes in the seventeenth century, and became integral to modern political thought.[33]

Having begun with the Aristotelian premise that humans are sociopolitical animals, endowed with reason and free will, and governed by natural law, Suárez then launches into his theory of the origin of society. He argues that political society is established by the coming together of families (not individuals) or what he describes as the multitude. In doing so, they create a new organic body: the *corpus mysticum* or mystical body. Suárez is clear that "power . . . resides . . . in the whole body of mankind . . . and it does not exist in each individual, nor any specific individual."[34] As a unit, moreover, the *corpus mysticum* includes powers which individual members never possessed. This is, according to the intellectual historian J. A. Fernández-Santamaría, one of the most intellectually revolutionary concepts to have emerged out of Thomism. And Skinner concurs; no one prior to Suárez had thought holistically about the legal dynamics of the people as a whole.[35]

The idea of the "mystical community" allowed Suárez to imagine the world in completely different terms than it had been previously. In his lifetime, Suárez witnessed the demise of the Church's hegemony over all of Europe, the reconfiguration of European societies, the rise of modern nation-states, and the development of international law. With this concept, writes Fernández-Santamaría, "I believe that here Suárez explicitly and most significantly intended to conjure up the image of society as something lying beyond the ordinary manner of knowing; an entity that, brought into being by the aforementioned act of the collective will, reached beyond the physical into a unique and inevitable reality in a way as novel as society itself."[36] If the emerging state was the new world unfolding in the sixteenth century, then Suárez devised a conceptual tool that allowed him to better understand this new, modern, political world.

Political authority thus emerges from the gathering of a multitude of families as they come together to create the mystical community. Suárez uses the Latin *potestas,* a Roman legal term meaning power or authority wielded over someone. The Spanish equivalent is *potestad* and is also the basis for *poder* ("power"); the English translation is "sovereignty." Fernández-Santamaría compares Suárez's efforts to his contemporary, Copernicus, who likewise offered a new theory of the cosmos: "*Potestas,* therefore, is the 'new physics' suitable to this 'new universe,' the instrument that in the totally novel environment that is society enables us to understand the novelty of social life."[37] But power rests not in a conglomerate of individuals, but in an undifferentiated, corporate sense of the people, of, specifically, groups of families coming together and creating a new entity. "Therefore," states Suárez, "we must say that this power, viewed solely according to the nature of things, resides not in any individual man but rather in the whole body of mankind."[38] But this power was transferred to a monarch, and once transferred, could not easily revert to the people. However, Scholastics did produce the seeds of insurrection by carefully debating the conditions in which the *corpus mysticum* could revolt against an unjust ruler.[39] And for this, as we have seen, Suárez and his fellow Jesuits became anathema to the late eighteenth-century Spanish Bourbon monarch.

Suárez's account does not theorize agency at the level of the individual but, rather, at that of the community. There is no *cogito ergo sum,* no Lockean subject, no possessive individualism. Agency, as we have seen, permeates the universe in this Catholic-Scholastic episteme, emanating from humans just as easily as it does from other entities, animate and inanimate alike. Suárez's concept of *potestas* invokes a new, productive, power that had not existed before; it is a collective, mystical power that does not emerge out of separate, individual, autonomous beings but only through their coming together as families.

While the Thomist account of the state of nature, proposed by sixteenth- and seventeenth-century Spanish Scholastics, was generally optimistic, wherein humans had always lived harmoniously and in perfect freedom, Protestants, such as Hobbes in the sixteenth and later John Locke in the seventeenth century, would revise the Spanish theory and respond with a much more somber, pessimistic, and Augustinian version of the state of nature. In what is now the dominant account of the state of nature (with the most influential accounts offered by Richard Hooker, Hugo Grotius, Hobbes, Samuel von Pufendorf, and Locke), the world was originally inhabited by lonely, random solipsistic individuals roaming the woods.[40]

In arguing in favor of divine right in order to divest the Catholic Church of power, the Protestant Reformation had, in effect, secured its ontological-political authority by splitting the world in two, into spiritual and temporal halves. They were able to establish their hegemony by relegating the temporal world not to the pope but to the domain of princes. Of course, sixteenth-century Protestant reformers sought to establish religious hegemony over the reconfiguring state; their goal certainly was not a secular society, but the long-term effect was one where religious and civil authority grew increasingly apart. Notwithstanding early Protestant attempts to the contrary, the divine eventually became confined to the spiritual realm.[41] From here, the path to secular societies within the West would diverge, one pursuing that of Protestant northern Europe, the other that of the Catholic Atlantic.

There is a growing, significant divergence, then, in sixteenth- and seventeenth-century European thought, a final cleft, perhaps, between Protestant and Catholic Europe. With the Reformation, as Skinner notes, "two rival political moralities . . . confront[ed] each other in every commonwealth of late sixteenth-century Europe. One was the natural-law theory [proposed by the Thomists]. . . . The other was the theory of 'Machiavelli and the *politiques*' *(los politicos)*, with its impious exhortation to our rulers to imitate both the lion and the fox." If, during the sixteenth and seventeenth centuries, Protestant and Catholic theologians engaged in passionate debate, there was now no doubt that a new competing moral universe had not only installed itself and grown in hegemony, but it could also now begin to ignore Catholic theological claims of sovereignty. As Skinner notes: "[T]he difficulty is that between these 'two political ways of thinking' there is virtually no common ground, since the truth of the one entails the falsity of the other, and each is claimed by its exponents to provide the only correct analysis of the moral standards to be applied in political life."[42] The bifurcation of Western modernity, into a Protestant-becoming-secular northern Europe and a minoritized Catholic southern Europe, has its origins in the Reformation.[43] And now the political legacies of this bifurcation were coming to the fore. Having traced this deep hidden history of Catholic sovereignty, we can now return to the broadsheet's powerful vision and, ultimately, comprehend the profound influence it had in remaking the social fabric in Texas and the rest of northern New Spain.

Revolutionary Catholic Visions of the Modern Political World

The broadsheet drinks deeply from this well of political thought. Having argued that God endowed humans with reason, it then claims that God "permitio a cada sociedad que eligiese, y formase el gobierno que le pareciese mas conveniente a sus intereses, conservacion, y costumbres [permitted each society to choose and form a government it thought most convenient for its interests, protection, and traditions]." Humans, then, have the capacity to use reason to decide on the most appropriate form of government. Anyone who dares suggest that God decreed monarchical rule the only legitimate form of government commits "la blasfemia mas grande que se ha dicho en politica; es una pretencion ridicula, y grosera, y el que la comete, no conoce la historia, ni sabe hacer uso de su razon [the most absurd, grandest blasphemy ever pronounced in politics; it is a ridiculously crude pretension; and he who commits it neither knows history nor how to make use of his reason.]" And Álvarez de Toledo knew his history, particularly the Scholastic theory of sovereignty articulated most effectively by Suárez.

Having thus established the origin of sovereignty as granted by God to the people, the broadsheet continues by developing its theory of the social contract: "Los primeros hombres dejaron á sus hijos en una total independencia entre si, y con igual derecho para procurarse por si mimos [*sic*] su particular subsistencia, y la de toda su familia, del modo que les fuese mas facil, menos peligroso, y mas conveniente [The earliest of mankind left their children in total independence amongst themselves, and with the same right to procure for themselves and their families their own subsistence, in the manner that was easiest, least dangerous, and most convenient for them to do so]."

Here, the language resembles Rousseau more than it does Locke. Rousseau, too, begins his theory of the social contract by comparing it to the family. Locke, on the other hand, does not entertain the familial allegory until chapter 6 of *The Second Treatise on Government.* Instead, throughout the first five chapters, his account of sovereignty emerges as a lonely, solitary affair of individuals struggling to protect their property and life, divorced and separated, it appears, from all social bonds.[44] Yet, though

Rousseau begins with the family, he does so in order to quickly proclaim that the bond between father (or sovereign) and child quickly "dissolves": "The children, exempt from the obedience they owe the father, all equally return to independence."[45] For both Locke and Rousseau (though slightly more emphasized in Locke), the emergence of society is a dialectical process: society emerges as a product of autonomous, sovereign *individuals,* and society produces autonomous individuals with fully developed concepts of *individual* rights to life, liberty, and property.[46]

The broadsheet, on the other hand, offers no concept of an autonomous individual with his or her own distinct rights. Rather, it delicately balances the role of the individual with that of the community in creating a social contract. The Protestant social contract begins with the premise of individuals with their individual right to property and liberty coming together and assigning those rights to a sovereign in order to be better protected. But the broadsheet is built on a fundamentally different premise. Rather than individuals, it begins with, and does not stray far from, families.

As society grew and differences became pronounced, so the broadsheet claims, families realized they had to:

> buscar arvitrios para evitar los desordenes que reynaban entre ellos, y para prevenir los que en los sucesivo ocurriesen. Determinaron pues, reunirse todas aquellas familias que mejor convenian en ideas, para formar un solo cuerpo, ó una pequeña nacion, á fin de establecer un sistema que les proporcionase del mejor modo posible su felicidad, sus comodidades, y que al mismo tiempo los defendiese de las tentativas que pudieran intentarse contra ellos, y sus hijos en lo venidero.

> [search for methods of adjudication in order to avoid the disorder that reigned over them and to prevent it from occurring in the future. They decided, then, to reunite all those families that most accorded in ideas, in order to form one single body, or a small nation, in order to establish a system that would provide them with happiness and comfort in the best manner possible, and that would simultaneously protect them from any future threats against them and their children.]

The account here is not that different from the more familiar Protestant version, except for the shifting subject "they" and "families." Unlike the Protestant social contract where children break their familial bonds in order to become autonomous individuals with rights,[47] in this account, it is patriarchal figures (literally "ancient Patriarchs" and later the "first of men," which could also be rendered as "the earliest of mankind"), that enter the social contract. It is these figures that ostensibly act not on their own behalf but, rather, on that of their families. Still, as the narrative unfolds, the subject becomes slippery: "patriarchs" become "they," which then defers to "families." That is, the subject starts out as "patriarchs," which, in theory, is limited to a specified number of individuals. Yet "patriarchs" morphs, and gives rise not to atomistic individuals with their own rights but to the yet more corporatist concept of the family.

Certainly, what I am describing as the Protestant tradition of the social contract is not representative of the entirety of the north Atlantic tradition of political thought; it is just as complex as that of Scholasticism. It contained just as powerful critiques of individualism over that of the common good. The eighteenth-century republican political tradition and especially the Scottish Enlightenment, for example, placed greater emphasis on the *res publica*. But these traditions would cede terrain, as we saw in Chapter 3, to the individualism of liberalism. And here, for our purposes in teasing out the differences between Protestant and Catholic thought, the focus remains on the tensions between individuals and the community to which they belong. Thus, though the Protestant social contract theorizes the formation of society as resulting in a corporate body (Hobbes's image of the composite monarch comes to mind), it is ultimately comprised of *autonomous individuals* (even if these individuals were still in the process of formation) prior to becoming the corporate body. In the broadsheet's account, the social body is produced by the coming together of families, not individuals.

The broadsheet proceeds to describe the origin of society, offering more evidence of its deep roots in Scholastic political thought:

> ved aqui el modo como empezó cada particular á depositar el derecho real que tenia de gobernarse así mismó; y ved al mismo tiempo el modo como empezó á formarse le [*sic*] soberanía que jamas puede residir sino en la suma total, del derecho particular, ó real que cada uno ha recibido del Autor de la Naturaleza.

> [one can see here the manner in which each one began to deposit the real right *(derecho real)* that they had to govern one's self; and see as well the manner in which sovereignty began to take shape, which can never reside other than in a complete and undivided sum of the particular or real right *(derecho particular ó real)* that each one has received from the Author of Nature.]

The grammatical subject becomes even more convoluted as the narrative unfolds; instead of using the less ambiguous noun (either "patriarchs" or "families"), the broadsheet turns instead to the third person plural "they" and third person singular "one," making it unclear as to whether it is referring to patriarchs or to families. In either case, the subject would still be plural. And this is the point: the first mention of rights of any kind emerges as collective rights or, since collective already denotes a "collection of individual persons or things." The concept of rights emerges *prior* to the clear articulation of a sense of an autonomous self; rather, rights emerge as something the family or corporate body possesses.

But the broadsheet also distinguishes between various kinds of rights: "real" and "particular." *Derecho real* or real right is derived from the Latin *ius in re,* a direct legal relationship existing between a person and a thing, as in ownership. *Derecho particular* or particular or personal right is a right one has over one's body. Thus, the broadsheet clarifies that sovereignty emerges only when "the complete and undivided sum of the particular or real right that each one has" is transferred to the state. Historians of political philosophy have demonstrated that the concept of rights—emerging from natural law and giving rise, in the eighteenth and nineteenth centuries, to the modern, contemporary concept of "human rights"—originated in the concept of property, and have traced this long, incredibly complex discursive history to the Romans.[48] Yet, in their accounts, once they arrive at the Reformation, historians often pursue the lineage through the Protestants and put aside the Catholic tradition. In the Protestant tradition of natural rights, reaching its apogee in Locke, rights centered on an individual's relationship to property, and the individual's ability to do what he wanted with it. Rights *in* property evolved into the modern concept of rights *as* property, as something possessed by individuals.[49]

But the Catholic history of natural law never fully resolved the concept of *ius in re,* of rights in property. The debate regarding the right to *own* property versus *using* property emerged as a debate in the thirteenth century between Franciscans (who had renounced all property) and Dominicans.[50] It vacillated between various rights in regards to property: as the right to own and control property *(dominium)* versus the right to use yet not own it *(usufruct).* It would continue to unfold with emphasis placed on individual versus communal property. Thus, if the Catholic account never fully resolved the concept of property as an individual's right (or resolved it differently), then it could not have developed the concept of rights as an individual's property, or, at least, not in the same way that Protestant philosophers developed it.

Even in early nineteenth-century Spanish-Mexican Texas, for example, the concept of private property rights remained just one facet of a larger, much more expansive continuum of rights. Andrés Tijerina has emphasized that the concept of common property or town commons, especially that of *propios,* continued to be an "important aspect of Tejano community life." *Propios* were lands owned communally by a municipality, and

> this communal ownership enhanced the sense of unity within the *vecindario* [a Spanish legal term referring to a neighborhood]. It offered a communal source of timber, communal or *pueblo* water rights, and common pasture or woodlands. The revenue from the *propios* made the community a fiscal entity as well. Thus, the programs supported by *ayuntamiento* expenditures were, in effect, community ventures which demanded the concern and contributions of all of the citizenry. And the management of the town's social functions—whether in recreation, social services, or in crises—lay almost exclusively in the hands of the *vecindario.*[51]

Other historians of colonial Mexico have argued that the concepts of *vida privada* ("private life") and *propiedad privada* ("private property"), cognates of possessive individualism, can not be found in pre-independence New Spain.[52] And it is the concept of an individual's rights that provides part of the basis for thinking of subjectivity as autonomous, separate, private, and contained within one's body.

In his carefully delineated history of the political philosophy of the Cortes of Cádiz, Suanzes-Carpegna has suggested that the debates at the Cortes failed to reveal a fully articulated individual with possessive rights.[53] Indeed, if literary and cultural historians have demonstrated that the eighteenth- and nineteenth-century novel in Britain, the United States, and France provided some of the intellectual scaffolding for thinking of an autonomous sense of self and of human rights,[54] then it may come as no surprise that the first Spanish-American novel, José Joaquín Fernández de Lizardi's *El periquillo sarniento* (published in Mexico in 1816), struggles throughout to produce a character with a sense of interiority. Instead, the most fascinating "character" to emerge is that of a community struggling to arrive at a sense of the common good.[55]

Rather than enumerating any kind of individual rights, the broadsheet places greater emphasis on articulating the structure of political society.

> De todo resulta, que los primeros gobiernos que establecieron los hombres, fueron fundados sobre la mas exacta, y distributiva justicia; sobre la prudencia, y moderacion; y ved aqui la causa, ó el origen de donde dimana la palabra Gobierno, Republica, ó Reyno legitimo. . . . Baxo este sistema de gobierno: es decir, en donde los individuos conservan el derecho sagrado de concurrir libremente á la formacion de la Ley que los ha de gobernar; es en donde han brillado mas la virtud, la sabiduria, y el amor de la Patria; por que es en donde la suma del interes particular hace crecer, ó aumentar en razon

directa el interes general; y de consiguiente el poder de toda la asociacion. Estos gobiernos que no estan sujetos al interes, y capricho de un solo hombre, son los que por mas largos años saben conservar el bien precioso, y dulce de la paz.

[From all this we may conclude that the first governments established by mankind were founded on the most exact and distributive justice, based on prudence and moderation; and we may see here the cause or origin from which arose the word Government, Republic, or legitimate Kingdom. . . . Under this form of government—that is, one where individuals preserve the sacred right to freely contribute to the formation of the Laws that are to govern them—is where virtue, knowledge, and love of the *Patria* have shone the brightest; because this is where the sum of particular interests allows the general interest to grow or augment in direct proportion; and, as a result, so too does the entire association's power. Those governments that are not subject to the interest or caprice of a single man are the ones that over the years have been able to preserve the precious common good and sweet peace.]

The language here rings of classic republican rhetoric: the coming together of civic-minded individuals in order to create a res publica based on the virtues of justice, prudence, moderation, and love of country. There is perhaps a gesture toward this emerging sense of individualism, but it develops only to quickly converge into "the sum of particular interests," and to give rise to "the general interest" or "common good."

Having provided an extensive account of sovereignty, the broadsheet turns to the present in order to imagine a better future. Sovereignty rests in the people; they alone have the right to determine the form of government under which they will live: "¿No os mueve ISLENOS y MEXICANOS, la pacifica felicidad que disfruta Venezuela, Santa Fé, Buenos Aires, Chile, el Perú, y la que pronto va á disfrutar Lima? Yo os aconsejo hijos ilustres del famoso Motesuma [*sic*], que no envaineís vuestras espadas hasta no haber restablecido el orden, y dado entera libertad á vuestro pais. [Does it not move you, ISLANDERS and MEXICANS, to see Venezuela, Santa Fé (de Bogotá), Buenos Aires, Chile, Peru, and, soon as well, Lima enjoy tranquil felicity? I advise you, illustrious sons of the famous Motesuma *(sic),* to not sheathe your swords until order and liberty have been reestablished in your country.]" From here, the broadsheet concludes by describing the formation of a provisional representative government:

expidase desde luego por los Generales, orden para que todos los Ayuntamientos de las Villas, Lugares, y Ciudades que estan baxo su mando, elijan un cabildante en quienes concurran las circunstancias de ser Americano de luces, ideas liberales, y amante de la libertad de su Patria. Estos representantes (así

> deben llamarse) deberan concurrir al parage mas seguro: y reunidos todos, deben resumir la soberania de los pueblos que representan . . . y establecer el gobierno legitimo. El interino se debe ir consolidando cada vez mas, al paso que los exercitos adelanten; pues deben agregarse á la Junta gobernativa, otros tantos vocales, quantos Cabildos se le reunan: este es el verdadero camino que os debe conducir al templo de la immortalidad y de la Gloria.
>
> [the Generals should immediately issue an order to all the Town Councils, Places, and Cities under their command to elect a council whose members have been shaped by the circumstances of being an enlightened *Americano*, liberal ideas, and lover of the liberty of one's Homeland *(patria)*. These representatives (this is how they should be called) should meet in the most secure place, and there, all reunited, they should resume the people's [*los pueblos*] sovereignty which they represent . . . and establish a legitimate government. The provisional government should consolidate itself with time and at the pace that the armies march forward; since other members will be added to the governing Council, according to the number of Town Councils that come into being: this is the true path that will lead you to the temple of immortality and glory.]

Unlike the documents discussed thus far, this broadsheet, at last, offers a preliminary vision of the future, based on the longer, now elided history of sovereignty under the Habsburgs, along with the now-dominant version of sovereignty that had circulated throughout the Atlantic world since the American Revolution.

The broadsheet appears to be most interested in the form of republican government recently created by the United States—defined by elections and, most significantly here, the name of these individuals, "representatives." The interest is at least in part because that form was the most familiar to Spanish Americans. But, much like *Amigo de los hombres,* the broadsheet also embraces the Habsburg tradition of electing town council members, while now calling them "representatives." Thus, it does not declare itself in favor of a democracy, far from it. Rather, it suggests either a republic or a constitutional monarchy. A democracy—in other words, rule by the "multitude" before these masses became the *corpus mysticum*—would entail the coming together of individuals with their particular political rights, a concept that had not fully developed in the Hispanic world. Instead, the broadsheet embraces a theory of sovereignty that is transferred in hierarchical fashion. Sovereignty emerges only when the people *(pueblo)* came together to produce that new entity, the *corpus mysticum,* and not as a result of *individuals* transferring their *individual* sovereignty. Sovereignty is then transferred from the multitude to a select few who know best how to create laws for the people.[56] In content, the broadsheet embraces a deeply, consistently Catholic political philosophical worldview of the people's rights, one that ultimately had to accord with a hierarchical conception of sovereignty.[57]

Spanish Americans, then, had their own intellectual tradition to draw from in order to develop their version of the social contract. They "did not need to read Rousseau or the Encylopedists," writes Miguel Molina Martínez. "It was enough to know Suárez and the sixteenth-century Scholastics."[58] Yet, it would be a mistake to think that elite Spanish Americans had no recourse to the thought of northern European social contract theorists such as Locke or Rousseau; the elite classes were able to circumvent the Inquisition, and read these authors.[59] But these were not the basis of university curricula, such as was the case with Suárez. That is, Scholastic thought formed the foundation of the Spanish-American social imaginary even as Spanish Americans continued to read non-Scholastic secular political philosophy from the north, such as Rousseau's. In fact, even when they utilized the *form* of Lockean or Rousseauian language, the *content* of their ideas remained Scholastic.[60]

For this generation of Spanish-American revolutionaries, argues Carlos O. Stoetzer, the most influential intellectuals were Scholastics and early modern thinkers, such as René Descartes and Isaac Newton. John Tate Lanning concurs, affirming that "Without them Raynal, Condorcet, Diderot, Benjamin Franklin, and Thomas Paine would scarcely have been heard and certainly not understood."[61] That Suárez continued to be even more influential in Spanish America than in Spain comes as no surprise, if one considers Alexander von Humboldt's observation in 1811 that those Spanish Americans living outside of metropolitan areas in New Spain, in peripheral areas such as Texas, for example,

> no conciben facilmente, que haya europeos que no hablen su lengua; consideran esta ignorancia como una prueba de baja extraccion, porque en cuanto les rodea, solo la última clase del pueblo deja de saber el español. *Mas instruidos en la historia del siglo 16°* que en la de nuestro tiempo, se imaginan que la España continua egerciendo una declarada preponderancia sobre lo demas de Europa; y la península es para ellos el centro de la civilizacion europea.
>
> [can not easily conceive that there are Europeans who do not speak their language; and they consider this ignorance (of the Spanish language) as proof of their lower class, since among the people with whom they live only those of the lowest class do not know Spanish. *They know better the history of the sixteenth century than they do of our present,* and they imagine that Spain continues to exercise hegemony over the rest of Europe; and the Peninsula is for them the center of European civilization.][62]

Even more to the point, Suárez had been a Jesuit, the very religious order responsible for the education of the Spanish-American elite. Thus, the Jesuits had been able to ensure the promulgation of Suárez's theories throughout Spanish-American universities. By the late eighteenth century, the Spanish monarch was no longer merely concerned with Rousseau and other Enlightenment political theories. He was just as "determined in his campaign against Suárez's 'subversive' theories."[63]

The broadsheet offers a social contract theory that is at once temporal, worldly, and also religious. It is inspired by the divine, though not divine in and of itself—because the divine cannot be known directly. This account of political society (of civil or positive law) must inevitably be related, in hierarchical order, to a Catholic God and worldview. And like Suárez's hierarchical account of law, the form and layout of the broadsheet mirror this view as well (see Figure 40).

Three crosses are spaced out evenly at the very top of the broadside, as we know, announcing to everyone (and anyone who may be illiterate) the document's very Catholic essence. The crosses convey the unknowability of divine reason even while serving as a contemplative image. Below each cross, forming the second nesting layer, are the names "JESÚS," "MARÍA," and "JOSÉ." Here, divine reason becomes expressed not in an image but in words, reflecting the approximate translation of divine reason into language. The names alone make no explicit claim, but they do invoke the holy family along with the concept of the trinity, and thus make an implicit argument of familial Catholic belonging. Another, third, layer of meaning is located immediately beneath the names: "En el nombre de DIOS, y de Nuestra SEÑORA de Guadalupe [In the name of GOD, and of Our LADY of Guadalupe]." Finally, the hierarchical sequencing of meaning—from the crucifixes, to the names of the members of the holy family, to the proclamation of faith in God and the Virgin of Guadalupe—surges into discursivity: the broadsheet spills forth its dense, clause-laden, efficient vision of the world to come.

As the broadsheet descends literally with each layer of meaning, it likewise descends from the symbolic to the literal. It moves from the unknowable divine to an account of the origin of sovereignty. In form and in content, the broadsheet proclaims that each realm of law, though related hierarchically to the others, functions independently. Thus, although civil law must accord with the common good, of following God's law in order to become one with him, it is ultimately separate from divine law, and thus is not ordained by God. The broadsheet, then, is able to convey symbolic meaning even to those who could not read the text, and does so through its layout, brilliantly reflecting the Suárez-inspired vision of the world.

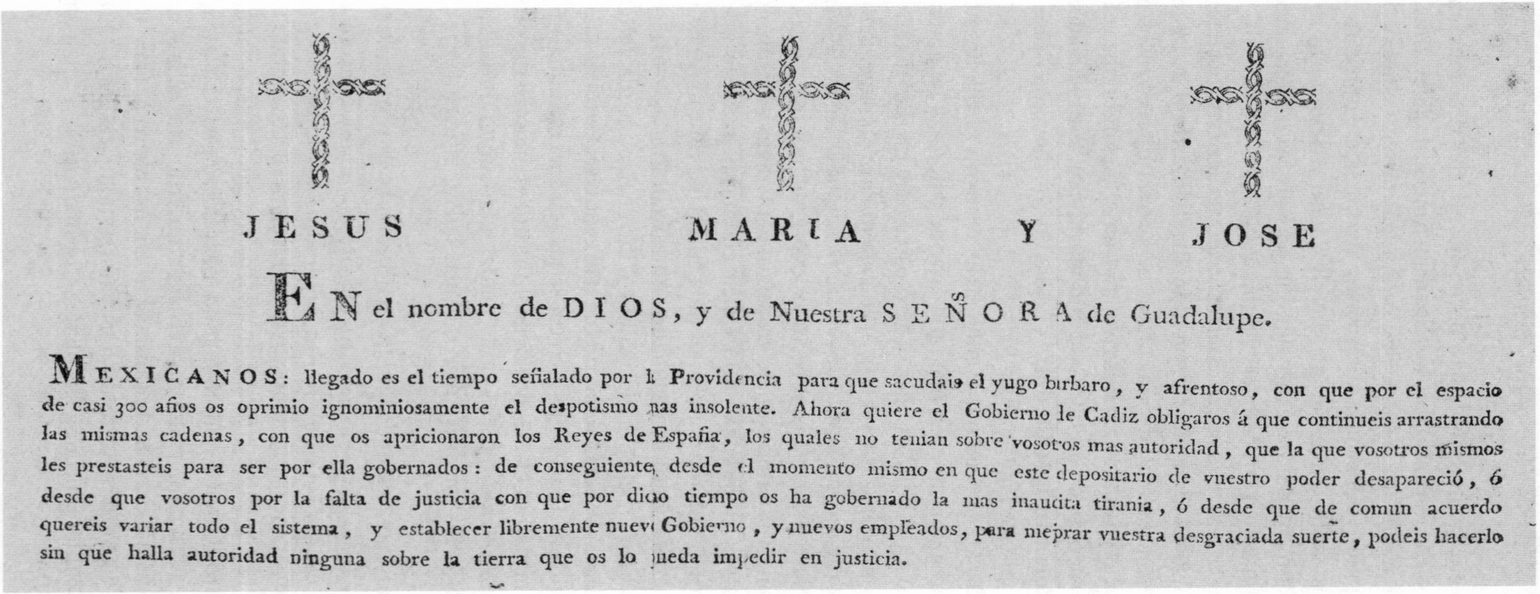
JESUS MARIA Y JOSE

EN el nombre de DIOS, y de Nuestra SEÑORA de Guadalupe.

MEXICANOS: llegado es el tiempo señalado por la Providencia para que sacudais el yugo barbaro, y afrentoso, con que por el espacio de casi 300 años os oprimio ignominiosamente el despotismo mas insolente. Ahora quiere el Gobierno de Cadiz obligaros á que continueis arrastrando las mismas cadenas, con que os apricionaron los Reyes de España, los quales no tenian sobre vosotros mas autoridad, que la que vosotros mismos les prestasteis para ser por ella gobernados: de conseguiente, desde el momento mismo en que este depositario de vuestro poder desapareció, ó desde que vosotros por la falta de justicia con que por dicho tiempo os ha gobernado la mas inaudita tirania, ó desde que de comun acuerdo quereis variar todo el sistema, y establecer libremente nuevo Gobierno, y nuevos empleados, para mejorar vuestra desgraciada suerte, podeis hacerlo sin que halla autoridad ninguna sobre la tierra que os lo pueda impedir en justicia.

Figure 40. Detail from José Álvarez de Toledo's *Jesús, María, y José* (Philadelphia, 1811).

Beinecke Collection Rare Book and Manuscript Library, Yale University.

Indigenous Literacies

Almost immediately, different Indian nations and Hispanicized Indians appeared to ascribe to the renewed ideas of sovereignty, and began to question the colonial order of things. If the Spanish royal governor of Texas, Manuel Salcedo, and more than a few historians since, have condescendingly dismissed the possibility that Spanish Texans could actively engage with these new ideas, then the attitude toward Native Americans is far worse. In April 1812, the Indians of the local Camargo mission, led by the Hispanicized Carrizo Indian José Julián Canales, rebelled against local authorities "in protest of the oppression of the Indians, the creole and the mestizo." Founded in 1749, the Camargo mission at one point had a congregation of 500 Indians, representing the nations of Tareguanos, Pajaritos, Tejones, Cueros Quemados, and Venados. But by 1816 it was reduced to twenty-five families, most of whom belonged to the Carrizo nation. Not withstanding his people's condition, Canales was literate, and he apparently produced stirring proclamations just as Bernardo's brother, Antonio, was making his. Though they have yet to be located, Canales's were read aloud to communities in the area, and, as a result, he enlisted the support of 500 Indians.[64]

A few months after the uprising, on June 9, 1812, Andrés Mendiola, the Spanish captain of Camargo, located in south Texas along the Rio Grande and some twenty-five miles from Bernardo's hometown of Revilla, encountered a group of these Indians. So dramatic was the encounter that Captain Mendiola had a scribe transcribe the conversation. Captain Mendiola had not been able to find a single Spanish-American resident willing to send an official message to this group of Indians, so much did the residents fear for their lives. Riding through the town of Camargo, he engaged in a conversation with a resident when all of a sudden a group of Indians, "vno con escopeta, y quatro de Arco, y flechas [one with a gun and four with bows and arrows]," appeared at a distance:

> dos de ellos conocidos y los otros tres desconocidos; inmediatam.[te] los llamé, y me respondieron con señas de mano que no querian, que fuera yó donde ellos estaban y entonces monte en mi cavallo y me fui a ellos, y preguntandoles quien de ellos hacia cabeza p.[a] que reciviera la orden del sor subdelegado que les llamaba dijo el Yndio Juan de Dios alos otros no crean nada de esa Orden, ni de lo que les diexere este, porque todas son mentiras y catelas y que les dixere ¿donde estaba el Rey? Y que supuesto no havia Rey cada uno podia estar donde su gana le diera, sin tener que obedecer a nadie.
>
> [two of them were familiar and the other three were not; I immediately called to them, but they replied with hand gestures indicating that they did not want

to, that I should go to them and, thus, I mounted my horse, and went to them; and asking them who among them was the leader so that they may receive the subdelegate's orders, the Indian Juan de Dios told the others do not believe a word of that Order, nor anything that this one has to say, because they are all lies and *catelas* (cheap gold chain Romans used to wear), and that I should tell them where the King is. That supposedly there was no King, and that in fact anyone could go as they pleased, without having to obey anyone.][65]

This is the only detailed encounter between Hispanics and Native Americans found in Governor Salcedo's archive.[66] The conversation was transcribed by Captain Mendiola's corporal, Juan Angel de la Garza, and forwarded to the captain of Laredo, who finally sent it to Salcedo. Where Indians had previously appeared in the archive in passing, as objects to be described, here Juan de Dios appears as a speaking subject, mediated though he was through de la Garza's pen. The description captures de Dios's language, and conveys his disdain for Spanish sovereignty. The irony of his name, "John of God," is unremarked upon. But his name and the names of the other Indians mentioned by Mendiola—Luciano, Matías, Ilario, and Julian—reveal that they were Hispanicized Indians.

The colonization of south Texas, the region from where the Gutiérrez de Lara brothers were from, had been quite different from that of Béxar and east Texas, where colonization followed the Spanish-American tradition of utilizing Catholic missions as a method of expansion. Throughout Spanish America, missions had been established at a remove from settled towns in order, in theory, to protect Native Americans from Spanish Americans and to ease their assimilation. But, as we saw in Chapter 1, the despotic government established by José de Escandón in the early eighteenth century had made sure that the Catholic mission system would not interfere with his plans for settlement, and he had the missions placed within the towns. Escandón preferred to incorporate Indians by force in order to exploit their labor, and he was able to do so largely without the interference of missionaries. Yet, once incorporated, the Indians not surprisingly suffered horribly, dying of torture, overwork, disease, or starvation.[67]

It is not clear to which Native nation de Dios and his party belonged; Mendiola never says. But the town of Camargo had been one of the largest in the area of south Texas, and had had one of the largest incorporated indigenous populations, comprised primarily of Carrizo Indians. These were the Indians that Canales a few months earlier had led in rebelling against Spanish rule in the name of "Indians, creoles, and mestizos." Given de Dios and his party's Hispanic names and their impudence, it is more than likely that they were part of the Camargo mission's indigenous community.

De Dios emerges in the archive defiantly, and does so because he participates in Mendiola's epistemological frame, moving in the discursive space between the subject and object of knowledge. By utilizing the language Mendiola is familiar with ("Where is the King?"), de Dios uses the very language of the aspiring colonizer to rhetorically undo the colonizer's world. Just as Hispanics had reduced Indians to objects of knowledge—to irrational, unintelligent beings incapable of understanding the world they inhabited and who, therefore, could only be talked and written about but who could not, themselves, participate in that very discourse—so too does de Dios reduce Mendiola to an object. That is, rather than address Mendiola directly, de Dios instead speaks to his party, and demands that they pose the question to Mendiola: "Where is the King?" It is a rhetorical question that de Dios immediately answers, but he likewise literally refers to Mendiola as an object, a thing to be talked about, when he refers to him using the demonstrative adjective "this one."

In posing the question "Where is the King?" de Dios calls into question Spanish sovereignty. In this, de Dios's rhetorical strategy resembles that of the broadsheet: it, too, uses the occasion of Napoleon's invasion of Spain and deposing of the king as the moment to call for revolution, for a reconfiguration of sovereignty. But in other parts of New Spain, revolutionaries had declared themselves in favor of the king and against the local peninsular rulers. For de Dios, revolution arrives precisely because the king no longer exists. How, then, must have Mendiola reacted to the suggestion that the *raison d'être* of New Spain no longer existed, that there no longer was a trinity of religion, king, and *patria*? But de Dios still had more bad news for Captain Mendiola.

De Dios admitted to traveling freely throughout the Rio Grande Valley in south Texas, defiantly breaking Governor Salcedo's stringent requirement of needing a passport to travel even short distances as a way to control the movement of people and ideas.

> Que havia ido hasta abajo de Camargo, y dando la buelta por Rebilla encontro un correo que benia de donde estaba D.ⁿ Bernardo Gutierrez y decia que un Palio traia apuntado el numero de gente que benia en su compañia y asi que las quatro armas biejas que tenia la tropa de Vallecillo por que no havia querido no havia benido por ellas, que el dia que quiciera bendria, pues le hera tan facil como comerse una tortilla.

> [That he had even traveled below Camargo; and on his return through Revilla he saw mail that had arrived from where Bernardo Gutiérrez was located (in Natchitoches); and he said that a notched Stick recorded the number of men that were in his (Bernardo's) company; and, thus, as for the four old

> weapons held by the troops at (the local garrison of) Vallecillo, that because he had not desired so he had not gone for them (the weapons). That the day that he wanted to, he would go for them. Well, that it would be as easy as eating a tortilla.][68]

De Dios and his world emerge much clearer here. But it is not his audacity to question Spanish colonial authority that is of interest, satirical and biting as it is ("eating a tortilla"). Rather, the archive leaves a trace of an alternative epistemology, a different way of making meaning in the world that has not emerged elsewhere in the archive, that is, his reference to a notched stick as a bearer of information. Given that they communicated in Spanish, that he went by the name of "Juan de Dios" (or at least that was one of his names), and that he apparently could read or at least understand the "mail" that Bernardo had sent to south Texas, de Dios serves as a historical synecdoche for the discursively (and materially) violent processes of colonization, of "becoming" Hispanicized and incorporated into Spanish-American society.[69] The notched stick signifies alternative literacies and ways of knowing; but these, unlike the documents and imprints desperately sought by royalists, were of no consequence for Mendiola and Salcedo, and thus there was no need to translate and incorporate them into the archive. In some instances, discursive violence and erasure from the historical record can approximate the devastating reality of brute force.

Catholic Republican Government

By early August, Bernardo believed these three documents had sufficiently paved the road to revolution. On August 11, 1812, some ten weeks after the documents began to circulate, Bernardo's Republican Army of the North, starting at less than 200 and eventually swelling to over 700 mostly Spanish-American, Anglo-American, and Indian soldiers, invaded and easily took Nacogdoches and its military fort.[70] As he prepared to march south from Nacogdoches toward the towns and military forts at Trinidad, La Bahía, and then Béxar, he issued, on August 31 and September 1, 1812, four different proclamations that were dispersed through Texas and beyond. Each proclamation was addressed to a different constituency: the first to the "gefes, soldados, y vecinos de San Antonio de Béxar [officers, soldiers, and *vecinos* of San Antonio de Béxar]"; the second to the "amados y honrados compatriotas los que abitais en la provincia de Texas [dear and honorable compatriots who live in the province of Texas]"; the third to the "amados compatriotas vezinos y habitantes del Reyno Mexicano [dear and honorable compatriots, *vecinos,* and inhabitants of the Mexican Kingdom]; and the fourth to Anglo-Americans, sent east to Louisiana and from there reprinted in various U.S. newspapers.[71] Like the literature that had circulated for months, these proclamations, too, endorsed the bold vision of independence, but these emphasized more the great emotional attachment that Bernardo felt both for the "Mexican Kingdom" and its inhabitants (see Figure 7).

The proclamations counter the outlandish claim made by Bernardo's onetime ally, the imperialist U.S. special agent William Shaler, who on August 18, 1812, had written to Secretary of State James Monroe stating that Bernardo appeared terrified and that he doubted the success of the revolution. As the historian Carlos Castañeda notes, "Shaler developed a rabid hatred for Gutiérrez after his success in San Antonio" because it excluded, in part, Anglo-American control of Texas. But Shaler's disdain for Bernardo was mutual; the latter would later describe Shaler as "a great scoundrel."[72]

Written with incredible ardor, the proclamations are love letters addressed to each of his imagined communities, all emerging concentrically, from Béxar, then Texas, and, finally, out to Mexico; and each utilizes the same language, at times the exact phrasing, as the broadsheet. By no means does Bernardo equivocate. "[L]legó el dia [the day has arrived]," he writes, "en q.e Yo; os la [*sic*] pudiera hablar con la claridad y seguridad, q.e mi corazon desea [in which I may speak to you with the clarity and security that my heart desires]." He has returned from the United States with military support and volunteers, he declares, who "[nos] alludar[án] a sacudir el llugo barbaro y afrentoso conq.e nos ha oprimido el Despotismo Ynsolente [will help us shake off the barbarous and outrageous yoke with which the most insolent despotism has oppressed us]"—lifting this line directly from the broadsheet.[73]

The documents must have been overwhelmingly convincing to his audience. Within a month, Bernardo's army easily took the fort at Trinidad, as soldiers and inhabitants welcomed the insurgents. But Salcedo had not remained inactive. By November, he and 800 reinforcements met the revolutionaries at La Bahía, the third largest town in Texas located some 100 miles downriver from Béxar. Established as a fort in 1749, La Bahía at one point had provided soldiers to fight in the American Revolutionary War under Bernardo de Gálvez.[74] Salcedo was able to keep the revolutionaries at bay until February 1813 when he retreated to Béxar. Everywhere around him, Salcedo saw his soldiers abandon the royal army and join the revolutionaries. Getting larger by the day, Bernardo's forces began to make their way toward Béxar. After a siege that lasted into the spring, the insurgent forces were able to take this symbolic heart of Spanish Texas on April 1, 1813.[75] At last, Salcedo's nightmare had come true. Texas had fallen; it was now only a matter of time before the rest of Spanish America, too, would succumb.

Four days later on April 6, 1813, the *pueblo* of Béxar declared their independence from all foreign powers. A council comprised of thirty different men, both citizens and soldiers, came together and collectively wrote their declaration (see Appendix 3). By April 17, the council had also produced a constitution, declaring itself the "state of Texas, forming part of the Mexican Republic." Throughout, they proudly proclaim the name of the nation, as Father Antonio and Bernardo had done, but there is no ambivalence: it is now clearly "la República Mexicana." But though the nation was born, nowhere in the documents do the new citizens refer to themselves as "Mexicans."[76] The project of nationalism, of replacing previous concentric senses of belonging, was only about to begin.

The Declaration of Independence articulates in the most moving of terms the revolutionaries' precise reasons for seeking independence. The republican council disseminated its Declaration of Independence along with the four other proclamations that Bernardo had written.

> Fuimos regidos por Ynsolentes Yntrusos, q. se valian de sus Empleos para despojarnos; y nos era negada toda especie de participacion en los negocios nacionales y munisipales.
>
> Sentimos con indignacion, la Tirania Exercitada, en excluirnos de toda comunicacion con otras Naciones, prohiviendo en nuestros Paises quanto pudiese servir á nuestra ilustracion, y a descillar nuestros ojos. Nos era prohivido el uso de los libros; la libertad de ablar y aun de pensar. Nuestro Pais era nuestra pricion. En una Provincia que la naturaleza ha favorcido con tanta prodigalidad; eramos pobres, hallandonos privados de Cultivar, aquellos frutos analogos á nuestro suelo, y aun los renglones de urgente nececidad.
>
> [We were ruled by Insolent Intruders, who took advantage of their Positions in order to dispossess us, and we were denied any and all type of participation in national and municipal affairs.
>
> We felt with great indignation, the Tyranny as Practiced, in excluding us from all communication with other Nations, prohibiting in our Countries anything that could serve toward our enlightenment and to opening our eyes. We were prohibited the use of books; the freedom to speak and even to think. Our Country was our prison. In a Province that nature has favored

> with so much abundance, we were poor, finding ourselves unable to and prevented from cultivating those fruits native to our land, and even those of urgent necessity.][77]

By early June, the proclamations had made their way deep into south Texas and even further into Mexico.[78]

The Declaration of Independence bears an obvious resemblance to that of the U.S. Declaration, and virtually all historians who have written about this document have attributed its sentiments to the "clear and evident influence of U.S. republican discourse."[79] The declaration begins:

> *Nos el Pueblo dela Provincia de Texas*
>
> Jurando al Juez Supremo del Vniverso la rectitud de nuestras intenciones, declaramos que los vinculos que nos mantenian, baxo de la Dominacion de la España Europea están p.ª siempre disueltos; que somos libres é Yndependientes; que tenemos el dro de establecér nuestro propio Gov.ⁿᵒ; y que en adelante toda autoridad lexitima, dimanará del Pueblo a quien Solam.ᵗᵉ pertenece este derecho; que desde ahora para Siempre jamas estamos absueltos de deber y obligacion a todo Poder Extrangero.
>
> Vna Relacion delas Causas que han atraido la urgencia de esta medida es debida á nuestra Dignidad y á las opiniones del Mundo.
>
> [*We the Pueblo of the Province of Texas*
>
> Swearing before the Supreme Judge of the Universe the rectitude of our intentions, we declare that the bonds that kept us under the Domination of European Spain are forever dissolved; that we are free and Independent; that we have the right to establish our own Government; and that henceforth all legitimate authority arises from the *Pueblo* in whom this right Only belongs; that from now on and forever we are absolved from all duty and obligation to all Foreign Powers.
>
> An Account of the Causes that have led to the urgency of this measure should be provided, in respect to our Dignity and opinions of the World.][80]

In form, the declaration does mirror that of the United States, but in content—the discursive trace of the *pueblo* and rights of the community, not of individuals—the language is adamantly Catholic political philosophy (see Appendix 3 for the transcription of the original and the translation).

There has been, however, a rather radical shift. Where the broadsheet begins with the symbolic representation of the divine, this declaration boldly alters the order. "Nos el pueblo [We the people]" has replaced the symbolic representation of God via the three crosses, placing God instead in the body of the text. Yet we should not assume that the terms here are synonymous. "People," as we have seen earlier, is an inadequate translation of the Spanish *pueblo. Pueblo* can also be translated as "town;" and, thus, conveys both the sense of a collective of people associated with a specific locale. As we saw in Chapter 1, the Spanish original has long connoted the sense of an indivisible group of people, a collective being—a concept that does not have an English equivalent. "People," on the other hand, conveys the sense of a conglomerate of individuals that could be separated into discrete persons; the word is typically translated into Spanish as *gente. Pueblo,* then, carries with it the Scholastic concept of the *corpus mysticum,* the mystical living body that can only emerge by the coming together of a mass of an indivisible people associated with a specific territory. Or, in Suárez's terms, the *corpus mysticum* is produced by the coming together of families. It is in this sense that *pueblo,* to this day, carries with it such political-emotional weight that it is commonly used in political slogans: "El pueblo unido! Jamás será vencido! [The people united! Will never be divided]!"

Thus, like the broadsheet, the declaration has no interest in offering an account of individual sovereignty or rights. In fact, it seems to refuse to do so: "los Goviernos están instituidos p.[a] el bien, y felicidad de las Comunidades y nó para el engrandecimiento de algunos Yndividuos [Governments are created for the benefit and happiness of Communities and not for the aggrandizement of certain Individuals]." Here, we may detect an overlap between political philosophies, one Catholic, the other republican, in that both argue that governments are instituted for the well-being of the people and not individuals. Though, as we have seen, in the case of the United States, this republican principle of community gave way to the value of self-interest of liberalism by the nineteenth century.

But the declaration refuses to entertain the political idea of democracy. In fact, it can not because democracy is not part of the language available to its authors. To invoke democracy would undo the very concept of the *pueblo.* Democracy requires the articulation of rights as residing within individuals who then come together to exercise their individual rights to participate in government. Rather, the declaration concludes:

> p.[a] evitar la Confucion y demora, de tomar la vos de cada un individuo del Pueblo, damos amplios Poderes en señal de nuestra gratitud á nuestro Ylustre libertador el señor D. Bernardo Gutierres, General en Gefe del Exercito Mexicano Republicano del Norte, para que nombre, y elija, incontinentemente, un Precidente, seis vocales, y un Secretario para componer, y constituir una Junta, investida de plenos poderes por nosotros, y para en nuestro nombre formár la

representacion Nacional: Establecer un Govierno para este estado . . . y alludar con perseberancia, y vigor la causa dela santa religion, y de la justicia, de la razon, y de los dros. Sagrados del hombre.

[in order to avoid Confusion and delay by tallying the voice of each individual in the Community *(pueblo)*, we give ample Powers as a token of our gratitude to our Illustrious liberator Don Bernardo Gutierres, General in Chief of the Mexican Republican Army of the North, so that he may name and choose, without constraints, a President, six members, and a Secretary to compose and create a Governing Board, invested by us with full power; and so that in our name they may create a National form of representation: to Establish a Government for this state . . . and to assist with perseverance and Vigor the cause of Holy religion, and that of Justice, of reason, and of the Sacred rights of man.][81]

The declaration proclaims the people's sovereignty, only to immediately and temporarily transfer it to Bernardo. He is asked to create a council, as a representation of the people, that would be charged with creating the new government. Here, the text gestures toward a growing awareness of individual rights, even if negatively. It begins by acknowledging the possibility that each individual has sovereignty, that is, that they each have the right to vote, but it does so only to immediately deny it for expedient reasons. Echoing, though, the nested structure of Catholic political thought, the declaration invokes the divine, moving down the descending levels of hierarchy to that of natural law, of reason, and finally to civil law.

The declaration draws from the same Scholastic thought that the broadsheet did, but it does so with a twist. It announces its sovereignty as arising in hierarchical order: it emerges from the people as a collective, but is immediately transferred to a president. Here, then, is the true revolution, the return to Scholastic thought in order to reimagine it for present purposes. If Scholastic philosophers had argued that sovereignty rested in the people, they had quickly moved to the next step. They argued that the people had permanently transferred their sovereignty to a monarch, and never contemplated a democratic republic as Texas was doing now. But this declaration melds Scholastic thought with republican philosophy. It brings together the Scholastic theory of sovereignty, the Spanish-American history of representation within *ayuntamientos* and contemporary republican thought in the figure of the president and council. In this, Texas was unlike the rest of Spanish America in following Suarezian political theories of sovereignty as resting in the *pueblo,* but it certainly veered to the radical in fully and immediately embracing a republican form of government over a monarchy.[82]

Texas may have declared itself independent, but it embraced a decidedly Catholic Hispanic epistemological worldview to do so. Revolution had arrived, but it was less a complete remaking of the social fabric than it was a return to what the revolutionaries saw as an uncorrupted form of sovereignty reconfigured for present purposes. Over the course of the eighteenth century, the Bourbon reforms had attempted to destroy the longstanding Scholastic model of sovereignty with its many-layered hierarchy. In its place, the Bourbons insisted on absolutism and the theory of divine right: of God's ordaining absolute monarchical rule. Thus, rather than destroying a Catholic vision of the world, these revolutionary republican documents seek instead a revolution, a full return to a centuries-old theory of sovereignty even as it was infused with new republican theories. It was premised on an unquestionable faith in a Catholic world, and a return to previous Habsburg principles of rule. What made Texas unique was that it was the first province in all of New Spain to declare itself independent with a republican form of government and a written constitution.[83] Even eight years later, in 1821, when Mexico finally gained independence, it did so because Mexican conservatives feared that liberal reform within Spain had gone too far. Thus, Mexican conservatives joined the revolutionaries, and Mexican became independent. But it would do so as a monarchy.

War and Terror

The war of social imaginaries unleashed by these documents was followed closely by an all-out war. Historians do not agree exactly on how events transpired after the declaration of independence. Once the insurgents took Béxar, historians disagree as to whether the Spanish commanders were pardoned and exiled or convicted and sentenced to death. Bernardo seems to have equivocated, but he finally handed Governor Salcedo and his officers over to a group of 100 men led by, among others, members of the Delgado and Menchaca families, who were the descendants of the original, elite Canary Islander founders of Béxar.[84]

On the evening of April 3, 1813, a few days after the capital was seized and a few days before the constitution was produced, revolutionary republicans marched seventeen royalists, including Salcedo, out of Béxar. The chained prisoners headed toward the Gulf Coast where they were to depart via ship to the United States or Mexico. Six miles outside of town, however, they were executed. According to contemporary testimony, the

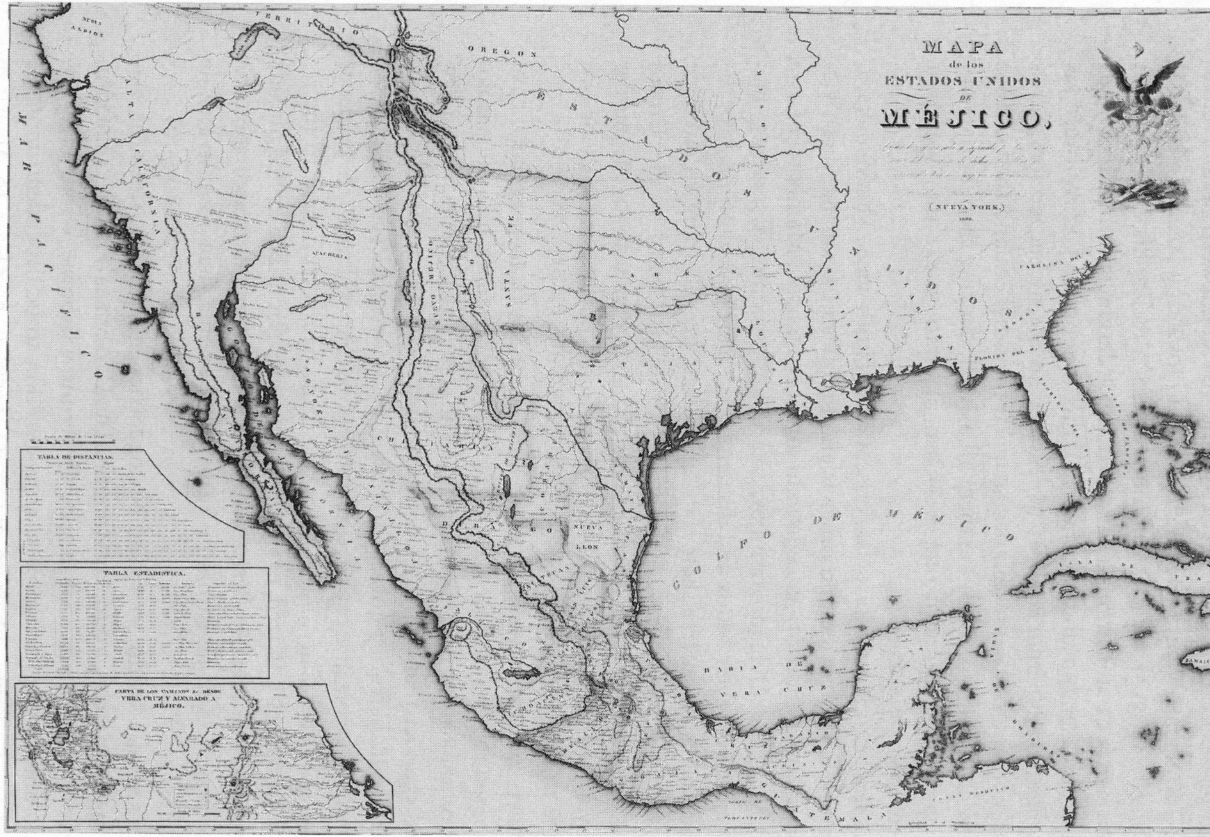

Figure 41. “Mapa de los Estados Unidos de Méjico, Según lo organizado y definido, por las varias actas del Congreso de dicha República; y construido por las mejores autoridades” (1828).

29.3×41.6 in. No. 76217. Texas General Land Office.

revolutionaries "los degollaron, negandoles los auxilios espirituales q. con áncia los pedian; y para hacér este sacrificio los desnudaron á todos y al Sr. Salcedo le sacaron la lengua, quitandoles a todos, las cabeyeras, sin permitir q. los enterraran, dexando en áquel desgraciado puesto Yndios para q. cuidasen que no se verificara les dieran sepulcro [slit their throats, denying them spiritual comfort which they anxiously begged for; and in order to make this sacrifice, they stripped them naked, and they cut out Mr. Salcedo's tongue, scalping them all as well, denying them burial, and leaving Indians to guard that wretched place to ensure they were not buried]."[85]

But terror and brutality, no surprise, worked both ways. The Menchaca, Delgado, Leal, Arocha, and other Isleño families in Béxar had been victims at the hands of Salcedo and other royalists. Members of the Menchaca and Delgado families, like countless other insurgents, had been executed, their heads and dismembered arms placed on pikes in the Bexareño town square; their only crime had been helping to circulate Bernardo's revolutionary literature.[86] Most historians in the United States and some in Mexico have placed blame on Bernardo for the murder of royal prisoners, claiming that either he acted out of vengeance or was unable to control his forces.

Other sources, including a good number of Mexican historians, have attributed the commanders' deaths to a variety of causes, including espionage on the part of the United States.[87] The standard accounts have understated the fact that Shaler, Natchitoches-based Indian agent John Sibley, and Orleans Territory governor William Claiborne had become incensed at Bernardo's role in creating a Texan republic that excluded U.S. influence (despite the fact that some Anglo-Americans had been named to the republican council). Indeed, even prior to the executions Shaler had already decided to help depose Bernardo in order to replace him with someone more pliable. And he would do so with none other than José Álvarez de Toledo.[88]

Álvarez de Toledo arrived in Nacogdoches in April 1813, just as Bernardo was marching into San Antonio. The U.S. officials had become infuriated with Bernardo's obstinacy. Governor Claiborne wrote that Bernardo and his "chiefs manifest no disposition to be dependent upon the American Government or to grant any peculiar privileges to American people."[89] We see here how "American" had already been co-opted by Anglo-Americans to refer to the United States. In effect, Bernardo's dream, expressed during his negotiations with the U.S. government while in Washington, D.C., of working toward the common good for "both Americas," will soon become a nightmare. As a result, Claiborne and his allies encouraged Álvarez de Toledo to enter Texas and, supported by other Anglo-Americans, depose Bernardo (see Figure 7).

Accompanying Álvarez de Toledo, however, was Juan Mariano Picornell, the revolutionary Spaniard who had been exiled from Spain to New Granada and who, in 1797, had printed and disseminated from the West Indies and into New Granada the first successful Spanish-American printing of the French Revolution's Declaration of the Rights of Man and of the Citizen. Historians have traced Álvarez de Toledo's vexed political career, relying on both U.S. and Spanish archives, and have documented what appears to be his rather personal pursuit of glory. Upon hearing of other U.S.-based revolutionary plots, Álvarez de Toledo "burn[ed] with impatience and [was] consumed with jealousy," writes Castañeda. "He seemed to think that he had a monopoly on filibustering and should be recognized as the sole leader and organizer."[90]

But, as early as January 1813, Bernardo had already been warned about Álvarez de Toledo. He had received letters dated December 29, 1812, from a Nathaniel Cogswell of Pittsburgh informing him that Álvarez de Toledo "was a traitor whose sole aim was to get control of the army and then deliver it to the Royalists." Indeed, Álvarez de Toledo had already set in motion a shift in his allegiances. He had written to the Spanish minister in Philadelphia seeking reconciliation with Spain. Minister Luis de Onís, in turn, would write to the infamous royal commandant general Joaquín de Arredondo on August 20, 1813, informing him that Álvarez de Toledo had offered to betray the insurgents. He would ultimately receive a pardon, and work as an informant against Spanish-American revolutionaries.[91]

Now, having arrived in Louisiana in April 1813 and working in concert with U.S. officials, Álvarez de Toledo, too, used printed documents to aid in his efforts to remove Bernardo from office. In Natchitoches, Álvarez de Toledo and Shaler published in May 25, 1813, what is known as the first Texan newspaper, the *Gaceta de Tejas* (see Figure 42), and they, too, dispersed the periodical into Texas. It was a double-sided Spanish-language gazette that criticized Bernardo's efforts and praised the U.S. and Anglo-American efforts to help secure Mexico's independence. A month later, on June 19, they issued a second double-sided newspaper, *El Mejicano*. This time, however, they turned to diatribe as they apologized to their "public for introducing . . . so insignificant and despicable a character as José Bernardo Gutierrez." They race-baited him by printing libelous news that 600 men, "composed principally of mulattoes, for years past exercised in every species of robbery and violence . . . [and] commanded by . . . a Frenchman of color from San Domingo," awaited off the coast of Texas, prepared "to reinforce the governor [Bernardo]." The Gulf of Mexico had been embroiled in a revolutionary maelstrom since the start of the Haitian revolution. Refugees—elite and impoverished; black, white, and mulatto; free and enslaved—had desperately sought to find new homes where they could start anew. And many of them had arrived in New Orleans, while a few had attempted to settle in what ultimately was a geographically inhospitable Galveston. But few if any had made their way further into Texas; thus, Álvarez de Toledo and Shaler merely sought to discredit Bernardo. Indeed, as it would turn out years later, Bernardo would actively solicit Haitian support for Mexican independence.[92]

Álvarez de Toledo and Shaler also sent their spies to Béxar, dispersing the defamatory newspapers, causing confusion to flourish.[93] Having planted the seeds of discord, Álvarez de Toledo entered Béxar on August 3, 1813. Poised, articulate, persuasive, and extravagantly dressed in a general's uniform, he "took by storm the hearts of the army, . . . extended his captivation to the population of San Antonio," and convinced the governing council to have Bernardo removed from office. The following day, the council appointed Álvarez de Toledo commander.[94]

His victory, though astounding, was short-lived. After the declaration of independence in April 1813, the Spanish royal army made its way up from Laredo, and was approaching Béxar only days before Álvarez de Toledo's arrival. On August 18, Arredondo met the republican forces in the sandy oak forest known as the *encinal de Medina*, some twenty miles south of the capital. In what became the bloodiest battle ever fought on Texas soil, the Battle of Medina, Arredondo led his royal forces of 1,830 soldiers to an easy defeat of Álvarez de Toledo's 1,400. (Among Arredondo's soldiers was the nineteen-year-old Antonio López de Santa Anna, who would return to Texas in 1836 to play a role at the Alamo.)[95] In fact, given Onís's letter to Arredondo (dated two days after the republicans' defeat) which implicated Álvarez de Toledo as a turncoat, it is more than clear that Álvarez de Toledo had contributed to the defeat of the insurgents. "Prisoners were shot as fast as they were brought from the battlefield," recounts Castañeda. "[The] next day the executions continued. By the end of the day 112 prisoners had been shot. Arredondo resumed his triumphant march to San Antonio, mopping up stragglers as he went. When he arrived in the city the following day he had 215 more prisoners, many of whom were civilians who had espoused the cause of the Revolution."[96] The remains of some 1,000 insurgents were left unburied. Álvarez de Toledo, however, abandoned his forces and the people of San Antonio, and barely escaped to New Orleans. Terror awaited those he left behind.[97]

Upon hearing of Álvarez de Toledo's defeat, the republican San Antonio families that had supported independence led a desperate, hurried retreat to the United States, abandoning all of their belongings. About 300 refugees

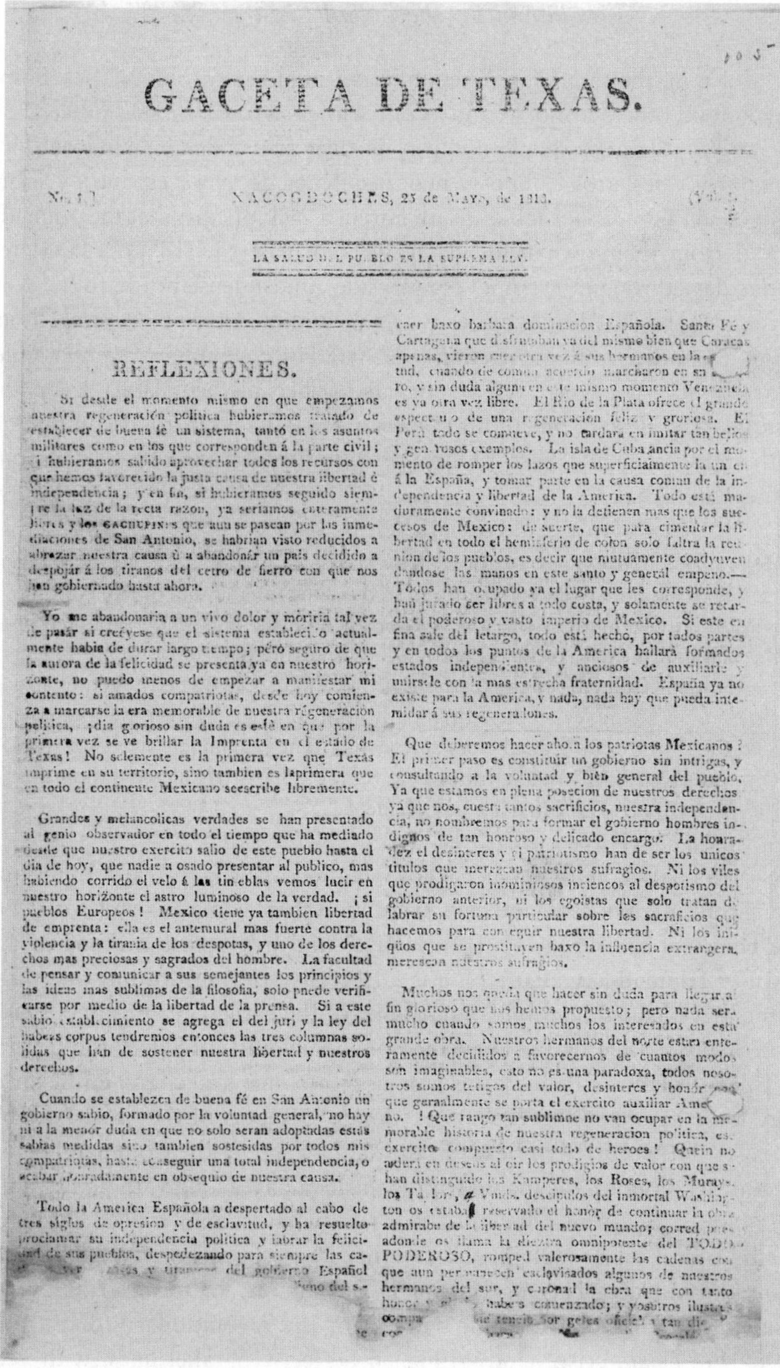

GACETA DE TEXAS.

No. 1.] NACOGDOCHES, 25 de Mayo, de 1813. [Vol. 1.

LA SALUD DEL PUEBLO ES LA SUPREMA LEY.

REFLEXIONES.

Si desde el momento mismo en que empezamos nuestra regeneración politica hubieramos tratado de establecer de buena fé un sistema, tantó en los asuntos militares como en los que corresponden á la parte civil; si hubieramos sabido aprovechar todos los recursos con que hemos favorecido la justa causa de nuestra libertad é independencia; y en fin, si hubieramos seguido siempre la luz de la recta razon, ya seriamos enteramente libres y los GACHUPINES que aun se pasean por las inmediaciones de San Antonio, se habrian visto reducidos a abrazar nuestra causa ù a abandonár un pais decidido a despojár á los tiranos del cetro de fierro con que nos han gobiernado hasta ahora.

Yo me abandonaria a un vivo dolor y moriria tal vez de pasár si creéyese que el sistema establecido actualmente habia de durar largo tiempo; péro seguro de que la aurora de la felicidad se presenta ya en nuestro horizonte, no puedo menos de empezar a manifestar mi contento: si amados compatriotas, desde hoy comienza a marcarse la era memorable de nuestra régeneración politica, ¡dia glorioso sin duda es estè en que por la primera vez se ve brillar la Imprenta en el estado de Texas! No solemente es la primera vez que Texás imprime en su territorio, sino tambien es laprimera que en todo el continente Mexicano seescribe libremente.

Grandes y melancolicas verdades se han presentado al genio observador en todo el tiempo que ha mediado desde que nuestro exercito salio de este pueblo hasta el dia de hoy, que nadie a osado presentar al publico, mas habiendo corrido el velo á las tin eblas vemos lucir en nuestro horiźonte el astro luminoso de la verdad. ¡si pueblos Europeos! Mexico tiene ya tambien libertad de emprenta: ella es el antemural mas fuerte contra la violencia y la tirania de los despotas, y uno de los derechos mas preciosas y sagrados del hombre. La facultad de pensar y comunicar a sus semejantes los principios y las ideas mas sublimas de la filosofia, solo puede verificarse por medio de la libertad de la prensa. Si a este sabio establecimiento se agrega el del juri y la ley del habeas corpus tendremos entonces las tres columnas solidas que han de sostener nuestra libertad y nuestros derechos.

Cuando se establezca de buena fé en San Antonio un gobierno sabio, formado por la voluntad general, no hay ni a la menór duda en que no solo seran adoptadas estás sabias medidas sino tambien sostesidas por todos mis compatriotas, hasta conseguir una total independencia, o acabar honradamente en obsequio de nuestra causa.

Todo la America Española a despertado al cabo de tres siglus de opresion y de esclavitud, y ha resuelto proclamar su independencia politica y labrar la felicidad de sus pueblos, despedezando para siempre las ca- [illegible] y [illegible] del gobierno Español [illegible] del s- [illegible]

caer baxo barbara dominacion Española. Santa Fé y Cartagena que disfrutaban ya del mismo bien que Caracas apenas, vieron otra vez á sus hermanos en la [illegible] tud, cuando de comun acuerdo marcharon en su [illegible] ro, y sin duda alguna en este mismo momento Venezuela es ya otra vez libre. El Rio de la Plata ofrece el grande espectaculo de una regeneracion feliz y groriosa. El Perú todo se conmueve, y no tardara en imitar tan bellos y generosos exemplos. La isla de Cuba ancia por el momento de romper los lazos que superficialmente la un en á la España, y tomar parte en la causa comun de la independencia y libertad de la America. Todo está maduramente convinado: y no la detienen mas que los sucesos de Mexico: de suerte, que para cimentar la libertad en todo el hemisferio de colon solo faltra la reunion de los pueblos, es decir que mutuamente coadyuven dandose las manos en este santo y generál empeno.— Todos han ocupado ya el lugar que les corresponde, y hañ jurado ser libres a todo costa, y solamente se retarda el poderoso y vasto imperio de Mexico. Si este en fina sale del letargo, todo está hechó, por tados partes y en todos los puntos de la America hallarà formados estados independientes, y anciosos de auxiliarle y unirsele con la mas estrecha fraternidad. España ya no existe para la America, y nada, nada hay que pueda intemidar á sus regeneradores.

Que deberemos hacer ahora los patriotas Mexicanos? El primer paso es constituir un gobierno sin intrigas, y consultando a la voluntad y bièn general del pueblo. Ya que estamos en plena posecion de nuestros derechos ya que nos, cuesta tantos sacrificios, nuestra independencia, no nombremos para formar el gobierno hombres indignos de tan honroso y delicado encargo. La honradez el desinteres y el patriotismo han de ser los unicos titulos que merezcan nuestros sufragios. Ni los viles que prodigaron ignominiosos inciencos al despotismo del gobierno anterior, ni los egoistas que solo tratan de labrar su fortuna particular sobre les sacraficios que hacemos para conseguir nuestra libertad. Ni los iniqüos que se prostituyen baxo la influencia extrangera, merescan nuestros sufragios.

Muchos nos queda que hacer sin duda para llegar al fin glorioso que nos hemos propuesto; pero nada será mucho cuando somos muchos los interesados en esta grande obra. Nuestros hermanos del norte estan enteramente decididos a favorecernos de cuantos modos son imaginables, esto no es una paradoxa, todos nosotros somos testigos del valor, desinteres y honór con que geraalmente se porta el exercito auxiliar Ame[illegible] no. !Que rango tan sublimne no van ocupar en la memorable historia de nuestra regeneracion politica, ese exercito compuesto casi todo de heroes! Quein no arderá en deseos al oir los prodigios de valor con que se han distinguido los Kamperes, los Roses, los Murays, los Taylor, a Vmds. descipulos del inmortal Washington os estaba reservado el honòr de continuar la obra admirabe de la liberdad del nuevo mundo; corred pues adonde os llama la diextra omnipotente del TODO PODEROSO, rompeld valerosamente las cadenas con que aun permanecen esclavisados algunos de nuestros hermanos del sur, y coronad la obra que con tanto honor [illegible] habers comenzado; y vosotros ilustres compa[illegible] tenido por gefes oficiel y tan di[illegible]

Figure 42. The first Texan newspaper, *Gaceta de Texas* (May 25, 1813).

Dispatches from Special Agents of the Department of State, 1794–1906, vol. 2, RG 59: General Records of the Department of State, U.S. National Archives.

left at 4 p.m. the same day Arredondo defeated the revolutionaries. Some fled on foot, others by horse, and as one witness wrote, "sin mas prevención que un saco de maíz que levantaron de su misma milpa, caminaron doce días por los desiertos campos y malezas, llenos de temor espanto, y sobre salto con el Jesús en los labios [with barely a sack of corn that they quickly picked from their own fields. They walked [east toward Louisiana] for twelve days through the empty countryside amidst dense brush, full of fear, terror, and shock, whispering Jesus's name and murmuring prayers]," hoping to avoid the wrath of Arredondo.[98] Avoidance would prove impossible.

Arredondo, the "one-eyed tyrant," unleashed his brutal fury upon the insurgents.[99] He sent one of his commanders, Ignacio Elizondo, in pursuit of the refugees, while he stayed in San Antonio to dispense justice. As one witness recollected:

> [H]ere my pen trembles in transcribing scenes of horror. . . . With infamous malice Arredondo ordered seven hundred pacific inhabitants of San Antonio without discrimination seized and imprisoned. In the house now tenanted by the Catholic priests, more than three hundred of these unfortunate beings were confined on the night of the 20th of August. Crowded together like sheep in the shambles, in the scorching heat of summer, eighteen were discovered the next morning dead from suffocation. The remainder were shot from day to day without other form of trial than the most trivial accusation that they were in favor of Mexican Independence.[100]

Meanwhile, Elizondo pursued those families fleeing toward Louisiana along the Camino Real, and caught up with them some 215 miles east, on the banks of the menacing Trinity River and just before arriving at the town of Trinidad (see Figure 7). It is a great historical misfortune that these events have led to the production of one of the earliest records about, and quite likely written by, the Spanish-American women of San Antonio.

Titled "Memoria de las cosas mas notables, que acaecieron en Bexar el año de 13 mandando el Tirano Arredondo" (Report of the Most Notable Things That Occurred in Bexar in the Year 13, under the Command of the Tyrant Arredondo), the manuscript is thirteen pages long with no attributable author (see Appendix 4). It is a terrifying account told in the third person plural by an individual, or perhaps a group, who were adamantly pro-independence. The manuscript is a testimony of the horrific events that unfolded after Arredondo's defeat of the revolutionary forces. It is written in clean, crisp handwriting, in perfectly parallel lines, with very few strikethroughs; the near-perfect quality suggests that perhaps the manuscript was recopied at a later time.

It begins by narrating the defeat of the revolutionary forces at the hands of the "crueldad é inaudita Tiranía de los defensores de un Monarca absoluto, en cuyas manos quedó indefenso este Pueblo Patriota [cruel and unprecedented tyranny of those defending the absolutist Monarch, and in whose hands this patriotic town was left]." The author expresses a clear desire to document these events for a larger audience:

> Lo que este Pueblo padecio, tolero, y sufrió no es facil sujertarlo á la pluma, ni menos narrarlo con exactismo y certeza, por haber muerto muchos de los que pudieran dar una noticia verás, porque otros que pudieran hacerlo por hallarse vivos, no presenciaron el echo; y [los] que lo vieron, tomaron parte en la opreción, y tiranía de su Patria en terminos de no poder declarar la verdad; y antes han tomado empeño en desfigurarlas p.r la parte que les toca. Este es á la verdad el motivo por que hta. el el [*sic*] día ignora el Público la parte que el Departamen.to de Texas tomó, y tubo en la libertad de la Patria, y gloriosa Yndependencia. . . . Vamos á la obra, y salga lo que saliere; con tal que el publico los cepa.
>
> [What this *Pueblo* underwent, tolerated, and suffered is not easy to put into writing, much less is it easy to recount with accuracy and certainty, since many of those who could have given a truthful account have died, and since others who are alive did not witness the events; and those who did witness them actually took part in the oppression and tyranny of their *Patria* and thus are incapable of telling the truth; and, in fact, they have actually attempted to distort the truth by lying about the roles that they actually played. This is indeed the reason why to this day the Public is unaware of the role played by the Department of Texas in pursuit of the *Patria*'s liberty and glorious Independence. . . . Let us begin our story then, come what may, so that the public may know what occurred here.][101]

The royalists caught up to the families on August 30, 1813, at 1 p.m. on the banks of the Trinity River. Most of the men crossed immediately, sent over by their wives in the hope that they would escape, but Elizondo had promised no retributions if the men returned. Over 270 men, including Antonio Delgado, the man who had led the execution of the Spanish commanders, decided to recross the bank. Upon doing so, however, Elizondo promptly shot and stabbed Antonio. The men were quickly allowed to confess, and over a hundred were executed, after which their bodies were left mutilated, stripped, and unburied.[102] The executions lasted through the afternoon and well into the night, while mothers, wives, and daughters held each other and wept. The following morning many of the women resolved to return to the killing field, and there found

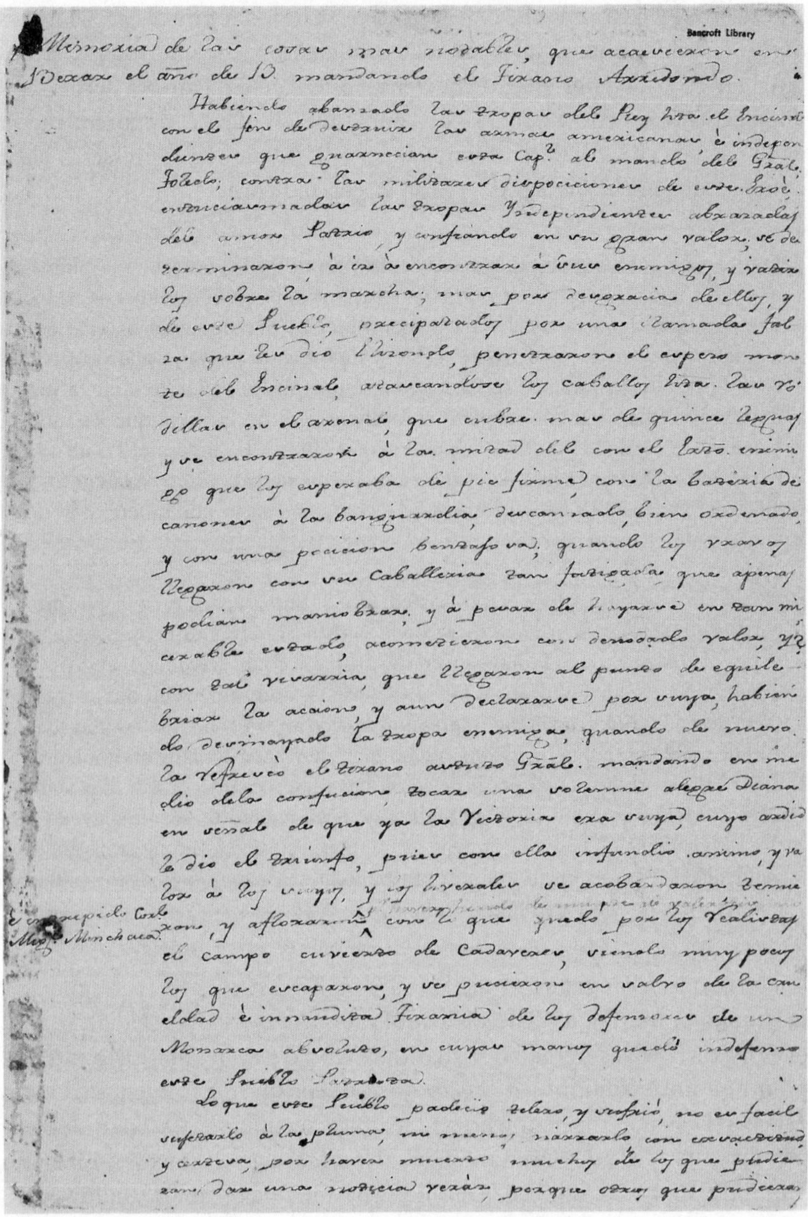
Bancroft Library

Memoria de las cosas mas notables, que acaecieron en Bexar el año de 13. mandando el Tirano Arredondo.

Habiendo avanzado las tropas del Rey hta. el Encinal con el fin de destruir las armas americanas è independientes que guarnecian esta Capl. al mando del Gral. Toledo; contra las militares disposiciones de este Gral. enunciavamadas las tropas Independientes arrastradas del amor Patrio, y confiando en su gran valor, se determinaron à ir à encontrar à sus enemigos, y batirlos sobre la marcha; mas por desgracia de ellos, y de este Pueblo, precipitados por una llamada falza que les dio l'ltronglo, penetraron el espeso monte del Encinal, atascandose los caballos hta. las rodillas en el arenal, que cubre mas de quince leguas y se encontraron à la mitad del con el Exto. enemigo que los esperaba de pie firme con la bateria de canones à la banguardia, descansado, bien ordenado, y con una posicion ventajosa; quando los nuestros llegaron con su Caballeria tan fatigada, que apenas podian maniobrar, y à pesar de hallarse en tan miserable estado, acometieron con denodado valor, [illegible] con tal bizarria, que llegaron al punto de equilebrar la accion, y aun declararse por suya, habiendo desvaratado la tropa enemiga, quando de nuevo la refuerzo el tirano avanzo Gral. mandando en medio de la confusion tocar una solemne alegre Diana en señal de que ya la Victoria era suya, cuyo ardid le dio el triunfo, pues con ella infundio animo, y valor à los suyos, y los liberales se acobardaron terminaron, y afloxaron con lo que quedo por los realistas el campo cubierto de Cadaveres, siendo muy pocos los que escaparon, y se pusieron en salvo de la crueldad è inaudita Tirania de los defensores de un Monarca absoluto, en cuyas manos quedó indefenso este Pueblo Inerme.

ê ocupado Corl. Migl. Menchaca.

Lo que este Pueblo padecio, lloro, y sufrio, no es facil referirlo à la pluma, ni menos narrarlo con exactitud y certeza, por haver muerto muchos de los que pudieran dar una noticia exacta, porque otros que pudieran

Figure 43. First page of "Memoria de las cosas más notables que acaecieron en Béxar el año de 13 mandando el Tirano Arredondo" (1813).

MSS P-O 811. The Bancroft Library, University of California.

> los cuerpos de sus hermanos muertos . . . tirados en el campo y comidos de los animales, y viendo tal inhumanidad se determinaron á pedirle al cruel Comand.[te] Elizondo les permitiera sepultarlos ellas mismas, mas no lo consiguieron diciendoles dho. Gefe: que estaban condenados p.[r] traidores al Rey, y ala Patria. . . . Algunos días pasaron estas infelices patriotas en tan infernal sitio con el alma atrabesada y sufriendo quanto males podían esperarse de los encarnizados defensores de un Rey absoluto Déspota, y tirano, hta. que por haverse corrompido la agua con los muertos que pasaron de ciento.
>
> [their dead brothers' bodies . . . thrown in the field and eaten by animals. Witnessing such inhumanity, they decided to ask the cruel Commander Elizondo permission to bury the bodies themselves. But this he refused, telling them that "the men were condemned as traitors to the King and *patria*." . . . These unfortunate patriotic women with their tortured souls remained at this infernal site for several days—suffering what horrid actions could be expected from the bitter, bloody defenders of an absolutist, Despotic, tyrant King. They remained there until the water became stagnant with the bodies of the dead, which surpassed a hundred.] (4)

Elizondo's blood-soaked retribution was so maddening, recalled another witness, that it affected even his own men. The day after the executions, Captain Manuel Serrano, "who felt grieved at the barbarious [*sic*] manner in which the men had been killed, deliberately walked into Elizondo's tent, shot him dead," and attempted to kill another commander before being captured. "They tied him and brought him to San Antonio a raving maniac."[103] The remaining men and 114 women and children were marched by the now commander-less royalists back to San Antonio.

Once in San Antonio, they faced "one-eyed" Arredondo, who forced them to wade across the San Antonio River on their way to jail while soldiers degraded them. The "Memoria de las cosas" quotes the soldiers' taunts: "tan tapaditas que van, que parece que tienen tanta vergüenza, ¿como no la tenían para andar con las pistolas matando gente [hah, now you cover yourselves so well, little ones, that you act almost as if you're ashamed. How is it that you didn't have any shame going around with guns killing people]?" For fifty-four cruel days the women were forced to live in the crowded jail known as the *quinta,* where they were forced to grind corn and make 3,500 tortillas a day for Arredondo's 1,000 troops (see Figure 44).[104] They worked from 2 a.m. until 10 p.m. and were prevented from resting. The soldiers also did not allow the boiled and limed corn to cool, forcing the women to grind the hot kernels with their bare feet.

The narrative refuses to conceal any detail. The women's feet were scalded, their toenails fell off, the skin on their feet and legs sloughed off, "y corriendo la viva sangre que se mesclaba con el maiz que refregaban, hta. hacer perdido la vida una muger [and the running blood mixed with the corn that they ground, until one woman finally lost her life]." But here, the author or authors later returned to the manuscript and revised it, and after the words "until one woman," inserted a caret and added the following text: "llamada Cribanta [a] quien [se le] ca[yó la piel de] las palmas y uñas de las manos [named Cribanta whose skin from her palms and her fingernails fell off]." The author was determined to bear witness to the horrid events, even revising the text so that the names of the victims would not be forgotten. Yet such cruelty was only the beginning.

The narrative continues in excruciating detail, forcing the reader to confront the unfolding trauma:

Figure 44. Sketchpad drawing of the *quinta* from the 1850s where the revolutionary women of San Antonio were imprisoned in 1813.

Morgan Wolfe Merrick Civil War journal and drawings. Gift of Mr. and Mrs. Stanley J. Miller Jr. in memory of Mrs. Lee B. Miller, Daughters of the Republic of Texas Library, SC504.27.

> Durante el día, y mientras ntras. mexicanas desempeñaban tan penosa fatiga el guardián Acosta no sesaba de imbentar medios para castigarlas, mortificarlas, é infamarlas, diciéndoles las mas descaradas desverguenzas, dándoles asotes á su antojo, y no dejando á las que se hayaban criando dar el pecho á sus niños; que lloraban de ambre, y aun uno de ellos murió á la vista; de este inhumano Nerón; que se complacía, en abergonsarlas afligirlas y mortificarlas, de mil modos, y con las palabras mas groseras, y acciones las impuras, indecentes y feas, que causa rubor decirlas, escribirlas, y ni aun el papel no las conciente. . . . [Al fin mandó los niños a la calle, y sus madres les dijeron,] Pidan limosna por hai en las casas. Con tan tierna dulce y amorosa despedida se separaron las madres de sus hijos, y estos de sus madres, hechos todos un mar de lagrimas, menos el tirano, que se complacía con tan hermoso cuadro, y con rabia las volvio á los metates diciéndoles con una furia infernal "*cárguense putas que aquí esta su Dios, yo soy el Dios de las putas.*["] Y corría de punta á punta de los metates azotándolas á todas, callando estas, sufriendo, y moliendo. Vengan mexicanas amantes de su Patria á aprehender a padecer por la libertad é Independencia.
>
> [During the day, and while our Mexican women discharged such painful toil, the guard Acosta worked arduously at inventing new methods of punishment in order to mortify and defame them, using the most brazen, shameless words, whipping them at his whim, and not allowing those with infants to breastfeed, whose children cried of hunger and one of whom died in plain view. From this inhuman Nero, who enjoyed embarrassing, afflicting, and mortifying them in a thousand ways, and with the crudest words and the most impure, indecent, and ugly actions, that they cause one to blush to say them, to write them, that not even the paper will permit them to be written down. . . . [At last he forced their children out into the street, and their mothers told them,] go beg house to house asking for alms for food. And with such a tenderly sweet and loving farewell they left their mothers, who were all left in a sea of tears, except the tyrant, who took great pleasure in viewing such a beautiful scene. He forced them back to [grinding corn on] the *metates,*[105] telling them with an infernal fury, "*get to praying, you whores, because your God has arrived; I am the God of the whores.*" And he ran from end to end of the *metates* whipping all of them, these, becoming silent, suffering, and grinding. [And he said to them:] Come now, my dear Mexican women, lovers of your *Patria,* come learn to suffer your liberty and Independence."] (8–9, 10–11, emphasis in original)

The narrative abounds with such concrete details—from the names of the individuals killed to extensive dialogue, especially between the women and royal officers—that the reader is forced to relive this sad eclipse of the revolution. The *Memoria* was written, the author or authors state at the beginning, so that the public would be aware of how the residents of Texas had suffered and struggled for independence. Tragically, however, this testimony had been lost virtually ever since it was composed. The manuscript resides in the archival collection of Herbert Eugene Bolton, the well-known early twentieth-century historian of the Spanish borderlands, and is part of the University of California Bancroft Library's collection. And yet Julia K. Garrett is one of the only historians, if not *the* only one, to have cited this testimony.[106] And in a rather bizarre act of historical documentation, considering the traumatic experiences these women underwent, Garrett merely states that the women were forced to "grind corn and make tortillas . . . while their children were driven into the streets to beg."[107]

For two centuries, their story had been nearly forgotten, their sacrifices in the name of liberty unnoticed. With Arredondo's victory, the revolutionary world of José Bernardo Gutiérrez de Lara reached a dead end. As we will see, like so many other world-transforming events in nineteenth-century Texas, the intellectual legacy of this period ended in an instant. This rupture, the suddenness of the revolutionaries' failure, is part of the reason that historians have long ignored these events. Independence in Texas failed to sustain itself and did not lead to the independence of Mexico. Yet the ideas that circulated in Texas would forever transform the lives of Spanish Americans. Decades later, as the Spanish-American Texans themselves transformed and began to identify as Texas Mexicans, they would still remember in detail the events of the period.[108]

The revolutionary documents that entered Texas let loose a whirlwind of old and new ideas. The resurrected Suarezian ideas of sovereignty and the *corpus mysticum* resonated profoundly for the *pueblos* of Texas, as did the innovative republican structures of the constitution. Yet while their social world had convulsed, their social imaginary had not yet settled, and the resurrected revolutionary ideas had not and would not seep deeply until decades later. As we have seen, the clash of ideas led to a brutality on all sides that was all too devastating. As for Bernardo, he would stay in Natchitoches and New Orleans until 1821, where he lived with his family, continuing to seek ways to gain Mexico's independence.[109] With Arredondo's boot on their neck, the *pueblos* would not attempt to fight for independence again. It would be another eight years before independence would arrive in Texas. This time it would come from the south, from Mexico City.

IV

THE ENTRANCE OF LIFE INTO HISTORY

CHAPTER SEVEN

"To the Advocates of Enlightenment and Reason"

From Subjects to Citizens

From Spanish Defeat to Mexican Independence

For nearly a decade, the bleached bones of the 1813 insurgent forces lay strewn across the fields outside San Antonio. The Spanish commandant general of the Eastern Interior Provinces, Joaquín de Arredondo, had unleashed his fury on the insurrectionists in Texas along with those in the surrounding provinces of Nuevo Santander, Nuevo León, and Coahuila, with mass executions, torture, rape, the confiscation of property, and the complete crippling of all towns in his path.[1] The four major Spanish-American centers in Texas were devastated.

Nacogdoches in east Texas was a virtual ghost town; most of the inhabitants had fled to Louisiana in August 1813, upon hearing of Arredondo's pending arrival (see Figure 7). Trinidad had been burned to the ground by the Spanish royal forces. La Bahía, located 100 miles downriver from San Antonio, and which had provided forces to aid Anglo-Americans during their revolutionary war, was left so destitute that its inhabitants repeatedly pleaded for support, and wrote that they were often forced to forage for food.[2] San Antonio had also been crippled by Arredondo's wrath.

Restoring Spanish rule came at a steep price. Soldiers and citizens had both supported the insurrection, and upon Arredondo's brutal conquest in 1813, many in Texas had fled to Louisiana. Those further south of Texas had abandoned their towns and lived in the surrounding depopulated mountains. The revolutionary battles had also disrupted the trade and treaties that had secured some peace with the ever-powerful Comanches from central and west Texas who had recently allied with Lipan Apaches. As a result, the tribes had renewed their devastating attacks on Spanish Americans. Yet even as the Spanish-American ranchers began to return to their homes in 1814, the news that José Bernardo Gutiérrez de Lara and José Álvarez de Toledo were planning more insurrections in Louisiana forced them to abandon their property and move into the neighboring towns. Royalists, revolutionaries, and Native Americans had all encroached upon cattle ranchers, who were the economic mainstay of the province. One rancher claimed he alone had lost more than 10,000 head of cattle. The battles and renewed Native American raids forced ranchers to leave their homes, leading to a meat shortage. Texas was now on the brink of starvation. Paranoia and fear swept over everyone. In an effort to calm fears and establish order, the new governor of Texas, Cristóbal Domínguez, in 1814 implemented new laws: trash was not to be burned, guns not to be discharged, strict curfews were put in place, all trade banned, yelling was forbidden, and changings of residence required approval from the *cabildo* (town council).[3]

As a way to restore order, Arredondo began offering pardons to many insurgents, forcing them to provide extensive testimony on their actions and to prove their loyalty. Others, however, he refused to pardon, such as the elite San Antonio families of the Arochas, Traviesos, Veramendis, and Seguíns. As punishment for having supported insurrection, he confiscated their property. But over the next several years, many slowly returned, and after testifying that they had been forced to support the insurrection, some were able to regain their property.[4]

Arredondo must have felt satisfied with himself. Not only had royal authority been reestablished in New Spain, but even in his *patria* the liberal Cortes of Cádiz with their liberal constitution of 1812 had all been put in their place. Spain at last defeated and expelled the French in March of 1814, and King Fernando VII promptly shred the Cortes and its constitution, arresting most of its liberal representatives. Absolutism had been restored in Spain, just as it had been in Spanish Texas. "From 1814 to 1820," writes Gabriel H. Lovett, "Spain was to live years of counterrevolutionary terror and black reaction, without any protest from those who supposedly wanted to 'renovate' the country. . . . The clock was turned back."[5] The situation was not that different in Texas.

Still, the residents of Texas persisted in spreading revolutionary ideas. Arredondo's plan to placate them by pardoning insurgents backfired: "Officials in San Antonio soon complained that the pardoned Insurgents in the city continued to spread their dangerous doctrines and aided [Anglo-] American prisoners to escape." As a result, officials forced many of them to immigrate to the interior of Mexico.[6] But the revolutionary ideas were never far away.

Exiled revolutionaries from throughout the Gulf of Mexico and abroad—Spaniards and Spanish Americans, along with French, Anglo-Americans, Haitians—had all descended upon New Orleans and other parts of Louisiana. New Orleans had become a beacon for exiles, just as Philadelphia had been a few years prior. Some thirsting for glory and wealth, others for liberty, these filibusters concocted several plans to help liberate Texas. From 1815 through 1821, the year Mexico gained independence, more than three serious yet ultimately failed attempts to declare Texas independent were launched from Louisiana. Some were well orchestrated, but most were confused, short-lived vainglorious efforts on the part of filibusters in search of land and fame.[7]

Notwithstanding the filibusters' efforts, Arredondo felt he had sufficiently pacified Texas. Or so he wrote to his superiors repeatedly through 1820, in an attempt to persuade them. Rumblings may have occurred off the Texas Gulf Coast, but all was placid in the interior towns of Texas. Still, as the historian Raúl A. Ramos notes, "peace came at a considerable price for Arredondo, requiring him to spend three-quarters of his military budget on Texas over the three other provinces under his command."[8] By the end of his reign of terror in 1821, the province of Texas had been reduced to a mere shadow of itself. The non-Native population in Texas had been reduced by more than half, from over 4,000 in 1803 to less than 2,000 in 1820.[9]

Independence arrived in Mexico in 1821. But unlike the short-lived republic of Texas in 1813, Mexican independence had been secured through an odd alliance between conservatives and revolutionaries. Absolutism had returned to Spain, but disaffection had grown to a pitch by 1820. Influenced by the liberal Cortes and newly created Spanish Masonic lodges, the royal army rose in rebellion, forcing the king to accept the liberal constitution of 1812. Back in Mexico, the conservatives feared the possible changes that would come under the liberal constitution. They hedged their bets, allied with the revolutionaries, and declared independence in 1821. Under the now famous Plan of Iguala of February 24, three guarantees were made: Mexico would now become a constitutional monarchy, social equality for all was guaranteed, and the Roman Catholic Church would be the official religion of Mexico. The treaty was confirmed on August 24, 1821, making Mexico independent, and the Mexican-born Agustín de Iturbide was crowned emperor of the Mexican empire. By August 1822, the first Mexican-appointed governor of Texas was making his way to the state.[10]

The new Texas governor, José Félix Trespalacios, had been, like Bernardo, a revolutionary from the northern provinces of New Spain. In 1811, Trespalacios was a royal soldier in Chihuahua when he learned of Father Miguel Hidalgo's insurrection. He immediately supported the revolution, was captured, arrested, and sent to the infamous fortress-prison of San Juan de Ulúa in Veracruz. He escaped twice, and managed to make his way to that bastion of exiles, New Orleans, where he, along with Bernardo and other ex-patriot Mexican revolutionaries, made several plans to gain Mexico's independence.[11] Now, in 1822, both of the revolutionaries had been appointed governors by the new government in Mexico City. Since his departure back in September 1811, Bernardo had not seen his home. But now, some eleven years later, he returned a recognized hero of independence. He accepted the position of governor of Tamaulipas (what had been the colonial province of Nuevo Santander) where he would remain active in politics until his death in 1841.[12]

Governor Trespalacios paused before entering the capital of San Antonio. There, on the outskirts of the city, one of his first acts was to bury the remains of the 1813 insurgents. "He gave burial to almost all the dead which were found," wrote a contemporary witness. "A cross carved in the trunk of [a] live oak indicates the site of the grave. Placed at the height of a man's head, renewed from time to time by the soldiers of the presidio who carve it as deep as the wood, it seems to be freshly engraved."[13]

Upon his arrival in San Antonio on August 25, 1822, Trespalacios immediately sent his aide, Juan Almonte, to New Orleans to procure much-needed supplies for an utterly impoverished Texas. One of the governor's most-desired items: a printing press. There had been very little interest—or financial means, for that matter—to acquire a press prior to Trespalacios. The documents that Bernardo dispersed into Texas, for example, had been handwritten or printed in Natchitoches, Louisiana, or on the East Coast. As to the fate of the press that Bernardo had brought to Natchitoches in 1812, nothing is known. But the first known press to have entered Texas came with Álvarez de Toledo in 1813 which he used, as we have seen, to print the first single-issue newspaper of Texas, the *Gaceta de Texas,* the defamatory paper used to help depose Bernardo. Then, in the course of the 1810s, a filibuster venture brought with it Texas's second known printing press. There would be, through 1835, no more than one press in operation however.[14]

The Spaniard Francisco Xavier Mina had risen against Napoleon Bonaparte in 1808, and he quickly joined Spanish liberals in their effort to save their nation. But upon the restoration of absolutism he was forced to flee to London. There, he met the famed Mexican insurgent Fray Servando

Teresa de Mier. Like Fathers José Antonio Gutiérrez de Lara and Miguel Ramos Arizpe, Mier was born and educated in Monterrey, and later became a fiery priest in Mexico City. There he had preached that the Americas had been converted to Christianity prior to the Spaniards' arrival, a blasphemous argument that undid the very rationale of Spanish colonization. Mier was arrested and sentenced to exile, but managed to escape, too, to London. He collaborated with Mina, and with British support they orchestrated an invasion of the sparsely populated Texas coast in late 1816. The filibusters landed in Galveston with a press, and, following well-established precedent, printed broadsides to disperse to a missing population. So, they continued down the coast to the populated Nuevo Santander coast, distributed their papers, and managed to defeat the local royal forces. Arredondo, however, quickly sprang into action. Mina and his forces were finally captured in October 1817. Arredondo quickly executed most of them, and shipped the rest off to Mexico City.[15]

But of all the prisoners, only one man was forced to march inland to Monterrey with Arredondo. The man was Samuel Bangs, an Anglo-American from Baltimore who was one of many to join the filibusters. He also happened to be the man who had served as the printer of the broadsides on the small press that Mina had acquired in London. Print technology in Europe and the Americas had only started to improve with the first cast-iron presses at the turn of the century, but these were still heavy, cumbersome equipment to transport. Mina's, then, was a standard wooden press with some iron components, and these presses would continue to be used well into the early twentieth century (see Figure 45).[16] For months Bangs lived in Monterrey in uncertainty, kept separate from other prisoners and forced to work as a cobbler. Finally, one day one of Arredondo's men allowed Bangs to bathe in the river and change clothes, before placing him in a room with something he quickly recognized: it was the small press that Mina had acquired in London. Arredondo had disobeyed an explicit order to send all books, documents, and printing presses to Mexico City. Clearly he thought the press was important, given that he spared Bangs's life and disobeyed the viceroy's orders. It had taken him months to locate the press among the filibusters' belongings on the coast. Now, Bangs and the press were reunited.[17]

The first two presses to enter Texas, Álvarez de Toledo's and Mina's, came from Louisiana. But Mina's, which had landed at Galveston and then made its way down the coast to Tamaulipas, was also the first press to enter Tamaulipas; it was now the first in Nuevo Leon, and, later, would be moved from Monterrey, Nuevo Leon, to Saltillo, Coahuila. Arredondo immediately put Bangs to work, forcing him to churn out a very different genre of imprints. From 1817 until 1822, Bangs would continue doing so as a prisoner, earning barely enough to feed himself.[18]

Several years later, in 1822, amidst profound poverty and desolation, Trespalacios used his government's scarce resources for a printing press. Both he and Arredondo, from near opposite ends of the political spectrum, recognized the importance of the press. What did print technology represent for Arredondo and Trespalacios? And what did it mean to the inhabitants of Texas?

Historians of print culture no longer take for granted the role of print technology in cultural formations. The narrative had long been established: print technology allowed for the democratization of writing and knowledge; it was the medium through which the Enlightenment and republican forms of government arose; and it was the foundation of our modernity.[19] As we assess the ideological importance of the printing press, it is easy to get carried away. The fact that the printing press facilitated the

Figure 45. Francisco Xavier Mina's 1817 press. The second press to enter Texas.

rise of the modern concepts of the public sphere, nationalism, individualism, and human rights has allowed for a certain kind of technological determinism; it is easy to assume that print technology's natural, essential ideological function is as a tool of liberal democratization.[20] As Michael Warner has argued: "By attributing social changes of great scale partly to printing, [certain] historians follow a model in which the logic of the technology is seen to 'press on and impress both on social activity and human consciousness.' This kind of technological determinism must suppose, therefore, that a technology could come about, already equipped with its 'logic,' *before* it impinged on human consciousness and *before* it became a symbolic action."[21] That is, print technology does not merely arrive and set out to transform societies, liberating them from darkness, as if these social worlds were passive objects upon which print technology did its work. Rather, the printed word is incorporated into a culture's already existing systems of symbolic signification. Though Mina's press was one of the first to enter Texas, the dissemination of imprints need not necessarily represent some significant shift in the inhabitants' social imaginary. We should turn instead to the meaning of the printing press and its relationship to already existing forms of communication.

Writing and print had long served as symbols of authority, and Arredondo had no intention of loosening his grip on that sovereignty. With Trespalacios, however, we begin to see a shift in the uses of the press and writing. Ideas that had once been considered abominations, worthy of execution, were now fully embraced by the governor. But this shift in thinking, though begun earlier with Bernardo, had not fully penetrated the social imaginary. By the 1830s, though, we begin to see a radical shift in the way the people of Texas thought about themselves. An epistemic shift, one that had been unfolding since Father Antonio Gutiérrez de Lara had taught the first modern philosophy course in Monterrey, had at last given way. The residual, fixed, hierarchical world gave way to a new modern episteme. Now, the social body and its longevity would take center stage. Where writing had once stood as the voice of an external sovereignty, one descending down from God, monarch, viceroy, to Arredondo, writing now becomes a means of producing sovereignty from the ground up. Let us begin, then, with how Arredondo and Trespalacios put the press to use.

Writing and the Word of the Sovereign

Arredondo and Trespalacios, as we will see, used the press in similar ways, but they did so with quite different notions of what the imprints should do. At first, Arredondo limited Bangs to more banal documents: various kinds of cards, letterhead, passports, and governmental forms, all of which he began printing in early 1820. Slowly, however, he expanded the press's repertoire, and had Bangs reprint official, royal announcements he received from Mexico City, such as the marriage between King Fernando VII and María Josefa Amalia of Saxony. As the historian Lota M. Spells notes, "Only slowly did the Commandant realize the wider use to which the press could be put."[22]

Indeed, the way Arredondo used the press responded to huge shifts in the Hispanic world. In mid-May 1820, Arredondo received news from the viceroy of New Spain announcing that King Fernando VII had taken an oath supporting the liberal constitution of 1812, thus ending absolutism and establishing a constitutional monarchy.[23] But rather than having the announcement reprinted as he usually had, Arredondo delayed publication.[24] Several weeks later, he received yet more news. All officials were to publicly support the liberal constitution. With that, Arrendondo did the unavoidable: he at last had the proclamation printed and dispersed throughout the Eastern Interior Provinces, and promptly went to church where he took the new oath and attended mass. From then on, Arredondo kept Bangs busy, having him print all of his proclamations and decrees, dispersing them, as well, to all four of the Eastern Interior Provinces under his command, including Texas.[25]

The printed proclamations, like most of the documents we discussed in Chapter 6, were meant to be read aloud to the inhabitants of the northern provinces. As in other parts of Spanish America, they would have been posted in public places. But they were also performed. The *pregonero* or town crier would have read them aloud in the town square or on the steps of the church, announcing the reading with the sound of a drum, trumpet, or church bells.[26] The same had occurred, as we have seen, with Bernardo's revolutionary literature, read aloud at the homes of prominent families.

Arredondo's imprints reveal that he used the press as an extension of the handwritten manuscript, the form that would have been utilized otherwise. As in other parts of Spanish America, handwritten documents had been the common practice of disseminating news. If official printed documents circulated, they would have been printed in Mexico City or Spain. In Texas, from the Spanish colonial period through the early Mexican period in the 1830s, the most common imprints to circulate were not books but rather decrees, circulars, and other official, state documents. And then these, along with the endless stream of royal manuscripts—official letters written on sealed, taxed, stamped paper—were publicized. From the colonial period through the early nineteenth century, manuscripts had circulated

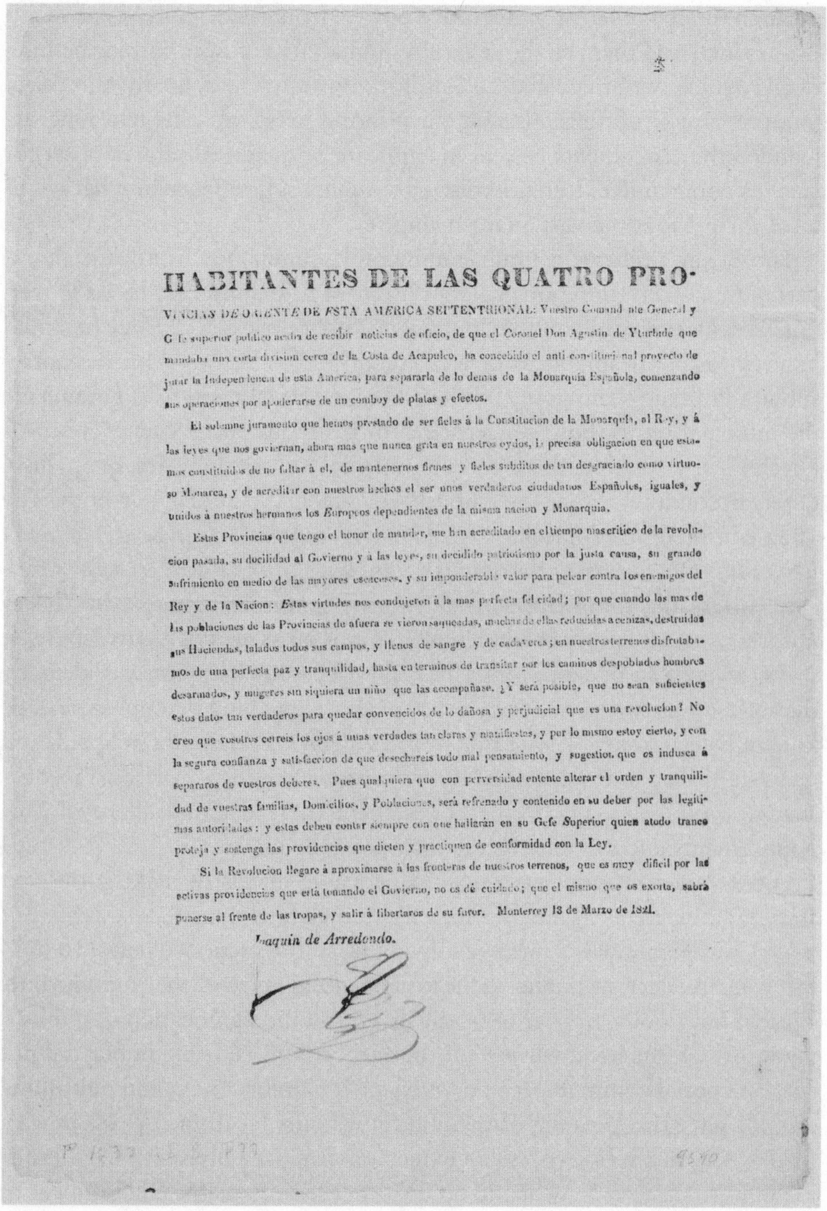

HABITANTES DE LAS QUATRO PROVINCIAS DE ORIENTE DE ESTA AMERICA SEPTENTRIONAL: Vuestro Comandante General y Gefe superior politico acaba de recibir noticias de oficio, de que el Coronel Don Agustin de Yturbide que mandaba una corta division cerca de la Costa de Acapulco, ha concebido el anti-constitucional proyecto de jurar la Independencia de esta America, para separarla de lo demas de la Monarquía Española, comenzando sus operaciones por apoderarse de un comboy de platas y efectos.

El solemne juramento que hemos prestado de ser fieles á la Constitucion de la Monarquía, al Rey, y á las leyes que nos goviernan, ahora mas que nunca grata en nuestros oydos, la precisa obligacion en que estamos constituidos de no faltar á el, de mantenernos firmes y fieles subditos de tan desgraciado como virtuoso Monarca, y de acreditar con nuestros hechos el ser unos verdaderos ciudadanos Españoles, iguales, y unidos á nuestros hermanos los Europeos dependientes de la misma nacion y Monarquia.

Estas Provincias que tengo el honor de mandar, me han acreditado en el tiempo mas critico de la revolucion pasada, su docilidad al Govierno y á las leyes, su decidido patriotismo por la justa causa, su grande sufrimiento en medio de las mayores escaceses, y su imponderable valor para pelear contra los enemigos del Rey y de la Nacion: Estas virtudes nos condujeron á la mas perfecta felicidad; por que cuando las mas de las poblaciones de las Provincias de afuera se vieron saqueadas, muchas de ellas reducidas a cenizas, destruidas sus Haciendas, talados todos sus campos, y llenos de sangre y de cadaveres; en nuestros terrenos disfrutabamos de una perfecta paz y tranquilidad, hasta en terminos de transitar por los caminos despoblados hombres desarmados, y mugeres sin siquiera un niño que las acompañase. ¿Y será posible, que no sean suficientes estos datos tan verdaderos para quedar convencidos de lo dañosa y perjudicial que es una revolucion? No creo que vosotros cerreis los ojos á unas verdades tan claras y manifiestas, y por lo mismo estoy cierto, y con la segura confianza y satisfaccion de que desechareis todo mal pensamiento, y sugestion que os indusca á separaros de vuestros deberes. Pues qualquiera que con perversidad entente alterar el orden y tranquilidad de vuestras familias, Domicilios, y Poblaciones, será refrenado y contenido en su deber por las legitimas autoridades: y estas deben contar siempre con que hallarán en su Gefe Superior quien atodo trance proteja y sostenga las providencias que dicten y practiquen de conformidad con la Ley.

Si la Revolucion llegare á aproximarse á las fronteras de nuestros terrenos, que es muy dificil por las activas providencias que está tomando el Govierno, no es dé cuidado; que el mismo que os exorta, sabrá ponerse al frente de las tropas, y salir á libertaros de su furor. Monterrey 13 de Marzo de 1821.

Joaquin de Arredondo.

Figure 46. Broadside meant to be read aloud. Joaquín de Arredondo, *Habitantes de las quatro provincias de Oriente de esta America septentrional* (printed by Samuel Bangs, November 20, 1820).

Vault F1232.I8 P77. The DeGoyler Library, Southern Methodist University.

through the centers of administrative power: from Madrid, to Mexico City, Chihuahua, and then, as the seat of administrative power within the Interior Provinces was relocated, to Saltillo, Monterrey, and, finally, San Antonio, the capital of Texas. Lacking a printing press, officials had long demanded that documents be sent in triplicate or quadruplicate, in order for various commanders to retain discursive, material evidence of what circulated throughout the vast Spanish empire.

The Bexar Archives contain innumerable commands from officials ordering that a certain report, whether in print or manuscript, be, as Governor Trespalacios commanded, "publicado" or "publicized" by "hac[iendola] fixar en los parajes publicos de esta ciudad y comunicarla aquienes corresponda [affixing them in the public places in this city and to communicate the information to those concerned]." In many instances, they were to be "hecho leer a los soldados [read aloud to the soldiers]."[27] Yet, in Spanish, *publicar* connotes either "to publish" or "to make public," or both. The 1822 edition of the *Diccionario de la lengua española de la Real Academia Española (Dictionary of the Spanish Language of the Royal Spanish Academy)* offers the following as the primary definition of *publicar:* "hacer notoria ó patente por voz de pregonero ó por otros medios alguna cosa que se desea venga a noticia de todos [to make well known or clearly evident, by the voice of the town crier or by other media, something that one desires be known by everyone]."[28] The role of the *pregonero* originates in Spain, and was established at the outset of the colonization of the Americas. *Pregoneros* were officials paid by the government to read aloud all royal pronouncements and any acts by the local town council.[29]

For Arredondo, printing a document was a means of making the text state-sanctioned, as in the printing of letterhead, passports, and so on. But it also, by default, was a means of divulging state-sanctioned news. To publish was, in effect, to publicize the synchronized voice of the Church-state. This, in fact, would appear to be the inverse of the signification of publishing in British America, where "for the early colonists, being public did not entail a special communicative context such as publication, and publishing did not have the meaning of making things public." In fact, publishing in British America was seen "as an extension of personal visitation."[30] Printing in northeastern New Spain, on the other hand, was the embodiment of the voice of sovereignty, of the Church and state. Yet printing in itself was not enough for a document to be considered published or publicized. It had to be read aloud and received communally by the townspeople.

As the eyes of Church officials dictated the laity's relationship to the word of God, so too with the secular word. Official state news was just as often disseminated within a church as it was in the town square. This had been the case, for example, with Arredondo's taking the oath to the 1812 Constitution. The printed proclamation was first posted and read aloud in the town square, after which Arredondo, members of the *ayuntamiento*, and the bishop crossed the square to the steps of the cathedral, where everyone took the oath.[31] The relationship between the written word, in handwritten manuscript or print form, and the community was not one of transparent representation; rather, it was one of authority. The written word represented the will of the Church and state, two institutions that had long served as mutually reinforcing forms of sovereignity.[32] Thus, in 1822, it was no contradiction whatsoever for Governor Trespalacios to receive an order from the minister of justice and ecclesiastical affairs of the newly independent Mexican empire to command all priests to educate the people as to their sociopolitical duties and to instill in them a sense of national belonging.[33]

This is not to say, however, that texts were always authoritative, or held total coercive control over the townspeople. Once a document was released, that is, read aloud, the ideas conveyed were mediated by the discursive world of each listener: murmurs, gasps, whispers, and gossip could quickly transform the intent of a text. This alternative discursive world, an oral one, is difficult, though not impossible, to trace. It exists within the written archive as traces, ghosts, darting in and around the visible, written script.[34]

The printing press under Arredondo, then, did not serve as a means to reconfigure social relations in any way, much less did it alter any sense of the public as it had existed prior to the press's arrival. Print technology served as a means to consolidate Church and state power. The most common printed documents to circulate throughout northern New Spain prior to independence were state-sanctioned, originating in Mexico City or Spain; no surprise then that Arredondo recognized the symbolic power of the printing press, and decided to harness that power, both discursive and political, for himself. Indeed, as we have seen, Arredondo, as the commandant general of the Eastern Interior Provinces, held just as much power, if not more, than the viceroy of New Spain. Ignoring the viceroy's order to ship the press and keeping it for himself, then, was a defiant conscious decision to seize the power of the press.

Arredondo refused to loosen his despotic grip on the Eastern Interior Provinces. Upon learning of the Plan of Iguala, he had Bangs print and distribute a proclamation throughout the provinces on March 13, 1821. In it, Arredondo arrogantly claimed that he knew he could count on his subjects' loyalty to the Spanish regime, and he pompously claimed that the insurgents (who in actuality were now the leaders of an independent Mexico) would be repelled. He, like Manuel Salcedo and other officials, viewed his subjects as an entity, as the *pueblo,* the *corpus mysticum.* They saw them as a mystical body that needed guidance and authority from above. Having superciliously informed the *pueblo* of their undying loyalty, he then took restrictive measures to ensure they followed through: travel was forbidden without passports and no type of writing, whether handwritten or in print, was allowed to circulate throughout the provinces. Within three months, however, as the insurgent troops approached, Arredondo, realizing resistance was futile, quickly abandoned Monterrey and easily slipped out of Mexico, heading for Cuba.[35]

With independence, the use of the press in Texas and northern Mexico did not alter radically. For several years after 1821, it continued to be used to disseminate the administrative needs of the newly established Mexican nation-state. Broadsides were printed announcing new regulations, the creation of various committees to produce a state constitution, the regulation of trade, and other state-sanctioned activities.[36] From the colonial period through early independence, therefore, the press functioned in northern New Spain as a metonym for official, Church and state-sanctioned political authority.

Under Spanish colonial rule, the printing press was univocal, synonymous with the official voice of the Church and state. The press became one of the tools used by the *caudillos,* the famous and infamous political-military rulers of Spanish America who imagined, through writing and action, the creation and spread of Spanish-American civilization across the Americas. Salcedo, for example, had desperately sought to prevent the revolutionary literature from "seducing" his subjects. Often, the Texas governors would catalogue the imprints received, creating a scrapbook-like notebook for each year, with the month noted in elegant script centered on a full page followed by a meticulous recording of each document's number, date, and a brief summary.[37]

Authorities did their best to secure the press's univocality, and though the officials of the state and Inquisition may have fared better in managing to prevent the printing of unauthorized documents, they failed to completely thwart the circulation of texts produced elsewhere. Thus, though the first periodicals emerged in New Spain in 1722, these were official, Church-sanctioned papers, under the control of the censor, and reported primarily ecclesiastical, economic, scientific, and governmental administrative news. Not until the era of independence would they become the tools of a far more expansive, diverse group of people beyond those associated with the Church and state.[38]

As we know, in Protestant northern Europe and British America, the eighteenth-century merchant class-cum-bourgeoisie slowly created a dis-

Figure 47. J. Finlayson, "Mexico and Internal Provinces" (1822). 17.8 × 22.5 in. No. 76189. Texas General Land Office.

cursive space for themselves in discussions central to the state. Following this northwestern European trajectory, Jürgen Habermas sees the advent of periodicals and creation of a reading public as central to the rise of a public sphere, a world where editors, journalists, and readers began publishing news related first to commerce, then to aesthetic questions and, finally, by the late eighteenth century, to the sociopolitical affairs of the state. Gradually, they used this growing political authority to take control of the state.[39]

In New Spain, by contrast, the press remained always within the control of the Church and state. Officials did everything in their power to regulate the dissemination of all nondoctrinal discourse, to prevent the free-flowing potential of the press. They were enemies, in other words, of multivocality, of the invariably messy presence of more than one printed perspective. For example, following the spread of rumors regarding a possible coup in postindependence Mexico, officials circulated in Texas and the rest of the Interior Provinces fifty copies of a broadside, instructing officials to publicize them so that the inhabitants would "cerrar los oidos a noticias exageradas [close their ears to exaggerated news]."[40]

In Spanish Texas, the spread of Church-state news (via print or manuscript) was the circulation of the most public, most supreme form of political authority. It was a hierarchical world where the *logos* descended down from God, and thus always mediated in order to assure appropriate interpretation by the masses. In this way, we may arrive at the significance of the Spanish-American political expression "obedezco pero no cumplo [I obey, but do not comply]." That is, the written word was never the sole authority. Its origin was divine and sovereign. But the divine, so the Church proclaimed, was also ethereal, intangible, sublime, affective, and nonlinguistic, as the Baroque aesthetic so wonderfully captures it.[41] The written word was respected, but its truth was always qualified, mediated by other nonscript systems of signification. Therefore, it was impossible to find knowledge just by reading the written word, as the Protestants so adamantly believed. The senses, the sublime, the spiritual, indeed, spirits, demons, saints, inhabited the world as well. They contributed to the understanding of the everyday, and participated in it.

The sign's dividing line between signified and signifier must be augmented, opening up (or returning to) a ternary level of meaning-making, as we saw in Chapter 1.[42] There, in that discursive gap between signified and signifier, is where spirits and the ineffably sublime coexist, participating just as much in the making of the sign. Printing and publication, then, did not wield total and complete authority. Printing was seen as originating hierarchically from supreme political powers, and represented the univocal authority of the Church-state. But it was always mediated by competing, though subaltern, discourses. Allowing freedom of the press meant the press would become multivocal; non-Church- and non-state-authorized voices would exist alongside the immutable word of God. To do this, though, would mean reconfiguring if not collapsing this episteme. It would tear asunder the ontological status between knowledge and the divine, placing humans as the sole authors of knowledge. This was the world that Salcedo, Arredondo, and countless others could not countenance or imagine.

Printing and the Making of Citizens in Postindependence Texas

On August 23, 1822, Governor José Félix Trespalacios set up camp on the Medina River, just twenty miles south of San Antonio. He was scheduled to arrive as the first governor of the postindependence province of Texas. The Medina had long served as the final resting point for travelers approaching San Antonio, and was, in fact, the same site where Arredondo had slaughtered more than 1,000 Texas revolutionaries in 1813. Now, ten years later, Trespalacios buried what remained of their bodies, as noted earlier, and also sent a letter in advance to the San Antonio town council informing them that he would arrive the following day prepared to "encargarme del Govierno Politico y Militar de esta Provincia que la Superioridad se ha dignado conferirme [take charge of the political and military governmental affairs of this Province with which the Superior powers have dignified me by conferring them to me]."[43]

Two days later, once in San Antonio, he wrote his first proclamation to the inhabitants of Texas (see Figure 48). The printing press had yet to arrive; thus, he sent handwritten copies to the town councils of San Antonio and La Bahía along with copies to the state's military forts, with an order that the officials "hara[n] publicar y fixar en los parajes publicos acostumbrados de cada ciudad [have them published and posted in the usual public spaces of each city]."[44] With all the optimism of a once-vilified revolutionary who had now been redeemed, Trespalacios addressed the residents of Texas:

> Sois libres: en tal concepto bien podeis criticar mis hechos sin temor de ser incomodados ni en buestras personas ni en btra opinion: si lo hicieseis con justicia cedere docilm.te a btras. razones y si lo hicieseis sin ella vos combencerse con las mias: vosotros debeis estar siempre atentos ami proceder y acercandose ami como a un amigo, adbertirme lo conduciente al acierto en que todos estamos interesados. Vais a tratar librem.te con las demas Naciones y espero q. con buestras virtudes sociales les infundais confianza y acreditais esta nueba que bá a pareser sobre la fáz del Universo.

> [You are free: as such, you may criticize my actions without fear of being inconvenienced neither in body nor in your opinion: if you should do it with justice I shall docilely cede to your reasons and should you do it without it I will convince you with mine: you should always be attentive to my actions

and consider me a friend, suggest to me that which will lead to the best decisions in matters in which we are all concerned. You are going to freely engage with other Nations, and I hope that your social virtues will instill confidence and make credible this new nation that will soon appear on the face of the Universe.][45]

With those two words, "sois libres [you are free]," Trespalacios attempted to create a rupture in historical time. But it was one that Bernardo had initiated with the circulation of revolutionary literature. The language in those documents certainly must have startled the people in Texas even as many embraced it, but it was one whose vision ultimately ended in brutal defeat. Yet, if that initial occasion was surreptitiously introduced by insurgents, this time it was proclaimed by none other than the figure of the sovereign. Trespalacios had arrived and imposed the language on the inhabitants of Texas. Like the broadsheet discussed in Chapter 6, his proclamation attempts to create an awareness among Spanish-American Texans that they had *previously* not been free. But for him freedom is only partly about physical mobility, an ability to do what one wants, to travel outside of Texas without the cumbersome process of applying for a passport, or to be able to engage in trade; rather, freedom is defined as a shift in consciousness, as an ability to think critically about the state's actions. He encourages the residents of Texas to engage in critical thinking by using their reason. He argues that the state, as represented in the position of the governor, should be liable to free examination by the residents of Texas. This was a radical shift from the Spanish governor Salcedo or the tyrannical commandant general Arredondo.

But to engage in reason or, as he characterizes it, reasonable debate, means relying on one's own internal logic, divorced from any other authority of meaning. In other words, Trespalacios is describing the idealized Cartesian subject, the individual as the sole author of knowledge. From this point on, the divine as political authority will slowly, though never completely, diminish. In its place will emerge the new citizen as subject of knowledge, and as this new subject of knowledge is produced so, too, will transcendental meaning begin to be reconfigured. Rather than knowledge and authority emanating from God and the sovereign, sovereignty will become internalized. Man, himself—always, not surprisingly, gendered male—will become the arbiter of meaning, of presence, of a self-sustaining form of knowledge that will serve as ontological foundation.

But this sense of "freeing," as we know, was merely a reconfiguring of forms of power, authority, and knowledge. As Martin Heidegger notes, for René Descartes, "liberation *from* the revelational certainty of salvation had to be intrinsically a freeing *to* a certainty *(Gewissheit)* in which man

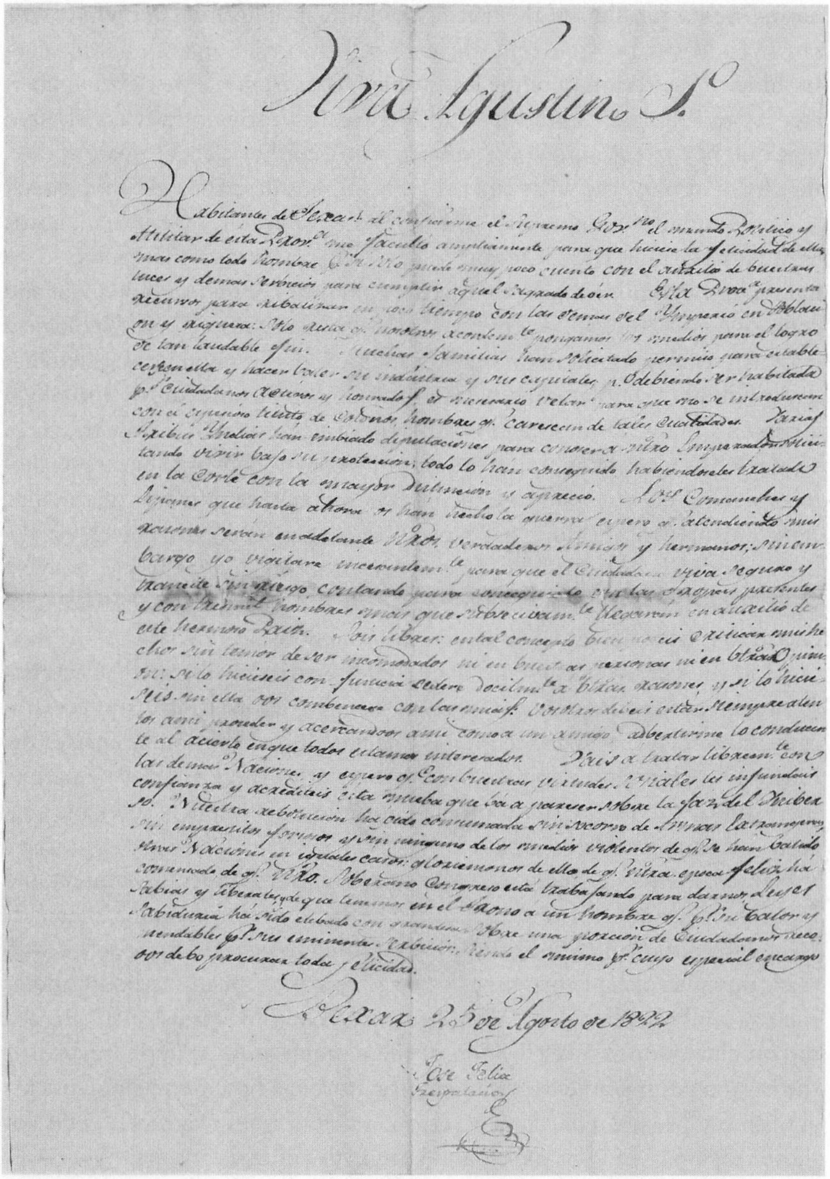

Figure 48. Governor Trespalacios informs Texas of the Mexican declaration of independence and installment of Iturbide of the Mexican Empire. José Félix Trespalacios, *Proclamation to the ayuntamientos of San Antonio and La Bahía* (August 25, 1822).

Bexar Archives. Image di_07440. Dolph Briscoe Center for American History, University of Texas at Austin.

makes secure for himself the true as the known of his own knowing *(Wissens)*. That was possible only through self-liberating man's guaranteeing for himself the certainty of the knowable." That is, the sense of being liberated from Scholastic authority and hierarchical forms of power required that one be "freed" into some other form of authority.[46] In this instance, that form of power is what Michel Foucault has described as "biopower."

At the end of the eighteenth century, writes Foucault, "Western man was gradually learning what it meant to be a living species in a living world, to have a body, conditions of existence, probabilities of life, an individual and collective welfare. . . . For the first time in history, no doubt, biological existence was reflected in political existence." If sovereign power, like that of Arredondo's, had worked before through the threat of death, of taking a person's life or letting them live, then the new form of power to which Trespalacios was encouraging the new citizens (no longer subjects) to submit to required that they see themselves as the raison d'être of the new state. In this world, biopower would no longer secure its power via the threat of death. Now, it will focus on ensuring the longevity of the living social body. "It was the taking charge of life, more than the threat of death, that gave power its access even to the body."[47]

But if the new Mexican citizens of Texas were now liberated, it was not so much because the political state, or sovereignty itself, had shifted radically. If the explicit language in Trespalacios's proclamation celebrates the birth of freedom and implores the inhabitants to validate the new nation, the form of the handwritten proclamation and its implicit language suggests a continuity with the past.

Handwritten on a single page, the proclamation conveys in content and form the solemnity of the occasion. The handwriting is immaculate, replete with ornamental flourishes. The heading, written in italic script with thick down strokes, is five times as large as the script in the body, and as such is symbolic. It reads: "Viva Agustín I [Long live Agustín I]." In fact, the proclamation is a celebration of the naming of Agustín de Iturbide as the first emperor of the Mexican empire. Iturbide, however, would quickly abolish the Mexican parliament, create a dictatorial government, and, for those reasons, would be exiled and executed within two years.[48]

Trespalacios says nothing regarding the shift in sovereignty from Spain to Mexico, and implies that, in form at least (that is, as a monarchical government) nothing had changed. Indeed, not once is the new nation of Mexico named nor its citizens' nationality mentioned; Mexico is nowhere to be found. Instead, sovereignty continues to rest in the emperor and, more specifically, in the "Supreme government" who appointed Trespalacios as governor. But even as the proclamation declares by insinuation—

that is, by the headline "Viva Agustín I"—that the nation-state is a constitutional monarchy, Trespalacios begins to reconfigure sovereignty. He encourages the inhabitants to begin to think differently about themselves and to see themselves as being able to shape sovereignty. Local sovereignty, in the guise of the governor, should neither be feared nor kept at a distance; rather, the inhabitants should see themselves as friends of, indeed, as equals to, the sovereign. The idiom of patriarchal belonging of monarchical rule that required one to submit to the patriarch has been reconfigured; the language of family, of brotherly love, has replaced the father. The language of amity, the discourse we explored in Chapter 5, is invoked here, and works to produce an egalitarian social world, where the citizens are now on the same plane as the sovereign.

A few weeks later, on September 3, 1822, Governor Trespalacios replied to a request from the Saltillo-based Commandant General Gaspar López for supplies to be acquired in the United States. At the top of the list: equipment for a printing press.[49] López was the new commandant general for all of northeastern Mexico, including Texas, replacing the despotic Arredondo. López also took control of the press on which Bangs had printed Arredondo's proclamations and other imprints (and Bangs, at long last, was allowed to return to his native Baltimore, only to return to Mexico years later with a handful of printing presses).[50] The old press had been seriously overworked, and López requested that Trespalacios acquire new type for it.

He held different ideas than Arredondo did as to how the press should be put to use. López had received tax exemptions on five printing presses to be imported from New York via Texas. These presses, he argued, would "facilitar la propagacion delas artes y las luces [facilitate the spread of the arts and Enlightenment]."[51] Trespalacios replied saying he would purchase the necessary type, and added that he, too, would buy a printing press for Texas. On September 11, he wrote an official letter commissioning his assistant, Juan Nepomuceno Almonte, as his commercial representative, and sent him to New Orleans to acquire these items. It would be months, however, before Almonte would return. Some six months later, Trespalacios would write to López informing him that a yellow fever outbreak in New Orleans had stalled Almonte's mission.[52]

Trespalacios arrived in Texas ready to inculcate a new sense of being and belonging for the residents of Texas, and the press was instrumental for this project. The press arrived at Matagorda Bay and was promptly loaded onto seven mules, and made its way to San Antonio by April 1823, only eight months after Trespalacios's arrival. The press may have been the acorn-shaped Washington hand press, a newly invented lightweight iron press that became incredibly popular and was easier to transport than the first iron press of 1800 (see Figure 49). Trespalacios set himself to work. On April 9, 1823, he published twenty copies of the first known imprint from this press. It is an elegant, bilingual, single-sided broadside prospectus for a newspaper, *El Correo de Texas* (see Figure 50). Though unsigned, the prospectus was surely authored by Trespalacios. He had, after all, sought to purchase the printing press, and he was more than likely at least bilingual. He had lived in New Orleans in exile where he certainly would have had opportunity to learn English, and he notes in a letter written to López that he was forwarding an English document translated into Spanish. Trespalacios published the prospectus in Spanish and English in recognition of the rapidly growing Anglo-American colony in southeast Texas, near present-day Houston. Anglo-American interest in Texas had not abated since the filibustering attempts of the 1810s. In 1821, Stephen F. Austin, the Anglo-American land contractor, received what would be the first of several colonizing contracts from Mexico allowing him to settle 300 Anglo-Catholic families.[53] The colony grew quickly, and the bilingual prospectus is testament to these changing demographics.

Figure 49. The widely popular Washington hand press, similar to the one used by Governor Trespalacios.

Tubac Presidio State Historic Park, Tubac, Arizona.

The prospectus develops many of the arguments Trespalacios made a year earlier in his proclamation. Written in both Spanish and English, with slight differences in the translation, the prospectus is directed to "los amantes de las luzes, de la razon, del bien de la Provincia de Texas, y del todo del Ymperio Mexicano / to the advocates of light & reason, the friends of the Province of Texas, and the Mexican Empire."[54] From the outset, Trespalacios inverts the sociopolitical hierarchical order of the Spanish colonial regime's imprints and manuscripts. In Arredondo's imprints, like so many before him (and even in Trespalacio's proclamation), the heading usually started by announcing the name of the sovereign (Arredondo and the viceroy and, later, Emperor Iturbide). It was understood that the sovereign was the author of the words, and the words were to be conveyed to his subjects. The prospectus, however, begins by addressing the anonymous "advocates of light and reason." The region's inhabitants remain the recipients of the text, yet they are no longer mere passive subjects of the state. Rather—in a literal translation of the Spanish—they are now described as "lovers of enlightenment, of reason, and of the well-being of the province of Texas and of all of the Mexican Empire."

From this radical beginning, the prospectus becomes an explicitly postcolonial political manifesto. Comprised of some 325 words, the imprint is more a declaration of intellectual, rather than political, independence. The author directs his ire at ignorance, specifically at Spain for preventing the circulation of knowledge regarding Texas and Spanish America, and for not establishing schools or supporting the arts and industry. The lack of knowledge, not the absence of a judicious political administrator, is what kept its inhabitants "reducidos a una misérable y précaria exîstencia/ reduced . . . to a scanty and precarious existence." But now, the editor proclaims, "la época de la razon y de las luces romp[io] para siempre las pesadas y degradántes cadénas que oprimian el nuevo hemisferio/ the epoch of reason and light [broke] forever the degrading chains which oppressed the new hemisphere." Paralleling the hierarchical inversion of sovereignty pronounced at the beginning of the prospectus, the editor demotes the ruler and places him below the new source of sovereignty: the people.

This rupture in historical time has broken "las pesadas y degradántes cadénas / the [heavy and] degrading chains." Now, Man (again, in all its patriarchal signification) will be "eleva[do] . . . á su verdadera dignidad y restableci[do] en el goce de sus sagrados é imprescriptibles derechos / rais[ed] to his true dignity, and establishing him in the enjoyment of his unalienable rights." The figurative and political language clearly resonates with that of the French and American Revolutions: the Enlightenment trope of light and knowledge, the celebration of reason, the elevation of knowledge as the basis of arriving at the common good, along with their declarations of the rights of Man. But Trespalacios's revolutionary language would have been interpreted within a Catholic political framework, as we have seen, where God deposits sovereignty in the people as a collective who then transfer it to the sovereign.

The question of sovereignty was not about democracy, with its concomitant notions of individual rights, but rather about local autonomy within a constitutional monarchy. Nowhere is the structure of the newly created state discussed; rather, it is merely referred to in passing as an "Ymperio Mexicano/Mexican Empire." How sovereignty will be reconfigured is not discussed either. Instead, Trespalacios yearns to convert the inhabitants of Texas into Cartesian citizen-subjects. If the previous "sistema despótico/ despotic system" preferred to "tener los pueblos aislados y sin la menor idéa de los acontecimientos politicos de los otros paises/deprive us of all knowledge, and keep us in ignorance of the political events in other countries," the new government's policy will be

> de comunicarles, con la mayor puntualidad, todas las noticias que puedan interesarles, y que se encuentren en la correspondencia y gacetas que se reciban de las naciones extrangeras y delas otras provincias del império; y adémas, de todo lo que concierna á la seguridad y Adelanto de esta provincia y al bien general del estado.
>
> [of communicating to you, with the utmost punctuality, all of the news that may be of interest to you, and that may be found in the correspondence and periodicals received from foreign nations and the other provinces of the empire; and, as well, everything that concerns the security and Advancement of this province and the well-being of the state.][55]

The citizens of Texas will now become the subjects of knowledge; they shall from here on be the sole authors of political discourse, and this knowledge will be cultivated and shaped not by God, king, or even the emperor (nowhere do they appear in the prospectus) but instead by "light and reason." In celebrating the sovereignty of the people, Trespalacios also inadvertently inaugurated the disenchantment of the world.

For Max Weber, living in a disenchanted world means that "there are no mysterious incalculable forces that come into play, but rather that one can, in principle, master all things by calculation. . . . One need no longer have recourse to magical means in order to master or implore the spirits."[56] Reason, emanating from the social body (which is not quite yet the same as emanating from *individuals* within that *corpus mysticum*), has begun to displace God and his representatives in the form of the sovereign. Here, then, is a trace of a shift from the Foucauldian notion of sovereign power to biopower. Or so Trespalacios would have it.

Trespalacios circulated the prospectus widely. Some six weeks later, on May 21, 1823, José Angel de Benavides of Monterrey wrote to Trespalacios congratulating him on establishing the *Correo de Texas*. It is not clear if the newspaper was ever printed, since there are no issues extant; nonetheless, it would have been only the third short-lived newspaper in all of northern Mexico.[57] For this reason alone, Benavides was thrilled. He was inspired to write, he said, because "no era bien que tan luminosas é instructivas ideas yacieran p.^r mas tiempo sepultadas en el abominable silencio; silencio pernicioso á estas Provincias del Oriente, y á las demas del vasto Septentrion [it was not right that such brilliant and informative ideas lay dormant any longer buried in the abominable silence, a pernicious silence to these Eastern Provinces along with the rest of the vast North]."[58] He requested a six-month subscription, and promised to forward any newspapers that arrived in Monterrey. On April 22, Trespalacios forwarded a copy of the prospectus along with another imprint to the town council of Sombrerete, Zacatecas, located some 200 miles southwest of Monterrey. The Sombrerete council replied to Trespalacios on May 26, and congratulated him as well on establishing the newspaper.[59]

The imprints reveal, the council argued, "el amor á la humanidad de que V.S. se halla poseido, y las luces nada communes que lo ilustran [the love for humanity with which Your Honor finds himself possessed, and the enlightenment, not at all common, which they (the imprints) exemplify]."[60] Stephen F. Austin was on business in Monterrey when he learned of the prospectus, and he, too, was thrilled to see it. Writing to his son who was living in San Antonio at the time, he said: "I am told you have a newspaper in Bexar which I am rejoiced to hear [;] it will be of incalculable advantage to Bexar and the whole Province."[61] Editors as far off as New Orleans and Saint Louis were ecstatic at receiving the prospectus, and reprinted it in their papers.[62]

Key to the enthusiasm the prospectus generated was Trespalacios's synthesis of the quest for knowledge with the printing press and education. Using the trope of illumination, he initiates a historical awareness of periodization, a movement from darkness to light, from tyranny to freedom, signaling the birth of historical consciousness itself, a consciousness that begins to see itself in linear, progressive terms. The implicit sense of rupture, a consciousness that becomes aware of a radical break between past and present, is itself a sign of modernity—not of modernity as an event, but of modernity as a narrative account—a narration whose ontological foundation is no longer rooted solely in God and hierarchical forms of

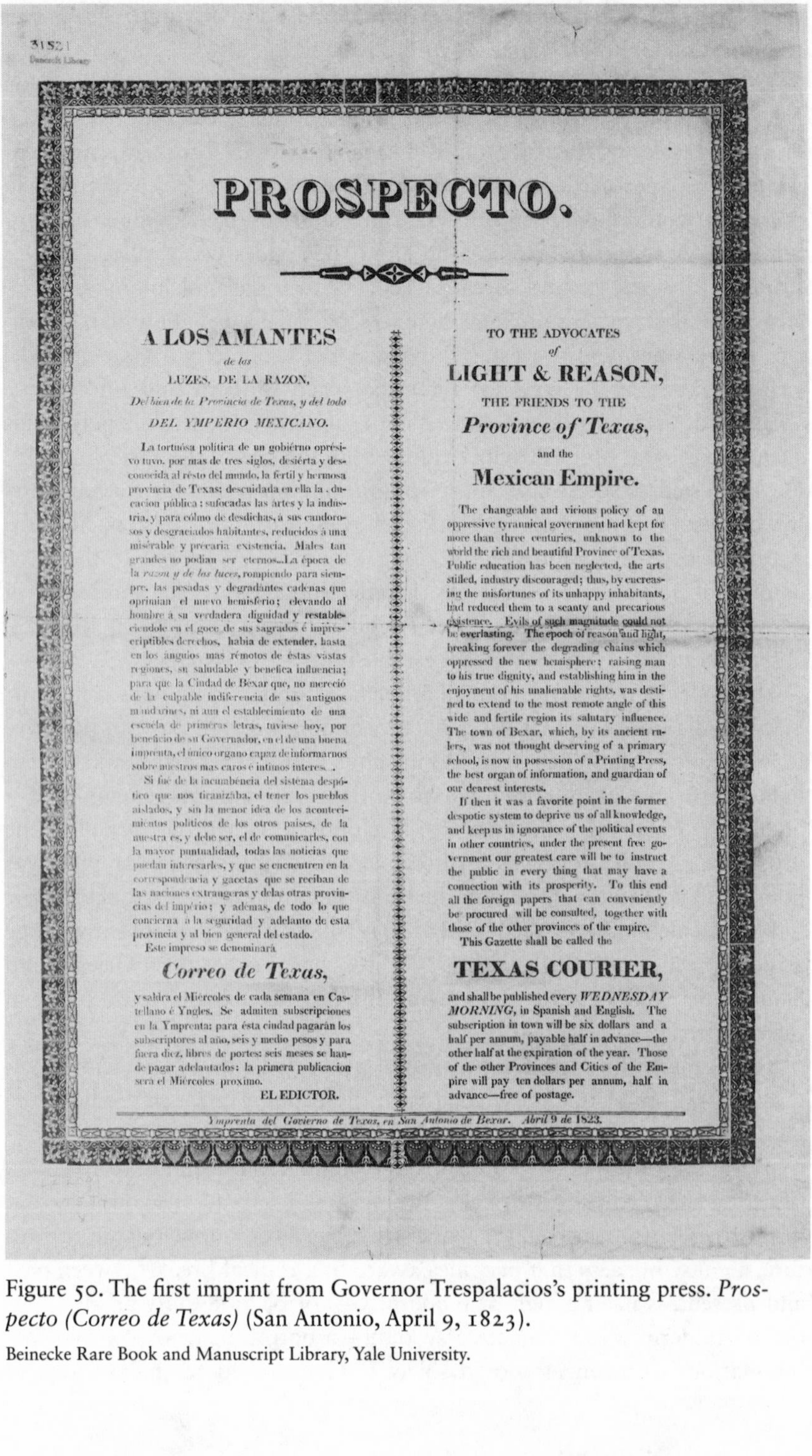

PROSPECTO.

A LOS AMANTES

de las

LUZES, DE LA RAZON,

Del bien de la Provincia de Texas, y del todo

DEL YMPERIO MEXICANO.

La tortuósa política de un gobiérno oprésivo tuvo, por mas de tres siglos, desiérta y desconocida al résto del mundo, la fertil y hermosa provincia de Texas: descuidada en ella la . ducacion pública : sufocadas las ártes y la indústria, y para cólmo de desdichas, á sus candorosos y desgraciados habitantes, reducidos á una misérable y précaria existencia. Males tan grandes no podian ser eternos...La época de la *razon y de las luces*, rompiendo para siempre, las pesadas y degradántes cadénas que oprimian el nuevo hemisfério; elevando al hombre á su verdadera dignidad y restableciendole en el goce de sus sagrados é imprescriptibles derechos, habia de extender, hasta en los ángulos mas rémotos de éstas vastas regiones, su saludable y benefica influencia; para que la Cindad de Béxar que, no mereció de la culpable indiferencia de sus antiguos mandarines, ni aun el establecimiento de una escuéla de priméras letras, tuviese hoy, por beneficio de su Governador, en el de una buena imprenta, el único organo capaz de informarnos sobre nuestros mas caros é intimos interes..

Si fué de la incumbéncia del sistema despótico que nos tiranizába, el tener los pueblos aislados, y sin la menor idéa de los acontecimiéntos politicos de los otros paises, de la nuestra es, y debe ser, el de comunicarles, con la mayor puntualidad, todas las noticias que puedan interesarles, y que se encuentren en la correspondencia y gacetas que se reciban de las naciones extrangeras y delas otras provincias del império; y adémas, de todo lo que concierna á la seguridad y adelanto de esta provincia y al bien general del estado.

Este impreso se denominará

Correo de Texas,

y saldra el Miércoles de cada semana en Castellano é Yngles. Se admiten subscripciones en la Ymprenta: para ésta ciudad pagarán los subscriptores al año, seis y medio pesos y para fuera diez, libres de portes: seis meses se hande pagar adelantados: la primera publicacion sera el Miércoles proximo.

EL EDICTOR.

TO THE ADVOCATES

of

LIGHT & REASON,

THE FRIENDS TO THE

Province of Texas,

and the

Mexican Empire.

The changeable and vicious policy of an oppressive tyrannical government had kept for more than three centuries, unknown to the world the rich and beautiful Province of Texas. Public education has been neglected, the arts stifled, industry discouraged; thus, by encreasing the misfortunes of its unhappy inhabitants, had reduced them to a scanty and precarious existence. Evils of such magnitude could not be everlasting. The epoch of reason and light, breaking forever the degrading chains which oppressed the new hemisphere; raising man to his true dignity, and establishing him in the enjoyment of his unalienable rights, was destined to extend to the most remote angle of this wide and fertile region its salutary influence. The town of Bexar, which, by its ancient rulers, was not thought deserving of a primary school, is now in possession of a Printing Press, the best organ of information, and guardian of our dearest interests.

If then it was a favorite point in the former despotic system to deprive us of all knowledge, and keep us in ignorance of the political events in other countries, under the present free government our greatest care will be to instruct the public in every thing that may have a connection with its prosperity. To this end all the foreign papers that can conveniently be procured will be consulted, together with those of the other provinces of the empire.

This Gazette shall be called the

TEXAS COURIER,

and shall be published every *WEDNESDAY MORNING*, in Spanish and English. The subscription in town will be six dollars and a half per annum, payable half in advance—the other half at the expiration of the year. Those of the other Provinces and Cities of the Empire will pay ten dollars per annum, half in advance—free of postage.

Ymprenta del Govierno de Texas, en San Antonio de Bexar. Abril 9 de 1823.

Figure 50. The first imprint from Governor Trespalacios's printing press. *Prospecto (Correo de Texas)* (San Antonio, April 9, 1823).

Beinecke Rare Book and Manuscript Library, Yale University.

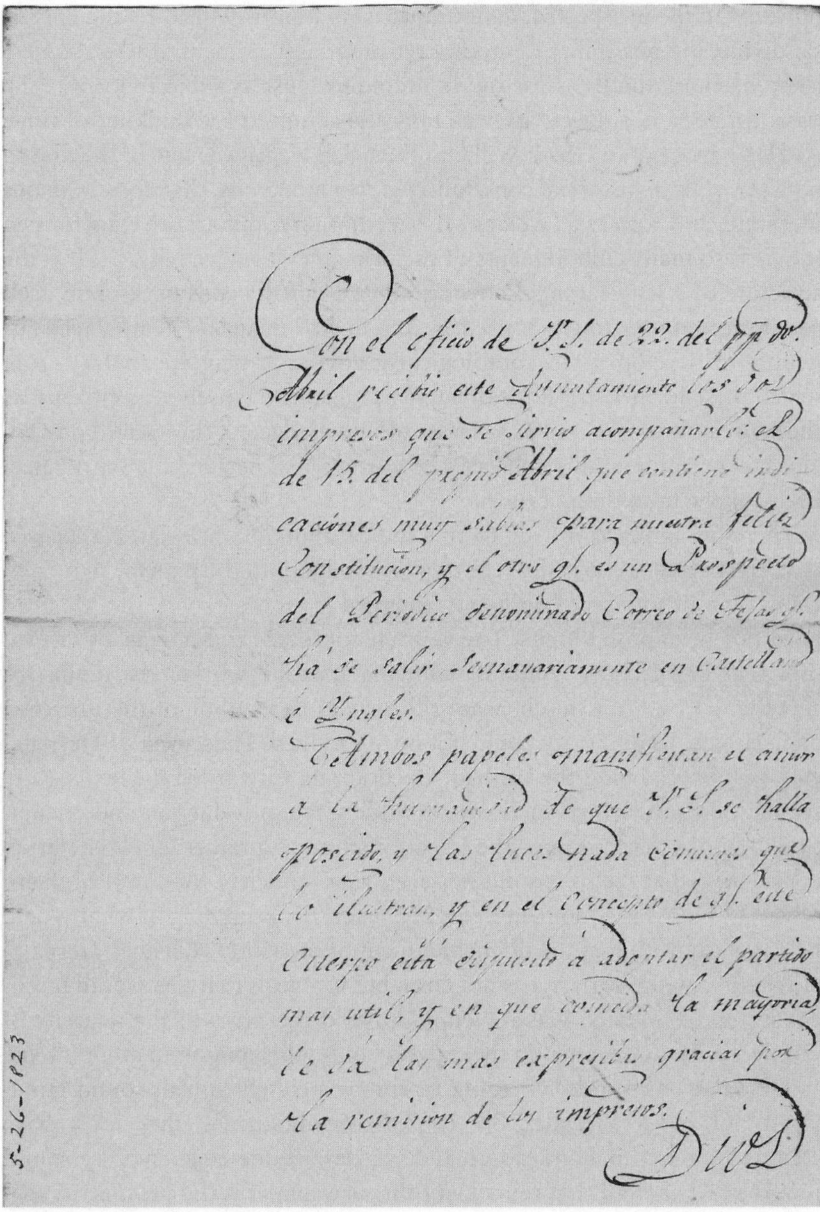

Con el oficio de V. S. de 22. del pp.do Abril recibió este Ayuntamiento los dos impresos que se sirvió acompañarle: el de 15. del prox.mo Abril que contiene indicaciones muy sabias para nuestra feliz Constitucion, y el otro q.e es un Prospecto del Periodico denominado Correo de Tejas q.e ha de salir semanariamente en Castellano é Ingles.

Ambos papeles manifiestan el amor á la humanidad de que V. S. se halla poseido, y las luces nada comunes que lo ilustran, y en el concepto de q.e este Cuerpo está dispuesto á adoptar el partido mas util, y en que convenga la mayoria, le da las mas expresivas gracias por la remision de los impresos.

D. y L.

5-26-1823

Figure 51. Upon receiving Governor Trespalacios's prospectus, the Sombrerete, Zacatecas, town council congratulated him on his "love for humanity." Ayuntamiento de Sombrerete, Zacatecas to Trespalacios (May 26, 1823).

Bexar Archives. Images di_07444. Dolph Briscoe Center for American History, University of Texas at Austin.

power.[63] In the prospectus, temporality is no longer defined by the universal divine, the possibility of eternal return at any moment. Rather, subjectivity becomes the basis for time's unfolding. Just as subjectivity was the basis for reason, subjectivity was now the standard for thinking of time. As Habermas notes, Georg Wilhelm Friedrich Hegel was one of the first to note this shift in historical consciousness: "In modernity, therefore, religious life, state, and society as well as science, morality, and art are transformed into just so many embodiments of the principle of subjectivity. . . . It is the structure of a self-relating, knowing subject, which bends back upon itself as object, in order to grasp itself as in a mirror image."[64] Trespalacios attempts to develop a new ontological grammar, a new vocabulary from which these former subjects can begin to imagine themselves as citizens, as the source of reason, and as subjects of knowledge. As the social body begins this imagining, this collective of citizens will become the ontological basis for the unfolding of time.

There are limits, however, to this radical thinking. Even as it appeared that Trespalacios yearned to open up sovereignty to the *pueblo,* that is, to claim that all sources of authority emerged from the people, the Mexican government imposed limits. The Church continued to serve as an institution that bridged the temporal with the spiritual world. The divine, as represented by the Church, was still seen as the author of the universe; and, as such, its authority could not be questioned. Thus, even as Trespalacios was proclaiming the birth of freedom, he forwarded a Mexico City regulation to the towns in Texas forbidding the introduction and circulation of books that critiqued the Catholic Church (a rather cruel regulation considering that the towns did not even have sufficient food to feed themselves).[65] This was a moment of ambivalence, the beginning of what would be a long transition in the disenchantment of the world. Whether Trespalacios agreed with the decree is not clear, but it reveals that the overall political system in Mexico was reluctant to yield the press to the anarchy of multivocality, of opening up the universe of public opinion to all opinions.

Trespalacios's words regarding reason and enlightenment sound familiar to the modern reader, but to his contemporaries, they must have sounded foreign, if not suspect. Indeed, despite the eager words from a few, the fact that all that remains of this newspaper is the prospectus suggests that the *pueblo* may not have been interested in his ideas. The conditions, in fact, were impossible, both materially and discursively. The towns in Texas had yet to recover from the devastating revolutionary battles; most were on the brink of starvation, and the battles had destroyed previous alliances with Apaches and Comanches who had, therefore, renewed their attacks. Likewise, the language Trespalacios used had long been associated with insurgency, and the consequences for those engaging with such language had been outright annihilation.

Trespalacios attempted to set this temporal rupture in motion, but was unable to succeed. The newly born Mexican empire had failed to take hold. Much like King Fernando VII on his return to the Spanish throne in 1814, Emperor Iturbide, too, dismissed the national Mexican assembly and instituted an absolutist monarchy a year after Mexican independence. Republicans, however, quickly forced him to abdicate on March 19, 1823. A three-man council took control of Mexico, and called for elections for delegates to the Constituent Congress, which would create Mexico's new constitution, not unlike the Supreme Central Junta and Cortes of Cádiz that had been created after Napoleon's invasion in 1808. But whereas the representatives at the Cortes had determinedly spoken up for their particular kingdoms, now the provinces that had produced the kingdom of Mexico were called to the Constituent Congress. As Timothy E. Anna has asserted, the impulse after independence had been for each province, such as the Eastern Interior Provinces of which Texas was a part, to assert its sovereignty even while calling for the coalescing of what had been the kingdom of New Spain into the nation of Mexico. This tension between local, provincial sovereignty and a strong executive would come to play itself out over the course of the century in the guise of liberal federalists versus conservative centralists. Where for centuries order had been imposed from above, with commands doled out from the Church and the monarch, now the people would struggle to assert their local sovereignties above those of any imposed will.[66]

While calling for elections to the Constituent Congress, the provisional government in Mexico City also called for each province to create a provisional governing *junta* or council in whom sovereignty would rest until the elected Constituent Congress produced the new constitution. But the provisional government also replaced all of Iturbide's appointments, including Trespalacios as governor of Texas. He resigned officially on April 17, 1823. The next day Trespalacios had the news published.[67]

Titled *A los Filantrópicos sin ambición,* the 20.25 by 14.75 inch single-sided broadside is elegantly designed, and is the second surviving document from the press (see Figure 52). The governor had called the troops, clergy, members of the "illustrious *ayuntamiento,*" and the citizens of Béxar to discuss the Mexican empire's dire circumstances. The document serves as a summary of the public gathering that had been held at the governor's palace. In effect, the broadside serves as a textual reproduction of public space, the gathering of the *pueblo* as represented by the four broad constituencies: troops, clerics, government officials, and citizens. Trespalacios sought to soothe his fellow citizens' nerves. They had, after all, experienced endless political upheaval and physical devastation for more than a decade.[68]

He reported on the unfolding events in Mexico City: first, Mexico would no longer be a monarchy but a federal republic, and, second, he proposed a "Plan to End the Bloody War in America," the ongoing wars of independence from Spain and the civil wars that were beginning to appear. But fearing violence and seeking stability, the Bejareños reluctantly refused to reject Iturbide's reign. Only a few months later—by which time they had accepted the shift in rule—they published a broadsheet explaining their reasoning: in a world where time had accelerated so rapidly, and where it took four to six weeks for news from Mexico City to arrive, they were hardly to blame for making decisions on dated information.[69] Still, the arguments in *Filantrópicos* reveal how clearly they had embraced the language of full constitutional monarchy.

Trespalacios insists in the inversion of the sociopolitical order: "son los pueblos los que para asegurar su mutual felicidad, han créado y organizado los gobiernos, y no los gobiernos á los pueblos [it is the *pueblos* who in order to secure their mutual happiness created and organized governments; governments did not create the *pueblos*]." As a result, "todo gobierno que no tiene por base la igualdad y libertad de todos y de cada uno de los ciudadanos que componen la nacion, es ilusorio [any government that is not based on the equality and freedom of everyone and of each citizen that comprises the nation, is illusory]." At last, the language of individual rights, "of each citizen," percolates through. But even at the exact moment that it is pronounced, it is placed in tension with the language of the collectivity, of the *pueblo,* of the "equality and freedom of everyone."

Throughout, Trespalacios relies on the suturing, emotional language of brotherhood, family, and belonging. Indeed, the central word in the title itself, "Filantrópicos," pops out immediately upon viewing the broadside. It is centered in a large, beautifully and intricately designed font at the top of the page. The word itself, "philanthropy," echoes that reconfiguring discourse from the eighteenth century that sought to reimagine a social world where the purpose of the state was not the well-being of the monarch and its elites; rather, the goal of "brotherly love" was to cement the bonds across the people, to care for the common good. Democracy is not mentioned, but it is clear that the language of brotherly love, of caring for the *pueblo*'s "mutual happiness," will no longer be something that is arbitrated by an "all-knowing" appointed official, as we saw in the case of Gaspar Melchor de Jovellanos, Pedro Rodríguez de Campomanes, and Salcedo. Now, the *pueblo*'s well-being will be cared for by themselves. Indeed,

A LOS

Filantropicos

SIN AMBICION.

NOTICIA DE LO ACAÉCIDO EN BEXAR, el dia 15 de Abril, de 1823.

EL SEÑOR D. JOSÉ FELIX TRÉSPALACIOS, *Gobernador de Texas*, despues de haber réunido el Ilustre Ayuntamiento, las tropas, el clero y un gran numero de ciudadanos distinguidos y del pueblo, en las casas consistoriales de ésta Ciudad, propuso, en atencion á las criticas circunstancias, en que se halla el Ymperio Mexicano, dos planes; uno para la organizacion de una República federada y otro titulado, *Plan de Abolicion de la Guerra sangrienta en America.* La introduccion que precedió á la lectura de dichos planes fué la siguiente.

La nacion Mexicana, antes tan oprimida por el mas orgulloso despótismo, despréndiendose para siempre, en el corto espácio de tres años, de todo lo que podia retardar su magestaosa y rápida marcha, y hallandose hoy restablecida en el goce de sus sagrados é inagenables derechos, ocupará bien pronto, entre las naciones, el distinguido rango que le está destinado; para que los años de libertad y gloria, señalen mas duracion en sus anâles, que señalaron, los de esclavitud y humillacion en los lamentables y ya pasados siglos de sus reyes y conquistadores.

Mas hallandose ésta en la situacion presente, segun consta por los oficios y démas documentos recibidos, en entera libertad para constituirse de nuevo por haberse disuélto, enteramente, el pacto social que nos ligaba, he créido que debo exponer con franqueza lo que sobre materia tan importante y delicada, me dictan la razon, la justicia, el honor, y mis propios sentimientos.

En el acto de convenir el Emperador, con el último voto pronunciado por la mayor parte de las provincias que desobedeciendole, reclaman su separacion del gobierno imperial, por no haberse restablecido la extinguida representacion nacional, quando convenia, ha dexado libre la opinion de todo ciudadano y le exime de la responsabilidad del juramento que le tenia prestado.

El Señor D. Augustin Yturbide aspira á la gloria de su pátria, mas no á reinar contra la voluntad de sus compatriotas. El se ha grangeado el renombre de grande, y lo será aun mas ocupando el cargo que la nacion le destine, paso que le hará mas memoráble que á todos los hombres celebres que nos refiere la historia.

Como quiera que son los pueblos los que para asegurar su mutua felicidad, han créado y organizado los gobiernos, y no los gobiernos á los pueblos, para que éstos en detrimento suyo, y con grave perjuicio de sus derechos, contribuyan á la élevacion y engrandecimiento de algunos, resulta que, todo gobierno que no tiene por base la igualdad y libertad de todos y de cada uno de los ciudadanos que componen la nacion, es ilusorio.

Paso pues á proponer el sistema Republicano que adémas de sér en mi opinion, el mejor que se conoce, es el que créo domina ahora el espíritu de toda la nacion.

1 Se formará una Junta Provicional guvernativa que entienda én lo economico y Politico de la Provincia, la qual se compondrá de los individuos que actualmente componen el Ayuntamiento de ésta Ciudad, como legitimamente nombrados por el Púeblo, de dos representantes de la Bahia del Espiritu Santo, uno del Colorado, otro de los Brasos y otro de Nacogdoches.

2. Se sostendran las tres garantias de Religion, Yndependencia y Union, como bases fundamentales del gobierno Republicano.

3. La Junta gubérnativa nombrará de sus proprios miembros quatro Jueses de paz que administren justicia en punto á deudas que no pasen de cien pesos.

4. La expresada junta deberá observar el Juicio de Jurados, mas no aplicara la pena de muerte en caso alguno.

5. En quanto á la administracion de justicia podra seguirse el metodo de conciliacion si la Junta lo tiene á bien.

6. Se nombrarán dos diputados por ésta Provincia que pasen á Monterrey y al Saltillo á la mayor brevedad, á tratár con sus gobiernos principales para formalizar uno superior, y adaptable á las quartro Provincias, de oriente, suponiendo que todas se decidan por el sistema propuesto.

7. Si se estableciese el gobierno superior para las quatro Provincias, éste no se disolberá hasta haber puesto la constitucion peculiar á ellas, en manos del congreso.

8. El cuerpo militar de las quatro Provincias, seguirá en el mismo orden que hasta aqui, escluyendo de las Leyes penales la pena de muerte, que se sustituirá con otra que declare una Junta de oficiales.

9. Cáda provincia de las quatro tendrá un comandante militar, los quales comandantes estarán sujetos al de mayor graduacion que se encuentre en ellas, y este podrá sér electo vocal de la Junta superior que gobierne las quatro provincias.

10. Se dará cuenta con una copia de éste Plan á todos los Ayuntamientos principales de la America, con la firme protexta de tener siempre por el primer hombre de ella al grande Yturbide, reconociendo dignamente sus meritos y servicios.

Sigue el Plan de Abolicion de Guerra Sangrienta.

1. Se establecerá en San Louis Potosi, una Junta, con lá denominacion de *Republica pacificadora*, y su objecto sera el de actuar como un *Tribunal de Arbitros*, en todas las disputas que puedan ofrecerse entre las provincias de nuestra America.

2. Se compondrá éste Congreso pacificador, de uno ó quando mas, dos disputados por cada provincia, los quales serán eléctos por los Ayuntamientos de las capitales, y se reuniran el proximo mes de Julio para comenzar sus interesantes funciones; y estando reunidos mas de la mitad de los vocales, podran comenzár sus sesiones.

3. Será el principal objécto de la Junta el evitár por quantos medios estén á su alcance, toda efusion de sangre entre los habitantes del Anahuac.

4. Se comprehenderan en las facultades de la República pacificadora, el arreglo de la convocatoria á Cortes en caso que haya sobre ésto discordancia en el parecer de las provincias.

5. Se comprehenderá, asi mismo, en las facultades de dicho cuerpo, el disponer si lo halla por conveniente, que los cuerpos militares, se retiren á sus respectivas provincias.

6. La Junta no se ocupará de otra cosa que de simentar la paz y la armonia y de uniformar la opinion de todas las provincias, y no se disolvera, hasta que púplicada la constitucion Mexicana, lo disponga el Congreso.

7. Si alguna provincia no quisiese sujetarse á las decisiones del cuerpo pacificador, todas las otras provincias, de acuerdo con él, se empeñaran en convencer, por los medios mas prudentes la provincia disidente.

8. Si por acaso, hubiese alguna provincia que no quisiese adherirse á éste plan de pacificacion, la Junta de Arbitros se hara cargo de sus razonès, para dexarla en libre eleccion de sus derechos.

BEXAR, Abril 15, *de* 1823.

Por desgracia éstos planes fueron desaprobados por la mayoria de votos en la Junta General, y solo convinieron en el del Excmo. Señor Echavarry, pronunciado en Casamata; mas si las otras provincias adoptasen siquiera el de *Abolicion de Guerra Sangrienta en America* llenarian de jubilo el corazon de su autor.

Ymprenta del Govierno de Texas, Abril 18, *de* 1823.—GEO. ASBRIDGE, *Impresór.*

Figure 52. The second imprint from Governor Trespalacios's press. José Félix Trespalacios, *A los Filantrópicos sin ambición* (San Antonio: Ymprenta del Govierno de Texas, April 18, 1823).

Beinecke Rare Book and Manuscript Library, Yale University.

not until June 17 would a newly appointed governor arrive. For two months, sovereignty rested fully in the *pueblo* of Texas.[70]

Trespalacios offered a detailed report that outlined the temporary structure of governance until a national constitution was developed. First, at the local level, a Provisional Governing Junta for Texas would be created, comprised of the eight members of Béxar's *ayuntamiento,* two representatives from La Bahía, and one each from Nacogdoches and the newly established Anglo-American colonies of Colorado and Brazos. Texas had now created its first representative body under Mexico. The Governing Junta declared itself sovereign over all economic, political, judicial, and ecclesiastical affairs in Texas, and would not accept any authority until the Mexican federal government made its constitution public to the world. Second, and in the concentric tradition in which Texas had long been part of the Eastern Interior Provinces, it would elect one representative to join the newly formed deputation (council) of the Eastern Interior Provinces. In this role, Texans elected Trespalacios as their representative. Finally, at the national level, Texas would also elect the Bexareño Erasmo Seguín, who had already held office under the Spanish crown and would later serve under the Texas Republic, as representative to the national Constituent Congress, which would produce the federal republic's new constitution. Above all, Trespalacios declared, their goal would be to "simentar la paz y la armonia y de uniformar la opinion de todas las provincias [cement peace and harmony and to standardize the opinion of all the provinces."[71]

It is not clear how his constituency felt about these ideas. Indeed, the texts discussed here were all authored by Trespalacios, and could suggest that he was at the vanguard of what had been only a decade earlier ideas worthy of annihilation. He had been, after all, a seditious insurgent soldier from Chihuahua, whose revolutionary travails had taken him throughout New Spain and the Gulf of Mexico, to Veracruz, Havana, and New Orleans, from where he had launched an attack on Galveston and continued struggling for independence by striking at the royal forces in Campeche on the Yucatán Peninsula. He had met countless other revolutionaries who had espoused these ideas as well. He was, in short, a cosmopolitan governor yearning to convert the subjects of Texas into citizens. Only years later, as we will see, do we arrive at textual evidence that reveals how much they had embraced this language to describe their world.[72]

Amidst all this instability, it is no surprise then that Trespalacios never refers to the citizens of Texas as "Mexicanos." He simply refers to them as "inhabitantes [inhabitants]," "ciudadanos [citizens]," and "vecinos [neighbors]" of Texas or the Mexican empire. That he does not refer to them as "Bexareños" is curious. But Trespalacios, originally from Chihuahua, was an outsider in a town that had a very long history and well-established familial networks. He had, after all, only been in Béxar for eight months; and, thus, he more than likely had never truly arrived at a comfortable way to bridge the difference in identification with his fellow citizens. "Mexicano," though had already been used before, as we saw in the case of the 1813 revolution and its defiant declaration of independence. By the 1830s, as we will see, the inhabitants of Texas would begin to refer to themselves interchangeably as "Mexicano," "Tejano," and, more consistently, even into the early twentieth century, as "Mejico-Tejano."[73]

On May 3, eight months after his arrival, Trespalacios was on his way to Monterrey to serve as representative to the deputation of the Eastern Interior Provinces; once there he sold his press to the deputation for 3,500 pesos. The Texas Governing Junta functioned as the sole source of political authority for several months; they in fact asserted their authority in a short double-sided broadsheet dated June 11, 1823, to the Eastern Interior Provinces' deputation. This document would be one of the last imprints by the junta; the press was shipped off to Monterrey five weeks later. There would be no printing press in Texas again until 1829.[74]

But sovereignty remained in flux. Six weeks later, on June 17, 1823, the Governing Junta received news from the commandant general of the Eastern Interior Provinces, Felipe de la Garza, that the provisional federal government had appointed a new governor. He ordered the local Governing Junta to cease all functions and to transfer authority to the new governor, Luciano García. And yet more orders arrived. The newly created federal government countermanded de la Garza's order; on August 18, the Constituent Congress of Mexico declared that all provinces should establish permanent provincial deputations. By September 8, elections had been held, and the newly created Provincial Deputation of Texas replaced the Governing Junta and ordered Governor García to relinquish all power. Sovereignty was affirmed, again, as resting in the people.[75]

At the national level, however, the Constituent Congress decided on May 7, 1824, to combine the provinces of Coahuila and Texas, notwithstanding the protests of their delegations. Given their small populations, however, Coahuila and Texas would have been reduced to territories instead of states. But Coahuila managed to have the capital located in their state, and the Texan deputation refused to recognize it. After a lengthy stalemate that veered on war, the deputation acquiesced, and sent their representative to Saltillo, Coahuila by early October.[76]

The inhabitants of Mexican Texas would now have to direct their concerns to a legislative body located some 300 miles to the south. The deputies of Coahuila had acted quickly. Even before the arrival of the Texas representative, they stripped Texas of all political autonomy, eliminating the position of governor and the deputation and ordered that the deputation's archive be forwarded to Saltillo. Clearly, the representatives from Coahuila sought to seize all political control of the new state of Coahuila y Texas. It was becoming all too clear that Texas's needs would continue to go ignored.[77]

On October 4, 1824, the Constituent Congress produced the Federal Constitution of the United Mexican States. Mexico was now a declared federal republic comprised of three branches of government, the executive, judicial, and legislative, but significant power had been allotted to the states, most of whose constitutions had yet to be written. Catholicism continued to be the official national religion. And yet, though elections were held and delegates represented the *pueblos,* nowhere did the new constitution declare the rights of citizens. Not only did the new constitution abjure the language of the rights of citizens, but it boldly declared that "the Mexican nation is composed of its provinces."[78] The Scholastic origin of sovereignty in the *corpus mysticum,* the concentric sense of belonging, from the *patria chica* of one's birth to the provinces, and then out to the young and wobbly Mexican nation, reverberates throughout. Yet even more curious, the constitution never makes mention of "Mexicans." Instead, it consistently refers to the inhabitants of Mexico as "Americans." The nation was, indeed, too young for it to offer that sense of transcendental meaning, that self-sustaining knowledge to which its inhabitants could cathect. It would take more than a mere decade for Mexico to be able to provide that foundational metaphysical feeling of belonging, such as the one long offered by the Catholic *patria* that united God and monarch.

Mexico had begun its painful process of modernity. For the next fifty years, until the dictator Porfirio Díaz took control in 1876, Mexico experienced interminable instability: an attempted reconquest by Spain in 1829; the Texas Revolution in 1835–1836; war, conquest, and annexation of half its territory by the United States (1846–1848); a French invasion and establishment of a French empire (1862–1866); and endless conflict between liberal federalists and conservative centralists.[79]

Caring for the Social Body

The citizens of Texas found themselves stuck between, on the one side, a national government dominated by centralists, and, on the other, a state legislature dominated by Coahuila deputies who were bent on excluding Texan interests. Even as sovereignty had been transferred to the people in

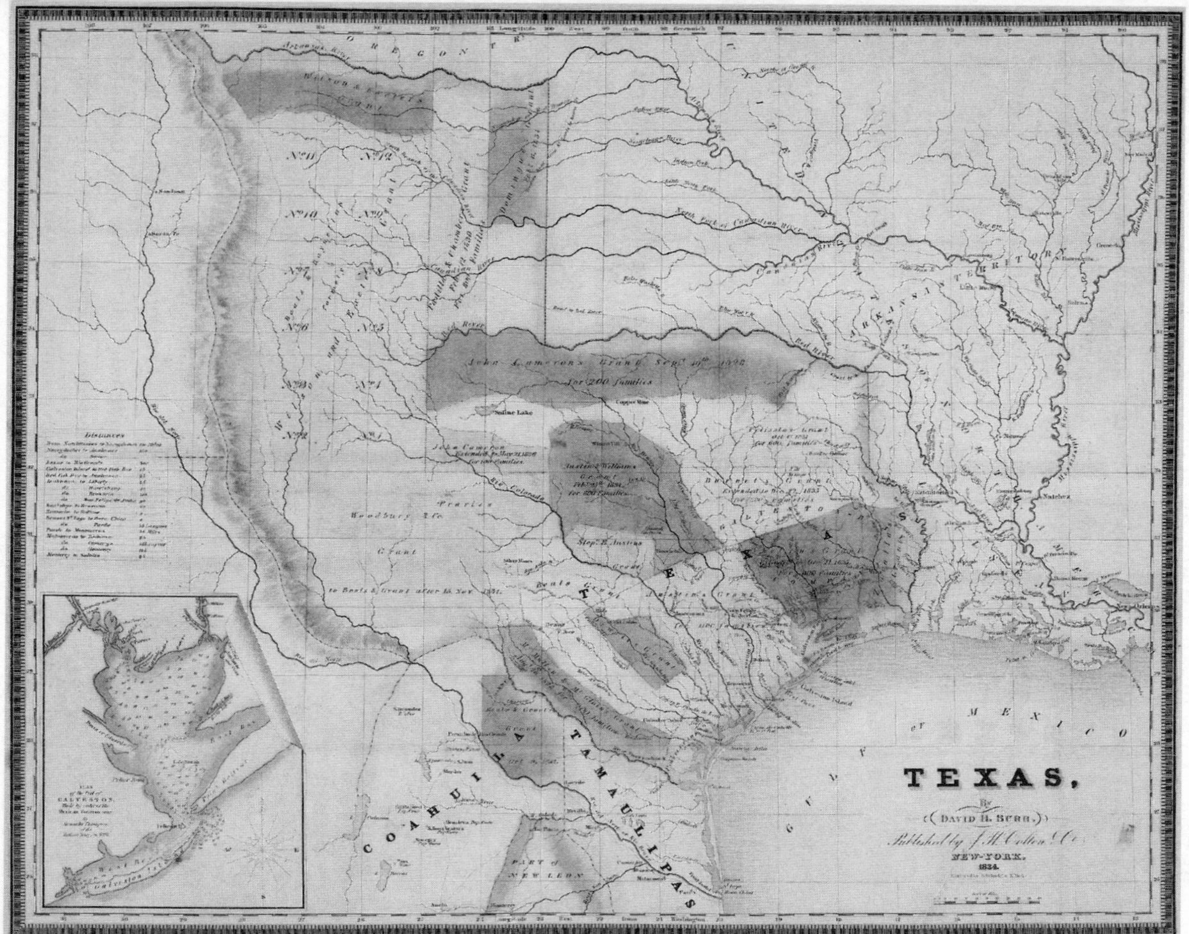

Figure 53. David H. Burr, "Texas" (1834).

22.7 × 18.9 in. No. 79292. Texas General Land Office.

the form of elected bodies, Tejanos were quickly learning the Machiavellian nature of power.

But they were facing a new, growing problem. Hoping to increase the population of Texas, the Spanish colonial government, in a complete policy reversal, began to slowly open the border to immigrants. In January 1821, just months before Mexican independence, Commandant General Arredondo authorized a colonization program. Indeed, Tejanos had long sought immigration as a means to economically develop Texas, and they had advocated in favor of Anglo-American immigration. After independence and a coup a few years later, Mexico and then the Coahuila y Texas legislature expanded the program, and by 1831 it had offered four more contracts to the Anglo-American empresario (land agent), Stephen F. Austin. The contracts stipulated that only "industrious Catholic families" be allowed to immigrate; they were to become Mexican, obey all Mexican laws, and, significantly, convert to Catholicism. The contracts opened the floodgates to a massive wave of Anglo-American immigrants yearning to escape the economic turmoil of the Panic of 1819, the United States' first major economic depression. By 1830, more than 2,000 families had settled in east Texas and the Gulf Coast where land was sold at a fraction of the cost of land in the United States and, even then, at a price to be paid at some indefinite date in the future. The vast majority of immigrants, 29 percent, were from Louisiana, with the rest coming from nearby Southern states. Staunchly Protestant, the majority were from humble backgrounds. They brought with them, as well, the institution of slavery, and immediately turned to raising cotton. But Mexico had long made its repugnance of slavery known to the world; the Coahuila y Texas legislature abolished the peculiar institution in 1827, and Mexican president Vicente Guerrero (himself of African-Indian heritage) made it illegal in 1829. This had been one reason why wealthy Southern planters had refused to emigrate to Texas. But Tejano politicians, yearning to attract more development, had worked to make sure that Texas was exempt from abolition.[80]

But where many of the empresarios, such as Austin, had successfully assimilated into Tejano society, the vast majority of the Southerners did not share the empresarios' enthusiasm for Tejanos. Much less were they willing to abandon Protestantism in favor of Catholicism. Still, in just a decade, Anglo-Americans had managed to do what Tejanos had long dreamt of: to attract colonists who could develop the land. The cotton plantation system of the South had successfully taken throughout east Texas and the Gulf Coast. But even as these colonies expanded exponentially, so, too, did their impatience with the centralist federal government of Mexico, and it appeared that many of them yearned to take matters into their own hands.[81]

It had become clear to the San Antonio de Béxar town council that this development had come at a price. Quickly, Tejanos learned that these new inhabitants had brought with them preconceived racial notions of Mexicans. They had become uncomfortable with what one Tejano official then described as the "superioridad con que se consideran [los Anglo-Americanos] en todo respecto de los mejicanos [superiority with which Anglo-Americans consider themselves in all respects to the Mexicans]."[82] Added to this racism was the newly arriving Anglo-Americans' rowdy, rambunctious, unruly behavior. As early as 1825, for example, a small group of foolhardy and recently arrived Anglo-Americans declared Nacogdoches independent. But they did so as a way to expropriate the Tejanos and Anglo-Americans that had long settled there of their land. Numerous other skirmishes would continue to unfold.[83]

Finally, in October 1832, frustrated with an autocratic federal government and their inability to affect the political affairs of Texas, fifty-eight Anglo-American delegates from sixteen districts met at San Felipe de Austin, the capital of Austin's colony. Not a single Tejano delegate attended. They drafted a petition urging that Texas separate from the state of Coahuila y Texas and become its own separate state within Mexico. Austin's colony wanted the San Antonio de Béxar town council, as the senior and most respected council in Texas, to review and sign the petition. Anglo-Americans knew they needed the San Antonio town council's approval in order for the petition to have any effect upon the Mexican government. But to the council, it was obvious that Austin's proposal was merely a step away from the tearing of Texas from the Mexican political body. The Mexicans in Texas had become a minority in their territory overnight, and yet they were only too familiar with the complaints outlined in the Austin colony petition.[84]

The town council responded swiftly and with tactful precision. The Anglo-American petition arrived at its doorsteps on December 3, 1832. Three days later some forty-nine Bexareño men signed a declaration authorizing a six-member committee to produce a response.[85] The committee remembered well the history of Spain's, and now Mexico's, snubbing of Texan concerns, and so they wrote their own petition to the Coahuila y Texas state legislature "solicitando el remedio de los males de los pueblos de Tejas [soliciting the remedy of the ills afflicting the towns in Texas]."

The committee was comprised of two city council members, Angel Navarro and José Cassiano, and four at-large citizens, José Antonio Navarro (Angel's son), Refugio de la Garza, José María Balmaceda, and Erasmo Seguín. All were members of prominent families, and had served and would continue to serve in various elected positions. Both Angel Navarro and Seguín had been former mayors, José Antonio Navarro supported Bernardo's insurrection and served as a representative to both the Coahuila y Texas state legislature and the Mexican congress, de la Garza and Seguín were former Texan delegates to the Mexican Constituent Congress that designed the federal constitution, and Cassiano was a prominent merchant who would become a city alderman.[86] That such a committee was created to produce a petition addressed to political superiors was nothing new. Such had been general practice since the colonial period whenever the town council had grievances. What makes the petition unique is that it is the one of the only documents of the period that self-consciously seeks to express the collective wishes of the Tejano community. Upon completing their work, the Béxar council circulated the sixteen-page handwritten petition to all the cities in Texas: Gonzales, San Felipe de Austin, Nacogdoches, and Goliad (the old town of La Bahía was renamed Goliad in 1829, an anagram in honor of the hero or "Goliath" of Mexican independence, Father Hidalgo). Once received, each council read it aloud in public squares, and unanimously approved it. Even more fascinating is that this representative body of Béxar and the Tejano community at large adopted in the petition the language that had been used by Trespalacios. The language of fraternal love and equality had seeped deeper into the social fabric of Mexican Texas.

Their petition, like nearly every record of this era, is almost always viewed—by scholars and laity alike—through the lens of the 1836 Texas revolt. It was then, a mere three and a half years after this petition was written, that Texas tore itself apart from Mexico and declared itself an independent republic. For a short period, Tejanos would share political power with Anglo-Americans, but the memory of the 1835–1836 Texas Revolution would quickly become soaked with a racializing rhetoric that would forever marginalize Tejanos. The regional differences that had long separated Tejanos from other Mexicans would be ignored; the alliances between elite Tejanos and the empresarios of the Anglo-American colonies would be broken; the fact that many Tejanos supported independence would be forgotten; and the complex sociopolitical structure that characterized the Tejano community would be elided.

It is no surprise then that the 1835–1836 revolution dominates historical accounts of Texas; the myth of the Alamo continues to exercise its ideological power over the minds of Texans and many Americans, and serves as one of the founding historical fictions of the origins of (Anglo-) Texas and, to a certain extent, Latina/o history.[87] But rather than continue to fetishize this war as a foundational moment, let us turn instead to the moments before the war, before independence was a foregone conclusion

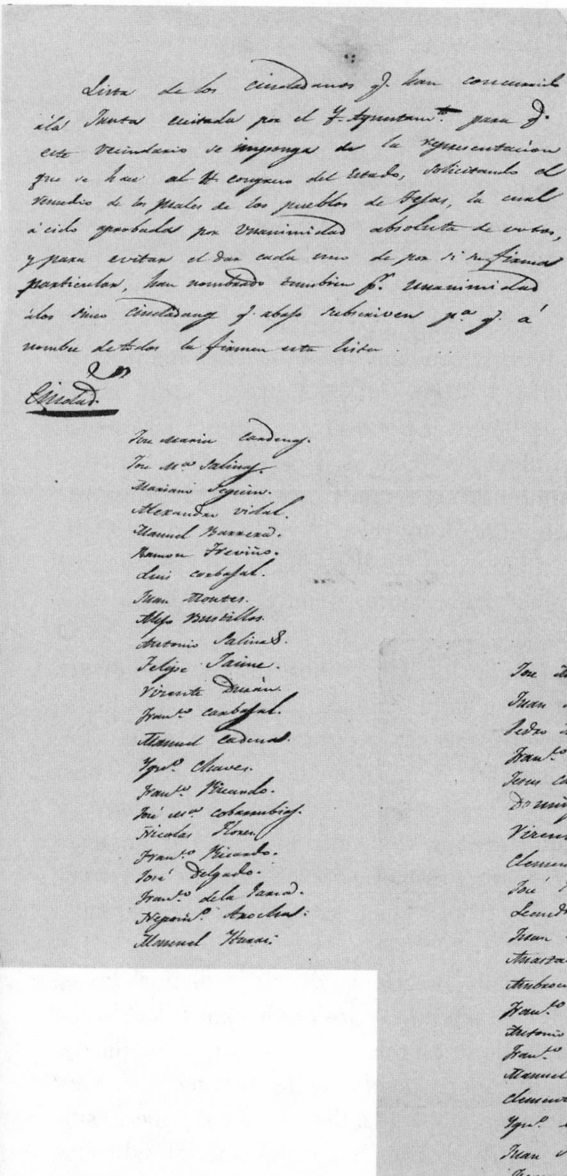
Lista de los ciudadanos q. han concurrido á la Junta citada por el Y. Ayuntam.to para q. este vecindario se imponga de la representacion que se hace al H. congreso del Estado, solicitando el remedio de los males de los pueblos de Tejas, la cual á sido aprobada por unanimidad absoluta de votos, y para evitar el que cada uno de por si su firma particular, han nombrado tambien p. unanimidad á los cinco ciudadanos q. abajo subscriben p.a q. á nombre de todos lo firmen esta lista.

Ciudad.

José Maria Cardenas.
José M.a Salinas.
Mariano Seguin.
Alexandro Vidal.
Manuel Barrera.
Ramon Treviño.
Luis Carbajal.
Juan Montes.
Alejo Bustillos.
Antonio Salinas.
Felipe Jaime.
Vicente Durán.
Fran.co Carbajal.
Manuel Cadena.
Ygn.o Chaves.
Fran.co Ricardo.
José M.a Cobarrubias.
Nicolas Flores.
Fran.co Ricardo.
José Delgado.
Fran.co de la Garza.
Nepomuc.o Arocha.
Manuel Flores.

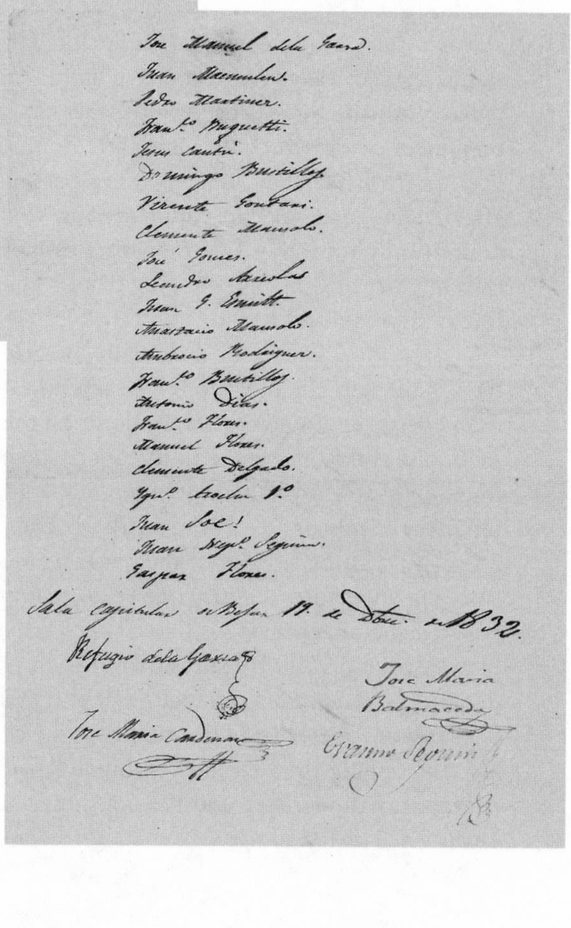
José Manuel de la Garza.
Juan Manchola.
Pedro Martinez.
Fran.co Bugnetti.
Jesus Cantú.
Domingo Bustillos.
Vicente Gortari.
Clemente Manolo.
José Gomez.
Leandro Arreola.
Juan G. Smith.
Anastacio Manolo.
Ambrosio Rodriguez.
Fran.co Bustillos.
Antonio Diaz.
Fran.co Flores.
Manuel Flores.
Clemente Delgado.
Ygn.o Arocha 1.o
Juan Soe!
Juan Nep.o Seguin.
Gaspar Flores.

Sala capitular de Bexar 19 de Dbre. de 1832.

Refugio de la Garza
José Maria Balmaceda
José Maria Cardenas
Erasmo Seguin

Figure 54. Signatures of those attending the town council meeting authorizing a committee to draft a petition to the Coahuila y Texas state legislature (December 19, 1832).

Bexar Archives. Images di_07446 (top) and di_07447 (right). Dolph Briscoe Center for American History, University of Texas at Austin.

and when the possibilities for the future seemed to be endless.[88] Thus, rather than turn to the narratives written by Tejanos after the revolt, many of which were written as a defense of Tejanos against what was becoming the dominant racial rhetoric among Anglo-Americans, we conclude this chapter by turning to what Tejanos had to say before the war.[89] How, that is, did they imagine their future before war would come to limit their visions?

The six-member committee deliberated for nearly two weeks. On December 19, 1832, they submitted sixteen densely handwritten manuscript pages to the town council, entitled "Representación dirijida por el ilustre Ayuntamiento de la ciudad de Béxar al honorable congreso del estado, manifestando los males que aflijen los pueblos de Texas, y los agravios que han sufrido desde la reunion de estos con Coahuila" ("Petition Addressed by the Illustrious Ayuntamiento of the City of Béxar to the Honorable Congress of the State, Expressing the Ills Afflicting the *Pueblos* of Texas, and the Grievances They Have Suffered since their Union with Coahuila").[90]

It is a rhetorically complex document. The authors are only too aware of the anguish Texas residents have had to endure. But they are just as familiar with the increasing Anglo-American separatist sentiment and the prejudices expressed by an increasing number of Anglo-Americans. Thus, in order to make their appeals more persuasive, the authors' employ an affective language of pain and suffering while also utilizing the language of political philosophy. What emerges from the document is a conceptualization of sovereignty as emerging from a living, social body, one that must be cared for and protected.

The petition begins by poetically describing the ills afflicting Texas, those "que han afligido á todos y cada uno de los desdichados Pueblos de Texas desde el momento mismo de su establecimiento [that have afflicted each and every one of the unfortunate *Pueblos* of Texas since their very founding]."[91] More than anything, they argue, the towns continue to suffer at the hands of "los bárbaros [barbarous Indians]," especially the Comanches, who had renewed their war against Texas.[92] "[T]odos estamos en el día amagados, á sufrir que se yó, nuestra total exterminacion por el nuevo levantamiento de los Comanches, tribu la mas numerosa y guerrera [we are all at present threatened with—who knows what—our total extermination due to the Comanche's new uprising, the most numerous and bellicose of tribes]" (4). The authors make clear that they have never been able to conquer the Comanches, Lipan Apaches, and several other Native American nations. War and the constant fear of death had characterized Texas since its founding:

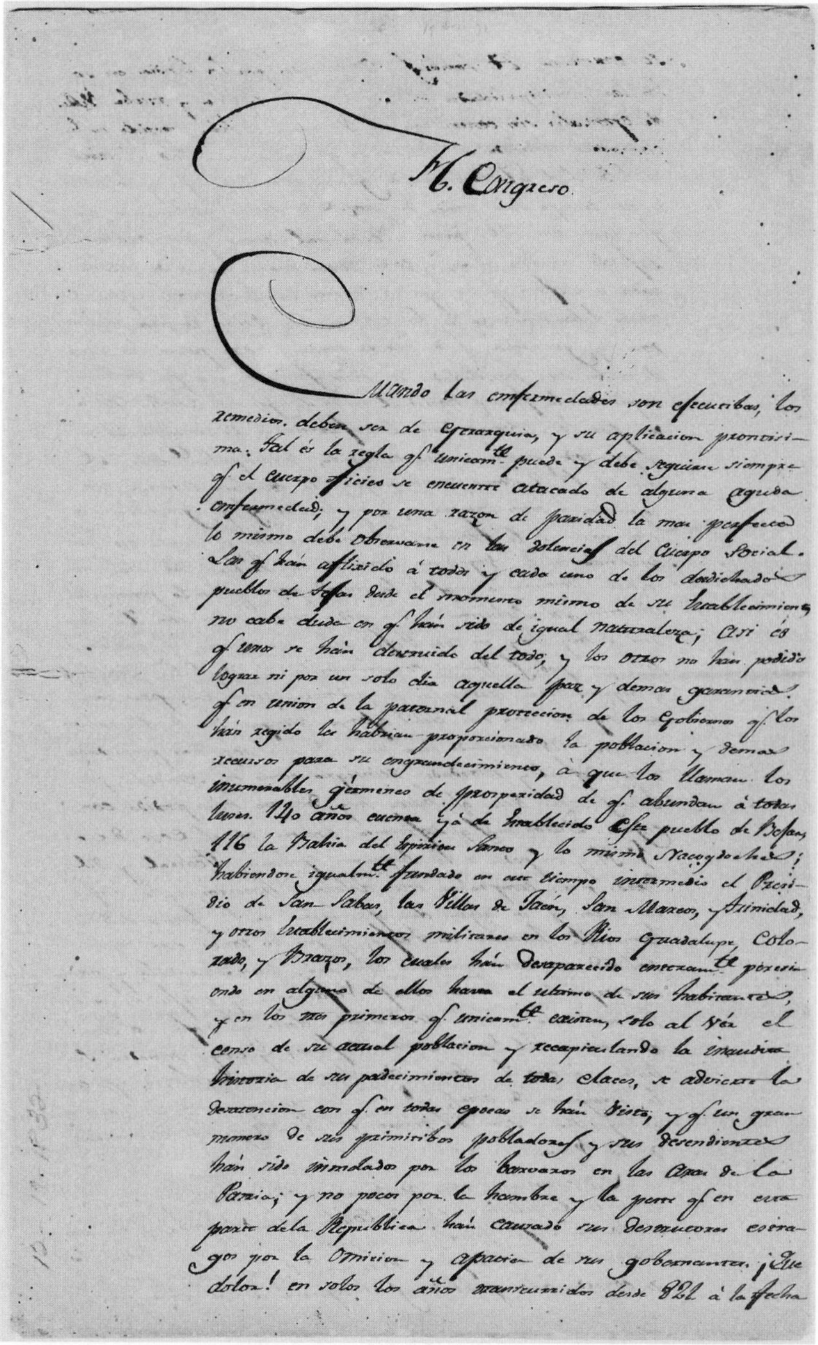

Figure 55. First manuscript page of "Representación dirijida por el ilustre ayuntamiento de la ciudad de Bexar al honorable congreso del estado" (San Antonio, December 19, 1832).

Bexar Archives. Image di_07448. Dolph Briscoe Center for American History, University of Texas at Austin.

> un gran numero de sus primitivos pobladores y sus descendientes han sido inmolados por los barbaros en las aras de la patria; y no pocos por la hambre y la peste que en esta parte de la Republica han causado sus destructores estragos por la omission y apatia de sus gobernantes. ¡Que dolor!
>
> [a great number of its early settlers and their descendants have been immolated by the barbarians at our *patria*'s altar; and not a few by the hunger and pestilence that in this part of the Republic have been wreaked by their devastation due to the government's omission and apathy. Oh, what pain!] (3)

What the Comanches could not do, starvation and lack of supplies would help accomplish, and this was all the due to the inaction of the Spanish colonial government and, now, the Coahuila y Texas state legislature in Saltillo. Both the colonial government along with the present state legislature had effectively impeded all trade and development at every turn. "Aunque nos pese deberemos decir que las miserables manufacturas de frazadas, sombreros y aun zapatos, jamás se han podido ver establecidas en los pueblos de Texas, siendoles necesario mendigarlas ó del estrangero ó á distancia de dos ó tres cientas leguas de lo interior de la republica [Although it pains us, we should say that the miserable manufacture of blankets, hats, and even shoes has never been able to be established in the towns of Texas, making it necessary to beg for them either abroad or in the interior at a great distance of two or three hundred leagues]" (6–7).[93] And they lacked commodities because there had been little incentive for capitalists to immigrate to Texas. Indeed, the authors proclaim, Mexico had taken several steps back.

Mexico was overwhelmed by the mostly illegal immigration of Anglo-Americans into Texas. The colonies in east and south Texas had grown rapidly, but they were not assimilating into Mexican society. As a result, in 1830, Mexico rescinded the colonization laws. In addition, Mexico began selling land in Texas at the exorbitant price of 100 to 300 pesos per lot, while land south of Texas was practically given away at fifteen pesos a lot. The authors respond with characteristic sarcasm, "What an admirable measure!" In either case, Texas had suffered complete depopulation with little chance of attracting settlers.[94]

Throughout, the authors emphasize the suffering their communities have endured, and, in doing so, build a foundation from which these Tejanos may view themselves as constituting an imagined community distinct from the rest of Mexico. Through the catharsis of communal suffering, members of the community begin to cathect to one another, as they imagine themselves coming together through pain and, together, alleviating that pain. The petition thus offers a narrative of communal suffering that must, one way or another, be alleviated; it is this suffering that Benedict Anderson shows is crucial to the emergence of nationalism.[95] Still, even if the narrative appears to construct the thesis of a community brought together through a painful past in order to arrive at the antithesis of national belonging as a way to alleviate that pain, the petition refuses that route. But it does offer a resolution.

It declares from the outset the purpose of government. It provides, in other words, a theory of the social contract. The opening lines of the petition offer a beautiful and double-edged metaphor:

> Cuando las enfermedades son executivas, los remedios deben ser de gerarquia, y su aplicacion prontisima. Tal es la regla que unicamente puede y debe seguirse siempre que el cuerpo fisico se encuentre atacado de alguna aguda enfermedad; y por una razon de caridad la mas perfecta lo mismo debe observase en las dolencias del cuerpo social.
>
> [When illnesses are critical, the remedies should be appropriate, and their application prompt. Such is the only rule that can and should be followed when the physical body finds itself attacked by some severe illness; and by the most perfect benevolence of reason, the same should be observed in dealing with ailments of the social body.] (2)

The authors begin with a gravely ill body and, as if desiring to instruct the listener, they describe how one should treat that sick body: the illness must first be identified, and having identified it, the appropriate treatment should be found and immediately applied. By starting with this image, the authors assert that caring for, and thus ensuring the longevity of, the living body should form the very basis of sociopolitical ethics. But the analogy serves as the basis for thinking about a new living entity: the social body. Thus, just as the human body suffers illnesses, the social body does as well.

Though the analogy is not original, it does reveal that the authors were thoroughly familiar with modern political philosophy, and more specifically with Jean-Jacques Rousseau, who developed the image of the living social body in his *Social Contract*. Yet, what is more significant is the influence of none other than Juan Pablo Viscardo and his *Carta a los españoles americanos*. As we saw in Chapter 4, the letter was published for the first time in Spanish in 1801 and then in several new editions throughout the Atlantic world. It circulated widely throughout Spanish America, including New Spain and the Gulf of Mexico, where it had a tremendous impact. And here, we witness the petition making the same argument using virtually identical language that Viscardo had used: "si sucede en las enfermedades políticas de un Estado, como en las enfermedades humanas, que nunca son más peligrosas que cuando el paciente se muestra insensible al exceso del mal que le consume, ciertamente la nación española en su situación tiene motivos para consolarse de sus penas [if it happens in political diseases as in those of the human body, that the symptoms are never so dangerous as when the patient seems insensible to the violence of his distemper, truly the Spanish nation, in its present condition, has some consolation for its misfortunes]."[96]

Yet, the metaphor serves to cut another way, and the published English translation of the petition fails to fully capture the double meaning. The petition begins, "When illnesses are critical [*executiva*], the remedies should be appropriate [*de gerarquía*], and their application swift" (2). "Executiva" and "gerarquía," however, may be translated in such a way as to reveal the council's political critique: "When illnesses are executive"—that is, alluding to the head of government—"the treatment must be one of hierarchy." Or, alternately, when the executive is ill the remedy must be one of treating the hierarchy. Here, illness afflicts the government or, more precisely, those in power (the executive); it is the upper political echelon, then, that injure the social body, and remedies must be applied to the hierarchical power relations.

Clearly, the authors were skilled rhetoricians. Seguín, the Texas representative to the Mexican Constituent Congress, was known for his love of books, and though it is not known what he read, there is evidence for what the other authors did. Navarro, for example, was educated in Saltillo, and was a self-taught lawyer who was thoroughly familiar with the foundations of Hispanic law, such as the fourteenth-century *Siete Partidas* and the sixteenth-century *Recopilación de las Leyes de Indias,* both of which continued to serve as the foundation of Spanish-American jurisprudence well into the nineteenth century. Navarro, like the elder Seguín, would become a preeminent Tejano statesman. He was active in the making of three different nation-states: serving as a representative to the Coahuila y Texas state legislature, the Mexican federal congress, the first congress of the republic of Texas, the 1845 convention on the proposal of the annexation of Texas to the United States, the convention that produced the first state constitution, and the Texas state senate. He would, as we will see later, write the first Tejano history of San Antonio, referencing everyone from Machiavelli to authors from antiquity, and comparing contemporary individuals to such historical figures as Socrates, George Washington, Simón Bolivar, Napoleon, Benjamin Franklin, and Benedict Arnold.[97]

With independence, it had become much easier for the residents of Texas to acquire books from New Orleans and the interior of Mexico

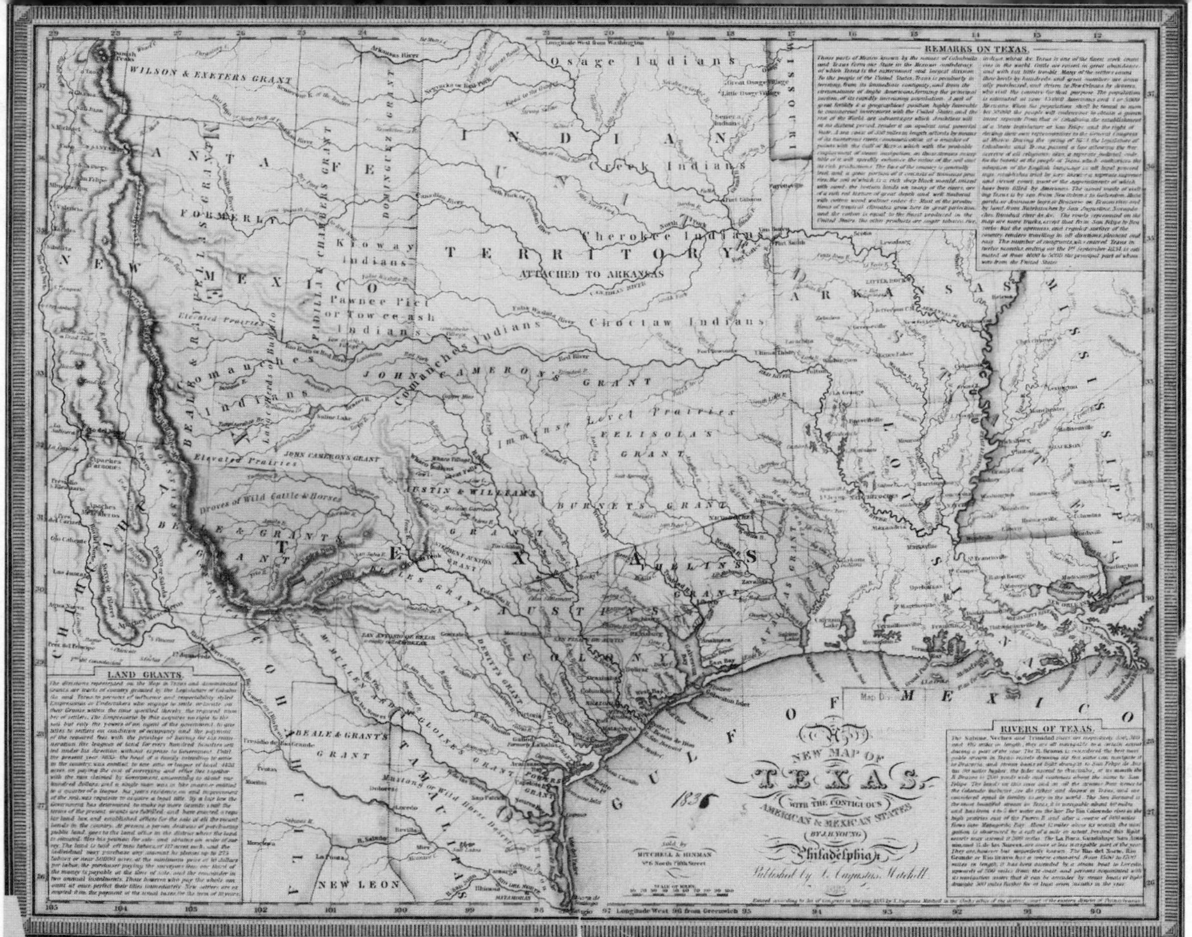

Figure 56. J. H. Young, "New Map of Texas with the Contiguous American and Mexican States" (1835).

13.3 × 15.9 in. Digital ID http://hdl.loc.gov/loc.gmd/g4030.ct002350, Geography and Map Division, Library of Congress.

(Saltillo, Monterrey, and Mexico City). Though more work must be done to unravel the various books that circulated during this period and the particular reconfiguration of theories of sovereignty, the petition reveals that the community now embraced the language that Trespalacios, as governor, had boldly sanctioned. Now, they conceived of their world (or, at least, their sociopolitical world) as one created solely by humans. They, and not God or some sovereign representation of the divine—indeed, God is rarely mentioned—were now the authors of their world. The authors' appeals are to civil law, not to some divinely ordained contract. The petition thus serves as evidence of an increasingly disenchanted consciousness.

Having diagnosed the social body's ailment, the petition must then identify the remedy: that is, who has the authority to heal the social body? The authors direct their criticism to the autocratic executive branch of the government, "la paternal proteccion de los gobiernos [the paternal protection of the governments]." However, if the sovereign is still described in a hierarchical, paternal way, the petition makes clear the origin of sovereignty and, more precisely, its specific role: to seek peace

> y demas garantias que en union de la paternal proteccion de los gobiernos que los han regido les habrian proporcionado [a] la poblacion y demas recursos para su engrandecimiento, á que los llaman los inumerables germenes de prosperidad de que abundan á todas luces.
>
> [and the other guarantees that, as a result of coming together under the paternal protection of the government that has governed them, would have provided to the population—along with the other resources needed for their development—those innumerable things that are described as the seeds of prosperity that, by all appearances, are plentiful.] (3)

Sovereignty originates in the people (*población,* derived from *pueblo*) who transfer it to the government that they themselves have built. It is not something that each individual possesses and voluntarily gives up, but, rather, is something that is a positive outcome of the people as a whole coming together. Thus, the petition opens with the powerful image of the social body, Francisco Suárez's *corpus mysticum,* not with the venerable concept of possessive individualism.

The council went to great lengths to demonstrate that its criticisms were shared by a much larger community, in fact, by all of the town councils in what was previously the autonomous province of Texas (2). Throughout, the language refers to communal interests in order to emphasize that what they ask for is for the common good. Through these sixteen densely written pages they refer to their particular, and expansive, social body as "corporación" (1), "municipalidad" (4), "ayuntamiento [town council]" (2), "un pueblo libre [a free *pueblo*]" (9), "el pueblo de Texas" (10), "este cuerpo [this body]" (10), "soberania del estado . . . y vindicta publica [sovereign state . . . and public vengeance]" (11), "un estado soberano y libre [a sovereign and free state]" (11), and "la representacion de Texas, en la persona de sus deputados [the representation of Texas, in the person of its deputies]" (12). These perpetual invocations of community also serve to emphasize that it is the community, not any specific individual, that has been insulted and disrespected by the government. Thus, when, in reference to a few years earlier when the Coahuila representatives of the state legislature refused to accept the representatives from Texas, the council writes: "se insulto a los pueblos de Texas . . . y a la soberania y los derechos del pueblo atropellado [the people *(pueblos)* of Texas were insulted . . . and the sovereignty and rights of the people *(el pueblo)* were trampled]" (12).

The purpose of government is to secure peace for the people, first, and then provide those "seeds of prosperity" that will allow them to flourish. The common good does not derive from the divine or any external authority; rather, it emerges from the increasingly secular concept of prosperity, which the petition has defined by now as peace, growth, development, and the satisfaction of the people's basic needs. The previous order, that of the Scholastic episteme, as we have seen, had been a finely woven tapestry, ordained by God and with a well-defined, fixed niche for man. In occupying their appropriate station, individuals as part of the social body were able to approximate transcendence, or what Charles Taylor describes as "human flourishing." In the emerging modern order, however, "the members of society serve each other's needs, help each other. . . . In this way, they complement each other. But the particular functional differentiation which they need to take on to do this most effectively is endowed with no essential worth. . . . [T]he modern order gives no ontological status to hierarchy."[98] What is happening at this moment, in other words, is the entrance of life into history, the shifting from sovereign power and its divinely ordained hierarchical episteme to biopower; ordinary human flourishing comes to supplant the appeal of the unchanging hierarchical whole.[99]

But this new episteme requires the reconfiguration of authority. If the traces of God's fingerprints were no longer to be sought out as a means to understanding the cosmos, as we have seen, then this modern world had to produce an alternative self-sustaining source of knowledge on which the social body could rest secure of its ontology. It had to be one that was no longer based solely in the certainty of God and his hierarchical sanctioning of the cosmos, which had long provided a sense of transcendence. That

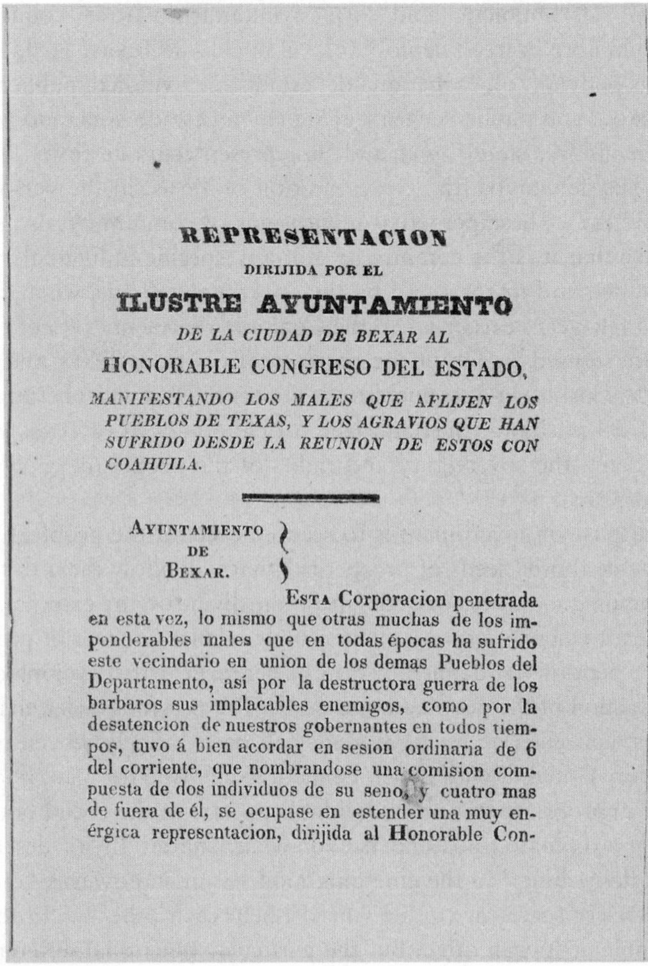

REPRESENTACION
DIRIJIDA POR EL
ILUSTRE AYUNTAMIENTO
DE LA CIUDAD DE BEXAR AL
HONORABLE CONGRESO DEL ESTADO,
MANIFESTANDO LOS MALES QUE AFLIJEN LOS PUEBLOS DE TEXAS, Y LOS AGRAVIOS QUE HAN SUFRIDO DESDE LA REUNION DE ESTOS CON COAHUILA.

AYUNTAMIENTO DE BEXAR.

ESTA Corporacion penetrada en esta vez, lo mismo que otras muchas de los imponderables males que en todas épocas ha sufrido este vecindario en union de los demas Pueblos del Departamento, así por la destructora guerra de los barbaros sus implacables enemigos, como por la desatencion de nuestros gobernantes en todos tiempos, tuvo á bien acordar en sesion ordinaria de 6 del corriente, que nombrandose una comision compuesta de dos individuos de su seno, y cuatro mas de fuera de él, se ocupase en estender una muy enérgica representacion, dirijida al Honorable Con-

Figure 57. San Antonio Ayuntamiento, *Representación dirijida por el ilustre ayuntamiento de la ciudad de Bexar al honorable congreso del estado* (Brazoria, TX: Imprenta del ciudadano Daniel W. Anthony, 1832).

Vault F394.S2 S19. The DeGoyler Library, Southern Methodist University.

source of self-sustaining knowledge had become the social body and the desire to secure its well-being. But if the social body is now an organic, living entity that may succumb to disease (and not because it sinned), then it may also be assumed that it can decay and die, which also means that it was born. "Ciento y cuarenta años cuenta ya de establecido este pueblo de Bexar, ciento diez y seis la Bahia del Espiritu Santo, y lo mismo Nacogdoches [It has been 140 years since the town of Bexar was founded, 116 since that of Bahía del Espiritu Santo (Goliad), and the same with Nacogdoches]" (3). Though the authors may have merely referenced the literal dates of the foundation of their towns, the previous narrative of origin—of Catholic Spain as the source of spiritual-political certainty—has been unmoored. But what is replacing it?

Their forebears would have related these dates to a providential narrative by appealing to God, king, and *patria*. But the collective authors of the petition refer to these dates as the birth of their social bodies, of their *pueblos,* for which the government must care. In this regard, the authors offer a narrative of origins that begins with the birth of a regional social body, comprised of the oldest towns in Texas. The settlement of Texas, not of Mexico, takes center stage here. But it is a conflicted, complex narrative. They desperately desire to remain a part of Mexico, but they have resorted to the petition in order to address their *pueblos'* suffering. In so doing, they write, the petition represents "los sentimientos que animan á su vecindario, que sin . . . que se piense . . . que trata de desmentir el dulce y appreciable renombre de Mexicano que posíe [the emotions that inspire its inhabitants, without it being thought that it tries to deny the sweet and valued glory of being Mexican]" (15). They insist on being referred to as "Mexicans" and never call themselves "Tejanos." But the insistence serves to mask an emergent Tejano-imagined community, one that would rival any sense of Mexican nationalism. In effect, the petition gives voice to a Tejano-imagined community.

The council insists that the *written* constitution serves as the social body's moral compass and the judiciary system as the moral enforcer. Yet when the legislature fails to abide by the law, as in the example above where the legislature barred a Texas representative, then the legislature has failed the social body. The contract being broken, the council veers close to declaring independence, warning:

> no cabe duda en que [la legislatura] violó abiertamente la constitucion del estado, y de derecho disolvió el pacto social Coahuiltejano. . . . El pueblo de Texas pudo haberse declarado en un estado natural procediendo desde luego á la organizacion de un gobierno particular adecuado á sus necesidades y á su situacion local; y el no haberlo hecho, teniendo el derecho en la mano, es, y debe ser una contestacion satisfactoria . . . á las calumnias con que algunos enemigos de Texas han intentado engañar al pueblo Mexicano esparciendo rumores vagos y falsos contra los colonos y demas habitantes de este pais.
>
> [Without any doubt whatsoever the legislature openly violated the state constitution, therefore dissolving the Coahuiltejano social pact . . . The people *(el pueblo)* of Texas could have declared themselves as in a natural state and

> could have gone on, therefore, to organize a special government adequate to its needs and local situation. That they did not do so, although it was their right, should be considered a satisfactory and conclusive answer to those charges and slander with which some enemies of Texas have tried to deceive the Mexican people by spreading vague and false rumors against the colonists and other inhabitants of this country.] (9–10)

Thus, if the legislature fails to heal the social body, the town councils of Texas must step in and seek the best remedy. For these "emergent" Tejanos, it is the law, along with education, that cultivates virtuous citizen-subjects. Sovereignty no longer functions as a threat of interdiction, as it had under Arredondo; rather, it has become productive, a means of *producing* and interpellating humans into citizens. Without a judicial system or educational system, Texas "no podrá . . . ni prosperar ni cimentar aquel respeto y sumision á las leyes que tanto se han menester para formar buenos ciudadanos [will be unable . . . to prosper or cement that respect and submission to the laws that is so necessary if people are to become good citizens]" (10). There is a domino effect here: when the constitution was violated, the social body was injured. The result is a community united through pain, but at the same time cognizant of the necessary balm offered by breaking the social contract with Mexico and creating its own.

Having offered such a dismal portrait of the towns in Texas, the petition concludes by offering fourteen numbered proposals addressed to the legislature of Coahuila y Texas. They are all related to encouraging immigration, developing the educational system, and supporting the capitalist development of Texas, but they all begin with the premise that the constitution must be followed. The authors declare that the power to remedy the situation is in the hands of the legislature (16). Through the spring of 1833, the petition made its way through the appropriate political channels. Austin took several copies with him to Mexico City, where it had a great effect and was reprinted several times. The Coahuila y Texas legislature attempted to address some of these issues. But it was too little, too late.[100]

In effect, the petition declares that the longevity of the social body in and of itself is the sole reason for the social contract. Sovereignty has been inverted: before, the state had existed for the well-being of the sovereign, as ordained by God; now, the health of the social body becomes the sole rationale for the social contract. And like the patient's organic cycle of life—its birth, growth, injuries, and decline—so, too, can one chart the life of the social body. History will now become the dominant narrative mode to tell this life story. The authors of the petition intuit this shift when they claim that the archive contains "Datos mas que suficientes . . . que en algun dia formarán en la posteridad la lamentable historia de Texas [More than sufficient facts . . . that will some day in the future produce the lamentable history of Texas]" (4). History and writing, itself, will become the source of transcendence. But rather than doing so as a symbolic representation of God, history and writing will begin to offer the means of finding an origin, of searching for, and, in the process, producing that foundational fiction of a self-sustaining knowledge.[101] Modernity has begun to sediment in Texas, modernity as historical awareness of rupture from the past and the birth of a world where biopower will begin to proliferate. History no longer begins with God and king—or any other sovereign figure for that matter. It begins instead with the birth of the Tejano social imaginary, the founding of this collectivity.

The Bexareños did not print the petition themselves, preferring instead to distribute handwritten copies to the town councils; it was Austin who had it published in Spanish.[102] However, their decision was necessitated by the fact that there was only one printer in Texas at the time, located in the Anglo-American town of Brazoria. Thus, even though Tejanos embraced the language of sovereignty that Trespalacios had used, they had not yet used the press as a means to promulgate their emerging sense of self. In order to cultivate this sentiment, they resorted instead to the means with which they had been most familiar: handwritten manuscripts and the public, collective reading of proclamations. But this was done with a difference. Rather than reading aloud declarations of the viceroy's or commandant's sovereignty which rang down to the *pueblos*, the *pueblos* responded and, at last, authorized the language of sovereignty that rang through the petition. But this unfolding discursive history would be forestalled. In the end, neither Mexico nor the Coahuila y Texas legislature would be able to improve the situation, and Texans—both Mexican and Anglo-American—would start a revolt in October 1835 that would lead to yet another birth: the independent Republic of Texas on March 2, 1836.

CHAPTER EIGHT

"Adhering to the New Order of Things"

Newspapers, Publishing, and the Making of a New Social Imaginary

Forced Peace

Tensions mounted on all sides as the 1830s unfolded. In Mexico, the government teetered dangerously back and forth between conservative centralist and liberal federalist factions. Antonio López de Santa Anna, the young man who had served under the despotic Spanish royal commandant general Joaquín de Arredondo against the revolutionaries in 1813 Texas, was elected president of Mexico as a liberal in 1833. But he practically handed the reins over to his vice president, Valentín Gómez Farías, who quickly enacted liberal reforms, divesting the Church and military of power, all while Santa Anna had retreated comfortably to his hacienda in Veracruz. By 1834, the conservatives ran to Santa Anna, begging him to stem the pace of change. Santa Anna returned, removed Gómez Farías, abolished the 1824 constitution, abandoned the federalist cause once and for all, and installed a dictatorship. He enacted wide-ranging repression throughout Mexico, having learned well from his mentor Arredondo, quashing provincial attempts to regain sovereignty. He would come to be known as the Napoleon of the West.[1]

In this sense, the 1835–1836 Texas Revolution was far from an aberration. Federalists throughout Mexico had sought more local sovereignty for their states, themselves having recently transformed from the provinces that had made up the kingdom of New Spain. Along with Texas, other

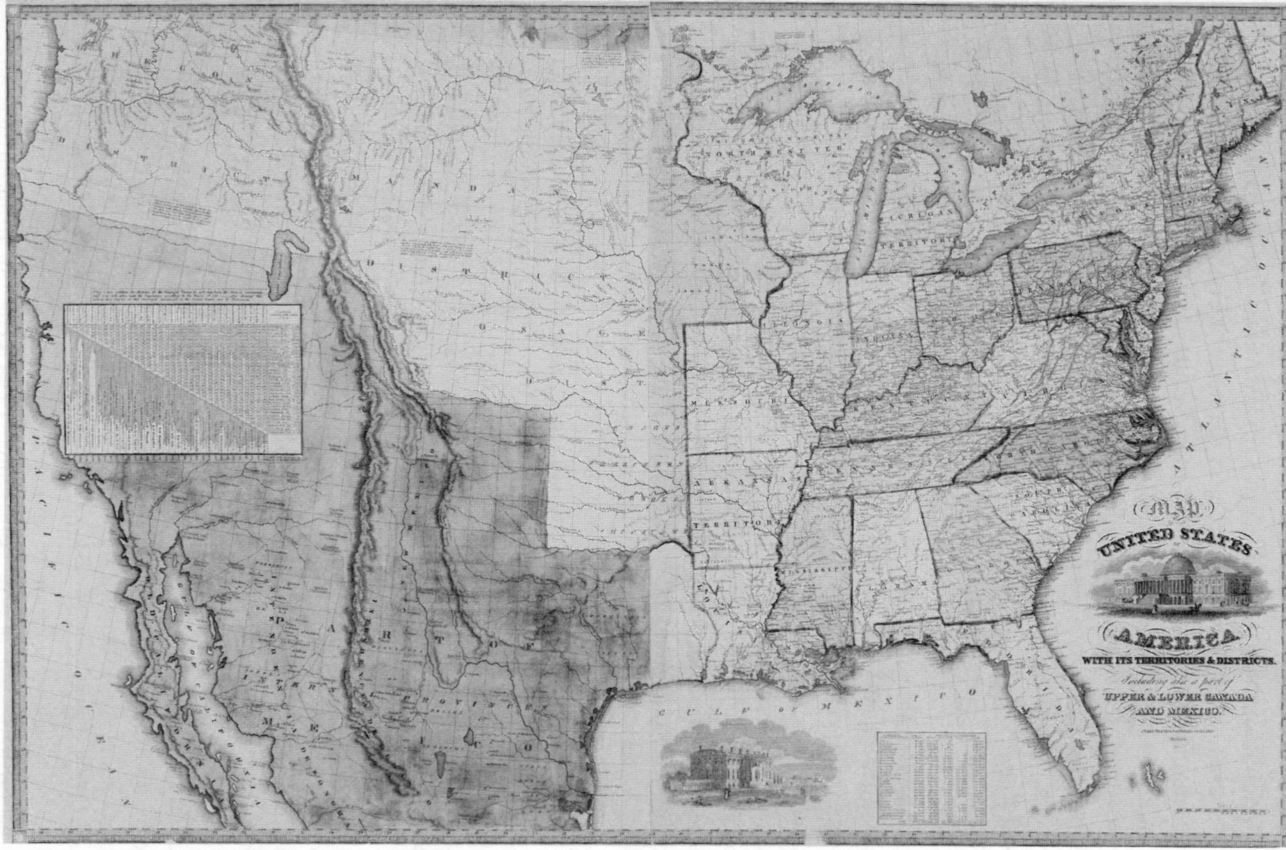

Figure 58. Bissell B. Barber and Asaph Willard, “Map of the United States of America with Its Territories and Districts, Including also a part of Upper and Lower Canada and Mexico” (1835).

43.2×30.3 in. No. 1449, Map Collection. Archives and Information Services Division, Texas State Library and Archives Commission, Austin.

provinces dreamt of creating independent republics, as was the case with the Republic of the Rio Grande in 1840. Federalists from what had been the Eastern Interior Provinces, and now the states of Coahuila, Nuevo León, and Tamaulipas met in none other than Revilla (now Ciudad Guerrero), the hometown of José Bernardo Gutiérrez de Lara in January 1840, and declared themselves the independent Republic of the Rio Grande. After an unsuccessful attempt to persuade the Republic of Texas to join them, the loose band of federalists were defeated disastrously by Mexican forces months later.[2]

Texas, then, certainly was not alone in desiring greater control over its destiny, but it was unique in successfully tearing itself away from the new nation and establishing itself as a republic in 1836. Those men and women who called themselves Mejico-Tejanos, however, had mixed reactions.[3] The majority yearned for a return to the 1824 Federal Constitution of the United Mexican States (itself modeled on the 1812 Spanish Constitution), and were thus divided on the question of Texan independence. In the end, most remained neutral, remembering well the devastation wrought by the 1813 struggle for independence. But many of the prominent Bexareños had supported Texan independence, including the statesmen Juan N. Seguín, son of Erasmo, and José Antonio Navarro. Mexico, however, refused to acknowledge Texan independence, just as it refused to acknowledge the Republic of the Rio Grande, and launched military forays into Texas in 1838 and 1842. Once again, and as would occur many times on the basis of mere rumor, families fled and abandoned towns in fear of retaliation, so brutal had Santa Anna been during the 1835–1836 Texas Revolution. Texan independence would not be secured until the United States annexed the Texas Republic in 1845. Annexation, in turn, prompted the U.S.-Mexican War the following year, resulting in the defeat of Mexico in 1848 and annexation of more than half of Mexico's territory. The 1848 Treaty of Guadalupe Hidalgo had guaranteed all Mexicans who remained in the conquered territories full citizenship rights and protection of property. But things would turn out differently.[4]

After the 1835–1836 Texas Revolution, the differences between Tejanos and Santa Anna's Mexican forces quickly became erased in the eyes of the ever growing Anglo-American population. Santa Anna's infamous success at the Alamo in March 1836 rang as a clarion call to Anglo-American immigrants. A new generation of immigrants arrived, this time not primarily from Louisiana, which now contributed 14 percent, but from further out in the South, from Alabama and Tennessee (12 and 14 percent respectively). The pattern of southern migration would continue; by 1860, most

Anglo-American immigrants came from Alabama (15 percent), Tennessee (18 percent), Georgia (10 percent), and Mississippi (9 percent).[5] Unlike the previous generation of Anglo-American immigrants, most of the newcomers failed to distinguish between Tejanos and Santa Anna's Mexican forces. Thus, upon the 1842 Mexican attempt to reconquer Texas, Anglo-American volunteers organized at once, but, as one volunteer would later remember, many of the men had "acted very badly, having ventured to force the Mexican families from their homes, [causing them] to droop about in the woods and seek shelter wherever they could find it. Moreover to gratify their beastly lusts [they have] compelled the women and Girls to yield to their hellish desires, which their victims did under the fear of punishment and death."[6] The anti-Mexican racial-sexual violence would only continue to escalate, producing a vexing indomitable racial discourse, one that combined the centuries-long Anglo-American anti-Catholic sentiment with emerging biological notions of racial inferiority.[7]

In the communities closest to Anglo-Americans in east Texas and along the coast, such as Goliad, Tejanos were summarily evicted from towns. Even the elite families who had supported Texan independence were not safe. Along the coast, Martín De León and his family, writes his biographer, "like other loyal Mexican families were driven from their homes, their treasures, their cattle and horses and their lands, by an army of reckless, war-crazy people. . . . These new people distrusted and hated the Mexicans, simply because they were Mexican, regardless of the fact they were both on the same side of the fighting during the war." Further out in east Texas, Anglo-Americans forced more than a hundred Tejano families to leave their homes and lands in Nacogdoches in 1839.[8]

Even San Antonio was not safe. Juan N. Seguín, captain in the Texas Revolutionary army, member of the republic's senate, and the last Tejano mayor of San Antonio in the nineteenth century, struggled to defend Tejanos and their property. He later recalled the turmoil:

> San Antonio claimed then, as it claims now, to be the first city of Texas; it was also the receptacle of the scum of society. My political and social situation brought me into continual contact with that class of people. At every hour of the day and night, my countrymen ran to me for protection, against the assaults or exactions of these adventurers. Some times by persuasion, I prevailed on them to desist; some times also, force had to be resorted to. How could I have done otherwise? Were not the victims my own countrymen, friends, and associates? Could I leave them defenceless, exposed to the assaults of foreigners, who, on the pretext that they were Mexican, treated them worse than brutes?

But Seguín, too, received numerous death threats, and was forced to flee to Mexico in 1842.[9]

By the late 1840s, the majority of Tejanos had fled the racial terror that had overtaken San Antonio. When many of them returned after the U.S.-Mexican War, they found their property taken over by squatters. An index of the extent of violence and conquest was marked by the virtually complete transfer of property: in 1840, 85 percent of the town lots were owned by Tejanos; ten years later that figure had been reduced to nine percent. When Tejanos refused to sell, however, they were forcibly expelled, as occurred in Austin in 1853 and 1855; in the town of Seguin in 1855; in the counties of Matagorda and Colorado in 1856; and in the county of Uvalde in 1857. Only along the Rio Grande, where Tejanos were in the numerical majority, was racial violence avoided. There, the postconquest transfer of land would take the form of Anglo-American manipulation of the law.[10]

Texas had changed dramatically since Mexican independence in 1821. Where Tejanos had once been the majority, they had become the minority. By 1850, the predominantly rural population of Texas was comprised of 25,000 Tejanos, 39,000 African-Americans (of whom only 300 were free), 124,500 Anglo-Americans, and 20,000 recently arrived Germans who had immigrated as part of various colonization projects and many of whom had escaped the failed liberal German revolutions of 1848. Native Americans were not counted in the U.S. census, but Comanches had been the largest group, followed by Kiowas, Wichitas, Lipan Apaches, Tonkawas, and Caddos. In the 1840s, there had been more than 20,000 Comanches alone, but that number dropped precipitously by more than half in the 1850s as Anglo-Americans launched a brutally successful war of extermination.[11]

Texas was also ethnically segregated. Anglo-Americans settled in east Texas and the Gulf Coast, where they completed the genocide of the Karankawas and developed a cotton-growing economy dependent on slave labor. The wave of German immigrants settled in central Texas and served as a buffer between Anglo-American and Tejano settlements. Meanwhile, San Antonio and the rest of south Texas remained steadfastly Tejano. Indeed, an Anglo-American visitor in 1846 described San Antonio as having "somewhat of a foreign appearance, altogether dissimilar to any other Texas city." San Antonio's population increased dramatically, more than doubling from 3,488 in 1850 to 8,235 ten years later, making it consistently the largest city in Texas. The number of Tejanos living there also doubled from 2,749 to 4,211. But at 45 percent of the population in 1850 and just one-third in 1860, Tejanos no longer comprised the majority.[12]

A new sense of order began to settle with the arrival of the U.S. Army after the U.S.-Mexican War ended in 1848. By 1851, the U.S. military had constructed the first roads and a regular stagecoach service stretching west from the Gulf Coast to San Antonio and on to El Paso, covering territory in central and west Texas that had long been under the control of Comanches and Apaches. By 1857, stagecoach service extended all the way to San Diego. The military also quelled Anglo-American mob violence and was well on its way to subduing and in many cases exterminating what remained of the Native Americans in Texas, pushing them into Indian Territory.[13] In central and south Texas, the forced Tejano-Anglo-American peace structure, as the historian David Montejano has described it, emerged from the forging together of the land-based Tejano aristocrats with the new capital-based Anglo-American elite via business and marriage.[14]

It was in this climate, during the 1850s, that Tejanos, for the first time, began to publish newspapers, histories, and memoirs. As we have seen, Tejanos had not resorted to using the printing press as a means of conveying their ideas to a larger community. Even as late as 1832, when the San Antonio town council distributed copies of its petition to the rest of the cities in Texas, they chose to do so by sending hand-copied versions and having them read aloud to their communities (it was Stephen F. Austin who had the petition printed). Their orientation to writing had shifted. It was no longer confined to the figure of the sovereign *letrado*. Deliberative thought in matters related to state formation was increasingly construed as something the *communitas* should engage in. Nonetheless, handwritten documents, instead of printed texts, were the chosen means of communication, notwithstanding José Félix Trespalacios's attempt in 1823 to use the press to do so. Even then, manuscripts were circulated to the representative bodies of other cities in Texas which were then read aloud and deliberated by what had long been referred to as *vecinos* or neighbors, a term with a very specific political definition that required one to follow the community's established moral, political, and social norms in order to participate in its affairs. Manuscripts, that is, may have been shared with a larger social body, but these had been directed toward a specific, quantifiable body; they were not meant for an anonymous, open-ended public.

With the arrival of the press in the 1850s, however, Tejanos turned to it as a means to publish or make public their ideas, especially as they related to the new solidifying state. As we know, during the late eighteenth century the bourgeoisie in the Atlantic world, especially the north, began to use the press as a means to intervene in and shape the modern state, giving rise to what Jürgen Habermas described as the "public sphere." The concept of the "public sphere," writes Nancy Fraser, "is the space in which citizens deliberate about their common affairs, hence, an institutionalized arena of discursive interaction. This arena is conceptually distinct from the state; it is a site for the production and circulation of discourses that can in principle be critical of the state." But it is also separate from economic market relations, "a theater for debating and deliberating rather than for buying and selling."[15] It is the bourgeois space where the language of possessive individualism becomes refined.[16]

In nineteenth-century Texas, Tejano newspapers and other publications, such as the first published Tejano history from 1869, served as one tool in helping to understand the world and its sociopolitical institutions as something that was contingent, a product of human ingenuity. The world became less a received order, one that had been ordained by God, as the Church dictated and the state endorsed. God certainly may have still inhabited their world, but he has left them to their own modern devices. And it is through the emergent public sphere that Tejanos participate in the remaking of their world. Newspapers, as a part of this public sphere that facilitated the circulation of ideas, were crucial in helping to create a consensus.

Prior to these newspapers, Tejanos had access to the world outside of their immediate locale either through travel, by word of mouth from others who had traveled, or through the infrequent circulation of texts. Now these journalists set out to produce a social imaginary at once concrete and imagined. But this social imaginary had yet to congeal into a particular kind of nation-based imagined community. Rather, editors first sought to map out this new world. As such, these papers offer an archive of "the ways people imagine their social existence, how they fit together with others, how things go on between them and their fellows, the expectations that are normally met, and the deeper normative notions and images that underlie these expectations."[17] In doing so, these newspapers sought to create a world onto which Tejanos could direct their social energies, one that would hopefully be long-lasting. Let us first explore the genesis of these papers and how they altered previous conceptions of community. By then turning to the first published Tejano history, we will then see how Tejanos sought to produce a foundational history that would hopefully serve as the origin for their imagined community. In Chapter 9, we will examine how Tejanos used the press to mitigate the vociferous racism that had engulfed them.

Interfacing with Writing and Print Culture

The handwritten word had long served as a symbol of political sovereignty throughout the Hispanic world, serving as the thread that sutured the hierarchical relationship between the Spanish crown and the various kingdoms that comprised the monarchy, all the way down to the local town councils. Spanish-American *letrados* in Texas sent and returned commands and correspondence through this chain, often in triplicate so that copies could be retained and stored in local archives. This textual world—more than 300,000 manuscript and printed pages of commands, reports, petitions, lawsuits, histories, personal letters, and proscribed documents—had been collected and carefully stored since 1717 in the voluminous archives of San Antonio de Béxar, the capital of Texas. They are, as one of the chief Bexar archivists has described them, "the single most important source for the history of Hispanic Texas up to 1836."[18]

But three years after Texas tore itself from Mexico, Anglo-Americans packed the archives into several wagons, and moved them and the capital to Austin. The move was also symbolic since the shift of sovereignty from Tejano to Anglo-American Texas meant that the painstakingly detailed documentation of Tejano life by *letrados* also ended. But of the 300,000 pages, however, a mere 4,000 are printed documents. Thus, just as political rule is transferred from Mexicans to Anglos, so too does the Tejano textual archive shift. Where manuscripts (especially in the form of the Bexar Archives) diminish almost to the point of nonexistence, Spanish-language communities turn to publishing as one way to shape the sociopolitical world that was to come.

The unstable political order, for sure, had hindered the development of an economy that could support a printing press. A small number of presses had entered Texas, as we have seen, from the 1812 press that Bernardo brought to the Louisiana-Texas border, the 1813 press that arrived with José Álvarez de Toledo's expedition via Louisiana, and several others had arrived with revolutionary Spanish-American expeditions or Anglo-American emigrants. Also notable, during the 1820s, were the few merchants from the United States willing to sell presses to the revolutionary Mexican councils in Tamaulipas, Coahuila, and Nuevo León.[19] Álvarez de Toledo's famed single-issue newspaper of 1813, *La Gaceta,* followed by another single-issue newspaper, *El Mexicano,* a month later, would be the only Spanish-American newspapers published in Texas for some forty years. Trespalacios, the first Mexican governor of Texas, did his utmost to secure a press in 1823, despite great poverty in the state. While he published in San Antonio a prospectus for the *Correo de Texas,* it appears that no issues were ever actually published. So dire were the economic circumstances that within months of having acquired the press, Trespalacios was forced to sell it to the local government in Monterrey, Mexico. It would be another thirty-two years, some eight years after the U.S.-Mexican War ended, before the political and economic conditions had stabilized enough for another Spanish-language newspaper to emerge.[20]

Besides the political-economic conditions, communities had to reorient themselves to print in ways that a more expansive community could see themselves actively participating in. Not until the 1850s, throughout the entire modern U.S. Southwest, do Latinos (to use an anachronistic term for Spanish Americans residing permanently in the United States) begin to publish newspapers on a regular basis, documents meant to be shared with a limitless audience.[21] The first Tejano imprints in the entire state since 1823 emerge in 1855. They started with the first continuously published Spanish-language newspapers established in San Antonio. The printing of documents by Tejanos had now been completely divorced from political sovereignty; they were no longer connected to the state. During the colonial period, as we saw with Arredondo, writing and printing were associated with univocal ideology, as a means to secure absolutist monarchical rule. Even under Trespalacios the press had been owned by the government, notwithstanding his rather different intentions of cultivating a new kind of citizen-subject. Yet even as sovereignty slowly expanded toward a larger social body, such as the state's first representative body, the Provisional Governing Junta of 1823, the imprints from Trespalacios's press do reveal a subtle shift.

In one of the publications from his press dated June 11, 1823, the Provisional Governing Junta of Texas published a double-sided broadsheet titled *Noticias del Govierno de Texas (News from the Government of Texas).* At 15.5 by 11 inches and laid out in two columns on each side, the broadsheet has lost the distinctive formatting that Arredondo had used (and that Trespalacios had used in his handwritten proclamation). Their formatting, with the name and title of Commandant General Arredondo or Emperor Agustín Iturbide at the top, reflected that they were pronounced from the voice of authority to the masses. Arredondo's imprints and Trespalacios's manuscript were formatted to reflect that sense of hierarchy, with the name of the sovereign placed at the top, followed by the name of the subjects to which the proclamation was directed. But here, in the 1823 imprint, there is no hierarchy of information, no sense that the imprint is a product of a sovereign speaking to his subjects.

The imprint instead is formatted more like a newspaper (see Figure 59). It appears that the Governing Junta modeled their formatting after the *Gaceta del Gobierno de Mexico,* the official state newspaper that had replaced the colonial-era *Gazeta de Mexico.* Rather than the hierarchy of a proclamation, the document is organized into two columns. Indeed, there is not even a masthead. The title is decentered, placed over the left column,

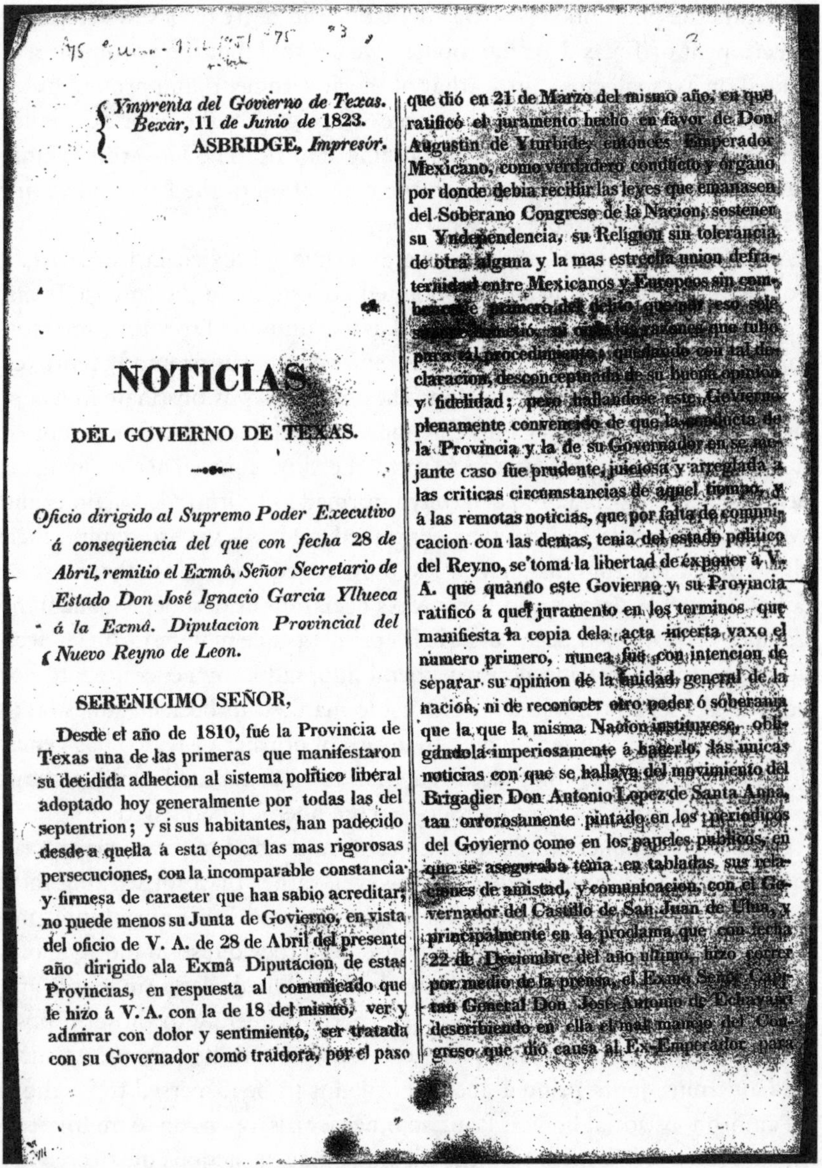

Ymprenta del Govierno de Texas.
Bexar, 11 de Junio de 1823.
ASBRIDGE, Impresór.

NOTICIAS

DEL GOVIERNO DE TEXAS.

Oficio dirigido al Supremo Poder Executivo á consequëncia del que con fecha 28 de Abril, remitio el Exmô. Señor Secretario de Estado Don José Ygnacio Garcia Yllueca á la Exmâ. Diputacion Provincial del Nuevo Reyno de Leon.

SERENICIMO SEÑOR,

Desde el año de 1810, fué la Provincia de Texas una de las primeras que manifestaron su decidida adhecion al sistema politico liberal adoptado hoy generalmente por todas las del septentrion; y si sus habitantes, han padecido desde a quella á esta época las mas rigorosas persecuciones, con la incomparable constancia y firmesa de caraeter que han sabio acreditar; no puede menos su Junta de Govierno, en vista del oficio de V. A. de 28 de Abril del presente año dirigido ala Exmâ Diputacion de estas Provincias, en respuesta al comunicado que le hizo á V. A. con la de 18 del mismo, ver y admirar con dolor y sentimiento, ser tratada con su Governador como traidora, por el paso que dió en 21 de Marzo del mismo año, en que ratificó el juramento hecho en favor de Don Augustin de Yturbide, entonces Emperador Mexicano, como verdadero conducto y órgano por donde debia recibir las leyes que emanasen del Soberano Congreso de la Nacion, sostener su Yndependencia, su Religion sin tolerancia de otra alguna y la mas estrecha union defraternidad entre Mexicanos y Europeos sin con[illegible] primero del delito que por eso sole [illegible] si [illegible] razones que tubo para tal procedimiento, quedando con tal declaracion, desconceptuada de su buena opinion y fidelidad; pero hallandose este Govierno plenamente convencido de que la conducta de la Provincia y la de su Governador en se mejante caso fue prudente, juiciosa y arreglada á las criticas circumstancias de aquel tiempo, y á las remotas noticias, que por falta de comunicacion con las demas, tenia del estado politico del Reyno, se toma la libertad de exponer á V. A. que quando este Govierno y su Provincia ratificó á quel juramento en los terminos que manifiesta la copia dela acta incerta vaxo el numero primero, nunca fue con intencion de separar su opinion de la unidad general de la nación, ni de reconocer otro poder ó soberania que la que la misma Nacion instituyese, obligandola imperiosamente á hacerlo, las unicas noticias con que se hallava del movimiento del Brigadier Don Antonio Lopez de Santa Anna, tan orrorosamente pintado en los periodicos del Govierno como en los papeles publicos, en que se aseguraba tenia en tabladas sus relaciones de amistad, y comunicacion, con el Governador del Castillo de San Juan de Ulua, y principalmente en la proclama que con fecha 22 de Deciembre del año ultimo, hizo correr por medio de la prensa, el Exmo Señor Capitan General Don José Antonio de Echavarri describiendo en ella el mal manejo del Congreso que dió causa al Ex-Emperador para

Figure 59. The San Antonio-based Provisional Governing Junta made public their response to the deputation of the Eastern Interior Provinces. Junta Gubernativa de la Provincia de Texas, *Noticias del Govierno de Texas* (San Antonio, 1823).

Dolph Briscoe Center for American History, University of Texas at Austin.

and bears the plain title "Noticias del Govierno de Texas [News from the Government of Texas]." At the top left, we are told that the document was printed on Trespalacios's press (that of the government) and printed by an Anglo-American printer named George Asbridge. Yet the imprint was far from being a newspaper, notwithstanding its title. The Governing Junta had in fact directed the contents to the deputation of the Eastern Interior Provinces, an elected representative body.

After Iturbide resigned, the new liberal regime in Mexico City ordered all provinces to remove Iturbide's appointed governors (in the case of Texas, Trespalacios). The deputation of the Eastern Interior Provinces, too, forwarded the orders to Texas. But Texas refused, and was promptly reproved by Mexico City and the deputation. They saw Texas as obstinate in its apparently conservative, tenacious clinging to monarchical rule. Texas refused to submit to such criticism and blamed the slow conveyance of mail for their actions. They had not been fully informed as to Iturbide's actions and those of the liberals. Indeed, they continued, and as a way to remind their fellow Mexicans from the interior lest they forget, since 1810 (that is, since Father Miguel Hidalgo's and Bernardo's declarations of independence) the province of Texas had been "una de las primeras que manifestaron su decidida adhecion al sistema politico liberal adoptado hoy generalmente por todas las del septentrion [one of the first to manifest its decided adhesion to the liberal political system, which today all of northern Mexico has generally adopted]." Texas, they declared, was fully committed—and perhaps more so than other parts of Mexico—to the liberal federal system.

Official communication had long been transmitted in manuscript form and addressed to specific officers. However, rather than forwarding their explanation through the appropriate channels, the Governing Junta preferred to print and publish their response. And they did so in the style of a newspaper. In doing so, the Governing Junta boldly declares (in words and format) that the information no longer pertains merely to those in positions in power. Rather, it is "news" to be shared with its citizens. As such, the Governing Junta printed and published it to be dispersed throughout the amorphous social body.[22] Print, in other words, opens up to multivocality, as we saw in Chapter 7, to the ideology that the actions of sovereignty were to be understood as being emitted by the social body.

Just as Tejanos were reimagining themselves as a sovereign living social body, they had started to use the press not only as a means to convey these ideas but also to actually produce that social body. That is, in order for them to go out into the world, and physically create the new nation-state, they first had to imagine its rhetorical-political structure, and persuade others to believe in that very real, lived construct as well. We are now at a far remove from the colonial world where authority and meaning had been located in the union of God and monarch. It had been a world imposed and accepted throughout the monarchy, from Spain, the Americas, and Philippines. Now, the new modern world called on the order to be reversed: the *pueblos* themselves were to come together and produce their social world. Authority would now be legitimated at the local level, building up toward the nation. Yet, as we have seen, the decades that followed the 1823 printing of this document unleashed further carnage. Even more troubling was the strengthening of a menacing Anglo-American racial rhetoric accompanied by even more disturbing violent attempts to dispossess Tejanos of their livelihood. As a result of two wars, the use of the printing press to circulate news had disappeared for more than thirty years.

War had at last ended, Texas had changed sovereignty once again, and the question of what kind of government should develop had been settled. The decidedly Southern Anglo-American majority meant pro-slavery Democratic Party interests dominated in political matters. Declared abolitionists risked life and property, and were run out of town if they were lucky. Such had been the case with the prominent liberal abolitionist German Adolph Douai. Having escaped the failed German revolutions of 1848, he (along with thousands of other Germans) arrived in San Antonio in 1853, where he set up the German-language *Zeitung*. But his unapologetic abolitionist views led to Anglo-American mob violence, forcing him to leave the state. In a world dominated by war-hungry, hotheaded Anglo-Americans who turned just as often to mob rule as they did to judicial institutions, life continued to be a precarious situation for Tejanos and anyone expressing a modicum of liberal views.[23]

In this world, Tejanos no longer controlled the political destiny of the state. Still, a new generation of Tejanos sought to continue that project of using writing and print to shape the social body. Beginning in 1855, the first Spanish-language newspapers appeared, and editors used them as a means to shape their community in two ways. They actively sought to consolidate their sense of communal identity at the local and regional level, but they also imagined themselves part of a larger, global, cosmopolitan world. Secondly, they used newspapers as a way to actively shape political affairs. They used them to help fashion their constituents into informed citizen-subjects who could participate in political-economic matters, and also to participate in the public sphere. In doing so, they would graft the new political language of citizenship onto previous political understandings of community. This was nothing short of extraordinary.

The Founding of Spanish-Language Newspapers

Publishing newspapers during this period, in any language, took great effort. The publisher more often than not served as both editor and journalist, and rarely made much income from it. The steam-powered press had arrived in the United States by the 1820s, but one would not arrive in Texas until 1857 and in San Antonio until 1859. Various types of hand presses were widely used, requiring human toil, and produced 240 impressions per hour (compared to 800 via steam). The manual labor was the least of their worries, though. Editors frequently complained that they were unable to publish because newsprint was unavailable. Indeed, a paper mill would not be built in Texas until after the American Civil War. Instead, newsprint was shipped in from New Orleans at an exorbitant price. One 1857 newspaper estimated that printers in the state had spent $180,000 alone on newsprint. These conditions meant, then, that most antebellum newspapers consisted of no more than four pages published weekly, and most were short-lived ventures lasting no more than a year or two.

Newspapers had been established in the Anglo-American communities of east Texas and the Gulf Coast since 1829. By the 1850s, there were at least thirty English-language newspapers. In San Antonio, the first press since 1823 arrived in 1848, and a second followed in 1850. English-language newspapers were immediately launched from these presses. The growing German immigrant community, in turn, brought the fourth press in 1853. From this press, Douai launched the liberal *San Antonio Zeitung,* and from it, too, would emerge the first Spanish-language newspaper.[24] These were the first imprints designed to be read by the Tejano community.

The *Bejareño* first appeared on February 7, 1855. Named after the city's original name, San Antonio de Béxar, it was published semi-monthly on Saturdays, changing to a weekly schedule on December 1. It would continue to publish until well after June 28, 1856, though no issues have been uncovered from after this date. A total of fifty-three issues are extant. A second weekly newspaper, *El Ranchero,* had a much shorter life span than the *Bejareño,* with only five surviving issues. But it emerged, as we will see, in response to the *Bejareño*'s political stance; its first issue was dated July 4, 1856. Then, in 1858, *El Correo* was launched, which ran to at least twelve issues although only three issues have been located. As a result, of course, the vast amount of information here is derived from the *Bejareño*.[25]

All three titles had similar formats, consistent with most of the other Texan newspapers. Each was four pages long, and each page was comprised of four columns. Other than a few small engravings of eagles, ships, shoes, guns, and pointing fingers—which were used in almost every issue—

there were no elaborate illustrations. The Civil War brought an abrupt stop to all publishing throughout the state. And yet while English-language newspapers quickly reemerged after the war, it was not until the 1880s that a Spanish-language newspaper would appear again.[26]

Who were these editors, who usually also served as publishers, that attempted to mold the Tejano community? If their primary audience were Tejanos, the editors were not necessarily all Tejano. To begin with the *Bejareño,* Xavier Blanchard Debray and Alfredo A. Lewis served as the newspaper's initial editors, and as such, they reveal the alliances that Tejanos had made in postwar Texas. Debray was a Frenchman who arrived in 1852 as part of a wave of French emigrants to Texas. He would later serve as a translator for the Texas General Land Office and as a general in the Confederate Army.[27] Less is known of Lewis's background, though his surname suggests he was Anglo-American. As for his first name, "Alfredo," he more than likely Hispanicized it, since his name later appears in newspapers as "Alfred." However, in the June 14, 1856, issue, the *Bejareño* noted that Lewis had married Josefa Seguín, daughter of the former mayor of San Antonio Juan N. Seguín. This marriage and the fact that Lewis had Hispanicized his name reveal that the editors were fully immersed in the world of Tejanos.

Though the *Bejareño* editors may initially not have been Tejanos, Tejanos were directly involved in the journal from its beginnings. Among the newspaper's correspondents were Narciso Leal and Mariano R. García of San Antonio. Then, in April 1856, Debray was replaced with one F. Villasana as publisher, and Angel Navarro (1828–1876) was added in June as both publisher and editor.[28] Navarro was the third son of Margarita de la Garza and José Antonio Navarro, who, as we have seen, was one of San Antonio's most prominent citizens and one of the authors of the 1832 petition discussed in Chapter 7. Angel had been educated at St. Vincent's College in Cape Girardeau, Missouri, and received a law degree from Harvard University in 1850; he returned to Texas where he worked as a lawyer, and would eventually serve in the state legislature.[29]

A year and a half after the founding of the *Bejareño,* José Agustín Quintero launched the *Ranchero.* The twenty-six-year-old Quintero, however, was not from San Antonio and not even of Mexican origin. He had arrived in San Antonio just before March 29, 1856. On that day, the *Bejareño* reported that

> Tuvimos el gusto de conocer al señor D. José A. Quintero, joven desterrado cubano, quien viene a ejercer la profesion de licenciado en esta ciudad. . . . Aunque muy joven, el Sor Quintero tiene un rango distinguido entre los

EL BEJAREÑO.

X. DEBRAY y A. A. LEWIS, EDITORES. OFFICINA—EN LA PLAZA DE ARMAS.

TOMO 1. SAN ANTONIO, MIERCOLES, FEBRERO 7, 1855. NO 1.

EDITORIAL.

Avisos de Abogados

DIRECTORIO COMERCIAL.

El Fallecido Capitan Don Salvador Flores

Censo de 1850.

Figure 60. First issue of *El Bejareño* (San Antonio, February 7, 1855).

Image di_07434. Dolph Briscoe Center for American History, University of Texas at Austin.

> poetas y escritores habaneros. Sus prendas y las recomendaciones halagüeñas que le han precedido en esta, le prometen un porvenir brillante.
>
> [We had the pleasure of meeting Mr. José A. Quintero, a young exiled Cuban who has arrived to practice law in this city. . . . Although quite young, Mr. Quintero has a distinguished rank among the poets and writers of Havana. His talents and the flattering recommendations that preceded his arrival promise him a bright future.]

Quintero had arrived from east Texas via New Orleans, following the commercial path long established since the colonial period.

Born in Havana on May 6, 1829, to a Cuban tobacco plantation owner and an English mother, Quintero had studied at the Colegio del Salvador, one of the premiere schools in Havana, under the esteemed intellectual José de la Luz y Caballero. Luz y Caballero had been a pupil of Father Félix Varela, a representative at the Cortes of Cádiz and, like Fathers Antonio Gutiérrez de Lara, Miguel Ramos Arizpe, and Servando Teresa de Mier, had revolutionized Scholastic philosophy by incorporating modern philosophy. According to the historian Darryl E. Brock, Quintero then spent some years at Harvard College, where he befriended Henry Wadsworth Longfellow and perhaps Ralph Waldo Emerson. The death of his father, however, prevented him from completing his degree. Quintero returned to Havana in early 1848 where he became involved in literary and revolutionary groups seeking Cuban independence. Having participated in a failed attempt at independence in 1852, Quintero was imprisoned, but he managed to escape to New Orleans, where he produced some of his well-known pro-Cuban independence poetry. In New Orleans, he befriended the former president of the Republic of Texas, Mirabeau B. Lamar. Lamar was taken by the young, affable Quintero, and he invited Quintero to his home near Houston to assist him in his compilation of Spanish historical documents (which became the basis for the University of Texas at Austin Lamar Papers). Quintero would also study law under Lamar, and became licensed to practice it in 1856. He moved to San Antonio, suggests Jorge Marbán, perhaps to gain a stable enough position to marry Eliza Bournos, his love interest from New Orleans. Only three months after his arrival in San Antonio, Quintero launched the *Ranchero* on, appropriately enough, July 4, 1856.[30]

More than a year and a half after the final issue of the *Ranchero,* José Ramos de Zúñiga began his journalistic enterprise *El Correo*. Nothing is known of the editor, but the newspaper continued the same format as its predecessors. While only three issues have been uncovered, we know at least twelve issues were published. In the final extant issue, Zúñiga notes that, due to his having to travel to Mexico, none other than Alfredo A.

Lewis, formerly of the *Bejareño,* will replace him as temporary editor. Another familiar name appears in the newspaper: among the agents listed is Quintero, now located in Austin, where he worked as a translator for a land office and served as an assistant clerk in the Texas House of Representatives.[31]

Editors enlisted agents within the city and throughout the region to help them with advertising and the circulation of their own and other newspapers. They served, in effect, as the foundation of the newspaper's communicative network. Among the *Bejareño*'s agents were members of San Antonio's prominent Tejano families. Many of them could trace their ancestry to the initial fifteen families who left Spain's Canary Islands and founded San Antonio in 1731. The *Bejareño,* in fact, reminded its public of this historic fact on the front page of its August 18, 1855, issue by publishing one of the original royal decrees dated November 28, 1730, authorizing "la conducion de quince familias Isleñas, para poblar el Real Presidio de San Antonio de Bejar [the conveying of fifteen Isleña families to settle the Royal Presidio of San Antonio de Bejar]."

Narciso Leal, one of the *Bejareño*'s first agents, as noted, was the direct descendant of Juan Leal Goraz, the founder and first mayor of San Antonio. (Leal Goraz's descendants would later support Bernardo's republican cause in 1813 and, as we saw, would pay dearly at the hands of Arredondo.)[32] Leal had developed several livestock, trading, and real estate businesses; traveled extensively to New Orleans for trade; owned several mercantile stores; became president of the Democratic Club of Mexico-Tejano Citizens in 1855; and would establish his own Spanish-language newspapers after the Civil War.[33]

The newspapers took advantage of the recently built wagon roads that connected the far-reaching corners of Texas, and they took advantage of state law that allowed them to send their newspapers through the mail service for free. The *Bejareño,* for example, established an elaborate array of more than ten agents in both Texas and Mexico, from San Antonio to El Paso in the west, Refugio near the port of Corpus Christi on the Gulf Coast, and Eagle Pass, Laredo, Coahuila, and Nuevo Leon, Mexico to the south. While most of the *Bejareño*'s agents had Spanish surnames, a handful were German, including the prominent San Antonio merchant Julius Berends. The newspaper, then, represented well the alliances that the Bexareño elite had already cultivated in the region as well as the new alliances with Germans, French, and Anglo-Americans.

Like the *Bejareño,* the *Ranchero* established a regional network of agents. The *Ranchero*'s, however, were different from those of the *Bejareño,* reflecting Quintero's own personal networks. He had traveled throughout

EL RANCHERO

PERIÓDICO DEMOCRÁTICO.

AÑO 1º. SAN ANTONIO, TEJAS: JULIO 4, DE 1856. Nº. 1.

BOLETA DEMOCRATICA.

PARA PRESIDENTE,
JAMES BUCHANAN,
DE PENNSYLVANIA.

PARA VICE-PRESIDENTE,
JOHN C. BRECKENRIDGE,
DE KENTUCKY.

ELECTORES POR EL ESTADO.
FRANK BOWDEN.
W. R. SCURRY.

ELECTORES POR EL DISTRITO.
A. J. HOOD,
A. J. HAMILTON.

INSPECTOR.
JAMES B. SHAW,

TESORERO.
JAMES H. RAYMOND.

ABOGADO-GENERAL,
JAMES WILLIE.

PARA JUEZ PRINCIPAL,
JOHN D. McLEOD.

PARA SECRETARIO DEL DISTRITO,
G. H. NELSON.

PARA SECRETARIO DEL CONDADO,
SAM. S. SMITH.

PARA SHERIFF,
JOHN DOBBIN.

PARA TESORERO DEL CONDADO,
LOUIS ZORK.

PARA ASESOR I RECAUDADOR,
HENRY L. RADAZ.

PARA COMISIONADOS DEL CONDADO,
J. A. CHAVEZ, | JOSEPH BEITLE
DR. HUSTON, | JOHN FRIES.

[Sujetos á la accion de las Convenciones de Distrito.]

PARA JUEZ DEL DISTRITO,
THOMAS J. DEVINE.

PARA ABOGADO DEL DISTRITO,
FRANK EGAN.

PARA AGRIMENSOR DEL DISTRITO,
FRANCIS GIRAUD.

Al aparecer nuestro periódico en el horizonte politico, confiamos que la bandera que enarbolamos dará á comprender desde luego, sin necesidad de un programa, cuales son sus tendencias i aspiraciones. Menester será, sin embargo, consignar aquí las razones que mal de nuestro grado, si bien con un corazon para hacer frente á cualquier destino, ponen hoy la pluma en nuestra mano. Por una parte el deseo de satisfacer las ecsigencias i suplicas de algunos mejicanos que no han podido permanecer mudos é indiferentes en las graves i vitales cuestiones que han surjido en estos ultimos tiempos i por otra parte las naturales simpatias que nos ligan á todos los pueblos de nuestra raza que hablan aquende los mares la lengua sonora de Castilla, nos han hecho prescindir de escrupulos de poco momento, al ver amenazada la paz i tranquilidad de este pais, para que nos decidieramos de un todo á mantener la lucha que en un dia no lejano ha de dar por resultado el triunfo de las ideas progresistas i principios democraticos.

No se nos oculta que habrá algunos cuyos sentimientos bastardos le haran encontrar doblez donde solo hai sinceridad; i ver engano donde solo hai noble-

deslumbrado con el resplandor del oro. A esos nos bastara decir que nuestra adhesion a los principios fue siempre de mas valia que la adhesion a los hombres i que entramos en las filas de la democracia, no como venales mercenarios, vendidos al poder, sino como soldados que cediendo a la fuerza de un sentimiento generoso i moral marchan hombro con hombro a la guerra, bajo un pendon de esperanza que simboliza la razon, la justicia i la gloria del porvenir.

No tememos los envenenados tiros que nos disparen los que vean en la independencia de nuestro caracter la condenacion viviente de su ductilidad de conciencia.—Entiendase que hemos desnudado ya la espada i arrojado la vaina de una vez i para siempre. La enemistad, la resistencia, la furia de nuestros contrarios no bastara a detener nuestra marcha.—Nuestra jornada sera breve; pero iremos hacia adelante en todos sentidos. No daremos un solo paso hacia atras, no cruzaremos los brazos sino despues de haber concluido.

¡MEJICO-TEJANOS!

La hora de la eleccion se acerca. Los que atacan la convencion democrática estan obrando de hecho con los Know-nothings que quieren engañaros, que han procurado siempre oprimiros i que intentan dividir nuestro partido para obtener el triunfo.

Ese es el estado actual, esa la significacion politica de los sucesos que vemos. ¿Les dareis vuestros votos? ¿Contribuireis a vuestra propia ruina?

¡Verguenza seria! Ese partido no ama el bien público sino su interes personal. Desconfia de sus fuerzas i os pide hoi ayuda representando principios que desconoce i sentimientos que no abriga, para destruiros mañana.

Nosotros os decimos que eso no puede ser, que jamas será. La alianza con los que abandonan las filas de la democracia es ya imposible.

Ellos os despojarian de vuestros derechos, se opondrian a vuestra fé religiosa, os considerarian como estrangeros, i os negarian hasta el empleo mas humilde.

Esa vanguardia desleal sintiendose derrotada teme la hora de la lucha i desea la desunion. Su politica es dividiros para dominar i oprimir.

La hora de la eleccion vá a sonar. No olvideis á los hombres que os defendieron en la que pasó. Son los mismos a quienes hoi quieren combatir otra vez. ¡Que cada Mejicano se prepare a hacer su deber! Que cada uno comprenda la santidad de su causa. Rechazad á los que os aconsejen lo contrario. Que no haya amigos ni compromisos, sino union, fraternidad i decision por vuestro partido. ¡La democracia ahora, la democracia despues, la democracia siempre!

Dos amantes en visperas de unirse se paseaban por las margenes del Danubio. Una flor azul celeste se balanceaba sobre las ondas que parecian querer arrastrarla: la joven admira su brillantez i se compadece de su destino. El amante se precipita al momento, se apodera de la rama florida: pero lo arrebata la corriente. Haciendo el último esfuerzo arrojó la flor a la orilla i en los instantes de desaparecer para siempre

LA CONVENCION DEMOCRATICA.

La circunstancia de haberse separado algunos miembros de la convencion democratica, que se constituyo legalmente el dia dos del pasado mes de Junio, i el convencimiento que tenemos de que, posteriormente, algunos malcontentos han tratado de desfigurar los hechos i presentarlos bajo un prisma poco favorable a la verdad i honradez de aquel partido, exigen que demostremos en pocas palabras el acierto i la propiedad con que el cuerpo principal de los democratas llevo a cabo el nombramiento de los candidatos.

La regla de la mayoria, que decide siempre todas las controversias, es tan conocida i tiene tal fuerza que en verdad nos sorprende que haya personas que lo nieguen i se opongan a que tenga efecto. Ni se diga tampoco que no eran admisibles los delegados que no residen en los precintos donde se les elijio—Esto es ridiculo en demasia—Desde que las Convenciones han tenido lugar, ha sucedido siempre lo mismo i en la ultima que se celebro en Austin, muchos de los delegados no residian en los condados que representaban—Si el principio es erroneo, dice con mucha propiedad uno de nuestros amigos, el error ha llegado a ser una regla por el derecho de la costumbre i su observancia es una doctrina necesaria al partido democratico. Creemos que existe una maxima juridica de que una persona no puede aprobar i reprobar el mismo hecho, i sin embargo esto sucede en el caso que nos ocupa, pues el derecho de dos de los que firman el informe de la minoria para votar en la convencion, cae bajo el peso de sus propias objeciones. Si no nos equivocamos uno de estos caballeros, delegado por el precinto numero 2, reclama el Atascoso como su residencia, i el otro fue elejido para un precinto en el cual no reside. Lo mismo podria decirse de algunos otros que votaron pocos momentos despues de haberse principiado la junta.

Las objeciones, pues, que presenta la minoria no tienen otro objeto que introducir la desunion en las filas democraticas. Confiamos que seran vanos todos sus esfuerzos. Los candidatos nombrados por la convencion seran elejidos i no temen el resultado de la contienda.

Guerra entre Espana i Mejico.—Por las últimas noticias recibidas de Madrid se sabe que el gobierno español habia dado orden a fin de que se hiciesen a la vela para el golfo de Mejico tres buques de la linea, tres fragatas, dos corbetas i cuatro vapores, lo cual aparece corroborado por los periodicos recibidos ultimamente de Paris en que se manifiesta terminantemente que Espana declarara la guerra a Mejico si este no satisface ciertas reclamaciones hechas por los subditos de aquella monarquia.—

Nosotros hemos conocido personalmente durante su destierro en New Orleans al Presidente de la Republica de Mejico, Sr. Comonfort, i tenemos motivos para creer que sabra repeler victoriosamente cualquiera agresion de parte del sanguinario i caduco lobo espanol. Los dias de su dominacion en America estan contados i mucho tememos que el primer canonazo disparado en las aguas del golfo mejicano los acelere. Nosotros que hemos nacido en una tierra de luz i amor que gime bajo el ferreo despotismo de Espaua, simpatizamos de todo corazon con la patria de los Morelos, Guerreros i Zavalas.

Un Irlandes fué al correo i pregunto si habia cartas para el. El administrador le preguntó por su nombre. Oh, dijo el, usted

HON. JAMES BUCHANAN.

CANDIDATO PARA LA PRESIDENCIA.

Mr. Buchanan nacio el 13 de Abril de 1791. en el Condado de Franklin, Estado de Pensylvania, Despues de haber tenido una educacion clasica i academica estudio derecho i entro en la profesion. Teniendo predileccion por la politica se le nombro en 1814 para la Casa de Representantes de la Legislatura de su Estado nativo i fue posteriormente elejido. Se le reeligio en el ano de 1815. Despues de haber servido dos se[siones] rehuso otra reeleccion. En 1820 s[e] le elijio para el Congreso i tomo asiento e[n] aquel cuerpo en Diciembre de 1821. Permanecio de miembro de la casa hasta el [4] de Marzo de 1831. Inmediatamente despues de su quinta eleccion se retiro a la vid[a] privada. En Mayo de 1831 se le ofrecio l[a] mision a Rusia por el Gen. Jackson i l[a] acepto. En el ano de 1831 despues de s[u] vuelta de Rusia se le elijio para el Senad[o] de los Estados Unidos para llenar la vacan[te] que habia con motivo de la renuncia d[e] Mr. Wilkins—En Diciembre de 1836 fu[e] elejido nuevamente i en 1843 se le reelijio. En Marzo de 1845 se le nombro Secretari[o] de Estado por el Presidente Polk en cuy[o] empleo estuvo hasta que termino la adm[i]nistracion de aquel caballero. Su carrer[a] en Londres como Ministro Plenipotenciari[o] de los Estados Unidos, bajo el nombramien[to] del presidente Pierce es bien conocida p[a]ra que nos ocupemos de ella, bastará s[in] embargo decir que represento los interes[es] del pais con dignidad i mantuvo en circun[s]tancias mui peligrosas el respeto que el c[a]racter americano demanda de las nacion[es] europeas—Como politico el Sor. Buchan[an] es una de las columnas mas fuertes del pa[r]tido democratico i probablemente se le [ha] censurado menos que a ningun otro de l[os] que recorren la espinosa senda de la politic[a].

Marina Española.—Decia el diputa[do] demócrata, Sr. Orense, en la sesion de Co[r]tes que tuvo lugar el 9 de Enero último:

"La Francia gasta 400 millones de real[es] y tiene una escuadra de 100 navios de lin[ea] ó su equivalente en vapores; la Inglaterr[a] con una escuadra de 200, gasta 700 millon[es] i nosotros con una escuadra que esta co[m]puesta de un navio, gastamos 90. Hace m[u]chos años que se nos dice que va aumenta[n]do la marina. Señores, creer que en el [...] podemos presentar una fuerza maritima, [se]ria hacerse una ilusion."

Por eso cree i con razon el diario ofic[ial] del apostadero de la Habana, que la Mari[na] *es la parte mas flaca del poder español.* [...]go dariamos nosotros por saber cual otra p[ar]te puede tener el tal poder que no adol[ezca] del mismo achaque, pues por mas que mi[ra]mos i remiramos, antojasenos que el llam[a]do *poder español esta flaco por todas par[tes]*. Descarnado, digámoslo asi, de las glorias [de] otros dias, hoy es un verdadero esqueleto [de] nacion que solo puede ofrecer, como mat[eria] de estudio, el asqueroso espectáculo de [su] carcomida osamenta. Solo para la *an[ato]mia* de la historia puede tener ya algun [in]teres esa momia exhumada del sepulcr[o].

[La Verda[d]

El mirto i el laurel.—Un dia dijó el laurel á un mirto vecino su[yo] Huye lejos de esta riberas vil arbu[sto] del amor, debil enemigo de la gl[oria] que mancillas con tus ramas la cor[ona] de los heroes i el árbol de la victo[ria] No sabes quien soi yo dijo el bondad[oso] mirto. Soi quien devuelvo a la tierr[a la] felicidad que tu destruyes i ¿eres q[ue] me insultas cuando hago felices sin [cu]ento i todos tus héroes famosos son [es]clavos mios?

Al pasar Henrique IV. de Francia [por] una aldea los habitantes se reunieron [para] felicitarle con motivo de su llegada. [Tan] pronto como el alcalde del lugar habia [prin]cipiado a hacer un discurso un burro e[mpezó] á rebuznar, i lo cual el rey volviendo hacia el lugar donde estaba el anima[l] gravemente. Señores, uno despues de[l] [...]

Figure 61. First issue of *El Ranchero* (San Antonio, July 4, 1856).

Image di_07435. Dolph Briscoe Center for American History, the University of Texas at Austin.

the East Coast and made contact with other Spanish Americans in New Orleans, including the exiled future president of Mexico Benito Juárez, and his network of agents expanded beyond the *Bejareño*'s Texas focus (though oddly, it did not include any from New Orleans).[34] They included Francisco Serano in Veracruz, Joaquin G. de la Huerta in Mexico City, José María G. Villareal in Camargo, Tamaulipas, and Rafael Guerra Cañamar in Mier, Tamaulipas, the last two being located on the Texas-Mexico border. But Quintero quickly developed adherents in San Antonio. He was initially listed as the sole editor with Guadalupe Leal as the only agent. With the final issue of July 28, 1856, however, Quintero was replaced with Guadalupe Leal, and none other than Narciso Leal, his brother, becomes the Ranchero's agent.[35] Why Narciso left the *Bejareño* to join the *Ranchero* is not fully clear, but, as we will see below, politics may have had everything to do with it. A few years later, the *Correo* had increased the number of agents to more than fifteen, more than those of the *Bejareño* and *Ranchero,* with agents in Austin, Laredo, and Rio Grande City in south Texas; Nacogdoches and Independence in east Texas; El Paso and San Elisario in west Texas; Santa Fe, New Mexico; and Piedras Negras, Coahuila, in northern Mexico.

Producing a New Social Imaginary

The editors laid down a foundation built on personal, commercial, and political alliances. Their networks reveal the expansiveness of a new sense of community covering Texas, New Mexico, the south Texas-Mexico border, and even deeper into Mexico. New Orleans, still commercially important to Texas, had no agents, a sign that Galveston, Indianola (near present-day Corpus Christi), and other ports had come into their own economically. Agents steadfastly worked to circulate newspapers from other parts of the world, supplementing this regional sense of community with a palpable awareness of events unfolding elsewhere. To help their readers comprehend this vast world, editors followed a standard format.

Keeping in mind the differences in the newspapers' durations, the *Ranchero* offered far more extensive editorials, usually encompassing the entire first page and portions of the second. But this was likely, as we will see in Chapter 9, because the *Ranchero* was launched in the midst of the highly contested election of 1856. During this period, the *Bejareño,* too, commented extensively on the elections. The three surviving issues of the *Correo* reveal a much more strident tone than the other two newspapers in defending Tejanos against escalating racial violence. Other important regional news, usually related to politics or the market, was included on the first page of all three newspapers. The second and third pages included local, state, national, and international news. On these pages, one could also find entertaining pieces. Interspersed throughout were letters to the editor. The fourth and final page contained advertisements, and these were usually reprinted unchanged in each issue.

Newspaper articles were reprinted regularly from cities throughout Texas, New Mexico, California, Louisiana, the Midwest, the East Coast, Spanish America, Europe, Africa, and India. They carefully attributed the source, even going as far as reprimanding other newspapers for not citing the original. But beyond attribution, editors included for their readers the tale of the newspapers' voyages. Introductory lines such as these would accompany news summaries: "llegada del vapor *Tejas* de New Orleans con noticias del 9 del pasado [arrived on the *Tejas* steamer with news from New Orleans dated from the 9th]," "las noticias de California llegadas por el *Prometeus* alcanzan el 20 del mes próximo pasado [the news from California arrived on the *Prometheus* dated from the 20th of last month]," or "el vapor *Persia* llegó a Nueva York con fechas de Londres del 26 de Enero [the *Persia* steamer arrived in New York with news from London dated January 26]." Each shipment from New Orleans, Havana, and Veracruz brought with it innumerable newspapers, and the names of newspapers and steamers and their routes abound in these pages: the *Western Texan, Gaceta de Santa Fé,* Los Angeles *Clamor Público,* Saint Louis *Republican, Courrier de la Louisiane,* Charleston *Courier, New York Times,* Monterrey (Mexico) *Restaurador de la Libertad,* Paris *Journal des Debats,* London *Punch,* Naples *Diario,* and *Correo de Bombay,* among numerous others. Editors were just as excited to receive news on the expanding steamer routes and the development of the railroad. The newspapers, in effect, map out an ever-expanding world, revealing how San Antonio was part of a global network of communication and commerce.

Given the dates cited in these newspapers, it took California newspapers about six weeks to arrive in San Antonio, those from Veracruz about three weeks, and those from Havana (often with news from Charleston and other Atlantic ports) two weeks. In consistently providing the precise dates of the news, readers were prompted to imagine time as unfolding uniformly, measured by the rhythms of commercial travel that facilitated the circulation of commodities and news. No longer did they rely on the pace of the state, as they had under Spain and Mexico, to comprehend an ever-expanding world. Nor did they need to rely only on the Church to provide a sense of existential belonging, though certainly this was still the dominant vehicle for achieving a sense of metaphysical presence. Rather, imagining this alternative, vast geography, readers could begin to see themselves as part of a larger metaphysical movement, one marked by the trope of progress and humanity, and one that we have come to describe as modernity.

Among the coverage, editors reported extensively on the increasing sectionalism and xenophobia in the United States, as the question of slavery and the rise of nativism radically reconfigured the relatively new political parties. Here, one learned not only of political upheavals, riots, speeches, and debates within Texas, but also of the violent clashes over slavery in Kansas now known as Bleeding Kansas, labor riots in New York, a fantastic ice bridge that had formed over Niagara Falls during a brutally cold winter throughout the North, the lynching of Chinese, Mexicans, Chileans, and Peruvians during the California Gold Rush, and the sale of the head and hand of the famous Joaquín Murieta. Equal coverage was provided to events unfolding in Mexico and the rest of Spanish America, as Mexico suffered political instability and Spain attempted to assert its authority over them. International news filled the pages as well with reports of William Walker's filibuster attempts in Central America, Haitian emperor Faustin I's attempt to conquer the Dominican Republic, the unfolding Crimean War between the Russian Empire and the French, British, and Ottoman Empires, and the expansion of the British Empire in India. Readers regularly learned quotidian information: the numbers of languages spoken in the world, the average life span in various parts of the world, the number of deaths in the world per year, day, hour, minute, and second, and the number of Catholics in the world.

The newspapers also sought to entertain. The second or third page of every issue included fables, poetry, humourous anecdotes, philosophical reflections, and excerpts from Miguel de Cervantes, Lord Byron, Voltaire, Jeans-Jacques Rousseau, and Dante Alighieri, selections from Quintero's friend the Cuban novelist and revolutionary Cirilo Villaverde, and Quintero's translations of Alexander Dumas, Washington Irving, and Longfellow. But they also included anonymous and locally produced texts, usually short fables, stories, or poems. One could find news on entertainment, such as the arrival of a circus from Mexico, the opening of a daguerreotype studio or a new bar, the staging of a play, or something as exotic as the exhibition of camels (the U.S. military attempted to use these on trips through arid west Texas). The last page was devoted to advertisements. Here, one learned of services offered, from lawyers, teachers, printers, and the arrival of the latest shipment of goods, from shoes and clothing to kitchenware, spices, and liquor. On the last page of the *Ranchero,* Ventura Reyes advertised her skills as a "profesora de harpa y guitarra [teacher of the harp and guitar]" who also taught dance, such as the French quadrille, Mexican contradanza, Cuban dance, and Mazurka polka. In the *Correo,* so too did "Madame Sieminski" advertise her pedagogical musical skills. Also included was evidence of the expanding textual world with Spanish-language ads for dictionaries, grammar books, medical handbooks, books and periodicals in Spanish, English, French, and German, including works by the "best Spanish authors" such as Miguel de Cervantes, the Spanish translation of Alain-René Lesage's 1735 *Gil Blas,* the complete works of Charles Dickens, the widely popular Philadelphia-based *Godey's Lady Book, Harper's Monthly, Edinburgh Review,* and *Westminster Review,* among others.

Through the medium of newspapers, editors took on a variety of tasks. Foremost in their minds was the need to organize Tejanos politically in order for them to participate in the electoral process. It is their expressed duty, they repeatedly remind their readers, to represent and advocate for their community of readers' interests. Through their editorials, editors worked arduously to educate Tejanos regarding their responsibility and the necessity to participate in a democratic government. As the *Bejareño* proclaimed in their first issue: "La falta de un agente de publicación dedicado á los Mejico-Tejanos los deja en la ignorancia de sus deberes y derechos ¿Quantos entre ellos no conocieron la existencia de alguna ley ó reglamento, sino despues de haber sido alcanzados por el golpe de la penalidad [The lack of a newspaper dedicated to the interests of Mejico-Tejanos leaves them ignorant of their rights and responsibilities. How many among them did not know the existence of some law or regulation until after the workings of the law caught up with them]?" The editors were responding to the Tejano landed elite's wholesale loss of land. Immediately after the 1835–1836 Texas Revolution, Tejanos throughout Texas lost their land through violence, squatters, or the evasive machinations of lawyers and judges. Between 1837 and 1842 alone, more than 1,368,000 acres owned by Tejanos were purchased by Anglo-Americans, and this did not include land taken from them illegally. Editors thus worked to educate their constituency in matters concerning the rapidly expanding Texas legal code by translating the most important laws affecting Tejanos, such as the penalty for not paying taxes—loss of land and property.

But newspapers did more than engage with the intricacies of laws. They also painted in broad strokes the philosophical foundation of the United States. The *Bejareño* launched immediately into this discussion on the front page of its first issue of February 7, 1855: "La Constitucion de los Estados Unidos es el objeto de admiracion y orgullo para todo hombre libre, y el terror y espanto de los tiranos que ven en las palabras: *Libertad y Igualidad* [The Constitution of the United States is the object of admiration and pride for all free men, and terror and fear is what tyrants see in the words: *Liberty and Equality*]." Liberty, continued the *Bejareño,* could be divided in three: that of the individual which "confiere á cada ciudadano el derecho de hacer y hablar, conformandose á las leyes establecidas [confers to each citizen the right to act and speak, according to established law]," that of political liberty which "permite á los ciudadanos el mezclarse en los asuntos politicos, discutiendo abiertamente las leyes, y confiriendoles el derecho libre de elejir los empleados publicos [allows citizens to become involved in political affairs, openly discussing laws, and granting them the free right to elect public servants]," and that of religion which "consagra el derecho de cada individuo de adorar á Dios y seguir el culto que le paresca, sin restriccion ninguna [consecrates the right for each individual to worship God and to follow the sect they so choose without any restriction]." Equality, on the other hand, was of two kinds: that of "derechos que se opone á los privilegios de rango y clase [rights opposed to privileges as to rank or class]" and that of "deberes que impone á todos los ciudadanos el tomar su parte respetiva de las cargas y tasaciones, y respetar los derechos individuales [duties imposed on all citizens to pay their respective part in fees and taxes, and respect individual rights]."

This new political foundation was one founded on political liberalism. At its core lay the principles of individual freedom and equality, as expounded by John Locke and enshrined in the foundational documents of the United States. In the first issue of 1856, dated January 5, the *Bejareño* translated the U.S. Declaration of Independence, instructing their readers that they should memorize it because it is the "Biblia política [political Bible]." It took for granted the idea of individualism as an innate, irreducible quality that defines modern political subjects and ascribes to them agency. This underlying agency emerges from the desires of each individual subject, and as they come together to create a government, they each give up certain rights—to do as one wants, to steal and kill, for example—in order to create the state. As a result, taxes had to be collected to build the state's infrastructure, such as the much-needed repairs to the dilapidated bridge in the center of San Antonio through which a young boy had fallen through to his death. All three papers argued in favor of new laws that would secure individuals' rights to their life, liberty, and property.

Or, as often was the case, they lambasted law enforcement officials for refusing to prosecute Anglo-Americans who robbed and killed Tejano oxcarters. Tejanos dominated the extremely lucrative freighting industry that transported goods to and from the Gulf Coast, and the incidents known as the 1857 Cart War prompted international attention, finally forcing state officials to intervene. But it was too little, too late. The fear of a race war and despoliation of Tejano carters led to their demise. Editors were just as furi-

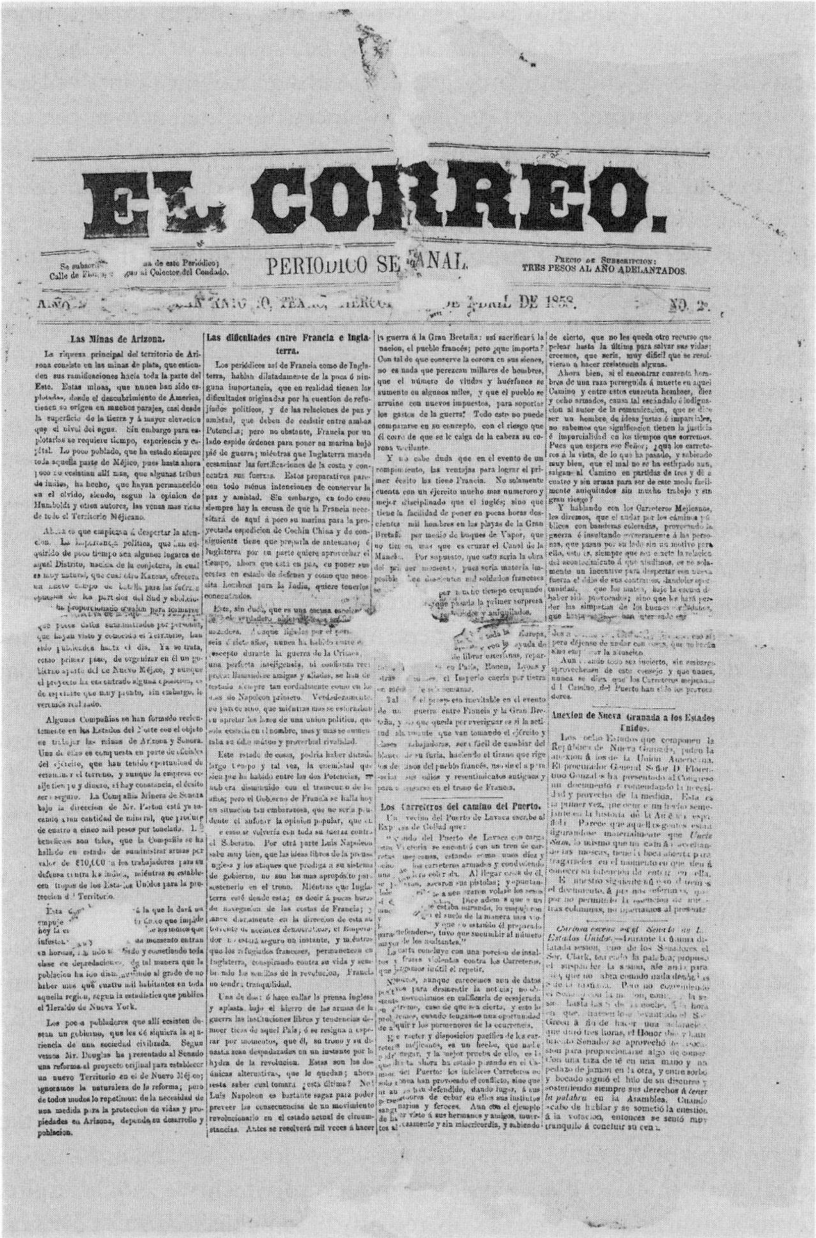

Figure 62. Second issue of *El Correo* (San Antonio, April 28, 1858).
Image di_07614, Dolph Briscoe Center for American History, University of Texas at Austin.

ous when east Texas and coastal towns forcibly expelled Tejanos from their land, only to find other Anglophone newspapers describe the incidents as Tejanos' choice to "migrate." Notwithstanding the failure of legal institutions to protect them in these instances, the three newspapers all agreed with the premise that government exists to ensure the freedom of each individual even as it requires each individual to contribute to the sustainability of that government. They vociferously demanded that legal institutions live up to their expectations even as they insisted that Tejanos participate in the making of them.

Along with the concept of liberty, the *Bejareño* also elaborated on the ideal of equality. It insisted that all privileges associated with rank and class be eliminated. Lost in this editorial is any reference to the *pueblo,* remnants of Francisco Suárez's *corpus mysticum,* or to any Catholic political philosophical sensibility. There is little conceptual hybridity here, unlike in the earlier documents that we have seen. The innate, hierarchical social order and the sense that God had fixed it and made change impossible have withered even more, surpassing the disenchantment that had been experienced by *letrados* such as the late eighteenth-century Hispanic Scholastics, the Gutiérrez de Lara brothers, Álvarez de Toledo, or Trespalacios. But to deny it did not mean that those sentiments, the collective spiritual feeling of the *pueblo,* the legal tradition of the commons (shared communal land), which had been the basis of the Hispanic social imaginary had disappeared completely. In fact, while the editorials made little explicit reference to non-U.S.-inspired political philosophy, one could find indirect allusions to it.

Buried on the back page of the April 16, 1856, issue of the *Bejareño* is a two-column article authored by the esteemed nineteenth-century conservative Catholic Spanish *letrado* Juan Donoso Cortés (1809–1853). A proud descendant of the Spanish conquistador Hernán Cortés, he had once embraced the radical liberalism of the Enlightenment, only to turn radically against it, especially after the 1848 European Revolutions. The reprint, titled "La biblia," is a much shorter, abridged version of Cortés's thirty-page "Discurso sobre la biblia." It is a panegyric of the Bible as an ur-text, the source of all of Western civilization's greatest works of art and one that offered ideal ethical and sociopolitical models to which we should aspire. Cortés's influential works had only recently been published in 1854–1855; thus, the editors easily could have had access to them.

Cortés's highly influential political thought altered the utopic, Thomist premises upon which Suárez had developed his theories. Rather than having always lived in society according to divinely inspired natural law, Cortés pursued the much more Augustinian, Puritan tradition: humans were depraved, wretched creatures incapable of rational thought, and therefore required that they be ruled with an iron fist. He, like most conservative European philosophers who were his contemporaries, embraced a fixed hierarchical view of the world. There was little of the Suarezian concept of the rights of the *corpus mysticum*.[36] Neither the *Bejareño* nor the other papers elaborated on Cortés's or other Catholic political ideas, but they certainly embraced the premises of liberalism which Cortés had dismissed. They also advocated for a heightened, reconfigured sense of the *corpus mysticum,* of the public.

Reconfigured Publics

The Tejano social imaginary began to be reconfigured even before Texas was annexed by the United States. It had already been called into question in the late eighteenth century when Spanish Americans protested the Bourbon reforms and, among the intellectual elite, with the debates between Scholastics and modern philosophers. Yet, the actual tearing apart of political and religious authority, that source of legitimacy that had been the very foundation of the Hispanic world, began with the events that unfolded after Napoleon's deposing of the Spanish king in 1808. With each shift in Texan sovereignty—from New Spain to the Mexican empire under Iturbide and then as the Mexican republic, to the Republic of Texas, and, finally, to the United States—that chain of political signifiers that had been cemented was loosened a bit further. Each time, the sense of stability, of an enchanted world, slipped further away. Each time, the idea that the social order was contingent and not fixed, able to shift, though often at a great price, emerged even clearer.

For most of the nineteenth century, Spanish Americans were in the midst of reconfiguring their social imaginary in at least two directions: (1) creating territorially bounded, nationally imagined communities that would supplant the concentric relationships of belonging that had been part of the Hispanic world, such as those we explored in Chapter 1; and (2) developing political arguments that would reconfigure sovereignty as something that was understood primarily as a product of human intention. To do so, however, meant tearing apart the very foundation that had legitimized the Hispanic world for centuries.

Traces of that world, however, could still be seen. Notwithstanding the *Bejareño*'s proclamation of liberty and equality of all individuals, sentiments that Trespalacios had pronounced thirty years earlier, these newspapers appealed to the concept of the *pueblo*. As we will see in Chapter 9, they did so as a means to politically unify the Tejano community, in the face of intransigent Anglo-American racism. The *Bejareño* and the *Ranchero,* for example, implored the *pueblo* to attend the meeting of the recently created organization named the "Ciudadanos Demócratas Méjico-Tejanos [Democratic Mejico-Tejano Citizens]" in order to defeat Anglo-American candidates who actively sought to eliminate their participation in the public sphere. A few years later, in 1858, their efforts would expand beyond the political arena as they created the Sociedad Méjico-Tejana. In effect, Anglo-American racism ensured that Tejanos would embrace the rhetoric of the Méjico-Tejano *pueblo* and its rights.

Yet declaring the rights of the individual and continuing to invoke the *pueblo* were not necessarily inconsistent. Rather, embracing the rights of the individual helped further the late eighteenth-century Hispanic reorientation of the *pueblo* that we witnessed in Chapter 3. Hispanic *letrados,* such as Campomanes and Jovellanos, sought to rethink the Hispanic monarch's responsibility as one whose primary duty was to secure the well-being of the *pueblo*. However, they did so without needing or desiring to resort to the rights of the individual, and they did so in a way that positioned the monarch and his *letrados* as the only ones capable of comprehending what the *pueblo* needed. But nineteenth-century Spanish Americans, including these Tejanos, begin to embrace the rights of the individual as a way to completely invert the rationale of the state. The monarch and his *letrados* and any such derivatives (like Emperor Iturbide) have been eliminated; now, it is the *pueblo* alone (comprised of individuals with rights) that legitimates the state.

By midcentury, the emphasis on the *pueblo* had begun to cede ground to liberalism and its attendant rights of the individual. Liberal Spanish Americans such as the towering political figure in Mexico, Father José María Luis Mora, struggled to eliminate the concept of corporate privileges and replace it with liberal concepts of individualism and private property. According to the historian Charles Hale, Mexican liberals believed corporate entities "exercise[d] a kind of tyranny over their members, which inhibit[ed] personal independence and the development of a community of citizens enjoying equal rights and responsibilities. The *espíritu de cuerpo* imposed not only juridical and administrative barriers to unity and progress but grave economic obstacles as well."[37] But this transformation was more immediate in the more metropolitan areas of Spanish America, such as Mexico City.[38]

In order to make the state legitimate, Tejanos had to participate in its making, and consciously used newspapers toward that end. As the *Bejareño*'s first editorial reads, "[H]abiendo comunicado nuestras miras é intenciones á muchos ciudadanos inteligentes y amigos del progreso, fuimos alentados y estimulados, y sin recelo nos propusimos llevar á cabo la empreza, lanzando nuestra barquilla en el mar de la publicidad [Having communicated our views and intentions to many intelligent citizens and friends of progress, we were encouraged and stimulated, and without hesitation we decided to carry out the enterprise, launching our tiny boat in the sea of publicity]."

The *Bejareño* invokes the concept of the public, but the "sea of publicity" had been removed from the very visible quarters of the public square. The concept of the public as a representation of the *pueblo* had existed before, certainly, but it had been subordinate to figures of the sovereign and had been limited in a quantifiable sense. The concept of the Tejano public had been a product of an oral and visual culture defined by the local town square. Such was the case when commandant general Arredondo printed a proclamation announcing the independence of Mexico, read it aloud in the town square, and then, afterward, crossed the square to the steps of the Cathedral, where he declared his oath to Mexico.[39] *Letrados,* the political officials and clergy who had long wielded authority over the written word,

Figure 63. The San Antonio Plaza de Armas had long served as the location for the public representation of the *pueblo*. William G. M. Samuel, *West Side Main Plaza, San Antonio, Texas* (1849).

Courtesy of the Witte Museum, San Antonio, Texas.

were left to inculcate dominant notions of the public good into their subjects.

As in the rest of Spanish America, the town square was the literal incarnation of the public. It was framed by the Church, the governor's quarters, and the market square. Yet the *pueblo* had not participated directly in the making of the state. They were called to witness the actions of the public figure of the sovereign (the general or governor). Still, the subaltern figure of the public *pueblo* was not without agency. The *pueblo*'s demands, including rumors, murmurs, and gossip, could all easily transgress the official sovereign authorities, and in doing so transformed and mediated the messages that were conveyed.[40] Alternative, non-state- or Church-sanctioned publics rivaled official processions, such as the well-documented history of dances known as *fandangos* in San Antonio, along with races and public bathing during the sweltering Texas summers.[41]

Figure 64. Theodore Gentilz, *Fandango* (late 1840s–1850s).
Yanaguana Society Collection. Daughters of the Republic of Texas Library.

Now, newspapers emerge as a way to ensure that the figure of the *pueblo* will participate in the making of the state. They thus help reconfigure the concept of the public in two ways. First, by printing their editorials and news, they make more concrete the *rhetorical* shape of the minoritized Tejano public as they seek to intervene in the dominant Anglo-American public sphere. But even as the rhetoric became distilled, the public itself became more disembodied than before. They were no longer confined to a locale or to a quantifiable number of *vecinos* in certain towns, as was the case with the public reading of the 1832 petition. Now, editors dispersed their newspapers throughout Texas, the Southwest, and Mexico, hoping to shape the broader consensus regarding Tejanos and their place in the public sphere. Second, and rather ironically, by cognitively mapping the world for their readership (and those who listened as it was read aloud), newspapers ended up constructing an alternative, imagined, geographic sense of the world. Their agents and the news they reprinted provide the framework for understanding that world. Their readers are now part of a produced order, one made by humans.

As for the other abstract concepts related to the *pueblo,* such as the management of their "well-being," this had long been considered the purview of *letrados.* Yet, even while newspapers sought to engage the public in configuring their well-being, editors and other elite Tejanos saw themselves as guiding the public in defining that sense of happiness even as they hoped that the individual members of the *pueblo* would become active citizens. But these *pueblos* were forced to separate themselves from the authority of the Church just as they realized that their world was a human construct. In effect, the sense of authority and belonging long offered by the unity of Church and state had been shattered.

But these newspapers also grafted themselves, quite literally, onto the space of these previous publics: the editors' offices were located in the San Antonio town square known as the Plaza de Armas. Previously, these official political-religious gatherings had been foundational to the *corpus mysticum,* providing a sense of metaphysical, spiritual belonging as participants imagined that other *pueblos,* too, were participating in similar gatherings. They offered a sense that the *pueblo,* as a witness to the functioning of sovereignty, was integral to the Catholic cosmos, to that string of sovereignty that ran from God, to Church, to monarch or emperor, to local commander or governor. Religion, certainly, continued to offer a sense of presence. However, Tejanos have now begun to use print as a means to shift from "the revelational certainty of salvation . . . to a certainty *(Gewissheit)* in which man makes secure for himself the true as the known of his own knowing."[42] Writing and the circulation of print will produce this alternative sense of presence, a presence that is the construct of self-liberating men (in all its gendered connotations), those "intelligent citizens and friends of progress, as the *Bejareño* had pronounced."

A New Temporality

Publics had inhabited an enchanted world embedded in what Charles Taylor describes as "higher time": hierarchically ordered, ordained by God, and thus fixed. They offered one the possibility of feeling secure in the world knowing that God had produced an intricately balanced, perfect universe and that one's role in that order was crucial to the maintenance of that world. Higher time was not defined by the activities of humans alone but, rather, by God. As Benedict Anderson describes it, in this world, there was "no conception of history as an endless chain of cause and effect or of radical separations between past and present." Rather, higher time was structured by the divine, was cyclical not linear, and saw time as "a simultaneity of past and future in an instantaneous present." Taylor spells out this sense of simultaneity in his discussion of St. Augustine, who sought to "participate in God's instant . . . [by] rising to eternity." It was through religious practice and ritual that one could approach this eternal sense of time.[43]

Newspapers appear to have wanted to produce a new social imaginary onto which the public could cathect. In removing themselves from a world that was understood to be a received order, they distanced themselves, too, from fully seeing themselves as only belonging to that sense of higher time. Increasingly, they are located within what Walter Benjamin described as "homogeneous, empty time," not structured by the divine but by humanity.[44] As Anderson has persuasively argued, by printing local news alongside international coverage, newspapers begin to move the social imaginary toward this concept of homogeneous time, away from the divine sense of simultaneity *along* time to simultaneity *across* time.[45]

Now, one could read about events unfolding simultaneously in Texas and across the world, and one could also read an extensive amount of history. It is as if the editors consciously sought to produce, through their reprinting of news, an imagined geographic space with which their readers could identify. Likewise, through their publishing of historical materials, the editors also inadvertently created an alternative narrative of origins and belonging, not unlike the 1832 petition discussed in Chapter 7. These newspapers, then, continued the arduous work inaugurated by the initial

Figure 65. Theodore Gentilz, *Entierro de un angel* (1850s).
Yanaguana Society Collection. Daughters of the Republic of Texas Library.

revolutionaries of the early nineteenth century, such as Father José Antonio Gutiérrez de Lara who pronounced the dawn of a new age when he declared independence in 1811. They produced narratives of progress, with its connotations of linear versus cyclical time, of life constantly moving forward, of life perpetually able to break free of the shackles of the past and start anew. Life has entered history, and will now determine the future.

Anderson's account of temporality and the modern emergence of history as a discipline tell us that this new sense of time is ordered along the nation. The time of eternity becomes "nation-time," and the modern discipline of history emerges as the biography of a nation.[46] The affect of belonging, the metaphysics of security that religion had once offered, is increasingly replaced with the love for one's nation. What was the history of this love affair, according to the *Bejareño?*

The *Bejareño* not only worked unconsciously to render this new temporality of simultaneity across time by juxtaposing in print events from around the world with those taking place locally. It also intuitively helped produce this modern temporality by dedicating so many pages to the publication of history. More than half of its extant fifty-five issues contain historical accounts on the front page that are at least half a page in length. The editors begin doing so with their second issue, in which they included excerpts from the Bexar Archives. The first reprinted record was a 1744 governmental document that described the geography, settlements, and inhabitants of Texas. In their fifth issue, they reprint Spanish royal commander Ignacio Elizondo's 1813 letter to Bernardo where Elizondo denounces Bernardo and revolutionaries as heretics, which we saw in Chapter 5.

In reprinting these records, the editors never introduce or offer commentary, and let the original language stand for itself. In all, thirteen of the twenty-six historical articles relate to Spanish or Mexican Texas. Another ten consist of long excerpts from an unnamed narrative history of the United States, from Christopher Columbus's arrival through the War of 1812, and several relate to Mexico. Still, though the *Bejareño* reprints items from the Bexar Archives, it does not weave these events into an integrated narrative history. They did not yet have available to them a unified, narrative account of their past, something akin to that of the history of the United States which they published. However, by bringing these together—the excerpts from the Bexar Archives and accounts from Mexico's past, along with the narrative history of the United States—it is as if the editors were seeking to produce an integrated whole, a narrative that could fully embody the Tejano *pueblo*. But the *Bejareño* was far from alone in working toward producing historical narratives, one where humans become central agents in the making of history rather than understanding the cosmos as divine in origin.

José Antonio Navarro—the former representative to the Coahuila y Texas legislature, one of three Tejano signers of the declaration of Texas's independence, and coauthor of the 1832 petition discussed in Chapter 7—had already attempted to produce such a historical narrative. He wrote it in response to the degradingly racist language in many English-language newspapers that dismissed Tejanos as "mongrels and greasers," and, more specifically, in response to the recently published, widely well-received history of Texas by Henderson Yoakum. Well-received, that is, by everyone except Tejanos. Yoakum had written that "Ignorance and despotism . . . hung like a dark cloud over [Texas's] noble forests and luxuriant pastures" until the arrival of Anglo-Americans.[47]

The *Bejareño* recognized the significance of Yoakum's effort, yet it also lamented "que deja mucho que desear en lo que refiere à los *primeros* años de la historia de Tejas, y mas bien deberia titularse 'Historia de los Americanos en Tejas [that it leaves much to be desired in respect to the *first* years of Texas' history, and that perhaps it should be titled 'History of the (Anglo) Americans in Texas']."[48] By "the first years of Texas's history," the *Bejareño* does not refer to the initial Spanish colonization of Texas; rather, the "first" years of Texas's history, that moment that severed with the past in order to begin anew, are the initial battles for Texan independence from Spain that occurred beginning in 1811. Not only did Yoakum include few details of those events, but the ones he did were erroneous. An Anglo-American participant in the events of 1812–1813 wrote exasperatedly about Yoakum, "I find such a multitude of misrepresentation and erroneous assertions . . . , it would exhaust my patience if it did not discompose my equinimity [*sic*] to persue [*sic*] his erroneous extracts."[49] Likewise, the *Bejareño* declared, "No hay excusa para vuestro crimen [There is no excuse for your crime]," since Yoakum never even consulted the eyewitness testimony of the highly esteemed Navarro. Born in 1795, Navarro was a teenager when he witnessed the bloody battles for Texan independence from Spain.

Navarro's accounts were written in 1853 and 1857, translated into English, and published by Anglo-sympathizers in English-language newspapers in order to combat Anglo-American racism. It was not until 1869, however, that his two accounts were collected by, among others, Narciso Leal, agent to both the *Bejareño* and *Ranchero* and president of the Sociedad Méjico-Tejana. They edited and rearranged the accounts to produce a cohesive history, and published them privately in Spanish. *Apuntes históricos interesantes de San Antonio de Béxar (Interesting Historical Notes regarding San Antonio de Béxar)* is the first published Tejano history.[50]

At twenty densely typed pages, the history narrates in often disturbing detail the events that began our book: the 1813 arrival of the insurgent Bernardo in San Antonio, the struggle on the part of Bexareño families to seek independence, their crushing defeat by the Spanish royal commander Arredondo, and the royal army's torture of the women whose families had supported insurrection. But the narrative actually begins with a rather personal exchange between Narciso Leal and Navarro. It is prefaced with two letters, one written by Leal, on behalf of several friends and himself, to Navarro asking for formal permission to: "publicarlos por la Prensa, para su mas estensa circulacion [publish them via the Press, in order to provide them with the widest circulation]." Navarro replied in turn, graciously granting permission to reprint his account. Yet, as Navarro informs them, he had published his narratives in 1853 and 1857, and "quedaron, desde luego al dominio público, los dichos opúsculos; por consiguiente, estan Vds en absoluta libertad de hacer de ellos el uso que les fuere placible [the

Figure 66. Anonymous, Portrait of José Antonio Navarro.
The Alamo Collection, San Antonio, Texas.

said pamphlets remained since then in the public dominion; thus, you are at absolute liberty to use them in whatever way would most please you.]"[51]

"Publishing," for these Tejanos, remains connected to the earlier denotation we have seen: the act of making something public. Thus, they choose to "publish them via the Press," implying that they could be "published" or made public via other means, such as the 1832 petition that was read aloud to the established towns in Texas. They suggest that printing had not displaced verbal communication or manuscripts as an important way of disseminating information. But if "publishing" was sufficient before, it no longer is, implies Leal. Leal actively seeks to gain the "widest circulation" because he and his friends believe, "firmemente que serán recibidos con júbilo por todos los ciudadanos mexicanos de Texas y principalmente por los hijos de San Antonio [firmly that they will be received with jubilation by all the Mexican citizens of Texas and especially by the sons of San Antonio]" (1). From here on, Leal claims, the memory of the revolutionary events that unfolded in San Antonio no longer pertains only to the "sons of San Antonio" but to all "Mexican citizens of Texas." That is, Leal and his friends do not see Navarro's accounts as Navarro saw them, as mere "historical notes." Rather, they become the basis upon which Tejanos can begin to construct a historical narrative of belonging, and the best way to make this narrative account accessible to this expansively imagined community was to publicize them, not through word of mouth or manuscripts, but via the medium of the printing press.

Despite the incredible racism (which we will see in Chapter 9) that surrounded them, these individuals do not emphasize it, merely mentioning it in passing. Instead, they seek to glorify what Navarro describes as

> las hazañas, sacrificios y trágico fin que tubieron sus ilustres ascendientes, por solamente conseguir la Independencia y libertad Mexicana . . . y donde por *primera* vez, los hijos de San Antonio de Bexar manifestaron su patriotismo é hicieron prodigios de valor y casi románticos tomando una parte activa los descendientes de aquellos nobles Isleños.
>
> [the deeds, sacrifices, and tragic end of their illustrious ancestors, for merely attempting to gain the Independence and freedom of Mexico . . . and where for the *first* time, the sons of San Antonio de Bexar manifested their patriotism and produced such wondrous, almost romantic, acts of valor, in which those descendants of those noble Islanders took an active part.] (2, emphasis added)

In the early nineteenth century, as we have seen, *patria* and patriotism could still connote love, in concentric circles, of Spain and its monarch, then of New Spain, all the way down to the province of Texas, and, finally, one's local community. But now, Navarro implies, a break has occurred. Now, "for the *first* time," patriotism is identified not only with country but, more importantly, with "Independence and freedom." *Patria* and *patriotismo* no longer connote a commitment to state and Church as the source of both political and ontological certainty, as the basis on which communities constructed meaning and acted in the world. *Patria* remains a key operative concept, despite its internal reconfiguration so as to signify, for the first time, the modern political concepts of freedom and independence. Here is a narrative of origins, one breaking from any Christian eschatological history that would trace their history back through the monarchy to the Bible.

There is no doubt as to these Tejanos' loyalty to the United States. Recounting the horrific 1813 Spanish defeat and torture of the Spanish-American-Tejano insurgents, Navarro describes how they lost all of their property and sacrificed their lives. Still, he continues:

> Nunca recibieron recompensa ó indemnizacion alguna y ni aun el respeto debido y gratitud de sus conciudadanos de México. Fué dado al olvido absoluto nuestro valor y heroismo por el Gobierno de la antigua y bien recordada Pátria. Por eso no creo que sorprenda á nadie el gérmen de descontento, que el pueblo de Texas abrigaba, y por cuya causa se adhiere al nuevo órden de cosas que nos brindaban las instituciones de una grande, poderosa, y agradesida República. Tal es el oríjen que dió márjen á la Independencia, de Texas, que para siempre se separó de aquel Gobierno.
>
> [They never received reward or compensation nor even the well-deserved respect and gratitude from their fellow Mexican citizens. Our valor and heroism were cast into oblivion by the Government of the ancient and well-remembered *Patria.* That is why I do not think it should surprise anyone that the seed of discontent that the people of Texas held is the reason for which they adhere to the new order of things, a new order granted to us by the institutions of a large, powerful, and grateful Republic. Such is the origin that led to the Independence, of Texas, which forever separated itself from that Government.] (20)

Having been abandoned by Mexico, Navarro claims, Tejanos turned instead to the "institutions" of a more powerful republic. But Navarro makes a distinction between "government" and "patria." It was the recently established "Gobierno," not the "Antigua y bien recordada Pátria [Ancient and well-remembered *Patria*]," that cast these Tejanos into oblivion.

Navarro does not disguise his disdain for the new "gobierno" of Mexico, and suggests that as a result Tejanos have shifted their emotional energies onto the "instituciones [institutions]" of that "larger, powerful Republic." Their energies have shifted, that is, to the government of the United States. But a palpable tension emerges here because Navarro's language also evokes nostalgia for that "Ancient and well remembered *Patria*" of Mexico. Yet, nostalgia, with its connotation of melancholia, means that Tejanos have not yet forgotten their *patria.* Indeed, they continue to "remember it well." Likewise, the name of their newly adopted parent (to invoke one of the connotations of *patria* that we saw earlier), the United States, does not emerge anywhere. Rather, it is simply metonymically referred to as "institutions," suggesting that the full transference of love to the United States has not occurred.

A nation and its attendant nationalism that could fully embrace these Tejanos have yet to form. But one can make out the contours of a hero. In

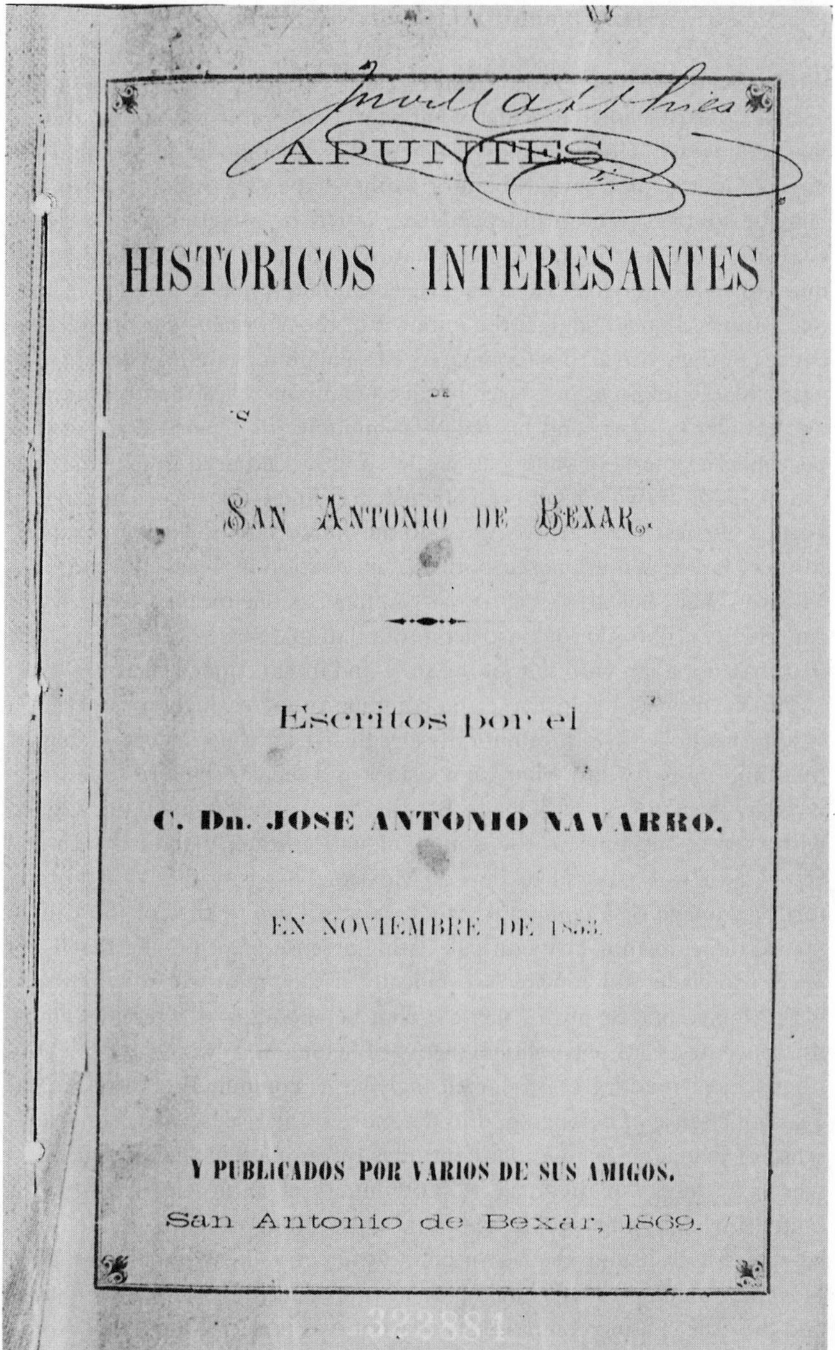

Figure 67. Title page of José Antonio Navarro, *Apuntes históricos interesantes de San Antonio de Béxar* (privately published 1869).

Image di_07615. Dolph Briscoe Center for American History, University of Texas at Austin.

their collectively written introductory essay to the *Apuntes,* Leal and his friends construct for the reader what can be seen as a foundational hero for an imagined nationalism. In Navarro they see a model citizen for Tejanos. He is not, they say, a liberator in the shape of a Simón Bolívar, the hero of South American independence; nor is he a legislator like Henry Clay, the esteemed Southern statesman who helped broker the Compromises of 1820 and 1850. He is not even a *caudillo* (political-military leader) like Father Miguel Hidalgo, the initiator of the Mexican War of Independence. Rather, Navarro is compared to Benjamin Franklin because Navarro, like Franklin, is possessed by an equanimous spirit that treats everyone equally (2). Leal and his fellow community of Tejanos draw from a hemispheric coterie of American heroes, and feel no need to explain their rationale for drawing from both Spanish and Anglo-Americans in order to adequately describe Navarro. (Nor do they remark on the ironic comparison to Clay, he who opposed both the annexation of Texas and the U.S.-Mexican War.) Navarro's history serves, then, as one means by which this community will begin to construct a foundational sense of belonging, one that may not align with that of the state and its sanctioned racism.

This history will help move the community increasingly away from a strictly Catholic world, temporally organized by the concept of higher time, and more toward what we consider as a secular sense of time structured by the activities of humans. But this sense of belonging is not aligned with that of the time of the dominant nation-state, that of the United States. Nor is it moored to that of Mexico. That is, rather than putting forth an image of a community that *only* belongs to that of the United States, these Tejanos insist on cultivating a sense of belonging that is, at once, rooted in San Antonio, specifically, Texas, more broadly, but also with Mexico and Spanish America. That belonging is also reminiscent of the concentric Catholic political theory of belonging in which one felt connected, in various degrees, to increasingly larger communities. It still retains a catholic sense of belonging, if in the more secular sense. This concentric sense of belonging is one that continues to resonate in the present, as in when one thinks of the imagined community of Latin America which is united through language, history, and culture but which is divided into countries each having their own concentric circles of national belonging. However, unlike Spanish Americans who produced nation-states, Tejanos and the other Latino communities of what was now the Southwest would be left with a national sense of belonging that would not be allowed to coalesce with that of the U.S. state.

The newspaper editors from 1855 to 1858, however, fought to incorporate Tejanos into the dominant public sphere. At no time did they express a desire to separate themselves from the U.S. polity. However, and in an effort to mitigate Anglo-American racism, they did attempt to steer the Tejano *pueblo* to acquiesce to Anglo-American moral standards. In doing so, newspapers, the *Bejareño* in particular, began to divest once-sanctioned public spaces of the authority they once had in giving shape to the public.

The *Bejareño,* for example, enthusiastically sided with Anglo-Americans in seeking to enforce the Sabbath and to legislate against what had been public spaces for Tejano entertainment. The legislation in regard to the Sabbath significantly curtailed Tejano Catholic celebrations on Sundays. Events such as *fandangos,* gambling, cockfighting, and public bathing in rivers during the scorching summers had long been common practice among Tejanos. But Anglo-Americans contemptuously looked upon these gatherings as morally corrupt and sought to regulate and, in some instances, criminalize them. Nonetheless, even as the *Bejareño* supported these legislative efforts, it was also quick to criticize Anglo-Americans' use of "greaser" and other racial slurs when discussing attempts to outlaw these spaces.[52]

In advocating for the suppression of previous Tejano publics, the *Bejareño* revealed its desire to forge elite, class alliances with the new Anglo-American majority. The name of the newspaper itself, in fact, insists that the Tejano community be recognized not as "Mexicans," with all the increasingly racial connotations of that term, but as "Bejareños," the legitimate founders of San Antonio de Béxar. The hierarchies of the Catholic world may have dissipated, but they were quickly replaced with new ones. Other newspapers, such as the *Ranchero,* would reveal competing interests that would call into question the *Bejareño*'s true loyalties. Still, no matter how much they debated one another, they quickly realized that no amount of effort would ever fully appease Anglo-American racism.

CHAPTER NINE

"The Natural Sympathies That Unite All of Our People"

Political Journalism and the Struggle against Racism

Putting Pen to Political Work

During the hot, humid summer of 1856, the San Antonio-based Spanish-language newspapers *El Ranchero* and *El Bejareño* engaged in heated debate over which political party would best serve the interests of Tejanos: the Democratic Party or the newly arrived Know-Nothing Party. José Agustín Quintero's *Ranchero* was an adamant supporter of the Democrats. The *Bejareño,* surprisingly, adopted a neutral position, disdaining the formation of partisan parties, especially where political parties often turned out to be nothing more than a competition of personalities. The rhetoric became inflamed when Quintero accused the *Bejareño* of colluding with the staunchly xenophobic, anti-Catholic Know-Nothing Party. Quintero had attempted to be patient and had tolerated, in the spirit of congenial debate, what he saw to be obvious contradictions in the *Bejareño*'s editorials. But in the face of increasing hostility toward Tejanos in San Antonio and throughout Texas, he could no longer hold back.[1]

Quintero thought that the *Bejareño*'s neutral position during the important election of 1856 would only lead to the political demise of Tejanos (whom newspapers also referred to as "Mejico-Tejanos" and "Mexicanos"). Finally, after repeated allusions to the *Bejareño*'s misplaced loyalties in previous issues, Quintero put, as he often described it, pen to political work. Unfortunately, the last surviving issue of the *Bejareño* is dated exactly one week before the *Ranchero* began publishing, so it is not known what the *Bejareño* had published. Nonetheless, on the front page of the July 19, 1856, issue, Quintero laid into the *Bejareño:*

> Vacilando entre una carcajada i un suspiro leimos el articulo que sobre nuestro periódico publica nuestro amable colega el Bejareño, en el cual, a pesar de sus pretensiones i del ligero tinte de modestia con que ha querido presentarlas a sus lectores se echa de ver, desde luego, cuales son sus aspiraciones i moralidad.
>
> [Vacillating between boisterous laughter and shocking gasps we read the article that our amiable colleague, the *Bejareño,* publishes about our newspaper, in which despite their pretensions and thinly veiled attempts at modesty with which they have wanted to present them to their readers, they make quite clear their true aspirations and ethics.]

Quintero had attempted to restrain himself in previous issues, but he knew "el dia del conbate se acercaba [the day of combat would soon arrive]." No longer could he "permanecer indiferentes al lado de un periodico que se olvida de los principios para abogar por las personas, i quiere sacrificar el bienestar general al interes de sus amigos [remain indifferent when confronted by a newspaper that had forgotten its principles to advocate for people, and wants to sacrifice the general well-being in favor of their friends' interests]."[2] Clearly, given the *Ranchero*'s editorials along with those of other newspapers', the *Bejareño* had continued to publish, but it is ultimately impossible to fully comprehend the *Bejareño*'s position. In Quintero's estimation, however, the editors of the *Bejareño* had shamelessly put their friends' interests before the people it ostensibly represented.[3]

Quintero turned to journalism as one way to defend his concept of the public above and against what he saw to be the *Bejareño*'s solipsistic interests. In essence, he began to define the contours of the relationship between journalism and the public sphere, and, to that extent, rehearsed a now-familiar argument on the metonymical relationship between newspapers and the collective interests of an imagined community. Newspapers, he contends, have the responsibility of "defending and advocating for people" and ensuring the "public's well-being." What we have here is no less than the making of a public sphere and, with it, of the concept of the public and of political authority, all as the elite sought with desperation to retain whatever power they could, in the midst of growing racial violence and the continuing displacement of Tejanos. For Quintero, newspapers are not mere neutral observers; they are, instead, the defenders of their

Figure 68. José Agustín Quintero. Photograph (ca. 1880).
Image di_07433, Dolph Briscoe Center for American History, University of Texas, Austin.

community of readers and listeners. They serve to shape that community rather than merely reflect its interests.

On the eve of their ultimate erasure from the public world of newspaper publishing, Tejanos turned to the medium as a way to both guarantee that their interests would be represented in the state and to cultivate a sense of community in Texas. Let us delve into the embattled electoral debate of 1856, one embroiled in the brutal anti-Mexican violence unfolding in the state. Yet, more than mere defensive posturing, these papers also articulate their ideal sense of community, one that had been built on the extensive networks they had cultivated throughout the Gulf of Mexico region.

Xenophobia and Anti-Mexican Violence

In the months prior to the debate between the *Bejareño* and the *Ranchero,* newspapers had reported on the escalating violence throughout central and south Texas; the formation of Anglo-American vigilante committees; the expulsion of Tejanos from central Texas counties; the theft of Tejanos' livestock and property; and the coercion, extortion, and lynching of Tejanos. The *Bejareño* vehemently criticized "la Ley Lynch," by which it was referring to a meeting of Anglo-Americans outside of San Antonio. The Anglo-Americans at the meeting had decided to establish a company of "Regulators" whose responsibility was to hang twelve Tejanos as a "lesson" for refusing to sell their land.[4] Then, again, on July 7, 1855, the *Bejareño* published a letter by Pedro Rodrigues in which he complained of an "outrage" committed by one J. J. Golman.

During the 1850s, as we have seen, Tejanos dominated the lucrative oxcart transportation route between the port of Indianola and San Antonio, due to their willingness to underbid Anglo-American carters. This indeed would become one of the central arenas of struggle between Anglo-Americans and Tejanos that would result in the Cart War, peaking in 1857 and concluding by December of that year. By then, however, Tejano cart companies had been systematically robbed and destroyed, and their carters lynched, culminating in their economic demise. After several years of unprosecuted violence against carters, the editors of both *El Bejareño* and *El Correo* were flabbergasted. They decried the lack of justice, and the *Correo* added, "No sabemos que significacion tienen la justicia é imparcialidad en los tiempos que corremos [We know not what meaning justice and impartiality have in these times]." So virulent and targeted was this war that the Mexican government officially protested, prompting the U.S. federal government to intervene.[5]

Rodrigues had owned one of these lines, and he had gone to the coastal town of Coleto to retrieve a team of oxen his carters had left at Golman's ranch. Upon his arrival, however, Golman claimed Rodrigues's carter owed him $50, adding that Rodrigues would not receive his oxen until he paid Golman the money, and promptly had Rodrigues's horse taken. "De repente [All of a sudden]," writes Rodrigues,

> se adelantó hacia mi, berduque en mano y me agarró, con amenazas de cortarme el pescueso; otro hombre se echó encima de mi por atras, me quitó mi pistola y veinte ó veinte y cinco otros, algunos con pistolas, se juntaron á mis agresores. Al mismo tiempo, Golman me amenazó de enviarme al calabozo ó

> de cortarme el pescueso si no le pagare al momento los cincuenta pesos. En vista de advertir mayores desgracias, en presencia de esa gente enfurecida que ya hablaba de *lincharme* tuvé que firmar un papel que me presentaron, diciendo que era un pagaré de 50 pesos, pagadero á tres meses de fecha. Golman dijó entre otras espreciones que siendo él Juez de Paz, no se le daba un bledo por mi, ni una centena de mi especia, y que no le importaba un c**** si tapara un arroyo con mi cuerpo.
>
> [he came up to me, knife in hand and grabbed me, threatening to slit my throat; another man jumped on me from behind and took my gun, while twenty or twenty-five others, some with guns, joined my aggressors. At the same time, Golman threatened to send me to jail or slit my throat if I didn't pay him fifty dollars on the spot. Wanting to avoid any other misfortunes, in light of the infuriated people who spoke of lynching me, I had to sign a paper they gave me, saying that it was a promissory note of fifty dollars, to be paid within three months. Golman said, among other expressions, that since he was Justice of the Peace, he could not care less for me, nor for even a hundred of my species, and that he did not give a d*** if they dammed up a stream with my body.]

After signing, Rodrigues was released and given back his horse, but not his oxen. In writing his letter, Rodrigues hoped the editors would "llamar la atencion publica sobre este ultraje cometido por una gente abandonada contra un ciudadano pacifico; no es el primer acto de agresion que se perpetró en esa parte del pais [give public notice of this outrage, committed by a depraved people against a peaceful citizen; it is not the first act of aggression that has been perpetrated in that part of the country]."[6]

A few months later, on September 15, 1855, the *Bejareño* criticized the citizens of Caldwell County (located between San Antonio and Austin) who had voted to expel the Tejanos living there under the pretext of their "seducing Negroes." For some time, working-class Tejanos—referred to then by the feudal term "peons"—had helped enslaved African-Americans escape south into South Texas and Mexico, infuriating Anglo-Americans and disconcerting elite Tejanos. Peons were located at the bottom of the social hierarchy; placed in a fixed, permanent position of subordination they lived at the whim of the landed-elite. Thus, it appears that they felt compassion for black slaves, and assisted them in escaping south into Mexico.[7]

Throughout the extant Spanish-language newspapers of the 1850s, a pattern emerges in the acts of violence reported: whether through systematic, organized attempts or through random, individual acts of violence, Tejanos were being dispossessed of their property and economic livelihood. To make matters worse, a rising tide of Anglo-Saxon Protestant xenophobic nativism had spread across the United States, making the situation even more precarious for Tejanos. While nativism spread across the country, provoking outbursts of violence in nearly every region and against a wide variety of immigrant groups, in Texas this only served to exacerbate the violently unstable social fabric that had come to dominate the lives of Tejanos, one that had started with the Spanish royal commandant general Joaquín de Arredondo's brutal repression of the 1813 revolution and had not ceded one bit.

The Know-Nothing Party made their grand entrance into Texas in December of 1854. Like the rest of the U.S. South, the pro-slavery Democratic Party reigned supreme in Texas. By the 1850s, however, it had become more than clear—in Texas and the rest of the United States—that the issue of slavery was tearing the nation apart. The Democrats had become virulently secessionist in their rhetoric, and the slavery question had caused the only other large national party, the Whigs, to fragment. In favor of slavery but against secession, the Know-Nothing Party was also driven by the xenophobic fear of "foreign ideas," such as those about abolition that were attributed to the Tejano and German communities, the latter of which, as we saw in Chapter 8, had grown to over 20,000 in less than a decade. It was then that the Know-Nothing Party entered Texas, persuading powerful Democrats to align themselves with the Know-Nothings. But other than their virulently anti-Catholic, anti-German, and, especially, anti-Mexican sentiments, they said little else about their platform. Thus, they surprised Texans by winning all of the municipal seats in San Antonio's 1854 election—the largest city in Texas at the time. The following spring, in March of 1855, they continued their success by electing a Know-Nothing candidate as mayor of Galveston.[8]

Political parties in Texas, as in the rest of the United States, had yet to develop into mature parties with clearly articulated platforms. They were driven by personalities and loyalty rather than fully developed ideologies. Indeed, political parties during this period were, as historians have pointed out, a form of mass entertainment, "a spectacle with rallies, parades, and colorful personalities." The Know-Nothing Party fit right in.[9]

In order to weaken the Democratic Party, the Know-Nothing Party used newspapers to great effect by painting staunch anti–Know-Nothing Democratic candidates as Know-Nothing members to defeat them. This, in turn, forced candidates to publish letters addressed to the public declaring their aversion to Know-Nothing principles and their loyalty to the Democratic Party. One prime example is that of the Irish Catholic district judge of San Antonio, Thomas Jefferson Devine, who was forced to publish several letters declaring his antipathy for the Know-Nothing Party and was, in turn, defended by several San Antonio newspapers, including the *Bejareño*. The Know-Nothings amplified the high drama of political affairs, preferring to operate secretively, via intrigue, holding unannounced political conventions, and persuading prominent Democratic leaders to switch parties, which all led to widespread mistrust and anxiety.[10]

But the Know-Nothings' extremism and highly secretive nature made many others wary. It was difficult for individuals to fully understand who was an actual Know-Nothing and what, precisely, they were advocating. Thus, during San Antonio's next elections, in August 1856, they resorted to infiltrating the Democratic Party convention in order to win the elections and pursue their xenophobic goals.

Representing Tejano Interests in the 1856 Election

The election of 1856, the Know-Nothing Party's vituperative anti-Mexican, anti-Catholic sentiment, and its influence in community affairs were reasons enough for Quintero to launch a newspaper. In the inaugural issue of the *Ranchero,* he enumerated "las razones que . . . ponen hoy la pluma en nuestra mano [the reasons for which . . . a pen has been placed in our hand today]." The most important was "el deseo de satisfacer las ecsigencias i suplicas de algunos mejicanos que no han podido permanecer mudos é indiferentes en las graves i vitales cuestiones que han surjido en estos ultimos tiempos [the desire to satisfy the pressing needs and requests of those Mexicans who have been unable to remain silent and indifferent to the vexing and vital issues that have arisen in recent times]."[11]

Quintero did not restrain himself in his caustic critique of the Know-Nothing Party, and fervently believed that only by uniting under the banner of the Democratic Party could Mexicans defend their interests:

> ¡Mejico-Tejanos! La hora de la eleccion se acerca. Los que atacan la convencion democrática estan obrando de hecho con los Know-nothings que quieren engañaros, que han procurado siempre oprimiros. . . . Ellos os despojarian de vuestros derechos, se opondrian a vuestra fé religiosa, os considerarian como estrangeros, i os negarian hasta el empleo mas humilde. . . . Su politica es diviviros para dominar i oprimir. . . . ¡Que cada Mejicano se prepare a hacer su deber! Que cada uno comprenda la santidad de su causa. . . . ¡La democracia ahora, la democracia despues, la democracia siempre!
>
> [Mejico-Tejanos! The hour of the election arrives. Those who attack the Democratic convention are conspiring with the Know-nothings who only want to deceive you, who have always sought to oppress you. . . . They would only

deprive you of your rights, they would oppose your religious faith, they would consider you foreigners, and they would deny you even the most menial of work. . . . Their politics are to divide us in order to dominate and oppress. . . . Let every Mexican prepare for his duty! Let each one know the sanctity of his cause. . . . Democracy today! Democracy tomorrow! Democracy forever!][12]

Quintero turned specifically to the various Know-Nothing newspapers that had begun to print inflammatory articles against Mexicans. These had repeatedly pointed to Germans as a reason for their electoral losses, but they were increasingly targeting their frenzied racial rhetoric at Mexicans. The *Ranchero* claimed that the Bastrop *Advertiser,* in particular, had become quite influential in the area, with dangerous repercussions for Mexicans. "[H]ace algun tiempo [For some time now]," the *Advertiser* has "declarado guerra a [*sic*] muerte a todo lo que no es americano,—i que por la hiel conque desahoga su ira contra los mejicanos, lo mismo que por la degradacion i cobardia de sus redactores, ha alcanzado algun renombre en la arena periodistica [declared war and death on everything not American. And because of its acrimonious venting of rage against Mexicans—the same as for the editors' degradation and cowardice—the newspaper has become quite renowned in journalistic circles]."[13] Quintero then printed a translated article from the *Advertiser* in which they warned of the abolitionist German influence at the ballot box. "[S]in embargo [Nevertheless]," noted the *Advertiser,* there is

otro elemento todavia mas peligroso i destructivo. Aludimos a los Mejicanos que votan. No tenemos documentos a mano para presentar a nuestros lectores el numero esacto de *greasers* a quienes se permite el derecho del sufrajio; pero suponemos por observacion personal que enla parte occidental del rio de San Antonio no hay menos de cuatro mil de estos cobrizos bribones que votan segun se lo mandan sus amos.

[another element yet more dangerous and destructive. We refer to the Mexicans who vote. We do not have the documents at hand to provide our readers with the exact numbers of *greasers* who are given the right to vote; but from personal observation we can estimate that west of the San Antonio River there are no less than four thousand of these copper-colored rascals who vote as their bosses tell them.][14]

The *Advertiser* continued by describing Mexicans as "ignorantes, venales, prostituidos, viles i estupidos [ignorant, corrupt, prostituted, vile, and stupid]," as a "raza donde ninguno es superior a vuestros negros en moral, educación o delicadeza, y con frecuencia aun mucho mas serviles [race where none is superior to your negroes in morality, education, nor refinement, and who are increasingly much more servile than your slaves]," and concluded by making what was already by then the well-rehearsed claim that Mexicans should be stripped of the franchise.[15]

By translating and publishing the article, Quintero underscored "cuan imperiosa la necesidad de que se unan todos como un solo hombre bajo la bandera democratica, para repeler los ataques de un enemigo implacable que no duerme i ha tiempo busca la ocasion de dividir a los democratas para obtener la victoria [how important it is that they (Mejico-Tejanos) all unite as one under the Democratic banner in order to repel the attacks of an implacable enemy who never sleeps and who searches for the occasion to divide the democrats in order to obtain victory]." If this was not enough to convince his readers, Quintero also accused the Know-Nothing Party of "empleando la fuerza, el engaño, el crimen i el asesinato [employing force, deception, crime, and murder]" in order to achieve success. Because of these tactics, Quintero emphasized: "El pueblo mejicano no puede, ni quiere, ni debe cooperar de ningun modo al exito de aquellos que no les tratan como conciudadanos sino como viles ilotas a quienes se niegan los derechos mas caros al hombre libre [The Mexican community can not, nor does it want to, nor should it cooperate in any way in the success of those who do not treat them as fellow citizens but rather as villainous Helots[16] who are denied the most cherished rights of free men]."[17]

The *Ranchero*'s clear opposition to the nativist Know-Nothing Party and fervent defense of Mexicans did not go unnoticed. Almost immediately, the *Ranchero* engaged in contentious exchanges with various Know-Nothing-sympathizing English-language newspapers. The pro-Know-Nothing San Antonio *Herald,* for example, sought desperately to identify the true identity of the author of various *Ranchero* articles that had criticized the Know-Nothing Party, and called on its readers to organize against the *Ranchero*.[18] The *Herald* was apparently persuasive: the Know-Nothing Party held an emergency meeting and concluded that they should assault Quintero and destroy the *Ranchero*'s property.

Anarchy seemed to descend upon San Antonio for almost a week, as newspapers of the period confirm. The pro-Democrat San Antonio *Texan,* for example, reported that "For several days after this article appeared [in the *Ranchero*] many threats were heard on the streets—some saying that the editor of the 'Ranchero' never wrote said article;—others that the scoundrel who wrote it, if he was a foreigner he should be driven out of the country; if a native he should be hung."[19] Quintero and the *Ranchero* apparently survived the incident. The upheaval, however, led to the death of one man, the arrest of several others, and destruction of property.[20]

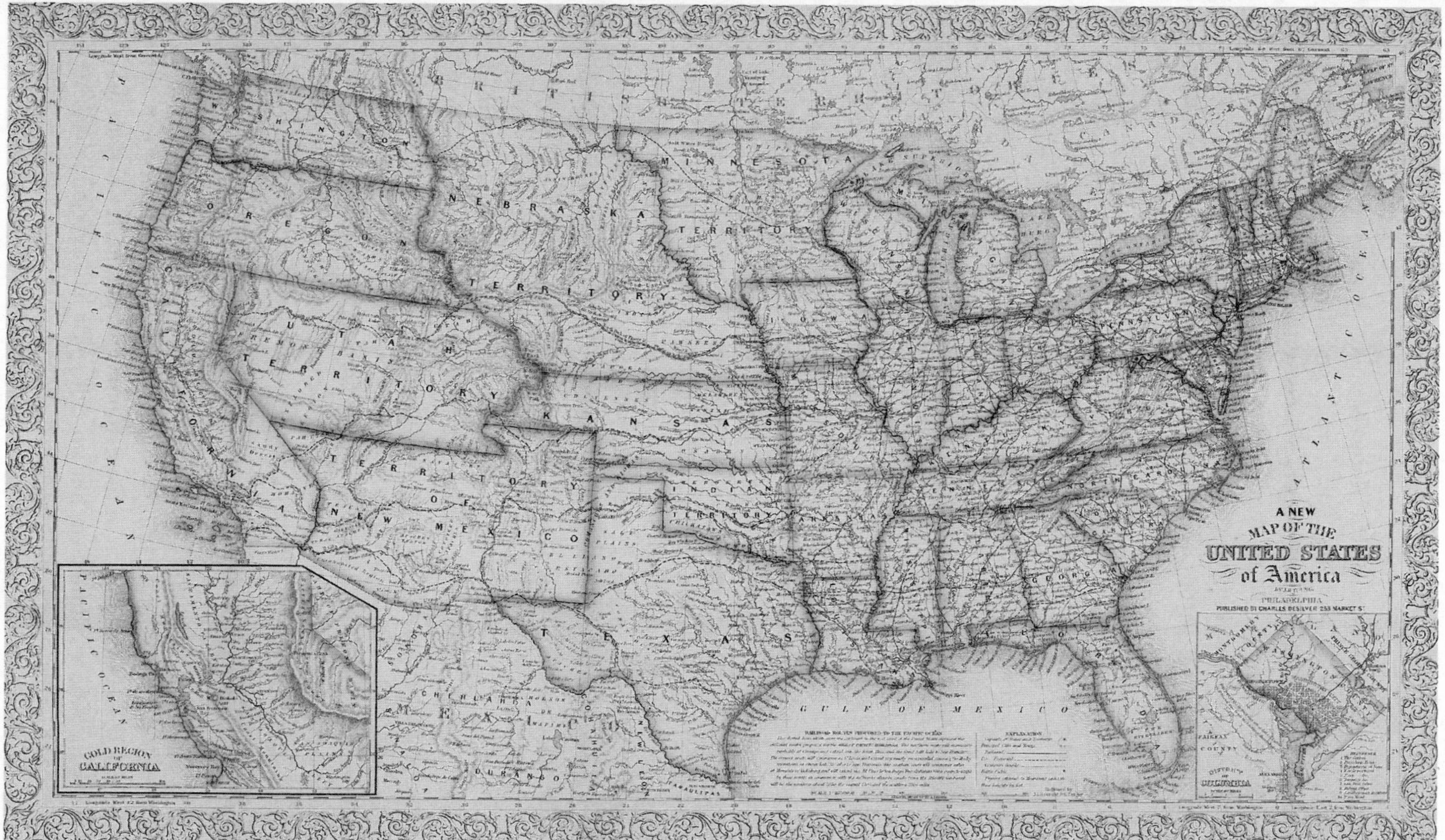

Figure 69. J. H. Young, "A New Map of the United States of America" (1856).

41 × 68 cm. No. 0405, Map Collection. Archives and Information Services Division, Texas State Library and Archives Commission, Austin.

Nevertheless, the diatribes of Know-Nothing newspapers did not go unchallenged. Along with the *Ranchero,* some Anglophone papers also criticized Know-Nothing newspapers' excessive rhetoric, castigating them for fomenting anti-Mexican sentiment. One such newspaper was the *Texan,* who used its editorial columns to defend the *Ranchero*'s freedom to criticize political parties and to remind the Know-Nothing *Herald* of proper journalistic etiquette:

> No public journalist dislikes more than we do to see any harsh epithets and low flung billingsgate in a newspaper; but still we can see no reason why the journal of one party [the Know-Nothing *Herald*] representing one portion of our fellow citizens can indulge in such language without limit or reserve while that of another party [the Democratic *Ranchero*] must be muzzled to suit the *ipse dixit* of a certain class.[21]

The *Bejareño* responded immediately to the *Ranchero*'s critique of the Know-Nothing Party. In the second issue of the *Ranchero*, Quintero acknowledges receipt of an issue of the *Bejareño* in which the editors apparently disagreed with the *Ranchero*'s political position. As noted above, the extant issues of the *Bejareño* end exactly one week prior to the *Ranchero*'s first issue, making it impossible to fully examine the debate.[22]

The differences between the *Bejareño* and the *Ranchero* appear to have originated with the Know-Nothings' attempt to infiltrate the Bexar County Democratic Party Convention in June 1856. Indeed, the editor of the *Ranchero* knew this to be the case, and suspected that the *Bejareño*'s neutral stance regarding the Democratic candidates for the Bexar County elections was tantamount to Know-Nothing support. The Know-Nothings succeeded, but only in forcing some of the delegates to bolt and create their own Democratic ticket: the Democratic Party would win most of the offices during the August 1856 elections.[23]

Over the next several weeks, newspapers rushed to investigate the source of political discordance during the convention and, indeed, found Know-Nothing members responsible.[24] Democratic Party members did not foresee the potential rift within their own party; and, if prior to the convention newspapers rallied their readers to support the Democrats, then, after, its editors mustered all their strength to defeat the Know-Nothings. "Never since the formation of our government has there been a more urgent necessity for the united efforts of all good citizens and honest patriots in defence of the Constitution of their country," wrote the *Texan* with dramatic flair. "Know-Nothingism like an evil spirit has overshadowed her [America's] fertile plains and dissipated the sunshine that had settled in placid sweetness on the brow of her tutelar Deity."[25] Division within the ranks, newspapers claimed, would certainly lead to the Know-Nothing's victory.

But to the editors of the *Bejareño* political lines could not be drawn so neatly. Prior to the convention, the *Bejareño* could match any other pro-Democratic Party newspaper's rhetoric. But the county convention, in the opinion of the *Bejareño,* "acabo en nada [resulted in nothing]." Indeed, "Menos whiskey y mas agua les hubiera hecho un gran servicio á varios représentantes del pueblo [less whiskey and more water would have done many of the town's representatives a great service]." If anything, the convention panned out to be a battle of egos in which both factions refused to compromise. At no time did "Los intereses del publico en general y del partido en particular . . . merecieron la atencion de los dos bandos [the public's interests in general nor of the party in particular ever receive either faction's attention]."

So disillusioned was the *Bejareño* that it preferred to remain neutral during the upcoming elections. "Como Democratas [As Democrats]," the editors concluded, "solo reconocemos principios; y como dos males no hacen un bien preferimos quedar estrictamente neutros; publicamente no favorecemos los intereses de ningun candidato y nos abstendremos de hacer comentarios que puedan construirse como parciales [we only recognize principles; and as two wrongs do not make a right we prefer to remain strictly neutral; publicly we do not support any candidate and we abstain from making any comments that may be construed as partial]." Hence, as a respectable "organo publico [public organ]," "[d]esde este momento quedan nuestras columnas abiertas para todas las comunicaciones ó otros escritos que deseen insertar los candidatos [from here on after our columns will remain open to all opinions and articles that the candidates may desire to have printed]."[26]

Curiously, though the *Bejareño* noted the creation of two factions they failed to mention the divisive activities of the Know-Nothing Party members during the Democratic convention. This was despite the fact that the *Ranchero* and other English- and German-language papers had investigated and published scathing critiques of the Know-Nothing infiltrators throughout the months of June and July.

Rumors and gossip apparently spread quickly, and within two weeks the *Bejareño* was forced to clarify its position. "[H]abiendo llegado á nuestros oidos que nuestra posicion es considerada como la de renegados politicos y que en ciertos corrillos se nos ha degradado del partido Democratico considerandonos indignos de el [It has been made known to us that our neutral position makes of us political renegades and that in certain corners we have been deemed unworthy of being called Democrats]." The

Bejareño was apparently referring to non-Spanish-speaking individuals: "Hay ciertos profetas de luengas barbas, voz ronca y grave que no entienden ni siquiera el idioma en que escribimos pero que con la pedanteria de todo ignorante se complacen ens [*sic*] meterse en lo que no entienden y sobre todo, no les importa [There are certain bearded-tongue prophets, with hoarse and sickly voices that do not even understand the language in which we write but who nevertheless, with all a pedant's ignorance, oblige themselves to become involved in things that they do not even understand and, above all, do not pertain to them]."[27]

The *Bejareño* took a clearly nationalist-linguistic stance on this, what appears to have been the same argument put forward by Anglophone papers: to use proficiency in a language as a means to include or exclude others from civic engagement. The *Bejareño* once again defended its right to abstain from endorsing any candidates. These are the *Bejareño*'s final words on the debate; only one more issue is extant, dated 28 June 1856, in which they say nothing about the ongoing debate. The *Ranchero* was launched immediately after the convention, and sought to castigate the *Bejareño* and the Know-Nothing party.

The *Bejareño* may have claimed neutrality, but the *Ranchero* and English-language papers insisted that the *Bejareño* represented the views of the defecting members of the Democratic Party. In the July 31 issue of the pro-Democratic Party *Texan,* the editors reported that after the split at the county convention, the "seceding party . . . formed a ticket of their own, and they secured to their use and benefit the 'El Bejareño,' a Spanish paper established in our city. The regular Democratic party, being aware that a large part of our Mexican population were with them immediately started another Spanish paper entitled 'The Ranchero.' Each of these papers of course [had] done all they could for their respective parties."[28]

Both San Antonio pro-Democratic Party papers, the *Texan* and the *Ledger,* readily described the *Bejareño* as a journal that represented the views of the defecting Democratic delegates. Even more compromising evidence regarding the *Bejareño*'s political stance comes from the *Bejareño* itself. In the June 28 issue, the editors included a brief announcement on the last page. There the editors rather nonchalantly endorsed M. A. Dooley's candidacy for judge of the fourth district.[29] But Dooley's candidacy was ripe with controversy, as several newspapers noted, for he was running against the celebrated, Democratic Irish Catholic Thomas Jefferson Devine. As it turns out, several of Dooley's campaign organizers had been (or were) members of the Know-Nothing Party.[30]

The *Ranchero* correctly perceived that here was yet another Know-Nothing attempt to defeat the Democrats, and immediately launched into an even more strident critique of the Know-Nothing Party and the *Bejareño*. For the reasons stated above, it is ultimately impossible to determine whether the *Bejareño* underwent some change in political allegiance. What is perhaps more likely is that the *Bejareño*, as the *Texan* surmised, remained loyal to the defecting candidates of the Democratic county convention, leading the *Ranchero* to declare in stark language that as "Jesucristo decia 'El que conmigo no es, contra mi está.' I ellos estan contra vosotros porque se han separado de las filas de la democrácia [Jesus Christ said, 'He who is not with me is against me.' And they are against you because they have abandoned the Democratic front-line]."[31]

Texas and the Gulf of Mexico Network

From the arrival of the first printing press in Texas, politics was always the primary motivation behind publishing. It was also politics that motivated Quintero to establish the *Ranchero*. He may have received threats from Know-Nothing sympathizers but he nonetheless continued his strident defense of Tejanos, and made clear his intent to publish critiques of the Know-Nothing Party. In the third issue dated July 19, 1856, the *Ranchero* reported on the chaos instigated by the *Herald* and Know-Nothing Party: "Se nos informa que varios de nuestros desafectos han asegurado que nuestro periodico cesaria esta semana [We have been informed that several of our adversaries have ensured that our newspaper would cease publication this very week]." The threat hardly dampened the *Ranchero*'s spirits. After reminding their would-be censors of previous vague and empty threats, it proclaimed: "Despues que tenga lugar la eleccion i cuando se hayan convencido de su impotencia i nulidad politica, entonces determinaremos si cesará nuestro periodico ó no, [*sic*] Por lo que hace al presente no retrocederemos un solo paso [Only after the election and only after the Know-Nothings are finally convinced of their political impotence and insignificance, then and only then will we decide whether we should cease publishing. For the time being, we will not retreat one step]."[32]

The empty threats, however, were quickly fulfilled. In the last extant issue of the *Ranchero*, dated July 28, 1856, and without any prior notice, Guadalupe Leal was announced as the new editor of the newspaper presumably due to Quintero's declining health. In the column adjacent to that announcement on the front page, however, the new editor reported in capital letters, "INDIGNACION!—JUNTA DE KNOW-NOTHINGS! [INDIGNATION! A KNOW-NOTHING PARTY MEETING!]" With a distinct sense of urgency, Leal wrote that that very morning, as the paper went to press at 10 a.m., tuvo lugar en la casa de Corte una junta compuesta por varios de los miembros del partido Know-Nothing. Su objeto era irritar al pueblo i cometer alguna violencia contra el Sr. Quintero, Editor del Ranchero, haciendole abandonar esta ciudad con motivo de la firmeza con que en la presente cuestion politica ha defendido el partido democratico i los derechos de los Mejicanos.

[several members of the Know-Nothing Party met at the Courthouse with the purpose of arousing the community to commit violent acts against Mr. Quintero, editor of the *Ranchero,* forcing him to flee the city only because of his indefatigable defense of the Democratic party and the rights of Mexicans.][33]

Leal called on Mexicans to rally behind Quintero "porque ha defendido vuestros derechos i *tiene nuestro mismo origen* [because he has defended your rights and because *he is of the same origin as us*]."[34] Despite the threats, the *Ranchero* persisted with their calls for the unity of Tejanos. It is doubtful that the Know-Nothing members followed through immediately on their threats. Only a year later we find Quintero married and living in Austin working as a translator for the state (he had married in New Orleans on April 13, 1857).[35] As for the *Ranchero,* neither the *Texan* nor the *Ledger* reported on its demise. Nonetheless, no further issues of the *Ranchero* are extant.

Yet who was part of this community of Mejico-Tejanos, as Quintero referred to it? And how is it that Leal could easily and without any sense of contradiction refer to Quintero, a Cuban who had only arrived in San Antonio four months prior, as someone who "is of the same origin as you"? The various invocations of Mejicano and Mejico-Tejano identity notwithstanding, the *Ranchero* did not advocate unity solely on the basis of Mexican-ethnic ancestry or of some incipient sense of Tejano nationalism. Likewise, despite Anglo-Americans' solidifying racial discourse on Tejanos during this period there is no sense of racial distinction—much less a sense of inferiority—articulated in these papers.

If neither a sense of Mexican or even Tejano nationalism bound this community, nor the counterdiscursive response to their racialization, what did unite it was its shared language and Spanish-American creole cultural heritage. The Spanish-American elites, however, were now engaged in a new historical project: the development of full-fledged capitalist, liberal democratic institutions in Texas. The *Ranchero* and the *Bejareño* had no other choice but to write specifically for an elite creole-identified community, since it was this class that had access to education and opportunities to become literate.

During the Spanish colonial era, and continuing through the postindependence Mexican one, education was hard to come by in Texas and throughout the far northern Mexican territories. This situation existed despite government documents revealing that San Antonio authorities repeatedly attempted to establish public schooling. Yet, as always, the steady economic demise of the Spanish crown and its increasing economic dependence on northern Europe during the colonial period, as well as Mexico's inherited political and economic instability after independence, guaranteed that the inhabitants of the northern frontier would see little economic aid. Likewise, the prohibitory trade laws that Spain had instituted and that Mexico attempted desperately to reform had prevented San Antonio from developing an economically sustainable community.[36]

After independence in 1821, Mexico attempted to institute liberal educational reforms but required local municipalities to pay for schooling. This meant that the local San Antonio community had to provide teachers' salaries and equipment and resulted in sporadic schooling at best.[37] If that were not enough, the chaotically revolutionary 1810s had obliterated any remnant of an educational system in Texas. This political-economic context can then explain the dismal literacy rate among Tejanos. During the 1850s, the estimated literacy rate among Mexicans over twenty years of age in south, central, and west Texas was just 25 percent, and the percentage of children attending school was a grim 16.7 percent (among Anglo-Americans, the rates were 97 percent and 33.9 percent respectively).[38] As a result of the poor educational system, many of the elite sent their children to be educated in the northern Mexican towns of Saltillo and Monterrey; some were even able to send their children to Catholic schools in Missouri, Kentucky, and elsewhere in the United States.[39] Eventually, as we have seen, some of these elite children would be educated at Ivy League universities, such as Harvard. Given these conditions, those who contributed to Spanish-language newspapers, those who appeared in newspaper articles as political representatives and delegates, those who were listed in the paper as leaders of various Spanish-language community groups, and in fact those who were able to read were more often than not descendants of elite Spanish-Mexican families.

San Antonio may have lacked the economic resources to have developed public schooling, but it was an integral part of a larger socioeconomic system that increasingly brought to it not only desperately needed commodities and goods but peoples with various experiences and backgrounds as well. The Mexican War of Independence brought Anglo-Americans, Spaniards, Cubans, South Americans, and Frenchmen to Texas in support of Mexico's cause. At the turn of the nineteenth century, Texas was at the international crossroads of three nations jockeying for imperial dominion of the area: the French had settled and developed a thriving community in

Figure 70. José Fermin Cassiano, Tomasa Flores de Cassiano, and children. Carte-de-visite (ca. 1868). Cassiano's father, Giuseppe Cassini, was born in San Remo, Italy, established himself as a merchant in New Orleans, and then relocated to San Antonio in the 1820s. He would change his name to José Cassiano, and was a member of the committee that drafted the 1832 petition to the Coahuila y Tejas legislature. His son José Fermin would continue his father's business, and was a prominent figure in San Antonio civic life. Tomasa Flores could trace her descendants to the original Canary Islander families that settled San Antonio.

Cassiano-Pérez Family Papers, 1741–1976, Col. 880, Box 13, Folder 319. Daughters of the Republic of Texas.

New Orleans and had set their eyes on the lucrative mercantile trade economy with residents in Texas and the Caribbean; Anglo-Americans had begun to migrate west toward Texas where land was plentiful; and Spain did its best to curtail foreign incursion. But the Mexican War of Independence altered the imperial dynamics of the entire area.

Cuba and New Orleans played crucial roles in facilitating the movements of people, the flow of capital, and the exchange of ideas during this period. The fever for independence that had spread throughout the Spanish colonies during the 1810s had also found its way to Cuba. Nevertheless, despite several attempts at independence on the part of Cubans, Cuba would remain under Spain's dominion until 1898. The result of these failed attempts to gain independence was the exile of liberal Cuban creoles and the eventual establishment of ex-patriot Cuban communities in New

Orleans and other U.S. cities. New Orleans, with its long history of Spanish and French colonization, had replaced Philadelphia as the haven for liberal Spanish Americans during the nineteenth century.[40] Hispanics often expatriated to New Orleans during Spanish America's battles for independence and turbulent early years. Quintero was far from being the only Cuban to have traveled from New Orleans to San Antonio. Other professional Cubans arrived ready to put their skills to use. In November 1855, Dr. Eduardo B. Montalvan, former professor of medicine at the University of San Carlos in Havana, settled in San Antonio and published in the *Bejareño* a prospectus for a home medical treatment book.[41]

The flow of Cubans, French, and Anglo-Americans into Texas via New Orleans, the west Louisianan town of Natchitoches, and the east Texas town of Nacogdoches was accompanied by the flow of commodities. That is, newspapers in San Antonio, Nacogdoches, and Brownsville often announced in celebratory language the arrival of clothing, furniture, jewelry, and books from New Orleans, Havana, and Veracruz. Likewise, they hailed the development of new steamboat lines, such as the one built in 1856 that brought New York, Havana, and Veracruz closer together.[42] For San Antonio and Texas, this nineteenth-century form of globalization would only integrate Texas further into the larger global economy since it had already established links with Havana and Veracruz.

We should think, then, of Texas's cultural geography during this period as a central hub of a network that encircled the Gulf of Mexico (see Figure 25). Established and solidified by trade routes and the recent, military-built stagecoach roads, this network was bounded on the west by El Paso and then on to New Mexico and California. It extended south to Monterrey and then further to Mexico City. Heading east, the nodes in this network included the Gulf Coast ports of Indianola and Galveston, as it extended further to the bustling port of New Orleans and from there to the Caribbean ports of Havana and Veracruz, before being integrated into other global economic networks. And it is this network that facilitated the flow of ideas, the frequent exchange and reprinting of newspaper articles from across the world, and the integration of Mejico-Tejanos into a larger imagined community of individuals committed to the new project described as "progress."

Reconfigured Imagined Communities

What binds together this imagined community of Tejanos is its shared Spanish-language and Spanish-American creole cultural heritage. Often, the preferred ethnic label of identification was Mejicano, for others Mejico-Tejanos, but the spirit is one of a pan-American identity based more on Spanish-language heritage and a recent conflictive history with Spain. In the inaugural issue of the *Ranchero,* Quintero enumerates the reasons for starting a newspaper. The first of these is the need to create a public forum through which "Mejicanos" could defend their interests. However, if "Mejicano" could be interpreted as an ethnic, nationalist identification, the second reason provided for establishing the paper mitigates this conclusion. The other reason, Quintero writes, is "las naturales simpatias que nos ligan a todos los pueblos de nuestra raza que hablan aquende los mares la lengua sonora de Castilla [the natural sympathies that bind us to all of our people's nations that speak that most melodious language of Castile on this side of the ocean]."[43]

These postindependence Americans (that is, the other Americans of the hemisphere) may have renounced Spain and proclaimed independence, but here there is no stated allegiance to a newly independent Mexican nation or even—in the case of Quintero—reference to the promise of an independent Cuba.[44] The "natural sympathies that bind" this community together have nothing to do with any sense of national identity. Instead, it is a residual Spanish cultural heritage that "binds" this community together. In naming this cultural heritage, the *Ranchero* would appear to struggle with its imperialist legacy of domination. It refuses to name Spain or identify its culture as Spanish. Rather, through a somewhat ambivalent metonymic displacement, Spain and Spanish culture is replaced with "that most melodious language of Castile." Castilian Spanish, deriving from the ancient kingdom of Castile, had long served as the official language of the Hispanic monarchy, and was the language utilized in the Spanish colonization of the Americas.

After independence, Spanish Americans could not arrive at a clear consensus for their future. Some, like Mexicans, entertained the idea of a Mexican monarchy under Emperor Agustín de Iturbide. Others, like Bolívar, had grand visions of a pan-American republic. While still others argued vociferously for the model of the young-though-remarkable democratic republic of the United States of America. But the issue is not so much that they had not developed the concept of a nation. It is that the idea itself was elastic. These nineteenth-century Spanish Americans, now Tejanos, now Cubans, used the concept of *nación* as it had long been used throughout the Hispanic world: to denote the inhabitants of a certain territory united by language, religion, and culture. And this is precisely how Quintero and Leal imagined their community of readers. What they had in common was the concentric circles of their imagined community, developed in the long course of Spanish colonization of the Americas, and from the deep well of Catholic notions of sovereignty. Nonetheless, though these Spanish Americans may have despised Spain for having obliterated the Mexican communities across Texas, what manages to unite them across their differences continues to be the "melodious language of Castile." There is no reference to any sense of a mestizo community, much less to anything having to do with pre-Columbian indigenous cultures. This was simply impossible to countenance during the nineteenth century when Tejanos continued to be at war with various Native American nations. It is only in the course of that century that *nación* would come to correspond to specific state formations.[45]

Throughout these newspapers, the defense of Tejanos does not take on racial overtones. Instead, differences emerge and are articulated via electoral politics and competing conceptions of the liberal public sphere. Unlike Mexicans in central Mexico, where the struggles between centralists and federalists would lead to coup and countercoup for decades, Mexicans in Texas had actively sought to develop a republican form of government; this had been the case since the first declaration of independence in 1813, when Texas declared itself a republic (the first province of Mexico to ever do so). However, rather than being derived solely from Anglo-American republican and liberal thought, the elite's arguments drew from an "American" rhetoric and iconology of liberalism more familiar to them: one derived from a Catholic Hispanic epistemology that sought to reconfigure Catholic notions of corporate rights into modern liberal ideas of individuality and private property. And precisely because they worked within this non-state identified framework of nationality, their concept of a national identity could not and would not be intelligible within the framework of the U.S. nation-state. This was the divergent path that modernity had taken in the other Americas.

In these newspapers, the elite voices its desire to participate as equals in a democratic republic through electoral politics. By uniting with the proslavery Democratic Party, the *Ranchero* thought it could counter anti-Mexican violence and defend its community's interests. "Cada nuevo sol alumbra una agresion, de parte de aquellos que quisieran estirparnos. Dividido i derrotado nuestro partido jamas podria organizarse ortra vez [Each new dawn gives light to yet another aggression, on the part of those who would like to annihilate us. Divided and conquered our party would never be able to organize itself again]." The "us," in this context, serves to collapse and combine both the Tejano community (that had certainly experienced a form of "annihilation") and the Democratic Party, which was under threat from the Know-Nothing Party. In effect, the *Ranchero* asserts that the only way Mexicans can survive as a community is by participating in U.S. electoral politics and uniting with the Democratic Party. The *Bejareño,* too, pleaded with Tejanos to organize and vote. Again, with great perspicacity the *Ranchero* evaluates the current state of political affairs: "No permitais: ¡oh mejicanos que la desunion se introduzca en nuestras filas. Nosotros os decimos i ponemos a Dios por testigo, que seria nuestra ruina i desolacion! [Don't let dissension be introduced into our ranks. We tell you and swear by God's word, that it will be our ruin and desolation!]"[46]

In the face of incredible physical violence and loss and as a way to surmount the heavy, leadened racialized discourse, these elite Tejanos turned instead to electoral politics and print culture as the most expedient defense of their interests, as was the case with the demonized former mayor of San Antonio, Juan N. Seguín, the last Tejano mayor of the nineteenth century. After the Texas Revolution and through the 1850s, Seguín became the target of Anglo-American racist violence and was forced to flee to Laredo. Frustrated by Anglo-American charges of treason, in 1858 he published an English translation of his memoirs explaining his actions and the virulent racism that had forced him to abandon his hometown.[47]

Quintero was fully aware of the differences between Mexicans and Cubans. Yet, this posed no obstacle in his eyes for his identification with Mexicans. The United States may have engaged in an unfortunate and unfair war with Mexico, but what had Mexico provided these northern frontier inhabitants other than neglect and abandonment? Many of these elites had yearned and struggled to establish a republic in Texas against the despotic and unstable government of Santa Anna. But now, before their very eyes, they were not only being described by Know-Nothings as marginal to the U.S. republican project, they were actually becoming so.

In one of his most impassioned editorials, in which he rallied Mexicans to defeat the Know-Nothings, Quintero pauses to reflect on Tejanos' dreary past and even more gloomy present. "Los momentos son siglos en el cuadrante de la humanidad [Mere moments are centuries in the annals of humanity]," he begins. "Tratamos de reconstruir en Tejas el poder de una raza a quien nos ligan no solo lazos de simpatias i amor sino los que son aun todavia mas fuertes para nosotros los del origen i la nacionalidad. No hai tiempo que perder [Let us try to rebuild in Texas the power of a people to whom we are bound not only by sympathy and affection but also by those bonds that are yet more powerful for us: those of origin and nationality. There is no time to spare]."[48] Using the metaphor of time to ingrain the urgency of action, Quintero emphasizes the importance of the present election ("mere moments") not only for his readers, but as his metaphor implies, for Tejanos' posterity ("the annals of humanity"). Quintero evaluates the situation with great astuteness. The present confrontation with the

Know-Nothing Party was not about a mere election. It was much more symbolic, and the outcome of the debate would foretell the future of Mexicans in Texas.

Together, Quintero exhorts, these particular *Americanos* could work to build anew a true republic. If the history of Mexico had demonstrated the difficulty for a republic to take hold, if the history of Cuba had revealed the intransigence of an Old World monarchy, and if the recent history of Texas had begun to manifest a troubling, antagonistic prejudice toward Mexicans, then perhaps here, "in Texas," these united Americans could regroup and "rebuild the power of" and promise of an alternate, liberal vision of America. The bond between this Cuban and his San Antonio Mexican community was not only sealed by the emotional sentiments of "sympathy and love," so Quintero tells us, but also by something much more rational and objective, something "even stronger": a common history of Spanish colonialism, a common heritage as Spanish-American creoles, and a common cause of national independence, "of origin and nationality." Here, however, nationality is not so much a present condition but a promise, a promise in which these Americans would work together with those other, northern (Anglo-)Americans in constructing a republic in Texas. And as a promise to be kept, Quintero warned, "there is no time to spare" in building it.

The *Ranchero*'s energy may have been focused on the success of the proslavery Democratic Party and the demise of Know-Nothing rhetoric, but its struggle was the continuation of one that had begun with Spain. The bloody battles against the Spanish crown had yet to congeal into a cold, distant memory, and instead continued to inspire great wrath. Across the issues of the *Bejareño* and *Ranchero,* the editors continually reported on Spain's repeated efforts to regain its American colonies, and this struggle against Spain also served as a unifying force among these Spanish Americans. Spain continued to attempt to assert its power over its former colonies, and during the 1850s attempted to force Mexico to compensate Spanish citizens for the loss of property during the war of independence.[49] These attempts at reconquest were cause for especially excoriating editorials.

Having received news that Mexico would not capitulate to Spain, the *Ranchero* lauded Mexico: "tenemos motivos para creer que sabra repeler victoriosamente cualquiera agresion de parte del sanguinario i caduco lobo español [we have reason to believe that Mexico will know how to victoriously repel any form of aggression on the part of that bloodthirsty and decrepit old wolf]." Indeed, the *Ranchero* warned that "Los dias de su dominacion en America estan contados [the days of her dominating America are numbered]." But this is no mere political alliance against Spanish colonialism. The *Ranchero* continues and elucidates the nature of this intimate relationship between Texans of Spanish-American descent and Mexicans or, perhaps we should say, all Americans: "Nosotros que hemos nacido en una tierra de luz i amor que gime bajo el ferreo despotismo de España simpatizamos de todo corazon con la patria de los Morelos, Guerreros i Zavalas [We, who were born in an enlightened and enchanted land that shines under Spain's iron-willed despotism, sympathize with all our hearts with the mother country of the Morelos, the Guerreros, and the Zavalas]."[50]

The familiar American trope (here, in the hemispheric sense) of invoking land and earth—that "enlightened and enchanted land"—as the source of American distinction makes its appearance here. While the American soil may serve as the germ of Americanness, what continues to count as civilized culture, what still unites these Spanish Americans, is a European-derived culture that unites those who "speak that most melodious language of Castile on this side of the ocean." Unlike their North American compatriots, they are tethered to a *southern* European culture characterized by the "idioma de Cervantes i Garcila[s]o [language of Cervantes and Garcilaso]."[51] But this sense of unity apparently does not correspond to one nation-state, since it is "all of our people's *nations*" that are bound together by Spanish culture. The *Ranchero,* then, gives voice to that colonial history of Hispanic belonging based on concentric imagined communities: from the *patria chica* (one's place of birth), to the kingdom (New Spain), to the Americas, and the monarchy (Spain). Though these Americans have attempted to undo the knot that ties them (politically though not culturally) to Spain, they have retained their hemispheric sense of belonging as Americans even while acknowledging their local sovereignties.

What has begun to emerge from these American seeds may not be as cultured and elevated as the writers of the Spanish Golden Age. After all, Quintero does not mention a single Spanish-American author. Nonetheless, what has begun to germinate is a distinctly *political* (as opposed to cultural) Americanness marked by "the Morelos, the Guerreros, and the Zavalas" of Mexico. Heroes of the Mexican war of independence, José María Morelos and Vicente Guerrero are logical icons of an emerging sense of Mexican nationality, but Lorenzo de Zavala is quite an odd choice for this political trinity. A radical liberal creole who embraced Enlightenment ideals, Zavala was born in Mérida on the Yucatán Peninsula, and had attempted to mold the young Mexican nation into a vision of Enlightenment-inspired republicanism. Zavala traveled extensively throughout the United States, first visiting New Orleans and traveling up the Mississippi and on to New England. He had grand visions of developing a U.S.-inspired government in Mexico.

But Mexico's chaotic early years were no place for a strident liberal. Zavala was forced into exile, fleeing to Texas where he supported the cause for Texas independence from Mexico and helped build the Republic of Texas's political infrastructure. Seen as a traitor by his contemporary Mexican citizens, Zavala would serve as the first vice president of the Republic of Texas. Admired by both his fellow liberal Anglo- and Mexican-Texans, Zavala would unfortunately resign in October 1836. He had contracted an interminable fever, and would succumb to pneumonia the following month.[52]

By embracing Zavala—without any sense of contradiction or need of explanation—the *Ranchero* (much like Leal comparing Navarro to heroes from North and South America, as we saw in Chapter 8) gives voice to an alternate nineteenth-century American vision of political nationalism, distinct from those that predominated in either the United States or Mexico. It was inspired and molded in the sociopolitical cauldron of the Circum-Gulf of Mexico network.

But this moment, and this vision, would fail to congeal. Rather than a fully spelled out political philosophy, we are left with remnants of an iconology of political liberalism (which is not to say that the textual remnants may not be teased out from other documents in the Circum-Gulf of Mexico). These newspapers give witness to that historical moment, not of a sedimentation of a different vision of belonging in the Americas, but, rather, of dead ends. They bear witness not to a history of origins, but to "one of division, of limits." They signal a history that is not "one of lasting foundations" because this vision of modernity would ultimately fail to take hold. In its place would be a "complete reversal" of this Circum-Gulf of Mexico vision of nationalism.[53] In Texas, the once dominant Catholic Hispanic concentric sense of imagined communities would be replaced with a thick racial discourse.

The *Ranchero* concludes its argument by turning to inspirational rhetoric, imploring Tejanos to "Haced que el pendon de la democracia cobije para siempre todo lo que de noble caballerezco se conserva en nuestra raza [let the banner of democracy always cover and shelter everything that is noble and chivalrous in our people]." The language used in making the argument of uniting under "the banner of democracy" strikes an odd chord and reveals the specifically other American rhetoric of liberalism. "Noble" and "chivalrous" have the ring of aristocratic rhetoric, a rhetoric that had been excised from dominant Anglo-American culture during the revolution but that continued to hold social and cultural force in Spanish America and the U.S. South.

The *Ranchero* does not stop here, however, and specifies *what,* precisely, should be protected by "the banner of democracy." It is those "noble and chivalrous" attributes comprised of "la pompa del rico idioma de Cervantes i Garcilao i los nobles atritutos [*sic*] del elemento latino que fluye en nuestras venas [the beauty of our mellifluous and splendid language of Cervantes and Garcila[s]o, and the noble attributes of the Latin element that flows through our veins]."[54] In effect, these Spanish Americans (the Cuban Quintero and his Tejano elite) utilized a rhetoric that was distinct from that of Anglo-Americans and yet familiar. For these elite, the culture that must be defended, the society that should be allowed to participate in U.S. electoral politics, is one that continues to be grounded in a Spanish-American culture. But here, as well, we see the shadow of cultural traits being biologized into an incipient racial language of blood, that "element flowing through our veins."

Now, rather than being of Spanish origin, they have transformed into something that may be described as "Latin." In using this language, Quintero reveals already what was becoming a dominant French influence in nineteenth-century Spanish America. France had sought to supplant Spain's and then Britain's political-economic influence in America, and had made the argument that Spanish Americans were bound to France through the history of "Latinness." "There existed, the French argued, a linguistic and cultural affinity, a unity of 'Latin' peoples for whom France was the natural leader and inspiration (and their defender against Anglo-Saxon, mainly US, influence and, ultimately, domination)."[55]

In these newspapers, what we find is a defense of a different worldview, one that had emerged from the Catholic Hispanic world, and was in the process of reconfiguring its own political tradition of liberalism, of the ideal relationship between community and individual, and of producing a Spanish-American culture that could sustain these reconfiguring Spanish-American nations. It is a world filled with Spanish-American noblesse, the idiom of Cervantes and Garcilaso, and the Latin tinge of southern Europe. But this different form of Occidental power, Western but not quite, had already been defeated. The Spanish empire, refusing to abandon its mercantilist policies, had long ceded its power and prestige to northern European nations. Left with an insufficiently developed capitalist culture and an economy that could not contend with the already industrializing United States and northern Europe, Mexico and the rest of Spanish America inherited their former colonizer's dependence. On a global scale, Spain and its former colonies in the Americas were quickly becoming peripheral in the transforming capitalist global order. At the more local level, in San Antonio, the elite continued to dream of producing a nation-state where they would retain their status. Now, they found themselves not just peripheral in a new nation-state, but obsolete.

Racialization and Colonization

As the racialization of Tejanos continued—that is, as the diverse, class-stratified Tejano community became an increasingly deterritorialized, terrorized, and pauperized population—their place within the public sphere became less secure.[56] The Bastrop *Advertiser* was far from alone in expressing its anti-Mexican sentiment. The famed nineteenth-century traveler and abolitionist Frederick Law Olmsted observed that Anglo Texans regarded Mexicans "in a somewhat unchristian tone, not as heretics or heathen, to be converted with flannel and tracts, but rather as vermin, to be exterminated."[57] For the Know-Nothing newspaper the *Advertiser,* the issue was not that Mexicans should be excluded merely because they were racially distinct; rather, it clarified that Mexicans did not have—and were incapable of acquiring—the requisite sociocultural accoutrements to participate in U.S. democracy. Hence, the *Advertiser* concluded that "any honest man regardless of political party, readily acknowledges that they [Mexicans] are *incapable* of appreciating the rights and privileges they have been granted; and no one will deny that they are ignorant, venal, prostituted, vile and stupid."[58]

The *Advertiser* was not alone in its views. Arnoldo De León has documented well this perniciously insidious Anglo-American racial discourse toward Mexicans. Anglos were disgusted by Mexicans' history of mestizaje, and viewed them as mixed-blood mongrels. Mexicans were seen as indolent and subservient, especially to the Catholic Church, and as having a defective morality.[59] These racial "others" had little place in the developing political life of Texas. Yet, Anglo Texans were far from unique in fomenting this racial rhetoric. It permeated Anglo-American society as well.

This Anglo-American ideology of racial superiority had developed as early as the 1830s, when Anglos and Mexicans met in the Southwest in significantly larger numbers than before. It had morphed from the discourse of Manifest Destiny, which also had roots in the Puritan notion of the providential nation. In fact, as Reginald Horsman documents, the 1836 Texas Revolution was described by Anglo-Americans in the United States "from its beginnings . . . as a racial clash, not simply a revolt against unjust government or tyranny." Indeed, the encounter between Anglos and Mexicans in the Southwest, the Texas Revolution, the war with Mexico, is what led Anglo "Americans [to] clearly formulate the idea of themselves as an Anglo-Saxon race." The U.S. press was full of anti-Mexican sentiment during both the Texas Revolution and, especially, the U.S.-Mexico War. Even those Anglos who were against the war and annexation of the contemporary Southwest made their arguments on the basis that there were too many Mexicans in the territory.[60]

This racial discourse naturalized Mexicans as biologically inferior, culturally backward, politically retarded, and, as a result, incapable of participating in a democratic republic. But this rhetoric, as we know, also had very real material consequences. A tangible elite had managed to survive the turmoil of U.S. annexation, and, as David Montejano describes it, a tenuous "peace structure" between elite Tejanos and Anglos had been achieved along the border. But even these small numbers of elites would dwindle, and the peace structure would collapse with the coming of the railroad in the 1880s. The shift from ranching to a modernized capitalist agricultural economy would once again alter the fabric of life for Tejanos. Montejano has charted the vexing late nineteenth-century and early twentieth-century juridical and political mechanisms put in place to ensure that Tejanos would remain, for the most part, in a position not unlike those of colonized peoples in the British and French empires. Tejanos became largely consigned to the purely economic sphere of colonization: as labor designed to incorporate the annexed land into the United States' capitalist economy.[61]

Participation in the U.S. public sphere required that one be interpellated as a citizen-subject, a process that required access to education. This, in turn, required the socioeconomic status that allowed one to devote time to education rather than, say, subsistence farming and ranching. Thus, when the *Advertiser* proclaims, "Educate them [Mexicans] and they will become traitors. Give them riches and power and they will abuse them," it is developing a rhetoric to insure that Mexicans do not become educated or have access to material wealth. The prophecy is self-fulfilling: absent economic resources, Tejanos were unable to receive the education required to participate in the public sphere. These ideas, needless to say, were not mere rhetoric. Tejanos were losing their land and property, and they were prevented from engaging in the labor market. This resulted in a flattening of the socioeconomic diversity among Tejanos and the decline, though not total demise, of the educated, elite Tejanos who had participated in the early sociopolitical formation of Texas.[62]

Two years after the 1856 debate between the *Bejareño* and the *Ranchero,* another Spanish-language newspaper emerged: *El Correo*. It would be the last gasp, the final opportunity for Tejanos to use newspapers as a way to intervene in the public sphere; not until 1886 would another paper emerge. The *Correo* reported on recent county legislation that established a committee to authorize funding for public schools, and congratulated the county for ensuring that students received an adequate education. Nonetheless, in "al consagrar aquí estas cortas líneas á negocio de tal interés [consigning here these brief lines to such matters]," writes the editor, José Ramos de Zúñiga, "permítasenos el emitir de paso, una lijera observacion, que se nos ocurre en este momento [allow us to make a light observation that comes to mind at the moment]." He then embarks on a critique, anything but a "light observation," noting that funds would be allotted "solo para el sostenimiento de las escuelas, en que el inglés se enseña con preferencia. . . . ¿Como puede esperarse que los niños mejicanos ó alemanes . . . lleguen . . . á espresarse con propiedad en [cualquiera] de las dos? [only for the maintenance of schools in which only English is taught. . . . How can one expect Mexican or German children . . . to ever . . . be able to express themselves properly in (either) language?]" Already, notes the *Correo,* so many Mexican and German children "que han sido educados en las escuelas públicas . . . no [saben] ní su idioma ni el inglés con perfeccion [who have been educated in public schools . . . neither know their language nor English with perfection]."[63] Such legislation only frustrated attempts to cultivate a literate and educated Tejano population.

But the *Correo* managed to exist for only three months, until July 1858. The Union firing on Fort Sumter in April 1861 would spur Texas to organize its forces, disrupting the state economy and ending all newspaper publishing for several years. Elites attempted to establish newspapers in the latter nineteenth century just as they began to organize mutual aid societies, but other than passing references to these titles they have yet to be discovered. Still, notwithstanding the efforts on the part of an ever-reduced Tejano elite, most Tejanos had been or (after the arrival of the railroad and capitalist incorporation of Texas into the national economy) would become thoroughly racialized and colonized. It was a brutal history that terrorized Mexicans in the United States, robbed them of their property, stripped them of their rights, and barred their children access to educational opportunities.[64] They were unable, in other words, to pass on their intellectual revolutions to their offspring, unable to fulfill that basic goal of leaving the world a better place than they had found it.

Publishing, then, was one of the few means that nineteenth-century Tejanos had as they struggled to continue to shape their new and increasingly fractured home. They had worked in tandem with elected officials to secure a position for Tejanos. But the number of elected officials, not surprisingly, also dwindled: no Tejanos were elected to statewide offices after 1846, and none held federal office until 1960. At the state level, only nineteen were elected between 1846 and 1961.[65]

The Know-Nothing Party's fierce rhetoric and the rising tide of racial violence against Tejanos did not sway them from voicing their critiques and embracing the democratic political system as the best method to protect their interests. Whether the *Bejareño* and the *Ranchero* eventually became victims of violence is uncertain, but the absence of a Spanish-language newspaper after 1858 meant that it was even more difficult for Tejanos to intervene in the social, economic, and political affairs of the state in order to ensure that Tejanos were integral to it. But, more importantly, in a world where print was crucial to communication, these newspapers offered an opportunity for Tejanos to cultivate a much larger sense of belonging, one that focused on Texas, yes, but that also had echoes of, and a longing for, a larger, catholic sense of belonging that transcended the nation.

It may only be with hindsight, with the perspective of time and history, that we are able to describe the conditions during and after this period as a form of U.S. colonialism. The 1848 Treaty of Guadalupe Hidalgo may have secured full citizenship rights for the Mexicans who remained in the conquered territory, but even then the U.S. Congress hesitated to bestow these rights on them. Instead, they preferred to rewrite in vague terms the treaty's article consigning citizenship to Latinos, those communities of Spanish-American descent living in the United States who would experience the tortuous process of racialization.[66] Technically speaking, Latinos may have had rights as citizens; nonetheless, this discursive and material history of conquest and colonization resulted in the territorial displacement of Tejanos, their economic demise and consequent impoverishment, and their erasure from the public sphere.

The Latinos involved in these newspapers may have thought that judicious and eloquent elocutions would temper the anti-Mexican sentiment they suffered, or that their speeches and editorials would foster a more congenial, multilingual public sphere. Yet, this generation of elite Tejanos was among the last of the preconquest generation to have the socioeconomic position, education, ability, and esteem to engage in the public life of the state. The erasure of Tejanos from the public sphere, the consequence of innumerable moments large and small, worked in tandem with an even more damning, though less intentional, effort: the erasure of Tejanos from the dominant narrative of history.

Conclusion

Surrounding Oneself with the Beauty of Life

In 1851, in the midst of the social turmoil that was redefining the future of Latinos in Texas, a school for young girls opened in San Antonio. After the United States annexed Texas in 1845, the Catholic Church made Texas its own diocese, and a Frenchman, Father Jean Marie Odin, after serving as bishop of New Orleans, was appointed bishop to the new state in 1847. In the years to come, he sought the assistance of religious orders wherever he traveled, including New Orleans, Quebec, and France. In 1851, that help came from New Orleans, when several Ursuline nuns joined three from the Galveston convent and opened the first girls' school in the state.

Founded in Italy in 1535 and dedicated to the education of young girls, the Ursuline Order, not unlike the Jesuits in Spanish America, were used to answering this plea. In 1639 in Quebec, then part of New France, they established one of the earliest girls' schools in all of the Americas. From there they continued their primary mission of educating girls in the Americas, both indigenous and of European origin, and established themselves, among other places, in New Orleans in 1727.

On November 3, 1851, six weeks after the arrival of the Ursulines in San Antonio, the doors of the Ursuline Academy opened. Within months, the nuns found themselves overwhelmed with families—Tejano, French, German, and Anglo-American—desiring to enroll their daughters. Students were "packed like sardines" in the four large classrooms on the first floor, while those from throughout Texas and northern Mexico who required room and board filled the sleeping quarters on the second floor to capacity. The French-speaking nuns and, later, Irish nuns, quickly learned Spanish. With time, the school attracted nuns from across the Americas and Europe, who eventually taught in Spanish, French, German, and English.[1]

Among their students was fifteen-year-old Florencia Leal. It is not clear when she enrolled, but she was studying at the academy by 1853. Born on February 22, 1838, in the Texas-Mexico border town of Mier, in Tamaulipas, Florencia was raised some ten miles from Revilla, the hometown of Father José Antonio Gutiérrez de Lara and his brother José Bernardo. Sometime in her early adolescence, her family sent her to San Antonio, and she found herself boarding at the Ursuline Academy, where she dutifully received lessons in Spanish grammar and rhetoric and began to learn English. Florencia had done what so many young Latinas would do: travel to San Antonio to be educated. The city had become the unofficial capital of what Américo Paredes famously described as "greater Mexico," the south Texas-northern Mexico borderlands. Less than a century later, in 1910, so, too, would the renowned novelist and folklorist Jovita González de Mireles leave her Rio Grande Valley to study in San Antonio.

San Antonio was not altogether a foreign city for Florencia. Her great, great, great, great grandfather was Juan Leal Goraz (1676–1743), leader of the families that had emigrated from the Canary Islands to found San Antonio in 1731. He had served as the town's first mayor.[2] From San Antonio, the Leal descendants had spread throughout the region, in Texas and Mexico; some became soldiers, others merchants. Her great-grandfather, Joaqúin Leal (1746–1819) of San Antonio, had been an esteemed patriot in support of independence in 1813. Florencia continued to have family in San Antonio. Among them were her two brothers, Narciso and Guadalupe, who as we have seen had both been involved with all three of San Antonio's first Spanish-language newspapers from the 1850s, *El Bejareño, El Ranchero,* and *El Correo*. In the 1880s, Narciso would edit *El Observador*. Along with their journalistic enterprises, they had set themselves up as merchants, trading in livestock and real estate, and opened several stores in San Antonio for which they traveled frequently to New Orleans to purchase goods.[3]

Sometime in 1853 Florencia acquired a handsome, leather-bound composition notebook, purchased perhaps by one of her brothers on one of their trips to New Orleans.[4] Her notebook served her several purposes. She had decided to learn the art of writing letters, and she transcribed, in perfect penmanship and with beautifully decorative bullet points, a Spanish-language epistolary manual. The manual covered every detail: from style ("how to address and begin a letter"), to rhetorical devices ("from prolepsis, analogy, metaphor, etc."), to the appropriate tone to use when writing to superiors.

Florencia spends the first twenty-three pages studiously learning the art of the written word. "El estilo es la manera de pintar sus pensamientos y sus sentimientos con palabras pronunciadas o escritas que son como los colores del estilo [Style is the manner by which one paints one's thoughts and feelings with spoken or written words, which are like the colors of style.]" Her manual describes three styles, of which the sublime, for example, "pinta los grandes pensamientos y los sentimientos elevados de una manera noble [paints grand thoughts and elevated feelings in a noble manner]" (5). She will put these to the test. Later, she will diagram her sentences by writing the sentence, one word at a time, down the left side of the page and defining the grammatical function of each word to its immediate right. The diagramming lesson concludes: "Con saber analizar todas estas palabras se pueden analizar todas las demas [By knowing how to analyze all of these words, one can then analyze all the rest]" (45). But in learning how to express herself through language by studying epistolary styles and grammar, she, too, comes to use language to paint her thoughts and feelings. She is able to use these skills in order to structure and analyze her interiority through language. Her journal—through her writing and her sketches—comes to be one of the ways that Florencia begins to unfold her subjectivity.

Having meticulously transcribed the manual, she then spent the summers of 1853 and 1854 putting those epistolary lessons to the test, filling over thirteen pages with letters. She first wrote drafts, painstakingly following the style manual's rules on proper address and etiquette. She set out to write letters to her girlfriends, family members, and teachers who lived in New Orleans, Mier, and elsewhere in Texas and Mexico, and, on one occasion, wrote from New Orleans herself. The notebook itself is testament to the flourishing of Florencia's subjectivity, and the epistolary manual becomes a model for styling her sense of self.

The first letters are no more than a page long, and they are short, bland, formulaic greetings. She acknowledges as much, writing, "El fin de la primera Carta que hise en el Convento de las Ursulinas no tiene fin . . . ni principio [The goal of the first Letter I wrote at the Ursuline Convent had neither end nor purpose]" (24). But she increasingly moves beyond the banal as she paints herself and her desires with words and images. "Querida amiga," she writes at the age of sixteen on June 5, 1854, "estoy sentida con Ud. por que a nomas a mi hermana le escribe [Dearest friend, I am upset with you because you only write to my sister]" (30). She had already

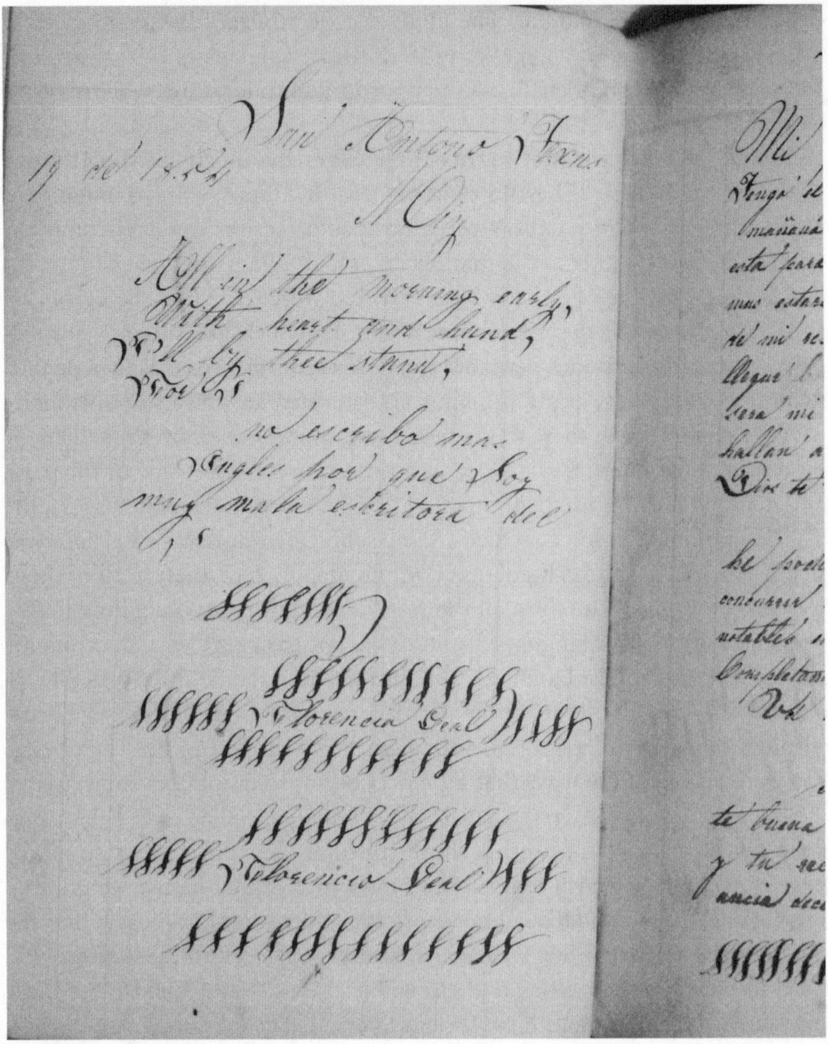
All in the morning early,
With heart and hand,
no escribo mas
Florencia Leal
Florencia Leal

Figure 71. Florencia Leal. Notebook (ca. 1853–ca. 1870), p. 54.
Manuscript Collection, the Nettie Lee Benson Collection, the University of Texas, Austin.

written to her younger sister that she had been “un poco triste de ver que no he tenido ningunas nuebas de ti [a little sad because I haven’t received any news from you]” (25). She becomes increasingly self-reflexive, able to ponder in writing the significance of her feelings. The letters are genuinely moving and reveal a young woman’s aspirations and longing for intimate friendships with friends and family. As she writes to friends and teachers, she often feels the need to apologize for what she felt was her poorly written prose. But after a dozen or so letters, she becomes occupied with her school lessons. She stops drafting letters, and spends the next thirty pages of the notebook carefully studying and transcribing the formal rules of Spanish grammar, organizing the pages into neat columns. Then, there is another shift.

Her writing begins to expand beyond the epistolary and grammatical lessons to engage with the poetic and aesthetics. It also is her first attempt to practice the English she was learning at the Ursuline Academy. On a new page, she begins:

San Antonio, Texas
19 de 1854 Mayo
All in the morning early,
With heart and hand,
I'll be thee stand,
For
no escribo mas [I won't write more]
ingles por que soy [English because I am]
muy mala escritora del [a bad writer of it] (53)

Florencia had started to transcribe an old Scottish love song, perhaps shared with her by some of the recently arrived Irish Ursuline nuns.[5] But she doubts her bilingual skills. Indeed, she would write to her teacher, Sister Josefa, "Yo quiero aprender esas lenguas tan dificiles [I want to learn those ever so difficult languages]" (100). But she grew increasingly frustrated: "me enojo todos los dias con los que las inventaron [I get angry every day with those who invented them]," and asked, again, for advice on how best to study. For the moment, however, Florencia instead resorted to practicing her signature, the first time she has done so in her notebook.

She signs her name twice in elegant script. Surrounding each signature are a series of continuous "S"-like flourishes that serve to buoy her names. The flourishes envelope each of her names and come to appear like clouds, soft and gentle. Her previous signatures, at the end of the letters, had included short curlicues at the end of her last name. But now, both of her signatures are surrounded by innumerable flourishes. From here on, the flourishes appear increasingly and with greater creative intensity. They are used as dramatic, decorative section breaks and graphic touches in the margins, peppered across the page as she transcribes her grammar lessons. Before, her orthography was crisp, perfect, and bereft of any stylistic variance. Now, it becomes much more confident as she begins to use various sizes of letters to emphasize transitions. The first letters of paragraphs, too, become artful and more calligraphic, amplified with cushiony spirals and thick down strokes. Unlike the immaculately copied epistolary lessons at the beginning of the journal, the transcribed grammar lessons had now expanded to incorporate Florencia's expressiveness. Weaving in and out between the words, Florencia integrated her aesthetic sensibilities.

The grammar lessons continue for thirty pages, and as they do, the flourishes become even more elaborate. Finally, script gives way to sketches. Her imagination takes her away from the grammar lessons and the desire to cultivate her friendships with others through letters. The lessons and letters end after a hundred pages, sometime around August 1854. She then fills more than ten pages with gorgeous sketches of interlaced hearts, one blue, the other red, and two-dimensional drawings of birdcages, roses, and homes surrounded by trees and brush. The flourishes, too, evolve and become almost like a tornado, an inverted triangle comprised of striated lines surrounded by smaller curlicues centered on a page. The attention to detail is impressive. Then she begins to paste striking decorative embossed foil onto the pages. The first is of a reposing matron in a bucolic setting with a staff in hand; the second is of what appears to be a gentleman in Scottish or Irish dress; and both are framed in delicately decorated borders. It is as if Florencia seeks to surround herself with all that is beautiful.

Several months before writing gave way to sketching, in May 1854 at the age of sixteen, Florencia had written to the Mother Superior asking for advice on her keen desire to join the convent and become a nun. What the advice was is not clear, but the result was that Florencia would leave the Ursuline Academy that summer and return to her native Mier. Nine months later, on February 24, 1855, she would marry José María García Villareal. But there are no more lessons, letters, or entries, and she says nothing of her engagement or marriage. Had she wanted to join the convent in order to avoid the patriarchal confines of marriage? Perhaps, given that not once does she mention her fiancé or husband. Instead, she includes in her notebook a short, touching speech she delivered on the occasion of her parents' anniversary (112). This is followed by the transcription of the Irish poet Thomas Moore's poem *The Last Rose of Summer* (114).

Written in 1805 and quickly set to music, the poem became widely popular and was included in operas. It has been performed by twentieth-century recording artists and is featured on television to the present. The poem allegorizes the beauty of life, even if fleeting. It is profoundly melancholic. Observing a rose bush, the speaker laments the solitary remains of a single, though still fragrant and blooming, rose. She has been left alone among the rest of the wilted flowers, their petals covering the ground beneath. Thus, the poem's speaker cuts the last remaining rose from the bush and scatters its petals to lie intermingled among her dead companions. The narrator, too, contemplates her own demise:

> so soon may I follow
> When friendships decay. . . .
> When true hearts lie withered,
> And fond ones are flown,
> Oh! Who would inhabit
> This bleak world alone?

But more than melancholic, the poem also embraces the sublimity of intimacy.

Life, the poem suggests, is not about possessing cherished objects, retaining youthful innocence, or cultivating an autonomous sense of self; the rose, after all, had been "left blooming alone; / All her lovely companions . . . faded and gone." Rather, the poem intimates that, like the rose, life emerges only in sociality, through a sense of interconnectivity, as the rose did among her companions. The mysticism of the social, of recognition by others who can "reflect back her blushes, / or give sigh for sigh," is what can approximate those fleeting moments of transcendence, equanimity, and the divine. In a sense, the divine is no longer solely seen as an external force operating on the masses. It emerges instead in the interstitial tissue of being.

Thus, quite appropriately, Florencia also surrounds herself with the beauty of life. Some ten months after her marriage, at the age of seventeen, Florencia returned to her notebook and began the last remaining entries. Now, however, she documented in careful detail the birth of her eight children, providing the exact time, date, day of the week, name, and weight of each one. Her first, "Nicolasito," was born around seven in the morning on December 4, 1855. Over the next twelve years, she would return to her journal and note the birth of each child, concluding with her eighth, Xulema, at eight in the morning on November 24, 1870. These would be her last entries. Perhaps she kept other diaries, but they have not been discovered. We do know that her daughter Xulema became a talented musician who studied and traveled in Europe before settling in San Antonio. Florencia herself would live to the age of fifty-six and would die of pneumonia in Washington, D.C., on January 4, 1894. It may be that Florencia contracted pneumonia while accompanying Xulema on one of her trips.[6]

Florencia had turned to writing in order to capture the poetics of life: its intimacies, beauty, knowledge, style. She never produced a diary-like entry where she addressed an anonymous reader, the modern form of journaling that clearly reveals a self-reflexivity in writing. But combined, the letters, the style manual, the grammar, the sketches, the poems, the inserted decorative paper, and, finally, the details of her children's births reveal Florencia's desire to use writing as a means of leaving traces, evidence of her life, one that would help sustain a sense of presence and belonging in the world, sedimented by her friends and family.

A History of Writing, a Search for Presence

Florencia's notebook is a stark aberration from the mass of documents that we have explored throughout this book. The notebook is, indeed, unique in at least two respects. It may be compared to José Bernardo Gutiérrez de Lara's travel narrative, but as I proposed earlier, he had a larger reading public in mind as he kept his journal. The vast majority, if not all, of the materials discussed here were meant to be read or heard by many, if not by a large public then by a coterie of political administrators or elite.

Florencia, on the other hand, did not intend for anyone else to read her notebook (other than those to whom she addressed her letters). It is intimate, private, an expressive lesson in cultivating one's sense of self. But it is more than that. In the twelve years I have spent conducting archival research, Florencia's notebook is one of only two nineteenth-century texts that I have been able to find written by a Tejana. The other is the horrific, unsigned testimony, discussed at the end of Chapter 6, of the experiences of the Bexareña women who were tortured by the Spanish royal commandant general Joaquín de Arredondo's forces in 1813.[7] Florencia had little to say about the events that were unfolding in San Antonio during the chaotic years leading up to emergence of the Know-Nothing Party and the increasing racialization of Mexicans. Instead, she dedicates the space to ensuring that her friendships will continue to deepen, to studying Spanish grammar, learning English, and transcribing images from her mind's eye.

Her text stands in contrast to the history of Latino writing we have studied here. Yet, at the same time, it also serves as a reminder of the necessity of our continued exploration. Literary scholars, myself included, have long focused on those well-established genres that we describe as literature: the novel, poetry, short fiction, drama, and other belletristic genres. But if literary history has fetishized these final forms, it has done so at the expense of the vast archive of writing that preceded, surrounded, and continues to surround the development of these genres.

A mutation occurred in the history of writing in the West (Catholic and Protestant), one originating in the eighteenth century and continuing

Figure 72. Florencia Leal, Notebook (ca. 1853–ca. 1870), p. 111.
Manuscript Collection, the Nettie Lee Benson Collection, the University of Texas, Austin.

through the nineteenth. It is during the nineteenth century that the category of the literary, as we know it, emerged as a recognizable genre distinct from other forms of writing.[8] But embedded in this notion of the literary was writing as a search for immanence and belonging, for what Derrida described as a yearning for a metaphysics of presence. Writing increasingly becomes a means of approximating a sense of the divine: "God is the name and the element of that which makes possible an absolutely pure and absolutely self-present self-knowledge. . . . [I]t can be *produced as auto-affection,* only through the *voice:* an order of the signifier by which the subject takes from itself into itself, does not borrow outside of itself the signifier that it emits and that affects it at the same time."[9] Rather than merely reflecting God's fixed meaning, language comes to be seen as a self-reflexive, flexible tool of understanding, much as Florencia's grammar book had suggested: learn to analyze these words, and all the rest will be easily understood.

As we have seen, these shifts become increasingly palpable after Mexican independence. The archive of nineteenth-century Latina/o writing unearthed here sought, above all, to reconfigure political morality in a disenchanted world, one that collapsed with Napoleon Bonaparte's 1808 invasion of Spain and one that continued to crumble with each social imaginary that failed to cohere—from Iturbide's short-lived empire, to the irreconcilable tensions between Santa Anna's autocratic centralism and Texas and other Mexican states' desire for federalism that allowed for more self-determination, to the tearing apart of Mexico after the Texas revolt and war with the United States. In 1820s and 1830s Texas, Tejanos turned to writing as a means to shape the material reality of the state, one that no longer depended on the metaphysical certainty of God and king. But this shift in writing was not only reflective of the shift in sovereignty; it was related to the much larger epistemic transformation that we have traced here, of seeing the world as a produced order.

As the nineteenth century continued to unfold, Latina/o writing sought to reconfigure political morality in a world that became increasingly hard to comprehend. For these writers, a world of certainty became a world of ambiguity; the previous Catholic vision of self and society as a beautifully woven tapestry was torn to shreds before their very eyes. And these writers slowly became aware that even those shreds that remained would have to be redesigned in order to remain integral to the now dominant liberal capitalist world of the United States. In the sovereign space that had once been dominated by God and king, humans will now use their own words as the foundation of a new world.

Latina/o writing would continue to flourish in a variety of genres, though the Latina/o novel and fiction in general do not begin to flourish until the late nineteenth century, if not the early twentieth century. It is in this sense, then, that we would be better served to focus on the development of Latina/o *writing* and the search for immanence, even as writing splintered, leading to new genres, new sources of authority that could both supplant the previous episteme's even while producing the ontological resources that would construct that which we hold so dear today: the modern, autonomous self.

I conclude my history with the 1850s, the moment when Tejanos were beginning to respond to the hardening of Anglo-American racism and the brutal experiences of being displaced, conditions that I argue should indeed be described as a form of colonialism. By returning to the moment prior to the U.S. annexation of what is now the Southwest, my goal has been to understand the world of nineteenth-century Latinas/os on their own terms, *prior* to their being colonized. Rather than begin with the *responses* of nineteenth-century Latina/os to their racialization and displacement, I found it imperative to unravel their worldviews, to appreciate the language and conceptual models they used to describe themselves and their world. Only after unearthing this discursive world, I argue, can we better appreciate the complex ways in which they responded to the historical processes of colonialism.

During the 1970s, Chicana/o historians and social scientists debated the appropriateness of colonialism as a conceptual model for Chicana/o history. They sought to counter the dominant social science paradigm that explained Chicanas/os' historical and contemporary socioeconomic status primarily through racist theories of inherent cultural and social deficiencies.[10] Instead, they argued that internal colonization offered a more accurate interpretation of the Mexican American experience. In doing so, they borrowed the notion of the internal colony from dependency theory.[11]

The theory, however, fell out of favor by the early 1980s. Tomás Almaguer seemingly laid the issue to rest in his provocative essay "Ideological Distortions in Recent Chicano Historiography: The Internal Colony Model and Chicano Historical Interpretation."[12] There he claimed that historians had ignored the complexity of pre- and post-conquest Mexican culture and society. Most importantly, Almaguer argues that Mexican Americans were legally considered white with ostensibly full citizenship rights and thus did not endure the more violent history that African Americans, Native Americans, and Asian Americans experienced. Due to these differences, that is, because of the social stratification of Mexicans, he contends that the internal colony model is not useful. With this article, Almaguer seemed to have settled the historiographical debate on whether Chicanos were ever colonized.

Yet the debate never developed to its full potential.[13] First, these scholars failed to provide a clear definition of colonialism. Second, Almaguer assumed a static model of colonization in which colonized people demonstrated little internal stratification, as if it were some utopian society absent of its own particular history of social domination. Historians of British and French colonialism, however, have long known that the concept of a homogenous colonized group is fictitious, noting that the existence of a small, elite colonized class facilitated the process of colonization. Finally, as alluded to here, a moment of great possibility was missed during this period. Contemporaneous to this debate, the school of postcolonial studies was developing out of the area studies of British and French imperial studies. From that school emerged vigorous debates among Marxist and poststructural theorists who offered rich conceptual frameworks for understanding the complex workings of power and oppression, not unlike the world of nineteenth-century Latinas/os. But these two areas of study, Chicana/o studies and postcolonial studies, never crossed paths during this period.[14]

If I have used the terms "Latino," "Spanish American," "Mexican," and "Tejano," among others, interchangeably, I have done so in the spirit of emphasizing the very contingency of these ways of describing one's self and one's community. During the nineteenth century, these national terms of identification were in flux and far from sedimented. Thus, in describing this history as "Latino" I have sought to move away from nationalist terminology (as only "Mexican American," for example), in order to revisit these much older catholic senses of belonging in the Hispanic world. These were imaginaries that transcended one's attachment to one's province, one's *patria chica,* in order to feel that one was part of a much larger world. This was Francisco Suárez's *corpus mysticum,* the sense of the *pueblo,* hierarchical and fixed as it was, coming together and producing something transcendental, something irreducible and divine. But in returning to this concept by invoking "Latino," I also choose to revise it, much as José Álvarez de Toledo and others did as they rethought Catholic political thought for their republican nations.

I am quite far from suggesting that this sense of Latina/o should be Catholic in any theological sense, but I am fascinated by this alternative nonnationalist universal desire to feel that ontological-spiritual sense of belonging. This concentric sense of community is one that continues to reverberate among Latin Americans—that sense of cultural-linguistic solidarity—even if intransigent nationalisms have desperately sought to undo it. Nationalism emerged in the nineteenth and twentieth centuries as overpowering ways to replace these previous understandings of belonging. But we have seen how quickly nationalisms have turned into rigid xenophobias where the nation cares for no one but itself. What is most tantalizing about the term "Latina/o" is that Latinas/os do not have one national origin. We come from all over Latin America, live in the United States, and have experienced, to varying degrees, the lived realities of racialization within the United States. But what is also noticeable here in my turn to "Latina/o" is my shift to the more explicitly gender-neutral "Latina/o." If I used the ostensibly gender-neutral "Latino" or "Tejano" before, I did so as a way to emphasize how thoroughly masculine the archive of Latino nineteenth century writing is.

In this regard, Florencia Leal's notebook should serve as a precaution. Though her writing is an exception, existing outside the formal structures of political sovereignty, it also serves to remind us that the official archives housed in libraries, even if long ignored, also need to be read against the grain. Any kind of written text produced by those ostensibly outside the workings of political power—such as women, peons, and indigenous peoples, or the Hispanicized Indians who produced the notched sticks discussed in Chapter 6—were usually of no consequence to those who produced and organized archives. Their texts may continue to exist in private collections, kept, perhaps, as family heirlooms. The writing studied here may have been collected and cared for, ready for the historian to access, but their significant visions and aspirations had long been unaccounted for. Their worlds now more familiar, we should continue to sift through the archive in order to pierce through other sedimented layers of textuality. Certainly, there are new worlds to uncover. We have seen what can be revealed when we upend our expectations, in order to approach a text anew, to read history from the unsure, unfolding perspective of its makers. By continuing our search, we will be able to discover other worlds, in texts both new and familiar, that can challenge us to see other glistening, brutal, tenuous desires to achieve a sense of immanence.

It has been, in part, the literary categories of genres that made it difficult to historicize nineteenth-century Latina/o writing. Rather than only search for the final form of the novel, for example, it would serve Latina/o literary and intellectual history better to historicize the development of Latina/o *writing* as a whole. We should hold at bay traditional categories of literary history in order to delve deeply into what and why nineteenth-century Latinas/os wrote. "To historians who wish to relive an era," Walter Benjamin reminds us, "they [should] blot out everything they know about the later course of history." Rather than focus on the end form—how a nineteenth-century text relates to the Latina/o novel, for example—Benjamin's method requires instead a deliberate, profoundly patient attention to the details within a piece of writing, in order to understand the world experienced and written about by the author of the text. If we are successful, such patient attention becomes an act of recognition, at once aesthetic and spiritual. It is an act of recognizing another person's vision of his or her world, and the manner in which another has sought to achieve that most basic sense of transcendence, that attempt at belonging and making meaning. For Benjamin, "it is a process of empathy whose origin is the indolence of the heart, *acedia,* which despairs of grasping and holding the genuine historical image as it flares up briefly."[15]

This sense of recognition is also a sense of loss for Benjamin, an impossible melancholic desire to grasp those fleeting moments of the past. My goal, however, has been to interpret these moments of loss as moments of possibility. The history recounted here, then, fleshes out more fully the imaginary of these authors. In doing so, it serves to expand our own imaginary today by giving us alternative models of being and belonging. If we blot out our own knowledge of the events that unfolded after these authors wrote—our own biases of the way history looks today—then we can acknowledge in these texts a string of alternate realities as disappointing as they are beautiful. They become, in the words of David Eng and David Kazanjian, "sites for memory and history, for the rewriting of the past as well as the reimagining of the future."[16]

Rather than an unbroken genealogy of Latina/o writing, what emerges from the diversity of materials we have studied is a history of false starts, of dreams that failed to cohere. These are precisely the remnants of the past that our typical study of history seems destined to forget. If history is, by default, written by the victors, these remnants are the visions of those who in their own universe may once have been elite; but theirs too, like those they had once dominated, became the visions of the voiceless, the indices of the irrelevant. Yet the very fact that they have been so thoroughly eclipsed is what makes them so valuable. As the field of Latina/o literary and intellectual history continues to unfold, our own visions will be more useful if we resist our own, often overpowering, categories of analysis—not only of literary form but of others as well, of nation and identity, for example—by historicizing the formations (and lack thereof) of other possibilities of imagining self and society.

The social imaginary that these nineteenth-century Spanish Americans sought to produce never came to fruition. To that extent, the account here is not of what nineteenth-century Latinas/os succeeded in producing. Rather, it is more in line with how the German historian Thomas Nipperdey characterized his version of history, as "an account of what happened in the light of what might have happened."[17] The emphasis here has been on those other possibilities, other visions of sovereignties, and imagined communities. They may have failed to cohere, but their discursive residues have continued to unfold underneath the dominant social formations of the last two centuries. Histories such as this one remind us of our own contingencies. The failures of these becomings remind us of the tenuousness of our own desires to flourish as well. They may also serve as ways to chip away at those behemoths that structure our lives, to see how xenophobic nationalisms, paralyzing racisms, and suffocating gender constructions may—indeed, will—cede ground to other imaginaries. That is, narrative histories work not unlike other forms of cultural production, the avant-garde poem or the brilliant filmmaker. Histories can enrich our own imaginaries by reintroducing concepts that had been discarded or, perhaps more accurately, existed only liminally. In recognizing those pasts, which seemed like eternities for those authors in the moment, and which now seem fleeting, nearly irrelevant, all-too easily forgotten, we too may learn new, more capacious ways of empathizing and thinking of our present.

APPENDIX ONE

José Antonio Gutiérrez de Lara, "Americanos"

(Proclamation, 1811; translation)

A transcription of the original is available in *Diario de lo ocurrido a las milicias del Nuevo Reino de León al mando de su comandante el Capitán Don Pedro Herrera Leyva en sus operaciones contra los Insurgentes* (Monterrey, Mexico: Archivo General del Estado de Nuevo León, 1985), 80–82.

AMERICANOS: THE FELICITOUS EPOCH we have anxiously desired for so many years has finally arrived. Now we can openly deal with the matters of our nation's interest. Yes, *Americanos,* our unquestioning Catholic faith is a testament of our allegiance to our majestic sovereign King Fernando VII; and the liberty of our beloved homeland [*patria*] is secured through the expulsion of the European traitors. The despotism, tyranny, and greed—which these individuals have exercised over us for three centuries—demand they receive the injustice of the offensive epithets of oppressors and misers. They have always attributed the causes [of our problems] to our supposed indolence without truly understanding their true source and reason. . . . [T]hey [European traitors] have woven the most horrific plots that go against the most sacred of natural laws. Thus, they are incriminated so much that it should provoke in us the most just indignation and desire for revenge. For they are worthy of their own iniquities. There is no doubt that after they conquered this New World they brought to it the Christian religion that we profess, the political laws that we follow, and the other arts that we practice for our happiness, government, and utility. In doing so, they removed the New World from the deep darkness in which it lived, and placed it instead under the rays of Diana's light,[1] in which it lives. But they committed innumerable betrayals as well, and now most recently—Oh, what pain!—they have tried to sell us to the King of England and to the worst monster in the world, our enemy Napoleon. Many have betrayed themselves to him, and as evidence we hold both correspondence and experience. There are so many notorious examples among us. These traitors argue and continue to try to rationalize their behavior. But their arrogance, ingratitude, and haughtiness, and in a word, their bad conduct render them undeserving of anything from us, least of all our love. How is it possible for us to love such treacherous men—such indolent, treacherous opportunists—with the tenderness and respect with which we used to love in another time?

No, sincere compatriots, neither divine law obligates us, nor human law allows us to tolerate those things that harm us all. Insofar as they can be detected, let that despicable breed, that wicked throng, be destroyed, waste away, and die, if it is necessary. They are much like spiders among the flowers in our kingdom; they will expel their venom only to hurt us.

Yes, *Americanos,* the nation has been born; its name has been declared. And she is being pursued by her ferocious, oppressive enemies. Already, on September 16, 1810, which we will forever remember, we began the glorious struggle for our liberty in the town [*pueblo*] of Los Dolores, and the village [*villa*] of San Miguel el Grande. We have captured the Europeans, and they are held in these towns according to the dictates of religion and humanity. No, they are not held according to those of injustice and tyranny, as our enemies have accused us in order to confuse and agitate our creole brothers, in effect so that they can defend themselves and pursue us. The noble city of Celaya submitted to discretion, as a representative of the nation, and declared in favor of our sage and gallant *caudillo* Don Miguel Hidalgo y Costilla as the nation's captain general. The rebellious and cagey city of Guanajuato has already tested the force of our arms, as did the rest of the surrounding area, and they felt the compassion of our mercy.

Valladolid, Pátzcuaro, Salamanca, San Felipe, Leon, Irapuato, Silao, and numerous other towns of New Spain have already sided with our salubrious party. The towns of Lagos, La Encarnacion, the grand Aguascalientes, and the majority of the other towns in this province of New Galicia have already sided with us. The great city of Zacatecas is leaning toward our side, and is looking forward to our arrival because they are aware of the just causes we defend and the propriety with which we conduct ourselves.

In the end, those who are not on our side with impatience desire to be so. Conquest travels with fast steps. Soon, Mexico will be ours, as will all of America, as long as we remain protected by the God of the armies and our divine patron the most Holy Mary of Guadalupe. Have courage, *Americanos*. With God's powerful protection and the Virgin Mary as our strong shield, we do not need anything more, neither a powerful nor a good friend. The wicked [Spanish bureaucrats like] Riaños[2] may have fortified themselves against us, but they soon suffered their punishment. In good time, we will rise up against the tyrannical, arrogant [Brigadier General Félix María] Callejas[3] and the seducers of Queretaro. In order to attack and destroy them we have the famous talent of the Hidalgos, the incomparable spirit of the [Ignacio] Allendes, the great resolve of the [Antonio] Canales, the grand expedition of the [Rafael] Iriartes,[4] and at last, the formidable force of the patriotic enthusiasm of the *Americanos*. Yes, dear patriots, we are committed to the cause, and we will be perpetually happy. But we must all do our part to defend a just and sacred war, if we do not want to end up unhappy. There is nothing better than courage! We must continue the venture, and place our trust in the Almighty and the Holy Patron [Virgin] Mother, who has favored us so much. Let us all join such a holy cause! Let us recruit people using our virtue, our influence, and with all our ability and strength. Courage! I repeat, courage and perseverance. Long live our Catholic religion! Long live Our Most Holy Patron [Virgin] Mary of Guadalupe! Long live our beloved [King] Fernando VII! Long live our noble *Americana*[5] nation! Long live our homeland [*patria*], and death to vice and bad government!

APPENDIX TWO

José Álvarez de Toledo, *Jesús, María, y José*

(Philadelphia, 1811; translation)

A reproduction of the broadsheet is available on microfilm. Thomas W. Streeter, ed., *Texas as Province and Republic, 1795–1845: As Based on the Bibliography by Thomas W. Streeter* (New Haven, CT: Research Publications, 1983), reel 17, no. 1048.

† † †

JESÚS MARÍA Y JOSÉ

In the name of God, and Our Lady of Guadalupe.

MEXICANOS: come is the time appointed by Providence to shake off the barbarous and offensive yoke with which for the space of almost 300 years the most insolent despotism has ignominiously oppressed you. Now the Government at Cádiz wants to force you to continue dragging the same chains with which the Kings of Spain imprisoned you, they who did not have over you more authority than that with which you yourselves let them borrow in order to be governed: consequently, from the moment when this depository of your power disappeared, or from the moment that you—due to the lack of justice with which they ruled you with the most unprecedented tyranny—decided through mutual agreement to change the entire system and freely establish a new Government with new servants, in order to improve your unfortunate luck, you may do it without any other authority on earth being able to justly impede you.

MEXICANOS: those of you who worry whether divine rule [*autoridad Regia*] is ordained by Heaven should contemplate [*reflexionad*] the fact that man existed before Kings came into being, and they existed under a more legitimate government. Who would deny for a single moment that the Author of Nature through his infinite goodness granted each individual man and to everyone in general the necessary liberty and enough reason in order to use it? Just as in the same manner that he permitted each society to choose and form a government it thought most convenient for its interests, protection, and traditions; and deposited sovereignty in one or more people, according to its needs, in order to merely limit the authority that can never be taken [*desprenderse*] from the people [*pueblos*], and that no one may legitimately usurp. The attempt to prove that God endorsed only one form of government—to which all men are subjected, according to the superstitious, and more than anyone the tyrannical monopolists of Cádiz—is the most absurd, grandest blasphemy ever pronounced in politics; it is a ridiculously crude pretension; and he who commits it neither knows history nor how to make use of his reason. To this day, there is not one form of government that is known to have been established and approved by God: to the contrary it is clearly documented that all forms of government that have been known to the present are nothing but the product of mankind, without the Divinity of the Almighty ever having had a part in it other than to allow mankind to work freely: and from this should be inferred that all forms of government are compatible with the ends of the Author of Nature.

Regarding that so desired monarchical form of government, and which the Sultans of Cádiz so highly recommend as an admirable and precise work of art because in it is suffused the religion that we profess, we know by the books of the Sacred Scripture that the ancient Patriarchs neither had nor ever attempted to establish divine rule [*autoridad real*]: neither through law nor action [*ni de derecho, ni de hecho*]: to the contrary, moral principles and the continuation of Divine rule [*poder real*] were incompatible to the Patriarchs, and no one ignores the opposition that exists between these two legal entities [*Potestades*]. The earliest of mankind left their children in total independence amongst themselves, and with the same right to procure for themselves and their families their own subsistence, in the manner that was easiest, least dangerous, and most convenient for them to do so. It was these same men who, while enjoying of this liberty and happiness and due to their small numbers, were able to come together and unite based on common ideas and interests: but after they multiplied, they began to separate, and their passions began to get excited, so that they began to fear one another. In this state they understood the necessity to search for methods of adjudication in order to avoid the disorder that reigned over them and to prevent it from occurring in the future. They decided, then, to reunite all those families that most accorded in ideas, in order to form one single body, or a small nation, in order to establish a system that would provide them with happiness and comfort in the best manner possible, and that would simultaneously protect them from any future threats against them and their children; and one can see here the manner in which each one began to deposit the real right [*derecho real*] that they had to govern one's self; and see as well the manner in which sovereignty began to take shape, which can never reside other than in a complete and undivided sum of the particular or real right [*derecho particular; derecho real*][1] that each one has received from the Author of Nature: thus, no one may usurp this sacred right from another person—which, if they did, would incline him to go against the very ideas designed to protect him and his natural liberty—without committing a fraud, not unlike the kind committed by a man who, armed with a knife, takes another's life in order to rob him of his riches. Anything forcing mankind to work against his interests is what one calls tyranny, despotism, etc., etc., etc. This is exactly what the Kings of Spain have done with you MEXICANOS, and this is what four miserable bandits in Cádiz want to continue doing, but with even more contempt of your rights and with even more prejudice toward your interests. Yet returning to the topic at hand, I say, that the earliest of mankind who distinguished themselves according to talent, prudence, knowledge, good customs, and valor were the first to be chosen to rule, and they were also the ones who labored the most for the benefit of the entire association, of the establishment of government, public works, and reform that the experience of all time and of humanity's knowledge could offer them; in this way, they acquired all of society's esteem and love . . . [about eight illegible words] . . . to the contrary, the ones who were weak, cowards, and did not know sentiments, and the manner in which they should be treated in order to contribute to the common good, and to the most proper justice, were unanimously subjected by the entire association's will to the first.

From all this we may conclude that the first governments established by mankind were founded on the most exact and distributive justice, based on prudence and moderation; and we may see here the cause or origin from which arose the words Government, Republic, or legitimate Kingdom. The first laws established by these governments by the accord and general will of the entire association are today called constitutional Laws of the

Monarchy, of the Republic, etc. etc., etc. Under this form of government—that is, one where individuals preserve the sacred right to freely contribute to the formation of the Laws that are to govern them—is where virtue, knowledge, and love of the homeland [*patria*] have shone the brightest; because this is where the sum of particular interests allows the general interest to grow or augment in direct proportion; and, as a result, so too does the entire association's power. Those governments that are not subject to the interest or caprice of a single man are the ones that over the years have been able to preserve the precious common good and sweet peace; and are simultaneously the ones that know how to make war in defense of its rights, as Rome, Holland, Switzerland, and the United States of America have done. To the contrary, Spain's most recent governments (including the current government in Cádiz) are founded on the most execrable violence, on the most contradictory principles, and on the most perfidious injustice; they are the ones who have always had the detestable and horrifying name of tyrants. In order to support themselves, this government's Mandarins [civil servants] and Agents have been placed in the cruel position of needing to protect scoundrels, foment vice, and employ machinations against the honor and wisdom of worthy men: and, in this way, these honorable men are reduced to opprobrium, degradation, and an untold number of calamities, to which bad luck has consigned them to live under such governments. These have been and are seen with horror and contempt, by reasonable men of wisdom and, most of all, by liberal and forthright governments founded on the majestic right of equality. I believe I have sufficiently proven that GOD has not declared a preference nor excluded any form of government: as a result, men can freely choose that which most accords with their interests, security, and conservation. This supposes as well that the Author of Nature has nothing to do with what men can freely do with the right that the same Author has consigned to them: I ask you, MEXICANOS, What have you promised that Cádiz government controlled by foreigners and monopolists? *Americans:* particularly those who live on the Islands, know, that if you neglect, if you abandon your interests and security, if you do not prevent in due time the means by which you may be placed under the control of some ambitious European Power, that perhaps, and maybe with the Cádiz government covertly working to deliver you, you will surely pass to another owner's hands who will continue to enslave you with the same or even greater tyranny than that of the Sultans of Spain. This of course is also part of the natural law and not Divine as the *Báxas* of Cádiz claim. Why not use this same right to form a wise, liberal government in order to secure your destiny and that of your future generations? Does it not move you, ISLAND-

ERS and MEXICANOS, to see Venezuela, Santa Fé [de Bogotá], Buenos Aires, Chile, and Peru, and, soon as well, Lima enjoy tranquil felicity? I advise you, illustrious sons of the famous Motesuma [*sic*], to not sheathe your swords until order and liberty have been reestablished in your country. And to you, Generals, keep in mind that you will not comply with the high charge confided to you by the people [*los pueblos*] if you do not contribute via various means to the establishment of a provisional government; without which, neither your efforts nor sacrifices nor the precious American blood shed with so much heroism and abundance on the battle camp, will have the desired effect. What may thwart the establishment of such a government? I see no easier way: the Generals should immediately issue an order to all the Town Councils, Places, and Cities under their command to elect a council whose members have been shaped by the circumstances of being an enlightened *Americano,* liberal ideas, and lover of the liberty of one's Homeland [*patria*]. These representatives (this is how they should be called) should meet in the most secure place, and there, all reunited, they should resume the people's [*los pueblos*] sovereignty which they represent, during the period that these can not freely name their representatives, and establish a legitimate government. The provisional government [*El interino*] should consolidate itself with time and at the pace that the armies march forward; since other members will be added to the governing Council [*junta*], according to the number of Town Councils that come into being: this is the true path that will lead you to the temple of immortality and glory. In this way that gang of petty tyrants will disappear, and your brothers will come together through the new government, through peace, and sweet harmony that always reigns among true Republicans. In this way, I repeat my dear Compatriots, will those days of horror disappear, and the desolation with which the new Silla [?] has covered with mourning and fright the opulent kingdòm of Mexico. I await in the not too far distance that glorious day in which each of you like Cato will direct [*ordirijaís*] yourselves to the grand palace and ask, "What is the Monster's name who has sacrificed so many illustrious Republicans?" Venegas! They will respond. Although I surely hope that by then you will not have to say, "Venegas has sacrificed them?" and "does Venegas still exist?" No, he will not exist if you follow my advice. But should you choose to ignore it, should you prefer your particular happiness over that of the good and glory of your Homeland [*patria*], if such petty passions impede your ability to firmly and resolutely move forward the grand project you have set upon building, I assure you that you will be enslaved even more than you were before because you should know that the Cádiz tyrants are trying (along with their supposed allies) to pass that Capital and place you in new chains and to oppress you with even greater ignominy than their ancestors had done. *Thus: valor, union, and conviction*. This, I entrust to you, from a disgraced *Americano*, persecuted by European scoundrels; but now safe in a free country [*país*], who will not lose occasion nor whatever means, though it may require the greatest of sacrifices, in order to contribute to the fortunate regeneration of the New World. This I offer and will carry out.

José Bernardo Gutierrez [script]
Philadelphia, I⁰ of October of 1811 J.A.T.
[José Álvarez de Toledo]

APPENDIX THREE

Governing Junta of Béxar, "We the *Pueblo* of the Province of Texas"

(San Antonio, Texas, April 6, 1813; transcription and translation)

Junta de Béxar, "Nos el pueblo dela provincia de Texas [Declaration of Independence]," April 6, 1813, BANC MSS M-A1, Operaciones de Guerra, José Joaquín de Arredondo, Brigadier 1811–1821, Selected Transcriptions from the Archivo General de la Nación. Documents for the History of Mexico (ca. 1524–1855), Bancroft Library, University of California, Berkeley, vol. 4, BANC FILM 3097: reel 2: 15–21.

JURANDO AL JUEZ SUPREMO del Vniverso la rectitud de nuestras intenciones, declaramos que los vinculos que nos mantenian, baxo de la Dominacion de la España Europea están p.[a] siempre disueltos; que somos libres é Yndependientes; que tenemos el dro de establecér nuestro propio Gov.[no]; y que en adelante toda autoridad lexitima, dimanará del Pueblo a quien Solam.[te] pertenece este derecho; que desde ahora para Siempre jamas estamos absueltos de deber y obligacion á todo Poder Extrangero.

Vna Relacion delas Causas que han atraido la urgencia de esta medida es debida á nuestra Dignidad y á las opiniones del Mundo.

Vna dilatada serie de Ocurrencias, originadas de la locura, dela maldad, y dela Corrupcion delos Governantes de España ha reducido aquella Monarquia á ser el Teatro de una Guerra Sangrienta entre dos Potencias Competidoras, pareciendo que deba ser el premio del vencedor: vn Rey en el Poder, y baxo la Autoridad de una de ellas; y los debiles restos de su Govierno en pocecion dela otra: ha perdido la Substancia, y casi la forma de Soberania. Yncapas de Defenderse en la Peninsula, menos podia amparar sus remotas Colonias. Estas Colonias, Abandonadas al Dominio de unos hombres perversos, que abusando de su Autoridad, sabian que podrian eludir el Ser responsables delas resultas de su rapacidad. Desde luego el dro. natural dela Concervacion propia el mas alto priuilegio dela Creacion humana ha hecho necesario nuestro procedim.[to]

El Mundo en su cinceridad reconoce que hemos tenido suficientes motivos en las opreciones y privaciones que nos tenian Sugetos desde tanto tiempo.

Los Goviernos están instituidos p.[a] el bien, y felicidad de las Comunidades y nó para el engrandecimiento de algunos Yndividuos: quando este fin no esta pervertido y que empiesa á ser un sistema de Oprecion: El Pueblo tiene dro. de Cambearle, por otro mejor adaptado á sus necesidades. Los hombres nacieron libres y todos Salieron de un mismo principio. Estan formados á la imagen de su Criador acia quien unicamente deben humillarse ¿Quien dirá, que la Justicia de nuestras quejas no ha llegado al Colmo de la paciencia, mas que Suficiente, para Justificarnos de elegir una nueva forma de Govierno, y descoger otros Governantes en quien podamos descansár del celo de nuestra felicidad.

Fuimos regidos por Ynsolentes Yntrusos, q. se valian de sus Empleos para despojarnos; y nos era negada toda especie de participacion en los negocios nacionales y munisipales.

Sentimos con indignacion, la Tirania Exercitada, en excluirnos de toda comunicacion con otras Naciones, prohiviendo en nuestros Paises quanto pudiese Servir á nuestra ilustracion, y a descillar nuestros ojos. Nos era prohivido el uso de los libros; la libertad de ablar y aun de pensar. Nuestro Pais era nuestra pricion. En una Provincia que la naturaleza ha favorcido con tanta prodigalidad; eramos pobres, hallandonos privados de Cultivar, aquellos frutos analogos á nuestro suelo, y aun los renglones de urgente nececidad.

El Comercio de nuestro Pais estaba vendido de los favorecidos de la Corte, y los Efectos nos eran suplidos, despues de haber Sufrido, unas exacciones execcivas [sic], por los Monopolistas. Vna barbara y vergonzosa Ynospitalidad se manifestaba por nuestros Gefes, á los Extrangeros, aun á nuestros vezinos mas Sercanos, Ligados con nosotros por la Sangre y los nudos mas Sagrados, á causa de la embidia que les tenian.

Era prohivido el extraer el producto de nuestro Suelo y de nuestra industria. Todo el Trafico se reducia á un Sistema de Contrabando.

Todas las Sendas Conducentes a la fama, y del honor nos eran inaccecibles, los empleos honorificos, nos eran negados en unos Exercitos, que se mantenian del fruto de nuestros Sudores. En el seno de nuestro Paiz, no podiamos esperar de ser promovidos á las Dignidades dela Yglecia, á la qual eramos fieles y obedientes hijos.

El vestuario siempre nos ha faltado y el terreno no lo daba por no haberse estimulado el fomento dela Agricultura delas fabricas. Los Estancos de varias clases y el sistema del Papel Sellado, entran en la lista delos abusos y de las iniquidades de nuestro infame Govierno.

Por menos fundados motivos El Pueblo de los Estados unidos, sacudió el Llugo dela Tirania, y declaró su independencia. Las resultas han sido su prosperidad, y su precente explendór.

Nuestras Leyes que tomaron su Origen en un Siglo de Corrupcion y en el tiempo del mallór despotismo del Ymperio Romano, estaban puestas en vigór por unos Tribunales Corruptos.

La Justicia abiertamente se vendía Vn Pleito criminal ocupaba la mitad del Espacio natural dela vida humana. Yndibiduos, con frequencia se arrestaban por las mas frivolas demandas, ó denuncias, o las mas lebes Sospechas; y su muerte era el olvido en las Tinieblas del Calaboso.

Vn Sueño Letargico y el Estado de Insencibilidad, que sucede á los largos Sufrimientos, nos Entorpecian, y Seguiamos humildes y rendidos á un Govierno, demaciadamente inhumano por pensar en mejorár nuestra suerte.

En este Estado de Cozas se trastornó [la] Monarquia Española. Vimos lo q.se llamaba la Me Patria, Asaltada p.[r] un Poderoso Monarca; inducida por otro apesar de su devilidad, á una defenza destructora; Olvidamos desde luego los Sufrimientos pasados; los innimerables [sic] agravios; los Vejamenes injustos é iniquos: Todos nuestros Seres fueron absorbados en Simpatia; volamos, á la ass.[a] dela Metropoli, como fieles y Submisos Vasallos.

En pago de nuestros leales servicios, Vn Tirano Sediento de Sangre humana, y que jamas se habia distinguido por ninguna accion virtuosa en su propia Patria, fué mandado entre nosotros: Desplegó en su administracion solo hechos de Crueldad con una insaciable Abaricia. Aumentó nuestro Estado de Oprecion; y tal era su Astucia que nos mantubo por largo tiempo indecisos, asegurandonos que las Cortes Tomarian en Consideracion nuestros derechos y Agravios y con estas expeciosas promesas nos induxo a que embiasemos nuestra Deputacion. La experiencia nos ha hecho ver claram.[te] que todo esto era ilusorio, pues su voto se hallaba ahogado por la Ynfluencia Europea.

Algunos miserables usurpadores del Setro dela Monarquia Española nos vendieron á una Potencia Extrangera, engañandonos en el momento delas mallores desgracias, para mejor someternos á su voluntad y Caprichos: Les fueron abiertos nuestros Tesoros y les entregamos el Provecho de un numero de años de Yndustria. El pago de esta conducta generosa en lo extremo; ha sido Oprecion, crueldad, y la mas vergonsosa esclavitud.

Las Colonias Españolas dela America del Sur primero que nosotros, abrieron los Ojos, y ellas se han declarado Yndependientes, y nos hallamos entre los ultimos, que adoptan esta importante medida.

Nos hallamos, pues, obligados tanto para nosotros como para el bien de nuestra posteridad, de aprovechar la ocacion oportuna que se nos brinda de Trabajar á la regeneracion del Pueblo Mexicano, separandonos del peso de toda dominacion Extrangera; tomando en nuestras propias manos las riendas de nuestro Govierno; formando Leyes Justas, Estudiadas del dro. natural; Erigiendo Tribunales, administrados por hombres honestos, y puros. Estos medios son los de asegurár la prosperidad de nuestra Patria, y una Estacion honrrada entre las de mas Naciones del Mundo.

Para prover, pues, el bien gral, y asegurar la Tranquilidad Domestica, dando dignidad y executando estas medidas, declaramos que p.[a] evitar la Confucion y demora, de tomar la vos de cada un individuo del Pueblo, damos amplios Poderes en Señal de nuestra gratitud á nuestro Ylustre libertador el Señor D. Bernardo Gutierres, General en Gefe del Exercito Mexicano Republicano del Norte, para que nombre, y elija, incontinentemente, un Precidente, seis vocales, y un Secretario para componer, y constituir una Junta, investida de plenos poderes por nosotros, y para en nuestro nombre formár la reprecentacion Nacional: Establecer un Govierno para este estado; Corresponder con las Naciones Extrangeras; Mantener la Corecion y Armonia con los Estados Colindantes, y de lo de mas de lo Ynterior dela republica Mexicana; alimentár un Exercito, y alludar con perseberancia, y Vigor la Causa dela Santa Religion, y de la Justicia, de la razon, y de los dros. Sagrados del hombre.

Sera de la Obligacion delos expresados siete Miembros de la Junta, nombrar a pluralidad de votos, un Governador, con el Titulo de precidente; Amparador del Govierno Provisional del Estado de Texas, y la Constitucion le prescrivirá la extencion de sus facultades.

Será igualmente dela Junta el encargo de franquear el Comercio, arreglar la Policia de lo interior imponer derechos; armar y dár vestuario, a los Exercitos del Estado de Texas, para lo cual podrá empeñar la fe y credito Publico.

Finalmente exercerá en Publico las funciones de tono lexitimo, hasta que en Congreso gral dela Republica Mexicana, se tomen otras dispociciones juzgadas por combenientes.

Para dar mas pezo a esta declaracion, y que inspire una justa confianza, tanto en nuestro Pais, como fuera de el, Juremos Solamen.[te] Sobre el Santo Evangelio todos en general, y cada uno de por si, á nuestros hermanos, de toda la extencion de esta Republica; y ala faz del Vniverso que defenderemos, y mantendremos, con nuestros haberes, y nuestras vidas hasta la ultima extremidad, nuestros principios y nuestra Patria.

San Antonio de Bexar, 6 de Abril de 1813. y 3.º dela Yndependencia Mexicana.

Por mandado del Sor. General en Gefe=Luis Masicote=Secretario

Es Copia conforme á los originales firmados, de todo el vezindario y Tropa.

Ciudad de S. Fern.[do] á 4 de Mayo de 1813. 3.[o]
de Nuestra Yndependencia.[1]

José M.[a] Guadiana (Rúbrica)	José Manuel Prieto (Rúbrica)
Sarg[to] Mayor	Ayud[te] May.[r] de Plasa
José Ygnacio de Abal (Rúbrica)	Jose Nicolas Benites (Rúbrica)
	Luis Cantu (Rúbrica)
Juan Melendez (Rúbrica)	
	Mig.[l] Cortinas (Rúbrica)
Rafael Alvarado (Rúbrica)	Juan José Tixerina (Rúbrica)
Tomas Oquillas (Rúbrica)	José Ant[o] Guerra (Rúbrica)
Crecencio Vargas (Rúbrica)	Bernardino Benavides (Rúbrica)
Jose Felis Peres (Rúbrica)	
	Pedro Arispe (Rúbrica)
Josef M.[a] Muñoz (Rúbrica)	
	Lucas Cantu (Rúbrica)

Swearing before the supreme judge of the Universe the rectitude of our intentions, we declare that the bonds that kept us under the Domination of European Spain are forever dissolved; that we are free and Independent; that we have the right to establish our own Government and that henceforth all legitimate authority arises from the *Pueblo* in whom this right Only belongs; that from now on and forever we are absolved from all duty and obligations to all Foreign Powers.

An Account of the Causes that have led to the urgency of this measure should be provided, in respect to our Dignity and opinions of the World.

A wide-ranging series of Events that originated from madness, evil, and Corrupt Spanish Governors has reduced the Spanish Monarchy to nothing more than the Theatre of a Bloody War between two Competitive Powers where it appears that the monarchy shall belong to the victor: either to a King [Fernando VII] in Power yet under the Authority of another [Napoleon Bonaparte], or to the weak remains of his Government [the Cortes of Cádiz] who declare to possess his authority. But the Cortes has lost the Substance and almost the form of Sovereignty. Incapable of Defending itself on the Peninsula, it could much less protect its remote [American] Colonies. These Colonies, Abandoned to the Dominion of some perverse men that, abusing their Authority, knew they could avoid being held responsible for all the fruits of their corruption. Certainly, the natural law of self-Preservation, that highest form of human Creativity, has made necessary our actions.

The World, in its sincerity, recognizes that we have had sufficient motives in the oppression and depravation that we have been subjected to for a long time.

Governments are created for the well-being and happiness of Communities, and not for the aggrandizement of some Individuals. When this goal is not met, it becomes perverted and becomes a system of Oppression. The *Pueblo* has the right to Change it for one better adapted to their needs. Men were all Born free and all have one common origin. They are shaped in the image of their Creator, the only one they should humble down to. Who will say that the Justice of our complaints has not reached the height of patience? It is more than Enough to justify the need of selecting a new form of Government, and to choose other Rulers who ensure the zeal of our happiness.

We were ruled by Insolent Intruders, who took advantage of their Positions in order to dispossess us, and we were denied any and all type of participation in national and municipal affairs.

We felt with great indignation the Tyranny, as Practiced, in excluding us from all communication with other Nations, prohibiting in our Countries anything that could serve toward our enlightenment and to opening our eyes. We were prohibited the use of books; the freedom to speak and even to think. Our Country was our prison. In a Province that nature has favored with so much abundance, we were poor, finding ourselves unable to and prevented from cultivating those fruits native to our land, and even those of urgent necessity.

Our Country's Commerce was controlled by those favored by the Court, and still the needed Commodities were not provided for, after we had suffered excessive levies by the Monopolists. Our Rulers manifested a barbarous and shameful lack of hospitality to Foreigners, even to our Closest neighbors [Louisiana and St. Louis], tied to us by Blood and the most Holy knots, due to the envy they had.

It was prohibited to extract the product of our Soil and our industry. All Commerce was reduced to a System of Contraband.

All the Paths that Lead to fame and honor were inaccessible. The honorific professions in some Armies, which were sustained by our sweat, were denied to us. In the heart of our Country, we could not expect to be promoted to the Dignities of the Church, to which we were loyal and obedient followers.

We have always been in need of proper clothing, and the land could not give it because of the lack of stimulation and development of Agriculture and factories. The various types of Monopolies and the system of Sealed

Paper [by which authority was wielded tightly by *letrados*] are under the list of abuses and iniquities of our infamous Government.

Under less established motives, the *Pueblo* of the United States freed itself from the yoke of Tyranny and declared its independence. The results have been its prosperity and current splendor.

Our Laws, which Originated in a Century of Corruption comparable to that of the greatest despotism of the Roman Empire, were put to work by Corrupt Tribunals.

Justice was openly sold. A criminal trial spanned half a lifetime. Individuals, frequently, were arrested for the most frivolous charges, reports, or the slightest Suspicions; and their death was secured in the abyss of the Darkness of the Dungeon.

A Lethargic Dream and the State of Insensitivity that are characteristic of the lengthiest Sufferings hindered us, and we Followed humbly and surrendered to a Government too inhumane to think about improving our fortune.

Under these conditions the Spanish Monarchy was then disrupted. We saw what was called the *Madre Patria* [Spain] assaulted by a Powerful Monarch [Bonaparte], induced, not withstanding [Bonaparte's] weakness, to a destructive defensive posture. Certainly we forgot the past Sufferings, the innumerable grievances, the unjust and wicked insults. All our Beings were absorbed in Sympathy. We flew to the assistance of the Metropolis, like loyal and Submissive servants.

A Tyrant Thirsty for human Blood [the viceroy of New Spain Francisco Javier Venegas] who had never been distinguished for a single virtuous act in his own *Patria,* was sent to us in return for our loyal services.[2] He Deployed in his administration only acts of Cruelty with insatiable Avarice. He increased our State of Oppression, and such was his Cunning that he kept us indecisive for a long time, assuring us that the Cortes [of Cádiz] would Take into Consideration our rights and Grievances. With these marvelous promises, he induced us to send our Deputation. The experience has made us see clearly that all this was illusory, because European Influence drowned our vote.

We were sold by some miserable usurpers of the Scepter of the Spanish Monarchy to a Foreign Power[3] who fooled us at the time of our greatest misfortunes, in order for us to better submit to their will and Caprice. Our Treasures were opened to them and we gave them the Advantage of a number of years of work. The result of this extremely generous conduct has been Oppression, cruelty, and the most shameful slavery.

The Spanish Colonies of South America were the first to open their Eyes, and they did so before we did. They have declared themselves Independent, and we find ourselves among the last that adopt this important measure.[4]

We find ourselves, then, obligated as much for ourselves as for the well-being of our posterity, to take advantage of the opportune occasion that presents itself of Working for the regeneration of the Mexican *Pueblo,* separating ourselves from the weight of all Foreign domination; taking the reins of our Government with our own hands; forming Just Laws, Studied from the natural right; Erecting Tribunals, administrated by pure and honest men. These means are to secure the prosperity of our *Patria,* and an honorable Status among the other Nations of the World.

To provide, then, the general well-being and to secure Domestic Tranquility, giving dignity and executing these measures, we declare that in order to avoid Confusion and delay by tallying the voice of each individual in the Community [*pueblo*], we give ample Powers as a token of our gratitude to our Illustrious liberator Don Bernardo Gutierres, General in Chief of the Mexican Republican Army of the North, so that he may name and choose, without constraints, a President, six members, and a Secretary to compose and create a Governing Board, invested by us with full power; and so that in our name they may create a National form of representation: to Establish a Government for this state; Correspond with the Foreign Nations; Keep in Communication and Harmony with the Adjoining States, and of the other affairs from the Interior of the Mexican Republic; to feed an Army, and to assist with perseverance and Vigor the cause of Holy religion, and that of Justice, of reason, and of the Sacred rights of man.

It will be the Obligation of the mentioned seven members of the board to name by a majority of votes a Governor, with the title of President; Assistant to the Provisional Government of the State of Texas, and the Constitution will prescribe the extension of their power.

It will also be the Board's responsibility to promote Commerce, fix the Policy of the interior, impose laws, and arm and clothe the Armies of the State of Texas, in order to cultivate faith and Public confidence.

Finally, it will execute in Public the legitimate functions of government, until the Congress of the Mexican Republic takes other dispositions judged most convenient.

To give more weight to this declaration, and for it to inspire a just confidence, as much in our Country as outside of it, We all, together and individually, Solemnly Swear on the Holy Gospel to our brothers, throughout the full extension of this Republic; and to the Universe that we will defend and protect, with our assets and our lives until the last extremity, our principles and our *Patria*.

San Antonio of Bexar, April 6, 1813, and 3rd of Mexican Independence.
By mandate of General in Chief=Luis Masicote=Secretary
This is a Copy according to the originals signed by the entire community and Troops.

City of San Fernando on May 4, 1813, 3rd of Our Independence.

José Maria Guadiana (Rubric)	Jose Manuel Prieto (Rubric)
Sergeant Major	Assistant Major of Plasa
José Ygnacio de Abal (Rubric)	Jose Nicolas Benites (Rubric)
	Luis Cantu (Rubric)
Juan Melendez (Rubric)	
	Miguel Cortinas (Rubric)
Rafael Alvarado (Rubric)	Juan José Tixerina (Rubric)
Tomas Oquillas (Rubric)	José Antonio Guerra (Rubric)
Crecencio Vargas (Rubric)	Bernardino Benavides (Rubric)
Jose Felis Peres (Rubric)	
	Pedro Arispe (Rubric)
Josef Maria Muñoz (Rubric)	
	Lucas Cantu (Rubric)

APPENDIX FOUR

Anonymous, "Remembrance of the Things That Took Place in Béxar in 1813 under the Tyrant Arredondo"

(transcription and translation)

Anonymous, "Memoria de las cosas más notables que acaecieron en Bexar el año de 13 mandando el Tirano Arredondo, 1813," MSS P-O 811, Herbert Bolton Papers (No. 711), Bancroft Library, University of California, Berkeley.

Note: The following account appears to have been narrated if not written by the female survivors of the short-lived republican revolution in Texas. The republicans had declared independence under José Bernardo Gutiérrez de Lara on April 1, 1813, only to be disastrously defeated by Spanish Royal forces months later. The narrative begins by recounting the revolutionaries' loss at the famed Battle of Medina that took place on August 18, 1813, in a sandy oak forest known as the *encinal de Medina* some twenty miles south of San Antonio. Under command of José Álvarez de Toledo (who had recently deposed Gutiérrez de Lara), the 1,400 revolutionary forces lost disastrously to Spanish Commandant General of the Eastern Interior Provinces Joaquín de Arredondo's forces of 1,830. Less than 100 republicans escaped with their lives. Upon their loss and hoping to escape Arredondo's wrath, the families of San Antonio (about 300 individuals) abandoned their town and made their way to Louisiana along the old Camino Real. While Arredondo secured San Antonio, he sent his commander, Ignacio Elizondo, and Second Lieutenant Fernando Rodríguez in pursuit of the families. They were captured some 215 miles away at the Trinity River, just before arriving at the town of Trinidad, which had already gone to the revolutionaries. See Figures 5 and 7 and Chapter 6 for details. All underlining and strike-throughs are in the original. In order to retain the feel and cadence of the original, as much of the original punctuation and syntax has been retained, except where doing so would have impeded comprehension. Quotation marks, for example, are rarely utilized. The authors rely instead on colons to mark off the beginning of dialogue.

HABIENDO AVANZADO las tropas del Rey hasta el Encinal con el fin de destruir las armas americanas, é independientes que guarnecían esta Capital al mando del Gral [General] Toledo; contra las militares disposiciones de este Exs [Excelentísimo] é entusiasmadas las tropas Independientes abrazadas del amor Patrio, y confiando en su gran valor, se determinaron á ir á encontrar a sus enemigos, y batirlos sobre la marcha; mas por desgracia de ellos, y de este Pueblo, precipitados por una llamada falsa que les dio Elizondo, penetraron el espeso monte del Encinal, atascándose los caballos hasta las rodillas en el arenal que cubre mas de quince leguas y se encontraron á la mitad del con el Exso [Excelentísimo] enemigo que los esperaba de pie firme con la batería de cañones á la vanguardia descansado, bien ordenado y con una posición ventajosa; cuando los soldados llegaron con su caballería tan fatigada que apenas podían maniobrar; y á pesar de hayarse en tan miserable estado, acometieron con denodado valor, y con tal bizarría que llegaron al punto de equilibrar la acción, y aun declararse por suya, habiendo desmayado la tropa enemiga, cuando de nuevo la refrescó el tirano astuto General mandando en medio de la confusión tocar una solemne alegre Diana en señal de que ya la Victoria era suya, cuyo ardido le dio el triunfo, pues con ella infundio animo, y valor a los suyos, y los liberales se acobardaron temieron y afloraron, por haber herido de muerte al valentísimo é intrepido Coronel Miguel Menchaca, con lo que quedó por los realistas el campo cubierto de cadáveres, siendo muy pocos los que escaparon, y se pusieron en salvo de la crueldad é inaudita Tiranía de los defensores de un Monarca absoluto, en cuyas manos quedó indefenso este Pueblo Patriota.

Lo que este Pueblo padecio tolero, y sufrió, no es facil sujetarlo á la pluma, ni menos narrarlo con exactitud y certeza, por haber muerto muchos de los que pudieran dar una noticia verás, por que otros que pudieran hacerlo por hallarse vivos, no presenciaron el echo; y [los] que lo vieron, tomaron parte en la opreción, y tiranía de su Patria en terminos de no poder declarar la verdad; y antes han tomado empeño en desfigurarlas por la parte que les toca. Este es á la verdad el motivo por que hasta el día ignora el Público la parte que el Departamento de Texas tomó, y tuvo en la libertad de la Patria, y gloriosa Independencia, y menos aparezcan algunos memorables hechos que dan gloria á sus Pueblos, como á Guadalajara, Valladolid, Zacatecas, Oaxaca, Puebla, Veracruz, y otros. Mas sin embargo, aun se pueden recoger algunos, que aun que pocos, se pondrán sin aliño ni elocuencia; pero si marcados con el Sello de la verdad, y sin exageración, hipérbole, ni triunfo. Vamos á la obra, y salga lo que saliere; con tal que el publico los cepa, y en premio de nuestro trabajo nos disimules los defectos.

De resultar de la derrota del Encinal de Medina se fugaron muchas familias enteras, con el fin de escapar la vida, tomando la dirección á los Estados Unidos del Norte, unos a pie y otros a caballo, pasando innumerables trabajos, congojas y penas, después de haber abandonado cuanto tenían, como casas, sembrados, ganado mayor menor, y otros bienes que gozaban en propiedad, entre las que se numera la familia del decidido Patriota Joaquín Leal, natural de esta Capital, con su Esposa Doña Ana María Arocha cuatro hijos varones, y tres mujeres que abandonaron su Patria natal el día 18 de Agosto á las cuatro de la tarde, sin mas prevención que un saco de maíz que levantaron de su misma milpa, caminaron doce días por los desiertos campos y malezas, llenos de temor espanto, y sobre salto con el Jesús en los labios, sin que los enemigos les diecen alcance, hasta que el día 30 del mismo dando vista á la Loma del Toro distante del río de la Trinidad como un tiro difícil yendo ya incorporados el ciudadano Miguel de Arocha, y la ciudadana Ángela Arocha saliendo al llano como a la una de la tarde oyeron el tremendo grito de las tropas del Rey que les dieron alcance diciendo el Alferer Fernando Rodríguez: "*párense Insurgentes, por que sino los mato traidores al Rey*," y apenas lo acabaron de decir cuando se vieron rodeados de catorce soldados, que como lobos carniceros con sola la vista querían devorarlos y al momento mataron de un balazo á Antonio Delgado y caído delante de la madre lo comenzaron á lancear, se tiró la madre al suelo, y le rogó al desapiadado Fernando no lo matara, pidiéndole por toda la corte celestial lo dejara confesar; y con indignación le respondió: "*que se confesara con los Diablos, que estaba condenado el y cuantos allí estaban*," y enfurecido con las cristianas piadosas suplicas de la madre, volteo la lanza por el cabo y le dio de palos hasta apartarla de su hijo ya muerto, al que dio orden lo desnudaran y dejaran para pasto de los fieras, como así se verificó.

Al momento mandó armar a los hombres y marcho en busca de Elizondo para presentarle la presa que había echo de hombres, y mujeres, quien luego que lo vio le dijo: que familias son estas, y Rodríguez le dijo: Los Leales, Arochas, y Delgados. *Pues todos deben morir que se dispongan.* Y al instante se puso el Padre Camacho á confesarlos. Las ciudadanas madres Ángela Delgado y Ana María Arocha intercedieron con Elizondo para que se les perdonara la vida, y las despidió con indignación diciéndoles: quítenseme de delante las insurgentas antes que las mande matar, buen ejemplo les ha dado á sus hijos, acá cuatro soldados con sus armas lleven estas mujeres y asegúrenlas.

Para las cuatro de la tarde del mismo día, ya estaban confesados los que habían de pasarse por las armas, como sucedió, en la misma hora, y al pasar á estos mártires de la Patria, por donde su madre, y hermanas estaban alzaron las cabezas y dijeron con valor y enteresa: *Adiós Madre adiós hermanas hasta el Valle de Josafad.* Apenas oyó la Madre el ultimo vale de sus hijos que morían por la Patria, cuando cayó de espaldas desmayada y una hija suya llamada María de la consolación Doncella le echó un brazo, y con el otro tomo una imagen del Señor de Esquipulas, pidiéndole desecha en lagrimas diese consuelo, y fortaleza á su angustiada madre.

Ya muertos los hombres pasaron aquella tristísima noche las mujeres con la amargura y aflicción que se deja entender solas desamparadas, con los verdugos de los liberales á la vista, y sin mas abrigo que el túnico y camisa, con que andaban, y apenas rayó la aurora el siguiente día, cuando entre ellas acordaron ir á buscar los cuerpos de sus hermanos muertos, y los hallaron tirados en el campo y comidos de los animales, y viendo tal inhumanidad se determinaron á pedirle al cruel Comandante Elizondo les permitiera sepultarlos ellas mismas, mas no lo consiguieron diciéndoles dicho Jefe: que estaban condenados por traidores al Rey, y a la Patria, cuando por esta derramaban su sangre en el campo de la gloria.

Algunos días pasaron estas infelices patriotas en tan infernal sitio con el alma atravesada; y sufriendo cuantos males podían esperarse de los encarnizados defensores de un Rey absoluto Déspota, y tirano, hasta que por haberse corrompido la agua con los muertos que pasaron de ciento determino el Jefe de la triunfante División dar la buelta á la Capital para dar cuenta al Tirano General Arredondo de la gran presa, que había hecho, y hombres que había muerto, con engaño é indefensos; mas apoco de andar fue herido de muerte con su hermano político Don Isidro, por mano de un Europeo Capitán que perdió el juicio al ver tan inhumana como cruel carnicería y en el río de Guadalupe tomo el mando el Coronel Quintero, quien por principio de su general tubo á las miserables mujeres de plantón al resistidero del Sol desde las 5 de la mañana hasta la una de la tarde; el numero de mujeres casadas Viudas, Solteras, y Doncellas llegaba á 114, muchas con sus hijitos que aun tomaban el pecho.

Pasado este tormento, como por vía de precaución y seguridad, el nuevo vecino mando hacer un registro general á hombres, y mujeres con el fin de recoger los papeles, y monedas; siendo comisionados para esta honrosa facción los oficiales que merecían su confianza, y aprecio, por su conocida adición al partido de los monarcas, y mas declarados enemigos de la Patria. Comenzaron al momento esta humillante y vergonzosa operación los tenientes José María Jiménez, y Tomás Saucedo, y los Alferraces Fernando Rodríguez y ____ Chapa, Diego Jiménez Leandro S. Miguel Cavazos, y otros, dando principio con los hombres con tanto vigor y escrupulosidad, que ni aun los zapatos escaparon; hicieron á las mujeres que se apearan del caballo, para hacer con ellas la misma operación, por ser también comprendidas en la orden del citado vecino Quintero; y lo desempeñaron tan bien y tan cumplidamente que hasta los senos los registraron sin que el pudor, y la honestidad de las Doncellas, escapase de tan obscena inspección; y desoluto manoces.

Al siguiente día para poder seguir la marcha a la capital con mas seguridad del Jefe, y mas martirizan á los verdaderos amantes de la Patria se dio la orden: que todos los prisioneros marchasen bien amarrados, y á pie, como se ejecutó al pie de la letra, caminando los mas de ellos descalzos, como los honrados Patriotas: Tomás Arocha, Fernando Veramendi y Clemente Delgado, todos muertos de sed hambre y cansancio llegaron como á las 3 de la tarde al Arroyo del Zirolo en donde apagaron nuestros hermanos la sed, echándolos los enemigos al agua todos de montón á palos y empujones, como tal vez no se hubiera hecho con un ato de cabras y manada de cerdos.

Al otro día, con las mismas precauciones y tormentos hicieron su jornada los patriotas, y llegaron al Zalado, mal comidos, peor bebidos y maltratados. En este punto, como que ya solo faltaba una jornada para llegar á la Capital determinó el *Dux* Quintero dar parte al General de su llegada, mas á poca distancia de Bexar, para hacer mas visible su triunfo, y mas atormentar difamar y avergonzar á los Independientes, ordenó separar á las mujeres de los hombres, y las hizo caminar por delante a pie y en cuerda, y fueron entregadas á la tropa del fiero, que las había salido á encontrar la que llegó con esta cuerda al Alamo, que se haya á los suburbios de esta ciudad del otro lado del Río al Oriente, como á las oraciones de la noche; mas para que la noche, no los privase del lucimiento de una brillante entrada para los tiranos, y cruel vergonsosima y amarga, para los mártires Patriotas, se mando, que hasta el siguiente día, no se hice como se efectúo al son de las cajas, pitos y tambores, á las diez del día habiéndose ya incorporado todos los prisioneros hombres, y mujeres y al pasar el río a pie y vestidos el Alferer Fernando Rodríguez á palos con la lanza hacía andar a las miserables mujeres que lo pasaron cayendo y levantando, dándoles el agua á la cintura.

Habiendo tomado la calle que desde el río guía ala plaza, se formó toda la tropa armada, y tomaron en medio á los prisioneros denostándolos, y cargándolos de injurias entre las cuales decían con ganga á las mujeres: "tan tapaditas que van, que parece que tienen tanta vergüenza, ¿como no la tenían para andar con las pistolas matando gente." Y las afligidas no hacían mas que sufrir, con los ojos puestos en el suelo, y llorar mudamente conteniendo sus lágrimas, y dejándolas caer al corazón, para que los tiranos no las vieran; y con esta aflicción, cangoja y pena que varonilmente ocultaban, llegaron á la Plaza en donde las esperaba el tirano Arredondo, acompañado de todos sus satélites y sátrapas, como Domínguez y demás oficialidad, y una concurrencia como de mil almas de espectadores, á quienes conducía la curiosidad; y luego que ya se hallaron en su presencia todos los presos, comenzó á burlarse de las afligidas mujeres diciéndoles con una vista gitana: "con que ustedes decían: hay viene el tuerto Arredondo / á pelear con los de Texas. / Pensará que son ovejas, / de las que trajo Elizondo—Para decir. Que se han buelto las ovejas Leones. Mírenme bien haber si soy tuerto, en donde está por aquí la que decía: que se había de comer mis huevos asados; crudos le harán mas provecho. Y la otra llamada Josefa Arocha, que prometía quinientos pesos por la cabeza de su marido, (Pedro Treviño que se hallaba entre las tropas del Rey) quiso responder la señora y no se lo permitió el, tirano, encendido en cólera, y tomando la palabra su segundo, esto es Domínguez dijo: ¿Dónde esta por aquí la que se le apareció San Francisco de Paula con unos pantalones de un americano en la mano? y todavía después dice la tal picarona: vengan acá señores, y verán el milagro, que ha hecho San Francisco que dice: que nosotros ganamos; y no los Gachupines.

Estando en esto una niña como de ____ años, viendo entre aquella comitiva de tiranos al Europeo Rosi, a quien de antemano conocía le dijo: Señor y yo me voy con usted? (pobre inocente á buen santo se encomendaba) muy pronto hayo su desengaño, pues con enfado le respondió: no por un punto pues hace tres años que por ustedes padesco. Esto lo hacia por agradar al tirano, y como por congraciarse con los espectadores. Y habiendo pasado el impío general revista á los hombres maltratando a las mujeres de mil modos se volvió y dijo á sus sátrapas: que será bueno hacer con estas? y sin esperar respuesta dio la cruel sentencia contra las desgraciadas decían en alta voz: *A la Quinta; á la Quinta; á moler maíz caliente para las tropas del Rey.*

Al momento los sanguinarios soldados las condujeron al paraje destinado, en donde ya las esperaba un feróz verdugo con la mayor ansia, para cebar en el su rabia, el que se nombraba, el Sargento Caballero Acosta quien una por una las fue reconociendo, con palabras obscenas é insultantes, y alzando la voz les dijo en tono magistral y campanudo: que pensaban putas, insurgentes como las traen, presentadas á cabeza de silla, siendo este trato el mas humano, y decente que uso con ellas. Al momento les puso una guardia de 8 hombres, y un cabo les aprontó veinte metates, y cuatro fanegas de maíz para que molieran siendo lo mas notable, que el maíz lo acarreaban de sus mismas milpas.

Tuvieron estas verdaderas hijas del Anahuac este martirio—días sin faltar uno comando desde las dos de la mañana hasta las diez de la noche destinando á unas á cocer el maíz dicho hasta hacerlo nistamal, otras á pisarlo ó refregarlo con los pies estando de aun caliente de suerte que muchas se pelaron los pies, y piernas perdiendo las uñas de los pies y corriendo la viva sangre que se mesclaba con el maiz que refregaban. hasta haber perdido la vida una mujer llamada Cribanta quien después de habercele caído las palmas y uñas de las manos con solo este inhumano ejercicio, y otras destinadas a moler, habiendo muchas que jamás lo habían hecho, y tenían muy delicado el cutis de las manos, y en cinta, como las benemeritas Ciudadanas que en esta Capital habían hecho el papel de Damas Principales, F. F. F. F. F.

Durante el día, y mientras nuestras mexicanas desempeñaban tan penosa fatiga el guardián Acosta no cesaba de imbentar medios para castigarlas, mortificarlas, é infamarlas, diciéndoles las mas descaradas desvergüenzas, dándoles asotes á su antojo, y no dejando á las que se hallaban criando dar el pecho á sus niños; que lloraban de hambre, y aun uno de ellos murió á la vista; de este inhumano Nerón; que se complacía, en avergonzarlas, afligirlas, y mortificarlas, de mil modos, y con las palabras mas groseras, y acciones las impuras, indecentes y feas, que causa rubor decirlas, escribirlas, y ni aun el papel no las conciente; sufriendo nuestras eroinas con firmeza y constancia, sin dar á torcer su brazo por solo el amor de su Patria cuantas tiranías y crueldades inventó el detestable Acosta, recogiéndose muy serenas á descansar á las diez de la noche, en su cama que era el vivo suelo.

Vamos ahora á examinar los alimentos que se daban á estas sirvientas, que daban que comer á tantos ambrientos, como era todo el Batallón del Fijo de Veracruz, y caballería de las Provincias. Cualquiera juzgará que seria fuerte y abundante para que se mantuviesen sanas y robustas, y no faltasen al interesante trabajo. En efecto se les daba su ración completa por la mañana; y en la noche sin falta, siendo la de por la mañana nada; al medio día dos tortillas, y una libra de carne cruda sin sal y de la que traían de su ganado, y en la noche dos solas tortillas, sin pasarse ni un solo día que se les pasara lista por mañana y noche en medio de dos filas de soldados armados, llamándolas por sus nombres y apellidos, del mismo modo, y en la misma forma que se pasa á los soldados.

Para que aquellos tiranos destituidos enteramente de todo sentimiento de humanidad ni una sola hora de descanso, ó desaogo permitieron á estas desgraciadas ni aun, dar el pecho á sus chiquillos; y cuando una sola vez se hallaron sin su vigilante Guardián, apuraron su tarea para tener juntas un momento de desahogo, como fue, pasando poco más de una hora en llorar su miserable suerte, y otro rato en reírse; pues ni uno ni otra les permitía el cruel Zelador, siendo para estas patriotas el mayor delito, el llorar ó reírse; mas ó "cuan caro les costó aquel rato de mutua consolación." Se dio parte al mayor D. Antonio Elozúa, quien para que no estuvieran ociosas; pues el tiempo perdido los santos lo lloran, para librarse de un escrúpulo tan fuerte, les mando sesenta camisas de soldados, para que las hicieran en los ratos que no molían; viendo lo muy gracioso, que hallándose sin los necesarios de costura, le pidieron á Acosta agujas para cocer, y su respuesta fue tumbarse los pantalones y decirles, que de allí tomasen. Este impuro y deshonesto hecho afligió hasta el extremo a nuestras hermanas, quienes ocurrieron al mudo llanto siendo tan bárbaro cruel é inhumano este caribe que a todas las azotaba cada, y cuando quería, sin mas causa ni motivo, que darle gana de hacerlo.

No encontrando este ministro infernal mandamientos con que martirizar á las patriotas le ocurrió el mas bárbaro que podía haber imaginado para consumar las penas, y fue: el de decir a las madres: que corrieran á sus hijos y no los tuvieran en su compañía; y que si así no lo hacían, los mandaría amarrar, y se los presentaría á Arredondo para que los castigara. Este espantoso golpe aniquiló á las mártires, les rompió las telas del corazón, y aun casi les boleo el juicio, y por tal de que sus inocentes tiernos hijos no sufriesen el castigo de los tiranos sin mas causa que ser ellas sus madres, con todo, y dolor los despidieron desechas en lagrimas diciéndoles estas memorables palabras "váyanse de aquí para donde los mandan, á las calles, pues así nos ha tocado la suerte." ¿"Y quien nos da que comer?" "Pidan limosna por hay en las casas." Con tan tierna dulce y amorosa despedida se separaron las madres de sus hijos, y estos de sus madres, hechos todos un mar de lagrimas, menos el tirano, que se complacía con tan hermoso cuadro, y con rabia las volvio á los metates diciéndoles con una furia infernal "*cárguense putas que aquí esta su Dios, yo soy el Dios de las putas*." Y corría de punta á punta de los metates azotándolas á todas, callando estas, sufriendo, y moliendo. Vengan mexicanas amantes de su Patria á aprehender a padecer por la libertad é Independencia.

Veinte días completos sufrieron tan penosa vida las que volvieron desde [el río de] la Trinidad, y las que no pudieron fugarse, padecieron cincuenta y cuatro días, en la nombrada Quinta, mas cuando les dieron la libertad, no encontraron, quien las reconociese en el ceno mismo de su Patria, ni un chamacuero en donde recogerse, ni quien un bocado les diese, ni donde tomarlo, pues ya les habían quitado sus casas sembrados, ganados, y cuantos bienes tenían, por el supuesto crimen de Independencia; y lo mas gracioso es que hasta el día carecen de sus propiedades, y las bien gozan á los que, ni padecieron, ni defendieron la justa causa y antes algunos de ellos cooperaron á su martirio.

En el alcance tuvieron la dicha de librarse las dos hijas del Patriota Manuel Delgado y Ángela Arocha, llamadas la una Cándida y la otra María Josefa, la primera de 20 años y la segunda de menos edad (15) y otra mujer hermana política de estas llamada Antonia Rodríguez quienes quisieron mas bien aventurar la vida echándose a nado en un caudaloso Río como es el de la Trinidad, que caer en manos de tan crueles enemigos y consiguieron en efecto salvarse á nado con la particularidad de haber salvado Cándida una sobrinita suya de pecho que aseguró con un brazo, quedándose la madre en poder del tirano Fernando, quien condujo en compañía de las demás hasta la Quinta.

The [spanish] king's troops advanced up to the sandy oak forest [near the Medina river] with the purpose of destroying the independent *Americano* armies under the command of General [José Álvarez de Toledo]. Confident, armed with great courage, and animated by their Patriotic love, the most excellent and enthusiastic independent troops advanced, determined to find their enemies and confront them during their march. But to their great misfortune, and to this town's as well, they were misled by a false call to arms given by [Spanish commander Ignacio] Elizondo.[1] They had penetrated the dense brush of the sandy oak forest where their horses became stuck up to their knees in the sandy deposit that covers more than fifteen leagues. There, they found themselves facing the most Excellent enemy halfway. Situated in an advantageous position, the enemy had awaited them on solid footing and with many well-placed cannons. The [revolutionary] soldiers arrived with their cavalry so fatigued that they could barely maneuver. Finding themselves in such a miserable state, they were still able to attack the royal forces, and did so with unflinching courage and with such a strength that they soon tired the enemy's troops. In fact, they appeared to have arrived at a turning point where victory could have been declared theirs. But in the midst of all the confusion, the astute tyrant General [Arredondo] ordered that a solemn happy military reveille be played, signaling that Victory was already his. This ultimately led him to victory, for with it he filled his army with courage and strength. Demoralized and witnessing the death of the valiant and intrepid Colonel Miguel Menchaca,[2] the liberals fled. The field was covered with cadavers, and only a few in number were able to escape the cruelty and unprecedented Tyranny of the defenders of an absolute Monarch, in whose hands this Patriotic *Pueblo*[3] was left defenseless.

What this *Pueblo* endured, tolerated, and suffered is not easy to put into writing, much less is it easy to recount it with accuracy and certainty, since many of those who could have given a truthful account have died, and since others who are alive did not witness the events; and those who did witness them actually took part in the oppression and tyranny of their homeland [*patria*]; and thus are incapable of telling the truth; and, in fact, they have actually attempted to distort the truth by lying about the roles that they actually played. This is indeed the reason why to this day the Public is unaware of the role played by the Department of Texas in the pursuit of the Homeland's [*Patria's*] liberty and glorious Independence, and the reason for which few accounts exist that tell about the memorable acts that give glory to their Towns [*Pueblos*], like those accounts of Guadalajara, Valladolid, Zacatecas, Oaxaca, Puebla, Veracruz, and others. However, one can still ask the few surviving individuals who will tell their story without seasoning or eloquence. But their account will at least be marked with the Seal of the truth, and without exaggeration, hyperbole, or triumph. Let us begin our story then, come what may, so that the public may know what occurred here. And in honor of our work we will not disguise our story's defects.

As a result of the defeat at the *encinal* of Medina entire families fled, with the hope of escaping with their lives, and headed toward the United States of the North, some on foot and others on horses, going through an infinite number of anguishing and distressing tasks. They abandoned everything they had: their homes, cultivated fields, livestock of all kind, and many other possessions. Among these was the family of the determined Patriot Joaquín Leal, a native of this capital, with his Wife Doña Ana María Arocha,[4] their four sons, and three women who all abandoned their native *patria* the 18th day of August at four in the afternoon. They fled with barely a sack of corn that they quickly picked from their own fields. They walked [east toward Louisiana] for twelve days through the empty countryside amidst dense brush, full of fear, terror, and shock, whispering Jesus's name and murmuring prayers, hoping the enemies would not reach them. The citizens Miguel de Arocha ~~with his three children~~ and Ángela Arocha[5] had caught up with them by then. But then, at one in the afternoon on the 30th of August, upon view of the Loma del Toro[6] not far from the Trinity River, like a bullet shooting across the plain, they heard the great cry of the King's troops who had caught up with them. The Second Lieutenant Fernando Rodríguez said: "*Stop insurgent traitors to the King, if not I will kill you.*" He had barely finished speaking when they found themselves surrounded by fourteen soldiers, who, like carnivorous wolves devoured them with their eyes.[7] At the same moment and with one shot, they killed [Angela Arocha's son] Antonio Delgado.[8] As he fell before his mother, they began to lance him. His mother threw herself to the floor, and pleaded with the pitiless Fernando to not kill him, beseeching him to let him confess, and with indignation he responded: *"that he should confess himself to the Devils. That he and all the others there were condemned."* Infuriated with the mother's pious Christian pleading, he turned the lance on its end and beat her with it until separating her from her dead son. He then gave orders to have Antonio's corpse disrobed, to be left as food for the wild animals, and so it was done.

He then had the rest of the men shackled, and set off in search of [his commander] Elizondo in order to present him with the loot he had captured. Upon seeing them, Elizondo said to him: which families are these, and Rodriguez said to him: The Leales, Arochas, Delgados. Well, said Elizondo in response, *they* [*the men*] *should all die; prepare them.* And instantly Father Camacho confessed them. The citizen mothers Ángela Delgado and Ana María Arocha—interceded with Elizondo for their lives to be forgiven, and he sent them off with indignation, saying to them: "get out of my way insurgents, before I order that you too be killed. What an excellent example you have given your children. Over here, you four armed soldiers take these women and secure them."

Those who were to be executed had already confessed by four in the afternoon of the same day. At that hour these martyrs of the *patria* were allowed to see their mother[9] and sisters. The martyrs lifted their heads, and said with complete courage and integrity: *"Goodbye Mother; goodbye Sisters; until* [*we meet in*] *the Valley of Jehoshaphat."*[10] As soon as the Mother heard her sons' last vows, those who were dying for their *patria,* she fell backwards fainting, and one of her young daughters named Maria de la Consolación lifted her with an arm and with the other took an image of the Lord Christ of Esquipulas.[11] In anguish, torn, and in tears, she begged him to offer consolation and strength to her anguished mother.

With the men already dead and within view of the tyrants, the women spent that wretched, bitter night with no more than a tunic and shirt to cover themselves. There, under the watch of their tyrants, the liberals spent the night full of the affliction that can only be best understood by those who have been forsaken. The rays of dawn had barely broken the following day when the women set out to look for their dead brothers' bodies. They found them thrown in the field and eaten by animals. Witnessing such inhumanity, they decided to ask the cruel Commander Elizondo permission to bury the bodies themselves. But this he refused, telling them: that the men were condemned as traitors to the King and *Patria;* they had shed their their blood in the field of glory.

These unfortunate patriotic women with their tortured souls remained at this infernal site for several days—suffering what horrid actions could be expected from the bitter, bloody defenders of an absolutist, Despotic, tyrant King. They remained there until the water became stagnant with the bodies of the dead that surpassed a hundred. The Chief [Elizondo] of the triumphant Division then decided to head toward the Capital to give an account to the Tyrant General Arredondo of the great prey he had caught, and the defenseless men he had killed through deception.[12] Shortly after parting, however, [Elizondo] was killed along with his brother-in-law Don Isidro, by the hand of a European Captain who had lost his judgment upon seeing such inhumane carnage. Coronel Quintero took command at the Guadalupe river,[13] who by orders from his general forced the miserable women to wait unprotected in the open field under the broiling sun from five in the morning until one in the afternoon. The number of widowed, married, and single women and maidens was about 114. Many of whom were with their dear sweet children who were still being breastfed.

The torturous ordeal having ended, and as a precautionary measure, the new *vecino*[14] ordered that a registry be made of the men and women with the real purpose of collecting all of their documents and coins. He commissioned for this honorable enterprise officials who deserved his trust and appreciation, and who were well known for their support of the king's faction [the royal troops] and were declared enemies of the *patria*. As soon as they began this humiliating and shameful operation, the lieutenants José María Jiménez and Tomas Saucedo and the Second Lieutenants Fernando Rodríguez and ____[15] Chapa, Diego Jiménez, Leandro S. Miguel Cavazos, and others. They began by inspecting the men. They were so detail-oriented and dedicated in their task that not even the shoes escaped scrutiny. They forced the women off the horses in order to do the same to them, such were the orders given by the previously mentioned *vecino* Quintero. So well and so dutifully did they carry out their order that even the women's breasts were registered. Not even the Maidens' modesty or innocence was allowed to escape such obscene inspection and depraved groping.

The next day, in order to continue the march to the capital and to ensure the Chief's safety, and as a way to torment even more the true lovers of the *Patria,* the order was given: that all the prisoners should march tied up and on foot. So it was executed word for word. Most of them walked barefoot, like the honorable Patriots: Tomas Arocha, Fernando Veramendi, and Clemente Delgado. All dying of thirst, hunger, and exhaustion, they arrived at the Zirolo stream at about three in the afternoon, where they quenched their thirst. The enemies threw them into the water all at the same time, and hit them with sticks, treating them worse than they would a herd of goats or a herd of pigs.

The following day, with the same torturous precautionary measures, the patriots made their journey. They arrived at the Salado creek,[16] badly fed, thirsty and battered. They were one day's journey from the Capital. At this point, the Doge Quintero decided to send General [Arredondo] notice of his short distance from Bexar. In order to make more visible his triumph and to better torment, defame, and humiliate those who were pro-independence, he ordered the women to be separated from the men, and made them walk in front on foot and tied to one another with ropes. They were then turned over to the troops of the Fierce One [Arredondo], who had come out to meet the women who, like the prayers of the night, had arrived at the Alamo (located in the suburbs of this city on the other side of the Guadalupe River to the east).[17] In order to prevent the night from depriving the tyrants of a brilliant entrance of the patriots, and in order to ensure a cruel, humiliating, and bitter return for the martyred Patriots, it was mandated that they cross the river the next day. So it occurred. At ten in the morning at the sound of beating drums and blowing horns and trombones, having already incorporated all the male prisoners and women, they crossed the river on foot. As they crossed the river on foot and fully dressed, the Second Lieutenant Fernando Rodríguez used a lance to beat the miserable women as they passed him, forcing them along, barely making it across as they constantly fell and lifted themselves, the water reaching their waists.

Having taken the street that leads from the river to the square, the armed troops formed in line. They surrounded the prisoners, yelling all kinds of shameful insults, freely telling the women: "hah, now you cover yourselves so well, little ones, that you act almost as if you're ashamed. How is it that you didn't have any shame going around with guns killing people?" And the afflicted women did not do more than suffer, their eyes staring at the floor, crying silently, holding back their tears, and letting them fall instead into their hearts, so that the tyrants would not see them. Valiantly, they hid the anguish and terrible shame they felt as they arrived at the Square where the tyrant Arredondo awaited them. He was accompanied by all of his minor officers and henchmen, like Domínguez and other officials, and an audience of about a thousand souls, who arrived out of curiosity. Once all the prisoners had made their way to Arredondo, he began to deride the afflicted women, saying to them with the look of a gypsy: "So you all were saying: there comes the one-eyed Arredondo[18]/to fight with the ones from Texas./He must think that they are sheep, brought to him by Elizondo—so to say/that they have become sheep turned into lions. Take a good look at me and see if I am one-eyed. Now, where is that woman who said: that she was to eat my testicles roasted. She would enjoy them much better raw." And the other one named Josefa Arocha, who promised five hundred pesos for her husband's head (Pedro Treviño who was among the King's troops).[19] The *señora* wanted to respond, but the tyrant did not allow it. He was lit with rage, and taking up the word his Second [lieutenant], that is Domínguez, said: Where around here is she that claims Saint Francis of Paola[20] appeared to her with some American's pants in his hands? And even then that wily one still has the nerve to say: Come over here, gentlemen, and you shall see the miracle that Saint Francis has made that says: that we won; and not the Gachupines.[21]

Among the prisoners was a girl of about ___ years, seeing among the tyrants' commotion the European Rosi, whom she knew from before. She said to him: Sir and how about me, can I go with you? (poor innocent one; may she have been entrusted to a good saint) She was quickly disappointed because, well, he replied to her with great annoyance: not by a long shot. For three years I have suffered because of you all.[22] This he did to please the tyrant and to ingratiate himself with the spectators. Having enjoyed watching his men mistreat the women a thousand ways, the impious general finally said to his henchmen: what should we do with these? And without waiting for an answer, he passed the cruel sentence upon the disgraced women. He said in a loud voice: *To the Quinta; to the Quinta; to grind hot corn for the King's troops.*[23]

Immediately, the bloodthirsty soldiers took them to the doomed destination, where a vicious tyrant awaited them with great anticipation in order to vent his anger out on them, the one named Sergeant Caballero Acosta. One by one, he recognized them, calling out to them with obscene and insulting words, and lifting his voice said to them in a magisterial and pompous tone: what did you insurgent whores think, the way they had you riding around straddling the saddle's horn? And these were the most humane, decent words he used on them. Then, he placed eight men to guard them while a corporal went for twenty *metates*[24] for grinding corn and four bushels of corn so they could grind. The most notable was that the corn was taken from their own crop.

These true daughters of Anahuac[25] experienced this martyrdom—without resting one day, working from two in the morning to ten at night. Some boiled the corn until it was made into *nixtamal*,[26] while others were forced to stomp and scrub it with their feet. But the maize was still hot, and many had the misfortune of having the skin peel from their feet and legs, losing the nails on their toes while the running blood mixed with the corn that they had ground, until one woman (named Cribanta, whose skin from her palms and her fingernails fell off)[27] lost her life, due to this inhumane work. Others were forced to grind, but many had never done so and had very delicate hands. Still others were pregnant. All of these women had comprised that distinguished section of our Captaincy's Citizenry; they had all been the Principal Ladies, etc., etc., etc.

During the day, and while our Mexican women discharged such painful toil, the guard Acosta worked arduously at inventing new methods of punishment in order to mortify and defame them, using the most brazen, shameless words, whipping them at his whim, and not allowing those with infants to breastfeed, whose children cried of hunger and one of whom died in plain view. From this inhumane Nero,[28] who enjoyed embarrassing, afflicting, and mortifying them in a thousand ways, and with the crudest words and the most impure, indecent, and ugly actions, that they cause one to blush to say them, to write them, that not even the paper will permit them to be written down. Our heroines suffered with strength and perseverance, without giving in, and they did so only for the love of their *Patria*. How many tyrannies and cruelties the detestable Acosta had created! The women serenely gathered themselves at ten at night and went to bed, spending the night on the dirt floor.

Let us now examine the food that was given to these servants, they who fed many hungry, such as the entire Battalion of the Fierce One of Veracruz and cavalry of the [Eastern Interior] Provinces.[29] Anyone would see that the food given to them would need to be plentiful and abundant in order to maintain them healthy and robust, capable of fulfilling their "interesting" job. In effect, they were given their complete ration in the morning; and at night nothing; at noon two tortillas and a pound of raw meat without salt which was brought from their cattle; and at night only two tortillas. They did this every single day as the guard called the roll each morning and night, and they marched between two lines of armed soldiers calling them by first and last name in the same way and form as with the soldiers.

Entirely destitute of all feelings of humanity, those tyrants did not even permit an hour of rest or relief for these unfortunate women; not even to breastfeed their little ones; and when only once they found themselves without their vigilant Guardian, they hurried to finish their work so they could have a moment of relief among themselves, as it happened, passing a little more than an hour crying and lamenting their miserable misfortune and then spent a few moments laughing. For neither one nor the other, crying or laughing, did the cruel prison guard allow them to do in front of him, since, according to the guard, the major crime these patriots could commit was to cry or laugh. Oh! But how expensive was that moment of mutual consolation. Command was then given to major Don Antonio

Elozúa,[30] who in order to prevent them from being idle—for the saints cry over lost time, he would say—and to free himself of such a heavy scruple, he sent them sixty of the soldiers' shirts, for them to mend while they were not grinding corn. Finding it rather humorous that they did not have the needed things for sewing, and after asking Acosta for needles to sew, Acosta's answer was to drop his pants and say to them to take them from here. This impure and shameless act brought extreme affliction to our sisters, who quietly cried at such barbarous, cruel, and inhumane behavior from this Caribbean[31] who would whip each and every one of them whenever he wanted, without more cause or motive than having a desire to do so.

This infernal minister did not find enough commands with which to martyrize the patriot women; thus, he came up with the most barbarous thing that he could have imagined in order to consummate their sorrow. This is what it was: he said to the mothers: to run their children off and not have them in their company; and if they did not do it this way, he would order that they be tied up, and he would present them to Arredondo to be punished. This horrendous blow annihilated the martyrs, it ripped the fabric of their heart, and almost drove them insane, and so that their innocent and gentle children would not suffer the tyrants' punishment, with no other fault than being their mothers, full of torment, anguish, and pain, bathed in a flood of tears, they sent them off with these memorable words: "leave from here. Go to where they send you, to the streets, for this is how fortune has come upon us."[32] "And who will feed us?" "Go beg house to house asking for alms for food." And with such a tenderly sweet and loving farewell they left their mothers, who were all left in a sea of tears, except the tyrant, who took great pleasure in viewing such a beautiful scene. He forced them back to [grinding corn on] the *metates,* telling them with an infernal fury, *"get to praying, you whores, because your God has arrived; I am the God of the whores."* And he ran from end to end of the *metates* whipping all of them, these, becoming silent, suffering, and grinding. [And he said to them:] Come now, my dear Mexican women, lovers of your *Patria,* come learn to suffer your liberty and independence.

For twenty full days they suffered such a terrible life, the women who returned from the Trinity River. And those women who were not able to escape [and had remained in San Antonio after the defeat of the revolutionaries], suffered fifty-four days, in the named Quinta. However, after they were freed, no one [in San Antonio] would acknowledge them, even here in the heart of their own *Patria*, not even a *chamacuero*[33] where one could go home to, nor someone to give them a bite, nor where to take it, for they [the royalists] had already taken away their homes, fields, cattle, and all the goods they had, because of the supposed crime of seeking Independence. And the funny thing is that up to this very day their property and belongings have yet to be returned to them. Instead, their property continues to be held by those who neither suffered nor defended the just cause. And, in fact, some of them actually contributed to the patriot women's martyrdom.[34]

In retrospect, the two daughters of the Patriot Manuel Delgado and Ángela Arocha had the good fortune of escaping [at the Trinity River]. One is named Cándida and the other María Josefa. The first is of twenty years of age and the second one under fifteen. Another woman, their sister-in-law named Antonia Rodríguez, also escaped. They preferred to risk their lives by swimming across the vast Trinity River than to fall into the hands of such cruel enemies. They effectively were able to save themselves by swimming across the river. And Cándida was able to save a small niece of hers who was still being breastfed. Cándida held her fast and swam across, while her mother stayed under the power of the tyrant Fernando, who arrived with the other women at the Quinta.

Notes

The Bibliography is available at http://www.hup.harvard.edu/supplementary/a-world-not-to-come.

Introduction

1. Thomas Blossom, *Nariño, Hero of Colombian Independence* (Tucson: University of Arizona, 1967), 1–21; Eduardo Ruiz Martínez, *La librería de Nariño y los derechos del hombre* (Bogotá, Colombia: Planeta, 1990), 187–208. "Spanish America" refers to the former Spanish colonies in the Americas. "Latin America" is a much more contentious term that emerged in the mid-nineteenth century. At the time, France attempted to extend its hegemony over Mexico under Napoleon III, and French intellectuals made the argument that "there existed . . . a linguistic and cultural affinity, a unity, of 'Latin' peoples for whom France was the natural leader and inspiration (and their defender against Anglo-Saxon, mainly U.S., influence and, ultimately, domination)." Leslie Bethell, "Brazil and 'Latin America,'" *Journal of Latin American Studies* 42, no. 3 (2010): 457. As Bethell notes, Brazil had long excluded itself from the category of "Latin America," and has only recently been included. For similar, vexing reasons, the former French colonies are sometimes considered to fall under "Latin America" as well. Today, "Latin America" is used more often than the term "Spanish America," despite the fact that "Latin America" continues to connote "Spanish America." See also Walter Mignolo, *The Idea of Latin America* (Oxford: Blackwell, 2004).
2. Antonio Nariño, *Proceso de Nariño: fiel copia del original que existe en el Archivo general de Indias de Sevilla* (Cádiz, Spain: Impr. de M. Álvarez, 1914; orig. 1796–1804), 89–145, contains Nariño's original testimony; Blossom, *Nariño*, 1–21; Enrique Santos Molano, *Antonio Nariño, filósofo revolucionario* (Bogotá,

Colombia: Planeta, 1999), 169–173, 203–230, describes the entire proceedings and sentencing of Nariño.

3. Harris Gaylord Warren, "The Early Revolutionary Career of Juan Mariano Picornell," *Hispanic American Historical Review* 22, no. 1 (1942): 72–73; Pedro Grases, *Derechos del hombre y del ciudadano. Estudio histórico-crítico sobre los Derechos del Hombre y del Ciudadano* (Caracas, Venezuela: Academia Nacional de la Historia, 1959), 120; Iris M. Zavala, "Picornell y la Revolución de San Blas: 1795," in *El texto en la historia* (Madrid: Nuestra Cultura, 1981), 240–243. Picornell's Atlantic travels are traced in Warren, "Early Revolutionary," 57–81; Harris Gaylord Warren, "The Southern Career of Don Juan Mariano Picornell," *Journal of Southern History* 8, no. 3 (1942): 311–333.
4. See the useful commentary on the usage of creole in the Americas in Ralph Bauer and José Antonio Mazzotti, "Introduction: Creole Subjects in the Colonial Americas," in *Creole Subjects in the Colonial Americas: Empires, Texts, Identities,* ed. Ralph Bauer and José Antonio Mazzotti (Chapel Hill: University of North Carolina, 2009), 3–7. On the formation of creole identities and creole patriotism, see Anthony Pagden, "Identity Formation in Spanish America," in *Colonial Identity in the Atlantic World, 1500–1800,* ed. Nicholas P. Canny and Anthony Pagden (Princeton: Princeton University Press, 1987), 51–94; David A. Brading, *The First America: The Spanish Monarchy, Creole Patriots, and the Liberal State, 1492–1867* (New York: Cambridge University Press, 1991), 53–54, 422–464, 535–540; Jorge Cañizares-Esguerra, *How to Write the History of the New World: Histories, Epistemologies, and Identities in the Eighteenth-Century Atlantic World* (Stanford: Stanford University Press, 2001), 204–210; Enrique Florescano, *Memoria mexicana,* 3rd ed. (Mexico City: Fondo de Cultura Económica, 2002), 469–498; Jaime E. Rodríguez O., *Nosotros somos ahora los verdaderos españoles: La transición de la Nueva España de un reino de la monarquía española a la República Federal Mexicana, 1808–1824,* 2 vols. (Zamora, Michoacán, Mexico: Colegio de Michoacán and Instituto Mora, 2009), 1:60–65.
5. The royal House of Bourbon dates to the thirteenth century in what is now southern France. In the sixteenth century, the Bourbon house ascended to the French throne, and by the eighteenth century the Bourbon dynasty held thrones throughout Europe, including Spain.
6. José Antonio Maravall, "El concepto de reino y los 'Reinos de España' en la Edad Media," *Revista de estudios políticos* 73 (1954): 81–144; John Lynch, *Spain under the Habsburgs: Spain and America, 1598–1700,* 2nd ed., vol. 2 (New York: New York University Press, 1984), 1–37, 218–250; John H. Elliott, *Imperial Spain, 1469–1716* (New York: Penguin, 2002), 15–99; Henry Kamen, *Empire: How Spain Became a World Power, 1492–1763* (New York: Perennial, 2004), 3–92; John H. Elliott, "A Europe of Composite Monarchies," in *Spain, Europe, and the Wider World, 1500–1800* (New Haven: Yale University Press, 2009), 3–24; Francisco Xavier Gil Pujol, "Un rey, una fe, muchas naciones. Patria y nación en la España de los siglos XVI–XVII," in *La monarquía de las naciones: Patria, nación, y naturaleza en la monarquía de España,* ed. Bernardo

José García García and Antonio Álvarez-Ossorio Alvariño (Madrid: Fundación Carlos de Amberes, 2004), 39–76.

7. John Lynch, *Spain under the Habsburgs: Empire and Absolutism, 1516–1598*, 2nd ed., vol. 1 (New York: New York University Press, 1984), 20–29; Brading, *First*, 213–227; Elliott, *Imperial Spain*, 99–110; David A. Brading, "La monarquía Católica," in *Inventando la nación: Iberoamérica, siglo XIX*, ed. Antonio Annino and François-Xavier Guerra (Mexico City: Fondo de Cultura Económica, 2003), 15–29.
8. Lynch, *Spain under the Habsburgs*, 1:51–58; John Lynch, *Bourbon Spain, 1700–1808* (Cambridge, MA: Blackwell, 1989), 1–66; Elliott, *Imperial Spain*, 164–181; Xavier Gil, "Republican Politics in Early Modern Spain: The Castilian and Catalano-Aragonese Traditions," in *Republicanism, a Shared European Heritage: The Values of Republicanism in Early Modern Europe*, ed. Martin van Gelderen and Quentin Skinner, vol. 2 (Cambridge, UK: Cambridge University Press, 2002), 265–270; Rodríguez O., *Nosotros somos*, 1:7–20.
9. Hamish M. Scott, ed., *Enlightened Absolutism: Reform and Reformers in Later Eighteenth-Century Europe* (Ann Arbor: University of Michigan, 1990); Gabriel Paquette, *Enlightenment, Governance, and Reform in Spain and Its Empire, 1759–1808* (New York: Palgrave Macmillan, 2008); Gabriel B. Paquette, ed., *Enlightened Reform in Southern Europe and Its Atlantic Colonies, c. 1750–1830* (Burlington, VT: Ashgate, 2009).
10. Jaime E. Rodríguez O., *The Independence of Spanish America* (New York: Cambridge University Press, 1998), 19, emphasis in original.
11. Captain General of Venezuela Pedro Carbonell, November 1, 1794, cited in Grases, *Derechos del hombre y del ciudadano*, 141.
12. Real Audiencia de Caracas, "La Real Audiencia de Caracas prohibe bajo terribles penas la introduccion y circulacion del libro Derechos del hombre y del ciudadano," in *Documentos para la historia de la vida pública del libertador de Colombia, Perú y Bolivia*, ed. José Félix Blanco, vol. 2 (Caracas, Venezuela: Imprenta de La Opinión Nacional, 1875), 327.
13. Walter Mignolo, "Citizenship, Knowledge, and the Limits of Humanity," *American Literary History* 18, no. 2 (2006): 313. See also Ana del Sarto et al., eds., *The Latin American Cultural Studies Reader* (Durham: Duke University Press, 2004); Mabel Moraña et al., eds., *Coloniality at Large: Latin America and the Postcolonial Debate* (Durham: Duke University Press, 2008); Walter Mignolo, *The Darker Side of Western Modernity: Global Futures, Decolonial Options* (Durham: Duke University Press, 2011).
14. Throughout, I use "Hispanic" to connote both Spain and Spanish America.
15. See Francisco Puy Muñoz, *El pensamiento tradicional en la España del siglo XVIII (1700–1760)* (Madrid: Instituto de Estudios Políticos, 1966), 31–32, where he denies that there was a Spanish Enlightenment; Asunción Lavrin, "Viceregal Culture," in *The Cambridge History of Latin American Literature: Discovery to Modernism*, ed. Roberto González Echevarría and Enrique Pupo-Walker, vol. 1 (New York: Cambridge University Press, 1996), 325–334; Jorge Cañizares Esguerra, "La Ilustración hispanoamericana: una caracterización," in *Revolución, independencia y las nuevas naciones de América*, ed.

Jaime E. Rodríguez O. (Madrid: Fundación MAPFRE Tavera, 2005), 87–89; Rodríguez O., *Spanish America,* 1, argues that the wars must be seen as part of a global Hispanic civil war.

16. Peter Gay, *The Enlightenment: An Interpretation,* 2 vols. (New York: Norton, 1977).

17. This is not to say that this documentation is not valuable; however, the interpretation of this evidence inevitably sees the development of revolutionary or liberal thought as an imported phenomenon that appears to have acted on a tabula rasa. See, for example, Michael González, *This Small City Will Be a Mexican Paradise: Exploring the Origins of Mexican Culture in Los Angeles, 1821–1846* (Albuquerque: University of New Mexico Press, 2005), 149–151; Louise Pubols, *The Father of All: The de la Guerra Family, Power, and Patriarchy in Mexican California* (Berkeley: University of California and Huntington Library, 2009), 151–155.

18. Harry Harootunian, "Some Thoughts on Comparability and the Space-Time Problem," *boundary* 2 32, no. 2 (2005): 30. See also Susan Gillman's work on the comparative literary history of the Americas. Eschewing the teleological logic of comparison, Gillman argues that adaptation "allows for thinking, simultaneously, of the multiple, formal interrelations between and among texts, along with other, different kinds of 'outsides' more conventionally associated with historical and social contexts." Susan Gillman, "Otra vez Calibán/Encore Caliban: Adaptation, Translation, Americas Studies," *American Literary History* 20, no. 1–2 (Spring–Summer 2008): 204.

19. O. Carlos Stoetzer, *The Scholastic Roots of the Spanish American Revolution* (New York: Fordham University Press, 1979), 20.

20. Harootunian, "Some Thoughts on Comparability," 29–36. Thus, in comparing the Spanish-American and British-American Enlightenments, John H. Elliott can not help but find that "the Spanish American Enlightenment lagged behind its British American equivalent." John H. Elliott, *Empires of the Atlantic World: Britain and Spain in America, 1492–1830* (New Haven: Yale University Press, 2006), 333.

21. This critique of Euro-America as the arbiters of universality has been at the heart of the South Asian Subaltern Studies school and its adherents. See, for example, Gayatri Chakravorty Spivak, *A Critique of Postcolonial Reason: Toward a History of the Vanishing Present* (Cambridge, MA: Harvard University Press, 1999); Dipesh Chakrabarty, *Provincializing Europe: Postcolonial Thought and Historical Difference* (Princeton: Princeton University Press, 2000); Ranajit Guha, *History at the Limit of World-History* (New York: Columbia University Press, 2002). No doubt, this was also the emergent critique among nineteenth-century Spanish Americans who, often following Montesquieu, argued that sociopolitical institutions could not be transplanted but had to be shaped by the particular local historical conditions.

22. John Tate Lanning, *Academic Culture in the Spanish Colonies* (New York: Oxford University Press, 1940), 61.

23. Michel Foucault, "Nietzsche, Genealogy, History," in *The Foucault Reader,* ed. Paul Rabinow (New York: Pantheon Books, 1984), 81.

24. Spanish America was officially divided into viceroyalties, "though the most enduring territorial units were those areas administered by the *audiencias* (high courts), often referred to as *reinos* (kingdoms)." Rodríguez O., *Spanish America,* 7. Lynch, *Spain under the Habsburgs,* 1:45–49.
25. William Spence Robertson, "The Juntas of 1808 and the Spanish Colonies," *English Historical Review* 31, no. 124 (October 1916): 573–585; Gabriel H. Lovett, *Napoleon and the Birth of Modern Spain: The Challenge to the Old Order,* vol. 1 (New York: New York University Press, 1965), 88–150, 290–294, 341–345; Lynch, *Spain under the Habsburgs,* 1:200; Rodríguez O., *Spanish America,* 51–64, 75–82; Elliott, *Imperial Spain,* 302–303.
26. "Por real resolucion cesan ya los nombres de colonias de los dominios españoles de Indias," *Gazeta de Mexico* 16, no. 49 (April 15, 1809): 325.
27. Lovett, *Napoleon and Spain,* 1:325–326; John Lynch, *The Spanish American Revolutions, 1808–1826,* 2nd ed. (New York: Norton, 1986), 302; José M. Portillo Valdés, *Crisis atlántica: Autonomía e independencia en la crisis de la monarquía hispana* (Madrid: Fundación Carolina Centro de Estudios Hispánicos e Iberoamericanos y Marcial Pons Historia, 2006), 29–53; Rodríguez O., *Nosotros somos,* 1:94. On revolution and print culture in the Spanish Philippines see Vicente L. Rafael, "Welcoming What Comes: Sovereignty and Revolution in the Colonial Philippines," *Comparative Studies in Society and History* 52, no. 1 (2010): 157–179.
28. Rodríguez O., *Spanish America,* 51–106; Rodríguez O., *Nosotros somos,* 1:199–223.
29. Stoetzer, *Scholastic,* 16–59.
30. François-Xavier Guerra, *Modernidad e independencias. Ensayos sobre las revoluciones hispánicas* (Mexico City: Fondo de Cultura Económica and Editorial MAPFRE, 1992), 149–175; María García Godoy, *Las Cortes de Cádiz y América. El primer vocabulario liberal español y mejicano (1810–1814)* (Seville: Diputación de Sevilla, 1998); Jeremy Adelman, *Sovereignty and Revolution in the Iberian Atlantic* (Princeton: Princeton University Press, 2006), 175–219.
31. Without drawing too fine a line, we can distinguish between "social imaginary" and "imagined community" by saying that an imagined community (as Benedict Anderson formulated it) develops from or is a particular incarnation of a social imaginary that takes the modern nation as its driving force. Charles Taylor offers a useful definition of social imaginary: it is "something much broader and deeper than the intellectual schemes people may entertain when they think about social reality in a disengaged mode. I am thinking, rather, of the ways people imagine their social existence, how they fit together with others, how things go on between them and their fellows, the expectations that are normally met, and the deeper normative notions and images that underlie these expectations." Charles Taylor, *A Secular Age* (Cambridge, MA: Harvard University Press, 2007), 171. For the classic theoretical formulation of imagined communities, see Benedict Anderson, *Imagined Communities: Reflections on the Origin and Spread of Nationalism* (New York: Verso, 1991).
32. Hugh Hamill Jr., *The Hidalgo Revolt: Prelude to Independence* (Gainesville: University of Florida, 1966); Ernesto de la Torre Villar, *La independencia de*

México (Madrid: Fondo de Cultura Económica and Editorial MAPFRE, 1992), 77–93; Rodríguez O., *Spanish America,* 107–109; Rodríguez O., *We Are Now the True Spaniards,* 60–67.

33. Hamill, *Hidalgo Revolt;* Torre Villar, *La independencia de México,* 77–93; Rodríguez O., *We Are Now the True Spaniards,* 118–142.
34. Félix D. Almaráz Jr., *Tragic Cavalier: Governor Manuel Salcedo of Texas, 1808–1813,* 2nd ed. (College Station: Texas A&M University Press, 1991), 122; Félix D. Almaráz Jr., "Texas Governor Manuel Salcedo and the Court-Martial of Padre Miguel Hidalgo, 1810–1811," *Southwestern Historical Quarterly* 96, no. 4 (April 1996): 455.
35. Adán Benavides Jr., "Loss by Division: The Commandancy General Archive of the Eastern Interior Provinces," *The Americas* 43, no. 2 (October 1986): 204; Donald E. Chipman and Harriett Denise Joseph, *Spanish Texas, 1519–1821,* 2nd ed. (Austin: University of Texas Press, 2010), 198–203.
36. David A. Cossío, *Historia de Nuevo León,* vol. 4 (Monterrey, Mexico: J. Cantú Leal, 1925), 243–273; David J. Weber, *The Spanish Frontier in North America* (New Haven: Yale University Press, 1992), 19–24; Jesús F. de la Teja, *San Antonio de Béxar: A Community on New Spain's Northern Frontier* (Albuquerque: University of New Mexico Press, 1995), 3–15; Elliott, *Imperial Spain,* 66–76.
37. Juliana Barr, *Peace Came in the Form of a Woman: Indians and Spaniards in the Texas Borderlands* (Chapel Hill: University of North Carolina Press, 2007).
38. Odie B. Faulk, *The Last Years of Spanish Texas, 1778–1821* (The Hague, Netherlands: Moulton, 1964), 83–99; Weber, *Spanish Frontier,* 174–177; de la Teja, *San Antonio de Béxar,* 97–117.
39. For the moment, I will leave "Latinos" in scare quotes. I offer a more elaborated working definition of this term below.
40. A case in point is José Antonio Navarro. Born in San Antonio, Texas in 1795, his life spanned four different nation-states (Spanish Texas, Mexican Texas, the Texas Republic, and the United States). As his biographer states, for more than a century historians have described Navarro variously as "a foolish man who let friendship prevent him from standing up for his best interests and those of his fellow Tejanos; or, at worst, he was a turncoat and a traitor to Tejanos." David R. McDonald, *José Antonio Navarro: In Search of the American Dream in Nineteenth Century Texas* (Denton: Texas State Historical Association, 2010), 7.
41. Eugene E. Loos et al., eds., "What Is Inchoative Aspect?" *Glossary of Lingusitic Terms* (http://www.sil.org/linguistics/GlossaryOfLinguisticTerms/WhatIsInchoativeAspect.htm), accessed May 19, 2006.
42. To date, the early nineteenth-century revolutionary period in Texas and its documents have attracted but little attention. For the best account see Julia K. Garrett, *Green Flag over Texas: A Story of the Last Years of Spain in Texas* (New York: Cordova, 1939). Garrett's captivating history is still, some seventy years after its publication, the only monograph on this period. Her work emerged from that early twentieth-century interest in Borderlands history

spearheaded by Herbert E. Bolton along with the transcription and acquisition of Hispanophone archives from Spain and Spanish America.

43. The eminent Mexican historian Josefina Zoraida Vázquez has made this point on numerous occasions, encouraging Mexican historians to develop the historiography on Texas and the U.S.-Mexican War (1846–148). Josefina Zoraida Vázquez, "Los años olvidados," *Mexican Studies/Estudios Mexicanos* 5, no. 2 (Summer 1989): 313–326; Josefina Zoraida Vázquez, "Un tema arrinconado por la historiografía mexicana," *Historia Mexicana* 42, no. 4 (1993): 827–835.

44. On writing postfoundational histories, see Gyan Prakash, "Writing Post-Orientalist Histories of the Third World: Perspectives from Indian Historiography," *Comparative Studies in Society and History* 32, no. 2 (April 1990): 383–408; Gyan Prakash, "Can the 'Subaltern' Ride? A Reply to O'Hanlon and Washbrook," *Comparative Studies in Society and History* 34, no. 1 (1992): 168–184.

45. Thus, the discursive web that relates the oral performance of a manifesto may be read in relation to a manuscript or book. This discursive world, in turn, will not be segregated from a certain kind of materiality. The method described here is a quite familiar one as articulated by New Historicists. The classic statement is that of Louis Montrose, who in 1986 wrote: "The new orientation to history in Renaissance literary studies may be succinctly characterized, on the one hand, by its acknowledgment of the *historicity of texts:* the cultural specificity, the social embedment, of all modes of writing—not only those texts that critics study but also the texts in which they study them; and, on the other hand, by its acknowledgment of the *textuality of history:* the unavailability of a full and authentic past, a lived material existence, that has not already been mediated by the surviving texts of the society in question—those 'documents' that historians construe in their own texts, called 'histories,' histories that necessarily but always incompletely construct the 'History' to which they offer access." Louis Montrose, "Renaissance Literary Studies and the Subject of History," *English Literary Renaissance* 16, no. 1 (1986): 8, emphasis in original. Montrose may have placed emphasis on the text as a material object (the book, the letter, the pamphlet), but I will also emphasize other less material forms of textuality, such as gossip, rumor, and oral culture.

46. Carlos Newland, "La educación elemental en Hispanoamérica: desde la independencia hasta la centralización de los sistemas educativos nacionales," *Hispanic American Historical Review* 71, no. 2 (1991): 357.

47. On alternative indigenous literacies see Elizabeth Hill Boone and Walter Mignolo, eds., *Writing without Words: Alternative Literacies in Mesoamerica and the Andes* (Durham: Duke University Press, 1994); Phillip H. Round, *Removable Type: Histories of the Book in Indian Country, 1663–1880* (Chapel Hill: University of North Carolina Press, 2010); Joanne Cummins and Thomas B. F. Rappaport, *Beyond the Lettered City: Indigenous Literacies in the Andes* (Durham: Duke University Press, 2012); Hilary E. Wyss, *English Letters and Indian Literacies: Reading, Writing, and New England Missionary Schools, 1750–1830* (Philadelphia: University of Pennsylvania Press, 2012).

48. The Protestant Reformation began as part of a much larger movement for reform within the Church. As a result, scholars now acknowledge that naming the Catholic Reformation as a "Counter-Reformation" ignores these internal, complex efforts at reform prior to and after the Protestant Reformation. Hubert Jedin, "Catholic Reformation or Counter-Reformation," in *The Counter-Reformation: The Essential Readings,* ed. David Martin Luebke (Malden, MA: Blackwell, 1999), 19–45; Diarmaid MacCulloch, *The Reformation* (New York: Viking, 2004), 3–102.
49. Angel Rama, *The Lettered City,* trans. John Charles Chasteen (Durham: Duke University Press, 1996), 1–28. Citing John Leddy Phelan, Roberto González Echevarría also makes this case. "The formula's origins go back to the Roman law concept that the prince can will no injustice. The 'I obey' clause signifies the recognition by subordinates of the legitimacy of the sovereign's power who, if properly informed of all circumstances, would will no wrong. The 'I do not execute' clause is the subordinate's assumption of the responsibility of postponing the execution of an order until the sovereign is informed of those conditions of which he may be ignorant and without a knowledge of which an injustice may be committed." John Leddy Phelan, "Authority and Flexibility in the Spanish Imperial Bureaucracy," *Administrative Science Quarterly* 5, no. 1 (1960): 59, cited in Roberto González Echevarría, *Myth and Archive: A Theory of Latin American Narrative* (Durham: Duke University Press, 1998), 196 n.37.
50. Rama, *Lettered,* 16. On the role of the *letrado,* see the extensive bibliography provided by González Echevarría, *Myth and Archive,* 193 n.12; see also Elsa M. Ramírez Leyva, *El libro y la lectura en el proceso de occidentalización de México* (Mexico City: Universidad Nacional Autónoma de México, 2001), 89–122.
51. The Bexar Archives contain a separate file of Spanish colonial printed documents that arrived in San Antonio. The great majority of them, if not all, are royal decrees sent from the centers of political authority, Spain or Mexico City. Bexar Archives, the Dolph Briscoe Center for American History, University of Texas at Austin (hereafter "Bexar Archives"), reels 1–7.
52. John Charles Chasteen, "Introduction," in *The Lettered City,* ed. Angel Rama (Durham: Duke University Press, 1996), viii–x.
53. Rama, *Lettered,* 25.
54. Lester G. Bugbee, *The Archives of Béxar* (Austin: University of Texas Press, 1899), quote is from p. 1; Adán Benavides Jr., *The Béxar Archives (1717–1836): A Name Guide* (Austin: University of Texas Press, 1989), xi–xiii; John Wheat, "Bexar Archives," *Handbook of Texas Online* (http://www.tshaonline.org/handbook/online/articles/lcb02), accessed July 30, 2011; "Bexar Archives Original Manuscripts and Printed Material, 1717–1836," the Dolph Briscoe Center for American History, University of Texas at Austin (http://www.lib.utexas.edu/taro/utcah/00179/00179-P.html), accessed December 25, 2012. Many of the Bexar Archives have been translated into English, and many more are available online at "Bexar Archives Online," the Dolph Briscoe Center for American History, University of Texas at Austin (http://www.cah.utexas.edu/projects/bexar/index.php), accessed December 30, 2011.

55. Harootunian, "On Comparability," 47.
56. Lynch, *Spain under the Habsburgs* 2:361–386; Elliott, *Imperial Spain,* 276–303. Quentin Skinner is one of the few historians of political thought to critically engage with the history of Hispanic political thought; his *Foundations of Modern Political Thought: The Age of the Reformation,* vol. 2 (New York City: Cambridge University Press, 1978) "integrat[es] it fully within a Europe-wide history of political thought, contrary to the tendency within Anglo-American historiography to discuss only those aspects and figures . . . that impinge upon a basically northern European and indeed Atlantic perspective." Annabel S. Brett, "Scholastic Political Thought and the Modern Concept of the State," in *Rethinking the Foundations of Modern Political Thought,* ed. Annabel S. Brett et al. (New York: Cambridge University Press, 2006), 141.
57. Norbert Lechner, "A Disenchantment Called Postmodernism," in *The Postmodernism Debate in Latin America,* ed. John Beverley et al. (Durham: Duke University Press, 1995), 149. Lechner takes this formulation from Marcel Gauchet, *The Disenchantment of the World: A Political History of Religion* (Princeton: Princeton University Press, 1997).
58. Otis H. Green argues that this epistemic shift—from viewing the world as a received order to one that humans actively produce—does not permeate the Hispanic world until perhaps the latter part of the nineteenth century. Otis H. Green, *Spain and the Western Tradition: The Castilian Mind in Literature from El Cid to Calderón,* vol. 4 (Madison: University of Wisconsin Press, 1966), v–vi.
59. Guerra, *Modernidad,* 85, emphasis added. For an earlier comparable argument see Richard M. Morse, "Toward a Theory of Spanish American Government," *Journal of the History of Ideas* 15, no. 1 (January 1954): 71–93.
60. Lanning, *Academic,* 61–89; Richard Herr, *The Eighteenth-Century Revolution in Spain* (Princeton: Princeton University Press, 1958), 163–172; Lavrin, "Viceregal Culture," 331–332.
61. According to Jürgen Habermas, Wilhelm Friedrich Hegel was the first to articulate this problem for (Protestant) modernity: how to constitute absolute or transcendental meaning in the wake of reason's critique of religion. Jürgen Habermas, "Hegel's Concept of Modernity," trans. Frederick Lawrence, in *The Philosophical Discourse of Modernity* (Cambridge, MA: MIT Press, 1987), 25–31.
62. A. Gabriel Meléndez, *So All Is Not Lost: The Poetics of Print in Nuevomexicano Communities, 1834–1958* (Albuquerque: University of New Mexico Press, 1997), 16–17.
63. No historian has offered a more convincing argument for understanding the revolts as part of a global Hispanic civil war than Jaime E. Rodríguez O. Among his many works, see Rodríguez O., *Spanish America,* 1–2, 36–74. However, the Colombian historian Nicolás García Samudio had already made the same argument as early as 1941. Nicolás García Samudio, "La misión de Don Manuel Torres en Washington y los orígenes suramericanos de la doctrina Monroe," *Boletín de historia y antiguëdades* 28 (1941): 475–476.
64. The same could be said in the case of France. On this epistemic shift in British America see Larzer Ziff, *Writing in the New Nation: Prose, Print, and Politics*

in the Early United States (New Haven: Yale University Press, 1991), 15–17, 121–125, where he describes the shift as one from immanence to representation.

65. Guerra, *Modernidad,* 275–296. "Imprint" here and throughout will refer to any document produced via a printing press; thus, this can mean anything from fliers to broadsheets, pamphlets, newspapers, and books.
66. Jürgen Habermas, *The Structural Transformation of the Public Sphere: An Inquiry into a Category of Bourgeois Society,* trans. Thomas Burger (Cambridge, MA: MIT Press, 1989), xi. As Michael Warner and others have pointed out, Habermas's original *Öffentlichkeit* (translated as "public sphere") does not refer so much to a tangible, physical entity as much as it does to a more abstract concept of "openness" or "publicness." Michael Warner, *Publics and Counterpublics* (New York: Zone Books, 2002), 47.
67. Guerra, *Modernidad,* 291–296; François-Xavier Guerra et al., eds., *Los espacios públicos en Iberoamérica: Ambigüedades y problemas, siglos XVIII–XIX* (Mexico City: Centro Francés de Estudios Mexicanos y Centroamericanos and Fondo de Cultura Ecónomica, 1998); Jean Franco, "Waiting for a Bourgeoisie: The Formation of the Mexican Intelligentsia in the Age of Independence," trans. Patricia Heid, in *Critical Passions: Selected Essays,* ed. Mary Louise Pratt and Kathleen Newman (Durham: Duke University Press, 1999), 478.
68. Jacques Derrida described this as a "metaphysics of presence," the desire to have stable, immediate access to meaning. "Self-presence" is another term he uses as a synonym: "God is the name and the element of that which makes possible an absolutely pure and absolutely self-present self-knowledge.... God's infinite understanding is the other name for the logos as self-presence." Jacques Derrida, *Of Grammatology,* trans. Gayatri Chakravorty Spivak (Baltimore: Johns Hopkins University Press, 1997), 98. In this, Derrida was influenced by Martin Heidegger, *Being and Time* (New York: HarperPerennial, 2008).
69. This is different, to be clear, from the eighteenth-century emergent creole quasi-national consciousness among the elite, educated sectors in Spanish America. In the case of Mexico, a cohesive nationalism capable of displacing one's regional attachment to their *patria chica* only emerged in the early twentieth century. See Florencia E. Mallon, *Peasant and Nation: The Making of Postcolonial Mexico and Peru* (Berkeley and Los Angeles: University of California Press, 1995), 310–330; Henry C. Schmidt, *The Roots of* lo mexicano: *Self and Society in Mexican Thought, 1900–1934* (College Station: Texas A&M University Press, 1978), 64–116; Eric Van Young, ed., *Mexico's Regions: Comparative History and Development* (San Diego: UCSD Center for U.S.-Mexican Studies, 1992); Alan Knight, "Peasants into Patriots: Thoughts on the Making of the Mexican Nation," *Mexican Studies/Estudios Mexicanos* 10, no. 1 (1994): 153–156; Alfredo Ávila, "México: Un viejo nombre para una nueva nación," in *Crear la nación: los nombres de los países de América Latina,* ed. José Carlos Chiaramonte et al. (Buenos Aires: Editorial Sudamericana, 2008), 271–284.

70. Suzanne Oboler et al., "Latino Identities and Ethnicities," *The Oxford Encyclopedia of Latinos and Latinas in the United States* (http://www.oxfordreference.com.proxy.uchicago.edu/view/10.1093/acref/9780195156003.001.0001/acref-9780195156003-e-493), accessed September 19, 2007.
71. And yet the term is not without its genealogical quagmires, given that the concept of Latin America originated out of mid-nineteenth-century French imperial impulses to dominate Spanish America. See Bethell, "Brazil and 'Latin America.'"
72. David J. Weber, *The Mexican Frontier, 1821–1846: The American Southwest under Mexico* (Albuquerque: University of New Mexico, 1982), 4, 10; Donald E. Chipman and Harriett Denise Joseph, *Spanish Texas, 1519–1821,* 2nd ed. (Austin: University of Texas Press, 2010), 255.

1. Anxiously Desiring the Nation

1. Founded in 1716, Nacogdoches was an outpost settlement established by the Spanish to prevent the French from expanding west from Louisiana. It is located some 170 miles southeast of present-day Dallas and 300 northeast of San Antonio. Archie P. McDonald, "Nacogdoches, Texas," *Handbook of Texas Online* (http://www.tshaonline.org/handbook/online/articles/hdn01), accessed June 1, 2011.
2. Governor Manuel Salcedo to New Orleans Spanish Consul Diego Murphy, April 21, 1812; Nacogdoches Spanish Agent Samuel Davenport to Bernardino Montero, May 6, 1812; Salcedo to New Spain Viceroy Francisco Xavier Venegas, May, 11, 1812; Montero to Salcedo, May 28, 1812; Interior Provinces Commandant General Nemesio Salcedo to Manuel Salcedo, June 9, 1812; Montero to Manuel Salcedo, August 14, 1812, Bexar Archives, the Dolph Briscoe Center for American History, University of Texas at Austin (hereafter "Bexar Archives"), reel 51, frames 30–36, 200–202, 236–243, 352–357, 492–505, 514–515; reel 52, frames 256–257; Manuel Salcedo to Viceroy Francisco Xavier Venegas, June 25 and July 8, 1812, Operaciones de Guerra, Manuel Salcedo, 1810–1812, BANC MSS M-A1 (FILM 3097: reel 3), Selected Transcriptions from the Archivo General de la Nación. Documents for the History of Mexico (ca. 1524–1855), Bancroft Library, University of California, Berkeley (hereafter "Operaciones de Guerra, Manuel Salcedo"), 83–128, 129–135.
3. Salcedo and other Spanish authorities in Texas continuously made reference to the scarce availability of paper. Félix D. Almaráz Jr., *Tragic Cavalier: Governor Manuel Salcedo of Texas, 1808–1813,* 2nd ed. (College Station: Texas A&M University Press, 1991), 77–79.
4. Salcedo to Venegas, June 3, 1812, Operaciones de Guerra, Manuel Salcedo, 62–81; "Proclamation Relating to the Revolution which took place at Bexar, Jan. 22, 1811," dated after April 1811, MF Reel 10, MS, No. 571, Nacogdoches Archives, Texas State Library, Austin; J. Villasana Haggard, "The Counter-Revolution of Béxar, 1811," *Southwestern Historical Quarterly* 43 (October 1939): 224–225; Frederick C. Chabot, ed., *Texas in 1811: The Las Casas and*

Sambrano Revolution (San Antonio: Yanaguana Society, 1941); Almaráz, *Tragic Cavalier,* 95–129.

5. Salcedo to Nuevo León Governor Ramón Bustamante, August 17, 1812, Operaciones de Guerra, Manuel Salcedo, 138.
6. Reinhart Koselleck, *Futures Past: On the Semantics of Historical Time,* trans. Keith Tribe (New York: Columbia University Press, 2004), 50.
7. The classic account of these two epistemes, if not a satisfactory account of *how* they changed, is that of Michel Foucault,*The Order of Things: An Archaeology of the Human Sciences* (New York: Vintage, 1994). Another quite persuasive account of these epistemes, though he does not use the concept or engage with Foucault's account, is that of Charles Taylor, *A Secular Age* (Cambridge, MA: Harvard University Press, 2007).

   Here and throughout I rely on Michel Foucault's definition of episteme as the conditions of possibility that allow for truth claims to be made. Foucault, *Order of Things,* xxii. He elaborates elsewhere: "By *episteme,* we mean, in fact, the total set of relations that unite, at a given period, the discursive practices that give rise to epistemological figures, sciences, and possibly formalized systems. . . . The episteme is not a form of knowledge *(connaissance)* or type of rationality which, crossing the boundaries of the most varied sciences, manifests the sovereign unity of a subject, a spirit, or a period; it is the totality of relations that can be discovered, for a given period, between the sciences when one analyses them at the level of discursive regularities." Michel Foucault, *The Archaeology of Knowledge,* trans. A. M. Sheridan Smith (New York: Barnes and Noble Books, 1972), 191.

   In this regard, we may heuristically say that the intellectual schemata of episteme, social imaginary, and imagined community have a concentric relationship with one another, where each emerges from the preceding.
8. Lorenzo de la Garza, *Dos hermanos héroes* (Mexico City: Editorial Cultura. Ex-Libris José Ramírez Flores, 1939; orig. 1913), 11–12; Gabriel Saldívar, *El primer diputado tamaulipeco al Congreso general, don José Antonio Gutiérrez de Lara* (Mexico City: Boletín de la Sociedad Mexicana de Geografía y Estadística, 1943); Lorenzo de la Garza, *La antigua Revilla en la leyenda de los tiempos: reseña histórica, geográfica y anecdótica del municipio de Cd. Guerrero, Tamaulipas, a contar desde el ciclo de su fundación 1750 a la época de 1952* (Ciudad Victoria, Mexico: Imprenta Oficial del Gobierno, 1944); Rie Jarratt, *Gutiérrez de Lara, Mexican-Texan: The Story of a Creole Hero* (Austin: Creole Texana, 1949), 1–4; Vidal Covián Martínez, "Don José Bernardo Maximiliano Gutiérrez de Lara. Primer diplomático Mexicano, héroe insurgente en Texas, primer gobernador constitucional de Tamaulipas," *Cuadernos de Historia (Ciudad Victoria, Tamaulipas),* no. 2 (1967): 5–7; Juan Fidel Zorrilla, "Los hermanos Gutierrez de Lara," in *Tamaulipas en la Guerra de Independencia* (Mexico City: Porrúa, 1972); James Clark Milligan, "José Bernardo Gutiérrez de Lara: Mexican Frontiersman, 1811–1841" (PhD dissertation, Texas Tech University, Lubbock, 1975), 1–8; Carlos González Salas, "El Padre José Antonio Gutiérrez de Lara," in *Historia de la literatura en Tamaulipas: Historiografía, geografía, y estadística,* vol. 1 (Ciudad Victoria, Tamaulipas,

Mexico: Instituto de Investigaciones Históricas, Universidad Autónoma de Tamaulipas, 1980), 101–116; Juan Fidel Zorrilla and Carlos González Salas, "Gutiérrez de Lara, José Antonio Apolinario (1770–1843) y Gutiérrez de Lara, José Bernardo Maximiliano (1774–1841)," in *Diccionario biográfico de Tamaulipas* (Ciudad Victoria, Mexico: Instituto de Investigaciones Históricas, Universidad Autónoma de Tamaulipas, 1984), 222–225.

9. Juan Fidel Zorrilla, *Integración histórica del noreste de Nueva España* (Ciudad Victoria, Tamaulipas: Instituto de Investigaciones Históricas, Universidad Autónoma de Tamaulipas, 1991); Patricia Osante, *Orígenes del Nuevo Santander (1748–1772)* (Mexico City: Universidad Nacional Autónoma de México, 1997), 119–151, 207–234; Patricia Osante, "Colonization and Control: The Case of Nuevo Santander," trans. Ned F. Brierley, in *Choice, Persuasion, and Coercion: Social Control on Spain's North American Frontiers,* ed. Jesús F. de la Teja and Ross Frank (Albuquerque: University of New Mexico Press, 2005), 227–233; Juan Fidel Zorrilla, *Tamaulipas y la guerra de Independencia: acontecimientos, actores y escenarios* (Ciudad Victoria, Mexico: Gobierno del Estado de Tamaulipas; Comisión Organizadora para la Conmemoración en Tamaulipas del Bicentenario de la Independencia y Centenario de la Revolución Mexicana, 2008; orig. 1972), 15–57.

10. Jarratt, *Gutiérrez de Lara,* 2–3; Milligan, "Gutiérrez de Lara," 4.

11. Escandón, however, would inevitably run afoul of royal authority, and was removed from power. See Patricia Osante, *Testimonio acerca de la causa formada en la colonia del Nuevo Santander al coronel Don José de Escandón* (Mexico City: Instituto de Investigaciones Históricas, Universidad Nacional Autónoma de México, 2000).

12. On the similarity of social conditions across the Eastern Interior Provinces, see Vito Alessio Robles, *Coahuila y Texas en la época colonial* (Mexico City: Editorial Porrúa, 1978; orig. 1938), 605–625; Jack Jackson, *Los Mesteños: Spanish Ranching in Texas, 1721–1821* (College Station: Texas A&M University Press, 1986), 223–523; Octavio Herrera Pérez, *Breve historia de Tamaulipas* (Mexico City: Colegio de Mexico and Fondo de Cultura Económica, 1999); Isidro Vizcaya Canales, *En los albores de la independencia. Las Provincias Internas de Oriente durante la insurrección de don Miguel Hidalgo y Costilla, 1810–1811,* 2nd ed. (Monterrey, Mexico: Fondo Editorial Nuevo León y Instituto Tecnológico de Monterrey, 2005; orig. 1976).

13. See, for example, the letters included throughout de la Garza, *Dos hermanos.*

14. De la Garza, *Dos hermanos,* 13.

15. Jarratt, *Gutiérrez de Lara,* 3.

16. Juan Agustín de Morfí, *History of Texas, 1673–1779,* trans. Carlos Eduardo Castañeda, vol. 2 (Albuquerque: The Quivira Society, 1935), 92. See also Jesús F. de la Teja, *San Antonio de Béxar: A Community on New Spain's Northern Frontier* (Albuquerque: University of New Mexico Press, 1995), 200 n.21. In this Morfí was not unlike most of his peninsular comrades who thought of American Spaniards as physically and morally inferior. David A. Brading, *The Origins of Mexican Nationalism* (Cambridge, UK: Centre of Latin American Studies, University of Cambridge, 1985), 10.

17. See, for example, David J. Weber, *The Spanish Frontier in North America* (New Haven: Yale University Press, 1992).
18. José Eleuterio González, *Apuntes para la historia eclesiástica de las provincias que formaron el obispado de Linares, desde su primer origen hasta que se fijó definitivamente la silla episcopal en Monterrey* (Monterrey, Mexico: Tip. Relig. de J. Chaves, 1877); Israel Cavazos Garza, *El Colegio Civil de Nuevo León: contribución para su historia* (Monterrey, Mexico: Ediciones del Centenario del Colegio Civil, Universidad de Nuevo León, 1957), 15–21; Israel Cavazos Garza, "Esbozo histórico del Seminario de Monterrey," *Anuario Humanitas (Universidad Autónoma de Nuevo León)* 8 (1969); Gerardo Zapata Aguilar, *Bibliotecas antiguas de Nuevo León* (Monterrey, Mexico: Universidad Autónoma de Nuevo León, 1996), 67–148; Zorrilla, *Tamaulipas e independencia,* 15–51.
19. Cavazos Garza, "Seminario de Monterrey," 413–414.
20. de la Garza, *Dos hermanos,* 11; Jarratt, *Gutiérrez de Lara;* Cavazos Garza, *El Colegio Civil de Nuevo León,* 15–21; Covián Martínez, "Gutiérrez de Lara," 6; Cavazos Garza, "Seminario de Monterrey," 412–415; Milligan, "Gutiérrez de Lara," 4.
21. Cited in de la Garza, *Dos hermanos,* 80–81.
22. Cavazos Garza, "Seminario de Monterrey," 414; Zapata Aguilar, *Bibliotecas,* 101.
23. Richard Herr, *The Eighteenth-Century Revolution in Spain* (Princeton: Princeton University Press, 1958), 163.
24. O. Carlos Stoetzer, *El pensamiento político en la América española durante el período de la emancipación, 1789–1825. Las bases hispánicas y las corrientes europeas,* vol. 1 (Madrid: Instituto de Estudios Políticos, 1966), 58; Dorothy Tanck de Estrada, "Aspectos políticos de la intervención de Carlos III en la Universidad de México," *Historia Mexicana* 38, no. 2 (1988): 182–184; David A. Brading, *The First America: The Spanish Monarchy, Creole Patriots, and the Liberal State, 1492–1867* (New York: Cambridge University Press, 1991), 497–503; François-Xavier Guerra, *Modernidad e independencias. Ensayos sobre las revoluciones hispánicas* (Mexico City: Fondo de Cultura Económica and Editorial MAPFRE, 1992), 169–170; Alejandro Cañeque, *The King's Living Image: The Culture and Politics of Viceregal Power in Colonial Mexico* (New York: Routledge, 2004), 51–78; Ugo Baldini, "Enlightenment and Renovation in the Spanish University," in *Universities and Science in the Early Modern Period,* ed. Mordechai Feingold and Víctor Navarro Brotons (Dordrecht, the Netherlands: Springer, 2006), 201–230.
25. The standard history on the Council of Trent is Hubert Jedin, *A History of the Council of Trent,* 2 vols. (London: T. Nelson, 1957–1961). But see as well John O'Malley's much anticipated *Trent: What Happened at the Council* (Cambridge, MA: Harvard University Press, 2013).
26. Margaret Ruth Miles, *Image as Insight: Visual Understanding in Western Christianity and Secular Culture* (Boston: Beacon, 1985); Margaret Ruth Miles, *The Word Made Flesh: A History of Christian Thought* (Malden, MA: Blackwell, 2005), 247–324; Carlos M. N. Eire, "The Reformation," in *The Blackwell Companion to Catholicism,* ed. James Joseph Buckley et al.

(Malden, MA: Blackwell, 2007), 63–80; Taylor, *Secular Age,* 61–89; O'Malley, *Trent,* 160, 241–284.

27. John Tate Lanning, *Academic Culture in the Spanish Colonies* (New York: Oxford University Press, 1940), 10–11; Bernice Hamilton, *Political Thought in Sixteenth-Century Spain* (London: Oxford University Press, 1963); Quentin Skinner, *The Foundations of Modern Political Thought: The Age of the Reformation,* vol. 2 (Cambridge, UK: Cambridge University Press, 1978), 113–184; Walter Rüegg, "Humanism and the Universities," in *A History of the University in Europe: Universities in Early Modern Europe (1500–1800),* vol. 2, ed., Hilde de Ridder-Symoens (Cambridge, UK: Cambridge University Press, 1996), 37–38; Ralph McInerny, *Aquinas* (Cambridge, UK: Polity Press, 2004), 128; Enrique Dussel, "Origen de filosofía política moderna: Las Casas, Vitoria, y Suárez (1514–1617)," *Caribbean Studies* 33, no. 2 (July–December 2005): 35–80; Ulrich Gottfried Leinsle, *Introduction to Scholastic Theology* (Washington, DC: Catholic University of America Press, 2010), 280–294.
28. Fernand van Steenberghen, *Aristotle in the West: The Origins of Latin Aristotelianism,* trans. Leonard Johnston, 2nd ed. (New York: Humanities Press, 1970). Plato, on the other hand, had been well known; in the fourth century, St. Augustine of Hippo, living in Roman Algeria and witnessing the collapse of the Roman empire, had already integrated Christianity with classical philosophy, especially Plato.
29. John W. O'Malley, *Four Cultures of the West* (Cambridge, MA: Harvard University Press, 2004), 98, 100.
30. Foucault, *Order of Things,* 42.
31. For useful, nonspecialist accounts of Scholasticism see Frederick Charles Copleston, *A History of Philosophy: Late Medieval and Renaissance Philosophy, Ockham, Francis Bacon, and the Beginning of the Modern World,* vol. 3 (New York: Doubleday, 1993), 1–23, 335–352; Leinsle, *Scholastic Theology;* H. M. Höpfl, "Scholasticism in Quentin Skinner's *Foundations,*" in *Rethinking the Foundations of Modern Political Thought,* ed. Annabel S. Brett et al. (New York: Cambridge University Press, 2006), 113–129; Josef Pieper, *Scholasticism: Personalities and Problems of Medieval Philosophy* (New York: Catholicism University of America Press, 2010).
32. Diego Valadés, *Rhetorica christiana* (Perugia, Italy: Petrutius, 1579).
33. Foucault, *Order of Things,* 17–44.
34. Ibid., 34.
35. Ibid., 27. I describe as a Scholastic episteme what Foucault characterizes as an episteme of resemblance, dominant in Western Europe until the sixteenth century. The periodization is not exact, but the Renaissance, Reformation, and new sciences reconfigured this episteme into one that Foucault describes as Classical, using the unique French periodization to describe the sixteenth and seventeenth centuries.
36. Taylor, *Secular Age,* 29–41.
37. Ibid., 32, 33, 35.
38. Servando Teresa de Mier, *Obras completas: Vol. 1, El heterodoxo Guadalupano* (Mexico City: Universidad Nacional Autónoma de México, 1981),

30–31, 221–255; Jacques Lafaye, *Quetzalcóatl and Guadalupe: The Formation of Mexican National Consciousness, 1531–1813* (Chicago: University of Chicago Press, 1987), 177–206; Servando Teresa de Mier, "Carta de despedida a los mexicanos," in *Obras completas: Vol. 4, La formación de un republicano,* ed. Edmundo O'Gorman and Jaime E. Rodríguez O. (Mexico City: Universidad Nacional Autónoma de México, 1988), 107–114.

39. Taylor, *Secular Age,* 35.
40. Writing about contemporary India, the historian Dipesh Chakrabarty makes a correlate argument when he critiques "modern European political thought and the social sciences," though the United States should definitely be included, for assuming "that the human is ontologically singular, that gods and spirits are in the end 'social facts,' that the social somehow exists prior to them." Instead, Chakrabarty, "take[s] gods and spirits to be existentially coeval with the human, and think[s] from the assumption that the question of being human involves the question of being with gods and spirits." Dipesh Chakrabarty, *Provincializing Europe: Postcolonial Thought and Historical Difference* (Princeton: Princeton University Press, 2000), 16. Indeed, one might suggest that the *real mágico* (magical realism) is genealogically related to this discursive ambivalence between signified and signifier, perhaps as traces of the conjuncture and ternary system of signs.
41. Foucault, *Order of Things,* 42–77. On the history of the sciences and rise of rationalism and skepticism in the more Protestant northern region of Europe (though attempting to pass itself off as universal), see the work of Georges Canguilhem, especially *Ideology and Rationality in the History of the Life Sciences,* trans. Arthur Goldhammer (Cambridge, MA: MIT Press, 1988). For comparable work on the Hispanic world, see Luis Rodríguez Aranda, *El desarrollo de la razon en la cultura española* (Madrid: Aguilar, 1962); Jeremy Robbins, *The Challenges of Uncertainty: An Introduction to Seventeenth-Century Spanish Literature* (Lanham, MD: Rowman and Littlefield, 1998); Jeremy Robbins, *Arts of Perception: The Epistemological Mentality of the Spanish Baroque, 1580–1720* (Abingdon, UK: Routledge, 2007).
42. Foucault, *Order of Things,* 296.
43. Ibid., 217–387.
44. Michel Foucault, *The History of Sexuality: An Introduction,* vol. 1 (New York: Random House, 1990), 136–141.
45. Walter J. Ong, "From Mimesis to Irony: Writing and Print as Integuments of Voice," in *Interfaces of the Word: Studies in the Evolution of Consciousness and Culture* (Ithaca: Cornell University Press, 1977), 287; Skinner, *Foundations,* vol. 2; J. G. A. Pocock, *The Machiavellian Moment: Florentine Political Thought and the Atlantic Republican Tradition* (Princeton: Princeton University Press, 2003); Miles, *Word Made Flesh,* 325–358; Taylor, *Secular Age,* 25–158. Angel Rama is simply incorrect in his adopting for Spanish America Foucault's periodization regarding the sixteenth and seventeenth century shifts from ternary to binary sign systems. Angel Rama, *The Lettered City,* trans. John Charles Chasteen (Durham: Duke University Press, 1996), 3.

46. Miles, *Image as Insight,* 95–125; Roger Chartier, ed., *History of Private Life: Vol. 3, Passions of the Renaissance* (Cambridge, MA: Harvard University Press, 1989), 111–159; quote is from Taylor, *Secular Age,* p. 70.
47. Dominique Julia, "Reading and the Counter-Reformation," in *A History of Reading in the West,* ed. Guglielmo Cavallo et al. (Amherst: University of Massachusetts Press, 1999), 261; Carmen Castañeda, "Los niños, la enseñaza de la lectura y sus libros," in *La infancia y la cultura escrita,* ed. Lucía Martínez (Mexico City: Siglo XXI-Universidad Autónoma de Morelos, 2001), 312–338; Eugenia Roldán Vera, "Lectura en preguntas y respuestas," in *Empresa y cultura en tinta y papel, 1800–1860,* ed. Laura Beatriz Suárez de la Torre and Miguel Angel Castro (Mexico City: Instituto Mora and Universidad Nacional Autónoma de México, 2001), 327–341.
48. Miles, *Image as Insight,* 95–125; Miles, *Word Made Flesh,* 300–314.
49. Olga Victoria Quiroz-Martínez, *La introducción de la filosofía moderna en España: el eclecticismo español de los siglos XVII y XVIII* (Mexico City: El Colegio de México, 1949); Robbins, *Arts of Perception.*
50. Bernabé Navarro, *La introducción de la filosofía moderna en México* (Mexico City: El Colegio de México, 1948).
51. O. Carlos Stoetzer, *The Scholastic Roots of the Spanish American Revolution* (New York: Fordham University Press, 1979), 40, 77–78. See also Lanning, *Academic,* 84–86; Samuel Ramos, *Historia de la filosofía en México* (Mexico City: Universidad Nacional Autónoma de México, 1943), 59–76; Jean Sarrailh, *La España ilustrada de la segunda mitad del siglo XVIII,* trans. Antonio Alatorre (Mexico City: Fondo de Cultura Económica, 1957), 194–229; Herr, *Revolution,* 163–172; José Antonio Maravall, *Teoría del estado en España en el siglo 17,* 2nd ed. (Madrid: Centro de Estudios Constitucionales, 1997), 411–417.
52. Historians have often remarked that Spanish America, even into the early nineteenth century, was still very much rooted in the *ancien régime.* Francois-Xavier Guerra, "The Spanish-American Tradition of Representation and Its European Roots," *Journal of Latin American Studies* 26, no. 1 (1994): 3; Annick Lempérière, "República y publicidad a finales del antiguo régimen (Nueva España)," in *Los espacios públicos en Iberoamérica: Ambigüedades y problemas, siglos XVIII–XIX,* ed. François-Xavier Guerra et al. (Mexico City: Fondo de Cultura Económica, 1998), 54. In his otherwise impeccable account of the period, Jaime Rodríguez O. overstretches the influence of modern philosophy in the Hispanic world by claiming, in pointing to one author, the eminent Spanish intellectual Benito Jerónimo Feijoo, that scientific skepticism had begun to chip away at the hegemony of Scholasticism in the late seventeenth century. Jaime E. Rodríguez O., *"We Are Now the True Spaniards": Sovereignty, Revolution, Independence, and the Emergence of the Federal Republic of Mexico, 1808–1824* (Stanford: Stanford University Press, 2012), 10–11.
53. Lorenzo de Zavala, *Ensayo histórico de las revoluciones de México desde 1808 hasta 1830,* vol. 1 (Mexico City: Fondo de Cultura Económica, 1985; orig. 1845), 40.

54. The classic statements are by Max Weber, "Politics as a Vocation," in *From Max Weber: Essays in Sociology,* ed. H. Gerth and C. Wright Mills (New York: Oxford, 1946), 77–128; Weber, "Science as a Vocation," in ibid., 129–156; Weber, "Religious Groups (The Sociology of Religion)," *Economy and Society,* ed. Guenther Roth and Claus Wittich (Berkeley and Los Angeles: University of California Press, 1978), esp. 422–438, 468–479; Weber, *The Protestant Ethic and the Spirit of Capitalism,* trans. Talcott Parsons (New York: Routledge, 1992; orig. 1930). See also Wolfgang Schluchter, *The Rise of Western Rationalism: Max Weber's Developmental History* (Berkeley: University of California Press, 1981), 139–174.
55. Copleston, *History of Philosophy,* 275–291.
56. Certainly, the Scholastic episteme in the Hispanic world underwent its own internal, dynamic reconfigurations. But this has yet to be examined thoroughly. Doing so would help flesh out more fully the development of the Hispanic Enlightenment.
57. Lanning, *Academic,* 61–89; Ramos, *Historia de la filosofía en México,* 55–76; Sarrailh, *España,* 155–167; Stoetzer, *Scholastic,* 60–105; quote is from Tanck de Estrada, "Aspectos políticos," 183 n.5.
58. Sarrailh, *España,* 501; quote is from Herr, *Revolution,* 177.
59. Lanning, *Academic,* 72–73.
60. Herr, *Revolution,* 169.
61. Ramos, *Historia de la filosofía en México,* 74; Karl Schmitt, "The Clergy and the Enlightenment in Latin America: An Analysis," *The Americas* 15, no. 4 (1959): 382–383.
62. Ramos, *Historia de la filosofía en México,* 74; Herr, *Revolution,* 168–172; Edward V. Coughlin and John F. Wilhite, "Some Notes on the Independence Movement at the Colegio del Rosario," in *Homenaje a Nöel Salomon: Ilustración española e independencia de América,* ed. Alberto Gil Novales (Barcelona: Universidad Autónoma de Barcelona, 1979), 358. On Jacquier, see Fourier Bonnard, *Histoire du couvent royal de la Trinité du mont Pincio à Rome* (Rome: Établissements français, 1933), 178–186; Gilles Montègre, "Un médiateur culturel français dans la Rome des Lumières: le père François Jacquier, 1744–1788," in *Anticléricalisme, minorités religieuses et échanges culturels entre la France et l'Italie : de l'antiquité au XXe siècle : hommage à Jean-Pierre Viallet, historien,* ed. Olivier Forlin (Paris: L'Harmattan, 2006), 181–202.
63. Herr, *Revolution,* 170.
64. Zapata Aguilar, *Bibliotecas,* 101–102.
65. Alzate had been one of the most ardent critics of Aristotelianism (a synonym for Scholasticism) in Mexico. A naturalist, he published extensively on scientific studies, geography, and natural history, and edited one of Mexico's earliest periodicals. José Antonio de Alzate y Ramírez, *Gacetas de literatura de Mexico,* 4 vols. (Puebla, Mexico: Reimpresas en la Oficina del Hospital de San Pedro, 1831; orig. 1788–89), 1:12–13. See Stoetzer, *Scholastic,* 90, where he describes Alzate as anti-Scholastic.
66. Harry Bernstein, "A Provincial Library in Colonial Mexico, 1802," *The Hispanic American Historical Review* 26, no. 2 (1946): 170; John Tate Lanning,

The Eighteenth-Century Enlightenment in the University of San Carlos de Guatemala (Ithaca: Cornell University Press, 1956), 98–99; Coughlin and Wilhite, "Colegio San Rosario," 358; Mercedes de Vega, "Bibliografías básicas de cohesión cultural: La biblioteca del Colegio de Guadalupe en Zacatecas," in *La Independencia de México y el proceso autonomista novohispano 1808–1824*, ed. Virginia Guedea (Mexico City: Universidad Nacional Autónoma de México, 2001), 416–417; Enrique González González, "Colegios y universidades: La fábrica de los letrados," in *Historia de la literatura mexicana: Cambios de reglas, mentalidades y recursos retóricos en la Nueva España del siglo XVIII*, ed. Nancy Vogeley and Manuel Ramos Medina, vol. 3 (Mexico City: Siglo XXI and Universidad Nacional Autónoma de México, 2011), 115.

67. Alzate y Ramírez, *Gacetas de literatura de Mexico*, 1:13.
68. Stoetzer, *Scholastic*, 81.
69. No references to the events leading up to and including the American Revolution could be found in the following: José Antonio de Alzate y Ramírez, ed., *Asuntos varios sobre ciencias y artes* (Mexico City: Imprenta de la Biblioteca Mexicana, 1772–1773); José Ignacio Bartolache, ed., *Mercurio Volante* (Mexico City: Felipe de Zúniga y Ontiveros, 1772–1773); Manuel Antonio Valdés, ed., *Gazeta de México* (Mexico City: Felipe de Zúniga y Ontiveros, 1784–1809); José Antonio de Alzate y Ramírez, ed., *Gazeta de literatura de México* (Mexico City: Felipe de Zúniga y Ontiveros, 1788–1795). For reports of Franklin's experiments, see Alzate y Ramírez, ed., *Gazeta de literatura de México*, 2.8:59, 2.10:78, 2.11:83, 2.18:140, 2.21:165, 3.14:104–110.
70. For similar claims, see Jorge Cañizares-Esguerra, "La Ilustración hispanoamericana: Una caracterización," in *Revolución, independencia y las nuevas naciones de América*, ed. Jaime E. Rodríguez O. (Madrid: Fundación MAPFRE Tavera, 2005), 87–98; Jorge Cañizares-Esguerra, *Nature, Empire, and Nation: Explorations of the History of Science in the Iberian World* (Stanford: Stanford University Press, 2006).
71. Emeterio Valverde Tellez, *Critíca filosófica: o, estudio bibliográfico y crítico de las obras de filosofía; escritas, traducidas o publicadas en Mexico desde el siglo XVI hasta nuestros dias; concluyen las "Apuntaciones históricas sobre la filosofía en México"* (Mexico City: Tipografía de los sucesores de Francisco Díaz de León, 1904), 88; Lanning, *Academic*, 65–79; Ramos, *Historia de la filosofía en México*, 77–88; Schmitt, "The Clergy and the Enlightenment in Latin America," 382–383; Stoetzer, *Scholastic*, 89–90; Pedro Álvarez de Miranda, *Palabras e ideas: El léxico de la ilustración temprana en España (1680–1760)* (Madrid: Real Academia Española, 1992), 457.
72. This information is based on an extensive online search on WorldCat and the National Library catalogues for Italy, Spain, France, Germany, the United Kingdom, the United States, and Mexico. The *British Periodicals* database includes hundreds of periodicals from the late seventeenth century to the early twentieth. *British Newspapers, 1600–1900* includes more than 3 million pages of digitized periodicals. The *Archive of Americana* includes the databases *Early American Imprints, Series I and II* and *America's Historical Newspapers*, covering the period of 1639–1922. On what Anglo-American revolutionaries read,

see Donald S. Lutz, "Appendix: European Works Read and Cited by the American Founding Generation," in *A Preface to American Political Theory* (Lawrence: University Press of Kansas, 1992), 159–164.

73. Stoetzer, *Scholastic,* 53 n.20. He paraphrases Karl Vossler, *Fray Luis de León* (Buenos Aires: Espasa-Calpa Argentina, 1946), 39. This is also the argument in Otis H. Green, *Spain and the Western Tradition: The Castilian Mind in Literature from El Cid to Calderón,* vol. 3 (Madison: University of Wisconsin Press, 1963), 3–4.

74. Compare Jaime E. Rodríguez O., *"Rey, religión, yndependencia y unión": el proceso político de la independencia de Guadalajara* (Mexico City: Instituto Mora, 2003); Mariana Terán Fuentes, "Por lealtad al rey, a la patria y a la religión. Los años de transición en la provincia de Zacatecas: 1808–1814," *Mexican Studies/Estudios Mexicanos* 24, no. 2 (2008): 289–323.

75. de la Garza, *Dos hermanos,* 11–109.

76. Pedro Herrera Leyva, *Diario de lo ocurrido a las milicias del Nuevo Reino de León al mando de su comandante el capitán don Pedro Herrera Leyva en sus operaciones contra los insurgentes* (Monterrey, Mexico: Archivo General del Estado de Nuevo León, 1985), 38. See also Vizcaya Canales, *En los albores,* 161–162.

77. See Appendix 1 for the translation of José Antonio Gutiérrez de Lara, "Americanos [1811]," in *Diario de lo ocurrido a las milicias del Nuevo Reino de León al mando de su comandante el Capitán Don Pedro Herrera Leyva en sus operaciones contra los Insurgentes* (Monterrey, Mexico: Archivo General del Estado de Nuevo León, 1985), 80–82.

78. François-Xavier Guerra, "De la política antigua a la política moderna. La revolución de la soberanía," in *Los espacios públicos en Iberoamérica: Ambigüedades y problemas, siglos XVIII–XIX,* ed. François-Xavier Guerra (Mexico City: Fondo de Cultura Económica, 1998), 119.

79. Carlos María de Bustamante, "Documentos relativos á la proclamacion de Fernando VII como rey de España [Julio–Agosto 1808, *Diario de Mexico*]," in *Historia de la Guerra de Independencia de México. Biblioteca de obras fundamentales de la Independencia y la Revolución,* ed. Juan E. Hernández y Dávalos, vol. 1 (Mexico City: Comisión Nacional para las Celebraciones del 175 Aniversario de la Independencia Nacional y 75 Aniversario de la Revolución Mexicana, 1985), 495–505; Hira de Gortari Rabiela, "Julio–agosto de 1808: La lealtad mexicana," *Historia Mexicana* 39, no. 1 (1989), 181–203; María José Garrido Asperó, *Fiestas cívicas históricas en la ciudad de México, 1765–1823* (Mexico City: Instituto Mora, 2006), 55–83.

80. Bustamante, "Proclamacion de Fernando VII," 496, emphasis added.

81. Mónica Quijada, "¿Qué nación? Dinámicas y dicotomías de la nación en el imaginario hispanoamericano," in *Inventando la nación: Iberoamérica, siglo XIX,* ed. Antonio Annino and François-Xavier Guerra (Mexico City: Fondo de Cultura Económica, 2003), 292–293; José Carlos Chiaramonte, *Nación y estado en Iberoamérica: el lenguaje político en tiempos de las independencias* (Buenos Aires: Sudamericana, 2004), 38–44. See also Joaquín Varela Suanzes-Carpegna, *La teoría del estado en los orígenes del constitucionalismo hispánico.*

Las Cortes de Cádiz (Madrid: Centro de Estudios Constitucionales, 1983), 221–245; Noemí Goldman and Nora Souto, "De los usos de los conceptos de 'nación' y la formación del espacio político en el Río de la Plata (1810–1827)," *Secuencia* 37 (Enero-abril) (1997), 35–56; François-Xavier Guerra, "Las mutaciones de la identidad en la América Hispánica," in *Inventando la nación: Iberoamérica, siglo XIX*, ed. Antonio Annino and François-Xavier Guerra (Mexico City: Fondo de Cultura Económica, 2003), 186–187; José Carlos Chiaramonte, *Ciudades, provincias, estados: orígenes de la nación argentina, 1800–1846* (Buenos Aires: Emecé, 2007); Mónica Quijada, "Sobre 'nación,' 'pueblo,' 'soberanía' y otros ejes de la modernidad en el mundo hispánico," in *Las nuevas naciones: España y México, 1800–1850*, ed. Jaime E. Rodríguez O. (Madrid: Fundación MAPFRE, 2008), 30–35.

82. Stoetzer, *Scholastic*, 78; Brading, *First America*, 543; Guerra, *Modernidad*, 159–160, 167; Roberto Castelán Rueda, *La fuerza de la palabra impresa. Carlos María Bustamante y el discurso de la modernidad, 1805–1827* (Mexico City: Fondo de Cultura Económica and Universidad de Guadalajara, 1997), 35; Guerra, "Mutaciones," 190–195, 201–202.
83. Gutiérrez de Lara, "Americanos," 81.
84. François-Xavier Guerra would describe this structure of imagined communities as a pyramid, with the monarch, kingdoms, and *pueblos* in descending order. Guerra, *Modernidad*, 157–158; Guerra, "Mutaciones," 188–197. But the metaphor of a pyramid, though implying a relationship between different levels, exaggerates the distinct notion of belonging. A concentric metaphor, on the other hand, better explains the nested, intimate, overlapping relationship between each expanding level of community. See, for example, Quijada, "Dinámicas," 290–299.
85. Edmund Burke, *Reflections on the Revolution in France: A Critical Edition*, ed. J. C. D. Clark (Stanford: Stanford University Press, 2001), 202.
86. Joan Corominas and José A. Pascual, *Diccionario crítico etimológico castellano e hispánico*, 6 vols. (Madrid: Gredos, 1980–1991), 4:202.
87. Benedict Anderson, *Imagined Communities: Reflections on the Origin and Spread of Nationalism* (New York: Verso, 1991), 187–206.
88. Gutiérrez de Lara, "Americanos," 80–81.
89. The changing denotations of *pueblo* can be traced using the online database of the Real Academia Española, which includes online facsimiles of all twenty-two editions of its dictionary since 1726, including the authoritative *Diccionario de autoridades*. Real Academia Española, "Dicciónarios de la lengua española (1726–1992)" (http://lema.rae.es/drae/), accessed January 22, 2006. This should be supplemented with the standard critical etymological dictionary, Corominas and Pascual, *Diccionario crítico etimológico*, 4:673.
90. On sovereignty emerging from the *pueblo*, see Varela Suanzes-Carpegna, *Teoría del estado*, 187–207; José Carlos Chiaramonte, *Ciudades, provincias, estados: orígenes de la nación Argentina, 1800–1846* (Buenos Aires: Ariel, 1997), 135–142. For related interpretations of *nación*, *pueblo*, and *patria*, see José Antonio Maravall, *Estado moderno y mentalidad social (siglos XV a XVII)*, vol. 1 (Madrid: Revista de Occidente, 1972), 461–500; Luis Monguió, "Palabras e Ideas:

'Patria' y 'Nación' en el Virreinato del Perú," *Revista Iberoamericana* 44, no. 104–105 (July–December 1978), 451–470; Álvarez de Miranda, *Palabras e ideas: el léxico de la ilustración temprana en España (1680–1760),* 211–261; Claudio Lomnitz-Adler, *Deep Mexico, Silent Mexico: An Anthropology of Nationalism* (Minneapolis: University of Minnesota Press, 2001), 3–34; François-Xavier Guerra, "La nación moderna: nueva legitimidad y viejas identidades," *Tzintzun: Revista de Estudios Históricos,* no. 36 (2002), 79–114; Guerra, "Mutaciones"; Quijada, "Dinámicas"; Chiaramonte, *Nación,* 27–57; José M. Portillo Valdés, *Crisis atlántica: Autonomía e independencia en la crisis de la monarquía hispana* (Madrid: Fundación Carolina Centro de Estudios Hispánicos e Iberoamericanos y Marcial Pons Historia, 2006), 159–209; Quijada, "Sobre 'nación,' "; Terán Fuentes, "Por lealtad al rey, a la patria y a la religión."

91. Real Academia Española, "Dicciónarios de la lengua española (1726–1992)."
92. Guerra, "Mutaciones," 204.
93. Gutiérrez de Lara, "Americanos," 80. On the sense of loyalty to the monarch as patriarch, see Guerra, *Modernidad,* 150–152.
94. Varela Suanzes-Carpegna, *Teoría del estado,* 189; Goldman and Souto, "De los usos de los conceptos de 'nación,' " 41–42.
95. Guerra also identifies this discursive shift from religious to nationalist messianism in the historical writing of this period. Guerra, *Modernidad,* 162–164, 239–250.
96. *El Semanario Patriótico* (Madrid, no. 3, September 15, 1808, p. 47) cited in Guerra, *Modernidad,* 242.
97. See the magisterial work on *patria, nación,* and other early modern Hispanic concepts of belonging in Maravall, *Estado moderno y mentalidad social (siglos XV a XVII),* 461–500.
98. Zapata Aguilar, *Bibliotecas,* 67–68, 89–90.
99. Machiavelli and Luther were seen as responsible for the demise of Catholic hegemony and were thus anathema in the Catholic world.
100. Zapata Aguilar, *Bibliotecas,* 71–75. This book provides a mine of archives that will yield fruitful research on the history of the book and intellectual history for years to come. On the history of the book in Spanish America, see the useful bibliographic essay: Hortensia Calvo, "The Politics of Print: The Historiography of the Book in Early Spanish America," *Book History* 6 (2003), 277–305.
101. Compare Andrés Reséndez, *Changing National Identities at the Frontier: Texas and New Mexico, 1800–1850* (New York: Cambridge University Press, 2005), 83–92. Persuasive as his theoretical account may be, Benedict Anderson is simply wrong when it comes to the power of print and the emergence of nationalism in Spanish America. Anderson, *Imagined Communities,* 9–38. For a critique of Anderson's historical claims, see Lomnitz-Adler, *Deep Mexico,* 3–34; Sara Castro-Klaren and John Charles Chasteen, *Beyond Imagined Communities: Reading and Writing the Nation in Nineteenth-Century Latin America* (Baltimore: Johns Hopkins University Press, 2004).

102. Real Academia Española, "Dicciónarios de la lengua española (1726–1992)"; Gutiérrez de Lara, "Americanos," 81.
103. Quijada, "Dinámicas," 293–296.
104. Gutiérrez de Lara, "Americanos," 80.
105. Ibid., 81.
106. Brading, *The Origins of Mexican Nationalism*, 3–23; Brading, *First America*, 53–54.
107. Gutiérrez de Lara, "Americanos," 81. "Nación" is feminine and takes "Americana."
108. *El Despertador Americano* of Guadalajara, Mexico (December 20, 1810) cited in Jaime E. Rodríguez O., *Nosotros somos ahora los verdaderos españoles: La transición de la Nueva España de un reino de la monarquía española a la República Federal Mexicana, 1808–1824*, vol. 1 (Zamora, Michoacán, Mexico: Colegio de Michoacán and Instituto Mora, 2009), 13.
109. Writes Myra Jehlen in her classic study, "In their energetic impatience to get to their futures, Americans have no interest in how they arrived at the present." Myra Jehlen, *American Incarnation: The Individual, the Nation, and the Continent* (Cambridge, MA: Harvard University Press, 1986), 6.

2. "Oh! How Much I Could Say!"

1. José Bernardo Gutiérrez de Lara, "1815, Aug. 1, J. B. Gutierrez de Lara to the Mexican Congress, an account of the progress of the revolution from the beginning," in *The Papers of Mirabeau Buonaparte Lamar, 1798–1859*, ed. Charles Adams Gulick Jr. and Katherine Elliott, vol. 1 (Austin: Texas State Library, 1920), 4–7; Elizabeth Howard West, "[Introduction to] Diary of Jose Bernardo Gutierrez de Lara, 1811–1812, I," *American Historical Review* 34, no. 1 (October 1928): 56; Lorenzo de la Garza, *Dos hermanos héroes* (Mexico City: Editorial Cultura. Ex-Libris José Ramírez Flores, 1939; orig. 1913), 11–14; Rie Jarratt, *Gutiérrez de Lara, Mexican-Texan: The Story of a Creole Hero* (Austin: Creole Texana, 1949), 5–7; Vidal Covián Martínez, "Don José Bernardo Maximiliano Gutiérrez de Lara. Primer diplomático Mexicano, héroe insurgente en Texas, primer gobernador constitucional de Tamaulipas," *Cuadernos de Historia (Ciudad Victoria, Tamaulipas)*, no. 2 (1967): 5–7; James Clark Milligan, "José Bernardo Gutiérrez de Lara: Mexican Frontiersman, 1811–1841" (PhD dissertation, Texas Tech University, Lubbock, 1975), 4–21; David E. Narrett, "José Bernardo Gutiérrez de Lara: *Caudillo* of the Mexican Republic in Texas," *Southwestern Historical Quarterly* 106, no. 2 (October 2002): 198–200.
2. Tomás Pérez Vejo, "El problema de la nación en las independencias americanas: Una propuesta teórica," *Mexican Studies/Estudios Mexicanos* 24, no. 2 (2008): 221–243. For a revisionist account see Eric Van Young, *The Other Rebellion: Popular Violence, Ideology, and the Mexican Struggle for Independence* (Stanford: Stanford University Press, 2001).

3. José Antonio Gutiérrez de Lara cited in José L. Cossio, ed., *Breve apología que el Coronel D. José Bernardo Gutiérrez de Lara hace de las imposturas calumniosas que se le articulan en un folleto intitulado: Levantamiento de un general en las Tamaulipas contra la República, o muerto que se le aparece al Gobierno en aquel Estado,* 2nd ed. (Mexico City: Imprenta del Niño Perdido Nüm. 10, 1915), 7.
4. Venezuela and Argentina had each deposed the local Spanish administrator in the spring of 1810, though they would not achieve independence until later. U.S. newspapers followed the events closely.
5. Indian agents were official government representatives and "were charged to watch the movements of the Indians and through the maintenance of trade to secure their good will toward the colonists." They were first appointed during the American Revolutionary War, as a way to ensure Native American loyalty. During the nineteenth century, the Indian agent system transformed and became the basis for the modern Indian reservation system. Frederick Webb Hodge, ed., *Handbook of American Indians North of Mexico,* vol. 1 (Washington, DC: Bureau of American Ethnology, Smithsonian Institute, 1907–10), 21–22.
6. Claiborne to Sibley, cited in Julia K. Garrett, *Green Flag over Texas: A Story of the Last Years of Spain in Texas* (New York: Cordova, 1939), 86.
7. Narrett, "Gutiérrez de Lara," 201.
8. Julia Kathryn Garrett, "Dr. John Sibley and the Louisiana-Texas Frontier, 1803–1814," *Southwestern Historical Quarterly* 45, no. 3 (January 1942): 288.
9. Garrett, *Green Flag,* 87.
10. José Bernardo Gutiérrez de Lara and Francisco Mariano Sosa, "Francisco Mariano Sora [*sic*], Mexican Curate, and José Bernardo Gutiérrez, Mexican Lieutenant Colonel, to James Monroe, Secretary of State of the United States, Natchitoches, LA, September 27, 1811," in *Diplomatic Correspondence of the United States concerning the Independence of the Latin-American Nations,* ed. William R. Manning, vol. 3 (Washington, DC: Oxford University Press), 1593.
11. Garrett, *Green Flag,* 83–88. The Neutral Ground had been designated by the United States and Spain in 1806. J. Villasana Haggard, "The Neutral Ground between Louisiana and Texas, 1806–1821," *Louisiana Historical Quarterly* 28 (October 1945): 1001–1128. The Orleans Territory was carved out of the Louisiana Purchase in October 1804, and would eventually become the state of Louisiana on April 30, 1812.
12. General Overton in Nashville gave him three letters: one to General James Winchester twenty-five miles outside of Nashville, the second to Overton's brother in Knoxville, and the third addressed to farmers. Garrett, *Green Flag,* 88–90.
13. The diary's remaining copy is housed at the Texas States Archives in Austin, and has never been published in its original Spanish. Elizabeth Howard West published a superb introduction and translation of the diary in 1928 and 1929. Still, West makes particular translation decisions that significantly alter

the political language that Bernardo used; thus, I offer my own translations here, as I do for most of the original Spanish-language materials. For cross-reference purposes, I cite the original followed by a citation to the corresponding page in West's translation. José Bernardo Gutiérrez de Lara, Diary, 1811–1812, Manuscripts Collections, Archives and Information Services Division, Texas State Library and Archives Commission, Austin; José Bernardo Gutiérrez de Lara, "Diary of José Bernardo Gutiérrez de Lara, 1811–1812, I," trans. Elizabeth Howard West, *American Historical Review* 34, no. 1 (October 1928): 55–77; José Bernardo Gutiérrez de Lara, "Diary of José Bernardo Gutiérrez de Lara, 1811–1812, II," trans. Elizabeth Howard West, *American Historical Review* 34, no. 2 (January 1929): 281–294.

14. "The trace was originally a game trail used by the Choctaw, Natchez, and Chickasaw peoples. In the late eighteenth century, boatmen who floated down the Mississippi River with flatboats of goods would sell both the goods and the boats and use the trace as an overland route back to the Ohio River valley. From 1800 to 1820 it was the most important highway in the Old Southwest." It stretches some 440 miles from Natchez, Mississippi (bordering Louisiana) up north-northeast to Nashville. "Natchez Trace Parkway," *Encyclopædia Britannica Online* (http://search.eb.com/eb/article-9054934), accessed May 10, 2008.
15. Though Spanish settlements were not established in what was the Old Southwest, Spanish explorers traveled through the region in the sixteenth century. In 1527, Álvar Núñez Cabeza de Vaca was a member of a failed attempt to colonize Florida. He and his surviving companions wandered through the southern Gulf Coast region from Florida across to modern-day Texas and down into Mexico where he arrived in 1536. Three years later, Hernando de Soto, fascinated by Cabeza de Vaca's stories of fortune to be found, set out for Florida and traveled through much of what is today the U.S. South. Then, twenty years after Bernardo, another prominent Mexican, Lorenzo de Zavala fled Mexico in exile, and followed his route.
16. Gutiérrez de Lara, Diary, 4E-5b; Gutiérrez de Lara, "Diary, I," 67.
17. David Crockett, *A Narrative of the Life of David Crockett, of the State of Tennessee,* 6th ed. (Philadelphia: E.L. Carey and A. Hart, 1834), 68–69; W. Bruce Wheeler, "Knoxville," *Tennessee Encyclopedia of History and Culture* (http://www.tennesseeencyclopedia.net/entry.php?rec=745), accessed October 18, 2008. On social conditions on the Natchez Trace and Old Southwest during this period, see William C. Davis, *A Way through the Wilderness: The Natchez Trace and the Civilization of the Southern Frontier* (New York: Harper Collins, 1995).
18. Gutiérrez de Lara, Diary, 4E-6a-b; Gutiérrez de Lara, "Diary, I," 68.
19. Gutiérrez de Lara, Diary, 4E-6b, emphasis added; Gutiérrez de Lara, "Diary, I," 68, emphasis added.
20. Gutiérrez de Lara, Diary, 4E-5b; Gutiérrez de Lara, "Diary, I," 67.
21. Gutiérrez de Lara, Diary, 4E-6b; Gutiérrez de Lara, "Diary, I," 68.
22. Allan Pred and Michael John Watts, *Reworking Modernity: Capitalisms and Symbolic Discontent* (New Brunswick: Rutgers University Press, 1992), 11.

23. François-Xavier Guerra, *Modernidad e independencias. Ensayos sobre las revoluciones hispánicas* (Mexico City: Fondo de Cultura Económica and Editorial MAPFRE, 1992), 155.
24. For a fascinating discussion on what she terms Catholic versus Protestant "ontologies of seeing" and its consequences for visuality, reading, and print culture, see Lois Parkinson Zamora, *The Inordinate Eye: New World Baroque and Latin American Fiction* (Chicago: University of Chicago Press, 2006), 1–59.
25. Gutiérrez de Lara, Diary, 4E-10a; Gutiérrez de Lara, "Diary, I," 71.
26. Gutiérrez de Lara, Diary, 4E-6b-4E-7a; Gutiérrez de Lara, "Diary, I," 68.
27. John F. Kasson, *Civilizing the Machine: Technology and Republican Values in America, 1776–1900,* 2nd ed. (New York: Hill and Wang, 1999), 139–142; Leo Marx, *The Machine in the Garden: Technology and the Pastoral Ideal in America,* 2nd ed. (New York: Oxford University Press, 2000), 165. But, already in 1784, on a tour of the United States, the revolutionary Spanish American Francisco de Miranda from Caracas would also write about the beauty of machines: "no puede negarse que la *maquina* esta, es un esfuerzo del genio, industria, y espiritu audáz del Pueblo que lo produxo!" Miranda was writing about a chain stretched across the Hudson river designed to prevent the passage of enemy vessels. Francisco de Miranda, *Diary of Francisco de Miranda: Tour of the United States, 1783–1784 (the Spanish Text)* (New York: Hispanic Society of America, 1928), 59.
28. Gutiérrez de Lara, Diary, 4E-9a; Gutiérrez de Lara, "Diary, I," 70.
29. Kasson, *Civilizing the Machine,* 33.
30. Gutiérrez de Lara, Diary, 4E-9a; Gutiérrez de Lara, "Diary, I," 70.
31. Real Academia Española, "Dicciónarios de la lengua española (1726–1992)" (http://www.rae.es/), June 21, 2008. The "arts" also had the same connotation in English during the early nineteenth century. Kasson, *Civilizing the Machine,* 146. See also Joan Corominas and José A. Pascual, *Diccionario crítico etimológico castellano e hispánico,* vol. 1 (Madrid: Gredos, 1980), 363, where it is defined as a set of rules for doing something well.
32. Here I draw on the philosophical account of the sublime as that which causes awe and terror simultaneously. See especially Frances Ferguson, *Solitude and the Sublime: Romanticism and the Aesthetics of Individuation* (New York: Routledge, 1992).
33. Joaquín Varela Suanzes-Carpegna, *La teoría del estado en los orígenes del constitucionalismo hispánico. Las Cortes de Cádiz* (Madrid: Centro de Estudios Constitucionales, 1983), 187–192; Annick Lempérière, "De la república corporativa a la nación moderna. México (1821–1860)," in *Inventando la nación: Iberoamérica, siglo XIX,* ed. Antonio Annino and François-Xavier Guerra (Mexico City: Fondo de Cultura Económica, 2003), 334.
34. Joyce Oldham Appleby, *Liberalism and Republicanism in the Historical Imagination* (Cambridge, MA: Harvard University Press, 1992); Gordon S. Wood, *The Creation of the American Republic, 1776–1787* (Chapel Hill: University of North Carolina Press, 1998), 606–615; Kasson, *Civilizing the Machine,* 36–42; J. G. A. Pocock, *The Machiavellian Moment: Florentine Political Thought*

and the Atlantic Republican Tradition (Princeton: Princeton University Press, 2003), 513–526.

35. Gutiérrez de Lara, Diary, 4E-9b; Gutiérrez de Lara, "Diary, I," 71; Kathryn Garrett, "The First Newspaper in Texas, *Gaceta de Texas,*" *Southwestern Historical Quarterly* 40, no. 3 (January 1937): 204.
36. Gutiérrez de Lara, Diary, 4E-10A; Gutiérrez de Lara, "Diary, I," 71.
37. François-Xavier Guerra, "El ocaso de la monarquía hispánica: revolución y desintegración," in *Inventando la nación: Iberoamérica, siglo XIX,* ed. Antonio Annino and François-Xavier Guerra (Mexico City: Fondo de Cultura Económica, 2003), 140–151; François-Xavier Guerra, "Las mutaciones de la identidad en la América Hispánica," in *Inventando la nación: Iberoamérica, siglo XIX,* ed. Antonio Annino and François-Xavier Guerra (Mexico City: Fondo de Cultura Económica, 2003), 185–220; Lempérière, "De la república a la nación"; Mónica Quijada, "¿Qué nación? Dinámicas y dicotomías de la nación en el imaginario hispanoamericano," in *Inventando la nación: Iberoamérica, siglo XIX,* ed. Antonio Annino and François-Xavier Guerra (Mexico City: Fondo de Cultura Económica, 2003), 287–315; Rafael Estrada Michel, *Monarquía y nación entre Cádiz y Nueva España: el problema de la articulación política de las Españas ante la revolución liberal y la emancipación americana* (Mexico City: Editorial Porrúa, 2006).
38. The first had been in 1792 when Secretary Thomas Jefferson recognized the French republic as a sovereign nation. William Spence Robertson, "The Recognition of the Hispanic American Nations by the United States," *Hispanic American Historical Review* 1, no. 3 (August 1918): 239. The second had been after 1804 when Haiti declared its independence. The United States would not recognize Haiti as independent until November 1864. Charles H. Wesley, "The Struggle for the Recognition of Haiti and Liberia as Independent Republics," *Journal of Negro History* 2, no. 4 (October 1917): 382.
39. On the rise of the Monroe Doctrine, see William Spence Robertson, *Hispanic American Relations with the United States* (New York: Oxford University Press, 1923); Jaime E. Rodríguez O. and Kathryn Vincent, *Common Border, Uncommon Paths: Race, Culture, and National Identity in U.S.-Mexican Relations* (Wilmington, DE: SR Books, 1997); Gretchen Murphy, *Hemispheric Imaginings: The Monroe Doctrine and Narratives of U.S. Empire* (Durham: Duke University Press, 2005).
40. Gutiérrez de Lara, Diary, 4E-12a; Gutiérrez de Lara, "Diary, I," 73.
41. Gutiérrez de Lara, Diary, 4E-21b; Gutiérrez de Lara, "Diary, II," 285.
42. Thomas Jefferson, too, was overwhelmed with what he saw upon his witnessing a new mill in 1787 England: "I could write you volumes on the improvements which I find made and making here in the arts." Jefferson cited in Kasson, *Civilizing the Machine,* 23. Gutiérrez de Lara, Diary, 4E-10a; Gutiérrez de Lara, "Diary, I," 71.
43. Gutiérrez de Lara, Diary, 4E-14b; Gutiérrez de Lara, "Diary, I," 76.
44. Gutiérrez de Lara, Diary, 4E-13a; Gutiérrez de Lara, "Diary, I," 74.
45. Mitchill enthusiastically had taken part in various scientific and scholarly exchanges throughout Spanish America, and advocated for the translation of

Spanish-language histories and natural histories of Latin America. Gutiérrez de Lara, Diary, 4E-14b; Gutiérrez de Lara, "Diary, I," 75–76; Harry Bernstein, *Making an Inter-American Mind* (Gainesville: University Press of Florida, 1961), 28–37, 74–79.

46. Gutiérrez de Lara, Diary, 4E-12a; Gutiérrez de Lara, "Diary, I," 73.
47. Gutiérrez de Lara, Diary, 4E-19B-20A; Gutiérrez de Lara, "Diary, II," 284.
48. Bernardo did, however, meet a Spaniard (an "Andalusian") somewhere in Virginia before arriving in Washington, D.C., who found it necessary to inform him that "the Creoles of the Kingdom of Mexico were a set of fools." Gutiérrez de Lara, Diary, 4E-8B; Gutiérrez de Lara, "Diary, I," 70.
49. Gutiérrez de Lara, Diary, 4E-11B; Gutiérrez de Lara, "Diary, I," 72.
50. Gutiérrez de Lara, Diary, 4E-15A, 15B; Gutiérrez de Lara, "Diary, I," 76.
51. Gutiérrez de Lara, Diary, 4E-13b, 14a, 15a; Gutiérrez de Lara, "Diary, I," 75–76.
52. Other sources reveal that Bernardo had continued to work with Toledo, and became acquainted with Ira Allen, a veteran of the American Revolution. Toledo wrote that he had 1,000 of his proclamations printed in Philadelphia, and that Bernardo was to disperse them throughout New Spain. Carlos Eduardo Castañeda, *Our Catholic Heritage in Texas, 1519–1936: Transition Period; the Fight for Freedom, 1810–1836,* vol. 6 (New York: Arno Press, 1950), 66–67. Yet Bernardo, as we will see, writes in his journal once he arrives at the Texas-Louisiana border that he had 1,000 proclamations printed in Natchitoches.
53. Gutiérrez de Lara, Diary, 4E-18A-19A; Gutiérrez de Lara, "Diary, II," 282.
54. Some of the earliest historians to cite Gutiérrez de Lara's voyage to the United States include Julio Zárate, ed., *México a través de los siglos: la guerra de independencia (1808–1821),* vol. 3 (Mexico City: Ballescá, 1887); Walter Flavius M'Caleb, "The First Period of the Gutierrez-Magee Expedition," *Southwestern Historical Quarterly* 4, no. 3 (1901): 218–231; West, "[Introduction to] Diary of Jose Bernardo Gutierrez de Lara, 1811–1812, I."; de la Garza, *Dos hermanos;* Garrett, *Green Flag;* Gabriel Saldívar, *El primer diputado tamaulipeco al Congreso general, don José Antonio Gutiérrez de Lara* (Mexico City: Boletín de la Sociedad Mexicana de Geografía y Estadística, 1943).
55. "theory, n.1," *OED Online* (http://dictionary.oed.com.proxy.uchicago.edu/cgi/entry/50250688), accessed April 6, 2008; "logos," *OED Online* (http://dictionary.oed.com.proxy.uchicago.edu/cgi/entry/50250688), accessed December 30, 2008.
56. By the 1820s, Niagara Falls had become one of the sublime objects of contemplation for American Romantic poets, north and south. See Kirsten Silva Gruesz, *Ambassadors of Culture: The Transamerican Origins of Latino Writing* (Princeton: Princeton University Press, 2002), 30–70.

3. Seeking the *Pueblo*'s Happiness

1. José Bernardo Gutiérrez de Lara, "Diary of José Bernardo Gutiérrez de Lara, 1811–1812, I," trans. Elizabeth Howard West, *American Historical Review* 34, no. 1 (October 1928): 70 n.51.

2. James Sterling Young, *The Washington Community, 1800–1828* (New York: Columbia University Press, 1966), 13–37; quotes are from Patricia L. Dooley, *The Early Republic: Primary Documents on Events from 1799 to 1820* (Westport, CT: Greenwood Press, 2004), 21.
3. James Robinson, *The Philadelphia directory for 1811* (Philadelphia: Wm. Woodhouse, 1811), viii; Edgar P. Richardson, "The Athens of America, 1800–1825," in *Philadelphia: A 300 Year History,* ed. Russell Frank Weigley et al. (New York: W.W. Norton, 1982), 208–223.
4. Cited in Richard A. Warren, "Displaced 'Pan-Americans' and the Transformation of the Catholic Church in Philadelphia, 1789–1850," *Pennsylvania Magazine of History and Biography* 128, no. 4 (2004): 344.
5. On Hispanopone publications in Philadelphia and the early United States, see Merle Edwin Simmons, "Spanish and Spanish American Writer Politicians in Philadelphia, 1790–1830," *Dieciocho* 3, no. 1 (1980): 27–39; Pedro Grases, "El círculo de Filadelfia," in *Obras de Pedro Grases: Preindependencia y emancipación. Protagonistas y testimonios,* vol. 3 (Barcelona: Seix Barral, 1981); Merle Edwin Simmons, *La revolución norteamericana en la independencia de hispanoamérica* (Madrid: Editorial MAPFRE, 1992); Anna Brickhouse, *Transamerican Literary Relations and the Nineteenth-Century Public Sphere* (New York: Cambridge University Press, 2004), 37–83; Debra A. Castillo, "Origins: Bird and *Jicoténcal,*" in *Redreaming America: Toward a Bilingual American Culture* (Albany: State University of New York Press, 2005), 15–53; Nicolás Kanellos, "José Alvarez de Toledo y Dubois and the Origins of Hispanic Publishing in the Early American Republic," *Early American Literature* 43, no. 1 (2008): 83–100; Rodrigo J. Lazo, "'La Famosa Filadelfia': the Hemispheric American City and Constitutional Debates," in *Hemispheric American Studies,* ed. Caroline F. Levander and Robert S. Levine (New Brunswick: Rutgers, 2008), 57–74; Nancy Vogeley, *The Bookrunner: A History of Early Inter-American Relations—Print, Politics, and Commerce in the United States and Mexico, 1800–1830* (Philadelphia: American Philosophical Society, 2011).
6. Hispanics used the term "modern" as a way to distinguish arguments that diverged from the Aristotelian method of Scholasticism. Pedro Álvarez de Miranda, *Palabras e ideas: El léxico de la ilustración temprana en España (1680–1760)* (Madrid: Real Academia Española, 1992), 644–649.
7. John Lynch, *Bourbon Spain, 1700–1808* (Cambridge, MA: Blackwell, 1989), 116–123; David J. Weber, *The Spanish Frontier in North America* (New Haven: Yale University, 1992), 172–203, 278–301; Henry Kamen, *Empire: How Spain Became a World Power, 1492–1763* (New York: Perennial, 2004), 466–485.
8. Gaspar Melchor de Jovellanos, *Biblioteca de autores españoles: Obras publicadas é inéditas,* vol. 2 (Madrid: Ribadeneyra, 1859), 38, emphasis added.
9. O. Carlos Stoetzer, *The Scholastic Roots of the Spanish American Revolution* (New York: Fordham University Press, 1979), 68; David A. Brading, *The First America: The Spanish Monarchy, Creole Patriots, and the Liberal State, 1492–1867* (New York: Cambridge University Press, 1991), 502–512.

10. Jean Sarrailh, *La España ilustrada de la segunda mitad del siglo XVIII,* trans. Antonio Alatorre (Mexico City: Fondo de Cultura Económica, 1957), 17–151; Richard Herr, *The Eighteenth-Century Revolution in Spain* (Princeton: Princeton University Press, 1958), 86–153; Robert Jones Shafer, *The Economic Societies in the Spanish World, 1763–1821* (Syracuse: Syracuse University Press, 1958), 3–23, 123–136; Lynch, *Bourbon Spain,* 196–246, quote is from p. 224; on conditions in America, 329–374; Immanuel M. Wallerstein, *The Modern World-System: Mercantilism and the Consolidation of the European World-Economy, 1600–1750* (Berkeley: University of California Press, 2011), 179–206.
11. Maravall invokes Karl Marx's *German Ideology* in claiming the historical emergence of the bourgeoisie in Spain: "first existed the bourgeois before the bourgeoisie." José Antonio Maravall, "Espíritu burgués y principio de interes personal en la Ilustracion española," in *Estudios de historia del pensamiento Español: Siglo XVIII* (Madrid: Centro de Estudios Políticos y Constitucionales, 1999), 351–356, quote from p. 356. See also José Antonio Maravall, "La formación de la conciencia estamental de los letrados," *Revista de estudios políticos,* no. 70 (1970): 53–82; Lynch, *Bourbon Spain,* 233–235; José Antonio Maravall, "Mentalidad burguesa e idea de la Historia en el siglo XVIII," in *Estudios de historia del pensamiento Español,* 163–197; José Antonio Maravall, "Las tendencias de reforma política en el siglo XVIII Español," in *Estudios de historia del pensamiento Español,* 93–96.
12. Peggy K. Liss, *Atlantic Empires: The Network of Trade and Revolution, 1713–1826* (Baltimore: Johns Hopkins University Press, 1983), 62–70, 127–154 172–192.
13. José Antonio Maravall, "La idea de la felicidad en el programa de la ilustración," in *Estudios de historia del pensamiento Español,* 231–268; Vivasvan Soni, *Mourning Happiness: Narrative and the Politics of Modernity* (Ithaca: Cornell University Press, 2010), 1–24.
14. Soni, *Mourning Happiness,* 424–431
15. Maravall, "Felicidad," 242.
16. María Carmen Iglesias, "Felicidad, política, y moral: Clásicos del siglo XVIII," *Boletín Informativo de la Fundación Juan March,* no. 172 (August–September 1987): 34–41; María Carmen Iglesias, "Política y virtud en el pensamiento político: Antecedentes de la filosofía política ilustrada," *Revista del Centro de Estudios Constitucionales,* no. 3 (May–August 1989), 115–142; Pedro Álvarez de Miranda, *Palabras e ideas: El léxico de la ilustración temprana en España (1680–1760)* (Madrid: Real Academia Española, 1992), 271–290; quote is from José Antonio Maravall, "El sentimiento de la nación en el siglo XVIII: La obra de Forner," in *Estudios de historia del pensamiento Español,* 69.
17. Maravall, "Felicidad," 240; quote is from Ludavico Antonio Muratori's "La pública felicidad, objecto de los buenos príncipes" (Madrid, 1790), 6.
18. Alessandro Roncaglia, *The Wealth of Ideas: A History of Economic Thought* (New York: Cambridge University Press, 2005), 18–52; quote is from p. 18.
19. Manuel Martín Rodríguez, "La institucionalización de los estudios de economía política en la universidad Española (1784–1857)," in *Elementos de*

economía política con aplicación particular a España (Madrid: Instituto de Estudios Fiscales, 1989), xi–lxxv; Vicent A. Llombart Rosa, "El pensamiento económico de la Ilustración en España (1730–1812)," in *Economía y economistas españoles: La ilustración,* ed. Enrique Fuentes Quintana, vol. 3 (Barcelona: Galaxia Gutenberg, 2000), 17–51. See also Gonzalo Anes Álvarez, *Economía e ilustración en la España del siglo XVIII* (Barcelona: Ediciones Ariel, 1969), and the magisterial nine-volume collection edited by Enrique Fuentes Quintana, *Economía y economistas españoles* (Barcelona: Galaxia Gutenberg, 1999–2004), especially vol. 2, *De los orígenes al mercantilismo* (1999), and vol. 3, *La ilustración* (1999). The collection traces the development of political economic thought from fourteenth-century Muslim Al-Andalus, mercantilism, through free trade, and includes the history of the academic discipline of political economy.

20. Brading, *First America,* 511; Rafael Anes Álvarez de Castrillón, "De las ideas de Jovellanos sobre la economía y la actividad económica," in *Economía y economistas españoles,* ed. Fuentes Quintana, 3:315–329; Vicent A. Llombart Rosa, "Campomanes, el economista de Carlos III," in Quintana, *Economía y economistas españoles,* 3:201–255.
21. Lynch, *Bourbon Spain,* 208–214.
22. Herr, *Eighteenth-Century Revolution,* 47–57; Shafer, *Economic Societies,* 3–23; Anes Álvarez, *Economía e ilustración,* 22–23; Stoetzer, *Scholastic,* 77.
23. Pedro Rodríguez de Campomanes, *Discurso sobre el fomento de la industria popular* (Madrid: en la Imprenta de D. Antonio de Sancha, 1774), 163.
24. Shafer, *Economic Societies,* 24–31; José Manuel Barrenechea, "Economistas vascos del siglo XVIII: Uztáriz, Uría Nafarrondo, Arriquíbar y Foronda," in *Historia del País Vasco, siglo XVIII,* ed. María Angeles Larrea et al. (Bilbao, Spain: Universidad de Deusto, 1985), 193–224; Salvador Almenar and Vicent A. Llombart Rosa, "Spanish Societies, Academies, and Economic Debating Societies," in *The Spread of Political Economy and the Professionalization of Economists: Economic Societies in Europe, America, and Japan in the Nineteenth Century,* ed. Massimo M. Augello and Marco E. L. Guidi (London: Routledge, 2001), 109–125; Gonzalo Anes Álvarez, "Los Amigos del País y las enseñanzas de economía," in *Homenaje a Pedro Saínz Rodríguez,* vol. 4 (Madrid: Fundación Universitaria Española, 1986), 451–460; Jesús Astigarraga, *Los ilustrados vascos: Ideas, instituciones y reformas económicas en España* (Barcelona: Crítica, 2003). These Economic Societies should not be confused with Masonic lodges or other secret societies. Richard Herr has attempted to put to rest the very old myth of freemasonry in eighteenth-century Spain. Herr argues that nineteenth-century historians, many of them freemasons, concocted histories where freemasons lurked everywhere in eighteenth-century Spain; yet when asked for evidence these historians would lament that the records had been destroyed or lost. Richard Herr, "The Twentieth Century Spaniard Views the Spanish Enlightenment," *Hispania* 45, no. 2 (1962): 183–193. Having conducted extensive archival research, Herr concludes that he simply has not seen "any indication of freemasonry in Spain before Napoleon's invasion in 1808 and feel[s] confident there was none." Sarrailh never mentions the

freemasons, and Shafer concludes that the "Societies were not a 'result' of masonic action." Herr, *Eighteenth-Century Revolution,* 326 n.42; Shafer, *Economic Societies,* 25–26. Virginia Guedea concurs, and says there were no Spanish-organized lodges in Spain until after 1814 and none in Mexico until around 1806. Virginia Guedea, "Las sociedades secretas durante el movimiento de independencia," in *The Independence of Mexico and the Creation of the New Nation,* ed. Jaime E. Rodríguez O. (Los Angeles and Irvine: UCLA Latin American Center Publications and UCI Mexico/Chicano Program, 1989), 46–48. Given the fascinating Servando-de-Mieresque "history" of freemasons (promulgated by both anti-mason Catholics and freemasons themselves), one might also want to call into question the history of freemason activity in Spanish America.

25. Shafer, *Economic Societies,* 68–73, 262–267; Anes Álvarez, *Economía e ilustración,* 22–26; Maravall, "Mentalidad burguesa," 169–170; José Luis Romero, *Latinoamérica: las ciudades y las ideas,* 2nd ed. (Buenos Aires: Siglo Veintiuno Editores, 2001), 159–172.

26. Sarrailh, *España,* 230–289; Herr, *Eighteenth-Century Revolution,* 154–163; Shafer, *Economic Societies,* 48–119, 253–344; Anes Álvarez, *Economía e ilustración,* 11–41; Vicent A. Llombart Rosa and Jesús Astigarraga Goenaga, "Las primeras 'antorchas de la economía': Las Sociedades Económicas de Amigos del País en el siglo XVIII," in *Economía y economistas españoles,* ed. Fuentes Quintana, 3:677–707. The late eighteenth-century flourishing of Spanish-American scientific expeditions must be seen as central to the diffusion of Hispanic Enlightenment thought. See Jorge Cañizares Esguerra, "La Ilustración hispanoamericana: una caracterización," in *Revolución, independencia y las nuevas naciones de América,* ed. Jaime E. Rodríguez O. (Madrid: Fundación MAPFRE Tavera, 2005), 87–98; Jorge Cañizares-Esguerra, *Nature, Empire, and Nation: Explorations of the History of Science in the Iberian World* (Stanford: Stanford University Press, 2006).

27. Herr, *Eighteenth-Century Revolution,* 183–200; Shafer, *Economic Societies,* 136–144; François-Xavier Guerra, *Modernidad e independencias. Ensayos sobre las revoluciones hispánicas* (Mexico City: Fondo de Cultura Económica and Editorial MAPFRE, 1992), 106–107.

28. For example, not one mention of the upheaval leading to and including the American Revolution could be found in the following: José Antonio de Alzate y Ramírez, ed., *Asuntos varios sobre ciencias y artes* (Mexico City: Imprenta de la Biblioteca Mexicana, 1772–1773); José Ignacio Bartolache, ed., *Mercurio Volante* (Mexico City: Felipe de Zúniga Ontiveros, 1772–1773); Manuel Antonio Valdés, ed., *Gazeta de México* (Mexico City: Por Don Felipe de Zúniga y Ontiveros, 1784–1809); José Antonio de Alzate y Ramírez, ed., *Gazeta de literatura de México* (Mexico City: Felipe de Zúniga y Ontiveros, 1788–1795).

29. Roncaglia, *Wealth of Ideas,* 43–44.

30. Adam Smith, *An Inquiry into the Nature and Causes of the Wealth of Nations,* 2 vols. (Indianapolis: Liberty Classics, 1981), 642–662; Manuel Martín Rodríguez, "Subdesarrollo y desarrollo económico en el mercantilismo español," in *Economía y economistas españoles: De los orígenes al mercantilismo,*

ed. Enrique Fuentes Quintana, vol. 2 (Barcelona: Galaxia Gutenberg, 1999), 359–402; Roncaglia, *Wealth of Ideas,* 41–46; Wallerstein, *Modern World-System,* 37–43.

31. Michel Foucault, *The Order of Things: An Archaeology of the Human Sciences* (New York: Vintage, 1994), 79.
32. Foucault, *Order of Things,* 169.
33. Smith, *Wealth of Nations,* 452–472, 642–662; Roncaglia, *Wealth of Ideas,* 115–154.
34. Maravall, "Espíritu burgués," 314.
35. This is indeed the association that Jesús Astigarraga finds. Late eighteenth-century Spaniards may have been fascinated with the modern discourse of political economy, but they quickly moved from questions of economy to the more specifically political questions of social contract, natural law, and political philosophy. Jesús 'Astigarraga, "*Iusnaturalismo* moderno de la mano de la economía política: Las "Apuntaciones al Genovesi' de Ramón de Salas," *Historia constitucional,* no. 9 (2008): 135–161.
36. Emma Rothschild, *Economic Sentiments: Adam Smith, Condorcet, and the Enlightenment* (Cambridge, MA: Harvard University Press, 2001), 27–28, 7–51. See also Susan Buck-Morss, "Envisioning Capital: Political Economy on Display," *Critical Inquiry* 21, no. 2 (1995): 434–467.
37. Jean-Jacques Rousseau, "Discourse on Political Economy," in *The Social Contract and Other Later Political Writings,* ed. Victor Gourevitch (New York: Cambridge University Press, 1997), 3, emphasis added.
38. Karl Polanyi, *The Great Transformation: The Political and Economic Origins of Our Time* (Boston: Beacon Press, 2001), 116–135.
39. Joyce Oldham Appleby, *Liberalism and Republicanism in the Historical Imagination* (Cambridge, MA: Harvard University Press, 1992), 23–28; Gordon S. Wood, *The Radicalism of the American Revolution* (New York: A. A. Knopf, 1992), 243–369; Eric J. Hobsbawm, *The Age of Revolution, 1789–1848* (New York: Vintage Books, 1996), 27–52, 234–264; Ranajit Guha, *Dominance without Hegemony: History and Power in Colonial India* (Cambridge, MA: Harvard University Press, 1997), 13–20; Michael Hardt and Antonio Negri, *Empire* (Cambridge, MA: Harvard University Press, 2000), 83–105; Polanyi, *The Great Transformation,* 136–170; T. H. Breen, *The Marketplace of Revolution: How Consumer Politics Shaped American Independence* (New York: Oxford University Press, 2004); Immanuel Maurice Wallerstein, *World-Systems Analysis: An Introduction* (Durham: Duke University Press, 2004), 23–59; Jeremy Adelman, *Sovereignty and Revolution in the Iberian Atlantic* (Princeton: Princeton University Press, 2006), 346–355.
40. John Rawls, *Political Liberalism,* expanded ed. (New York: Columbia University Press, 2005), 29–35; John Rawls, *A Theory of Justice,* 1st ed. (Cambridge, MA: Harvard University Press, 2005), 433–440, 513–520, 560–567.
41. J. B. Schneewind, *The Invention of Autonomy: A History of Modern Moral Philosophy* (New York: Cambridge University Press, 1998), 483–530; C. B. Macpherson, *The Political Theory of Possessive Individualism: Hobbes to Locke* (New York: Oxford University Press, 2011), 263–277.

42. John H. Elliott, *Empires of the Atlantic World: Britain and Spain in America, 1492–1830* (New Haven: Yale University Press, 2006), 335.
43. J. G. A. Pocock, *The Machiavellian Moment: Florentine Political Thought and the Atlantic Republican Tradition* (Princeton: Princeton University Press, 2003), 523.
44. The literature on liberalism is vastly complex. For a useful conceptual overview, see Alan Ryan, "Liberalism," in *A Companion to Contemporary Political Philosophy*, ed. Robert E. Goodin et al. (Malden, MA: Wiley-Blackwell, 2012), 360–382. On the relationship between personal interest, liberalism, and republicanism in the Anglophone world, see Isaac Kramnick, *Republicanism and Bourgeois Radicalism: Political Ideology in Late Eighteenth-Century England and America* (Ithaca: Cornell University Press, 1990); Gillian Brown, *The Consent of the Governed: The Lockean Legacy in Early American Culture* (Cambridge, MA: Harvard University Press, 2001).
45. Maravall cites "Aranguren," but fails to provide further bibliographical information on the source. Maravall, "Tendencias," 95.
46. Marcel Gauchet, *The Disenchantment of the World: A Political History of Religion* (Princeton: Princeton University Press, 1997), 64–66; Charles Taylor, *A Secular Age* (Cambridge, MA: Harvard University Press, 2007), 90–145.
47. Max Weber, *The Protestant Ethic and the Spirit of Capitalism*, trans. Talcott Parsons (New York: Routledge, 1992; orig. 1930), 104.
48. Maravall, "Tendencias," 95–97; Maravall, "Felicidad," 241–243.
49. Lynch, *Bourbon Spain*, 350–366, quote is from p. 352; Stanley J. Stein and Barbara H. Stein, *Apogee of Empire: Spain and New Spain in the Age of Charles III, 1759–1789* (Baltimore: Johns Hopkins University Press, 2003), 223–266; Graciela Márquez, "Commercial Monopolies and External Trade," in *The Cambridge Economic History of Latin America: The Colonial Era and the Short Nineteenth Century*, ed. Victor Bulmer-Thomas et al., vol. 1 (New York: Cambridge University Press, 2006), 395–422; Barbara H. Stein and Stanley J. Stein, *Edge of Crisis: War and Trade in the Spanish Atlantic, 1789–1808* (Baltimore: Johns Hopkins University Press, 2009), 250–260.
50. Herr, *Eighteenth-Century Revolution*, 239–268; Shafer, *Economic Societies*, 22, 57–59; Iris M. Zavala, "Picornell y la Revolución de San Blas: 1795," in *El texto en la historia* (Madrid: Nuestra Cultura, 1981), 202–203; Lynch, *Bourbon Spain*, 375–421.
51. Light Townsend Cummins, *Spanish Observers and the American Revolution, 1775–1783* (Baton Rouge: Louisiana State University Press, 1991), 99–167; Vicente Ribes Iborra, *Don Juan de Miralles y la independencia de los Estados Unidos* (Valencia, Spain: Generalitat Valenciana, 2003), 19–85. As early as the mid-eighteenth century, however, Sephardic Jewish communities could be found in Charleston, South Carolina, and New Amsterdam. The Sephardim (from the Hebrew word for Spain) are descendants of Jews who were expelled from Spain, along with the Moors, in 1492. A community of Sephardim from London immigrated to Charleston in 1748. They appear to have been descendants of Jews expelled from Spain and Portugal. Barnett A. Elzas, *The Jews of*

South Carolina, from the Earliest Times to the Present Day (Philadelphia: J. B. Lippincott Company, 1905), 30–35.

52. "Spain, along with its traditional ally France, was intermittently at war with Great Britain for almost a century [1689–1763], during which it fought the British in four major international conflicts." The final conflict, the Seven Years' War (also known as the French-Indian War in the United States), concluded in 1763 with a "resounding humiliation for France and Spain," in which Spain was forced to cede Florida to Britain. Cummins, *Spanish Observers,* ix–x.
53. Enrique Fernández, "Spain's Contribution to the Independence of the United States," *Revista/Review Interamericana* 10, no. 3 (Fall 1981); Weber, *Spanish Frontier,* 265–266; Thomas E. Chavez, *Spain and the Independence of the United States: An Intrinsic Gift* (Albuquerque: University of New Mexico Press, 2004), 70–88, 105–106.
54. Cummins, *Spanish Observers,* 105–109, 116–137; quote is from pp. 105–106.
55. Stein and Stein, *Edge of Crisis,* 16.
56. Enrique Fernández y Fernández, "Esbozo biográfico de un ministro ilustrado, Diego de Gardoqui y Arriquibar (1735–1798)," *Hispania (Madrid)* 49, no. 172 (1989): 290–304; Reyes Calderón Cuadrado, *Empresarios españoles en el proceso de independencia norteamericana: La Casa Gardoqui e Hijos de Bilbao* (Madrid: Instituto de Investigaciones Económicas y Sociales "Francisco de Vitoria," 2004), 188–304; Chavez, *Spain and the U.S.,* 15, 61–68.
57. Samuel Flagg Bemis, *Pinckney's Treaty: America's Advantage from Europe's Distress, 1783–1800* (New Haven: Yale University Press, 1960); Griffin, *Disruption,* 18–20; José A. Armillas Vicente, "El Mississippi, frontera de España: España y los Estados Unidos ante el tratado de San Lorenzo" (PhD thesis, Institución Fernando El Católico, Zaragoza, Spain, 1977).
58. Miguel Gómez del Campillos, ed., *Relaciones diplomáticas entre España y los Estados Unidos según los documentos del Archivo Histórico Nacional,* vol. 1 (Madrid: Consejo Superior de Investigaciones Científicas, Instituto Gonzalo Fernández de Oviedo, 1944), 223; Eric Beerman, "Spanish Envoy to the United States (1796–1809): Marques de Casa Irujo and His Philadelphia Wife Sally McKean," *The Americas* 37, no. 4 (April 1981): 447.
59. The *Diccionario de la lengua española de la Real Academia Española* first includes "diplomático" in the 1791 edition. While the *OED* cites 1813 as the first entry for "diplomat," it does note that its cognate, "diplomatic," developed during the French Revolution. Real Academia Española, "Dicciónarios de la lengua española (1726–1992)"; "diplomatic, adj. and n.," *OED Online* (http://www.oed.com/view/Entry/53206), accessed July 20, 2012.
60. Linda Salvucci, "Development and Decline: The Port of Philadelphia and Spanish Imperial Markets, 1783–1823" (PhD dissertation, Princeton University, 1985); Cummins, *Spanish Observers,* 125–131; Linda Salvucci, "Supply, Demand, and the Making of a Market: Philadelphia and Havana at the Beginning of the Nineteenth Century," in Franklin W. Knight and Peggy K. Liss, eds., *Atlantic Port Cities: Economy, Culture, and Society in the Atlantic World,*

1650–1850 (Knoxville: University of Tennessee, 1991), 40–56; Linda Salvucci, "Merchants and Diplomats: Philadelphia's Early Trade with Cuba," *Pennsylvania Legacies* 3, no. 2 (November 2003): 6–10; Calderón Cuadrado, *Empresarios.*

61. Sandra Sealove, "The Founding Fathers as Seen by the Marqués de Casa-Irujo," *The Americas* 20, no. 1 (1963): 37–42; Beerman, "Spanish Envoy"; José A. Armillas Vicente, "Carlos Martínez de Irujo. Apunte biográfico de un embajador de Carlos IV," in *Estudios de historia moderna y contemporánea: homenaje a Federico Suárez Verdeguer,* ed. Federico Suárez (Madrid, Spain: Ediciones Rialp, 1991), 51–60.

62. Carlos Martínez de Irujo, *Letters of Verus, addressed to the Native American* (Philadelphia: Benjamin Franklin, 1797); "Appendix: Latin American and Iberian Corresponding and Honorary Members of North American Learned Societies," in Bernstein, *Inter-American Mind,* 178–186.

63. Robert Sidney Smith, "*The Wealth of Nations* in Spain and Hispanic America, 1780–1830," *Journal of Political Economy* 65, no. 2 (1957): 108.

64. Carlos Martínez de Irujo, *Compendio de la obra inglesa intitulada Riqueza de las Naciones, hecho por el Marques de Condorcet y traducido al castellano con varias adicciones del original* (Madrid, Spain: La Imprenta Real, 1792), iv–v. By "Empire's mistake" Casa Irujo is referring to Spain's mercantile system.

65. Jefferson Rea Spell, *Rousseau in the Spanish World before 1833: A Study in Franco-Spanish Literary Relations* (New York: Octagon Books, 1969), 40.

66. Smith, "*The Wealth of Nations* in Spain," 105; Herr, *Eighteenth-Century Revolution,* 69–85, quote from p. 77; Gabriel Bonno, "The Diffusion and Influence of Locke's *Essay concerning Human Understanding* in France before Voltaire's *Lettres Philosophiques,*" *Proceedings of the American Philosophical Society* 91, no. 5 (1947): 421; Gabriel Bonno, "La culture et la civilisation britanniques devant l'opinion française de la Paix d'Utrecht aux Lettres philosophiques (1713–1734)," *Transactions of the American Philosophical Society* 38, New Series, no. 1 (1948): 4–5. At the turn of the eighteenth century in France, for example, French instructors made sure their pupils studied Italian, German, and Spanish; English was not mentioned as worthy of study and would not be recommended until 1732. Indeed, while Spanish and Italian grammars proliferated in the first half of eighteenth-century France, not one English grammar was published. Bonno, "Culture," 5–6. However, the 1713 War of Spanish Succession (which secured the Spanish crown for the Bourbons) had not only altered the international political state of affairs but also produced a cultural rift, one where English culture—and the English language—would rise in status as the century unfolded. The 1713 Treaty of Utrecht, write the historians Stanley and Barbara Stein, "spelled out what would become, in the long run, subordination of imperial Spain to English naval and economic hegemony." Liss, *Atlantic Empires,* 1–25; Stanley J. Stein and Barbara H. Stein, *Silver, Trade, and War: Spain and America in the Making of Early Modern Europe* (Baltimore: Johns Hopkins University Press, 2000), 136–144, quote from p. 137.

67. "In France [Pierre] Coste's translation [of the *Essay*] was circulated by Locke himself among his French friends . . . to whom he sent copies of the book, fresh from the press, with a pressing appeal for their comments." Bonno, "Diffusion," 421–422; Bonno, "Culture," 80–96; Herr, *Eighteenth-Century Revolution,* 41–85.
68. Vicent A. Llombart Rosa, "Traducciones españolas de economía política (1700–1812): catálogo bibliográfico y una nueva perspectiva," *Cromohs* 9 (2004): 1–14.
69. Spell, *Rousseau,* 282; John C. Attig, "Appendix: Language Index to Translations of Locke's Works," *John Locke Bibliography* (http://www.libraries.psu.edu/tas/locke/bib/lang.html), accessed January 28, 2010. The influence of Locke and Rousseau has been highly debated. See Luis Rodríguez Aranda, "La recepción e influjo de la filosofía de Locke en España," *Revista de filosofía* 14 (1955): 359–381; Joaquín Varela Suanzes-Carpegna, *La teoría del estado en los orígenes del constitucionalismo hispánico. Las Cortes de Cádiz* (Madrid: Centro de Estudios Constitucionales, 1983), 55 n.162; Miguel Molina Martínez, "Pactismo e independencia en Iberoamérica, 1808–1811," *Revista de estudios colombinos,* no. 4 (2008): 61–74.
70. Herr, *Eighteenth-Century Revolution,* 69–70.
71. Attig, "Appendix: Language Index to Translations of Locke's Works." Pedro Grases, however, notes that Andrés Bello or his brother may have translated this text before 1810, though it apparently was never published and no copy has been found. Pedro Grases, "Traducciones de interés politico-cultural en la época de la independencia de Venezuela," in *Escritos Selectos* (Caracas, Venezuela: Biblioteca Ayacucho, 1989), 112.
72. Cotton Mather's *La fe del christiano* (1699) is the first, and Santiago F. Puglia's *El desengaño del hombre* (1794), as we will see later, is the second.
73. Anonymous, *Reflexiones sobre el comercio de España con sus colonias en America, en tiempo de guerra. Por un Español, en Philadelphia* (Philadelphia: James Carey, 1799), 12, 36, 57, 77–78, 82, 87; Anonymous, *Observations on the commerce of Spain with her colonies, in time of war* (Philadelphia: James Carey, 1800), viii, 25, 39, 55, 58, 62; Spanish then English editions hereafter cited in text; Anonymous, "Review. *Observations on the Commerce of Spain with her Colonies,*" *Monthly Magazine and American Review* 3, no. 2 (August 1800): 137; attribution to Foronda by Stein and Stein, *Edge of Crisis,* 240, and Robert Sidney Smith, "Valentín de Foronda: Diplómatico y Economista," *Revista de Economía Política* 10 (1959): 427; attribution to Torres by Charles H. Bowman Jr., "Manuel Torres, a Spanish-American Patriot in Philadelphia, 1796–1822," *Pennsylvania Magazine of History and Biography* 94 (1970): 29; attribution to Casa Irujo by Simmons, "Hispanic Writers in Philadelphia," 28.
74. Smith, "Foronda," 429.
75. Aurelio Báig Baños, "¿Qué se requirió para ser don Valentín de Foronda Caballero de la Orden de Carlos III?," *Revista de Archivos, Bibliotecas, y Museos* Tercera Época, Año 31, no. 10–12 (October–December 1928): 393–420; Jefferson Rea Spell, "An Illustrious Spaniard in Philadelphia, Valentín de

Foronda," *Hispanic Review* 4, no. 2 (April 1936): 136–140; José de Onís, "Valentin de Foronda's Memoir on the United States of North America, 1804," *The Americas* 4, no. 3 (1948): 353; Smith, "Foronda," 425–443; José Manuel Barrenechea, *Valentín de Foronda: reformador y economista ilustrado* (Vitoria, Spain: Diputación Foral de Alava, Departamento de Publicaciones, 1984); Manuel Benavides, *Valentín de Foronda, los sueños de la razón* (Madrid: Editora Nacional, 1984); José Manuel Barrenechea González, "Valentín de Foronda y el pensamiento económico ilustrado," in *Economía y economistas españoles,* ed. Fuentes Quintana, 3:529–567. For a recent collection of Foronda's writings, see Ignacio Fernández Sarasola, *Escritos políticos y constitucionales: Valentín de Foronda* (Bilbao, Spain: Servicio Editorial de la Universidad del País Vasco, 2002).

76. Thomas Jefferson, "Letters from Jefferson to Foronda (1807–1814)," in *The Writings of Thomas Jefferson,* ed. Andrew A. Lipscomb and Albert Ellery Bergh, vols. 11, 12, 14 (Washington, DC: Thomas Jefferson Memorial Association, 1905), 11:326–327; 12:318–321; 14:30–33; Onís, "Foronda's Memoir," 358.
77. Valentín de Foronda, "Apuntes ligeros sobre los Estados Unidos de la America Septentrional (1804)," *The Americas* 4, no. 3 (1948): 380. On Foronda's frustration with the United States, see E. Wilson Lyon, "The Closing of the Port of New Orleans," *American Historical Review* 37, no. 2 (1932): 280–281; Onís, "Foronda's Memoir," 355–356; Smith, "Foronda," 430.
78. Valentín de Foronda, *Cartas sobre los asuntos más exquisitos de la economía-política, y sobre las leyes criminales* (Madrid: Imprenta de M. Gonzalez, 1789), vi–vii.
79. Cited in Smith, "Foronda," 427 n.8.
80. Valentín de Foronda, *Cartas sobre la obra de Rousseau titulada: Contrato social en las que se vacía todo lo interesante de ella, y se suprime lo que puede herir la religion católica apostólica romana* (Coruña, Spain: Oficina de Don Antonio Rodriguez, 1814).
81. In Foronda, one finds the traces of an alternate idiom of natural rights philosophy, one that synthesizes Catholic political philosophy with British, French, Italian, and, to a lesser degree, Anglo-American political thought. Valentín de Foronda, *Carta sobre el modo que tal vez convendría a las Cortes seguir en el examen de los objetos que conducen a su fin, y dictamen sobre ellos* (Cádiz, Spain: Imprenta de Manuel Ximenez, 1811). See also Fernández Sarasola, *Foronda,* 21–22, 33.
82. Valentín de Foronda, *Carta sobre lo que debe hacer un príncipe que tenga colonias a gran distancia* (Philadelphia: American Philosophical Society, 1803), 3.
83. Ibid., 9.
84. Ibid., 15.
85. Otis H. Green, *Spain and the Western Tradition: The Castilian Mind in Literature from El Cid to Calderón,* vol. 4 (Madison: University of Wisconsin Press, 1966), 19–76; Stein and Stein, *Apogee of Empire,* 338–350.
86. José Antonio Maravall, *Estado moderno y mentalidad social (siglos XV a XVII),* vol. 1 (Madrid: Revista de Occidente, 1972), 467–492; Varela

Suanzes-Carpegna, *Teoría del estado,* 59–74; François-Xavier Guerra, "Las mutaciones de la identidad en la América Hispánica," in *Inventando la nación: Iberoamérica, siglo XIX,* ed. Antonio Annino and François-Xavier Guerra (Mexico City: Fondo de Cultura Económica, 2003), 204–206; Mónica Quijada, "¿Qué nación? Dinámicas y dicotomías de la nación en el imaginario hispanoamericano," in *Inventando la nación,* ed. Annino and Guerra, 295–301; José Carlos Chiaramonte, *Nación y estado en Iberoamérica: el lenguaje político en tiempos de las independencias* (Buenos Aires: Sudamericana, 2004), 27–57.

87. Taylor, *Secular Age,* 180.
88. François-Xavier Guerra, "De la política antigua a la política moderna. La revolución de la soberanía," in *Los espacios públicos en Iberoamérica: Ambigüedades y problemas, siglos XVIII–XIX,* ed. François-Xavier Guerra (Mexico City: Fondo de Cultura Económica, 1998), 120.
89. Iglesias, "Política y virtud en el pensamiento político," 131 n.40, emphasis added.

4. From Reform to Revolution

1. David A. Brading, *The First America: The Spanish Monarchy, Creole Patriots, and the Liberal State, 1492–1867* (New York: Cambridge University Press, 1991), 535–560; Barbara H. Stein and Stanley J. Stein, *Edge of Crisis: War and Trade in the Spanish Atlantic, 1789–1808* (Baltimore: Johns Hopkins University Press, 2009), 200–258.
2. Numerous examples exist, such as the attempt to establish a black monarchy in New Granada in 1555 and again in 1711; the Pueblo Indian revolt of 1630 which effectively ended Spanish rule in New Mexico for twelve years; and the creation of autonomous communities, such as the creation of the Cimarron community in Panama by former slaves in the sixteenth century. See, for example, David J. Weber, *Bárbaros: Spaniards and Their Savages in the Age of Enlightenment* (New Haven: Yale University Press, 2005); Jane Landers and Barry Robinson, eds., *Slaves, Subjects, and Subversives: Blacks in Colonial Latin America* (Albuquerque: University of New Mexico Press, 2006). For primary sources see Miguel León Portilla and Earl Shorris, eds., *In the Language of Kings: An Anthology of Mesoamerican Literature, Pre-Columbian to the Present* (New York: Norton, 2001); Kathryn Joy McKnight and Leo Garofalo, eds., *Afro-Latino Voices: Narratives from the Early Modern Ibero-Atlantic World, 1550–1812* (Indianapolis: Hackett, 2009).
3. As early as the 1730s, however, creole Spanish Americans had led several uprisings against mercantile restrictions. Peggy K. Liss, *Atlantic Empires: The Network of Trade and Revolution, 1713–1826* (Baltimore: Johns Hopkins University, 1983), 147–171. For a cogent review of studies on these rebellions, see Victor M. Uribe-Urán, "The Birth of a Public Sphere in Latin America During the Age of Revolution," *Comparative Studies in Society and History* 42, no. 2 (April 2000): 428–436. For a comparative perspective of rebellion in the Spanish and British Americas, see John H. Elliott, *Empires of the Atlantic*

World: Britain and Spain in America, 1492–1830 (New Haven: Yale University Press, 2006), 325–368.

4. Virginia Guedea, "Las sociedades secretas durante el movimiento de independencia," in *The Independence of Mexico and the Creation of the New Nation,* ed. Jaime E. Rodríguez O. (Los Angeles and Irvine: UCLA Latin American Center Publications and UCI Mexico/Chicano Program, 1989), 46.
5. Robert Jones Shafer, *The Economic Societies in the Spanish World, 1763–1821* (Syracuse: Syracuse University Press, 1958), quote is from 263; Guedea, "Las sociedades secretas," 45–62; Virginia Guedea, *En busca de un gobierno alterno. Los Guadalupes de México* (Mexico City: Universidad Nacional Autónoma de México, 1992); François-Xavier Guerra, *Modernidad e independencias. Ensayos sobre las revoluciones hispánicas* (Mexico City: Fondo de Cultura Económica and Editorial MAPFRE, 1992), 92–102; François-Xavier Guerra and Annick Lempériere, "Introducción," in *Los espacios públicos en Iberoamérica: Ambigüedades y problemas, siglos XVIII–XIX* (Mexico City: Centro Francés de Estudios Mexicanos y Centroamericanos and Fondo de Cultura Ecónomica, 1998), 5–21; Carole Leal Curiel, "Tertulia de dos ciudades: modernismo tardío y formas de sociabilidad política en la provincia de Venezuela," in *Los espacios públicos en Iberoamérica: Ambigüedades y problemas, siglos XVIII–XIX,* ed. François-Xavier Guerra and Annick Lempériere (Mexico City: Fondo de Cultura Económica, 1998), 168–195; Rénan Silva, "Prácticas de lectura, ámbitos privados y formación de un espacio público moderno. Nueva Granada a finales del Antiguo Régimen," in *Los espacios públicos en Iberoamérica: Ambigüedades y problemas, siglos XVIII–XIX,* ed. François-Xavier Guerra and Annick Lempériere (Mexico City: Fondo de Cultura Económica, 1998), 80–106; Uribe-Urán, "Public Sphere," 438–440.
6. Carlos Newland, "La educación elemental en Hispanoamérica: Desde la independencia hasta la centralización de los sistemas educativos nacionales," *Hispanic American Historical Review* 71, no. 2 (1991): 357; Guerra, *Modernidad,* 106–108; Uribe-Urán, "Public Sphere," 440–443; Carmen Castañeda, "Periódicos en la ciudad de México: Siglo XVIII," in *Historia de la literatura mexicana: Cambios de reglas, mentalidades y recursos retóricos en la Nueva España del siglo XVIII,* ed. Nancy Vogeley and Manuel Ramos Medina, vol. 3 (Mexico City: Siglo XXI and Universidad Nacional Autónoma de México, 2011), 128–149.
7. Gabriel Torres Puga, "Inquisición y literatura clandestina en el siglo XVIII," in Vogeley and Ramos Medina, *Historia de la literatura mexicana,* 3:167.
8. Casa Irujo cited in Harris Gaylord Warren, "The Early Revolutionary Career of Juan Mariano Picornell," *Hispanic American Historical Review* 22, no. 1 (1942): 61. Though overstretching the case, Peggy K. Liss provides evidence that news regarding the American and French Revolutions did circulate in Spanish America. Liss, *Atlantic Empires,* 130–131. For the 1830s complaint on lack of information on the United States, see the Mexican ambassador to the United States, José María Tornel, *Manifestación del C. José María Tornel* (Mexico City: A. Valdés, 1833), 42. On Spain's fear see Thomas E. Chavez, *Spain and*

the Independence of the United States: An Intrinsic Gift (Albuquerque: University of New Mexico Press, 2004), 133.

9. Valentín de Foronda, *Cartas para los amigos y enemigos de Don Valentín de Foronda, encargado de negocios y consul general de S.M.C. Fernando VII, cerca de los Estados Unidos de la América septentrional, relatívas à lo acontecido en España, con el motivo de haber nombrado el Emperador Napoleon I a su Hermano Joseph, rey de las Españas e Yndias,* 3rd ed. (Philadelphia: Thomas y Jorge Palmer, 1809), 14.
10. Rodrigo J. Lazo, "'La Famosa Filadelfia': the Hemispheric American City and Constitutional Debates," in *Hemispheric American Studies,* ed. Caroline F. Levander and Robert S. Levine (New Brunswick: Rutgers, 2008), 57–59; Nancy Vogeley, *The Bookrunner: A History of Early Inter-American Relations—Print, Politics, and Commerce in the United States and Mexico, 1800–1830* (Philadelphia: American Philosophical Society, 2011), 83–87.
11. In 1699, after apparently "learning" Spanish in an incredulous three weeks (more than likely merely relying on a bilingual dictionary), Cotton Mather published *La fe del christiano* (Boston: B. Green and J. Allen, 1699). His pamphlet was meant to aid in the conversion of Spanish-American Catholics to Protestantism. For an English translation and a brief, useful introduction, see Thomas E. Johnston, "A Translation of Cotton Mather's Spanish Works: La Fe del Christiano and La Religion Pura," *Early American Literature Newsletter* 2, no. 2 (1967): 7–21. A well-known polyglot, Mather would publish a similar pamphlet in French in 1704. Cotton Mather, *Le vrai patron des saines paroles* (Boston: Timothy Green, 1704). See also Howard C. Rice, "Cotton Mather Speaks to France: American Propaganda in the Age of Louis XIV," *New England Quarterly* 16, no. 2 (1943): 198–233.
12. On clandestine literature in eighteenth-century New Spain, see Torres Puga, "Inquisición y literatura clandestina." For a useful comparison see Robert Darnton, *The Literary Underground of the Old Regime* (Cambridge, MA: Harvard University Press, 1982).
13. Mauro Paez-Pumar, *Las proclamas de Filadelfia de 1774 y 1775 en la Caracas de 1777* (Caracas: Centro Venezolano Americano, 1973), 9–11, 20–22.
14. David J. Weber, *The Spanish Frontier in North America* (New Haven: Yale University Press, 1992), 266–267.
15. The ship's captain decided to bypass Charleston, much to Miranda's frustration. Karen Racine, *Francisco de Miranda: a Transatlantic Life in the Age of Revolution* (Wilmington, DE: SR Books, 2003), 7–29. Racine cites Bolívar on p. 27.
16. Francisco de Miranda, *Diary of Francisco de Miranda: Tour of the United States, 1783–1784 (the Spanish Text)* (New York: Hispanic Society of America, 1928), 78, 95, 118; Racine, *Miranda,* 31–64. See also William Spence Robertson, "Francisco de Miranda and the Revolutionizing of Spanish America," in *Annual Report of the American Historical Association,* ed. American Historical Association, vol. 1 (Washington, DC: Government Printing Office, 1908), 189–539; Carmen L. Bohórquez M., *Francisco de Miranda: precursor*

de las independencias de la América Latina (Caracas: Universidad Católica Andrés Bello, 2001).

17. Padrón's testimony is found in Spanish Cortes, *Discusión del proyecto de decreto sobre el tribunal de la Inquisición* (Cádiz, Spain: Imprenta Nacional, 1813), 328–373. See also José Trujillo Cabrera, *Mi Don Antonio José Ruiz de Padrón* (Santa Cruz de Tenerife, Canary Islands: Goya Artes Gráficas, 1971), 35–47; José I. Alguerό Cuervo, "Antonio José Ruiz de Padrón: sacerdote, diputado, ilustrado, y liberal," *Espacio, tiempo y forma,* series 5, vol. 3 (1990): 51–64.
18. Thomas Blossom, *Nariño, Hero of Colombian Independence* (Tucson: University of Arizona Press, 1967); Eduardo Ruiz Martínez, *La librería de Nariño y los derechos del hombre* (Bogotá, Colombia: Planeta, 1990).
19. Lucía Fox, "Dos precursores de la independencia hispanoamericano y sus obras editadas en Filadelfia entre 1794 y 1799," *Inter-American Review of Bibliography* 19 (1969): 407–414; Lucía Fox, "Un documento ignorado en el movimiento de emancipación americana," *Razón y fábula,* no. 31 (Jan–Mar 1973): 13–32; Merle Edwin Simmons, *La revolución norteamericana en la independencia de hispanoamérica* (Madrid: Editorial MAPFRE, 1992), 73.
20. Santiago Felipe Puglia, *El desengaño del hombre* (Philadelphia: En la imprenta de Francisco Bailey, calle alta no. 116, 1794), x–xi; Merle Edwin Simmons, *Santiago F. Puglia, an early Philadelphia propagandist for Spanish American independence* (Chapel Hill: University of North Carolina Press, 1977), 13–15. The third known publication is Casa Irujo's anonymously published *Reflexiones sobre el comercio de España con sus colonias en America, en tiempo de guerra. Por un Español, en Philadelphia* (Philadelphia: James Carey, 1799).
21. Merle E. Simmons is the only scholar to have studied Puglia's writings in any detail. Simmons, *Puglia,* 13–24, 41–48; Merle Edwin Simmons, "Santiago F. Puglia de Filadelfia (y de Caracas)," *Montalbán,* no. 19 (1987): 205–255; Simmons, *Revolución,* 72–79. Simmons was unable to discover much detail about Puglia's life. Puglia continued to publish in English and Spanish and worked as a teacher of Spanish and other languages. In 1822 he translated Thomas Paine's *Rights of Man* into Spanish. But in 1831, at the age of seventy-one, Puglia committed suicide in Charleston. Simmons, *Puglia,* 69.
22. Simmons, *Puglia,* 45–46.
23. Iris M. Zavala, "Picornell y la Revolución de San Blas: 1795," in *El texto en la historia* (Madrid: Nuestra Cultura, 1981), 212–219; quote is on p. 219. Zavala has produced one of the most thorough studies on the San Blas revolutionary plot, based on over 20,000 pages of archival material.
24. One wonders, however, about Picornell's activities in the Basque Economic Society. He became a member in 1787, precisely during the period that Foronda was a professor at the seminary sponsored by the Basque Economic Society. Surely they must have crossed paths, though historians have not suggested so. Mariano Tirado y Rojas, *La masonería en España. Ensayo histórico,* vol. 1 (Madrid: E. Maroto, 1892), 289; Warren, "Early Revolutionary," 59, 61; Richard Herr, *The Eighteenth-Century Revolution in Spain* (Princeton: Princeton University Press, 1958), 325–327. Warren follows Tirado y Rojas in ascribing

the plot to freemasons, but Richard Herr disputes the possibility of freemasons existing in Spain prior to 1808. Herr, *Eighteenth-Century Revolution,* 326 n.42. To Herr's credit, the literary historian Iris M. Zavala found copies of the original San Blas conspiracy archive, and she never mentions freemason activity. On Picornell's intellectual influences and activities, see also Casto Fulgencio López, *Juan Picornell y la conspiración de Gual y España,* 2nd ed. (Caracas: Academia Nacional de la Historia, 1997); María Jesus Aguirrezábal, "La conspiración de Picornell (1795) en el contexto de la prerrevolución liberal Española," *Revista de Historia Contemporánea,* no. 1 (1982): 7–38; María Luisa Alares Dompnier, "Un ilustrado liberal en la América de la emancipación," *Studi di Letteratura ispano-Americana* (1983): 109–124.

25. Warren, "Early Revolutionary," 62; Zavala, "Picornell," 216, 233.
26. Warren, "Early Revolutionary," 67.
27. Ibid., 72–73; Pedro Grases, *Derechos del hombre y del ciudadano. Estudio histórico-crítico sobre los Derechos del Hombre y del Ciudadano* (Caracas, Venezuela: Academia Nacional de la Historia, 1959), 105–121, 150–161; Zavala, "Picornell," 240–243. Juan Bautista Mariano Picornell y Gomila, *Derechos del hombre y del ciudadano, con varias máximas republicanas y un discurso preliminar dirigido a los americanos* (Guadeloupe: En la imprenta de la Verdad, 1797). *Derechos* is reprinted in Grases, *Derechos del hombre y del ciudadano.*
28. Zavala, "Picornell," 241 n.51.
29. Very little is known of Picornell's activities in the United States, though surely some trace may still be found buried in the archive. Harris Gaylord Warren, "The Southern Career of Don Juan Mariano Picornell," *Journal of Southern History* 8, no. 3 (1942): 311–333.
30. Charles W. Bowman Jr. has provided the most comprehensive biography of Torres, though he, at times, appears to be too liberal in interpreting his sources. William Duane, "Death of Mr. Torres," *Niles' Weekly Register,* July 27, 1822; Enrique Olaya and W. Freeland Kendrick, "In Honor of the Patriot Don Manuel Torres," *Bulletin of the Pan-American Union* 60, no. 10 (1926): 951–957; Nicolás García Samudio, "La misión de Don Manuel Torres en Washington y los orígenes suramericanos de la doctrina Monroe," *Boletín de historia y antiguëdades* 28 (1941): 474–484; Guillermo Hernández de Alba, "Origen de la Doctrina Panamericana de la Confederacion: Don Manuel Torres, precursor del panamericanismo," *Revista de Historia de América,* no. 22 (1946): 367–398; José de Onis, *The United States as Seen by Spanish-American Writers, 1776–1890* (New York: Hispanic Institute, 1952), 34–35; Charles H. Bowman Jr., "The Activities of Manuel Torres as Purchasing Agent, 1820–1821," *Hispanic American Historical Review* 48, no. 2 (1968): 234–246; Charles H. Bowman Jr., "Manuel Torres in Philadelphia and the Recognition of Colombian Independence, 1821–22," *American Catholic Historical Society* 80 (1969): 17–38; Charles H. Bowman Jr., "Manuel Torres, a Spanish-American Patriot in Philadelphia, 1796–1822," *Pennsylvania Magazine of History and Biography* 94 (1970): 35; Charles H. Bowman Jr., "Antonio Caballero y Góngora y Manuel Torres: La cultura en la Nueva Granada," *Boletín de historia y*

antiguëdades 58 (September 1971): 415–452. On Antonio Caballero y Góngora see José Torre Revello, "La biblioteca del Virrey-Arzobispo del Nuevo Reino de Granada Antonio Caballero y Gongora," *Boletín del Instituto de Investigaciones Históricas* 9 (July–September 1929): 27–45; Victor Frankl, "La estructura barroca del pensamiento político, histórico, y económico del arzobispo-virrey de Nueva Granada Antonio Caballero y Gongora," *Revista Bolívar* 2, no. November (1951): 805–873; José Manuel Pérez Ayala, *Antonio Caballero y Góngora, virrey y arzobispo de Santa Fe, 1723–1796* (Bogotá, Colombia: Impr. Municipal, 1951).

31. Duane, "Death of Mr. Torres," 347; Bowman Jr., "Caballero y Góngora y Manuel Torres," 429–430, 437–438.
32. Duane, "Death of Mr. Torres," 347; William Duane, *A Visit to Colombia, in the years 1822 & 1823, by Laguayra and Caracas, over the Cordillera to Bogota, and thence by the Magdalena to Cartagena* (Philadelphia: T.H. Palmer, 1826), 608–609.
33. Bowman cites García Samudio, "Torres." He adds that perhaps Torres helped Duane reorganize the *Aurora,* as Duane did several times as editor. Bowman Jr., "Torres, Patriot," 28.
34. Duane, "Death of Mr. Torres," 347; Bowman Jr., "Torres, Patriot," 28.
35. One wonders, as in the case of Picornell's and Foronda's involvement in the Basque Economic Society, whether Puglia and Torres knew one another. Surely they must have, given that both were teachers of Spanish, lived in Philadelphia during the same period, and were dedicated to the independence of Spanish America. Nonetheless, the studies on Puglia do not mention Torres, and vice versa. Manuel Torres and L. Hargous, *Dufief's Nature displayed in her mode of teaching language to man* (Philadelphia: T. & G. Palmer, 1811); Manuel Torres and Hargous L., *La naturaleza descubierta en su modo de enseñar las lenguas á los hombres* (Philadelphia: T. y G. Palmer, 1811).
36. Bowman Jr., "Torres, Patriot," 29.
37. Francisco de Miranda and Vicente Dávila, eds., *Archivo del General [Francisco] Miranda,* vol. 17 (Caracas: Editorial Sur-América, 1929–1950), 282. Cited in Bowman Jr., "Torres, Patriot," 30.
38. Manuel Torres, *An exposition of the commerce of Spanish America with some observations upon its importance to the United States, to which are added, a correct analysis of the monies, weights, and measures of Spain, France, and the United States, and of the new weights and measures of England, with tables of their reciprocal reductions, and of the exchange between the United States, England, France, Holland, Hamburg, and between England, Spain, France, and the several states of the Union* (Philadelphia: G. Palmer, 1816), viii.
39. Racine, *Miranda,* 156–165.
40. Alberto Miramón, "Los diplomáticos de la libertad," *Boletín de historia y antiguëdades* 36, no. 414–416 (1949): 256–285; Bowman Jr., "Torres and Colombian Independence"; Gabriel Jaime Arango Toro, "Orígenes de las relaciones diplomáticas con los Estados Unidos de Norte América," *Cancillería de San Carlos,* no. 25 (January–April 2000): 51–60.

41. New Orleans, too, would become in the early nineteenth century a central meeting place for revolutionaries from throughout the Gulf of Mexico. Already in 1797, we can identify José Antonio Rojas, a former professor of math at the College of Guanajuato who had fled to New Orleans. The ideologically conservative Mexican historian Lucas Alamán writes that Rojas had become an "addict" of Enlightenment political thought and had been sentenced by the Inquisition, only to escape to New Orleans from where he sent letters to New Spain denouncing the Inquisition and celebrating republican forms of government. Lucas Alaman, *Historia de Mexico,* vol. 1 (Mexico City: Victoriano Agüeros, 1883), 106, 141, 146; Pablo González Casanova, *La literatura perseguida por la Inquisición* (Mexico City: Libros de Contenido, 1992), 118–130.
42. On the process and effects the elections had in New Spain, see Nettie Lee Benson, "Texas Failure to Send a Deputy to the Spanish Cortes, 1810–1812," *Southwestern Historical Quarterly* 64 (July 1960): 14–18; Nettie Lee Benson, ed., *Mexico and the Spanish Cortes, 1810–1822: Eight Essays* (Austin: University of Texas Press, 1966); Virginia Guedea, "Los procesos electorales insurgentes," *Estudios de Historia Novohispana* 11 (1991): 201–249; Guerra, *Modernidad,* 177–225; Nettie Benson, "The Elections of 1809: Transforming Political Culture in New Spain," *Mexican Studies/Estudios Mexicanos* 20, no. 1 (2004): 1–20. On the category of *vecinos,* see Tamar Herzog, *Defining Nations: Immigrants and Citizens in Early Modern Spain and Spanish America* (New Haven: Yale, 2003).
43. Gabriel H. Lovett, *Napoleon and the Birth of Modern Spain: The Challenge to the Old Order,* vol. 1 (New York: New York University Press, 1965), 292, 323–370; Marie Laure Rieu-Millán, *Los diputados americanos en las Cortes de Cádiz: igualdad o independencia* (Madrid: Consejo Superior de Investigaciones Científicas, 1990), 1–21; Jaime E. Rodríguez O., *The Independence of Spanish America* (New York: Cambridge University Press, 1998), 59–65, 75–77.
44. Lovett, *Napoleon and Modern Spain,* 370–414; Rieu-Millán, *Diputados,* 58–62, 273–294; Rodríguez O., *Spanish America,* 78–83; Manuel Chust Calero, *La cuestión nacional americana en las Cortes de Cádiz (1810–1814)* (Mexico City: Universidad Nacional Autónoma de México, 1999); Federico Suárez, *Las Cortes de Cádiz* (Madrid: Rialp, 2002), 13–68.
45. Clarice Neal, "Freedom of the Press in New Spain, 1810–1820," in *Mexico and the Spanish Cortes, 1810–1822,* ed. Nettie Lee Benson (Austin: University of Texas Press, 1966), 87; Guerra, *Modernidad,* 227–274; Rafael Rojas, *La escritura de la independencia. El surgimiento de la opinión pública en México* (Mexico City: Taurus y el Centro de Investigación y Docencia Económica, 2003), 49–63; Nancy Vogeley, "Espacios públicos descolonizados: la hoja volante," *Revista Iberoamericana* 73, no. 218–219 (January–June 2007): 137–158.
46. Spain's population numbered 10.5 million in 1811, while Spanish America had 14 million. José Álvarez de Toledo, *Manifiesto ó satisfaccion pundonorosa, todos los buenos españoles europeos, y todos los pueblos de la America, por un diputado de las Cortes reunidas en Cádiz* (Philadelphia, 1811), 30–32; Carlos Manuel Trelles y Govín, *Un Precursor de la independencia de*

Cuba: Don José Álvarez de Toledo. Discursos leídos en la recepción pública del Sr. Carlos M. Trelles y Govín (Havana: Imprenta El Siglo XX, 1926), 11; Lovett, *Napoleon and Modern Spain,* 415–490; Rodríguez O., *Spanish America,* 61.

47. María García Godoy, *Las Cortes de Cádiz y América: El primer vocabulario liberal español y mejicano (1810–1814)* (Seville: Diputacion de Sevilla, 1998); Richard Hocquellet, "La publicidad de la Junta Central Española (1808–1810)," in *Los espacios públicos en Iberoamérica: Ambigüedades y problemas, siglos XVIII–XIX,* ed. François-Xavier Guerra and Annick Lempériere (Mexico City: Fondo de Cultura Económica, 1998), 140–167; Rodríguez O., *Spanish America,* 75–106.
48. Benson, "Texas Failure to Send Deputy," 14–19; Rodríguez O., *Spanish America,* 108.
49. William Spence Robertson, "The Juntas of 1808 and the Spanish Colonies," *English Historical Review* 31, no. 124 (October 1916): 574–576; Lovett, *Napoleon and Modern Spain,* 123–124.
50. John Lynch, *The Spanish American Revolutions, 1808–1826,* 2nd ed. (New York: Norton, 1986); Brading, *First America,* 540–560; Rodríguez O., *Spanish America,* 107–109; Elliott, *Empires,* 374–391.
51. Onis, *United States,* 31–35; Elizabeth Rezner Daniel, "Spanish American Travelers in the United States before 1900: A Study in Inter-American Literary Relations" (PhD dissertation, University of North Carolina, 1959). The social base of the actual rebellions, however, was quite diverse. Eric Van Young, *The Other Rebellion: Popular Violence, Ideology, and the Mexican Struggle for Independence* (Stanford: Stanford University Press, 2001), 65.
52. Duane, "Death of Mr. Torres," 348.
53. Bowman Jr., "Torres, Patriot," 31, 39; George Erving, "George Erving to James Monroe, 4 Jan 1816," in *A Comprehensive Catalogue of the Correspondence and Papers of James Monroe,* ed. Daniel Preston, vol. 2 (Westport, CT: Greenwood Press, 2001), 616.
54. On Spanish-American revolutionaries in the United States and the United States' response to them, see Charles Carroll Griffin, *The United States and the Disruption of the Spanish Empire, 1810–1822: A Study of the Relations of the United States with Spain and with the Rebel Spanish Colonies* (New York: Octagon Books, 1968), 42–68. Their diplomatic correspondence may be found in William R. Manning, ed. *Diplomatic Correspondence of the United States Concerning the Independence of the Latin-American Nations,* vol. 2 (New York: Oxford University Press, 1925), 1141–1158; Cristóbal L. Mendoza, ed., *Las Primeras misiones diplomaticas de Venezuela. Documentos,* vol. 2 (Caracas, Venezuela: Academia Nacional de la Historia, 1962), 15–100.
55. José Bernardo Gutiérrez de Lara, Diary, 1811–1812, Manuscripts Collections, Archives and Information Services Division, Texas State Library and Archives Commission, Austin, 4E–11b, 4E–15b; José Bernardo Gutiérrez de Lara, "Diary of José Bernardo Gutiérrez de Lara, 1811–1812, I," trans. Elizabeth Howard West, *American Historical Review* 34, no. 1 (October 1928): 72, 76.

56. Gutiérrez de Lara, Diary, 4E–19a; José Bernardo Gutiérrez de Lara, "Diary of José Bernardo Gutiérrez de Lara, 1811–1812, II," trans. Elizabeth Howard West, *American Historical Review* 34, no. 2 (January 1929): 283.
57. Torres and Hargous, *Dufief's Nature;* Torres and Hargous, *La naturaleza descubierta.* Another possible candidate may be the Irishman Matthias James O'Conway (also Santiago Matthias O'Conway). He emigrated to Spain in the late eighteenth century where he learned Spanish, then traveled to Havana, New Orleans, and finally Philadelphia. All of his sons died fighting for the independence of various Spanish-American nations. In Philadelphia, in 1809, he published an anthology of articles taken from the most prominent Enlightenment-era Spanish newspapers. The anthology was designed to be used for the "instruction and entertainment of students of Spanish." Santiago Matthias O'Conway, *Rasgos historicos y morales sacados de autores célebres de diversas naciones y destinados para la instruccion y entretenimiento de los estudiantes del idioma español* (Philadelphia: Thomas and William Bradford, 1809). It is not likely that Puglia was the teacher, despite his advertising such services in the 1790s. Puglia himself acknowledged his Spanish was poor (his native tongue was Italian); Simmons also discovered that Puglia served as Health Officer for Philadelphia from 1809 to 1817. "During the eight years covered by this appointment, the erstwhile author apparently published nothing, and, indeed, except for his work as Health Officer, the only event in his life that seems to have left any traces at all is another unimportant court suit that occurred in 1815–1816." Simmons, *Puglia,* 53–54.
58. These presses were owned primarily by Anglo or Irish Catholics, and all within five blocks of one another. Among these were Thomas Bradford, Thomas and George Palmer, Andrew Blocquerst, and Mathew Carey. On the history of these publishers, see Vogeley, *Bookrunner,* 35–107. Anglo-American publishing markets were expanding considerably during this period. Where they had focused on publishing and printing for local markets before, the expanding economy and competition during the early nineteenth century demanded that they "gain access to markets outside Philadelphia." Rosalind Remer, *Printers and Men of Capital: Philadelphia Book Publishers in the New Republic* (Philadelphia: University of Pennsylvania, 1996), 69.
59. Merle Edwin Simmons, "Spanish and Spanish American Writer Politicians in Philadelphia, 1790–1830," *Dieciocho* 3, no. 1 (1980): 30; Vogeley, *Bookrunner,* 110–158. Other significant imprints include Manuel Garcia de Sena, *La independencia de la Costa Firme justificada por Thomas Paine treinta años* (Philadelphia: En la imprenta de T. y J. Palmer, 1811); Manuel García de Sena, *Historia concisa de los Estados Unidos, desde el descubrimiento de la América hasta el año de 1807* (Philadelphia: T. y J. Palmer, 1811); Anonymous, *Manual de un republicano para el uso de un pueblo libre* (Philadelphia: T. y J. Palmer, 1812); Juan Germán Roscio, *El triunfo de la libertad sobre el despotismo en la confesión de un pecador arrepentido de sus errores políticos, y dedicado a desagraviar en esta parte a la religión ofendida con el sistema de la tiranía* (Philadelphia: Imprenta de Thomas H. Palmer, 1817).

60. Manuel Salcedo, *Hacemos saber á todos los vasallos del Rey Nuestro señor de qualquiera clase y condición que sean ha resuelto S.M. se haga la retrocesion de la Provincia de la Louisiana* (New Orleans, 1803); Un Viejo Castizo Español, *España ensangrentada por el horrendo corzo, tyrano de la Europa, auxiliado de su iniqüo agente el vilisimo Godoy, (alias) el choricero* (New Orleans: En casa de Juan Mowry, Nueva-Orleans, 1808); William H. Johnson, ed., *El Misisipí* (New Orleans: William H. Johnson, 1808–1810); Anonymous, *Manifestacion de la legitima autoridad de la Junta suprema de Sevilla. Sobre las colonias Españolas de America. Obra patriótica de un letrado Asturiano, que dan a luz unos amigos del autór en esta cuidad* (New Orleans: De la oficina del Mensagero Luisianes, 1810); Joaquin de Lisa, ed., *El Mensagero Luisianes* (New Orleans: Joaquin de Lisa, 1810 [October 13]). On Onís see Julia K. Garrett, *Green Flag over Texas: A Story of the Last Years of Spain in Texas* (New York: Cordova, 1939), 244 n.8. On the Hispanophone print culture in Louisiana, see Douglas C. McMurtrie, *Early Printing in New Orleans, 1764–1810, with a Bibliography of the Issues of the Louisiana Press* (New Orleans: Searcy & Pfaff, 1929); Douglas C. McMurtrie, *Louisiana Imprints, 1764–1803* (Hattiesburg, MS: Book Farm, 1942); Kirsten Silva Gruesz, *Ambassadors of Culture: The Transamerican Origins of Latino Writing* (Princeton: Princeton University Press, 2002); Kirsten Silva Gruesz, "The Gulf of Mexico System and the 'Latinness' of New Orleans," *American Literary History* 18, no. 3 (2006): 468–495.
61. José Manuel Villavicencio, *Constitución de los Estados Unidos de America* (Philadelphia: En la Imprenta de Smith & M'Kenzie, 1810). As early as 1802, however, a Spanish translation of the U.S. Declaration of Independence and an English-language copy of the U.S. Constitution had circulated in Chile. Anglo-American maritime entrepreneurs had taken these with them. Richard J. Cleveland, *A Narrative of Voyages and Commercial Enterprise* (Cambridge, MA: J. Owen, 1842), 184. A year after Villavicencio's translation, in 1811, three other Spanish translations of the Constitution were published: by the Venezuelan Manuel García de Sena in Philadelphia, the Colombian Miguel de Pombo in Bogotá, and a third in the port of Cádiz in Spain. Pedro Grases, "Introducción," in *Primera traducción castellana de la Constitución de los Estados Unidos de América, Filadelfia 1810* (Caracas, Venezuela: Ministerio de Relaciones Exteriores, 1987), 17–18. See also David Armitage, *The Declaration of Independence: A Global History* (Cambridge, MA: Harvard University Press, 2007), 117–122.
62. Grases, "Introducción," 16, 23–27.
63. Álvarez de Toledo, *Manifiesto,* 32. See also Rieu-Millán, *Diputados,* 69–73.
64. Antonello Gerbi, *The Dispute of the New World: The History of a Polemic, 1750–1900,* trans. Jeremy Moyle (Pittsburgh: University of Pittsburgh Press, 1973); Jorge Cañizares-Esguerra, *How to Write the History of the New World: Histories, Epistemologies, and Identities in the Eighteenth-Century Atlantic World* (Stanford: Stanford University Press, 2001).
65. Ramos Arizpe ultimately served as representative for all of the Eastern Interior Provinces because the other provinces were unable to send representatives. He

dated the document November 11 on the penultimate page. Miguel Ramos Arizpe, *Memoria que el Doctor D. Miguel Ramos de Arispe, cura de Borbon, y Diputado en las presentes Cortes Generales y Extraordinarias de España por la Província de Cohauila* [*sic*], *una de las cuatro Internas del Oriente en el Reyno de Mexico, presenta á el augusto Congreso sobre el estado natural, político, y civíl de su dicha provincia, y las del Nuevo Reyno de Leon, Nuevo Santander, y los Texas: con exposicion de los defectos del sistema general, y particular de sus gobiernos, y de las reformas, y nuevos establecimientos que necesitan para su prosperidad* (Cádiz, Spain: En la imprenta de D. José María Guerrero, 1812), 59, hereafter cited in text.

66. Vito Alessio Robles, ed. *Miguel Ramos Arizpe: Discursos, memorias e informes,* 2nd ed. (Mexico City: Universidad Nacional Autónoma de México, 1994), ix–lxv; Estrada Michel, *Monarquía,* 595–604.

67. According to the University of Chicago librarian Sarah G. Wenzel, "The only mention of it, to which every other bibliography refers (including a long article on the history of printing in Spanish and French in Charleston), is in Spell's book. As Spell is relying not only on second-hand knowledge, but also on the memory of an auction catalog record (not always the most reliable), I'm doubtful [it exists]." Email to the author, March 10, 2010. Wenzel references Jefferson Rea Spell, *Rousseau in the Spanish World Before 1833: A Study in Franco-Spanish Literary Relations* (New York: Octagon Books, 1969), 282–283.

68. Rousseau begins his text with the well-known opening lines: "Man is born free, and he is everywhere in chains." The comparison to slaves and sheep is in bk. 1, ch. 2. Jean-Jacques Rousseau, *The Social Contract and Other Later Political Writings* (New York: Cambridge University Press, 1997), 41–43.

69. José María Miquel i Vergés, "Álvarez de Toledo, José," in *Diccionario de Insurgentes,* 2nd ed. (Mexico City: Editorial Porrúa, 1980), 27; David E. Narrett, "José Bernardo Gutiérrez de Lara: *Caudillo* of the Mexican Republic in Texas," *Southwestern Historical Quarterly* 106, no. 2 (October 2002): 206.

70. Trelles y Govín, *Toledo,* 8–13; Harris G. Warren, *The Sword Was Their Passport: A History of American Filibustering in the Mexican Revolution* (Baton Rouge: Louisiana State University Press, 1943), 10–13; Pascual O'Dogherty Sánchez, "Historia de la Escuela Naval Militar," *Temas de historia militar: Ponencias del Primer Congreso de Historia Militar, Zaragoza* 1 (1983): 628–643; José María Blanca Carier, "La Escuela Naval Militar, su origen histórico," *Revista de Historia Naval* 9, no. 32 (1991): 11–44.

71. Useful sources, in addition to those cited above, include Joseph B. Lockey, "The Florida Intrigues of José Alvarez de Toledo," *Florida Historical Society Quarterly* 12, no. 4 (April 1934): 145–178; Harris Gaylord Warren, "José Álvarez de Toledo's Initiation as a Filibuster, 1811–1813," *Hispanic American Historical Review* 20, no. 1 (1940): 56–82; Harris G. Warren, "José Álvarez de Toledo's Reconciliation with Spain and Projects for Suppressing Rebellion in the Spanish Colonies," *Louisiana Historical Quarterly* 23, no. 3 (July 1940): 827–863; Arturo Santana, *José Álvarez de Toledo: el revolucionario cubano en*

las Cortes de Cádiz y sus esfuerzos por la emancipación de las Antillas (San Juan, PR: Centro de Estudios Avanzados de Puerto Rico y el Caribe, 2006); Nicolás Kanellos, "José Alvarez de Toledo y Dubois and the Origins of Hispanic Publishing in the Early American Republic," *Early American Literature* 43, no. 1 (2008): 83–100. Toledo, like many American representatives to the Cortes, had been a member of the secret society Caballeros Racionales in Cádiz, a group designed to aid the Americans. However, Nicolás Kanellos claims that once Toledo was in Philadelphia, "the local chapter of Caballeros succeeded in putting him into contact with [other] resident revolutionaries." Kanellos, "Toledo," 87. He suggests there existed an extensive, underground, trans-Atlantic network of revolutionary lodges. But the sources he cites say nothing of the existence of a Philadelphia-based lodge. See Warren, *Sword,* 11; José R. Guzmán, "Una Sociedad Secreta en Londres al Servicio de la Independencia Hispanoamericana," *Boletín del Archivo General de la Nación* 8, no. 1–2 (1967): 114–115; Estela Guadalupe Jiménez Codinach and María Teresa Franco González Salas, eds., *Pliegos de la diplomacia insurgente* (Mexico City: LIII Legislatura, Senado de la República Mexicana, 1987), 490–491. Likewise, citing Warren, Kanellos claims that Toledo arrived in Philadelphia via London in 1811. Kanellos, "Toledo," 86–87. He may have misread Warren, since on p. 11 Warren writes that Toledo had been in London in 1808 as an officer in the Spanish navy; however, Warren writes that after Toledo's arrest in Cádiz, Toledo "fled from Spain on June 25, 1811, and arrived at Philadelphia in September." Warren says nothing of Toledo stopping in London. Warren, *Sword,* 11. In what is an otherwise impeccably researched essay, Virginia Guedea also claims that Toledo stopped in London on his way to Philadelphia, but goes further by claiming that he, along with Servando Teresa de Mier, founded a chapter of the Caballeros Racionales. Virginia Guedea, "Autonomía e independencia en la provincia de Texas. La junta de gobierno de San Antonio de Béjar, 1813," in *La Independencia de México y el proceso autonomista novohispano 1808–1824,* ed. Virginia Guedea (Mexico City: Universidad Nacional Autónoma de México, 2001), 151. Guedea misread her sources; they state that Mier and other Spanish Americans founded the lodge in London, and that Toledo, a member of the lodge *in Cádiz* had left for Mexico (never passing through London). Estela Guadalupe Jiménez Codinach and María Teresa Franco González Salas, "Introducción," in *Pliegos de la diplomacia insurgente,* ed. Estela Guadalupe Jiménez Codinach and María Teresa Franco González Salas (Mexico City: LIII Legislatura, Senado de la República Mexicana, 1987), xxiv, xxix–xxx.

While lodges of the Caballeros Racionales were established in Cádiz, London, Jalapa, Mexico, Havana, and Buenos Aires, there is little clear concrete evidence of their activities, and I have found no mention at all of a lodge in Philadelphia. Nonetheless, the lodge may be less important, given that the individuals who were said to be members did circulate throughout the Atlantic. One should keep in mind, however, that the history of secret societies in the Hispanic world is confounded with conspiracy and dubious sources. Many secondary sources rely on testimonies given by captured insurgents to the Inquisition, such as the oft-cited testimony given by Servando Teresa de Mier, yet one should remember that this testimony was often given under the duress of torture. Likewise, as in the case of the Masonic lodges described above, historians like Richard Herr and William Spence Robertson claim that much of the history of secret societies is "hardly more than a legend." William Spence Robertson, *Rise of the Spanish-American Republics, as Told in the Lives of Their Liberators* (New York: D. Appleton and Company, 1918), 53. On the dubious history of Hispanic Masonic lodges, see Richard Herr, "The Twentieth Century Spaniard Views the Spanish Enlightenment," *Hispania* 45, no. 2 (1962): 183–193. One of the most substantiated sources on Spanish-American secret societies is Guedea, "Las sociedades secretas."

72. Hereafter cited in text. His first publication, however, was a broadside dated October 1, 1811. This will be discussed in detail in Chapter 6.

73. Jaime E. Rodríguez O., *Nosotros somos ahora los verdaderos españoles: La transición de la Nueva España de un reino de la monarquía española a la República Federal Mexicana, 1808–1824,* 2 vols. (Zamora, Michoacán, Mexico: Colegio de Michoacán and Instituto Mora, 2009), 13. A revised, translated version was published as Jaime E. Rodríguez O., *"We Are Now the True Spaniards": Sovereignty, Revolution, Independence, and the Emergence of the Federal Republic of Mexico, 1808–1824* (Stanford: Stanford University Press, 2012). He takes the title from the December 20, 1810, edition of the Guadalajara, Mexico newspaper, *El Despertador Americano.*

74. Harry Harootunian, "Remembering the Historical Present," *Critical Inquiry,* no. 33 (2007): 486. For a fascinating account of a similar impasse in the present, see Lauren Berlant, *Cruel Optimism* (Durham: Duke University Press, 2011), 51–68.

75. Miguel Díez et al., *Las Lenguas de España,* 2nd ed. (Madrid: Ministerio de Educación, 1980), 204; John H. Elliott, *Imperial Spain, 1469–1716* (New York: Penguin, 2002), 245–246; Fernando R. de la Flor, "On the Notion of a Melancholic Baroque," in *Hispanic Baroques,* ed. Nicholas Spadaccini and Luis Martín-Estudillo (Nashville: Vanderbilt University Press, 2005), 3–19.

76. John D. Browning, "Cornelius de Pauw and Exiled Jesuits: The Development of Nationalism in Spanish America," *Eighteenth-Century Studies* 11, no. 3 (1978): 289–307; Brading, *First America,* 497–513, 535–540; Miguel Batllori, *El abate Viscardo: historia y mito de la intervención de los jesuitas en la independencia de Hispanoamérica* (Madrid: Editorial MAPFRE, 1995); Luis Varela, ed. *Juan Pablo Viscardo y Guzmán (1748–1798): el hombre y su tiempo,* 3 vols. (Lima: Fondo Editorial del Congreso del Perú, 1999); Cañizares-Esguerra, *History of the New World,* 234–265. While writing about other Jesuits, Cañizares-Esguerra fails to mention Viscardo.

77. David A. Brading, "Introduction: Juan Pablo Viscardo y Guzmán, Creole Patriot and *Philosophe,*" in *Letter to the Spanish Americans, a Facsimile of the Second English Edition (London, 1810)* (Providence, RI: The John Carter Brown Library, 2002), 3–59.

78. Burton Van Name Edwards, "Bibliographical Note," in Viscardo y Guzmán, *Letter to the Spanish Americans,* 89–92.

79. Bernard Bailyn, *The Ideological Origins of the American Revolution* (Cambridge, MA: Harvard University Press, 1992), 160–229.
80. See, for example, Jeff Osborne, "American Antipathy and the Cruelties of Citizenship in Crèvecoeur's *Letters from an American Farmer*," *Early American Literature* 42, no. 3 (2007): 529–553; Todd Estes, "The Voices of Publius and the Strategies of Persuasion in *The Federalist*," *Journal of the Early Republic* 28, no. 4 (2008): 523–558; Ed White, "The Ends of Republicanism," *Journal of the Early Republic* 30, no. 2 (2010): 179–199.
81. J. Hector St. John de Crèvecoeur, *Letters from an American Farmer and Sketches of Eighteenth-Century America* (New York: Penguin, 1986).
82. Benedict Anderson, *Imagined Communities: Reflections on the Origin and Spread of Nationalism* (New York: Verso, 1991), 199–201.
83. For a reading of the trope of forgetting in early Anglo-American culture, see Myra Jehlen, *American Incarnation: The Individual, the Nation, and the Continent* (Cambridge, MA: Harvard University Press, 1986), 1–21.
84. Brading, *First America*, 538, 593–595.
85. The English translation offers "Spanish Americans" whereas the original French has "Espagnols Américain," which translates as "American Spaniards." Juan Pablo Viscardo y Guzmán, *Lettre aux espagnols-americains* (London (false imprint of Philadelphia): A Philadelphie, 1799); Viscardo y Guzmán, *Letter to the Spanish Americans;* Juan Pablo Viscardo y Guzmán, *Carta dirigida a los españoles americanos* (Mexico City: Fondo de Cultura Económica, 2004). Page numbers of the 2004 and 2002 editions are respectively cited in text hereafter. I cite the English translation, unless noted.
86. Anthony Pagden, "Old Constitutions and Ancient Indian Empires: Juan Pablo Viscardo and the Languages of Revolution in Spanish America," in *Spanish Imperialism and the Political Imagination: Studies in European and Spanish-American Social and Political Theory, 1513–1830* (New Haven: Yale University Press, 1990), 118–120. See also Karen Stolley, "Writing Back to Empire: Juan Pablo Viscardo y Guzmán's *Letter to the Spanish Americans*," in *Liberty! Egalité! Independencia!: Print Culture, Enlightenment, and Revolution in the Americas, 1776–1838: Papers from a Conference at the American Antiquarian Society in June 2006*, ed. David S. Shields (Worcester, MA: American Antiquarian Society, 2007), 117–131.
87. César Pacheco Vélez, "Bibliografía Crítica de Juan Pablo Viscardo," in *Obra completa: Juan Pablo Viscardo y Guzmán*, vol. 2 (Lima: Ediciones del Congreso de la República del Perú, 1998), 444–448; Edwards, "Bibliographical Note," 90.
88. Pedro Grases, "La trascendencia de la actividad de los escritores españoles e hispanoamericanos en Londres, de 1810 a 1830," in *Obras de Pedro Grases: Instituciones y nombres del siglo XIX*, vol. 6 (Caracas: Editorial Elite, 1943), 157–200; Guzmán, "Sociedad Secreta"; Rieu-Millán, *Diputados*, 365–367, 380–381; Guerra, *Modernidad*, 227–318; Jeremy Adelman, *Sovereignty and Revolution in the Iberian Atlantic* (Princeton: Princeton University Press, 2006), 181–185.
89. Guerra, *Modernidad*, 285–289.

90. On the relationship between print and the creation of publics, see Michael Warner, *Publics and Counterpublics* (New York: Zone Books, 2002), 65–124.
91. Anonymous, *Objeciones satisfactorias del mundo imparcial al folleto dado á luz por el marte-filosofo de Delaware Don José Alvarez de Toledo* (Charleston, SC, 1812).
92. José Álvarez de Toledo, *Contestacion á la carta del Indio Patriota con algunas reflexiones sobre el dialogo—entre el Entusiasta Liberal, y el Filosofo Rancio—y sobre las notas anonymas con que ha salido reimpreso el Manifiesto de dn. José Alvarez de Toledo* (Philadelphia: A. J. Blocquerst, 1812); Un Indio Patriota, *Dedicada a los nuevos refutadores del manifiesto de Dn. Jose Alvarez de Toledo, aparecidos en las margenes del Delawarre* [*sic*] (Washington, DC, 1812).

5. Seduced by Papers

1. Julia K. Garrett, *Green Flag over Texas: A Story of the Last Years of Spain in Texas* (New York: Cordova, 1939), 102; Carlos Eduardo Castañeda, *Our Catholic Heritage in Texas, 1519–1936: Transition Period; the Fight for Freedom, 1810–1836,* vol. 6 (New York: Arno Press, 1950), 66–67.
2. José Bernardo Gutiérrez de Lara, Diary, 1811–1812, Manuscripts Collections, Archives and Information Services Division, Texas State Library and Archives Commission, Austin, 4E–23b–24a; José Bernardo Gutiérrez de Lara, "Diary of José Bernardo Gutiérrez de Lara, 1811–1812, II," trans. Elizabeth Howard West, *American Historical Review* 34, no. 2 (January 1929): 287.
3. Gutiérrez de Lara, Diary, 4E–23b–24a; Gutiérrez de Lara, "Diary, II," 287.
4. This is the thesis in Gabriel H. Lovett, *Napoleon and the Birth of Modern Spain,* 2 vols. (New York: New York University Press, 1965).
5. An oft-quoted citation attributed to Michel Foucault's *Madness and Civilization,* it is actually found in Hubert L. Dreyfus and Paul Rabinow, *Michel Foucault: Beyond Structuralism and Hermeneutics,* 2nd ed. (Chicago: University of Chicago Press, 1983), 187. The authors cite "personal communication" as the source. "People know what they do; frequently they know why they do what they do; but what they don't know is what what they do does."
6. Garrett, *Green Flag,* 86; David E. Narrett, "José Bernardo Gutiérrez de Lara: *Caudillo* of the Mexican Republic in Texas," *Southwestern Historical Quarterly* 106, no. 2 (October 2002): 206–208.
7. Gutiérrez de Lara, Diary, 4E–29b; Gutiérrez de Lara, "Diary, II," 292; James Clark Milligan, "José Bernardo Gutiérrez de Lara: Mexican Frontiersman, 1811–1841" (PhD dissertation, Texas Tech University, Lubbock, 1975), 46–57.
8. Broadsheets are printed on both sides of a single sheet of paper; broadsides are printed on only one side. Remarkably, Julia Garrett is the only historian to cover in extensive detail the events that unfolded during this period in her *Green Flag.* Her narrative should be supplemented with the abbreviated accounts in Castañeda, *Catholic Heritage,* 6:1–120; Jack Jackson, *Los Mesteños: Spanish Ranching in Texas, 1721–1821* (College Station: Texas A&M

University Press, 1986), 525–552. Almaráz's biography of Governor Manuel Salcedo offers a much more focused and insightful perspective. Félix D. Almaráz Jr., *Tragic Cavalier: Governor Manuel Salcedo of Texas, 1808–1813*, 2nd ed. (College Station: Texas A&M University Press, 1991).

9. Gutiérrez de Lara, Diary, 4E–30a; Gutiérrez de Lara, "Diary, II," 292–293.
10. Gilbert C. Din, "Spanish Control over a Multiethnic Society: Louisiana, 1763–1803," in *Choice, Persuasion, and Coercion: Social Control on Spain's North American Frontiers*, ed. Jesús F. de la Teja and Ross Frank (Albuquerque: University of New Mexico Press, 2005), 65. See also H. Sophie Burton, "Vagabonds along the Spanish Louisiana-Texas Frontier, 1769–1803: 'Men Who are Evil, Lazy, Gluttonous, Drunken, Libertinous, Dishonest, Mutinous, etc. etc. etc.—And Those are Their Virtues,'" *Southwestern Historical Quarterly* 113, no. 4 (2010): 438–467.
11. As in other frontier regions in the Americas, intermarriage between European men and Indian women was common, but intermarriage, as the historian Juliana Barr has noted, was just as often a political tool. Juliana Barr, "Beyond Their Control: Spaniards in Native Texas," in *Choice, Persuasion, and Coercion: Social Control on Spain's North American Frontiers*, ed. Jesús F. de la Teja and Ross Frank (Albuquerque: University of New Mexico Press, 2005), 154–158.
12. H. Sophie Burton and F. Todd Smith, *Colonial Natchitoches: A Creole Community on the Louisiana-Texas Frontier* (College Station: Texas A&M University Press, 2008), ix–xiii, 92. The social dynamics that emerged in this region prior to the congealing of nation-states may be compared to that described in Richard White, *The Middle Ground: Indians, Empires, and Republics in the Great Lakes Region, 1650–1815* (New York: Cambridge University Press, 1991).
13. Gutiérrez de Lara, Diary, 4E–30b; Gutiérrez de Lara, "Diary, II," 293.
14. F. Todd Smith, *The Caddo Indians: Tribes at the Convergence of Empires, 1542–1854* (College Station: Texas A&M University Press, 1995), 85; David La Vere, *The Caddo Chiefdoms: Caddo Economics and Politics, 700–1835* (Lincoln: University of Nebraska, 1998), 126–144; F. Todd Smith, "Dehahuit: An Indian Diplomat on the Louisiana-Texas Frontier, 1804–1815," in *Nexus of Empire: Negotiating Loyalty and Identity in the Revolutionary Borderlands, 1760s–1820s*, ed. Gene A. Smith and Sylvia L. Hilton (Gainesville: University Press of Florida, 2010), 140–159.
15. La Vere, *Caddo*, 10–15; David La Vere, *The Texas Indians* (College Station: Texas A&M University Press, 2004), 104, 146, 153–176; F. Todd Smith, *From Dominance to Disappearance: The Indians of Texas and the Near Southwest, 1786–1859* (Lincoln: University of Nebraska Press, 2005), 4–5, 26–27, 67–100; Juliana Barr, *Peace Came in the Form of a Woman: Indians and Spaniards in the Texas Borderlands* (Chapel Hill: University of North Carolina Press, 2007), 211–229; Raúl A. Ramos, *Beyond the Alamo: Forging Mexican Ethnicity in San Antonio, 1821–1861* (Chapel Hill: University of North Carolina Press, 2008), 69–79.
16. Smith, *Dominance*, 98; Pekka Hämäläinen, *The Comanche Empire* (New Haven: Yale University Press, 2008), 182–190; Smith, "Dehahuit," 152–155.

17. Gutiérrez de Lara, Diary, 4E–30b; Gutiérrez de Lara, "Diary, II," 293.
18. Narrett, "José Bernardo Gutiérrez de Lara," 224.
19. Adriana Terán Enríquez, "La ley como enemiga de la libertad: El caso de Fray Melchor de Talamantes," in *Juicios y causas procesales en la independencia Mexicana,* ed. Francisco A. Ibarra Palafox (Mexico City: Universidad Nacional Autónoma de México, 2010), 47–73; Jaime E. Rodríguez O., *"We Are Now the True Spaniards": Sovereignty, Revolution, Independence, and the Emergence of the Federal Republic of Mexico, 1808–1824* (Stanford: Stanford University Press, 2012), 47–48.
20. Peter Gerhard, *The North Frontier of New Spain,* rev. ed. (Norman: University of Oklahoma Press, 1993), 335; Isidro Vizcaya Canales, *En los albores de la independencia. Las Provincias Internas de Oriente durante la insurrección de don Miguel Hidalgo y Costilla, 1810–1811,* 2nd ed. (Monterrey, Mexico: Fondo Editorial Nuevo León y Instituto Tecnológico de Monterrey, 2005; orig. 1976), 175–193.
21. Manuel Salcedo to Governor of Coahuila Bustamante, August 17, 1812, Bexar Archives, the Dolph Briscoe Center for American History, University of Texas at Austin (hereafter "Bexar Archives"), reel 52:268–270; Salcedo to Viceroy, June 2, 1812, Operaciones de Guerra, Manuel Salcedo, 1810–1812, BANC MSS M-A1 (FILM 3097: reel 3), selected transcriptions from the Archivo General de la Nación. Documents for the History of Mexico (ca. 1524–1855), Bancroft Library, University of California, Berkeley (hereafter "Operaciones de Guerra, Manuel Salcedo"), 53.
22. Manuel Salcedo, "A Governor's Report on Texas in 1809," trans. Nettie L. Benson, *Southwestern Historical Quarterly* 71 (April 1968): 603–605; Almaráz, *Cavalier,* 22–28.
23. Donald E. Chipman and Harriett Denise Joseph, "José Bernardo Gutiérrez de Lara/Joaquín de Arredondo: Ill-Fated Insurgent/Vengeful Royalist," in *Notable Men and Women of Spanish Texas* (Austin: University of Texas Press, 1999), 227.
24. The Cortes of Cádiz stipulated that representatives had to be natives of the province they were representing. Nettie Lee Benson, "Texas Failure to Send a Deputy to the Spanish Cortes, 1810–1812," *Southwestern Historical Quarterly* 64 (July 1960): 19–25.
25. Manuel Salcedo, "Puntos que conviene tenga presentes el sujeto elegido por Diputado del Reino de Nueva España," Operaciones de Guerra, Manuel Salcedo, 25; Salcedo, "Governor's Report," 615.
26. Salcedo to Viceroy, November 21, 1810; Salcedo to Governor of Coahuila, Operaciones de Guerra, Manuel Salcedo, 5, 136–137.
27. Natchitoches-based Spanish vice consul Félix Trudeaux to Nacogdoches Commander Bernardino Montero, May 3, 1812, Operaciones de Guerra, Manuel Salcedo, 57.
28. Salcedo to Commandant General of the Interior Provinces Nemesio Salcedo, June 3, 1812, Bexar Archives, reel 51:412–413; Trudeaux to Montero, May 3, 1812, Case 17, No. 589, reel 17, Nacogdoches Archives, Archives & Manuscripts, Texas State Library and Archives Commission, Austin (hereafter

"Nacogdoches Archives"). Notwithstanding the extensive research on the printing press in Texas, some historians have dismissed the possibility of this press or failed to mention it entirely. Henderson mentions that "some authorities contend that Gutiérrez had a printing press, [but] it is doubtful." Kathryn Garrett does not mention the press in her otherwise thorough account. But M'Caleb, Cox, and Moore had already documented its existence. Walter Flavius M'Caleb, "The First Period of the Gutierrez-Magee Expedition," *Southwestern Historical Quarterly* 4, no. 3 (1901): 221 n.4; Isaac J. Cox, "Monroe and the Mexican Revolutionary Agents," *American Historical Association Annual Report* I (1911): 207; Ike H. Moore, "The Earliest Printing and First Newspaper in Texas," *Southwestern Historical Quarterly* 39 (1935): 92; Garrett, *Green Flag;* Harry M. Henderson, "The Magee-Gutiérrez Expedition," *Southwestern Historical Quarterly* 55 (July 1951): 45.

29. James Moran, *Printing Presses: History and Development from the Fifteenth Century to Modern Times* (Berkeley: University of California Press, 1973), 30–40.
30. Gutiérrez de Lara, Diary, 4E–31b; Gutiérrez de Lara, "Diary, II," 293–294. Castañeda writes that 1,000 copies of a pamphlet were printed in Philadelphia prior to Bernardo's departure, but does not mention the 1,000 copies of the proclamation that Bernardo writes about in his diary once he is in Natchitoches. Castañeda, *Catholic Heritage,* 6:67.
31. Gutiérrez de Lara to Luis Grande, Nacogdoches, September 4, 1812; Gutiérrez de Lara, "Mis amados compatriotas vezinos y abitantes, del Reyno Mexicano," Nacogdoches, September 1, 1812, Operaciones de Guerra, Manuel Salcedo, 147, 149–150; Moran, *Printing Presses,* 32–35.
32. Salcedo to Viceroy, September 24, 1812, Operaciones de Guerra, Manuel Salcedo, 144–146.
33. Salcedo to Viceroy, August 17, 1812, Operaciones de Guerra, Manuel Salcedo, 136.
34. Salcedo to Governor Bustamante, August 17, 1812, Operaciones de Guerra, Manuel Salcedo, 140.
35. Salcedo to Viceroy, June 2, 1812; Bustamante to Salcedo, July 26, 1812, Bexar Archives, reel 51:389–392, 986–988; Salcedo to Nemesio Salcedo, August 14, 1811; Salcedo to Viceroy, June 2, 1812, Operaciones de Guerra, Manuel Salcedo, 66–68, 53–54.
36. This had been the case with the Las Casas revolt in San Antonio in January 1811. Salcedo to Venegas, June 3, 1812, Operaciones de Guerra, Manuel Salcedo, 62–81; "Proclamation Relating to the Revolution which took place at Bexar, Jan. 22, 1811," dated after April 1811, MF Reel 10, MS, No. 571, Nacogdoches Archives; J. Villasana Haggard, "The Counter-Revolution of Béxar, 1811," *Southwestern Historical Quarterly* 43 (October 1939): 224–225; Frederick C. Chabot, ed. *Texas in 1811: The Las Casas and Sambrano Revolution* (San Antonio: Yanaguana Society, 1941); Almaráz, *Cavalier,* 95–129.
37. Montero writes "desnaturalizado," which could be translated as "unnatural" in the sense that a family member lacks the natural obligations they owe to

their family. Montero to Salcedo, May 12, 1812, Operaciones de Guerra, Manuel Salcedo, 55.

38. Ibid.
39. Ibid.
40. O. Carlos Stoetzer, *El pensamiento político en la América española durante el período de la emancipación, 1789–1825. Las bases hispánicas y las corrientes europeas,* vol. 1 (Madrid: Instituto de Estudios Políticos, 1966), 58.
41. O. Carlos Stoetzer, *The Scholastic Roots of the Spanish American Revolution* (New York: Fordham University Press, 1979), 113–121; Jaime E. Rodríguez O., *The Independence of Spanish America* (New York: Cambridge University Press, 1998), 19–26, 34–35.
42. John Lynch, *Bourbon Spain, 1700–1808* (Cambridge, MA: Blackwell, 1989), 98–109; Gabriel Paquette, *Enlightenment, Governance, and Reform in Spain and Its Empire, 1759–1808* (New York: Palgrave Macmillan, 2008), 70–92.
43. Otis H. Green, *Spain and the Western Tradition: The Castilian Mind in Literature from El Cid to Calderón,* vol. 2 (Madison: University of Wisconsin Press, 1964), 3–30; Joaquín Varela Suanzes-Carpegna, *La teoría del estado en los orígenes del constitucionalismo hispánico. Las Cortes de Cádiz* (Madrid: Centro de Estudios Constitucionales, 1983), 182; Colin M. MacLachlan, *Spain's Empire in the New World: The Role of Ideas in Institutional and Social Change* (Berkeley: University of California Press, 1988), 1–19; Vicente L. Rafael, "Welcoming What Comes: Sovereignty and Revolution in the Colonial Philippines," *Comparative Studies in Society and History* 52, no. 1 (2010): 157–179. Aquinas derived his hierarchical view of the cosmos from the fifth-century anonymous Christian author known as Pseudo-Dionysius. Aquinas developed his views especially in the treatises on angels and on man (part I, question 50, answers 1–3; question 75, answer 2). Saint Thomas Aquinas, *Summa Theologica (1265–74)* (http://www.ccel.org/ccel/aquinas/summa.html), accessed January 19, 2006. See also Mary Cecelia Wheeler, *Philosophy and the* Summa theologica *of Saint Thomas Aquinas* (Washington, DC: Catholic University of America, 1956), 26–27; Roger Haight, *Christian Community in History* (New York: Continuum, 2004), 315.
44. Charles Taylor, *A Secular Age* (Cambridge, MA: Harvard University Press, 2007), 32–35.
45. Montero to Salcedo, June 27, 1812, Operaciones de Guerra, Manuel Salcedo, 131–132. The Spanish officers in Texas wrote on many occasions of their attempts to prevent the circulation of these documents. Montero to Salcedo, May 28 and June 8, 1812; Salcedo to Junta of Nuevo Leon, Governor Diaz de Bustamante, June 8, 1812; Nemesio Salcedo to Manuel Salcedo, June 9, 1812; N. Salcedo to Salcedo, June 19, 1812; Montero to Salcedo, July 6, 1812; Salcedo to troops of Bexar, July 7, 1812; José Antonio Benavides to Salcedo, July 14, 1812; Jose María Peña to Salcedo, July 20, 1812, Bexar Archives, reel 51:352–354, 482–487, 492–505, 620–627, 781–784, 797–798, 839–841, 909.
46. Salcedo, "Fieles habitantes de esta Capl.," August 18, 1812, Bexar Archives, reel 52:273–275. Raúl A. Ramos interprets Salcedo's declaration against the

insurgents along ethnic lines, that is, that the "heretics" are the Anglo-Americans. Yet Salcedo never mentions any national or ethnic difference. Likewise, this ethnonational interpretation would be difficult given the fact that Bernardo was seen as the leader and that Spanish Americans had been involved in the insurgency since Hidalgo in 1810 and Las Casas in 1811. Ramos, *Beyond,* 43.

47. José Bernardo Gutiérrez de Lara and Ignacio Elizondo, "Comunicación de don Bernardo Gutiérrez de Lara y contestación de don Ignacio Elizondo, de 6 y 16 de abril [1813]," *Colección de documentos para la historia de la guerra de independence de México de 1808 a 1821* (http://www.pim.unam.mx/catalogos/juanhdzt5.html), accessed May 10, 2010. Elizondo's letter was later published in the San Antonio Hispanophone paper *El Bejareño* (San Antonio, 1855–1856), March 31, 1855, vol. 1. no. 5, p. 3.

48. Historians have identified this millenarian-messianic rhetoric throughout early nineteenth-century Latin America (including Brazil) but have been, as Eric Van Young points out, unsure how best to interpret it. They "often pose answers as ambiguous as the ideas and movements themselves." Eric Van Young, *The Other Rebellion: Popular Violence, Ideology, and the Mexican Struggle for Independence* (Stanford: Stanford University Press, 2001), 25.

49. José Luis Romero, *Las ideas políticas en Argentina,* 2nd ed. (Mexico City: Fondo de Cultura Económica, 1956), 58–59. Cited in Stoetzer, *Scholastic,* 81.

50. This was the classic statement articulated by the influential nineteenth-century conservative Spanish Catholic political philosopher Donoso Cortés. Juan Donoso Cortés, Marqués de Valdegamas, *Selected Works of Juan Donoso Cortés,* trans. Jeffrey P. Johnson (Westport, CT: Greenwood, 2000), 95–100.

51. Mariano Picón-Salas, *A Cultural History of Spanish America: From Conquest to Independence,* trans. Irving A. Leonard (Berkeley: University of California Press, 1962), 107.

52. Taylor, *Secular Age,* 25–89. This is also a version of the world to which Dipesh Chakrabarty refers in wanting to think outside of Eurocentric historical frameworks. See Dipesh Chakrabarty, *Provincializing Europe: Postcolonial Thought and Historical Difference* (Princeton: Princeton University Press, 2000), 16.

53. Walter Benjamin, "Theses on the Philosophy of History," trans. Harry Zohn, in *Illuminations: Essays and Reflections,* ed. Hannah Arendt (New York: Schocken Books, 1969), 261, 263; Jacques Le Goff, *Medieval Civilization, 400–1500,* trans. Julia Barrow (New York: Basil Blackwell, 1989), 165–187; Benedict Anderson, *Imagined Communities: Reflections on the Origin and Spread of Nationalism* (New York: Verso, 1991), 22–26; Reinhart Koselleck, *Futures Past: On the Semantics of Historical Time,* trans. Keith Tribe (New York: Columbia University Press, 2004), 222–255; Taylor, *Secular Age,* 54–74.

54. Montero to Salcedo, Nacogdoches, June 8, 1812; Montero to Salcedo, June 27, 1812; Montero to Salcedo, Nacogdoches, July 6, 1812; Felipe de la Garza to Manuel Salcedo, Trinidad, July 19, 1812, Bexar Archives, reel 51:482–485, 694–701, 781–784, 891–897.

55. Montero to Salcedo, June 8, 1812, Bexar Archives, reel 51:482–87; Montero to Salcedo, June 8, 1812, Operaciones de Guerra, Manuel Salcedo, 91–92. Vanegas's name appears in the archive as "Bagenas" or "Banegas." The standardized name now used is "Vanegas." Adán Benavides Jr., *The Béxar Archives (1717–1836): A Name Guide* (Austin: University of Texas Press, 1989), 1047.
56. Salcedo to Montero, August 4, 1812, Bexar Archives, reel 52:129–135; Montero to Salcedo, June 27, 1812, Operaciones de Guerra, Manuel Salcedo, 131–132.
57. Salcedo to Viceroy, June 25, 1812, Operaciones de Guerra, Manuel Salcedo, 83.
58. This should not be confused with the colonial caste term of "gente de razón [people with reason]," which emerged in the seventeenth and eighteenth centuries as a way to describe Indians who had converted to Christianity. "Reason," in this indigenous context, refers to one's acquiescing to Christian colonialism. Gloria E. Miranda, "Racial and Cultural Dimensions of *Gente de Razón* Status in Spanish and Mexican California," *Southern California Quarterly* 70 (Fall 1988): 265–278.
59. "seduce, v.," *OED Online* (http://www.oed.com.proxy.uchicago.edu/viewdictionaryentry/Entry/174721), accessed July 20, 2009; Real Academia Española, "Dicciónarios de la lengua española (1726–1992)" (http://www.rae.es/).
60. Sigmund Freud, "The Splitting of the Ego in the Processes of Defence," in *The Standard Edition of the Complete Psychological Works of Sigmund Freud,* ed. James Strachey et al. (London: The Hogarth Press and The Institute of Psychoanalysis, 1953), 271–278.
61. Salcedo to Viceroy, September 24, 1812, Operaciones de Guerra, Manuel Salcedo, 144. Bernardo provides instructions on how and where to circulate the documents on pp. 147–148.
62. Montero to Salcedo, June 27, 1812, Operaciones de Guerra, Manuel Salcedo, 131.
63. Montero to Salcedo, June 8, 1812; Salcedo to Viceroy, June 25, 1812, Operaciones de Guerra, Manuel Salcedo, 91–92, 83–84.
64. Gutiérrez de Lara, Diary, 4E–31b; Gutiérrez de Lara, "Diary, II," 293–294.
65. Castañeda, *Catholic Heritage,* 6:75; Henry P. Walker, "William McLane's Narrative of the Magee-Gutierrez Expedition, 1812–1813," *Southwestern Historical Quarterly* 66, no. 4 (1963): 581; Ted Schwarz and Robert H. Thonhoff, *Forgotten Battlefield of the First Texas Revolution: The Battle of Medina, August 18, 1813* (Austin: Eakin Press, 1985), 13.
66. José Bernardo Gutiérrez de Lara and Bernardo Despallier, "El coronel Don José Bernardo Gutiérrez de Lara desea que todos los Criollos avitantes en las Provincias de Mexico sepan lo siguente," Operaciones de Guerra, 101–102.
67. Elizabeth West attributes it to Álvarez de Toledo in Gutiérrez de Lara, "Diary, II," 294 n.38.
68. H. Glenn Brown and Maude O. Larsen Brown, *A Directory of the Book-Arts and Book Trade in Philadelphia to 1820, Including Painters and Engravers* (New York: New York Public Library, 1950), 12, 20; Emilio Rodríguez Demorizi, *La imprenta y los primeros periódicos de Santo Domingo,* 3rd ed. (Santo

Domingo, Dominican Republic: Taller de Impresiones (Publicación de la Biblioteca Nacional), 1973), 13–14; Sibylle Fischer, *Modernity Disavowed: Haiti and the Cultures of Slavery in the Age of Revolution* (Durham: Duke University Press, 2004), 180.

69. José Álvarez de Toledo, *Manifiesto ó satisfaccion pundonorosa, todos los buenos españoles europeos, y todos los pueblos de la America, por un diputado de las Cortes reunidas en Cadiz* (Philadelphia, 1811).

70. Eighteenth-century philosophers were engaging with a well-established philosophical discourse on friendship, one originating with the classics. See, for example, Laurie Shannon, *Sovereign Amity: Figures of Friendship in Shakespearean Contexts* (Chicago: University of Chicago Press, 2002).

71. Fred Morrow Fling, *Mirabeau and the French Revolution* (New York: G. P. Putnam's, 1908), 91.

72. Jacques Derrida, *The Politics of Friendship,* trans. George Collins (London: Verso, 2005), 253.

73. J. B. Schneewind, *The Invention of Autonomy: A History of Modern Moral Philosophy* (New York: Cambridge University Press, 1998), 508–515.

74. On novels and the cultivation of a new sense of intrapersonal ethics that had helped cultivate a sense of autonomy, see Nancy Armstrong, *How Novels Think: The Limits of British Individualism from 1719–1900* (New York: Columbia University Press, 2005); Lynn Avery Hunt, *Inventing Human Rights: A History* (New York: W. W. Norton, 2007). The concept of friendship would be picked up again by the English Romantic poets: see, for example, Samuel Taylor Coleridge's highly influential journal *The Friend* from 1809 to 1810.

75. José Blanco White, ed., *El Español* (London, 1810–1814), vol. 3, no. 16, July 10, 1811; Álvaro Flórez Estrada, *Exámen imparcial de las disensiones de la America con la España, de los medios de su reconciliacion, y de la prosperidad de todas las naciones,* 2nd ed. (Cádiz, Spain: Imprenta de Don Manuel Ximenez Careño, 1812).

76. Flórez Estrada, *Exámen imparcial,* 59–60.

77. José Álvarez de Toledo, *Amigo de los hombres, a todos los que habitan las islas y el vasto continente de la America española; obrita curiosa, interesante, y agradable seguida de un discurso sobre la intolerancia religiosa* (Philadelphia: Andres José Blocquerst, 1812), 1, hereafter cited in text.

78. Fredrick B. Pike, "The Cabildo and Colonial Loyalty to Hapsburg Rulers," *Journal of Inter-American Studies* 2, no. 4 (1960): 405–420; Tamar Herzog, *Defining Nations: Immigrants and Citizens in Early Modern Spain and Spanish America* (New Haven: Yale University Press, 2003).

79. On these political strategies of exclusion in eighteenth-century British political thought, see Uday Singh Mehta, *Liberalism and Empire: A Study in Nineteenth-Century British Liberal Thought* (Chicago: University of Chicago Press, 1999), 46–76. See also Dana D. Nelson, *National Manhood: Capitalist Citizenship and the Imagined Fraternity of White Men* (Durham: Duke University Press, 1998).

80. Nancy Vogeley, *The Bookrunner: A History of Early Inter-American Relations—Print, Politics, and Commerce in the United States and Mexico, 1800–1830* (Philadelphia: American Philosophical Society, 2011), 54.

81. José María Heredia, "En una tempestad: Oda al huracán (in Spanish)/In a Tempest: An Ode to the Hurricane (in English)," trans. Raúl Coronado and Armando García, in *The Heath Anthology of American Literature,* ed. Paul Lauter et al., vol. B (Boston: Wadsworth, 2013), 160–163. See also Raúl Coronado, "The Poetics of Disenchantment: José María Heredia and the Tempests of Modernity," *J19: The Journal of Nineteenth-Century Americanists* 1, no. 1 (Spring 2013): 184–189.
82. In their correspondence, insurgents in New Spain, including Texas, continued to use the Gregorian calendar but added to it the year or years from independence, as in "1813, 2nd year of independence."
83. I take this ontological-political conundrum to be at the heart of the first known Spanish-American (if not the first Hispanophone) historical novel (published in Philadelphia). Félix Varela's *Jicotencal* may be read as an attempt to synthesize various political moralities: Catholic and republican ones along with their antitheses, Catholic political claims to divine right and Machiavellian cynicism, for example. Félix Varela, *Jicoténcal* (Houston: Arte Publico Press, 1995); Anonymous, *Xicoténcatl,* trans. Guillermo I. Castillo-Feliú (Austin: University of Texas Press, 1999; orig. Boston, 1826). I follow Luis Leal and Juan Cortina's persuasive attribution of the novel to Varela. Not only does Castillo-Feliú not address Leal and Cortina's claim regarding Varela's authorship, but in his otherwise good translation he makes significant stylistic changes in verb tense that alter the theatrical feel of the original Spanish.

6. "We the *Pueblo* of the Province of Texas"

1. José Álvarez de Toledo, *Jesús, María, y José* (Philadelphia, 1811), hereafter cited in text; José Bernardo Gutiérrez de Lara, Diary, 1811–1812, Manuscripts Collections, Archives and Information Services Division, Texas State Library and Archives Commission, Austin, 4E–31b; José Bernardo Gutiérrez de Lara, "Diary of José Bernardo Gutiérrez de Lara, 1811–1812, II," trans. Elizabeth Howard West, *American Historical Review* 34, no. 2 (January 1929): 294. Governor Manuel Salcedo forwarded the broadsheet to Mexico City, and it is stored in Mexico's National Archives. A copy of the broadsheet was also collected by Thomas Winthrop Streeter sometime in the early twentieth century as part of his bibliographical project on Texas imprints; the Streeter Collection is now part of the Yale Beinecke Library's Western Americana Collection, all available on microfilm. Thomas W. Streeter, *Bibliography of Texas, 1795–1845,* vol. 1, part 1 (Cambridge, MA: Harvard University Press, 1955); Thomas W. Streeter, ed. *Texas as Province and Republic, 1795–1845: As Based on the Bibliography by Thomas W. Streeter* (New Haven, CT: Research Publications, 1983), reel 17, no. 1048. Oddly enough, the imprint has not been collected as part of the Early American Imprints series, the most thorough database of early U.S. imprints, despite the fact that it is a part of the Streeter Texana Collection.
2. For "pompous disquisition" and "pretentious tract," see Carlos Eduardo Castañeda, *Our Catholic Heritage in Texas, 1519–1936: Transition Period;*

the Fight for Freedom, 1810–1836, vol. 6 (New York: Arno Press, 1950), 75. For "tirade," see Harris G. Warren, *The Sword Was Their Passport: A History of American Filibustering in the Mexican Revolution* (Baton Rouge: Louisiana State University Press, 1943), 25. Garrett condescendingly ascribes the political ideals espoused in the literature to Anglo-American and French "doctrine." Kathryn Garrett, "The First Constitution of Texas, April 7, 1813," trans. Kathryn Garrett, *Southwestern Historical Quarterly* 40, no. 4 (1937): 291–292, 295. Guedea, citing Garrett, likewise attributes the political philosophy to Anglo-Americans. Virginia Guedea, "Autonomía e independencia en la provincia de Texas. La junta de gobierno de San Antonio de Béjar, 1813," in *La Independencia de México y el proceso autonomista novohispano 1808–1824*, ed. Virginia Guedea (Mexico City: Universidad Nacional Autónoma de México, 2001), 153. See also James Clark Milligan, "José Bernardo Gutiérrez de Lara: Mexican Frontiersman, 1811–1841" (PhD dissertation, Texas Tech University, Lubbock, 1975), 76.

3. Walter Flavius M'Caleb, "The First Period of the Gutierrez-Magee Expedition," *Southwestern Historical Quarterly* 4, no. 3 (1901): 229; Guedea, "Autonomía en Texas," 176; David E. Narrett, "José Bernardo Gutiérrez de Lara: *Caudillo* of the Mexican Republic in Texas," *Southwestern Historical Quarterly* 106, no. 2 (October 2002): 209.
4. James Gaines, "1835, (M. B. Lamar, Sabine River). Information from Capt. Gaines," in *The Papers of Mirabeau Buonaparte Lamar,* ed. Charles Adams Gulick Jr. and Katherine Elliott, vol. 1 (Austin: Texas State Library, 1920), 281; José Antonio Menchaca and Antonio Barrera, "Notes Taken from Menchaca and Barrera [regarding 1811–1813 insurrections, taken in 1857]," in *The Papers of Mirabeau Buonaparte Lamar,* ed. Harriet Smither, vol. 6 (Austin: Texas State Library, 1927), 340; José Antonio Navarro, *Defending Mexican Valor in Texas: José Antonio Navarros' Historical Writings, 1853–1857* (Austin: State House Press, 1995), quote from pp. 57, 74 (*Defending Mexican Valor* includes the English translation followed by a facsimile of the Spanish original.
5. Patriota sensible, *El triunfo de la virtud y del patriotismo proclama* (Philadelphia, 1813).
6. Gutiérrez de Lara to Luis Grande, September 4, 1812, Bexar Archives, the Dolph Briscoe Center for American History, University of Texas at Austin (hereafter "Bexar Archives"), reel 52:414–416; Operaciones de Guerra, Manuel Salcedo, 1810–1812, BANC MSS M-A1 (FILM 3097: reel 3), selected transcriptions from the Archivo General de la Nación. Documents for the History of Mexico (ca. 1524–1855), Bancroft Library, University of California, Berkeley (hereafter "Operaciones de Guerra, Manuel Salcedo"), 125.
7. Gutiérrez de Lara to Luis Grande, September 4, 1812, Bexar Archives, reel 52:414–416.
8. Angel Rama, *The Lettered City,* trans. John Charles Chasteen (Durham: Duke University Press, 1996), 24.
9. Cited in Roger Chartier, "Reading Matter and 'Popular' Reading: From the Renaissance to the Seventeenth Century," in *A History of Reading in the West,* ed.

Guglielmo Cavallo et al. (Amherst: University of Massachusetts Press, 1999), 276.

10. Arnoldo De León, *The Tejano Community, 1836–1900* (Albuquerque: University of New Mexico Press, 1982), 188–189; Arnoldo De León and Kenneth L. Stewart, *Tejanos and the Numbers Game:A Socio-Historical Interpretation from the Federal Censuses, 1850–1900* (Albuquerque: University of New Mexico Press, 1989), 36; Carlos Newland, "La educacion elemental en Hispanoamérica: Desde la independencia hasta la centralizacion de los sistemas educativos nacionales," *Hispanic American Historical Review* 71, no. 2 (1991): 357; Kenneth L. Stewart and Arnoldo De León, *Not Room Enough:Mexicans, Anglos, and Socio-Economic Change in Texas, 1850–1900* (Albuquerque: University of New Mexico Press, 1993), 66–67.
11. The ethnocentric concept that illiterate people did not engage symbolically with textuality was aptly criticized by Derrida in his review of Lévi-Strauss's logocentrism. Jacques Derrida, *Of Grammatology,* trans. Gayatri Chakravorty Spivak (Baltimore: Johns Hopkins University Press, 1997), quote is from pp. 55, 109; for Derrida's critique of Lévi-Strauss, see pp. 101–140.
12. Margit Frenk, "Lectores y oidores: La difusión oral de la literatura en el Siglo de Oro," in *Actas del Séptimo Congreso de la Asociación Internacional de Hispanistas, celebrado del 25 al 30 de agosto de 1980* (Rome: Bulzoni, 1982), 115–116.
13. Dominique Julia, "Reading and the Counter-Reformation," in Guglielmo Cavallo et al., *History of Reading,* 238–239, emphasis added.
14. Alfredo Ávila, "México: un viejo nombre para una nueva nación," in *Crear la nación: los nombres de los países de América Latina,* ed. José Carlos Chiaramonte et al. (Buenos Aires: Editorial Sudamericana, 2008), 277; Dorothy Tanck de Estrada, "En búsqueda de México y los mexicanos en el siglo XVIII," in *Crear la nación: los nombres de los países de América Latina,* ed. José Carlos Chiaramonte et al. (Buenos Aires: Editorial Sudamericana, 2008), 260–263.
15. Jesús F. de la Teja, *San Antonio de Béxar: A Community on New Spain's Northern Frontier* (Albuquerque: University of New Mexico Press, 1995), 152–156.
16. For an illuminating analysis on the etymological shifts in "rebellion" and "revolution," see Hannah Arendt, *On Revolution* (New York: Penguin Books, 2006), 11–48.
17. Otis H. Green, *Spain and the Western Tradition: The Castilian Mind in Literature from El Cid to Calderón,* vol. 2 (Madison: University of Wisconsin Press, 1964), 75–104; Paul E. Sigmund, "Law and Politics," in *The Cambridge Companion to Aquinas,* ed. Norman Kretzmann and Eleonore Stump (New York: Cambridge University Press, 1993); Saint Thomas Aquinas, *Political Writings,* trans. R. W. Dyson (New York: Cambridge University Press, 2002), 5–51, 83–95.
18. Quentin Skinner's account remains the most cogent analysis of the Protestant Reformation's political philosopy. See his *Foundations of Modern Political Thought: The Age of the Reformation,* vol. 2 (Cambridge, UK: Cambridge University Press, 1978), 3–108.

19. Ibid., 184; José Antonio Maravall, *Teoría del estado en España en el siglo 17*, 2nd ed. (Madrid: Centro de Estudios Constitucionales, 1997); J. A. Fernández-Santamaría, *Natural Law, Constitutionalism, Reason of State, and War: Counter-Reformation Spanish Political Thought*, 2 vols. (New York: Peter Lang, 2005); Annabel S. Brett, "Scholastic Political Thought and the Modern Concept of the State," in *Rethinking the Foundations of Modern Political Thought*, ed. Annabel S. Brett et al. (New York: Cambridge University Press, 2006), 137–138.
20. Writing in the early fifth century and witnessing the collapse of the Roman empire, Augustine developed a profoundly pessimistic account of human nature and of the earthly world, while celebrating the spiritual, heavenly City of God. Saint Augustine, Bishop of Hippo, *The City of God against the Pagans* (New York: Cambridge University Press, 1998). Aquinas, on the other hand, lived in the thirteenth century, a period of relative peace where the Church enjoyed hegemony, and his writings evince a generally more optimistic account of human nature and of the earthly world. Aquinas, *Political Writings*. Augustine would come to have a more significant impact on Protestant reformers while Aquinas experienced a revival among Catholic Reformers.
21. Bernice Hamilton, *Political Thought in Sixteenth-Century Spain* (London: Oxford University Press, 1963); Skinner, *Foundations*, 2:144–166; Maravall, *Teoría del estado en España en el siglo 17*, 115–150; J. A. Fernández-Santamaría, *Natural Law, Constitutionalism, Reason of State, and War: Counter-Reformation Spanish Political Thought*, vol. 1 (New York: Peter Lang, 2005), 79–109.
22. For a recent reengagement of these scholars along these lines, see Enrique Dussel, "Origen de filosofía política moderna: Las Casas, Vitoria, y Suárez (1514–1617)," *Caribbean Studies* 33, no. 2 (July–December 2005): 63–64; Miguel Molina Martínez, "Pactismo e independencia en Iberoamérica, 1808–1811," *Revista de estudios colombinos*, no. 4 (2008): 61–74; Mónica Quijada, "From Spain to New Spain: Revisiting the *Potestas Populi* in Hispanic Political Thought," *Mexican Studies/Estudios Mexicanos* 24, no. 2 (2008): 185–219.
23. Skinner, *Foundations*, 2:174.
24. Skinner, *Foundations*, 2:138. Skinner is perhaps one of the few Anglophone scholars to seriously engage with Catholic political philosophers in writing about the broader history of Western political thought. One senses, however, that he barely scratches the surface. Skinner, *Foundations*, 2:113–184. The most useful overviews of the School of Salamanca are Hamilton, *Political Thought;* Maravall, *Teoría del estado en España;* Fernández-Santamaría, *Natural Law.* The revival of Thomism was primarily a Spanish affair; however, their influence spread throughout Europe, and there were other important Thomists writing in Italy and France. Along with Skinner, useful overviews of Suárez's oeuvre include Heinrich Rommen, "Francis Suarez," *Review of Politics* 10, no. 4 (1948): 437–461; Reijo Wilenius, *The Social and Political Theory of Francisco Suárez* (Helsinki: Societas Philosophica Fennica, 1963); Frederick Charles Copleston, *A History of Philosophy: Late Medieval and Renaissance*

Philosophy, Ockham, Francis Bacon, and the Beginning of the Modern World, vol. 3 (New York: Doubleday, 1993), 353–405; José Pereira, *Suárez: Between Scholasticism and Modernity* (Milwaukee: Marquette University Press, 2007).

25. Francisco Suárez cited in Wilenius, *Suárez,* 76; Francisco Suárez, *Defensa de la fe católica y apostólica contra los errores del anglicanismo,* trans. José Ramón Eguillor Muniozguren, S.I., vol. 2 (Madrid: Instituto de Estudios Políticos, 1970), 218 (bk. 3, ch. 2, art. 5). See also Hamilton, *Political Thought,* 35–43; Skinner, *Foundations,* 2:161.
26. Wilenius, *Suárez,* 79, 85; Lee Ward, *The Politics of Liberty in England and Revolutionary America* (New York: Cambridge University Press, 2004), 23–47.
27. For relevant representative work see Francisco Suárez, *Selections from Three Works: De legibus, ac deo legislatore, 1612; Defensio fidei catholicae, et apostolicae adversus anglicanae sectae errores, 1613; De triplici virtute theologica, fide, spe, et charitate, 1621* (Oxford: Clarendon Press, 1944); Francisco Suárez, *Tratado de las leyes y de Dios legislador en diez libros,* trans. José Ramón Eguillor and Luis Vela Sánchez, 6 vols. (Madrid: Instituto de Estudios Políticos, 1967); Francisco Suárez, *Defensa de la fe católica y apostólica contra los errores del anglicanismo,* trans. José Ramón Eguillor Muniozguren, S.I., 4 vols. (Madrid: Instituto de Estudios Políticos, 1970).
28. O. Carlos Stoetzer, *El pensamiento político en la América española durante el período de la emancipación, 1789–1825. Las bases hispánicas y las corrientes europeas,* vol. 1 (Madrid: Instituto de Estudios Políticos, 1966), 65, 72.
29. Joaquín Varela Suanzes-Carpegna, *La teoría del estado en los orígenes del constitucionalismo hispánico. Las Cortes de Cádiz* (Madrid: Centro de Estudios Constitucionales, 1983), 25–38.
30. Though Lanning and Stoetzer had made these claims earlier, few have heeded them. For more recent work that develops these claims, see Richard Morse, "Claims of Political Tradition, *New World Soundings: Culture and Ideology in the Americas* (Baltimore: Johns Hopkins University Press, 1989), 95–130; Manuel Chust Calero, ed., *Revoluciones y revolucionarios en el mundo hispano* (Madrid: Universitat Jaume I, 2000); José Carlos Chiaramonte, "Fundamentos Iusnaturalistas de los movimientos de independencia," in *Las guerras de independencia en la América española,* ed. Marta Terán et al. (Morelia, Michoacán, Mexico: El Colegio de Michoacán, 2002); José Carlos Chiaramonte, "The Principle of Consent in Latin and Anglo-American Independence," *Journal of Latin American Studies* 36, no. 3 (2004): 563–586; José Carlos Chiaramonte, *La ilustración en el Río de la Plata: cultura eclesiástica y cultura laica durante el Virreinato* (Buenos Aires: Editorial Sudamericana, 2007); Quijada, "From Spain to New Spain"; Jaime E. Rodríguez O., "Sobre la supuesta influencia de la independencia de los Estados Unidos en las independencias hispanoamericanas," *Revista de Indias* 70, no. 250 (2011): 691–714.
31. Suárez, *Selections,* 143–360. For critical reviews of his political philosophy, see Hamilton, *Political Thought,* 11–29; Wilenius, *Suárez,* 50–65; Skinner, *Foundations,* 2:148–154; Fernández-Santamaría, *Natural Law,* 75–148.

32. Skinner, *Foundations,* 2:155–167.
33. In referring to Thomas Hobbes as Protestant I mean to emphasize that he was a product of a Protestant world. That is, his intellectual genealogy stems from the long discursive history of the concept of rights in the West, one that parted from the Catholic concept of rights during the Reformation and had developed, especially, around the concept of the right to resist tyrannical rulers. Skinner, *Foundations,* 2:327–348; Brian Tierney, *The Idea of Natural Rights* (Grand Rapids, MI: William B. Eerdmans, 2001), 288–289, 329–342; Brett, "Scholastic Political Thought," 137–138.
34. "A Treatise on Laws and God the Lawgiver," in Suárez, *Selections,* 375 (bk. 3, ch. 2, art. 4); Francisco Suárez, *Tratado de las leyes y de Dios legislador en diez libros,* trans. José Ramón Eguillor and Luis Vela Sánchez, vol. 2 (Madrid: Instituto de Estudios Políticos, 1967), "Ley civil" (bk. 3, ch. 2, art. 4). See also Copleston, *History of Philosophy,* 393–395.
35. Skinner, *Foundations,* 2:165–166; Fernández-Santamaría, *Natural Law,* 175–193.
36. Fernández-Santamaría, *Natural Law,* 187.
37. Ibid., 188.
38. "A Treatise on Laws and God the Lawgiver," in Suárez, *Selections,* 373 (bk. 3, ch. 2, art. 3); Suárez, *Tratado,* vol. 2, "Ley civil" (bk. 3, ch. 2, art. 3).
39. Skinner, *Foundations,* 2:177–178, 183.
40. For a useful overview of these philosophers and their theories, see Leo Strauss, ed., *History of Political Philosophy* (Chicago: University of Chicago Press, 1987).
41. Skinner, *Foundations,* 2:20–108; Talal Asad, *Formations of the Secular: Christianity, Islam, Modernity* (Stanford: Stanford University Press, 2003), 174. Beginning in the eighteenth century, the Spanish Bourbon monarchy would try to follow the path of England and France, and attempted to wrest temporal power from the Church. Colin M. MacLachlan, *Spain's Empire in the New World: The Role of Ideas in Institutional and Social Change* (Berkeley: University of California Press, 1988), 1–7.
42. Skinner, *Foundations,* 2:172. See also Tierney, *The Idea of Natural Rights,* 288ff. Stoetzer makes a related claim in arguing that Spain had its own Renaissance and Reformation. O. Carlos Stoetzer, *The Scholastic Roots of the Spanish American Revolution* (New York: Fordham University Press, 1979), 53 n.20.
43. The Reformation, as Enrique Dussel has noted, coincides not coincidentally with the arrival of Europeans in the Americas and the consequent expansion of imperialism. Enrique Dussel, "Europe, Modernity, and Eurocentrism," *Nepantla: Views from South* 1, no. 3 (2000): 465–478. While Dussel here appears to be too quick to homogenize all of European modernity, and oddly enough ignores the modernity he is actually most interested in (a Catholic, Indo-Hispanic modernity that emerged in the southern Atlantic and Pacific), his more recent publications demonstrate a keen interest in this intellectual formation. See, for example, Dussel, "Origen"; Enrique Dussel, "'Being-in-the-World-Hispanically': A World on the 'Border' of Many Worlds," trans. Alexander Stehn, *Comparative Literature* 61, no. 3 (2009): 256–273.

44. For a reading of the trope of solitude in late eighteenth-century United States culture, see "Being Alone in the Age of Social Contract," in Slauter, *The State as a Work of Art,* 215–240.
45. Jean-Jacques Rousseau, *The Social Contract and Other Later Political Writings* (New York: Cambridge University Press, 1997), 42.
46. On the history of autonomy and possessive individualism, see Charles Taylor, *Sources of the Self: The Making of the Modern Identity* (Cambridge, MA: Harvard University Press, 1989), 185–198; J. B. Schneewind, *The Invention of Autonomy: A History of Modern Moral Philosophy* (New York: Cambridge University Press, 1998); Lynn Avery Hunt, *Inventing Human Rights: A History* (New York: W. W. Norton, 2007), 70–112; C. B. Macpherson, *The Political Theory of Possessive Individualism: Hobbes to Locke* (New York: Oxford University Press, 2011).
47. See the classic study by Jay Fliegelman, *Prodigals and Pilgrims: The American Revolution against Patriarchal Authority, 1750–1800* (New York: Cambridge University Press, 1982). On the patriarchal origins of the social contract, see Carole Pateman, *The Sexual Contract* (Stanford: Stanford University Press, 1988), 19–38.
48. Richard Tuck, *Natural Rights Theories: Their Origin and Development* (New York: Cambridge University Press, 1979), 11–17. Also see Tierney, *The Idea of Natural Rights.*
49. Tuck, *Natural Rights Theories,* 5–31, 59–61; Schneewind, *The Invention of Autonomy,* 78–81; Tierney, *The Idea of Natural Rights,* 78–89, 131–169; Ward, *Politics of Liberty,* 1–6, 80–81, 213–246; Macpherson, *Possessive Individualism.*
50. Tuck, *Natural Rights Theories,* 17–24.
51. Andrés Tijerina, *Tejanos and Texas under the Mexican Flag, 1821–1836* (College Station: Texas A&M University Press, 1994), 47.
52. Varela Suanzes-Carpegna, *Teoría del estado,* 62–66, 182; Annick Lempérière, "República y publicidad a finales del antiguo régimen (Nueva España)," in *Los espacios públicos en Iberoamérica: Ambigüedades y problemas, siglos XVIII–XIX,* ed. François-Xavier Guerra et al. (Mexico City: Fondo de Cultura Económica, 1998), 72–79.
53. Varela Suanzes-Carpegna, *Teoría del estado,* 66, 182.
54. Gillian Brown, *Domestic Individualism: Imagining Self in Nineteenth-Century America* (Berkeley: University of California Press, 1990); Nancy Ruttenburg, *Democratic Personality: Popular Voice and the Trial of American Authorship* (Stanford: Stanford University Press, 1998); Cathy N. Davidson, *Revolution and the Word: The Rise of the Novel in America* (New York: Oxford University Press, 2004), 306–355; Nancy Armstrong, *How Novels Think: The Limits of British Individualism from 1719–1900* (New York: Columbia University Press, 2005); Hunt, *Inventing,* 35–69.
55. For a fascinating account of the difficulty in forming possessive individualism (though she does not use this term) via the tearing apart of the family in *Periquillo,* see Nancy Vogeley, *Lizardi and the Birth of the Novel in Spanish America* (Gainesville: University Press of Florida, 2001), 83–107.

56. Varela Suanzes-Carpegna, *Teoría del estado,* 182–202.
57. Jeremy Adelman likewise places the Latin American revolutions within the political philosophical framework of sovereignty rather than democracy. Jeremy Adelman, *Sovereignty and Revolution in the Iberian Atlantic* (Princeton: Princeton University Press, 2006), 6, 370–372.
58. Molina Martínez, "Pactismo e independencia," 64.
59. Stoetzer, *Pensamiento político,* 1:52.
60. Jean Sarrailh, *La España ilustrada de la segunda mitad del siglo XVIII,* trans. Antonio Alatorre (Mexico City: Fondo de Cultura Económica, 1957), 291–321; Richard Herr, *The Eighteenth-Century Revolution in Spain* (Princeton: Princeton University Press, 1958), 63–66, 168; Jefferson Rea Spell, *Rousseau in the Spanish World Before 1833: A Study in Franco-Spanish Literary Relations* (New York: Octagon Books, 1969). While Spell's book is impeccably researched, he attributes expressions of the social contract to Rousseau without any mention of Scholastic philosophers' influence; Stoetzer, *Scholastic,* 20, 42–43, 51, 80–83; Boleslao Lewin, *Rousseau en la independencia de latinoamérica* (Buenos Aires: Ediciones Depalma, 1980); Varela Suanzes-Carpegna, *Teoría del estado,* 29; Molina Martínez, "Pactismo e independencia." Locke and Rousseau would not have a significant impact on Spanish-American thought until after the initiation of the first Spanish-American declarations of independence in 1811, and even then these non-Hispanic philosophers would meld with, rather than replace, Scholastic social contract theory. Manuel Giménez Fernández, *Las doctrinas populistas en la independencia de Hispano-América* (Sevilla: La Escuela de Estudios Hispano-Americanos, 1947), 3; Stoetzer, *Pensamiento político,* 1:25–38; Stoetzer, *Scholastic,* 84; Varela Suanzes-Carpegna, *Teoría del estado,* 26–31; Molina Martínez, "Pactismo e independencia," 73.
61. John Tate Lanning, *Academic Culture in the Spanish Colonies* (New York: Oxford University Press, 1940), 87; Stoetzer, *Scholastic,* 81–84.
62. Alexander von Humboldt, *Ensayo político sobre el reino de la Nueva-España,* trans. Vicente González Arnao, vol. 1 (Paris: Rosa, 1822), 225, emphasis added.
63. Stoetzer, *Pensamiento político,* 1:81; Stoetzer, *Scholastic,* 73, 121–122.
64. Gabriel Saldívar, *Historia compendiada de Tamaulipas* (Tamaulipas, Mexico: Editorial Beatriz de Silva, 1945), 135–137; quote is from Spanish captain Pedro López Priettô, "An Indian Uprising in Camargo, 1812: A Military Report by Captain Pedro López Priettô," trans. and ed. Clotilde P. García, *Southwestern Historical Quarterly* 78, no. 4 (1975): 432–436, 443; Juan Fidel Zorrilla and Carlos González Salas, "Gutiérrez de Lara, José Antonio Apolinario (1770–1843) y Gutiérrez de Lara, José Bernardo Maximiliano (1774–1841)," in *Diccionario biográfico de Tamaulipas* (Ciudad Victoria, Mexico: Instituto de Investigaciones Históricas, Universidad Autónoma de Tamaulipas, 1984), 72; on the ethnohistory of the Carrizo nation, see Martín Salinas, *Indians of the Rio Grande Delta: Their Role in the History of Southern Texas and Northeastern Mexico* (Austin: University of Texas Press, 1990), 91–94.

65. Mendiola to Bustamante, June 15, 1812, Operaciones de Guerra, Manuel Salcedo, 124.
66. The archive dates from 1810 to 1812 and consists of Salcedo's correspondence and correspondence sent to him from his officers, governors of surrounding provinces, and other officials throughout the region. All of this correspondence was then forwarded to his immediate superior (and uncle) Commandant General Nemesio Salcedo in Chihuahua, Mexico.
67. Gilberto M. Hinojosa and Anne A. Fox, "Indians and Their Culture in San Fernando de Béxar," in *Tejano Origins in Eighteenth-Century San Antonio,* ed. Gerald E. Poyo and Gilberto M. Hinojosa (Austin: University of Texas Press, 1991); Patricia Osante, *Orígenes del Nuevo Santander (1748–1772)* (Mexico City: Universidad Nacional Autónoma de México, 1997), 146–151, 226–234; Patricia Osante, "Colonization and Control: The Case of Nuevo Santander," trans. Ned F. Brierley, in *Choice, Persuasion, and Coercion: Social Control on Spain's North American Frontiers,* ed. Jesús F. de la Teja and Ross Frank (Albuquerque: University of New Mexico Press, 2005), 238–241.
68. Mendiola to Bustamante, June 15, 1812, Operaciones de Guerra, Manuel Salcedo, 125.
69. Indians, not Spanish Americans, continued to exert superior military strength in Texas through the mid-nineteenth century. But the phenotypic line between both groups was often blurred and indistinguishable. As José Antonio Menchaca recalled in his memoir, Indians would raid San Antonio, kill its residents at random, and "would dress themselves with the clothes of the victim, and would promenade the streets at will." José Antonio Menchaca, *Memoirs* (San Antonio: Yanaguana Society, 1937). On the difficulty of finding archival evidence of indigenous voices in Spanish-Mexican Texas, see Raúl A. Ramos, *Beyond the Alamo: Forging Mexican Ethnicity in San Antonio, 1821–1861* (Chapel Hill: University of North Carolina Press, 2008), 78–79.
70. John Villars, "Report on Battles for Independence [1812–1813]," in Gulick and Elliott, *Papers of Mirabeau Buonaparte Lamar,* 1:145–146, 150–151; Julia K. Garrett, *Green Flag over Texas: A Story of the Last Years of Spain in Texas* (New York: Cordova, 1939), 145; Harry M. Henderson, "The Magee-Gutiérrez Expedition," *Southwestern Historical Quarterly* 55 (July 1951): 145; Félix D. Almaráz Jr., *Tragic Cavalier: Governor Manuel Salcedo of Texas, 1808–1813,* 2nd ed. (College Station: Texas A&M University Press, 1991), 159, 168–169; Guedea, "Autonomía en Texas," 153–155; Narrett, "Gutiérrez de Lara," 202, 209, 212.
71. "Mis amados compatriotas vezinos y abitantes, del Reyno Mexicano," "Gefes, soldados y vecinos de San Antonio de Bexar," "Amados, y honrados, compatriotas los que abitais en la provincia de Texas," September 1, 1812, Operaciones de Guerra, Manuel Salcedo, 149–154; José Bernardo Gutiérrez de Lara, "The following is the address, (by proclamation) of Colonel Barnardo, to the Republican Volunteers at Nachogdoches [*sic*]," *Louisiana Herald,* August 31, 1812. *Vecinos* was a political category established during the Spanish medieval period and used in the Americas that accorded individuals rights and

membership of a town. Tamar Herzog, *Defining Nations: Immigrants and Citizens in Early Modern Spain and Spanish America* (New Haven: Yale University Press, 2003).

72. José Bernardo Gutiérrez de Lara, "1815, Aug. 1, J. B. Gutierrez de Lara to the Mexican Congress, an Account of the Progress of the Revolution from the Beginning," in Gulick and Elliot, *Papers of Mirabeau Buonaparte Lamar,* 1:17; Castañeda, *Catholic Heritage,* 6:100, 102; Narrett, "Gutiérrez de Lara," 218. In an otherwise impeccably researched history, Garrett in 1939 cites Shaler in claiming that Bernardo lacked adequate leadership skills, and "appeared to be under the influence of fear, that he was the only person in Natchitoches who doubted the success of the enterprise, and that Gutiérrez reluctantly took his departure after many expressions of gratitude to the United States Government and its agents for their countenance and kindness." Garrett, *Green Flag,* 150. Ironically, Garrett herself had documented Shaler's condescending, culturally supremacist attitudes toward Spanish America.

73. "Mis amados compatriotas vezinos y abitantes, del Reyno Mexicano," "Gefes, soldados y vecinos de San Antonio de Bexar," September 1, 1812, Operaciones de Guerra, Manuel Salcedo, 149, 151.

74. Jeri Robison Turner, "Goliad, TX," *Handbook of Texas Online* (http://www.tshaonline.org/handbook/online/articles/hjg05), accessed October 27, 2011.

75. Gutiérrez de Lara, "To the Mexican Congress," 13–17; Garrett, *Green Flag,* 167–174; Castañeda, *Catholic Heritage,* 6:86–100; Milligan, "Gutiérrez de Lara," 52–75; Almaráz, *Cavalier,* 164–173; Guedea, "Autonomía en Texas," 151–160.

76. Garrett, "The First Constitution of Texas, April 7, 1813"; Castañeda, *Catholic Heritage,* 6:102–104; Milligan, "Gutiérrez de Lara," 76–90. The fact that the declaration was signed by thirty men and that Bernardo's signature does not appear on any of these documents belies the claim made by several historians that Bernardo singlehandedly declared independence with little to no support from the residents of San Antonio.

77. Junta de Béxar, "Nos el pueblo dela provincia de Texas [Declaration of Independence]," April 6, 1813, BANC MSS M-A1 (FILM 3097: reel 2:15–21), Operaciones de Guerra, José Joaquín de Arredondo, Brigadier 1811–1821, Selected Transcriptions from the Archivo General de la Nación. Documents for the History of Mexico (ca. 1524–1855), Bancroft Library, University of California, Berkeley (hereafter "Operaciones de Guerra, José Joaquín de Arredondo"), vol. 4, reel 2:16.

78. On June 7, the commandant general of the Spanish royal forces of the Eastern Internal Provinces, Joaquín de Arredondo, forwarded to the Spanish viceroy all of Bernardo's proclamations. Joaquín de Arredondo to Viceroy Félix María Calleja, June 7, 1813, Operaciones de Guerra, José Joaquín de Arredondo, vol. 4, reel 2:2.

79. Guedea, "Autonomía en Texas," 164. See especially Garrett, "The First Constitution of Texas, April 7, 1813"; Milligan, "Gutiérrez de Lara," 76.

80. Junta de Béxar, "Nos el pueblo de Texas," 15. Mexico would not declare its own independence for another seven months, on November 6, 1813.

81. Ibid., 19–20.
82. For arguments that modern Spanish-American political culture is rooted in Suarezian theories, see also, among the sources above, Timothy E. Anna, *Forging Mexico, 1821–1835* (Lincoln: University of Nebraska Press, 1998), 44–50.
83. Carlos E. Castañeda had made this bold claim in 1950; however, historians have apparently not been aware of this. In 2001, the Mexican historian Virginia Guedea made the same claim, apparently not aware that Castañeda had done so fifty years prior (though she does cite him on other matters). Castañeda, *Catholic Heritage,* 6:viii; Virginia Guedea, "Autonomía e independencia en la provincia de Texas: La junta de gobierno de San Antonio de Béjar, 1813," in *La Independencia de México y el proceso autonomista novohispano 1808–1824,* ed. Virginia Guedea (Mexico City: Universidad Nacional Autónoma de México, 2001), 135; Virginia Guedea, "La primera Declaración de independencia y la primera Constitución novohispana," in *Las guerras de independencia en la América española,* ed. Marta Terán and José Antonio Serrano (Morelia, Michoacán, Mexico: El Colegio de Michoacán, Instituto Nacional de Antropología e Historia, Universidad Michoacana de San Nicolás de Hidalgo, 2002).
84. Among the most reliable accounts, though with varying interpretations, is Garrett, *Green Flag;* Castañeda, *Catholic Heritage,* 6:86–120; Milligan, "Gutiérrez de Lara," 76–105; Ted Schwarz and Robert H. Thonhoff, *Forgotten Battlefield of the First Texas Revolution: The Battle of Medina, August 18, 1813* (Austin: Eakin Press, 1985); Almaráz, *Cavalier;* José Antonio Navarro, "Apuntes Históricos Interesantes de San Antonio de Béxar, escritos por el C. Dn. José Antonio Navarro, en noviembre de 1853," in *Defending Mexican Valor in Texas: José Antonio Navarro's Historical Writings, 1853–1857,* ed. David R. McDonald and Timothy M. Matovina (Austin: State House Press, 1995). Many historians in the United States had, until relatively recently, relied on the imperialist nineteenth-century historian Henderson Yoakum as a reliable source. That Yoakum had fought against Mexicans during the U.S.-Mexican War and that this experience may have informed his writing of *The History of Texas* seems to have gone unnoticed by historians. Henderson Yoakum, *History of Texas from Its Settlement in 1685 to Its Annexation to the United States in 1846,* 2 vols. (New York: Redfield, 1855). For one of the few critical readings of Yoakum, see Carroll Van West, "Democratic Ideology and the Antebellum Historian: The Case of Henderson Yoakum," *Journal of the Early Republic* 3, no. 3 (1983): 334–339.
85. Testimony taken from fourteen men by José Antonio Benavides, April 8 and 15, 1813, Operaciones de Guerra, José Joaquín de Arredondo, vol. 3, reel 2:249–250, 331–332. See also Garrett, *Green Flag,* 180–181; Castañeda, *Catholic Heritage,* 6:99; Almaráz, *Cavalier,* 171; Navarro, "Apuntes," 15–16.
86. Gaines, "1835, (M. B. Lamar, Sabine River)," 281; Menchaca and Barrera, "Notes," 340; Garrett, *Green Flag,* 180–181; Almaráz, *Cavalier,* 171.
87. For a discussion of the various interpretations of these events, see Guedea, "Autonomía en Texas," 61–62; Narrett, "Gutiérrez de Lara," 196–198.

88. Castañeda, *Catholic Heritage,* 6:100, 108–109; Narrett, "Gutiérrez de Lara," 218.
89. Garrett, *Green Flag,* 191.
90. Castañeda, *Catholic Heritage,* 6:129. See also Eric John Bradner, "José Álvarez de Toledo and the Spanish American Revolution" (PhD dissertation, Northwestern University, Evanston, Illinois, 1931); Harris Gaylord Warren, "José Álvarez de Toledo's Initiation as a Filibuster, 1811–1813," *Hispanic American Historical Review* 20, no. 1 (1940): 56–82; Harris G. Warren, "José Álvarez de Toledo's Reconciliation with Spain and Projects for Suppressing Rebellion in the Spanish Colonies," *Louisiana Historical Quarterly* 23, no. 3 (July 1940): 827–863; Kristin A. Dykstra, "On the Betrayal of Nations: José Alvarez de Toledo's Philadelphia *Manifesto* (1811) and *Justification* (1816)," *CR: The New Centennial Review* 4, no. 1 (2004): 267–305.
91. Onís to Arredondo, August 20, 1813, Bexar Archives, reel 53:140–141; Bradner, "Toledo," 23.
92. José Álvarez de Toledo and William Shaler, eds., *Gaceta de Texas* (Natchitoches, LA, 1813); José Álvarez de Toledo and William Shaler, eds., *El Mexicano* (Natchitoches, LA, 1813); Marilyn McAdams Sibley, *Lone Stars and State Gazettes: Texas Newspapers before the Civil War* (College Station: Texas A&M University Press, 1983), 15–27; Sara E. Johnson, *The Fear of French Negroes: Transcolonial Collaboration in the Revolutionary Americas* (Berkeley and Los Angeles: University of California Press, 2012), 91–114.
93. Gutiérrez de Lara, "To the Mexican Congress," 18.
94. Anonymous, "Early History of San Antonio [1853]," in *The Papers of Mirabeau Buonaparte Lamar,* ed. Charles Adams Gulick Jr., vol. 4, part 2 (Austin: Texas State Library, 1925), quote is from p. 9; Bradner, "Toledo," 37–39; Lorenzo de la Garza, *Dos hermanos héroes* (Mexico City: Editorial Cultura. Ex-Libris José Ramírez Flores, 1939; orig. 1913), 64–69; Garrett, *Green Flag,* 217–221; Castañeda, *Catholic Heritage,* 6 :106–112; Narrett, "Gutiérrez de Lara," 223. For Bernardo's account see José Bernardo Gutiérrez de Lara, "1815, Aug. 1, J. B. Gutierrez de Lara to the Mexican Congress, an account of the progress of the revolution from the beginning," in Gulick and Elliott, *Papers of Mirabeau Buonaparte Lamar,* 1:17–19; José Bernardo Maximiliano Gutiérrez de Lara, *Breve apologia que el Coronel D. Jose Bernardo Gutierrez de Lara hace de las imposturas calumniosas que se le articulan en un folleto intitulado: Levantamiento de un general en las Tamaulipas contra la Republica, o Muerto que se le aparece al gobierno en aquel estado* (Monterrey, Nuevo Leon, Mexico: Ymprenta del ciudadano Pedro Gonzalez y socio, 1827).
95. Joaquin de Arredondo, "Joaquín de Arredondo's Report of the Battle of the Medina, August 18, 1813," trans. and ed. Mattie A. Hatcher, *Southwestern Historical Quarterly* 11, no. 3 (January 1908): 220–236; Garrett, *Green Flag,* 224.
96. Castañeda, *Catholic Heritage,* 6:115–116. Arredondo reports 1,000 insurgents were killed. For detailed reports on the battle, see Juan Gutiérrez to Joaquín de Arredondo, August 25, 1813; Arredondo to Félix Trudeaux, Sep-

tember [no date given] 1813; Arredondo to Viceroy Calleja, September 13, 1813; Ignacio Elizondo to Arredondo, September 2, 1813, Operaciones de Guerra, José Joaquín de Arredondo, vol. 4, reel 2:130–133, 136–138, 143–162, 181–186.

97. Garrett, *Green Flag,* 223–229; Schwarz and Thonhoff, *Forgotten Battlefield of the First Texas Revolution,* 97–115. On Álvarez de Toledo's activities in Louisiana, his attempts to disrupt other revolutionary plots, and his ultimate reconciliation with Spain, see Warren, "Toledo's Reconciliation"; Castañeda, *Catholic Heritage,* 6:129–142.

98. Anonymous, "Memoria de las cosas más notables que acaecieron en Bexar el año de 13 mandando el Tirano Arredondo, 1813," MSS P-O 811, Herbert Bolton Papers (No. 711), Bancroft Library, University of California, Berkeley, 1. Castañeda reports 300 individuals fled. Castañeda, *Catholic Heritage,* 6:116. See Appendix 4 for transcription and translation.

99. Arredondo had a cataract in one eye. Menchaca and Barrera, "Notes," 338.

100. Anonymous, "Early History of San Antonio [1853]," 10–11.

101. Anonymous, "Memoria de las cosas," 1–2; hereafter cited in text.

102. One of the other few testimonies of these horrific events is that of José Antonio Menchaca, who was thirteen at the time. Menchaca, *Memoirs,* 18.

103. Ibid., 19. Another account states that Serrano stabbed and killed the second captain. Villars, "Report on Battles for Independence [1812–1813]," 154. On Menchaca's memoirs see Timothy M. Matovina, "José Antonio Menchaca: Narrating a Tejano Life," in *Tejano Leadership in Mexican and Revolutionary Texas,* ed. Jesús F. de la Teja (College Station: Texas A&M University Press, 2010), 171–193.

104. Menchaca, *Memoirs,* 18.

105. A *metate* is a traditional Mesoamerican flat mortar.

106. Castañeda cites Garrett's summary. Jackson appears to quote from the testimony but provides no source. Castañeda, *Catholic Heritage,* 6:119; Jack Jackson, *Los Mesteños: Spanish Ranching in Texas, 1721–1821* (College Station: Texas A&M University Press, 1986), 537.

107. Garrett, *Green Flag,* 228.

108. Some forty years later, José Antonio Menchaca and Antonio Barrera would also remember well the events. In 1813 they were thirteen and ten years old, respectively, and still recollected that Arredondo "warned them [the women] that they should make 10,000 tortillas daily and if they did not do it promptly, Sergeant Acosta, who was the overseer, would give them the lash during the day and during the night the officials of the Army went to the *Quinta* and ordered Acosta to bring some of the most decent of the women to them." Menchaca and Barrera, "Notes," 339. See also the first published Texas-Mexican history: Navarro, *Defending Mexican Valor.* Navarro was critical of many of the revolutionary actors, yet this does not diminish the influence of the ideas that had circulated, as some historians have claimed.

109. Gutiérrez de Lara, "To the Mexican Congress," 26–29; de la Garza, *Dos hermanos,* 85–109; Milligan, "Gutiérrez de Lara," 106–134.

7. "To the Advocates of Enlightenment and Reason"

1. David A. Cossío, *Historia de Nuevo León,* vol. 4 (Monterrey, Mexico: J. Cantú Leal, 1925), 272–273; Juan Fidel Zorrilla, "Los hermanos Gutierrez de Lara," in *Tamaulipas en la Guerra de Independencia* (Mexico City: Porrúa, 1972), 91–98; Jack Jackson, *Los Mesteños: Spanish Ranching in Texas, 1721–1821* (College Station: Texas A&M University Press, 1986), 537–557.
2. Arredondo to Texas Governor Armiñan, June 29–30, 1814, Bexar Archives, the Dolph Briscoe Center for American History, University of Texas at Austin (hereafter "Bexar Archives"), reel 53:1027–1036; La Bahía Ayuntamiento Minutes, May 23, 1822, in Malcolm Dallas McLean and John R. McLean, eds., *Voices from the Goliad Frontier: Municipal Council Minutes, 1821–1835* (Dallas: William P. Clements Center for Southwest Studies, Southern Methodist University, 2008), 23–24.
3. Juan N. Almonte, "Statistical Report on Texas, [1835]," trans. Carlos Eduardo Castañeda, *Southwestern Historical Quarterly* 28, no. 3 (1925): 181; José Antonio Menchaca, *Memoirs* (San Antonio: Yanaguana Society, 1937), 19–20; Carlos Eduardo Castañeda, *Our Catholic Heritage in Texas, 1519–1936: Transition Period; the Fight for Freedom, 1810–1836,* vol. 6 (New York: Arno Press, 1950), 121–123; Pekka Hämäläinen, *The Comanche Empire* (New Haven: Yale University Press, 2008), 184–189.
4. Raúl A. Ramos, *Beyond the Alamo: Forging Mexican Ethnicity in San Antonio, 1821–1861* (Chapel Hill: University of North Carolina Press, 2008), 46–47.
5. Gabriel H. Lovett, *Napoleon and the Birth of Modern Spain: The Struggle, without and Within,* vol. 2 (New York: New York University Press, 1965), 809–842, quote is from p. 833.
6. Castañeda, *Catholic Heritage,* 6:123.
7. Ibid., 128–173; A. Carolina Castillo Crimm, *De León, a Tejano Family History* (Austin: University of Texas Press, 2003), 168–169. "A filibustering expedition is an irregular, unauthorized attack which proceeds from the territory of one state against that of a friendly state." Harris G. Warren, *The Sword Was Their Passport: A History of American Filibustering in the Mexican Revolution* (Baton Rouge: Louisiana State University Press, 1943), vii.
8. Ramos, *Beyond the Alamo,* 47.
9. Castañeda, *Catholic Heritage,* 6:121–129, 145–146; David J. Weber, *The Spanish Frontier in North America* (New Haven: Yale University Press, 1992), 299.
10. Trespalacios to San Antonio and La Bahía ayuntamientos, August 25, 1822; Trespalacios to Eastern Internal Provinces Mexican Commander Gaspar López, September 3, 1822, Bexar Archives, reel 72:629–34, 751; Castañeda, *Catholic Heritage,* 6:308; Lovett, *Napoleon,* 2:841; Timothy E. Anna, *Forging Mexico, 1821–1835* (Lincoln: University of Nebraska Press, 1998), 66–72; Luis Villoro, "La revolución de Independencia," in *Historia general de México,* ed. Centro de Estudios Históricos (Mexico City: El Colegio de México, 2000),

511–523; Michael C. Meyer et al., *The Course of Mexican History,* 8th ed. (New York: Oxford Univesity Press, 2007), 259–261.

11. Mirabeau Buonaparte Lamar, "Life of James Long," in *The Papers of Mirabeau Buonaparte Lamar,* ed. Charles Adams Gulick Jr. and Katherine Elliott, vol. 2 (Austin: Texas State Library, 1922), 93–96; Vito Alessio Robles, *Coahuila y Texas, desde la consumación de la independencia hasta el tratado de paz de Guadalupe Hidalgo,* 2nd ed., vol. 1 (Mexico City: Editorial Porrúa, 1945), 117–118; Castañeda, *Catholic Heritage,* 6:170–175.

12. Lorenzo de la Garza, *Dos hermanos héroes* (Mexico City: Editorial Cultura. Ex-Libris José Ramírez Flores, 1939; orig. 1913), 133–134; David E. Narrett, "José Bernardo Gutiérrez de Lara: *Caudillo* of the Mexican Republic in Texas," *Southwestern Historical Quarterly* 106, no. 2 (October 2002): 227–228.

13. James Gaines, "1835, (M. B. Lamar, Sabine River). Information from Capt. Gaines," in *The Papers of Mirabeau Buonaparte Lamar,* ed. Charles Adams Gulick Jr. and Katherine Elliott, vol. 1 (Austin: Texas State Library, 1920), 285; quote is from Jean Louis Berlandier, *Journey to Mexico during the Years 1826 to 1834,* vol. 1 (Austin: Texas State Historical Association, 1980), 284. For an informative account of the procedures in transitioning from Spanish to Mexican rule, see Félix D. Almaráz, *Governor Antonio Martínez and Mexican Independence in Texas: An Orderly Transition* (San Antonio: Bexar County Historical Commission, 1979).

14. Trespalacios to Béxar and La Bahía ayuntamientos, August 25, 1822; Trespalacios to Gaspar López, September 3, 1822, Bexar Archives, reel 72:629–634, 760; Thomas W. Streeter, *Bibliography of Texas, 1795–1845,* vol. 1, part 1 (Cambridge, MA: Harvard University Press, 1955); Juan Nepomuceno Almonte, *Almonte's Texas: Juan N. Almonte's 1834 Inspection, Secret Report and Role in the 1836 Campaign,* trans. John Wheat (Austin: Texas State Historical Association, 2003), 21.

15. William Davis Robinson, *Memoirs of the Mexican Revolution* (Philadelphia: Lydia R. Bailey, 1820), 57–122; Warren, *Sword Was Their Passport,* 146–172; Alessio Robles, *Coahuila y Texas,* 117–138; Castañeda, *Catholic Heritage,* 6:140–147; Luis Aboites, "La primera transición (1790–1830)," *Breves historias de los estados de la República Mexicana: Breve historia de Chihuahua* (http://bibliotecadigital.ilce.edu.mx/sites/estados/menu.htm), accessed December 30, 2011. Among the imprints were Joaquín Infante, *Cancion patriotica que, al desembarcar el general Mina y sus tropas en la Barra de Santander* (Soto la Marina, Mexico: Samuel Bangs, 1817); Francisco Xavier Mina, *Proclama del General Mina* (Galveston, TX: Imprenta de Juan J.M. Lara, 1817); Francisco Xavier Mina, *Compañeros de armas* (Galveston, TX: Imprenta de Juan J.M. Lara, 1817). A third press arrived with the failed James Long filibuster attempt in 1819 Nacogdoches. They printed a short-lived newspaper, the *Texas Republican,* for less than a month, though there are no extant issues. Marilyn McAdams Sibley, *Lone Stars and State Gazettes: Texas Newspapers before the Civil War* (College Station: Texas A&M University Press, 1983), 32–37.

16. Lota M. Spell, "Samuel Bangs, the First Printer in Texas," *Hispanic American Historical Review* 11, no. 2 (May 1931): 250; James Moran, *Printing Presses: History and Development from the Fifteenth Century to Modern Times* (Berkeley: University of California Press, 1973), 31–40.
17. Lota M. Spell, *Pioneer Printer: Samuel Bangs in Mexico and Texas* (Austin: University of Texas Press, 1963), 12–38.
18. Vito Alessio Robles, *La primera imprenta en las provincias internas de oriente: Texas, Tamaulipas, Nuevo León, y Coahuila* (Mexico City: Antigua Librería Robredo, de José Porrúa e Hijos, 1939), 31–48, 57–63; Spell, *Pioneer Printer,* 39–57.
19. This indeed is the tone of much of the historiography on the history of the press in Texas. See, for example, E. W. Winkler, "Notes and Fragments: The First Newspaper in Texas," *Southwestern Historical Quarterly* 6, no. 2 (October 1902); Eugene C. Barker, "Notes on Early Texas Newspapers, 1819–1836," *Southwestern Historical Quarterly* 21, no. 2 (October 1917): 127–144; Ike H. Moore, "The Earliest Printing and First Newspaper in Texas," *Southwestern Historical Quarterly* 39 (1935): 83–99; Kathryn Garrett, "The First Newspaper in Texas, *Gaceta de Texas,*" *Southwestern Historical Quarterly* 40, no. 3 (January 1937): 200–215.
20. Roger Chartier, ed., *History of Private Life: Vol. 3, Passions of the Renaissance* (Cambridge, MA: Harvard University Press, 1989), 111–159; Jürgen Habermas, *The Structural Transformation of the Public Sphere: An Inquiry into a Category of Bourgeois Society,* trans. Thomas Burger (Cambridge, MA: MIT Press, 1989), 43–51; Benedict Anderson, *Imagined Communities: Reflections on the Origin and Spread of Nationalism* (New York: Verso, 1991); Lynn Avery Hunt, *Inventing Human Rights: A History* (New York: Norton, 2007), 35–69.
21. Michael Warner, *The Letters of the Republic: Publication and the Public Sphere in Eighteenth-Century America* (Cambridge, MA: Harvard University Press, 1990), 6–7.
22. Spell, *Pioneer Printer,* 39.
23. Ibid., 42, 168.
24. Reprint of Viceroy Juan Ruiz de Apodaca's proclamation, June 13 1820, in Spell, *Pioneer Printer,* 168.
25. Spell, *Pioneer Printer,* 41–42. See, for example, Joaquin de Arredondo, *Proclamation which publishes 1812 decrees of the Spanish Cortes, relating to elections to be held in the four Internal Provinces of the East, July 6* (Monterrey, Mexico: Samuel Bangs, 1820); Diputación Provincial, *Habitantes de las quatro provincias de Oriente, 20 Noviembre* (Monterrey, Mexico: Samuel Bangs, 1820); José Eustaquio Fernández, *Aviso* [*election of deputies to the Diputacion Provincial, October 3*] (Monterrey, Mexico: Samuel Bangs, 1820); Viceroy Juan Ruiz de Apodaca, *A los habitantes de esta nueva España* (Monterrey, Mexico: Reimpreso en Monterrey, 1821); Joaquin de Arredondo, *Habitantes de las quatro provincias de Oriente de esta America septentrional, Marzo 13* (Monterrey, Mexico: Samuel Bangs, 1821).

26. Spell, *Pioneer Printer,* 43; Bernardo P. Gallegos, *Literacy, Education, and Society in New Mexico, 1693–1821* (Albuquerque: University of New Mexico Press, 1992), 77–81; Annick Lempérière, "República y publicidad a finales del antiguo régimen (Nueva España)," in *Los espacios públicos en Iberoamérica: Ambigüedades y problemas, siglos XVIII–XIX,* ed. François-Xavier Guerra et al. (Mexico City: Fondo de Cultura Económica, 1998), 67; François-Xavier Guerra, "El escrito de la revolución y la revolución del escrito: información, propaganda, y opinión pública en el mundo Hispánico (1808–1814)," in *Las guerras de independencia en la América española,* ed. Marta Terán and José Antonio Serrano (Morelia, Michoacán, Mexico: El Colegio de Michoacán, 2002), 125–147; Andrés Reséndez, *Changing National Identities at the Frontier: Texas and New Mexico, 1800–1850* (New York: Cambridge University Press, 2005), 230–231.
27. Trespalacios to Ayuntamientos of Béxar and La Bahía, August 26, 1822; Trespalacios to López, March 17, 1823, Bexar Archives, reel 72:629, 74:390–408; Almaráz, *Governor Martínez,* 5.
28. Real Academia Española, "Dicciónarios de la lengua española (1726–1992), accessed June 21, 2011.
29. Luis Reed Torres, "Los pregoneros," in *El periodismo en México: 450 años de historia,* ed. María del Carmen Ruiz Castañeda et al. (Mexico City: Editorial Tradición, 1974), 7–12; María del Pilar Paleta Vázquez, "Pregones y pregoneros de Puebla en el siglo XVI: Comunicación oficial en la plaza pública," *Graffylia: Revista de la Facultad de Filosofía y Letras,* no. 4 (2004): 131–139.
30. Warner, *Letters,* 35.
31. Spell, *Pioneer Printer,* 42.
32. John H. Elliott, *Empires of the Atlantic World: Britain and Spain in America, 1492–1830* (New Haven: Yale University Press, 2006), 205–207.
33. José Dominguez to Trespalacios, December 23, 1822; López to Trespalacios, February 8, 1823, Bexar Archives, reel 73:787, reel 74:175–190.
34. Of this tension between the documentation of oral and written culture Michel de Certeau has poetically observed: "These voices can no longer be heard except within the interior of the scriptural systems where they recur. They move about, like dancers, passing lightly through the field of the other." Michel de Certeau, *The Practice of Everyday Life* (Berkeley: University of California Press, 1988), 131. One place one could begin to search in the Bexar Archives would be in the many legal depositions taken by scribes. Walter J. Ong's work, compared to that of Derrida's, offers a more elaborate historical-theoretical account of the structuring of consciousness in oral cultures along with its relationship to writing and print culture. See, for example, Walter J. Ong, *Interfaces of the Word: Studies in the Evolution of Consciousness and Culture* (Ithaca: Cornell, 1977); Walter J. Ong, *Orality and Literacy: The Technologizing of the Word* (New York: Routledge, 1991). See also the excellent review by Johannes Fabian, "Keep Listening: Ethnography and Reading," in *The Ethnography of Reading,* ed. Jonathan Boyarin (Berkeley: University of California Press, 1993).

35. Arredondo, *Habitantes de las quatro provincias;* Spell, *Pioneer Printer,* 47–48.
36. See the extensive bibliography of imprints listed in Spell, *Pioneer Printer,* 167–199; John Holmes Jenkins, *Printer in Three Republics: A Bibliography of Samuel Bangs, First Printer in Texas, and First Printer West of the Louisiana Purchase* (Austin: Jenkins, 1981).
37. Bexar Archives, reel 73:879–886; in the early nineteenth century, the imprints were removed from the notebook and categorized with all other imprints.
38. Juan Ignacio María de Castorena Ursúa y Goyeneche, ed. *Gaceta de México y Noticias de Nueva España* (Mexico City, 1722–1742). On printing and the emergence of a bourgeoisie, see Jean Franco, "Waiting for a Bourgeoisie: The Formation of the Mexican Intelligentsia in the Age of Independence," trans. Patricia Heid, in *Critical Passions: Selected Essays,* ed. Mary Louise Pratt and Kathleen Newman (Durham: Duke University Press, 1999).
39. Habermas, *Structural,* 14–43. For the case of British America, see Warner, *Letters,* 34–72.
40. López to Trespalacios, October 23, 1822, Bexar Archives, reel 73:237.
41. On the Baroque's extralinguistic, especially visual, sources of meaning, see Lois Parkinson Zamora, *The Inordinate Eye: New World Baroque and Latin American Fiction* (Chicago: University of Chicago Press, 2006).
42. On the shift from a ternary to a binary sign system, see Michel Foucault, *The Order of Things: An Archaeology of the Human Sciences* (New York: Vintage, 1994), 42–77.
43. Trespalacios to San Antonio ayuntamiento, August 23, 1822, Bexar Archives, reel 72:589–90.
44. Trespalacios to San Antonio and La Bahía ayuntamientos, August 25, 1822, Bexar Archives, reel 72:633, 639–641, 694, 703, 753, 814.
45. Ibid., reel 72:632.
46. Martin Heidegger, *The Question Concerning Technology and Other Essays* (New York: Harper Perennial, 1977), 148–149. For a similar account, that of Hegel's search for ontological foundation after reason's critique of religion, see Jürgen Habermas, "Hegel's Concept of Modernity," trans. Frederick Lawrence, in *The Philosophical Discourse of Modernity* (Cambridge, MA: MIT Press, 1987).
47. Michel Foucault, *The History of Sexuality: An Introduction,* vol. I (New York: Random House, 1990), 142, 143.
48. Meyer et al., *Course of Mexican History,* 259–272.
49. Trespalacios to López, September 3, 1822, Bexar Archives, reel 72:760.
50. Bangs returned to the United States in 1823, but, according to his biographer, "he had lived too long in a Latin world . . . [and] had realized that he wanted to go back to Mexico, which had cast her peculiar spell on him, and had written to Monterrey offering to return as government printer at thirty-five pesos a month." He decided to buy several presses in order to sell them in Mexico, and returned in early 1827. Spell, *Pioneer Printer,* 53–67.
51. López to Antonio Martínez, August 5, 1822, Bexar Archives, reel 72:437–438.

52. Trespalacios to Almonte, September 11, 1822; García to Trespalacios, January 19, 1823; Trespalacios to López, March 17, 1823, Bexar Archives, reel 72:836–837, 74:63–64, 390–408. Almonte was the illegitimate though recognized son of one of the leaders of the movement for Mexican independence, José María Morelos y Pavón. In 1815, and in the midst of the war of independence, Morelos sent his twelve-year-old son Almonte to New Orleans to be educated and to escape the strife in Mexico. Almonte, *Almonte's Texas,* 11–23.
53. Luciano García to Felipe de la Garza, July 17, 1823; invoice on printing costs, July 10, 1823; Trespalacios to López, March 17, 1823, Bexar Archives, reel 75:246–247, 179–180; reel 74:390–408; José Félix Trespalacios, *Prospecto (Correo de Texas)* (San Antonio: Ymprenta del Govierno de Texas, 1823); Spell, *Pioneer Printer,* 63–67; Moran, *Printing Presses,* 79–81; David J. Weber, *The Mexican Frontier, 1821–1846: The American Southwest Under Mexico* (Albuquerque: University of New Mexico Press, 1982), 158–178; Marilyn McAdams Sibley, *Lone Stars and State Gazettes: Texas Newspapers before the Civil War* (College Station: Texas A&M University Press, 1983), 40; Gregg Cantrell, *Stephen F. Austin: Empresario of Texas* (New Haven: Yale University Press, 1999), 119–163; Ramos, *Beyond the Alamo,* 81–107.
54. The original Spanish and English from the prospectus is offered here and separated by a slash. Translations appearing in brackets are mine.
55. The original English abridged the Spanish; thus, I offer my translation in brackets.
56. Max Weber, "Science as a Vocation," in *From Max Weber,* ed. H. Gerth and C. Wright Mills (New York: Oxford University Press, 1946), 139.
57. As we saw in Chapter 6, José Álvarez de Toledo published the single-issue *Gaceta de Texas* on May 25, 1813, and, three weeks later, *El Mexicano* on June 19, 1813. In 1826 Monterrey, the first newspaper with more than a prospectus or single issue to be published in all of northern Mexico, including Texas, would be *La Gazeta Constitucional.* Historians of Texan print culture have divorced the events that unfolded in Texas prior to 1836 (that is, prior to the 1835–1836 Revolution) from the history of northern Mexico, and have not seen the development of print culture in Texas as related to that of Mexico.
58. José Angel de Benavides to Editor of the Correo de Texas, May 21, 1823, Bexar Archives, reel 74:832–833.
59. José Félix Trespalacios, *A los Filantropicos sin ambición* (San Antonio: Ymprenta del Govierno de Texas, 1823). Sombrerete ayuntamiento to Trespalacios, May 26, 1823, Bexar Archives, reel 74:856–857.
60. Ibid., 74:856.
61. Austin to James B. Austin, May 20, 1823, in Eugene C. Barker, ed. *The Austin Papers: Moses Austin and Stephen F. Austin,* vol. 2, part 1 (Washington, DC: Government Printing Office, 1924), 644.
62. Sibley, *State Gazettes,* 40–41.
63. On modernity as a narrative account rather than as an event, see Fredric Jameson, *A Singular Modernity: Essay on the Ontology of the Present* (New York: Verso, 2002), 20–25.

64. Jürgen Habermas, "Modernity's Consciousness of Time and Its Need for Self-Reassurance," trans. Frederick Lawrence, in *The Philosophical Discourse of Modernity. Twelve Lectures* (Cambridge, MA: MIT Press, 1987), 18.
65. Trespalacios to La Bahía, November 5, 1822, Bexar Archives, reel 73:417–420.
66. Anna, *Forging Mexico,* 34–72; Christon I. Archer, "Fashioning a New Nation," in *The Oxford History of Mexico,* ed. Michael C. Meyer and William H. Beezley (New York: Oxford University Press, 2000), 301–337; Meyer et al., *Course of Mexican History,* 269–280.
67. Anastacio Bustamante to Trespalacios, April 15, 1823; Trespalacios to Junta Provisional Gubernativa, April 4, 1823, Bexar Archives, reel 74:563–565, 571–575; Andrés Tijerina, *Tejanos and Texas under the Mexican Flag, 1821–1836* (College Station: Texas A&M University Press, 1994), 93–98. Sibley mistakenly states that Trespalacios resigned because Bexareños disapproved of the provisional government. Sibley, *State Gazettes,* 41.
68. Trespalacios, *Filantropicos.*
69. Junta Gubernativa de la Provincia de Texas, *Noticias del Govierno de Texas* (San Antonio: Ympr. del Govierno de Texas, 1823).
70. Juan Martín de Veramendi to Texas Governor Luciano García, July 8, 1823, Bexar Archives, reel 75:169. See also Beatriz González Stephan, "On Citizenship: The Grammatology of the Body-Politic," in *The Latin American Cultural Studies Reader,* ed. Ana Del Sarto et al. (Durham: Duke University Press, 2004), 384–405.
71. Trespalacios to the Junta Provisional Gubernativa, May 3, 1823, Bexar Archives, reel 74:742–743; Alessio Robles, *Coahuila y Texas,* 150–154; Jesús F. de la Teja, "The Making of a Tejano," in *A Revolution Remembered: The Memoirs and Selected Correspondence of Juan N. Seguín* (Austin: State House Press, 1991), 3–13; Tijerina, *Tejanos and Texas,* 96
72. Alessio Robles, *Coahuila y Texas,* 118; Commandant Gaspar López to Iturbide, December 7, 1821, in McLean and McLean, *Voices from the Goliad Frontier,* 620–621.
73. Spanish-language newspaper editors in 1850s San Antonio consistently describe themselves as "Mejico-Tejanos." This term continued to be used well into the twentieth century, as when the failed 1915 Plan de San Diego revolutionaries described themselves as the "Ejercito Libertador de los Mexico-Texanos [the Liberating Army of the Mexico-Texans]." Richard R. Flores, "The Corrido and the Emergence of Texas-Mexican Social Identity," *Journal of American Folklore* 105, no. 416 (1992): 166–182; Emilio Zamora, *The World of the Mexican Worker in Texas* (College Station: Texas A&M University Press, 1993), 81
74. Trespalacios to the Junta Provisional Gubernativa, May 3, 1823; Luciano García to Felipe de la Garza, July 17 and 22, 1823, Bexar Archives, reel 74:742–743; reel 75:246–247, 289–291; Junta Gubernativa de la Provincia de Texas, *Noticias del Govierno de Texas;* Streeter, *Bibliography,* xxxvii.
75. Commandant Felipe de la Garza to Texas Governmental Junta, June 16, 1823; Juan Martín de Veramendi to Governor Luciano García, July 8, 1823; Governor García to Manuel Iturri Castillo, September 24, 1823; Governor García to

Béxar Ayuntamiento, September 25, 1823, Bexar Archives, reel 75:25–26, 169, 575–587, 591–615; Junta Gubernativa de la Provincia de Texas, *Circular announcing the arrival of newly appointed governor Luciano García* (San Antonio: Ympr. del Govierno de Texas, 1823); Tijerina, *Tejanos and Texas,* 96.

76. Alessio Robles, *Coahuila y Texas,* 155–195; Tijerina, *Tejanos and Texas,* 98–101; Anna, *Forging Mexico,* 165–166.
77. Tijerina, *Tejanos and Texas,* 99.
78. Anna, *Forging Mexico,* 101, 161–175.
79. Meyer et al., *Course of Mexican History,* 264–361.
80. Cantrell, *Austin,* 104–170; Randolph B. Campbell, *Gone to Texas: A History of the Lone Star State* (New York: Oxford University Press, 2003), 100–114; Ramos, *Beyond the Alamo,* 193–196; Sean M. Kelley, *Los Brazos de Dios: A Plantation Society in the Texas Borderlands, 1821–1865* (Baton Rouge: Louisiana State University Press, 2010), 22; David R. McDonald, "Juan Martín Veramendi: Tejano Political and Business Leader," in *Tejano Leadership in Mexican and Revolutionary Texas,* ed. Jesús F. de la Teja (College Station: Texas A&M University Press, 2010), 36.
81. Alessio Robles, *Coahuila y Texas,* 95–116; Weber, *Mexican Frontier,* 242–248; Tijerina, *Tejanos and Texas,* 93–112; Campbell, *Gone to Texas,* 100–104; Ramos, *Beyond the Alamo,* 111–165.
82. Ramón Músquiz to Veramendi, January 10, 1833, Bexar Archives, reel 154:586–588; Músquiz to Veramendi, January 10, 1833, in Eugene C. Barker, ed. *The Austin Papers: Moses Austin and Stephen F. Austin,* vol. 2 (Washington, DC: Government Printing Office, 1928), 913.
83. Campbell, *Gone to Texas,* 108–109.
84. *Proceedings of the Convention of Texas at San Felipe de Austin* (San Felipe de Austin: Daniel W. Anthony, 1832); David J. Weber, "Introduction," in *Troubles in Texas, 1832: A Tejano Viewpoint from San Antonio* (Austin: DeGolyer Library of Southern Methodist University, 1983), 2–3.
85. David J. Weber has written an excellent account of these events. Weber, "Introduction," 1–12. See also Alessio Robles, *Coahuila y Texas,* 428–452.
86. List of citizens authorizing committee to write petition, December 19, 1832, Bexar Archives, reel 154:358–359, quote is from frame 358. The final petition, however, was signed by José Antonio de la Garza, Angel Navarro, José Cassiano, Manuel Ximenes, Juan Angel Seguín, José María Sambrano, and Ignacio Arocha. Bexar Archives, reel 154:367. Angel Navarro's father was from Corsica and lived in Barcelona and Cádiz before making his way to New Spain in 1769. He eventually made his way to Béxar in 1777 where he would become a successful merchant. Cassiano had arrived from Italy via New Orleans in the 1820s. Bernice Strong, "Cassiano, José," *Handbook of Texas Online* (http://www.tshaonline.org/handbook/online/articles/fcaan), accessed June 1, 2011; David R. McDonald, *José Antonio Navarro: In Search of the American Dream in Nineteenth Century Texas* (Denton: Texas State Historical Association, 2010), 12–14.
87. For only the most recent Tejano responses to the discursive history of the Alamo, see Richard R. Flores, *Remembering the Alamo: Memory, Modernity,*

and the Master Symbol (Austin: University of Texas Press, 2002); Emma Pérez, *Forgetting the Alamo, or, Blood Memory: A Novel* (Austin: University of Texas Press, 2009).

88. Indeed, as the historian Arnoldo De León remarks, "The history of nineteenth century Tejanos, and the experience of Mexican Americans at other times, is not solely a story of people victimized by oppression. It is much more the history of actors who have sought to take measures in their own behalf for the sake of a decent living." Arnoldo De León, *The Tejano Community, 1836–1900* (Albuquerque: University of New Mexico, 1982), 203.
89. See, for example, José María Rodríguez, *Rodríguez Memoirs of Early Texas*, 2nd. ed. (San Antonio: Standard Printing Co., 1961; orig. 1913); Menchaca, *Memoirs;* David J. Weber, ed., *Foreigners in Their Native Land: Historical Roots of the Mexican Americans* (Albuquerque: University of New Mexico Press, 1973); Juan Nepomuceno Seguín, *A Revolution Remembered: The Memoirs and Selected Correspondence of Juan N. Seguín* (Austin: State House Press, 1991; orig. 1858); Timothy M. Matovina, ed. *The Alamo Remembered: Tejano Accounts and Perspectives* (Austin: University of Texas Press, 1995); José Antonio Navarro, *Defending Mexican Valor in Texas: José Antonio Navarros' Historical Writings, 1853–1857* (Austin: State House Press, 1995).
90. The original manuscript version is in the Bexar Archives. Stephen F. Austin had it published in Spanish in February 1833 along with a now lost English translation. The original Spanish was published along with a modern translation in 1983. "Representación," December 19, 1832, Bexar Archives, 154:360–367; Ayuntamiento de Béxar, *Representación dirijida por el ilustre ayuntamiento de la ciudad de Bexar al honorable congreso del estado, manifestando los males que aflijen los pueblos de Texas, y los agravios que han sufrido desde la reunion de estos con Coahuila* (Brazoria, TX: Imprenta del Ciudadano D.W. Anthony, 1833); Ayuntamiento de Béxar, *Troubles in Texas, 1832: A Tejano Viewpoint from San Antonio with a Translation and Facsimile,* trans. Conchita Hassell Winn and David Weber (Dallas: Degolyer Library of Southern Methodist University, 1983).
91. Ayuntamiento de Béxar, *Representación,* 2; translations are mine, hereafter cited in text. The facsimile available in *Troubles in Texas* is used here; citations are to the pamphlet's original page numbering. *Troubles in Texas* also includes a translation; however, the translators altered the meaning significantly in several passages, and I thus offer my own translations.
92. Hämäläinen, *Comanche,* 194–198.
93. Two to three hundred leagues is the equivalent of 520 to 800 miles.
94. For historical events surrounding the petition, see Weber, "Introduction."
95. Anderson, *Imagined Communities,* 187–206.
96. Juan Pablo Viscardo y Guzmán, *Letter to the Spanish Americans: A Facsimile of the Second English Edition (London, 1810)* (Providence, RI: John Carter Brown Library, 2002), 77; Juan Pablo Viscardo y Guzmán, *Carta dirigida a los españoles americanos* (Mexico City: Fondo de Cultura Económica, 2004), 186.

97. Tijerina, *Tejanos and Texas,* 97; McDonald, *Navarro,* 16–18. Another Tejano statesman, Juan Martín Veramendi, governor of Coahuila y Texas in 1832, had a collection of more than thirty books, including Francisco de Lizardi's *El periquillo sarniento* (the first Spanish-American novel) and *La Quixotita, French and Spanish Grammar, Rights of Man,* and *Life of Napoleon.* McDonald, "Veramendi," 38. McDonald misidentifies Lizardi's *La Quixotita* as Cervantes's *Don Quixote.*
98. Charles Taylor, *A Secular Age* (Cambridge, MA: Harvard University Press, 2007), 164–165.
99. Foucault, *History of Sexuality,* 141–143; Taylor, *Secular Age,* 16–21.
100. Weber, "Introduction," 9.
101. Foucault, *Order of Things,* 219. See also Joyce Oldham Appleby et al., *Telling the Truth about History* (New York: Norton, 1994), 15–128; Robert Young, *White Mythologies: Writing History and the West,* 2nd ed. (New York: Routledge, 2004), 32–52.
102. The petition is one of the earliest Texan imprints of more than a few pages. Weber, "Introduction," 8.

8. "Adhering to the New Order of Things"

1. Michael Costeloe, *The Central Republic in Mexico, 1835–1846: Hombres de Bien in the Age of Santa Anna* (Cambridge, UK: Cambridge University Press, 1993), 31–45; Timothy E. Anna, *Forging Mexico, 1821–1835* (Lincoln: University of Nebraska Press, 1998), 257–260.
2. Joseph Milton Nance, *After San Jacinto: The Texas-Mexican Frontier, 1836–1841* (Austin: University of Texas Press, 1963), 252–315; Josefina Zoraida Vázquez, "La supuesta república del Río Grande," *Historia Mexicana* 36, no. 1 (July–September 1995): 49–80; Josefina Zoraida Vázquez, "Los primeros tropiezos," in *Historia general de México,* ed. Centro de Estudios Históricos (Mexico City: El Colegio de México, 2000), 544–549.
3. As we have seen, the origins of a Tejano sense of self emerged in the 1830s. By the 1850s and through the early twentieth century, Tejanos referred to themselves variously as "Mejico-Tejanos," "Mejicano-Tejanos," and "Mejicano."
4. Nance, *After San Jacinto,* 68–77, 420–430, 481–498; Richard Griswold del Castillo, *The Treaty of Guadalupe Hidalgo: A Legacy of Conflict* (Norman: University of Oklahoma Press, 1990); Randolph B. Campbell, *Gone to Texas: A History of the Lone Star State* (New York: Oxford University Press, 2003), 187–189; Timothy J. Henderson, *A Glorious Defeat: Mexico and Its War with the United States* (New York: Hill and Wang, 2007); Raúl A. Ramos, *Beyond the Alamo: Forging Mexican Ethnicity in San Antonio, 1821–1861* (Chapel Hill: University of North Carolina Press, 2008), 133–165.
5. Sean M. Kelley, *Los Brazos de Dios: A Plantation Society in the Texas Borderlands, 1821–1865* (Baton Rouge: Louisiana State University Press, 2010), 22.
6. Henry Alexander Adams, "[Journal of an] Expedition against the Southwest, 1842," the Dolph Briscoe Center for American History, University of Texas at Austin, 18.

7. Raymund A. Paredes, "The Origins of Anti-Mexican Sentiment in the United States," in *New Directions in Chicano Scholarship*, ed. Ricardo Romo and Raymund A. Paredes (La Jolla: University of California at San Diego, 1978), 139–165; Reginald Horsman, *Race and Manifest Destiny: The Origins of American Racial Anglo-Saxonism* (Cambridge, MA: Harvard University Press, 1981), 208–248; Arnoldo De León, *They Called Them Greasers: Anglo Attitudes toward Mexicans in Texas, 1821–1900* (Austin: University of Texas Press, 1983); David J. Weber, "'Scarce More than Apes': Historical Roots of Anglo-American Stereotypes of Mexicans in the Border Region," in *Myth and History of the Hispanic Southwest* (Albuquerque: University of New Mexico Press, 1988), 153–167.
8. A. B. J. Hammett, *The Empresario Don Martín de León* (Waco: Texian Press, 1973). Cited in David Montejano, *Anglos and Mexicans in the Making of Texas, 1836–1987* (Austin: University of Texas Press, 1987), 26–27.
9. Montejano, *Anglos and Mexicans,* 28; Juan Nepomuceno Seguín, *A Revolution Remembered: The Memoirs and Selected Correspondence of Juan N. Seguín* (Austin: State House Press, 1991; orig. 1858), 90.
10. Joseph Milton Nance, *Attack and Counter-Attack: The Texas-Mexican Frontier, 1842* (Austin: University of Texas Press, 1964), 384, 403; Arnoldo De León, *The Tejano Community, 1836–1900* (Albuquerque: University of New Mexico Press, 1982), 14–15; Montejano, *Anglos and Mexicans,* 28; Timothy M. Matovina, *Tejano Religion and Ethnicity: San Antonio, 1821–1860* (Austin: University of Texas Press, 1995), 50–52; Campbell, *Gone to Texas,* 187.
11. Terry G. Jordan, "A Century and a Half of Ethnic Change in Texas, 1836–1986," *Southwestern Historical Quarterly* 89, no. 4 (1986): 408; Arnoldo De León and Kenneth L. Stewart, *Tejanos and the Numbers Game: A Socio-Historical Interpretation from the Federal Censuses, 1850–1900* (Albuquerque: University of New Mexico, 1989), 15; Kelly F. Himmel, *The Conquest of the Karankawas and the Tonkawas, 1821–1859* (College Station: Texas A&M University Press, 1999); Campbell, *Gone to Texas,* 159, 207–214; Pekka Hämäläinen, *The Comanche Empire* (New Haven: Yale University Press, 2008), 303.
12. Matovina, *Tejano Religion,* quote from p. 49; Ramos, *Beyond the Alamo,* 207.
13. Campbell, *Gone to Texas,* 194–206; F. Todd Smith, *From Dominance to Disappearance: The Indians of Texas and the Near Southwest, 1786–1859* (Lincoln: University of Nebraska Press, 2005).
14. Montejano, *Anglos and Mexicans,* 34–49. Jovita Gonzalez and Eve Raleigh's beautifully illuminating historical novel takes this theme as its focus. Written in the 1930s and 1940s, the novel is set in south Texas shortly after the U.S.-Mexican War. Jovita González and Eve Raleigh, *Caballero: A Historical Romance* (College Station: Texas A&M University Press, 1996).
15. Nancy Fraser, "Rethinking the Public Sphere: A Contribution to the Critique of Actually Existing Democracy," in *Habermas and the Public Sphere,* ed. Craig J. Calhoun (Cambridge, MA: MIT Press, 1992), 111.

16. Jürgen Habermas, *The Structural Transformation of the Public Sphere: An Inquiry into a Category of Bourgeois Society,* trans. Thomas Burger (Cambridge, MA: MIT Press, 1989), 51–56; Michael Warner, *Publics and Counterpublics* (New York: Zone Books, 2002), 94–96.
17. Charles Taylor, *A Secular Age* (Cambridge, MA: Harvard University Press, 2007), 171.
18. John Wheat, "Bexar Archives," *Handbook of Texas Online* (http://www.tshaonline.org/handbook/online/articles/lcb02), accessed July 30, 2011; "Bexar Archives Original Manuscripts and Printed Material, 1717–1836," the Dolph Briscoe Center for American History, University of Texas at Austin (http://www.lib.utexas.edu/taro/utcah/00179/00179-P.html), accessed December 25, 2012.
19. Vito Alessio Robles, *La primera imprenta en las provincias internas de oriente: Texas, Tamaulipas, Nuevo León, y Coahuila* (Mexico City: Antigua Librería Robredo, de José Porrúa e Hijos, 1939); Lota M. Spell, *Pioneer Printer: Samuel Bangs in Mexico and Texas* (Austin: University of Texas Press, 1963), 69; Marilyn McAdams Sibley, *Lone Stars and State Gazettes: Texas Newspapers before the Civil War* (College Station: Texas A&M University Press, 1983), 28.
20. After Trespalacios's 1823 press, another press would not be set up in San Antonio until 1848. Sibley, *State Gazettes,* 213. Several other short-lived efforts at establishing newspapers, mostly bilingual, occurred in the early nineteenth century, though no copies are extant, such as the 1819 *Texas Republican* and the 1823 *Mexican Advocate,* both of Nacogdoches. Eugene C. Barker, "Notes on Early Texas Newspapers, 1819–1836," *Southwestern Historical Quarterly* 21, no. 2 (1917): 127–144; Sibley, *State Gazettes,* 34–46. There were also Spanish translations of Anglophone newspapers along the Texas-Mexico border during the 1840s, especially during the U.S.-Mexican war. But these were more often than not war propaganda with little to no participation on the part of Tejanos. Conchita Hassell Winn, "Spanish-Language Newspapers," *Handbook of Texas Online* (http://www.tshaonline.org/handbook/online/articles/ees18), accessed May 8, 2011; Sibley, *State Gazettes,* 200–205; Nicolás Kanellos and Helvetia Martell, *Hispanic Periodicals in the United States, Origins to 1960: A Brief History and Comprehensive Bibliography* (Houston: Arte Público, 2000), 300–306.
21. The press entered New Mexico and California in 1834. As in Texas, the early attempts to establish newspapers in New Mexico during the 1830s were short-lived. The East Coast, on the other hand, saw the first regularly published Hispanophone newspapers as early as 1824 with Father Félix Varela's Philadelphia-based *El Habanero.* Varela later moved it to New York City. David J. Weber, *The Mexican Frontier, 1821–1846: The American Southwest under Mexico* (Albuquerque: University of New Mexico, 1982), 230–231; A. Gabriel Meléndez, *So All Is Not Lost: The Poetics of Print in Nuevomexicano Communities, 1834–1958* (Albuquerque: University of New Mexico Press, 1997), 16–21; Nicolás Kanellos and Helvetia Martell, *Hispanic Periodicals in the United States, Origins to 1960: A Brief History and Comprehensive*

Bibliography (Houston: Arte Público, 2000), 76–77; Félix Varela, *Obras,* ed. Eduardo Torres-Cuevas, Jorge Ibarra Cuesta, and Mercedes García Rodríguez, vol. 2 (Havana, Cuba: Imagen Contemporánea, 2001), contains transcriptions of *El Habanero;* Kirsten Silva Gruesz, *Ambassadors of Culture: The Transamerican Origins of Latino Writing* (Princeton: Princeton University Press, 2002), 100–102.

22. Junta Gubernativa de la Provincia de Texas, *Noticias del Govierno de Texas* (San Antonio: Ympr. del Govierno de Texas, 1823).
23. On Douai see Sibley, *State Gazettes,* 230–237; On Anglo mob violence see Campbell, *Gone to Texas,* 166–182, 232–233.
24. James Moran, *Printing Presses: History and Development from the Fifteenth Century to Modern Times* (Berkeley: University of California Press, 1973), 49–53, 113–114; Sibley, *State Gazettes,* 5–6, 213–217.
25. All three newspapers have been microfilmed and are available via interlibrary loan. The *Bejareño* is available online at the University of North Texas Libraries, The Portal to Texas History, http://texashistory.unt.edu; crediting the Dolph Briscoe Center for American History, the University of Texas at Austin.
26. Narciso Leal apparently edited the semiweekly 1886 *El Observador.* Though no issues have been found to date, the *San Antonio Express* reported on the paper in 1886: "It will represent and protect the rights of the Mexican people and the Latin speaking races in general in a dignified manner." De León, *Tejano Community,* 197.
27. Anne J. Bailey and Bruce Allardice, "Debray, Xavier Blanchard," *Handbook of Texas Online* (http://www.tshaonline.org/handbook/online/articles/fde02), accessed August 27, 2011; Xavier Blanchard Debray, *A Sketch of the History of Debray's (26th) Regiment of Texas Cavalry* (Austin: E. von Boeckmann, 1961; orig. 1884); Stewart Sifakies, "Xavier Blanchard Debray," in *Who Was Who in the Civil War* (New York: Facts on File, 1988).
28. *El Bejareño* (San Antonio, 1855–1856), April 26, 1856, vol. 2., no. 17, p. 2; June 14, 1856, vol. 2, no. 24, p. 2.
29. Camilla Campbell, "Navarro, José Angel (the Younger)," *Handbook of Texas Online* (http://www.tsha.utexas.edu/handbook/online/articles/view/NN/fna8.html), accessed June 1, 2011; David R. McDonald, *José Antonio Navarro: In Search of the American Dream in Nineteenth Century Texas* (Denton: Texas State Historical Association, 2010), 158–160; Helen P. Trimpi, "Navarro, (José) Angel," in *Crimson Confederates: Harvard Men Who Fought for the South* (Knoxville: University of Tennessee Press, 2010), 224–225.
30. Jorge Marbán, *José Agustín Quintero: Un enigma histórico en el exilio Cubano del ochocientos* (Miami: Ediciones Universal, 2001), 12–23; Darryl E. Brock, "José Agustín Quintero: Cuban Patriot in Confederate Diplomatic Service," in *Cubans in the Confederacy: José Agustín Quintero, Ambrosio José Gonzales, and Loreta Janeta Velazquez,* ed. Phillip Thomas Tucker (Jefferson, NC: McFarland, 2002), 12–28. Quintero's poetry appeared in a collection by revolutionary exiled Cubans published in New York City in 1858. See Matías Montes Huidobro, *El laúd del desterrado* (Houston: Arte Público, 1995).

31. José Ramos de Zúñiga and Alfred A. Lewis, eds., *El Correo* (San Antonio, 1858). The last remaining issue is numbered vol. 1, no. 12, July 8, 1858; Marbán, 22; Brock, "Quintero," 31.
32. Randell G. Tarín, "Leal, Joaquín," *Handbook of Texas Online* (http://www.tshaonline.org/handbook/online/articles/fle98), accessed August 25, 2011; Frederick C. Chabot, *With the Makers of San Antonio: Genealogies of the Early San Antonio Families* (San Antonio: Artes Gráficas, 1937), 147–152; Jesús F. de la Teja, *San Antonio de Béxar: A Community on New Spain's Northern Frontier* (Albuquerque: University of New Mexico Press, 1995), 17–48.
33. *El Bejareño,* February 7, 1855, vol. 1, no. 1, p. 1; July 7, 1855, vol. 1 no. 12, p. 3; November 24, 1855, 1.23, p. 2; January 12, 1856; February 16, 1856, 2.7, p. 2; May 31, 1856, 2.22, p. 2; Chabot, *Makers of San Antonio,* 329; De León, *Tejano Community,* 97.
34. Brock, "Quintero," 27.
35. Chabot, *Makers of San Antonio,* 152.
36. Juan Donoso Cortés, *Obras,* ed. Gavino Tejado, 5 vols. (Madrid: Imprenta de Tejado, 1854–1855); Juan Donoso Cortés, Selected Works, ed. and trans. Jeffrey P. Johnson (Westport, CT: Greenwood Press, 2000). See also Carl Schmitt's well-known exposition on Cortés in *Political Theology: Four Chapters on the Concept of Sovereignty,* trans. George D. Schwab (Chicago: University of Chicago Press, 2004; orig. 1922), and Paul Piccone and Gary Ulmen, eds., "Carl Schmitt and Donoso Cortés," *Telos* 125 (Fall 2002).
37. Charles A. Hale, *Mexican Liberalism in the Age of Mora, 1821–1853* (New Haven: Yale University Press, 1968), 114. See also Pamela Voekel, *Alone before God: The Religious Origins of Modernity in Mexico* (Durham: Duke University Press, 2002), 146–170.
38. Annick Lempérière, "De la república corporativa a la nación moderna. México (1821–1860)," in *Inventando la nación: Iberoamérica, siglo XIX,* ed. Antonio Annino and François-Xavier Guerra (Mexico City: Fondo de Cultura Económica, 2003), 319–330. On the development of Spanish-American liberalism, see Andrés Lira, *Espejo de discordias. Lorenzo de Zavala, José Ma. Luis Mora, Lucas Alamán* (Mexico City: Secretaría de Educación Pública, 1984); Josefina Zoraida Vázquez and Antonio Annino, *El primer liberalismo mexicano, 1808–1855* (Mexico City: Museo Nacional de Historia, 1995); José Antonio Aguilar and Rafael Rojas, eds., *El republicanismo en hispanoamérica: ensayos de historia intelectual y política* (Mexico City: Fondo de Cultura Económica, 2002); Antonio Annino, "Pueblos, liberalismo, y nación en México," in *Inventando la nación: Iberoamérica, siglo XIX,* ed. Antonio Annino and François-Xavier Guerra (Mexico City: Fondo de Cultura Económica, 2003), 399–430.
39. For an account of the merging of political, religious, and mercantile interests in the making of a public religious festival in Saltillo (some 300 miles south of San Antonio), see Jesús F. de la Teja, "St. James at the Fair: Religious Ceremony, Civic Boosterism, and Commercial Development on the Colonial Mexican Frontier," *The Americas* 57, no. 3 (2001): 395–416.

40. See, for example, Céline Desramé, "La comunidad de lectores y la formación del espacio público en el Chile revolucionario: de la cultura del manuscrito al reino de la prensa (1808–1833)," in *Los espacios públicos en Iberoamérica: Ambigüedades y problemas, siglos XVIII–XIX,* ed. François-Xavier Guerra and Annick Lempériere (Mexico City: Fondo de Cultura Económica, 1998), 273–299; François-Xavier Guerra and Annick Lempériere, "Introducción," in *Los espacios públicos en Iberoamérica: Ambigüedades y problemas, siglos XVIII–XIX* (Mexico City: Centro Francés de Estudios Mexicanos y Centroamericanos and Fondo de Cultura Ecónomica, 1998), 9; Annick Lempérière, "República y publicidad a finales del antiguo régimen (Nueva España)," in *Los espacios públicos en Iberoamérica: Ambigüedades y problemas, siglos XVIII–XIX,* ed. François-Xavier Guerra et al. (Mexico City: Fondo de Cultura Económica, 1998), 66–72.
41. De León, *Tejano Community,* 172–186; Lawrence Phillip Knight, "Becoming a City and Becoming American: San Antonio, Texas, 1848–1861" (PhD dissertation, Texas A&M University, College Station, 1997), 18–32; Timothy M. Matovina, "Sacred Place and Collective Memory: San Fernando Cathedral, San Antonio, Texas," *U.S. Catholic Historian* 15, no. 1 (1997): 33–50; Jesús F. de la Teja, "Discovering the Tejano Community in 'Early' Texas," *Journal of the Early Republic* 18, no. 1 (1998): 73–98; Teja, "St. James at the Fair"; Jesús F. de la Teja, "'Buena gana tenía de ir a jugar': The Recreational World of Early San Antonio, Texas, 1718–1845," *International Journal of the History of Sport* 26, no. 7 (2009): 889–905.
42. Martin Heidegger, *The Question concerning Technology and Other Essays* (New York: Harper Perennial, 1977), 148.
43. Benedict Anderson, *Imagined Communities: Reflections on the Origin and Spread of Nationalism* (New York: Verso, 1991), 24; Taylor, *Secular Age,* 57.
44. Walter Benjamin, "Theses on the Philosophy of History," trans. Harry Zohn, in *Illuminations: Essays and Reflections,* ed. Hannah Arendt (New York: Schocken Books, 1969), 261.
45. Anderson, *Imagined Communities,* 24–36.
46. Hayden V. White, *Metahistory: The Historical Imagination in Nineteenth-Century Europe* (Baltimore: Johns Hopkins University Press, 1973), 135–139; Anderson, *Imagined Communities,* 192–199, 204–206; Joyce Oldham Appleby et al., *Telling the Truth about History* (New York: Norton, 1994), 91–125.
47. Henderson Yoakum, *History of Texas from Its Settlement in 1685 to Its Annexation to the United States in 1846,* vol. 1 (New York: Redfield, 1856), 208. Notwithstanding his ethnocentric biases (he participated in the 1846–1848 U.S.-Mexico War), Yoakum's history has long served as a foundational history of Texas, one that continues to serve as a primary and secondary source for many historians. For an analysis of Yoakum's Manifest Destiny ideology, see Carroll Van West, "Democratic Ideology and the Antebellum Historian: The Case of Henderson Yoakum," *Journal of the Early Republic* 3, no. 3 (1983): 319–339.
48. *El Bejareño,* vol. 2, no. 16, p. 2, cols. 2–3, emphasis added.

49. Henry P. Walker, "William McLane's Narrative of the Magee-Gutierrez Expedition, 1812–1813," *Southwestern Historical Quarterly* 66, no. 4 (1963): 569.
50. José Antonio Navarro, "Apuntes Históricos Interesantes de San Antonio de Béxar, escritos por el C. Dn. José Antonio Navarro, en noviembre de 1853," in *Defending Mexican Valor in Texas: José Antonio Navarro's Historical Writings, 1853–1857,* ed. David R. McDonald and Timothy M. Matovina (Austin: State House Press, 1995), 2, 5–6. For a detailed publishing history of *Apuntes,* see David R. McDonald and Timothy M. Matovina, "José Antonio Navarro: Tejano Advocate and Historical Chronicleer," in McDonald and Matovina, *Defending Mexican Valor in Texas,* 15–32.
51. Navarro, "Apuntes," 1–2. The edition used here is the reprinted facsimile, and the page references refer to the original numbering. Hereafter cited in text; all translations are mine.
52. *El Bejareño,* February 7, 17, March 3, 1855, vol. 1, nos. 1–3, 7–8; January 12, May 17, vol. 2, nos. 2, 20. On the criminalization of these public spaces, see De León, *They Called Them Greasers,* 36–48; Knight, "Becoming a City," 18–47; Larry Knight, "The Cart War: Defining American in San Antonio in the 1850s," *Southwestern Historical Quarterly* 109, no. 3 (2006): 322.

9. "The Natural Sympathies That Unite All of Our People"

1. The *Bejareño* reported on June 7 that "the first three days of this week have been the hottest we have had this year" and on June 21 the "insufferable" hot weather is mentioned. On June 28 news of 100-degree-plus weather and a month-long drought was reprinted from a Laredo newspaper. *El Bejareño,* vol. 2, nos. 23, 25.
2. *El Ranchero,* Friday, July 19, 1856, vol. 1, no. 3, p. 1, col. 3.
3. The last known editors of the *Bejareño* are Alfredo A. Lewis and Angel Navarro. Listed beneath the masthead as publishers are Lewis, Navarro, and F. Villasana. *El Bejareño,* June 28, 1856, vol. 2, no. 26, p. 2, col. 1.
4. *El Bejareño,* June 7, 1856, vol. 2, no. 23, p. 2, col. 2. The *Ranchero* likewise reported on the creation of vigilante committees, violence, and lynching of Mexicans on July 19, 1856, vol. 1, no. 3, p. 1, col. 2.
5. The *Bejareño* reported on attacks on Tejano carters, criticized legal jurisdictions for failing to prosecute attackers, and offered carters advice as to how to protect themselves. *El Bejareño,* February 17 vol. 1, no. 2, p. 2, col. 2; December 15, 1855, vol. 1, no. 26, p. 1, col. 3; and March 29, 1856, vol. 2, no. 13, p. 2, col. 3. The San Antonio *Correo* took the Goliad *Express* to task for claiming that Tejanos had attacked Anglo-American carters when, the *Correo* editors claimed, it was Anglo-Americans who had attacked Tejanos. *El Correo,* May 26, 1858, vol. 1, no. 2, p. 1, cols. 3–4. On the Cart War see J. Fred Rippy, "Border Troubles along the Rio Grande, 1848–1860," *Southwestern Historical Quarterly* 23, no. 2 (1919); Larry Knight, "The Cart War: Defining American in San Antonio in the 1850s," *Southwestern Historical Quarterly* 109, no. 3 (2006): 319–336. Knight claims there were only five attacks on cart men resulting in only three deaths and only in 1857. But these newspapers reported

on attacks occurring from as early as 1855 to as late as 1858. Even more startling, he does not cite any of the Spanish-language newspapers that defended Tejano carters.

6. *El Bejareño,* July 7, 1855, vol. 1, no. 12, p. 3, col. 1.
7. Father Miguel Hidalgo had declared slavery illegal in Mexico in 1810. President Guadalupe Victoria declared slavery illegal as well in 1824. But it was President Vicente Guerrero who decreed it illegal and emancipated all slaves in 1829. After Mexican independence, elite Tejanos petitioned the federal government to allow slavery in Texas in order to attract Anglo-American immigrants. Nonetheless, Tejanos as a whole appeared to be much less supportive of the institution, much to the consternation of Anglo-American slave owners. In 1832, "a group of former black slaves lived and worked in San Antonio as free persons in spite of vociferous protestations from their former owners and supported by Mexican authorities. . . . [I]n that same year of 1832, Texas [Mexican] officials initiated criminal proceedings against a posse of Anglo-Texans . . . [who] kidnapped five emancipated former slaves from the streets of San Antonio." Andrés Reséndez, *Changing National Identities at the Frontier: Texas and New Mexico, 1800–1850* (New York: Cambridge University Press, 2005), 162–163. The history of Tejano and African American slave relations is a seriously understudied topic. See also Randolph B. Campbell, *An Empire for Slavery: The Peculiar Institution in Texas, 1821–1865* (Baton Rouge: Louisiana State University Press, 1991); James E. Crisp, "José Antonio Navarro: The Problem of Tejano Powerlessness," in *Tejano Leadership in Mexican and Revolutionary Texas,* ed. Jesús F. de la Teja (College Station: Texas A&M University Press, 2010), 150–151; Andrés Reséndez, "Ramón Múzquiz: The Ultimate Insider," in *Tejano Leadership in Mexican and Revolutionary Texas,* ed. Jesús F. de la Teja (College Station: Texas A&M University Press, 2010), 134–137; Bruce A. Glasrud, ed., *African Americans in South Texas History* (College Station: Texas A&M University Press, 2011).
8. Walter L. Buenger, "Whig Party," *Handbook of Texas Online* (http://www.tshaonline.org/handbook/online/articles/wawo1), accessed May 12, 2011; Roger A. Griffin, "American Party," *Handbook of Texas Online* (http://www.tshaonline.org/handbook/online/articles/waa01), accessed May 12, 2011.
9. Ernest William Winkler, "Beginnings of Political Party Organizations in Texas," *Bulletin of the University of Texas: Special Issue, Platforms of Political Parties in Texas,* no. 53 (1916): 11–41; Joel H. Silbey, *The American Political Nation, 1838–1893* (Stanford: Stanford University Press, 1991), 46–71; Eric Foner, *Free Soil, Free Labor, Free Men: The Ideology of the Republican Party before the Civil War* (New York: Oxford University Press, 1995), 1–10, quote on p. 7.
10. Litha Crews, "The Know Nothing Party in Texas" (MA thesis, University of Texas, Austin, 1925), 11–68; Sister Paul of the Cross McGrath, "Political Nativism in Texas, 1825–1860" (PhD dissertation, Catholic University of America, Washington, DC, 1930), 79–106; Ralph A. Wooster, "An Analysis of the Texas Know Nothings," *Southwestern Historical Quarterly* 70, no. 3 (January 1967): 414–423; Yancey L. Russell, "Devine, Thomas Jefferson," *Handbook*

of Texas Online (http://www.tshaonline.org/handbook/online/articles/fde50), accessed December 19, 2011. For contemporary defenses of Democratic candidates against Know-Nothing claims, see *El Bejareño* December 22, 1855, p. 1; June 21, 1856, p. 2; *San Antonio Texan,* July 10, 1856, p. 2, August 28, 1856, p. 2; *San Antonio Ledger,* August 2, 1856, p. 2; *El Ranchero,* July 28, 1856, p. 1.

11. *El Ranchero,* July 4, 1856, vol. 1, no.1, p. 1, col. 1.
12. Ibid., p. 1, col. 2.
13. Ibid., p. 1, col. 1.
14. This article, originally appearing in the Bastrop *Advertiser,* was translated by and reprinted in the San Antonio *El Ranchero,* Friday, July 4, 1856, vol. 1, no. 1, p. 2, cols. 1–2. This issue of the *Advertiser* could not be located at the Dolph Briscoe Center for American History Newspaper Project; therefore, I rely on the reprinted and translated article. The Center for American History undertook the enormous task of collecting and archiving every extant paper ever printed in what is today Texas, and thus has the most reliable collection of Texan newspapers.
15. *El Ranchero,* Friday, July 4, 1856, vol. 1, no. 1, p. 2, col. 2.
16. "Helots" refers to one who has been stripped of citizenship rights. Its origin is from antiquity, used to describe Sparta's serfs.
17. *El Ranchero,* Friday, July 4, 1856, vol. 1, no. 1, p. 2, col. 2.
18. *San Antonio Herald* article reprinted in *San Antonio Texan,* Thursday, July 31, 1856, vol. 8, no. 41, p. 2, cols. 3–4.
19. Ibid., col. 3.
20. *San Antonio Ledger,* Saturday, August 2, 1856, vol. 6, no. 28, p. 2, col. 3.
21. *San Antonio Texan,* Thursday, July 31, 1856, vol. 8, no. 41, p. 2, col. 4.
22. The July 28, 1856 (vol. 1, no. 5, p. 2, col. 1) issue of *El Ranchero* cited receipt of the July 19, 1856, edition of *El Bejareño.* The latest extant issue of *El Bejareño* is dated June 28, 1856. Yet a month later, in its Thursday, July 31, 1856 (vol. 8, no. 41, p. 2, cols. 3–4), issue, the *San Antonio Texan* reported on the heated exchanges between the *Ranchero* and *Bejareño* but said nothing of the *Bejareño* ceasing publication.
23. Though the Know-Nothings divided the Democratic Party, they apparently were unable to take it over. The election results appear in the *San Antonio Texan,* Thursday, August 7, 1856, vol. 8, no. 42, p. 2, col. 2; Thursday, August 14, 1856, vol. 8, no. 43, p. 2, col. 3.
24. According to the *San Antonio Texan,* "The persons who took the lead in fomenting this spirit of discord although they called themselves democrats, yet it is singular but significant fact that at every important city county and State election for the last three years, these *very persons* have invariably been the aiders, abetters and often *leaders* of the *very party* [the Know-Nothings] opposing the democracy. But they are now desirous to acquire the influence and confidence of the democratic party which some of them had of yore, and too without purifying themselves—but it is no go; by their works we must know them," *San Antonio Texan,* Thursday, June 5, 1856, vol. 8, no. 33, p. 2, col. 2, emphasis in original. Then, on June 12, the *Texan* took "notice [of] a very able

article" by the German-language San Antonio *Texas Staats Zeitung* in which the *Zeitung* alleged that former Know-Nothing members, "feeling their influence diminished under the new state of things, had determined to bring about a split in the democratic party," by infiltrating and disrupting the convention. *San Antonio Texan,* Thursday, June 12, 1856, vol. 8, no. 34, p. 2, cols. 3–4.

25. *San Antonio Texan,* Thursday, June 12, 1856, vol. 8, no. 34, p. 2, col. 3.
26. *El Bejareño,* Saturday, June 7, 1856, vol. 2, no. 23, p. 2, col. 3.
27. *El Bejareño,* Saturday, June 21, 1856, vol. 2, no. 25, p. 2, col. 3.
28. *San Antonio Texan,* Thursday, July 31, 1856, vol. 8, no. 41, p. 2, col. 2.
29. *El Bejareño,* Saturday, June 28, 1856, vol. 2, no. 26, p. 4, col. 2.
30. *El Ranchero,* Monday, July 11, 1856, vol. 1, no. 2, p. 1, cols. 2–3 and Monday, July 28, 1856, vol. 1, no. 5, p. 2, col. 2; *San Antonio Texan,* Thursday, August 7, 1856, vol. 8, no. 42, p. 2, col. 2.
31. *El Ranchero,* Monday, July 28, 1856, vol. 1, no. 5, p. 1, col. 3.
32. *El Ranchero,* Friday, July 19, 1856, vol. 1, no. 3, p. 2, col. 2.
33. *El Ranchero,* Monday, July 28, 1856, vol. 1, no. 5, p. 1, col. 2.
34. Ibid., col. 3, emphasis added.
35. Jorge Marbán, *José Agustín Quintero: Un enigma histórico en el exilio Cubano del ochocientos* (Miami: Ediciones Universal, 2001), 22–23.
36. I. J. Cox, "Educational Efforts in San Fernando de Béxar," *Southwestern Historical Quarterly* 6 (July 1902): 27–63; Georgia Lee Dorsey, "A History of the Education of the Spanish-Speaking People in Texas" (MA thesis, North Texas State Teachers College, Denton, 1941); Max Berger, "Education in Texas during the Spanish and Mexican Periods," *Southwestern Historical Quarterly* 51 (July 1947): 41–53; Daniel Tyler, "The Mexican Teacher," *Red River Historical Review* 1, no. 3 (Autumn 1974): 207–221.
37. Cox, "Educational Efforts in San Fernando de Béxar," 37; Tyler, "The Mexican Teacher," 209.
38. In 1850 Texas and New Mexico, for example, the literacy rates for Mexicans hovered around 25 percent. This appears rather high compared to the 15 percent literacy rate for the rest of Spanish America, according to Carlos Newland. Gender differences may explain the discrepancies (some of the studies only reported on literacy rates among men). Arnoldo De León, *The Tejano Community, 1836–1900* (Albuquerque: University of New Mexico Press, 1982), 188–189; David J. Weber, *The Mexican Frontier, 1821–1846: The American Southwest under Mexico* (Albuquerque: University of New Mexico Press, 1982), 234; Arnoldo De León and Kenneth L. Stewart, *Tejanos and the Numbers Game: A Socio-Historical Interpretation from the Federal Censuses, 1850–1900* (Albuquerque: University of New Mexico Press, 1989), 36; Carlos Newland, "La educacion elemental en Hispanoamérica: Desde la independencia hasta la centralizacion de los sistemas educativos nacionales," *Hispanic American Historical Review* 71, no. 2 (1991): 357; Bernardo P. Gallegos, *Literacy, Education, and Society in New Mexico, 1693–1821* (Albuquerque: University of New Mexico Press, 1992), 43–53; Kenneth L. Stewart and Arnoldo De León, *Not Room Enough: Mexicans, Anglos, and Socio-Economic Change*

in Texas, 1850–1900 (Albuquerque: University of New Mexico Press, 1993), 66–67.

39. Tyler, "The Mexican Teacher," 211; Weber, *Mexican Frontier,* 232–234; Jesús F. de la Teja and John Wheat, "Béxar: Profile of a Tejano Community, 1820–1832," in *Tejano Origins in Eighteenth-Century San Antonio,* ed. Gerald E. Poyo and Gilberto M. Hinojosa (Austin: University of Texas Press, 1991), 13; Joseph E. Chance, *José María de Jesús Carvajal: The Life and Times of a Mexican Revolutionary* (San Antonio: Trinity University Press, 2006), 17–20.
40. Kirsten Silva Gruesz describes New Orleans during this period as a city bustling with transnational, multilingual literary and intellectual activity. See Kirsten Silva Gruesz, *Ambassadors of Culture: The Transamerican Origins of Latino Writing* (Princeton: Princeton University Press, 2002), 108–160; Kirsten Silva Gruesz, "The Gulf of Mexico System and the 'Latinness' of New Orleans," *American Literary History* 18, no. 3 (2006): 468–495.
41. *El Bejareño,* Saturday, November 24, 1855, vol. 1, no. 23, p. 2, col. 1.
42. *El Bejareño,* Saturday, January 5, 1856, vol. 2, no. 1, p. 2, col. 3.
43. *El Ranchero,* Friday, July 4, 1856, vol. 1, no. 1, p. 1, col. 1.
44. Quintero, as noted in Chapter 8, had participated in various struggles for Cuban independence. He had also printed various patriotic essays celebrating Cuban revolutionaries. See, for example, his "Patriotas Cubanas," in *El Bejareño,* April 19, 1856, vol. 2, no. 16, p. 1, cols. 2–3.
45. Real Academia Española, "Dicciónarios de la lengua española (1726–1992)" (http://www.rae.es/), accessed May 10, 2011; Mónica Quijada, "¿Qué nación? Dinámicas y dicotomías de la nación en el imaginario hispanoamericano," in *Inventando la nación: Iberoamérica, siglo XIX,* ed. Antonio Annino and François-Xavier Guerra (Mexico City: Fondo de Cultura Económica, 2003), 287–315; José Carlos Chiaramonte, *Nación y estado en Iberoamérica: el lenguaje político en tiempos de las independencias* (Buenos Aires: Sudamericana, 2004); Mónica Quijada, "Sobre 'nación,' 'pueblo,' 'soberanía' y otros ejes de la modernidad en el mundo hispánico," in *Las nuevas naciones: España y México, 1800–1850,* ed. Jaime E. Rodríguez O. (Madrid: Fundación MAPFRE, 2008), 19–51.
46. *El Ranchero,* Friday, July 19, 1856, vol. 1, no. 3, p. 1, col. 2.
47. Juan Nepomuceno Seguín, *Personal Memoirs of John N. Seguín, from the Year 1834 to the Retreat of General Woll from the City of San Antonio in 1842* (San Antonio: Ledger Book & Job Office, 1858). For a transcription of the original and a useful introduction, see Juan Nepomuceno Seguín, *A Revolution Remembered: The Memoirs and Selected Correspondence of Juan N. Seguín,* ed. Jesús F. de la Teja (Austin: State House Press, 1991; orig. 1858).
48. *El Ranchero,* Friday, July 19, 1856, vol. 1, no. 3, p. 1, cols. 1–2.
49. *El Ranchero,* Friday, July 4, 1856, vol. 1, no. 1, p. 1, col. 3.
50. Ibid.
51. *El Ranchero,* Friday, July 19, 1856, vol. 1, no. 3, p. 1, col. 2.
52. Raymond Estep, "The Life of Lorenzo de Zavala" (PhD dissertation, University of Texas at Austin, 1942), 1–11, 378–383. Estep's is still the best biography of

Zavala. See also Lorenzo de Zavala, *Ensayo histórico de las revoluciones de México desde 1808 hasta 1830,* 2 vols. (Mexico City: Fondo de Cultura Económica, 1985; orig. 1845); Lorenzo de Zavala, *Journey to the United States of America*=Viaje a los Estados Unidos del Norte de America, trans. Wallace Woolsey (Houston: Arte Público, 2005).

53. Michel Foucault, *The Archaeology of Knowledge,* trans. A. M. Sheridan Smith (New York: Barnes and Noble Books, 1972), 5; Michel Foucault, "Nietzsche, Genealogy, History," in *The Foucault Reader,* ed. Paul Rabinow (New York: Pantheon Books, 1984), 81.

54. *El Ranchero,* Friday, July 19, 1856, vol. 1, no. 3, col. 2.

55. Leslie Bethell, "Brazil and 'Latin America'," *Journal of Latin American Studies* 42, no. 3 (2010): 457–485. Walter Mignolo also argues that the concept of Latinness allows elite Spanish Americans to emphasize their common European white roots as opposed to those of mestizos, Indians, and blacks. Walter Mignolo, *The Idea of Latin America* (Oxford: Blackwell, 2004).

56. Here, of course, I rely on the classic account of racialization in Michael Omi and Howard Winant, *Racial Formation in the United States: From the 1960s to the 1990s,* 2nd ed. (New York: Routledge, 1994).

57. Frederick Law Olmsted, *The Cotton Kingdom: A Traveller's Observations on Cotton and Slavery in the American Slave States,* vol. 2 (New York: Mason Brothers, 1862), 19.

58. Translated and printed in *El Ranchero,* Friday, July 4, 1856, vol. 1, no. 1, p. 2, cols. 1–2, emphasis added.

59. Arnoldo De León, *Apuntes Tejanos: An Index of Items Related to Mexican Americans in Nineteenth-Century Texas Extracted from the San Antonio* Express *(1869–1900) and the San Antonio* Herald *(1855–1878),* vol. 1 (Austin: Texas Historical Association, 1978); Arnoldo De León, *Apuntes Tejanos: An Index of Items Related to Mexican Americans in Nineteenth-Century Texas Extracted from the Corpus Christi* Weekly Caller *(1883–1899), the Corpus Christi (Matamoros and Brownsville)* Ranchero *(1859–1870), the El Paso* Times *(1883–1899), the El Paso* Daily Herald *(1881–1899), and the Austin* Statesman *(1871–1899),* vol. 2 (Austin: Texas Historical Association, 1978); Arnoldo De León, *They Called Them Greasers: Anglo Attitudes toward Mexicans in Texas, 1821–1900* (Austin: University of Texas Press, 1983). See also Reginald Horsman, *Race and Manifest Destiny: The Origins of American Racial Anglo-Saxonism* (Cambridge, MA: Harvard University Press, 1981), 208–249.

60. Horsman, *Race and Manifest Destiny,* 208, 213. See the highly influential essays by John O'Sullivan, the man who coined the term "Manifest Destiny" in his 1845 essay "Annexation." John O'Sullivan, "The Democratic Principle," *United States Magazine and Democratic Review* 1, no. 1 (October 1837): 1–15; "The Great Nation of Futurity," *United States Magazine and Democratic Review* 6, no. 23 (November 1839): 426–430; "Territorial Aggrandizement," *United States Magazine and Democratic Review* 17, no. 88 (October 1845): 241–48; "Annexation," *United States Magazine and Democratic Review* 17, no. 85 (July–August 1845): 5–10.

61. David Montejano, *Anglos and Mexicans in the Making of Texas, 1836–1987* (Austin: University of Texas Press, 1987), 75–219.
62. The Cassiano-Pérez Family Papers at the Daughters of the Republic Texas Library contain a wealth of documents on late nineteenth-century bourgeois Tejano civic life, such as it was given the challenging racial contexts. Among the Cassiano descendants is one Esther Adela Carvajal. Having been educated in San Antonio and Durango, Mexico, she would receive both her BA (1920) and MA (1929) in Romance Languages and Literatures and Comparative Literature, respectively (both with honors) from the University of Chicago. Cassiano-Pérez Family Papers, 1741–1976, Col 880, Manuscript Collection (San Antonio: Daughters of the Republic of Texas Library), Pérez Family Papers (Esther Pérez Carvajal Professional Papers), Folder 185.
63. José Ramos de Zúñiga and Alfred A. Lewis, eds., *El Correo,* Wednesday, May 26, 1858, vol. 1, no. 6, p. 2, cols. 1–3. As for their German counterparts, with the exception of a handful of liberals who had escaped the failed 1848 revolutions, most Germans had in fact been much more amenable to slavery than contemporary sources and some historians since then had noted. Their general acceptance of slavery, their European origin, and, in many cases, their Protestant background made it much easier for them to assimilate. Terry G. Jordan, *German Seed in Texas Soil: Immigrant Farmers in Nineteenth-Century Texas* (Austin: University of Texas at Austin, 1966), 108–109.
64. See, for example, Tomás Almaguer, *Racial Fault Lines: The Historical Origins of White Supremacy in California* (Berkeley: University of California Press, 1994); Laura E. Gómez, *Manifest Destinies: The Making of the Mexican American Race* (New York: New York University Press, 2007).
65. Roberto R. Calderón, "Tejano Politics," *Handbook of Texas Online* (http://www.tshaonline.org/handbook/online/articles/wmtkn), accessed December 26, 2012.
66. Richard Griswold del Castillo, *The Treaty of Guadalupe Hidalgo: A Legacy of Conflict* (Norman: University of Oklahoma Press, 1990), 46–67.

Conclusion

1. Patrick Foley, "Odin, Jean Marie," *Handbook of Texas Online* (http://www.tshaonline.org/handbook/online/articles/fodo2), accessed December 12, 2011; Sister M. Claude Lane, O.P., and Sister Ignatius Miller, O.S.U., "Ursuline Sisters," *Handbook of Texas Online* (http://www.tshaonline.org/handbook/online/articles/fne19), accessed December 21, 2011; Sister Ignatius Miller, O.S.U., "Ursuline Academy, San Antonio," *Handbook of Texas Online* (http://www.tshaonline.org/handbook/online/articles/kbu04), accessed December 21, 2011; Robert E. Wright, O.M.I., "Catholic Church," *Handbook of Texas Online* (http://www.tshaonline.org/handbook/online/articles/icc01), accessed December 12, 2011; Ettie Madeline Vogel, "The Ursuline Nuns in America," *Records of the American Catholic Historical Society* 1 (1884–1886): 214–216, 219, 229–233; M.A., "The Ursulines of Texas," *St. Louis Catholic Historical Review* 4, no. 1–2 (January–April 1922): 16–19; Catherine McDowell,

ed. *Letters from the Ursuline, 1852–1853: From Our Beloved Sisters, Who Quitted St. Mary's, April 17th, 1852, to Commence the Mission at San Antonio* (San Antonio: Trinity University Press, 1977); Emily Edwards, *Stones, Bells, Lighted Candles: Personal Memories of the Old Ursuline Academy in San Antonio at the Turn of the Century* (San Antonio: Daughters of the Republic of Texas Library, 1981), 3; Emily Clark, *Masterless Mistresses: The New Orleans Ursulines and the Development of a New World Society, 1727–1834* (Chapel Hill: University of North Carolina Press, 2007).

2. Frederick C. Chabot, *With the Makers of San Antonio: Genealogies of the Early San Antonio Families* (San Antonio: Artes Gráficas, 1937), 147–152.
3. According to baptismal records from the Tamaulipas parish records (available online through www.ancestry.com), Narciso Leal was baptized on October 31, 1830, and Guadalupe Leal on December 21, 1835, both in Mier, Tamaulipas, Mexico. See also Randell G. Tarín, "Leal, Joaquín," *Handbook of Texas Online* (http://www.tshaonline.org/handbook/online/articles/fle98), accessed February 22, 2012.
4. Florencia Leal, Notebook, ca. 1853–ca. 1870, Manuscript Collection, Benson Latin American Collection, University of Texas at Austin, hereafter cited in text. Other Tejanas who attended the Ursuline academies in San Antonio and Galveston would also keep notebooks. See, for example, Adina Emilia de Zavala, Adina Emilia de Zavala Papers, 1766 (1831–1955), Box 2M161, the Dolph Briscoe Center for American History, University of Texas at Austin. The collection contains her late nineteenth-century notebooks.
5. The full text of the song is: "Come over the heather, we'll trip thegither/All in the morning early;/With heart and hand I'll by thee stand,/For in truth I lo'e thee dearly,/There's mony a lass I lo'e fu' well,/And mony that lo'e me dearly,/But there's ne'er a lass beside thysel'/I e'er could lo'e sincerely,/Come over the heather, we'll trip thegither, All in the morning early; / With heart and hand I'll by thee stand,/For in truth I lo'e thee dearly." Charlotte Taylor Blow Charless, *A Biographical Sketch of the Life and Character of Joseph Charless, in a Series of Letters to His Grandchildren* (St. Louis: A.F. Cox [Echo Library, 2008], 1869), 14.
6. Chabot, *Makers of San Antonio*, 152.
7. Anonymous, "Memoria de las cosas más notables que acaeceron en Bexar el año de 13 mandando el Tirano Arredondo, 1813," MSS P-O 811, Herbert Bolton Papers (No. 711), Bancroft Library, University of California, Berkeley.
8. Michel Foucault, *The Order of Things: An Archaeology of the Human Sciences* (New York: Vintage, 1994), 42–44, 81–92, 299–300; Michael T. Gilmore, "The Literature of the Revolutionary and Early National Periods," in *Cambridge History of American Literature,* ed. Sacvan Bercovitch and Cyrus R. K. Patell, vol. 1 (New York: Cambridge University, 1994), 541; Pierre Bourdieu, *The Rules of Art: Genesis and Structure of the Literary Field* (Stanford: Stanford University Press, 1996); Roberto González Echevarría, *Myth and Archive: A Theory of Latin American Narrative* (Durham: Duke University Press, 1998), 1–42; Julio Ramos, *Divergent Modernities: Culture and Politics in Nineteenth-Century Latin America,* trans. John D. Blanco (Durham: Duke University, 2001), xl–xli.

9. Jacques Derrida, *Of Grammatology,* trans. Gayatri Chakravorty Spivak (Baltimore: Johns Hopkins University Press, 1997), 98, emphasis in original.
10. For a review and critique of these sociohistorical studies, see Mario Barrera, Carlos Muñoz, and Charles Ornelas, "The Barrio as an Internal Colony," in *People and Politics in Urban Society,* ed. Harlan Hahn, vol. 6 (Beverly Hills: Sage, 1972), 465–498.
11. See, for example, Tomás Almaguer, "Toward the Study of Chicano Colonialism," *Aztlán* 2, no. 1 (Spring 1971): 7–21; Joan W. Moore, "Colonialism: The Case of the Mexican Americans," *Social Problems* 17, no. 4 (1971): 473–472; Frank Bonilla and Robert Girling, eds., *Structures of Dependency* (East Palo Alto, CA: Nairobi Bookstore, 1973); Tomás Almaguer, "Historical Notes on Chicano Oppression: The Dialectics of Racial and Class Domination in North América," *Aztlán* 5, no. 1–2 (1974): 25–56; Rudolph Gómez, "Mexican Americans: From Internal Colonialism to the Chicano Movement," in *The Social Reality of Ethnic America,* ed. Kathleen Jackson (Lexington, MA: D. C. Heath & Co., 1974), 317–336; Mario Barrera, *Race and Class in the Southwest: A Theory of Racial Inequality* (Notre Dame, IN: University of Notre Dame Press, 1979).
12. Tomás Almaguer, "Ideological Distortions in Recent Chicano Historiography: The Internal Model and Chicano Historical Interpretation," *Aztlán* 18, no. 1 (1989): 7–28. See also Mario T. García, "Inside the Beast: Internal Colonialism and the Chicano," *La Luz* (November 1974): 27–28; Mario T. García, "Internal Colonialism: A Critical Essay," *Revista Chicano Riqueña* 6, no. 3 (1978): 38–41.
13. For a perceptive yet underappreciated productive critique made during this period, see Frederick A. Cervantes, "Chicanos as a Post Colonial Minority: Some Questions concerning the Adequacy of the Paradigm of Internal Colonialism," in *Perspectivas en Chicano Studies I: Papers Presented at the 3rd Annual Meeting of the National Association of Chicano Social Science, 1975,* ed. Reynaldo Flores Macías (Los Angeles: National Association of Chicano Social Science, 1977), 123–135.
14. It is profoundly ironic that those working within the field of contemporary Chicana/o cultural studies often use postcolonial theory without acknowledging how Chicanas/os became postcolonial, to say nothing of how they were colonized to begin with. More recently, a few historians have returned to this framework, but the discussion has yet to make a rapprochement with that of the 1970s. See, for example, María E. Montoya, "Beyond Internal Colonialism: Class, Gender, and Culture as Challenges to Chicano Identity," in *Voices of a New Chicana/o History,* ed. Refugio I. Rochín and Dennis N. Valdés (East Lansing: Michigan State University Press, 2000), 183–195; Laura E. Gómez, *Manifest Destinies: The Making of the Mexican American Race* (New York: New York University, 2007).
15. Walter Benjamin, "Theses on the Philosophy of History," trans. Harry Zohn, in *Illuminations: Essays and Reflections,* ed. Hannah Arendt (New York: Schocken Books, 1969), 256.

16. David L. Eng and David Kazanjian, "Introduction: Mourning Remains," in *Loss: The Politics of Mourning*, ed. David L. Eng and David Kazanjian (Berkeley: University of California Press, 2003), 4.
17. Nipperdey's work is characterized in this manner in Donal Ó Drisceoil, "Framing the Irish Revolution: Ken Loach's *The Wind That Shakes the Barley*," *Radical History Review* 104 (Spring 2009): 10.

Appendix 1

1. Diana is the Roman goddess of the hunt, wildlife, and the moon. She is associated with the light, the divine, and the unknown.
2. Juan Antonio Riaño y Bárcena was a Spanish coronel who fought in the American Revolutionary War and was then stationed as intendant of Guanajuato, New Spain. He died in battle on September 10, 1810, as Hidalgo's forces took Guanajuato. The Bourbon reforms created the administrative office of the intendant as a way to systematize the governance of Spanish America.
3. Callejas was famous for his ruthlessness in conquering his enemies. He would eventually subdue Hidalgo's forces and would be named viceroy of New Spain.
4. These were all leaders of the wars of independence.
5. "Nación" is a feminine noun and takes the feminine "Americana."

Appendix 2

1. The term *Derecho real* or real right is derived from the Latin *ius in re*, a direct legal relationship existing between a person and a thing, as in ownership. *Derecho particular* or particular or personal right is a right one has over one's body. Richard Tuck, *Natural Rights Theories: Their Origin and Development* (New York: Cambridge University Press, 1979), 11–17.

Appendix 3

1. The city now known as San Antonio was established in 1731 as San Fernando de Béxar. It was settled by Canary Islanders adjacent to the San Antonio de Béxar Presidio, the center of Spanish defense for Texas, which was established in 1718. The distinction made here is that the military base was at the San Antonio presidio and the civilian signatories represented the city of San Fernando. The city was also widely referred to as Béxar through the 1830s, when it became referred to as San Antonio.
2. Venegas served as viceroy from September 14, 1810, to March 4, 1813, and sought to quash Father Miguel Hidalgo's insurrection.
3. Reference to the forced abdication of King Fernando VII to Bonaparte.
4. The *ayuntamientos* of Buenos Aires, Bogotá, and Caracas had already declared independence.

Appendix 4

1. Ignacio Elizondo, along with Spanish governor of Texas Manuel de Salcedo, had helped capture Father Miguel Hidalgo and his revolutionary forces on March 21, 1811, at the Wells of Baján, some 200 miles southeast of present-day Laredo, Texas. Arredondo had ordered Elizondo to join his forces as Hidalgo approached San Antonio.
2. Miguel Menchaca had been a soldier stationed at Nacogdoches. He, along with Juan Galván, helped distribute José Bernardo Gutiérrez de Lara's revolutionary literature in San Antonio in the summer of 1812. Jack Jackson, "Menchaca, Miguel," *Handbook of Texas Online* (http://www.tshaonline.org/handbook/online/articles/fme/15), accessed December 31, 2012.
3. *Pueblo* and *patria* have various connotations that are lost in English translation. *Pueblo* can be translated as "the people," "the community," or "town." *Patria* can be translated as "fatherland," "homeland," or "country." See Chapters 1 and 2 for how these terms shifted during this period.
4. Both Juan Antonio Joaquín Delgado Leal (1746–1813) and Ana María de Arocha (1754–1830) came from two of the most wealthy, prominent families of San Antonio. They were each descendants of the original Canary Islander settlers who founded San Fernando (what became known as San Antonio) in 1718. Joaquín Leal was a cousin of Juan Leal (1735–?), who was the great-great-grandfather of Narciso, Guadalupe, and Florencia Leal. Narciso and Guadelupe had helped establish the earliest continuously published Spanish-language newspapers in Texas during the 1850s. See Chapters 8 and 9 for a discussion of Narciso and Guadalupe and the Conclusion for a discussion of Florencia. Randell G. Tarín, "Leal, Joaquín," *Handbook of Texas Online* (http://www.tshaonline.org/handbook/online/articles/fle98), accessed August 25, 2011; Frederick C. Chabot, *With the Makers of San Antonio: Genealogies of the Early San Antonio Families* (San Antonio: Artes Gráficas, 1937), 147–152.
5. Also a descendant of the original Canary Islander settlers of San Antonio, Ángela Curbelo de Arocha was born around 1748 in San Antonio. She married Manuel Martín Delgado around 1737, with whom she had twelve children. Governor Salcedo ordered Manuel's execution in 1813 for having participated in the revolution. He was beheaded, and his head placed on a pike. Angela and Manuel's son Antonio Delgado, in turn, participated in the execution of Governor Salcedo and other royal commanders. See Chapter 6 and the extensive genealogical sources on the Moya-Delgado family at http://wc.rootsweb.ancestry.com/.
6. Loma del Toro or Bull's Hill was located at the Trinity River where the old Camino Real and Camino de la Bahía met before continuing on to Nacogdoches (see Figure 5). The town of Trinidad was located on the east bank of the river. After the Bexareño refugees were captured, Elizondo waited several days for the Trinity water level to recede. Once it did, he entered the now-abandoned town of Trinidad and destroyed it. Though archaeologists have been unable to find the precise location of Trinidad or Loma del Toro, it is believed to have

been located near where State Highway 21 meets the Trinity River. Jack Jackson, ed., *Texas by Terán: The Diary Kept by General Manuel de Mier y Terán on His 1828 Inspection of Texas* (Austin: University of Texas Press, 2000), 224–225; Bradley Folsom, "Santísima Trinidad de Salcedo," *Handbook of Texas Online* (http://www.tshaonline.org/handbook/online/articles/hvs43), accessed December 31, 2012.

7. The authors do not mention that many of the revolutionary men had crossed the Trinity River in order to be saved, knowing that the women would not be harmed. Lieutenant Rodríguez promised not to harm the men if they voluntarily gave up. The men did and swam back across the river, and many were promptly executed.
8. As noted above, Antonio had participated in the slaying of Governor Salcedo and other Spanish commanders.
9. The narrative shifts attention to Ana María Arocha and her children. Arocha and her husband had at least eighteen children, though only five lived past infancy. Of these, Maria de la Consolación (b. 1795) was one of their daughters.
10. The Valley of Jehoshaphat is mentioned once in the Bible in Joel 3:11–12. It is believed that God's final judgment will take place there.
11. Jesus of the Esquipulas is an image of Christ carved out of wood that has darkened over the centuries. It has been venerated in Central America and Mexico since the late sixteenth century.
12. The authors allude to Fernando Rodríguez's having deceived the men in telling them their lives would be spared if they gave up.
13. They had traveled approximately fifty miles from the Trinity to the Guadalupe River.
14. *Vecino* is an old Spanish political category given to individuals who inhabit a town that grants them full rights as members of that town. The authors sardonically refer to Quintero as a *vecino* of their camp.
15. The authors left an underscored blank space here with the intention of later returning and including the first name, as they had done in other instances.
16. The Salado creek runs south-southeast from northeastern San Antonio, mostly on the eastern part of the city, to where it meets the San Antonio River.
17. The Alamo mission and the city of San Antonio had been separate though adjacent establishments, separated by the San Antonio River and less than a mile from one another.
18. Arredondo had a cataract in one eye.
19. The parenthetical note refers to Arocha's husband, who appears to have sided with the royalists. Clearly, the revolution had pitted family members against one another, much as the 1836 Texas Revolution, like all wars certainly, would do as well.
20. Saint Francis of Paola (1416–1507) was the founder of the Catholic Order of Minims and was known for his prophesies.
21. Derogatory term for Peninsular-born Spaniards.
22. Rosi is referring to the start of the insurrection in 1810. The revolution had pitted American-born Spaniards against European-born Spaniards.

23. The words in italics were written in letters twice as large as the rest of the text.
24. A *metate* is a traditional Mesoamerican flat stone mortar.
25. Anahuac was the Aztec term for the valley of central Mexico. By this time, creoles had co-opted Aztec mythology and history into their emergent nationalist Mexican history.
26. *Nixtamal* is maize cooked with lime that is then ground to make tortillas.
27. The authors used a caret to insert the words in parentheses.
28. Infamous as a tyrant, the Roman emperor Nero was known for burning Christians in his garden as a source of light.
29. Arredondo had been commander of the infantry regiment of Veracruz, a state on the Gulf Coast of Mexico, and was commander of the Eastern Interior Provinces. The Eastern Interior Provinces were comprised of the northeastern provinces of Mexico, including Texas. See Chapter 1.
30. Born in Cuba, Antonio Elozúa was a brevet lieutenant-colonel, the highest-ranking officer in Arredondo's forces. He would serve in various posts in the Eastern Interior Provinces. His final commission was that of commander of the military troops in Texas, based in San Antonio from 1827 to 1833. Adán Benavides Jr., "Elozúa, Antonio," *Handbook of Texas Online* (http://www.tshaonline.org/handbook/online/articles/fel34), accessed February 12, 2012.
31. Elozúa was from Cuba; Acosta may have been as well.
32. This is one of the few instances where quotation marks instead of colons are used to set off dialogue.
33. *Chamacuero* is a Tarascan or Purepechan word from Michoacán in central Mexico meaning "place where the wall fell" or "place of ruins."
34. For decades after, the revolutionary women and their children would file lawsuits seeking the return of their property.

Acknowledgments

I thank my parents, Leonor Coronado and Raúl Coronado Mendoza, for giving me the tools for surviving in this world. My mother gave me the language of introspection, of emotions, and therapy. For that, Ma, I will be eternally grateful. Pa instilled in me a different way of being *Americano,* one that could easily traverse the psychological and physical borders of the Americas. He also taught me his work ethic, without which I never would have finished this book. To my sisters, Anna and Lisa, I thank you from the bottom of my heart for all of your love and support over the years, for listening and helping out, and for all those wonderful memories of being in the moment and living life. To Anna, thanks for the incredible amount of time and energy you spent in making the gorgeous maps. To my precious nieces Aleah, Sofía, and Bianca, I adore you more than you'll ever know.

This project started when I was an undergraduate at the University of Texas at Austin and trying to make sense of the world, who I was, and why I felt like I never belonged. It began as a desire to write a history of Latina/o sexuality. For teaching me how to integrate a personal journey, intellectual passion, and political commitment, I thank my MEChistas Louis Mendoza, Deb Vargas, Sandy Soto, and the rest of the gang. I was an undergraduate when I first met Louis, who was an English graduate student; he opened my eyes to academia as a possible career path. My undergraduate mentors provided me with the tools that would help me launch this work: Lisa Moore, José Limón, David Montejano, and Ann Cvetkovich. For their continuing support in my archival research, thanks to Margo Gutiérrez and Adán Benavides.

In graduate school at Stanford, I realized that so much of contemporary Latina/o studies rests on the assumption that Latinas/os are some kind of postcolonial people or that sexuality is a product of biopower. If that was the case, I wondered, then shouldn't we know something about those historical processes? The book has taken quite a different shape, but I see it as central to my initial commitment. Stanford's Modern Thought and Literature Program provided both intellectual rigor and lifelong friends. Thanks to Monica Moore and Jan Hafner for helping me make my way across Stanford. Let it be known: your fellow grad students not only become great friends but also some of your best interlocutors. Thanks, of course, to Jackie Olvera and Rich Benjamin, to Lisa Arellano, Magdalena Barrera, Ericka Beckman, Yael Ben-Zvi, María Cotera, Manishita Dass, Nicole Fleetwood, Mishuana Goeman, Marcial Gonzalez, Karina Hodoyan, Mari Negrón, Celine Parreñas Shimizu, Lisa Thompson, and last but not least Kyla Tompkins. My professors and friends guided me through the arduous process of graduate school. Thanks to Ramón Saldívar, Yvonne Yarbro-Bejarano, Norma Alarcón, Paulla Ebron, Jane Collier, Arnold Rampersad, Ann Stoler, and Nick DeGenova. Jay Fliegelman came out of the blue when I was lost in a sea of archives, and enthusiastically helped me make sense of it all. It came as no surprise when I later learned that he had produced a whole generation of early Americanists. Cherríe Moraga came into my life when I was drowning in a world of authority. She taught me how to claim my voice and to tell my version of the story.

The University of Chicago opened up a new world to me. My colleagues helped me to radically rethink my book project. Through both casual conversation and rigorous in-depth discussions, I never cease to be amazed by how fortunate I am to be among such generous colleagues. Thanks to Lauren Berlant, Bill Brown, Jim Chandler, Leela Gandhi, Jackie Goldsby, Ramón Gutiérrez, Elaine Hadley, the late Miriam Hansen, Beth Helsinger, Janice Knight, Emilio Kourí, Loren Kruger, Agnes Lugo-Ortiz, Debbie Nelson, Lisa Ruddick, Josh Scodel, Eric Slauter, Richard Strier, Robin Valenza, and Ken Warren. My junior colleagues eased the pressures of being an assistant professor immensely. Thanks to Adrienne Brown, Tim Campbell, Hillary Chute, Patrick Jagoda, Rachel Jean-Baptiste, Heather Keenleyside, Cesar Melo, Benjamin Morgan, John Muse, Chicu Reddy, and Jen Scappetone. My Chicago-area friends gave me much needed balance in life.

To do this work requires interlocutors in a variety of fields, from Latina/o studies and Latin American studies, to U.S.-American Studies. Thanks to Jesse Alemán, José F. Aranda Jr., Richard Bauer, Mary Pat Brady, Carrie Tirado Bramen, Debbie Castillo, Ernie Chávez, John Alba Cutler, Emily García, Susan Gillman, Nicole Guidotti-Hernández, Robert McKee Irwin, Rodrigo Lazo, Marissa Lopez, Nancy Mirabal, Juan Poblete, Gerry Poyo, Jaime E. Rodríguez, Juan Rodríguez Diaz, Nancy Vogeley, and Michael Warner. For asking thoughtful questions and supporting my work, thanks to audiences at the University of California at Los Angeles, Northwestern University, the University of Illinois at Urbana-Champaign, the University of Texas at Austin, Southern Methodist University, Yale, Columbia, the University of California at Berkeley, Stanford, the University of California at Irvine, Cornell, the University of Louisville, Leipzig University, and El Taller Chicana/o at the University of North Texas. Thanks, especially, to my extraordinary readers at Harvard University Press, Kirsten Silva Gruesz and Debbie Castillo. David Lobenstine came in at the last minute as my structural editor and helped me transform this book into what it is.

Generous financial support made this work possible. The Ford Foundation supported me from the start with a three-year Pre-Doctoral Fellowship. I was fortunate enough to also receive their two other fellowships, including a postdoctoral fellowship. The Ford Foundation conferences exposed me early on to a vibrant world of faculty of color. Notwithstanding our dismal numbers in the academy, it is good to know that the Ford Foundation is as committed as ever to diversifying academia. At Stanford, fellowships from the College of Humanities and Sciences, the Richard Weiland Research Fund, El Centro Chicano, the Center for the Comparative Studies in Race and Ethnicity, and the Humanities Center provided funding, space, and immense intellectual support for my work. A Fulbright–García Robles Fellowship changed my life by allowing me to spend seven months in Mexico City. An NEH Summer Fellowship exposed me to the world of late nineteenth-century Latina/o political thought. My former humanities dean at Chicago, Janel Muller, believed in me from the beginning, and my current dean, Martha Roth, has supported me all the way. I thank them and the Humanities Division for two paid yearlong sabbaticals and a book subvention that made including the images possible. The Center for the Study of Race, Politics, and Culture, the Center for the Study of Gender and Sexuality, and the Latin American Studies Center all provided much-needed funding that allowed me to hire research assistants. For helping me track down materials and to scan, organize, and translate many of them, thanks to José Estrada, James Estrella, Christina Priscilla Flores, Kevin Kimura, Shannon Thompson, Dalia Yedidia, and Omaris Zamora. Thanks to Melissa Galván for transcribing the 1813 *Memoria.*

I'm a native of Dallas, and I could not wait to get out of that conservative city after high school. Imagine my surprise and great fortune when I received a fellowship in 2010 at the Clements Center for Southwest Studies at Southern Methodist University in Dallas. I was reluctant to return, given my feelings for the city. As it turns out, the fellowship turned my world upside down. The time spent there was immeasurably rich in so many ways. Not only did I write more than half of the manuscript there, but I had the great fortune to become friends with David Weber. His warmth, generous spirit, and enthusiasm, including the gentle prodding to remove unnecessary jargon, made my time there memorable. He was lost too soon. For generous feedback during the manuscript workshop, thanks to Anna Brickhouse, Cathleen Cahill, Jorge Cañizares-Esguerra, John R. Chávez, Sarah Cornell, Ben Johnson, and David Narrett. Rick Bozorth convinced me that Dallas had changed for the better. More than anything, I am grateful for the time spent with my family: to my father, who brought me meals during the day so that I could write into the night; to my mother, who took me out to dinners and movies and continues to teach me how to take care of the little boy inside me; to my sisters and nieces, who visited me on weekends for much-needed play time. They made the ideas in this book real. Among them I've learned to see how interconnected we all are, how living in the now and seeing the world with more compassion and love allows us to fully feel those fleeting moments of spiritual transcendence.

Index